The
Home
Handyman
Encyclopedia

Edited by Harold King

OCTOPUS
Octopus Books

This edition published 1978 by
Octopus Books Limited
59 Grosvenor Street London W1

Seventh impression 1983

© 1974 Octopus Books Limited

ISBN 0 7064 0684 2
Printed in Czechoslovakia
50307/7/br.

Contents

Planning décor: colour planning your home

Two homes, externally identical, may look totally different within—as a result of the varied use of colour, textures, furniture and fittings. The use of colour in home décor and furnishing schemes is a way of expressing individuality. Do not be too hesitant in experimenting with colour; while there must be rules, these should only be regarded as general guidelines.

Natural light, or white light, is composed of all the colours of the spectrum. The spectrum, or wheel of colours, is made up of all the colours of the rainbow. These are red, orange, yellow, green, blue, indigo and violet.

Primary colours

The colours red, yellow and blue are known as the primary colours. Strong, vibrant colours, especially red, cannot be produced by mixing any other colours together. If equal parts of red, yellow and blue are mixed together they will make a neutral shade of grey.

From this, two equal parts of yellow and blue mixed together will produce green and two equal parts of green and blue will produce blue-green.

Colour disc

Warm, advancing colours

Cool, receding colours

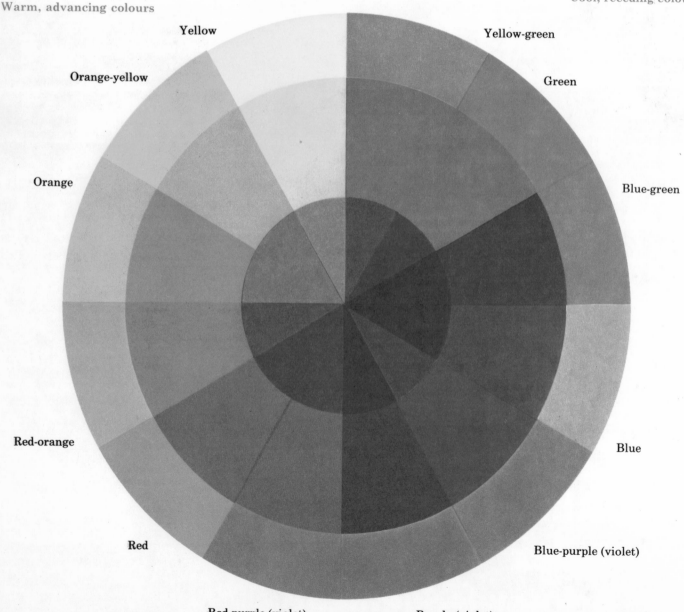

Yellow

Orange-yellow

Orange

Red-orange

Red

Red-purple (violet)

Purple (violet)

Blue-purple (violet)

Blue

Blue-green

Green

Yellow-green

It is possible to mix well over 2,000 distinct colours, using the primary colours in varying proportions.

Colour balance

When decorating a home, the object should be to try to achieve a balanced mixture of primary colours, shades and tints. Shades are produced by adding black; tints by adding white to the base colour.

White, black and grey are considered as 'non-colours'. White reflects light, black absorbs it and grey can be used to give a muted or receding effect. White is used extensively in modern décor to reflect light and colour, giving contrast and creating a sense of space.

Colour disc

In all this wealth of colour it may be difficult to decide on a harmonious colour scheme. A colour disc is the standard way of differentiating between the colours of the spectrum. Yellow is always placed at the top of the disc and grey in the middle, to give a reference point, when planning a colour scheme.

From yellow the colour range proceeds, clockwise, through the 'cool' colours on the right of the wheel to the 'warm' colours on the left.

Harmony

Colour can be used to produce harmony or disorder. It is better to use too few colours than to try to cope with too many.

There are some guide lines to follow when planning colour schemes. One method is to choose one colour and use it with shades and tones of that same colour.

This scheme can be difficult to achieve successfully, for unless carefully balanced it can produce a rather dull effect. Black, white and grey can be used to give added interest.

Two related colours, such as blue and blue-green, can be used together if one colour is used in a greater proportion than the other. Again, white, black or grey can add interest. Opposite colours used in unequal proportions will give a visually interesting scheme. Used in equal proportions, opposite colours, orange and blue, for instance, will clash.

Another way is to use three different colours set at equal distances apart on the colour wheel – for example, orange, violet and green. There are, of course, different permutations of this scheme.

Other varied colour schemes can be devised by dividing the colour wheel into cool and warm colours. Take yellow-orange and red-orange, miss out orange between them and pair them with their opposite colours on the cool half of the disc. Here, the opposite colours are blue-violet and blue-green, blue being omitted.

Experimenting in colour

One needs to experiment with colours. Try, as far as you can, to see how colours will mix and blend. Obtain colour cards of paint colours, get samples of wallpaper and swatches of material to give you some idea of the finished effects of blending

colour. Look at the colours in artificial and natural light and appreciate the fact that some colours, in proximity with others, alter in hue. Colours may 'steal' from each other.

The aim should be to achieve a modulated blending or a complementary contrast but never discord. The latter can be difficult to live with and may create a cluttered, restless feeling.

Using colour

Red is a vibrant colour which should be used sparingly. It is suitable for use in such places as hallways, to give a bright, warm, welcoming feeling; in children's rooms; and in living areas, to highlight focal points.

Orange is another vibrant colour which creates a warm feeling, but it can be overpowering if used extensively – particularly in a small room.

Yellow mixes well with red but needs the contrast of a cool colour. Lemon-yellow contrasts well with greens and blues. Blue is a cold colour and may create an atmosphere of remoteness and chill. Blue and red tend to fight each other although they can, with skill, be used effectively together.

Purple is a rich colour but can be rather overpowering if used too extensively. Used sparingly, it can make a valid contribution to a décor scheme. Shades and tints of purple can make very attractive colour combinations. Black and white, though non-colours, are used as contrast mediums.

Contrast

Black contrasts well with white, yellow and pale tints. White is a very important 'colour'. Extremely versatile, it can be used for the main colour scheme with highlights in other colours. Alternatively, it becomes the contrast part of a scheme using colour.

All-white bedrooms are very popular – white walls, ceiling, fitted cupboards, carpet, bedspreads, blinds and so on. Colour may provide highlights in, for example, lampshades, cushions, occasional chair covers, a bedside rug or books on a shelf. To take another example, white used as a ceiling 'colour' and for woodwork, doors and window frames provides an effective contrast for carpets, furniture, soft-furnishing and ornaments in other colours, tints or shades.

If you want a restful scheme, you should include such colours as oatmeal, beige, gold, soft greens, browns and cream. More stimulating, but correspondingly less easy to live with, are colours such as orange, blue, purple, red, yellow and pink, contrasted with white or black.

Colour deception

Camouflage of unattractive or obtrusive features can be achieved by the clever use of colour. Grey mixed with any colour will cause that colour to recede. In this way, angular, ugly shapes that tend to intrude visually can be made to recede.

A number of doors breaking up a wall area can be made less obtrusive by painting the doors and frame in the same

shade as the surrounding wall. If you are using wallpaper, take a non-dominant, receding colour from the paper and paint the doors and frames in this. In this way, the door will blend into the background. Radiators and pipes can also be similarly disguised. Paint them the same colour as the walls behind them.

Shapes within a room that are angular, such as chimney breasts, tend to be less attractive as features than rounded recesses.

To lessen their impact, paint or decorate them with receding colours and use bright focal colours or pastel shades, adjacent to the object, to draw the eye. The converse works if you wish to highlight a particular feature.

Colour can be used to deceive the eye and help to redress the balance of badly proportioned rooms. This needs additional planning, but much can be done with colour alone.

Proportions

In a narrow room, where one exists, leave the picture rail and bring the ceiling right down to it. Concentrate colour on the lower part of the walls; this will bring the eye down to the colour level and give an impression of width.

Paint the long walls in cool, receding colours and the short walls in a warm colour. Cool colours, like blue and green, make the walls appear further apart. The room will appear to be wider and shallower.

Flooring can also add to this illusion. Patterned carpet, lino, tiles or woodblock flooring should be laid with the lines running across the width of the room. Alternatively, a carpet with a diagonal pattern or carpet tiles arranged in this way will also make the room appear wider.

Another widening trick is to paint the ceiling in a colour that tones with the flooring and paint the walls white. The eye is drawn to the walls which gives an immediate impression of width.

One problem may be that the room needs an illusion of height. The eye needs to be drawn upwards; one way of doing this is to use vertical striped wallpaper. A plain floor covering in a matching or toning colour should then be used.

As cool colours recede and give an impression of depth and space, they can be used to make a wide room look narrower. The long walls should have a warm-coloured finish, while the shorter walls should be painted in a receding colour.

The floor covering should be laid with the pattern running from the front to the back of the room, emphasizing any lines on the walls.

A large floor that appears too spacious can be stained or painted. Highlight the centre with a bright rug or carpet. The carpet becomes the focal point and the surrounding area merges into the background.

Grand illusion

Conversely, fitted carpet gives an illusion of space. This illusion can be carried further by painting the skirting board in a colour that matches the carpet. In a small house, it may be possible to use the same-colour carpet throughout one floor. Qualities may vary, dependent upon the usage required in differing rooms, but when doors are open one will get the impression of an endless vista.

If this is not possible, carpet or floor-covering colours should be linked. Think of the visual assault of ill-matching carpets meeting in a hall or landing. Any linking hall or landing carpet should attempt to continue the adjacent colours.

Carpets are an expensive item and should be chosen to blend with schemes of décor and make a positive contribution to the overall effect.

Carpets and colours

Whether to have patterned or plain carpet is often debated. From the standpoint of colour scheming, plain carpets may be easier to furnish around. A costly item that may have to last for years, a carpet is less easily changed than the more versatile curtains and other soft furnishings.

However, plain carpets, especially if pale, do show specks and mark more easily than patterned carpets. The latter may be better in rooms where there are children or pets.

If in doubt when choosing a carpet colour, choose one that will blend well with several décor schemes. Colours such as brown, grey, moss green and beige might be suitable.

The carpet colour should be one shade darker than the walls – if they are the same colour, or used to give stability, a darker shade of the main furnishing colour – this will help to unify the scheme.

A room can be made to appear larger than it is by using a fitted, plain carpet in a receding colour and texture, or a carpet with a subdued pattern and colour.

Patterned carpets, in strong colours, will make the room look smaller but the danger here is a conflict between the carpet, the rest of the décor scheme, and the furniture, which may produce a cluttered effect. Soft furnishings, particularly, need to be chosen with great care.

Texture can be introduced through carpets and a textured carpet or a shaggy rug may provide a focal point to a room. Again, there is a danger of introducing too many textures in flooring, upholstery and soft furnishings. Nothing is worse than a multitude of textures, fighting it out together.

Well used, texture can add interest to a room. Textured wallpaper, such as hessian or woodchip, may make an attractive background against which to display pictures or ornaments.

Colour and texture

Colour is affected by texture. On a flat surface some colours will seem dull, while the same colours used on a textured surface will seem interesting and alive.

Smooth surfaces reflect light, while a rough surface absorbs light and gives a darker tone. A dark, matt surface absorbs light but a light, matt surface reflects light and is, therefore, suitable for use in rooms that lack a great deal of natural light.

Patterned fabric looks attractive against a white or cool background. Strong pattern tends to dominate and should be used sparingly. Less-definite patterns tend to merge into the background and are easier to live with.

Pattern, too, combined with the choice of colour, can be used to disguise problem features. Intrusive doors can be papered to match the wallpaper, matching wallpaper and fabric can help rectify a badly proportioned or ugly window.

Small, fussy windows can be hidden behind a wall of curtaining, or made to look quite stately by using long patterned floor-length curtains.

Patterned material can also be used to co-ordinate areas of a room – for example, in linking together curtains, bedspread, furniture covers and cushions.

Furniture can be used to help correct the proportions of a room. Try to avoid a cluttered room that is neither comfortable to live in nor pleasing to look at.

A long, low room can be quite depressing. Look at the entire area as one and then subdivide it, using colour, modular storage divider units or tall pieces of furniture. These units should reach the ceiling to give an illusion of height. Long curtains will also help to create a sensation of vertical height.

Tall furniture tends to give a feeling of height, while furniture arranged at a lower level brings focus down in a high-ceilinged room.

Space project

Many people want to create an impression of space in their homes. Much can be done with colour, pattern and texture but actual physical proportions, furniture and soft furnishings play an important part in the overall effect.

In other areas, modular furniture can be used, leaving floor space free. Wall units and shelves can be made of light material, so that they do not dominate the wall area. For example, glass shelves mounted on light brackets merge into the background. Picture rails can be removed, low radiators or skirting radiators can be used.

Often, two small rooms can usefully be combined into one living area. Instead of two cluttered boxes, one can have two functional areas, linked by flooring and décor colouring.

Dark walls need not necessarily make areas look small if they are combined with plenty of white on the ceiling and floor and in the furnishings.

Glazed look

Mirrors can be used to give an added dimension and feeling of spaciousness. A mirror backing a recessed alcove reflects light and gives a sense of space.

To widen a narrow hallway use mirrors or mirror tiles on one side. Use wall to wall carpeting and extend the colour of the carpet by 50mm or so up the wall.

Hallways, can afford to be decorated in bright colours. They need to be welcoming entrances, well lit and inviting.

Around the home

Homes are usually divided into particular activity areas. One room, where one may spend much of one's leisure time is the living room. This is a room that should be restful enough for relaxation yet stimulating enough for entertaining.

It is important when choosing colour schemes, particularly for a living area, to visualize the scheme under natural and artificial light. In fact, if you do a lot of entertaining, a colour scheme that looks its best in artificial light may be more successful.

Fluorescent light tends to bleach out colour, while ordinary tungsten lamps give a warmer glow to most colours.

Unless there is the opportunity to start from scratch, most décor schemes have to be built around existing furniture and flooring. There are two ways of doing this. The first is to take one predominating colour and create a colour scheme, using shades and tones of that colour.

The second is to use one fixed colour and a contrast. In the first case, an example is a blue-green carpet, complemented by varying shades and tones of green, used on the walls and soft furnishings.

A white ceiling would contrast the greens. Alone, this could be a boring scheme and would need to be livened up with splashes of colour in cushions and lampshades.

In the second instance, one fixed colour and a contrast can be used in a two-colour scheme. A scheme can be built up, using complementary colours. With green, one can add soft yellows, shades of orange and brown. The original colour might be echoed or repeated in window furnishings or carpets.

A natural woodblock floor, or a wood-panelled wall, rich in colour, could provide the basis of a natural-coloured, neutral-toned scheme. Here texture would play a big part in making a success of a scheme that is dependent on shades of oatmeal, black, grey and off-white. The whole scheme might need a focal point of more definite colour, perhaps in lampshades or cushion covers.

Aspect

Aspect affects the choice of room colour schemes. A room facing north will have a cold aspect with cold light. Orange, yellow, red, the warm colours, help to counteract any cold feeling and create a feeling of warmth.

On the other hand a west- or south-facing room, which will have a warmer light, can be decorated in cool greens, blues and greys.

Colour scheming tends to be rather subjective, so really it is a choice for the individual. Bedrooms are a personal choice and range from the feminine colour schemes, pale and pastel, to the very masculine room.

Children's rooms grow with them and while a pastel-shaded room is restful for a small baby, children enjoy the vibrant primary colours that adults may tend to find over-stimulating.

Teenagers tend to experiment with their own schemes, often achieving a discordant but successful clash of colours.

Decorating: the right tools for the job

It is important to choose your painting weather as carefully as you choose your paints and brushes.

There is one limiting factor when you paint exterior surfaces–the weather. The ideal day to paint outdoors is a dry warm slightly overcast day with a drying breeze blowing. This weather is most likely in late spring or early autumn.

Very hot or wet weather does not produce conditions suitable for painting. It is first necessary to look at the properties of paints and the effect of temperature and moisture on paint.

An ordinary gloss paint used on exterior wood or metal work consists of a pigment, a binder and a solvent. The pigment gives the colour and covering capacity, or opacity, of the paint. The binder, a sticky fluid, 'binds' the pigment particles together to provide an adherent, a weather-proof layer, and the solvent helps to lubricate the binder and make it run easily under the brush to provide an even 'cover' coat.

As the paint dries the solvent evaporates leaving a sticky layer which flows into a smooth film. Paint dries by taking in oxygen from the air; a chemical reaction is set up which causes the paint to set into a smooth, hard film.

If the weather is very hot, the solvent dries rapidly, preventing the paint film from flowing and levelling out properly. This means that some parts of the film, particularly at the end of brush marks, will be thinner than others. The finished surface will be patchy and the paint life only as long as the thinnest parts.

Strong sunlight

Strong sunlight can cause paint to blister. This happens when sunlight on still-wet paint causes any air or water trapped under the surface to expand and push the surface up in blisters.

Blisters or stickiness may also become apparent when timbers with a high resin content are exposed to strong sunlight. The trouble may occur immediately or appear sometime later. This is caused by the natural resin in the wood and particularly in the knots. Although it consists of the same type of resin as in the binder, the natural resin does not combine with oxygen and dry, as does resin in paint. The result is a wet patch which, as time passes, turns brown and disfigures the paint surface as more resin oozes from the knots. The remedy is to treat knots and any suspect areas with two thin coats of a knotting compound. Allow this to dry before priming the surface.

Low temperatures

Low temperatures also affect painted surfaces. If the weather is cold the paint will become thick and difficult to brush out. It is more difficult in cold weather to apply a smooth, even film of paint. The solvent will dry out but the danger is that although the surface will appear to be dry the lower layers will still be wet and soft. The result is that the hard top surface may wrinkle or even crack.

Fog and frost leave a film of moisture on the surface. Attempts to wipe this off may not be successful, especially if the surface timber, possibly only undercoated, has absorbed some of the moisture.

Water under the paint surface can cause a great deal of trouble. A paint film is not impervious to water and in a shaded position the water will slowly evaporate through the paint surface, without causing blistering.

If the surface to be painted is even slightly wet, the top coat may not adhere to the undercoat. While it may appear to dry normally, with fluctuations in temperatures the top and undercoats will expand and contract, causing the paint film to crack and peel off. To prevent this, make sure the surface to be painted is absolutely dry.

No one chooses to paint in the rain. If rain should fall on newly painted work it will depend on how dry the paint film is as to any damage. A quick shower on 'touch-dry' paint should do no harm, but rain on a very liquid paint film may thin certain areas and produce a very patchy appearance when dry.

The same rules apply when using any of the newer, polyurethane-based paints which do not require special priming or undercoating when used on timber. These paints are applied 'coat on coat'.

On metal, a base primer must always be used, whatever paint is applied.

Outdoor finishes

Hard-wearing surface finishes applied from the can are available in a number of forms.

One is a durable paint made of plastic resin reinforced with small particles of mineral aggregate and minute nylon fibres. Another is an emulsion-based masonry paint, also with nylon reinforcement, plus an anti-mould additive. Another type of stone finish is made of plastic polymer resin combined with finely crushed marble. This finish is waterproof and is very durable. A product suitable for both exterior and interior surfaces is made of a dense mixture of synthetic resin base mixed with finely crushed minerals.

Another is a water-based textured masonry finish based on an emulsion polymer containing titanium oxide, graded mica-loaded aggregate and mineral quartz. This is suitable for cement rendering, brick-work, asbestos cement, concrete, pebble-dash and any other types of masonry.

With any of these 'stone' finishes on an unstable surface, sealer should be used before applying the stone finish.

Woodwork treatments

There are many preparatory treatments for exposed woodwork, including wood stains and dyes. Clear polyurethane varnishes also help to protect the colour and grain of the wood. If the wood is discoloured, a number of preparations are made to remove discolouration and to strip wood back to its original colour. Stain or dye wood finishes help to preserve timber and provide a water-repellent surface.

Household paints

Household paints can be divided into two main types–emulsion-based and oil-based paints. The latter includes those which are polyurethane based. Emulsion-based paint or PEP (plastic emulsion paint) is used now in place of water paint and distemper. Particles of synthetic resin, acrylic or vinyl are suspended in water. As the water evaporates the particles flow together to form a film of resin on the surface.

Emulsion paint can be used in areas of hard wear, for these can be washed or even scrubbed. Some emulsion paints are used as primers and undercoats. Emulsion paint dries fairly quickly; depending on temperature, you can repaint within an hour or two. The characteristic smell of paint is reduced to a faint odour which disappears quickly. Many people find emulsion paint easy to use, particularly over a large area. It is thinned with water and any splashes can be wiped up with a damp cloth.

For use indoors where you require a quick drying, low-sheen decorative cover, emulsion is suitable for both walls and ceilings. Some emulsions are suitable for both inside or outside use.

Coverage

The number of coats of paint needed varies

on the surface to be covered. Generally, more coats will be needed going from a dark to a light colour than the other way. On new plaster at least two coats will be needed. A thinned coat, diluted with water, should be applied as a sealant before painting with two coats. If you brush out too thoroughly it will not cover too well and an extra coat may be needed.

On a good surface where colours approximate, only one coat may be needed. Cracks should be filled and rubbed down before repainting. A thinned coat of the new colour should be applied to the repaired area before the final decorative coat is applied.

Porous paint should be used for early decoration on new plaster. The wall ideally should be completely dry. This will normally take several months. As it is not practical to leave undecorated plaster for this length of time, you should use a porous paint that will let the wall continue to dry out. They can be used as soon as efflorescence (a crystalline deposit white and fluffy, sometimes hard, especially on cement-based materials when it is known as lime bloom) has ceased.

Emulsion paint is of two types; PVC (homopolymer or co-polymer) or acrylic. These paints decrease in porosity as the

sheen increases. They are hard wearing and can be cleaned easily and allow efflorescent salts to pass through.

Vinyl distemper (water paint) is an inexpensive form of emulsion paint. It has a low sheen but is porous. This paint has no great resistance to wear.

Gloss paint or any other that is not porous will prevent the wall plaster from drying out. Trouble may follow if both sides of a newly plastered wall are painted or if one side is tiled and the other painted before the wall has dried out properly. When using porous paint as a temporary decoration, choose one that will suit the permanent decoration. Either use a decoration that can easily be removed or, if planning an oil paint, use emulsion that can be painted over. When repainting use paint of the same type as that originally used. Some types of paint will not 'take' over another paint–for example, a bitumen paint will 'bleed' through oil paint.

Oil-based paints all have the characteristic 'paint' smell. This includes primers, undercoats, gloss and eggshell finishes. Synthetic resins, alkyd and polyurethane combined with drying oils give a tough flexible finish.

These are slower drying than emulsion paint and need longer drying periods be-

The decorator's 'tool kit':

1 Paint kettle

2 Paint roller and tray

3 Filling and stripping knives

4 Paint pads

5 Shave hook

6 Ceiling brush

7 Paint brushes for larger and smaller areas

8 Cutting-in brush

9 Crevice brush

10 Dusting brush

tween coats. Thinning is done with white spirit, which is also used for cleaning up any splashes.

Oil-based paint gives you a wide range of sheen from matt to high gloss. These paints provide hard-wearing surfaces, but the degree of resistance depends on the level of gloss. Oil-based paint is excellent for outside wood and metal work.

Oil-based paint can be obtained in gloss, matt or eggshell finish. Eggshell gives a lower level of gloss. These paints should be used internally in areas of hard wear, such as bathrooms and kitchens. Gloss paint only should be used externally.

It is possible to buy two types of gloss paint; liquid and gell (thixotropic). Liquid gloss needs a little more care in application. Gell is for the less experienced painter. It drips less during application, gives a heavier coat and minimizes the risk of runs and curtaining. Other paints include additives such as silicones and polyethylene.

Distempers – oil-bound and washable. These are used mainly for interior work and will stand light washing. They are not suitable for areas subject to high condensation. Oil-free, size-bound distemper is sometimes used on ceilings. It will not take rubbing and must be washed off before redecorating.

Tools for painting

It is a golden rule to buy the best tools you can afford. A good paint brush, pad, or roller, given reasonable care, will give many years of service. Always compare the length and thickness of the bristles on a brush. A 75mm brush should have bristles 75mm long and be at least 20mm thick. A cheaper 75mm brush would tend to have only 50mm bristles perhaps 15mm thick.

Cheap brushes tend to shed bristles and may spoil your work. Test the quality of the bristles by flexing them in your hand. Good-quality bristles should feel soft.

Bristle, which comes from hog-hair, has at the end of each bristle countless invisible barbs which hold the paint and cut down on the number of times you dip into the paint kettle. Genuine bristles have a natural taper which makes the brush a manageable shape.

Many experienced painters will only use bristle brushes although brushes with synthetic bristles are available. The synthetic bristle does not have the same paint-holding qualities as it lacks the barbs.

You will need brushes of various widths for particular jobs. A useful width for many jobs is 65mm–75mm wide. Door panels walls, and even larger areas can be painted with a brush of this size. For bigger areas, such as ceilings, you need a 100mm–150mm brush, and a dry dusting brush to dust off mouldings.

Smaller brushes–38mm to 50mm–are used for skirting boards, mouldings and window frames, while a 13mm brush is useful for glazing bars and other narrow paint surfaces.

A cutting-in brush, which has a bevelled edge, is useful for painting mouldings or around awkward corners. A wire-handled crevice brush is useful for tackling tight corners, such as behind radiators, where an ordinary flat brush cannot be used.

A round brush, called a sash brush, is used for painting round pipes and railings. A long thin-headed fitch, a brush made of hog's hairs, is useful for picking out intricate details. Also useful is a flat brush designed for lining work. This can be used to achieve straight edges at corners and where walls of different colours abut.

Stippling brushes for stone paint, distemper brushes and varnish brushes are among other types. You can build up a selection of brushes in the same way you might build up a tool-kit.

Paint rollers. Paint rollers are used for painting large areas. The roller head may be made of lamb's wool, foam plastic or felt. A lamb's wool roller is by far the most expensive, but the best. Rollers are ideal for decorating with water-based paints as the paint will wash out easily.

Gloss paint is much more difficult to remove completely and it may be better to use a brush even on a large area. When using a roller, paint is poured into a paint tray, and the brush tracked into this; this applies the paint evenly to the roller head.

Long-handled rollers are also available, enabling you to paint at a distance.

Paint pads. Paint pads are made of foam or mohair and are obtainable in various widths. They are suitable for interior work. Some types of pad are renewable.

Paint kettles. Paint kettles are made of metal or plastic. A working quantity of paint should be decanted from the main tin into the kettle. Among advantages are that you are not carrying a large heavy tin of paint, possibly up a ladder, with risk of spillage. A paint kettle can also be secured to a ladder with an S-hook. Skin will form on paint on which the lid is not secured. A kettle prevents this.

Blowtorch. One of the butane torches with disposable or exchange canisters is suitable for removing paint from timber or metal. Avoid using near glass.

Shave hooks. The multi-edge shave hook and the triangular hook are used for stripping paint from mouldings and difficult corners, in conjunction with a blow torch or chemical stripper.

Filling or stripping knife. The filling knife has a more flexible blade than the stripping knife. Both are used to apply filler to cracks in plaster.

Scrapers. These are used in conjunction with chemical paint removers or blow torches.

Sanding block. This can be a piece of timber, with glasspaper wrapped round, or a proprietary sanding block which 'locks' the glasspaper round it.

Sponge and tack rag. The sponge is used for cleaning and wiping down and the tack cloth to remove surface dust from paint surfaces.

Step ladder. This should be in good condition and safe to use. Two ladders can be used in conjunction with a scaffold board about 3m long. Below a height of 2·50m, a pair of hop-ups, which can be hired or made, may be a better platform. Multi-purpose ladders can be used as trestles or converted to a general-purpose ladder.

Trestles. These can be made, bought or hired. The trestle can be a working platform or used with a second trestle and a scaffold board. Trestles and boards should be in sound condition and not likely to give way.

Extendable ladders and scaffold towers. A light-weight aluminium ladder, with two or three extensions, will tackle a wide range of jobs. A wooden ladder is heavier to manipulate. Check all ladders for safety before use. Ladder stays prevent the ladder from resting on guttering, which may give way.

Scaffold towers can be built up to varying heights and wheels can be fitted to move them around. A pair of towers with bridging staging can provide a working platform along the width or depth of the house. Some types of scaffolding can be used indoors.

Power aids These include disc and orbital sanders, paint stirrers and power sprays.

TABLE 1

Material	Kind of Material	Primer
Timber	Ordinary softwoods used in building construction	Wood primer
	Most hardwoods used in furniture construction	Wood primer, slightly thinned with white spirit
	Porous wood such as oak	Wood primer thinned about 15% by white spirit followed by a normal coat
	Highly resinous wood, i.e. Columbia pine	Aluminium primer sealer
	Oily woods such as teak	Teak sealer
Building boards	Standard hardboard	Plaster primer, hardboard primer or emulsion paint thinned with the same quantity of water
	Tempered hardboard	Thinned emulsion paint
	Chipboard	Plaster primer
	Fire-resisting board	Alkali-resisting primer
	Plasterboard	Alkali-resisting primer
	Asbestos (when can be kept dry)	Alkali-resisting primer
Plaster	Old	Plaster primer
	New	Alkali-resisting primer
Metal	Iron and steel	Zinc chromate, red lead or zinc-rich primer
	New galvanized iron (showing bright silvery colour)	Calcium plumbate primer
	Old galvanized iron (showing a dull grey)	Zinc chromate or calcium plumbate primer
	Zinc-sheeting	As galvanized iron which actually is iron coated with zinc by a hot-dip process
	Aluminium	Zinc chromate primer
	Brass, copper, lead	No primer at all

TABLE 2

Surface	First choice	Second choice	Third choice
Walls and ceilings	Emulsion paint	Washable distemper (water paint)	Eggshell or matt alkyd-resin paint
Wood	Gloss alkyd-resin paint	Eggshell alkyd-resin paint	Matt alkyd-resin paint
Metal (including guttering)	Gloss alkyd-resin paint	Bituminous paint	Cellulose paint (small surfaces only)
Concrete and cement rendering	Stone paint, nylon-fibre based emulsion	Outdoor-grade emulsion paint (not waterproof)	Cement paint (waterproof)
Stucco	Deoresinous or vegetable oil paint	Limewash	
Asbestos (gutters and sheds)	Outdoor-grade emulsion paint (not waterproof)	Bituminous paint (waterproof)	
Wooden fences	Proprietary wood preservative	Creosote	Bituminous or gloss alkyd-resin paint
Where there is a steamy atmosphere such as in bathrooms and kitchens	Gloss alkyd-resin paint	Outdoor-grade emulsion paint	Eggshell alkyd-resin paint (on no account matt or distemper)
Kitchen and bathroom furniture	Gloss polyurethane paint	Matt polyurethane paint	Gloss alkyd-resin paint
Nurseries	Use lead-free paints throughout		

TABLE 3

Paint type	Coverage m²
Alkali-resisting primer	8·36
Undercoat	7·50
Co-polymer acrylic	90
Emulsion paint	95
Thixotropic paint	55
Oil-based paint	100
Whitewash, limewash, distemper	90
Quantities all 500ml (millilitres)	

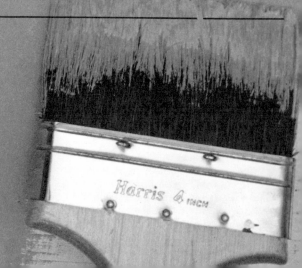

New paintwork, however carefully applied, is only as good as the surface beneath it. Careful preparation of the surface, whether exterior or interior, is essential. Paint can be applied to a variety of surfaces such as wood, metal, plaster, lining paper, plastic, polystyrene and stonework.

Preparation may count for three quarters of the time taken to do a job, but the result will be worthwhile. If work is rushed the result may be poor and not durable.

Surfaces to be painted must always be clean, dust and grease-free. Paint will stick to whatever is immediately below it. It will stick to dust and come away with it. If paint is applied to a greasy surface, the grease may combine with the oil present in the paint and lengthen the drying time.

If the surface is basically in good condition it may only need washing down with a paint cleaner, such as sugar soap or detergent. When washing down, particularly on walls and large areas, such as doors, start washing from the bottom and work upwards. In this way streaks of concentrated cleaning fluids will not run down the surface and form patchy areas which make for an uneven surface.

When the first wash is completed wash again, starting at the top, with clean water. This is to remove any remaining dirt and ensure that there is no residual detergent left which might react with the chemical constituents of the paint. After washing, the surface must be allowed to dry completely before paint is applied. If necessary, rub down with a fine glasspaper and use a soft brush to remove any dust.

New plaster should always be allowed to dry out completely before a final decorative coat is applied. Some take anything up to a year to do this. If decorated during this time, use a water-based emulsion paint which will not seal the surface but will allow it to continue drying out.

In many cases, if old paint is in good condition and the new coat will marry with the old, it is not necessary to remove it. The surface may need rubbing down with a wet-and-dry paper, used wet. Rubbing down will slightly roughen the surface and provide a good key for the new undercoat.

Blistered or flaked paint must be scraped back to a firm edge. 'Feather' the edges with the abrasive paper until they are level with the surrounding surface.

Any indentations, cracks or joins in interior woodwork should be filled with cellulose filler before priming.

All distemper should be completely removed by being washed off thoroughly with warm water. Distemper and non-washable distemper used on ceilings, consisting of glue and whiting, are very hard to remove and difficult patches may have to be scraped away with a paint scraper.

Before applying a new coat of water-based paint, the surface should be sealed with a primer.

If the distemper is covering ceiling paper, the paper may need soaking two or three times. Scrape off the paper with a broad stripping knife. Take care not to dig too deeply, or you may gouge out a hole in the plaster.

Emulsion or any water-based paint should be sponged down with detergent and warm water. Again, work from the bottom upwards for the first wash and then wash down with clean water from the top.

If the surface feels rough when dry, rub it carefully down with fine glasspaper. Remember to dust down the surface before painting.

Other paints, such as enamel paints, oil paints, oil-based gloss paints and water-based gloss paints should also be washed down with detergent and warm water to remove grease and dirt.

After rinsing with clean water, allow the surface to dry and then smooth it with wet-abrasive paper, held over a sanding block or a conveniently sized piece of wood.

To remove very bad imperfections on woodwork, such as sags and runs, a soda block, which is very coarse, can be used to rub down the surface. After rubbing down with abrasive paper or soda block, finish with a fine glasspaper or a fine wet-and-dry paper.

Basically, the surfaces that need to be

painted can be divided into two categories: internal and external surfaces which may be old paint surfaces that need preparation and repainting; and new internal and external surfaces that need treatment. These surfaces may be wood, metal, plaster, stonework, rendering or paper.

Externally, paint is normally applied to wood, metal or rendering.

Unexposed wood or metal will soon deteriorate if left to the elements. It has to be protected from the action of frost and rain. New wood should be well seasoned and matured. Softwood needs planing as paint brings out the irregularities in the grain. Hardwood, used for sills and door thresholds, can be given a clear finish. Stop any joints or indentations with oil-based putty stained to match the wood.

Door and window frames made of softwood should be rubbed down or planed smooth. Patent knotting should be applied to knots and on resinous areas. Wood primer should then be applied, ensuring that it is well brushed in so that the grain is filled.

Hardwood window sills and door thresholds provide a good surface for paint.

Wood primer is oily. Some of the oil is absorbed into the wood and helps to give good adhesion. Oily wood primer should not be thinned unless it is being used on highly porous wood. This should saturate the pores of the timber. If this does not happen, air will be trapped in the pores by the thick primer.

As the temperature rises, the air expands, causing bubbles to rise in the primer and burst through the paintwork. To avoid this on porous wood use a thin saturation coat of primer, then when dry apply a second primer coat.

An aluminium sealer is effective. It prevents seepage of resin in highly resinous timbers and problems such as creosote bleeding through the surface. The ends of window sills and thresholds should be stopped to seal the open grains. This should be done before undercoating.

Sound wood surfaces that need repainting still need preparation. The surface should be washed down and lightly glass-papered. Brush down to remove dust. Often a coat of primer, well applied, may last several paintings without being renewed. Exterior wooden surfaces that have cracks or indentations should be filled with hard-stopping after priming, then rubbed down before either undercoat or finish coats are applied.

Metal door and window frames and lead pipes need preparation. They are liable to be dirty, and coated with rust. Large areas should be scraped or brushed down with a wire brush and emery paper. It is important to protect the eyes when brushing down metal as particles of rust may cause discomfort and even damage.

Next, use rust solvent to remove the rust particles, microscopic in size, which will cause further trouble. In difficult-to-reach areas a proprietary rust curative, a preparation that turns rust to iron-oxide, can be used. This can, on gutters, be painted over with bituminous-based paint. If the surface is good but smooth, it should be roughened to form a good key.

On window frames rust should be removed from metal with a wire brush. Rub down with emery paper and paint with a rust solvent. If the windows need reputtying, remove the old putty, treat the window frame for rust, prime the metal and then replace with metal glazing putty.

Walls can be protected against damp with cement or stone paints. Cement-based emulsion paints provide a damp-resistant layer but they are only as good as the wall beneath. This must also provide a waterproof barrier.

Before applying cement or stone paint the surface must be sound, dry and clean. If the rendering has blown (come away from the brickwork) it must be hacked back and re-rendered. Brush down the surface with a stiff brush and, if required, apply a clear sealant coat before covering with the decorative coats. Before applying an external wall cover coat, the wall should be quite dry.

Internally, surfaces that need preparation may be of wood, metal, plaster or paper on plaster. Plaster surfaces should be dry before painting. If painting a new wall, a water-based paint should be used to allow the plaster to dry out. Any cracks should be cut back and filled before painting or papering. Unless a papered surface is smooth it is advisable to remove the old paper before relining and repapering.

Wood surfaces, if sound, can be washed, rubbed down and painted. Badly pitted or blistered surfaces should be stripped back to the bare wood.

Where damage is only localized, treat the area separately–rubbing down and filling if necessary. If a complete change of colour is required, such as stripping a dark paint to repaint in a light colour, it is necessary to strip the paint back to the wood. Varnish should be removed before replacing with paint. It does not provide a good surface for new paint as adhesion, even after sanding down, is not good. Remove the varnish and treat as new wood.

Polish, wax and silicone adhering to a surface can be removed with white spirit. Rub off the wax or silicone with a rough cloth and sand down. If the paint separates, the surface is not clean enough. French polish can be removed with methylated spirit applied with a rough cloth.

There are three ways of stripping paint. It is a tedious job but the effort involved is worthwhile to achieve a good surface. Paint can be removed using heat, chemical or mechanical means.

Heat is most effectively applied to oil-based paints. You can use a blow-lamp or gas blow torch. A paraffin blow torch is quite difficult to use as it needs priming with methylated spirit. No form of heat should be used near glass, as this may cause it to crack. Heat should not be used near asbestos or plaster walls.

The modern blow torch may either be one that incorporates a replaceable canister of gas or an attachment joined by a flexible cord to a gas cylinder. The latter

Fill any cracks in interior woodwork with cellulose filler before priming

Where conventional, oil-based paint is to be used, bare timber should be primed

Rub down rusted metal with wire brush; treat chemically and apply metal primer

is useful for reaching awkward corners, but is not quite so portable.

Various fittings are available with gas blow torches, from pin-head to wide flames. A paint-stripping head, which spreads the flame, should be fitted to the blow torch. As the flame produced is non-luminous it is necessary to watch the work carefully. Used in conjunction with a stripping knife, the flame must be kept well ahead of the knife.

The flame should be played from side to side. At no time should the flame set the paint alight as this will char the wood. Hold the stripping knife at an angle so that the shreds of hot paint do not fall on the hand. Place something to catch the pieces. When stopping work turn the torch away from the surface to avoid accidental burning.

Start stripping at the bottom of the areas to be treated, covering only a small area at a time. Once the wood is completely bare, use glasspaper to smooth the surface, fill any indentations or cracks and then dust down carefully before priming. Electric strippers are slower and should not be used on damp surfaces.

Chemical strippers can be home-made or commercially produced. Simple strippers can be used on paints that dry by evaporation but not on bituminous cement or chlorinated rubber paints.

Methylated spirits will remove water-based paints, distemper or emulsion; ammonia dissolved in warm water will help remove the glue in non-washable distemper; cellulose coating can be removed by cellulose thinner.

Modern chemical strippers are spirit-based and should be brushed on to the surface with an old paint brush and left until the paint starts to bubble, when it can then be removed with a paint scraper. It is wise to wear protective clothes and old gloves when using chemical strippers, as these may irritate or burn the skin. If there are several layers of paint to be removed, more than one application of stripper may be needed.

A jelly-type stripper is easier to use than a liquid as it will stay in one place and not run down the surface. Never use a chemical stripper near a naked light as it gives off highly flammable vapour.

Always ensure adequate ventilation when working. Chemical strippers are very useful when stripping window frames –especially metal frames. Burn all the stripped waste. After the paint is stripped wipe down with white spirit and treat as new wood or metal.

There are various types of paint scraper. One has a double-sided blade, one side of which is serated to cut through the paint film. A shave-hook should be used for scraping mouldings. Using a paint scraper is a skilled job and takes time. It is also possible to sand off old paint using a hand block sander with fine, medium or coarse-grained glasspaper.

A sanding attachment to a power tool will make quick work of the old paint but has the disadvantage of producing clouds of fine dust. Always use with the window open and protect the eyes with goggles. There is also the danger that the wood may be scored too deeply and additional making good will be necessary. If using a sander on large areas it is advisable to use a sand belt or orbital sander.

Try to work in a dust-free room and use lead-free priming paint. In decorating any wooden surface, preparation may include the replacement of sections of wood. This may be due to wet or dry rot. Remove the sections of infected wood and treat the surrounding areas. If new sections of wood are used this wood must be knotted and primed before paint is applied.

There are several faults that appear in old paint surfaces. These include crazing, mould, cracks, flaking, blistering and bubbling, as well as the normal dents and chips of everyday wear.

Chips can be rectified by first removing the old paint, rubbing down or 'feathering' with glass paper and filling the hole with a cellulose filler. A hard-stopper would be used for external use, applied after the primer coat, and a soft-stopper used in-ternally. This is allowed to harden and then rubbed down and primed.

When one coat of paint is applied over a coat of an entirely differently constituted paint the result may be crazing. The new and original coats of paint contract at different rates. If badly crazed, the entire surface must be stripped back to the bare wood which should be knotted and primed before painting. Small areas may be locally treated by rubbing down with a wet-and-dry paper before applying a new top coat.

A small area of blistering may be treated, by lifting the eruption with a knife, knotting the cavity, priming, filling with stopper and allowing to dry before rubbing down level with the surrounding surface. Once the surface has been allowed to dry the repaired areas can be primed.

Cracks in ceilings, walls and plaster according to size can be filled with plaster or cellulose filler. Make sure the crack to be filled is clean, clear out loose material and cut back if needed. Cracks should be dusted and damped before filling. Press the filler in and smooth off with a knife. Sand down to achieve a smooth surface.

If the plaster surface is to be painted it is a good idea to add a little of the chosen colour to the filler. This helps the filled area to blend under the colour coat.

Very wide or deep cracks should be cleared out and filled in layers, allowing each layer to dry before putting in the next.

Efflorescence, or the permeation of alkaline salts through the plaster, can only be cured if the wall is allowed to dry out. Use an alkaline-resistant primer and then redecorate.

Mould should be scraped off before redecorating. This can be caused by damp and lack of ventilation. Wash down with an anti-fungicidal preparation, allow to dry and then redecorate.

Primer and undercoating fulfil two functions: primer is used to seal a new or newly prepared surface; it is used on unpainted surfaces. Undercoat is used to fill in the wood before the top coats are added.

When repainting sound surfaces, rub with abrasive paper to remove 'bloom'

When using blow torch, play flame from side to side to avoid charring the wood

Patent knotting should be applied to knots in wood and on any resinous areas

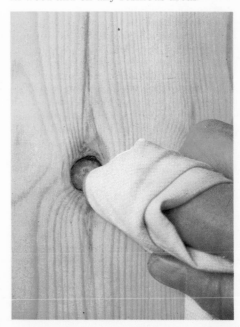

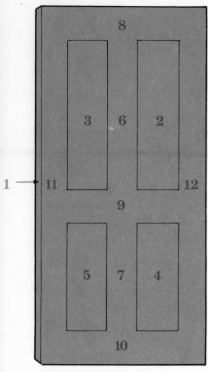

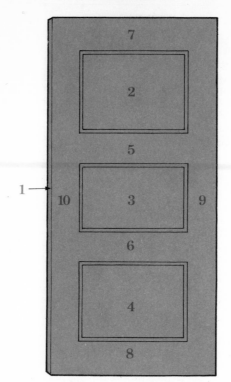

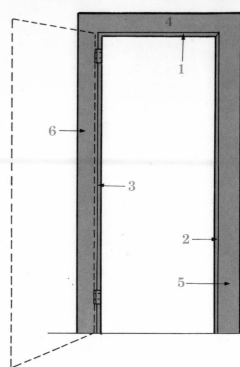

1. Cruciform door

Painting: order of sequence

2. Panelled door

3. Door surround; the faces of door stops are painted the colour of the outer face of the door

The finished effect in painting can only be as good as the work of preparation which went into it. Time spent in preparing the work and the careful choice of materials and 'tools', may possibly seem tedious but should enable you to achieve results of which you may be justly proud.

Preparation

Before beginning to paint, first clear the area as much as possible. Carpets should be rolled up and, if possible, removed. Curtains should be taken down and any furniture covered with dust sheets or paper.

Collect together all the equipment you will need. This includes brushes, paint kettles, clean rag, dusting brushes, a tack cloth and bigger items such as ladders, steps or trestles and, of course, the paint.

All equipment should be as clean as possible and dust-free. After pre-painting preparation there is likely to be quite a lot of dust in the air and on sills, picture rails and skirtings. A vacuum cleaner will remove the dust on the floor. Wipe down all doors, window sills, rails and skirtings. Before opening the paint tins, wipe the lids to remove dust. If the paint is not new, stand the tins upside down for a couple of days before using, to help loosen the settled pigment.

A well-ventilated environment is essential when painting as some paints have pungent odours. Unless it is very windy and dust is likely to be blown in, keep a window or door open to ensure circulation of air.

Paint, other than thixotropic paint (gell), should be stirred before use to mix together the pigment, thinners and bind-ing agents in the correct proportions.

When opened, the paint should have a layer of oil or thinners on the top. If it is old paint, there may be a layer of skin which must be removed. Do not attempt to mix it in with the paint. Stir the paint from the bottom of the tin using a piece of clean wood or a paint-mixing attachment on a power tool.

The paint is at the right consistency when it flows evenly from the tip of the stirrer or stick without leaving lumps adhering. If lumps remain, the paint needs further stirring.

It is important to work with small amounts of fresh paint. To do this, paint can be dispensed from the tin into a paint kettle. Strain paint through a fine mesh, such as an old nylon stocking, into the kettle. Dispense about a 25mm depth of paint at a time. A kettle is easier to handle while working. Replace the lid of the main tin to keep the paint clean and prevent a skin forming.

Paint can be thinned with the solvent recommended for the particular type of paint. Usually, paint is supplied in the correct working consistency.

When painting a room, the areas are usually painted in the following sequence: picture rails, if any, window frames, skirtings and, lastly, doors.

If the surface is stripped bare or previously unpainted, a primer or sealer should be applied to the surface.

Separate primers are made for wood and metal. Some polyurethane paints can be applied straight on to wood surfaces, but metal must always be primed.

Obtain enough paint to complete the job. It is better to over-estimate as spare paint can always be used for touching in afterwards.

Painting should not be undertaken in a moist or frosty atmosphere. Surfaces to be painted should always be dry. When painting outside do not prepare a greater area than can be painted in one day or spell of work.

Unprotected wood is particularly affected by rain, dew and frost and should be primed if left overnight. Primers do not weather well and ideally surfaces should be undercoated if they have to be left for any period.

Polyurethane paints have a limited 'wet-edge' time. If there is paint drag on the brush the remedy is to add a little paraffin to the paint.

Rubbing down between the coats of paint will give good inter-coat adhesion. If painting on to an existing gloss surface, this should be smoothed with a wet-and-dry abrasive paper or fine glasspaper to give a matt, slightly roughened, surface.

There are two methods of using topcoat paints. It is easier to use one coat of eggshell finish, followed by one gloss coat. Two gloss coats give a higher sheen but are slightly harder to apply.

Full gloss, semi-gloss, eggshell and flatfinish paints can be used on interior woodwork. Areas of paint that are subject to condensation and sunlight, such as sashes, window ledges, frames and reveals will last longer if a full-gloss paint is used.

External woodwork that has to stand up to weather should be painted with hard gloss paint, using the appropriate undercoat recommended by the manufacturer.

Undercoating

In general new paintwork on soft wood will last longer if a four-coat system of painting is used. This consists of one coat of primer, one or two coats of undercoat and one or two coats of top coat. A paint

How to do an undercover job

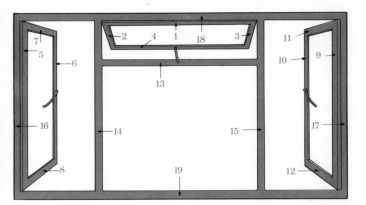

4. Casement window

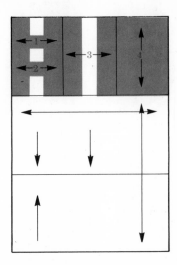

5. Large areas, such as a flush door. Divide the area into three. The colour indicates direction of brush strokes. Lay paint off well into previously painted areas

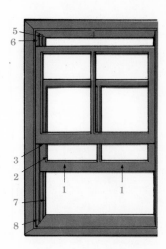

6. Sash window. Sashes should be temporarily fixed, at each stage of painting, with small wedges

system that is used internally should not contain a lead primer or any other toxic material, particularly where children may be present, since lead is poisonous. Avoid using lead-based paints on such surfaces as sills, stairways, nursery woodwork or furniture.

Undercoat should be applied after the primer coat has been allowed to dry for at least 48 hours. Before applying the undercoat, check that the primer is dry, but not too hard, and that any filling or stopping necessary is done. Lightly rub down the surface with a wet-abrasive paper, and then wipe off with a leather.

Once the surface is completely dry, apply the undercoat. Undercoat has more colour pigment than the top coat and should be similar to, but not match, the top coat.

The quality of the top coat is dependent on a sound undercoat. To achieve a dense base for the top coat, it is preferable to apply two undercoats. If there are uneven patches in the undercoat they will show through the top coat. This should be an opaque covercoat, free as far as possible, from brush marks.

Avoid putting on too much paint too lightly which could cause sagging or 'curtaining'. The skill comes in spreading the paint as far as possible, while keeping the density of colour. When the undercoat is completely dry, after about 16–20 hours, rub down lightly, clean with a tack cloth, and apply the top coat.

Wood
Use a brush slightly narrower than the area to be painted. Hold the brush in a flexible position. The movement of the brush is controlled by the wrist and hand

and should be relaxed. Painting of detailed features such as beading requires the firm control of the forefinger, second finger and thumb. Any grip in painting should be relaxed, or the movement will be tiring and lead to fatigue.

Use of brushes
If you are using a new brush, first brush the bristles against the palm of your hand to remove any stray bristles or dust. Charge the brush by dipping the bristles into the paint for two-thirds of their length. Touch the bristles lightly against the side of the kettle to remove excess paint. After this initial dipping, it should not be necessary to dip the bristles more than a third of their length into the paint.

There are a number of aids to prevent the brush accidentally falling into the tin, from a magnetic device which fits on the side of the tin and is obtainable commercially, to a piece of string stretched across the top of the tin on which to rest the brush.

Work over an area of about 300mm² at a time. Brush firmly, but lightly, over the area. Brush up and down, then diagonally and finally across the grain to produce an even spread.

To obtain a clean, smooth finish 'lay off' across the grain one brush width at a time. If painting the stile of a door lay off with a downward stroke. Do not start to lay off in the centre of the area as brush marks will be left.

Work in a continuous sequence, and do not let one area become too dry before starting the next. If this happens the paint will not blend and a demarcation line will show. Painting in awkward areas such as corners is dealt with by jabbing the paint

into the corner with the tip of the brush and then brushing the paint downwards.

It is important to work in a good light. Natural light is by far the best working light. Artificial light can cast shadows, particularly when using white gloss paint, since thin patches may be left which spoil the finished effect. If work has to be done under artificial light, use the best light available.

With many modern paints, brush marks will disappear when the paint dries.

While it is a great temptation to use one thick coat of paint, it is not wise as the paint is likely to run or 'curtain' and look unsightly. Two thinner coats give a better finish. Two topcoats are essential for external use, to give adequate protection.

Gloss topcoat is stiffer than undercoat and needs to be applied firmly. Most types of gloss paint take three to six hours to dry but will not dry completely for up to 24 hours.

Gelled (thixotropic) paints are used straight from the tin. The paint is only stirred if it is to be applied with a roller or has been stored for some time and a layer of oil has formed on the surface. When using a roller, stir the paint until it is really fluid before pouring it into a paint tray. If painting in the conventional way, stir up paint that has separated, replace the lid and allow to re-gell.

Gell paints have a good covering or obliterating quality. One coat is equivalent to one thin undercoat and one top coat of the conventional paint. Gell paint is applied and laid off in the same way as gloss paint. Less movement is required than when brushing gloss paint but the brush needs to be charged more frequently.

Old paint should be strained; discarded stocking makes a useful mesh for this

Piece of string stretched over top of a paint kettle provides rest for brush

Use masking tape or a piece of card to keep as much paint as possible off the glass

Using a rust inhibitor on a metal surface, then apply a metal primer

Paint one area in one movement and lay off immediately. Brush from left to right, then right to left in a slightly downwards movement. Without applying any more paint, brush up and down. This fourway movement gives an even spread of paint. Paint one area at a time, working towards edges and the wet edge. When painting stiles or panels, work towards the edge and lay off with a smaller brush.

Doors
First, remove window catches, stays, door handles and letter boxes. Once splashed with paint these are often difficult to clean.

Doors should be painted in a definite sequence. On conventional panelled doors first paint the mouldings and then the panelled area. The top panel should be painted first, avoiding the door edges and glazing beading. Then paint the lower panel or panels.

The wider sections dividing the panels are called stiles. These are painted next, again working down the door. The top, middle or lock rail, and the bottom rail are then painted in that order. Paint the inner panels then the stiles on each side.

The edge of the door showing from the painted side should then be painted in the same colour. If the door opens to the exterior the top and, if possible, the bottom edges as well should be painted to make the timber both weatherproof and waterproof. Water may collect under the door and, through capillary action, be absorbed into the wood which may cause the paint eventually to peel off.

Next, paint the architrave. This order of work helps to give an even coat and cuts down the risk of paint runs and visible lines of demarcation.

Flush doors present a large area which it is difficult to paint in one section. Divide the door horizontally, into three equal sections.

Using a 75mm brush, start in the top left hand corner of the door. First, paint a vertical strip, about 450mm wide, then paint another 450mm strip, parallel with the first. Cross brush the two strips evenly into each other and then lay off the paint vertically. This pattern is repeated for the entire door, section by section. Once the three sections are painted, finishing is completed by brushing lightly upwards and downwards to join the sections.

This method requires quick careful work, particularly with some of the quick-drying paints. Once started, the door must be completed in one operation.

Casement Windows
Windows should also be painted systematically. Casement windows may be fixed, or consist of a combination of fixed windows and windows that swing open or out. The closing surfaces of the opening windows should not be painted too thickly as this may cause difficulty in closing. This is most important on metal window frames.

Paint the least accessible parts first. Start with the glazing bead, then open the window and paint the top and bottom bar of the window, then the sides of the frame. The hinged upper surface should be painted at the same time as the top bar. Paint the inner faces of the surround to the frame next. Large, opening casement windows are similarly painted.

If the fanlight or long casement window is fixed, paint the glazing beads first, and then the part of the frame facing into the room. Paint the edges, top, bottom and sides, the horizontal bars, the vertical bars and the sill in that order.

When painting windows, use masking tape or a piece of card to keep as much paint as possible off the glass. The glazing putty should be covered with paint, especially on metal frames where moisture may seep between the putty and the frames, causing corrosion. Take the paint to the edge of the glass. If the paint dries on to the glass, use a paint scraper to remove the excess paint.

Sash windows
Start painting with the window closed. Paint the outer sash glazing beads at the top, bottom and sides. Then paint the side frame faces. Next, paint the parting beads but do not apply the paint too thickly. Open the sash and slide it down a little. Next paint the top bar, then slide the inner sash up and paint the lower bar beneath it.

Paint the inner sash in the same sequence as the outer sash, beginning with the beads. Complete the painting sequence as for a casement window. When painting the inner frame surround, first paint the outer mouldings then the upper and lower faces and then the two side faces. Finally, paint the sill.

When decorating a room first paint the skirting and picture rails. Make quite sure they are clean and dust-free and paint the top edge first. Take care not to brush the paint out too hard as the paint covering on the outer curve or edge of the moulding may work thin.

Metal
Metal window and door frames should be coated with metal primer. Before priming, make absolutely certain that all rust is removed and apply a rust inhibitor if necessary. Badly affected surfaces should be rubbed down first with a wire brush, to remove loose rust.

The choice of finishing coat is optional but as this is a vulnerable area a hard gloss paint would give good protection. Metal window frames and doors need to be maintained carefully and regularly. The protective coat should not be too porous. Alkyd undercoats and gloss paints are suitable.

If used externally, lead and copper are rarely painted. Internal plumbing pipes are often painted to improve appearance. After rubbing down with wet-and-dry abrasive paper, wipe down with white spirit to remove metal dust which can be poisonous. Lead pipes and gutterings can be painted with bituminous paint which imparts a rubberized protective surface.

Iron gates and railings should be rubbed down and cleaned off with white spirit. Do not wash them down before painting as water may be lodged in crevices and lead to fresh rusting.

Paint finishes are often marred by faults in technique, poor surfaces, inadequate or incorrect preparation. Recognizing the likely flaws in painting, described in this section's glossary of faults, will help you to achieve better results. It is also essential to choose the right paint for the work in hand.

A lid should be replaced firmly on a paint tin, or a skin may form. Use the foot or a block of wood to exert an even pressure to shut the tin. Avoid distorting the lid, or air may enter and skin will form. All paint should be kept airtight, to prevent skinning.

Bristles should always be cleaned thoroughly. If you have been using an oil-based paint, white spirit or a proprietary brush cleaner will be satisfactory. Paraffin can be used, but take care to see that the bristles are completely paraffin-free, since this, left in the bristles, could slow down the drying time of future paintwork.

If you are merely stopping work overnight, the brushes may be stood in white spirit. A word of warning—do not let the brush rest on the bristle tips. Sediment will collect at the bottom of the kettle and clog the bristles.

Terms used in painting

Cutting in
Cutting in is the technique of painting up to an adjoining surface. This is done where walls of different colours meet, at the edges of cupboards or round window frames and doors. To achieve a straight edge, use a 25mm brush in which the bristles are worn at an angle, or a special, angled 'cutting-in' brush. Charge the brush with paint but do not overload it. Remove excess paint by touching the bristles lightly against the side of the container.

Draw the brush down in one continuous movement, steadying the heel of the hand against the clear surface. Masking tape can be used to prevent paint from spreading on to an adjacent surface, but remove it before the paint has dried.

Laying off
Apply paint in one direction with carefully controlled strokes, lifting the brush gently at the end of the stroke. You should not need to recharge the brush during this, though sometimes a little extra paint on the brush may aid the laying off. Laying off helps to avoid brush marks, to achieve an even flow, and to eliminate runs or curtaining on the surface.

Wet edge
The wet edge is the furthest edge of the area being painted. When the next section is painted, the two edges are merged together, without dragging, to avoid a demarcation line. Quick-drying paints restrict the amount of paint that can be applied at one time. If the paint is fast drying, do not work to a wet edge. Apply the first coat in one direction; the next in the other direction. Work across the grain for the first coat, and with the grain for the second.

Common faults

Bittiness
Small pimples on the surface caused by dust or particles of paint skin in the finish coat. Rub down with fine glass-paper and apply a further coat of fresh paint.

Bleaching

The premature fading of new paint caused by fumes which attack ultramarine. The cure is to remove the source of the fumes or change the colour. Alkali salts, merging through new plaster, also cause bleaching. Use an alkali-resistant paint to allow the plaster to 'breathe'.

Bleeding

This occurs when a sub-layer of paint bleeds through the surface, causing staining of the top-coat. This may be caused by the reaction of the constituents of old paint with new, if, for example, oil-based paint is applied over a bituminous paint. To treat, rub down, apply a layer of stop-tar knotting, followed by a coat of aluminium primer, then repaint. Another cause is where inks used in a wallpaper design bleed through a covering paint. Strip the wallpaper to the plaster and repaint.

Blistering

Small 'blisters' on the paint surface are caused by moisture which prevents adhesion between old and new paint layers.

This may be caused by painting on a moist surface, or in moist conditions, and can be remedied by scraping off the blistering and repainting in dry circumstances.

It is also caused by seepage of water along the grain of the wood from other areas. Remedy by sealing the weak spots. If caused by water seepage from poorly primed woodwork, adjacent to brickwork, seal the gaps between wall and frame with a mastic.

Blistering on new timber, painted for the first time, is treated by stripping the paint surface, glasspapering smooth and allowing the timber to dry out thoroughly before repainting.

Blistering may also be caused by resinous knots. Apply a patent knotting or cut out the knots, prime the holes, fill with hard-stopping, rub down, prime and repaint.

Blooming

This is a whitish haze on the paint, or, more often, varnished surface, caused by a damp atmosphere or draught during drying. The remedy is to rub down with glasspaper and repaint in dry conditions. Blooming, after drying, is caused by a damp atmosphere. Rub down with a chamois leather. If this does not help, rub down with a mixture of raw linseed oil and vinegar.

Brush marks

Brush marks, which show in the form of ribs in the finished paint, may be caused by brushing out after the paint has started to dry or show through from an inadequately prepared undercoat. In both cases, rub down the surface and apply a new finish.

Chalking

This is a white, powdery film on the surface, which powders as the paint film wears away, leaving the dry pigment. It can be rubbed down with a damp cloth and repainted. Chalking may also be caused by the porosity of the surface. Brush down, wash clean and apply an undercoating, adding a little linseed oil.

Crazing, cracking

The formation of fine hair cracks or fissures in the paint surface. There are four causes:

● Where a hard-drying paint has been used on a wet or oily undercoat;
● Through painting over a sized surface;
● As a result of using quick-drying cellulose paint over an oil-based undercoat;
● Where a hard-drying paint was applied over a bituminous paint.

Minor blemishes can be cured by gently rubbing down the surface and repainting. Badly affected surfaces should be stripped to the bare wood, re-prepared and repainted.

Cheesiness

This is an unstable surface condition, caused by alkaline salts affecting the paint

surface. It can be remedied by stripping back the paint completely then applying an porous paint, unless the surface is completely dry. It is also caused by too much linseed oil in the undercoat. The remedy is to strip the coats and repaint.

Cissing

This generally occurs on varnished surfaces in the form of circular patches, drawn away from paint surfaces. It is caused by painting over a waxy surface; or painting an old varnish that has not been roughened. In both cases, clean the surfaces with white spirit, and use abrasive paper to flatten the surface before repainting.

Efflorescence

This is caused by alkaline salts, in the plaster or walls, reaching the surface and producing a white crystalline deposit. The remedy is to give the surface adequate time to dry out and then to apply an alkali-resistant primer and porous paint. Non-permeable decoration should be left until the wall has dried out.

Fatty-edge

A fatty-edge occurs where two paint coats, painted at different times, meet at an angled edge. The ridges must be rubbed down before repainting the whole surface.

Flaking

Flaking is where paint falls away from the surface. It is often caused where there is dirt or moisture in the undercoat, size on the surface or where old paint has been inadequately removed. This may be remedied by stripping off the coat, cleaning and repainting in dry conditions.

Another cause is efflorescence. Strip down, allow to dry and apply an alkali-resistant primer and paint. Apply a porous paint unless the surface is completely dry.

Paint fatigue, where paint is used in rooms subject to high condensation, may also cause flaking. The paint film expands

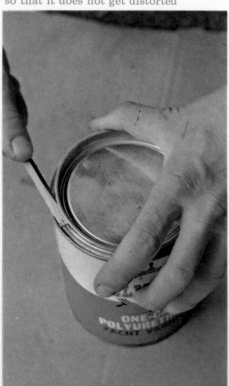

Prise the lid carefully from a pot of paint so that it does not get distorted

Lid can be replaced firmly using block of wood so that tin is properly sealed

and contracts, and may be remedied by removing old paint and repainting with a porous paint.

Corrosion on metal surfaces, and rust breaking through the paint film, is another cause. To remedy, strip down the paint, apply a rust inhibitor, prime with a metal primer and repaint.

Gelling
This occurs when stored paint turns to jelly. It is caused by frost or the addition of an unsuitable thinning agent. Paint affected in this way is useless and should be thrown away.

Grinning
This is when the undercoat shows through the finish coat. It is caused by an undercoat of an unsuitable colour being used or by changing from a contrast colour too quickly–from a dark to a light colour. The remedy is either to strip off the paint, rub down and apply the correct coloured undercoat and top coat, or rub down and apply further finishing coats.

Lifting
A condition where a new coat of paint pulls away from the surface. It is caused when the top coat has been applied to a still-wet undercoat, or where the solvent in the new coat affects the base coat.

It is possible to rub down the surface, touch in the parts that have lifted and apply a fresh finish coat.

Misses
These are gaps in the finishing coat, usually as a result of poor workmanship or through working in a poor light. The only remedy is to rub down and repaint the finish coat.

Mildew-mould-fungicide growths
These occur in damp, humid conditions. If mould appears on the surface, rub down the affected parts with a solution of one part of bleach to three parts of water, wash off and allow to dry before repainting. Repaint with fungicidal-resistant paint. Treat the underlying cause of the growth.

Orange peel
This describes a wrinkled appearance of a sprayed paint surface, caused by incorrect thinning of paint or paint applied at the wrong pressure. Treatment is to rub down and respray.

Pinholes
Pinholes are tiny holes in the paint surface and are caused by imprisoned air bubbles which expand with heat and then burst. This should be treated by rubbing down and recoating the entire surface. Where a quick-drying paint has been applied to a porous surface, the surface should be roughened and a sealer applied, followed by an undercoat and a finishing coat.

It may also be caused by oil or moisture in the air line of a spray gun. The paint coat should be removed and the surface resprayed.

Sags, runs or curtains
These are lines of paint or drips on a painted surface. There are four causes:

- A paint coat applied too thickly;
- Insufficient brushing out;
- A wet-edge left too long and starting to set before the next area is painted and the wet-edge picked up;
- Paint bristles catching on an irregularity and leaving a paint deposit.
  In all cases the surface should be rubbed down until it is smooth and a finish coat applied.

Saponification
A condition where the paint surface goes spongy. It is caused by the oil in the paint mixing with the alkaline salts present in the surface to produce a soapy solution. Treat by stripping down the paint coats and applying an alkali-resisting primer and then repaint.

Sheeriness (flashing)
Sheeriness occurs when gloss appears uneven, or there are glossy patches in a flat or eggshell finish. Five causes are:

- A surface with porous patches which has been painted over;
- Use of an unsuitable thinner which may cause uneven drying;
- Failure to keep the wet-edge when painting;
- Paint insufficiently stirred;
- Mixing resin and oil-based paints that do not 'marry'.

The remedy is to roughen the surface and apply a fresh finishing coat.

Skinning
Skin forms over paint when it is trapped in the can. Remove the skin–never attempt to stir it in–and reseal the lid of the tin tightly. A layer of white spirit can be floated over some paints to prevent skinning but care must be taken to see that the spirit does not mix with the paint.

Wrinkling
Wrinkling occurs if the paint dries too quickly. It happens where paint coat is applied too thickly; when the sun is hot or where old putty is painted.

Treat by removing all paint, rub down the bare surface, then prime, undercoat, and apply a finish coat.

Slow drying
Paint may dry slowly for several reasons:

- Painting over an undercoat that is not completely dry or using an unsuitable thinner. The coat must be stripped and repainted;
- Painting in cold or damp conditions. Allow the paint to dry, then rub down if necessary and apply a finish coat;
- Paint applied over a dirty or greasy surface. The surface must be stripped and cleaned thoroughly before repainting.

Once the brush is charged, touch lightly against side of kettle to remove excess

Laying off helps to avoid brush marks, to achieve an even flow, and to eliminate runs

Wallpaper can be a costly decorative material and to achieve a finished result of which you are justifiably proud, careful attention should be paid to the preparation of the wall surfaces. This is necessary to ensure a good base for the decorative paper. Estimating the amount of paper needed, choice of paper and the techniques of preparatory lining are important aspects of this highly popular handyman job.

Paperhanging: preparing to do a good job

When choosing wallpaper it is important to choose a paper of good quality; cheap papers are expensive in the long run as they tend to tear easily, fade and stretch. If the wall surface shows irregularities a thicker paper will cover blemishes and conceal minor defects.

The job of paper-hanging falls into three sections:

● Preparation of surfaces;

● Lining the wall;

● Final paper-hanging and finishing off.

The right tools for the job make progress smooth and the task much easier.

Preparation
Equipment needed

Two step ladders or a trestle; two scaffold boards at least 1830mm long and 230mm wide; some dust sheets, old newspaper or polythene sheeting; an old distemper brush; bucket and sponge or a coarse cloth; stripping knife; filling knife; scraper; waterproof abrasive paper, glass-paper or a hand sander.

As walls are rarely true, it is also useful to have a spirit level to check the verticals.

An 'extra' that saves time and effort is an apron, with large pockets to carry the small tools.

It will save time and muddle if the floor area is covered before work starts. Use old newspaper when stripping wallpaper, then, as the work progresses, the stripped paper can be rolled up in the newspaper and disposed of.

Polythene dust sheets are useful as the job of stripping paper is inclined to be wet and messy.

All clear

Working is easier if the space is clear. If all the furniture cannot be removed, stack it in the centre of the room and cover with a dust sheet. Roll up the carpets or cover fitted carpets with polythene dust sheets.

The room should be warm, clean and as dust-free as possible. Choose the best working light available.

Surface preparation

Good surface preparation is essential to achieve a perfect, finished job. Newly plastered wall surfaces should not be papered. The surface should be allowed to dry out for at least six months. If a decorative finish is required sooner than this, a porous paint finish, such as an emulsion, should be applied.

A prematurely papered wall will be unsatisfactory. The moisture in the plaster weakens the adhesive properties of the adhesive used and alkali salts, present in plaster, may stain the surface of the paper.

Walls that have been decorated with

emulsion or washable distemper, once the drying-out process has stopped, can be papered over. This is not possible over non-washable distemper, which should be removed before papering.

Sound surfaces

A surface should be sound. If any areas are crumbly or flaking, scrape them clean and then wash down. Finish by rubbing over with glass-paper.

Oil-based paint surfaces, which are non-porous, can be papered but the area must be rubbed first with a wet, waterproof abrasive paper. Rub down bare plaster with a coarse, damp cloth to remove any surface deposits and then coat with a weak solution of glue size if the paste to be used is water-based.

A cellulose paste requires a thinned coat of cellulose used as a size. Size is used to seal the surface and provide a smooth area on which to slide the paper.

When preparing a surface that has been previously painted with an oil-based paint, add about a handful of whiting to a basinful of size.

Filling

If an old plaster surface is cracked, the cracks must be filled before the surface is papered. Cut back the unstable plaster to a v-shape, using a scraper. Damp the area and fill with a non-shrink cellulose filler. This must be allowed to dry and then

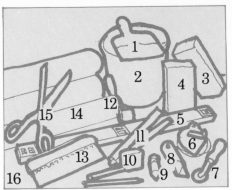

Tools and equipment

1 Paste and brush
2 Paste pail
3 Sponge
4 Adhesive
5 Spirit level
6 Chalk-o-Matic
7 Cutting wheel
8 Cutting knife
9 Plumb bob
10 Steel tape
11 Boxwood rule
12 Seam roller
13 Smoothing brush
14 Lining and wall paper
15 Shears
16 Paste table

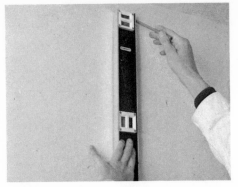

Establish and mark vertical working line. Ideally, start hanging near a window

Use paste table and apply paste evenly to paper. Paste at angle out to edges

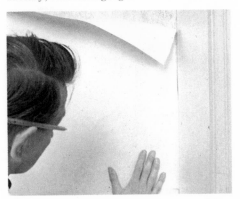

Poor wall surfaces should be covered by lining paper. Cross-line very bad walls

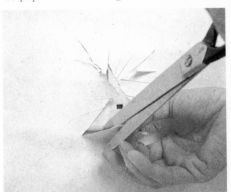

When papering round obstacles, make star-shaped cut and trim paper to fit

rubbed down lightly with glass-paper.

Where large areas of the plaster are unstable – if these sound hollow, when tapped, plaster has 'blown' and has no adhesion to the wall behind – the entire area must be hacked back and replastered. Wallpaper will not retain unstable plaster.

Let's strip
It is never wise to hang new paper over a previous covering. The two layers of adhesive may react together, causing both layers of paper to peel off. Also old joins may show through the new paper.

While there are commercially produced paper-strippers that hasten the job, most wallpaper can be removed after it has been thoroughly soaked with water. Start at the bottom of the area, and, with a distemper brush, scrub and soak the paper.

As work progresses, the area first treated should become removable. Repeated treatment may be necessary on thick papers or where adhesion is strong. The soaking-off process can be helped, on washable or particularly tough surfaces, by scoring the surface to allow the water to soak in. Over large areas it may be worth while to hire a steam-stripper.

Stripping is done with a broad-bladed stripping knife. Care should be taken not to dig the knife into the plaster as blemishes will need filling. Once the wall is stripped, wash it with a sponge and warm water and allow the area to dry. Before starting the next stage, ensure that any rough projections are rubbed down with glass-paper.

Wallpaper
A roll of wallpaper is 10m long by 520mm wide. Continental papers may be narrower and special papers are available in non-standard sizes.

A standard roll of paper will cover an area of 5m². More paper must be allowed for pattern matching and cutting in. Machine-printed papers are usually supplied ready trimmed. If not, the unprinted 'selvedge' on each side should be cut off with a trimming knife and a metal-edged ruler. These papers can usually be trimmed when purchasing as most decorating shops have a trimming machine which will trim the paper in minutes.

Estimating
When calculating the amount of paper that will be needed for an area, always allow extra to ensure that there will be enough to complete the job. For large patterns this could add 610mm to the length of each run.

With a very expensive paper, it is necessary to measure accurately the precise amount of paper that will be needed. Divide the walls into 520mm widths round the room. Count the number of widths and multiply this figure by the height of the paper required. When using this method, remember to allow for pattern matching.

An alternative is to measure the entire distance round the room, including doors and windows. While less detailed, this allows for wastage in pattern matching.

First, measure the height of the room from the skirting board to ceiling. Divide the length of a roll of paper (10m) by the height of the room. A room with a height of 2440mm will allow four lengths to a roll.

Measure the distance all round the room and divide the total figure by the width of a roll. Divide this figure by the number of lengths to give the total number of rolls needed.

Rooms with ceilings that may differ in height over the area, or stairwells, should be measured by the first method, establishing the differing heights and adding the totals to find the paper required.

Colour matching
During printing, papers of the same batch may vary slightly, in colour and tone, from roll to roll or even from one edge to the other, within a roll. Before attempting to cut any paper, unroll short lengths from each roll and look for differences in tone value of colour.

When using plain paper or one with a small overall pattern, edge-to-edge variations may be overcome by hanging every other length upside down. In this way light edges will abut light edges.

On floral patterns there may be shadowing on the underside of the pattern. These should always be placed to the bottom. A length that does vary in shade or tone should be used at a corner over a door or under a window where it will blend in and be less obvious to the eye.

Pattern matching
Pattern matching is most important. There are two types of pattern: a set pattern where the pattern is repeated horizontally; and a drop pattern in which the design runs diagonally.

The bigger the pattern sequence, the greater will be the paper wastage. Patterns which match diagonally are more extravagant than horizontal patterns.

When hanging paper from left to right the left edge of the second piece of paper should line up with the right edge of the first piece and so on along the area. The converse applies when working in the reverse direction.

It is important that a paper with a definite pattern should match. While, with fairly muted overall patterns or plain paper, work should start from a window area and proceed inwards, when using a defined pattern, on a feature such as a chimney breast, the hanging sequence

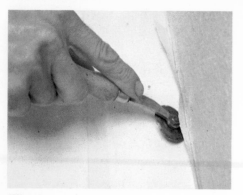

Wheel cutter has advantage of trimming paper closely to the contours of walls

Cut paper slightly longer than needed. With patterns, match 'repeat' carefully

To cut paper neatly, square up the edges and then fold down to a sharp crease

Paper can then be cut along line of the crease, using a pair of cutting shears

An alternative is to fold paper flat and slit along crease line with sharp blade

A knife and straight edge can be used. Paper can be torn neatly along steel edge

alters. The centre of the main design must start at the centre of the chimney breast or focal feature to prevent the room looking out of balance.

Cutting

Cutting a plain, striped or textured paper presents no problems of pattern matching. Cut sufficient lengths to paper at least half the room. (Some people advocate cutting all the lengths, including shorter lengths to go over doors, fireplaces and over and under windows.) When cutting each length, allow between 50mm and 75mm at each end for trimming.

A paper with a definite pattern needs cutting carefully. Place a length of paper, design upright, on the paste table and find the main motif or pattern. Cut the paper 75mm above this pattern, measure the length required and then add on an extra 75mm at the bottom. This gives the standard pattern drop.

Move this paper across the table, unroll the paper again and match up the next length to be cut. If the pattern has a big 'drop' there will be some wastage. It may be more economical to take another roll and match the next length from that, taking alternate lengths from two rolls. Manufacturers normally give guidance on the particular pattern drop for each design.

Adhesives

It is important to use the adhesive specified by the manufacturer, for the type of wall covering to be used. Paste should be mixed exactly as specified and used while it is still fresh. Generally, the thicker the paper the thicker the paste.

There are two main types of paste:

starch flour paste, which is mixed with hot or cold water; or water-soluble cellulosé paste. Tub paste, sold in containers, comes into the latter category and is thinned with cold water. Cellulose pastes are easier to use and if accidentally spilt on the paper surface, will dry out without marking.

Unless you are using a vinyl paper or special wall-covering material, the paste should be allowed to soak in. The time allowed for this, as a general guide line, is the time taken to repeat the pasting sequence with the next length of paper.

While starch flour or cellulose pastes are suitable for most normal papers, these should not be used in kitchens or bathrooms.

In kitchens and bathrooms, where there may be high condensation, vinyls and washable papers, which have an impervious or nearly impervious finish, should be hung with a fungicidal paste. There are various heavy-duty fungicidal pastes available.

Tools
Paper-hanging

The following equipment is needed: A bucket, a plum bob or long spirit level, a pasting brush, a sponge, a stripping knife, a trimming knife, a boxwood seam roller, a pair of 305mm long scissors or paper-hanger's shears at least 255mm long, a steel straight edge, a sharp pencil and a smoothing brush.

Other items needed: A paste table and access equipment—either a trestle or two step ladders and a suitable plank to act as a catwalk.

Lining paper

To achieve a high-quality surface finish

when hanging wallpaper, it is important to use lining paper. This is available in varying weights, and qualities, and provides an even surface of the correct porosity for maximum adhesion.

On good wall surfaces, a lightweight paper will be satisfactory. If the surface is uneven, a thicker lining paper will help to cover minor blemishes and irregularities in the plaster surface. When using a thick wallpaper, choose a corresponding lining paper. Lining paper can be used to line a porous wall.

When used purely as an under-paper, lining paper should be laid horizontally so that at no time will the joins align with the vertical joins of the decorative paper. The joins should be butt-jointed. Lining paper is pasted and concertina-folded before hanging.

Wall surfaces that are badly covered with hairline cracks should be lined twice, using heavy brown or white glazed lining paper. The first lining paper is applied horizontally, the second vertically.

Where cross lining, with long lengths of paper, lay the beginning of the length on the pasting table, leaving the rest to hang over one edge. Paste the exposed length carefully, ensuring that all the paper is covered to within 25mm of the end.

Take the end and fold back the paper, with paste to paste, making a fold or pleat of about 380mm in length. Continue pasting and folding in the same way until the entire length is pasted and folded into a 'concertina'.

Starting at one end of the room, hold the concertina section in one hand and, releasing a fold at a time, apply the lining paper with a roller or brush to smooth it out. All joins should be butt-jointed and excess paper at ceilings and skirtings trimmed.

There is more to paperhanging than meets the eye if you wish to achieve first-class results. Care at every stage of work, using a few sound rules, is the recipe for success. 'Awkward' areas, such as reveals, chimney breasts and papering around fittings may seem a problem, but, tackled systematically, are not necessarily difficult.

The art of paperhanging

Pasting

Stand the pasting table near the light source. Good light is important when checking pattern matching, measuring and ensuring an even spread of paste.

A plastic bucket is a suitable paste container. A piece of string, stretched tautly between the handle sockets, will be useful for wiping surplus paste from the brush.

When you have measured the length of the drop, cut, in one operation, several strips of the same length; this will save you time. Use a pair of scissors or a metal straight-edge and knife, or tear the paper along the straight-edge. This gives a neat, quick, accurate cut.

Paperhanging

Place the first length of paper, pattern side down, on the paste table. Line up the far end of the paper with the end of the table, allowing a slight overlap. At the other end, let the excess paper fall on to the floor.

Dip the paste brush into the adhesive until the paste is one third of the way up the bristles, wipe it against the string and start pasting, working from the centre of the paper outwards to the far edge.

Ensure that the paste is spread evenly. Never brush in from the edges as the paste will seep under the paper and on to the patterned surface.

Next, move the paper towards the near edge of the table and brush the paste towards you. Half the length is now pasted. Take hold of the pasted end of the paper and loop it over to the centre, paste to paste, making sure the top and bottom edges match. Do not fold in a crease which will mark the paper.

Move the folded loop along the table so that the loop overhangs the end. Apply paste to the other section in the same way. When this is completed, loop this end over to the centre so that the two looped edges meet.

Checking verticals

Start working at a window area. Take a point about 900mm from the window and mark in a vertical line. Use a chalked plumb-bob or vertical spirit level to mark the vertical from ceiling or picture rail height to the skirting.

Hold the bob firmly in one hand and 'twang' the chalked string so that it marks the wall, or use the level as a straight edge and pencil in the line. This marking should be repeated at every corner of the room.

Begin work at one side of the window, dividing the room into two sections. Hang the paper in sequence on both sides of the room, working towards the door. The advantage of this method is that joins and overlaps that occur will be in shadow and not so obvious to the eye.

This hanging sequence is suitable for plain or overall patterned wall coverings. Where a bold motif is used, the paper should first be applied to room features, such as chimney breasts and alcoves.

Hanging technique

Lift the looped, pasted paper over one arm and carry it to the wall. With the pasted inner side facing the wall, offer the top end to the wall at the junction of the wall and ceiling or picture rail.

Allowing about 50mm overlap at the top, slide the paper into position. Line it up with the chalk line, marking the perpendicular. Supporting the rest of the paper with the knee, brush down the centre of the paper and then outwards towards the edges to push out any entrapped air.

Open out the bottom loop and smooth this into position, using a similar brushing sequence – leaving a 50mm overlap at the skirting edge.

Trimming

With the back of the shears, press the paper into the angle between ceiling or picture rail and wall to ensure a neat fit. This will give a crease line at the point of trimming.

Gently pull the paper away from the wall and, from the back, cut away the surplus along this line, then push back the paper; a similar trimming method is used at the skirting edge.

If the paper appears wrinkled, this means the air has not been brushed out.

Peel the paper back gently, re-position and brush out that section. Any surplus paste on skirting or picture rails should be wiped off.

Butt joints

Butt joints should be used when hanging paper. The two edges should meet exactly. This is done by brushing the side of the piece of paper being hung into line with the last piece of paper. When the paper has been hung for ten minutes gently roll the seams with a boxwood roller.

Small or awkwardly shaped pieces of paper, needed for filling in odd widths, can be measured and cut on the flat surface of the paste table.

Corners

There are two types of corners to be papered:

● A projecting corner
● An inner corner.

Corners are not difficult to paper but do not attempt to hang a whole width round or into the corner. Irregular walls will almost certainly give an unsightly result.

Projecting corners

Measure the distance between the last full length hung and the corner, adding 25mm to this measurement. Cut off the paper, making sure that the edge is cut straight.

Hang the wider part of the length first, trim top and bottom and then position the overlap trim and brush out. This overlap will butt joint to the remainder of the length, which is hung next.

After pasting, loosely fold one end of the sheet of paper into the middle »

Similarly fold in half way from other end. Paper can now be taken to wall and hung »

Unroll top half of fold and support the paper with a foot while you position it »

Brush paper well into the wall at both the ceiling and at the skirting level »

Back of shears can be used to mark the cutting line at ceiling and at skirting »

Butt second length to first. Allow top and bottom overlap; check pattern match »

Make joints above a door or window where it is less obtrusive on pattern join »

Cut in around light fittings and trim; Plate can be removed to aid neatness »

At window, paper into vertical reveal. Space above is filled with matched piece »

Inner corners

Inner corners can be treated in two ways. One is to offer the paper to the corner, and mark the position of the corner crease with the back of the shears. Cut the paper along this line; paste the two sections and draw together to make a butt joint.

In the second method, measure the distance between the last complete length and the corner, adding a 25mm overlap. Mark the next length to be hung. Cut off the excess and hang the first piece of paper so that the overlap turns the corner; trim top and bottom. Hang the remainder of the length to match the pattern and to be perpendicular.

In all cases, the paper should be pasted before cutting to fit round or into corners. The only exception is when using pre-pasted papers. These should be cut before the paste is activated.

Door frames

A neat fit round a door is achieved in the following way. The last full width is pasted and hung, then trimmed roughly, leaving a 25mm overlap at the top and frame side edge.

Make a diagonal cut, about 6mm long, in the paper, at the top corner of the door frame. Use the smoothing brush to press the paper into the angle between the wall and the door frame. Score along the top and bottom of the length with the shears and the top and bottom of the frame.

Peel back the paper carefully, cut off excess, then press it back. On a wide opening it will be necessary to match in a short length of paper over the centre of the door.

Windows

When papering round an obstacle, such as a window, a long narrow gap is often left. Measure the length and breadth of this strip, taking the measurement of the gap from the last complete width hung to the window frame.

Place the paper, pattern uppermost, on the table and cut off a strip of the required size, adding 50mm to the length, to allow for pattern matching.

Paste the paper and butt-joint it to the last piece of hung paper. Excess paper at the trim should be cut off and the paper pushed into place. To camouflage the joins at top and bottom, tear off the excess paper to give a feathered edge and gently brush the paper in.

Light fittings

Before papering round any light fitting, such as a switch, it is wise to turn off the electricity at the mains.

Light switches may be either flush or projecting. Unless the fitting cover is removed, paper over a flush switch. Use scissors to make a hole in the centre of the switch position and cut diagonal lines beyond each corner. Crease the paper, on all four sides, with the back of the shears, and trim off the excess. Press the paper into position.

With a projecting light switch, hang the paper over the switch; this will cause a bulge in the paper, marking the outline of the switch. Next, make a small hole in the centre of the switch area, then peel back the paper.

Cut vertically and diagonally; make each cut about twice the length and radius of the fitting. Replace the paper, and crease round the fitting, peel the petal-like strips back gently again, and cut round these marks. Finally, press the paper back into position round the fitting.

Chimney breasts

A paper with a bold pattern should be hung centrally on a chimney breast. The centre of a pattern in wallpaper will either be on the paper edge or somewhere within the width of the pattern. Measure to find the central position of the chimney breast, then mark in the vertical.

Where the pattern is on the edge of a length, paste the paper then hang it with the pattern centre, flush with the vertical. Trim top and bottom and hang the second length on the other side of the centre line.

If the pattern centre is not on the paper edge, the method of hanging is slightly different. Mark in the centre vertical on the chimney breast, then measure on the paper the distance between the pattern centre and the left-hand edge of the paper.

Transfer that measurement to the chimney breast, and mark in the new vertical the measured distance on the left of the centre line.

The first piece of paper is hung to the right of this line. Butt-joint the second piece to the left of the line, flush with the first length.

Recessed areas

A bay window which presents a recessed area is dealt with when the wall above is papered. Do not attempt to fold the whole paper width round the corner, into the reveal; separate cut pieces will be needed.

There are two ways to paper a reveal: either outwards from the reveal or inwards. This depends on whether work is progressively towards or away from the reveal.

In working outwards from the reveal, measure, in one operation, from the inner edge of the reveal and round the corner.

Allow for trimming if the uprights are not true. Align the outer edge of a length

Hold paper with one hand and untuck the bottom fold and smooth down into place

Hang paper to vertical line on wall. Slide it finally into place to adjust

Brush paper outwards at angle to remove air bubbles; check correct alignment

After brushing out and trimming, smooth the joints flush with the seam roller

When hanging paper round door, cut out wedge so that paper can be fitted

Paper can then be trimmed into the architrave with shears or the cutting wheel

Leave gap and paper into the top of the reveal next to this unpapered section

Tear in trimmed piece of paper, 6mm above angle, to disguise line of join

Similarly, tear in around projections, such as the edges of window sills

of paper vertically and mark a working line down the wall.

Paste and hang the length, then cut the paper to the depth of the reveal, allowing about 6mm above. Smooth the paper into the reveal and trim the vertical edge as necessary.

A slight overlap will be left at the top of the reveal. Trim carefully round window sills or boards and the bottom horizontal edge of the reveal.

When working inwards, hang the paper in the normal way, butt-jointed to the adjacent section. Cut the top and bottom of the paper so that the paper butts into the reveal, where the vertical edge can be trimmed. Again, allow a 6mm gap above the reveal.

The procedure, whether working inwards or outwards, is the same for the next section. Cut a further length, making sure that any pattern matches, to fit to the length of the wall drop and reveal, and allow for trimming.

Hang this vertically and smooth into the reveal. Finally, cut an oversize piece of wallpaper to fill the gap alongside. Trim this to fit accurately into the reveal but overlapping at the front by 25mm.

Tear the overlap edge carefully; this will leave a ragged edge and conceal the join when pasted into position. Check carefully that the pattern is matched when cutting the infill piece.

Since the point above a door or window is often unobtrusive, any pattern disparity, caused by falling short of a complete length or width, may occur here.

Stair wells

Papering a stair well should logically start at the light source – either the front door or a stair-well window. This presents problems when the join of the stair-well

wall and the head wall, which returns across the stairs, is reached.

Cutting this length would be difficult and the length of paper required would be unwieldy to handle. Therefore, start on the stair-well wall adjacent to the head wall.

Mark the vertical line on the stair-well wall. Hang the first length of paper, allowing a 50mm overlap on to the head wall. This will give room for adjustment if the wall is not true. A 50mm overlap should be allowed at the top and bottom of the length for trimming.

At the stair edge it may be a good idea to trim the paper roughly at the cutting angle, to prevent the weight of paper pulling at the pasted length and causing stretching.

As this is a long length of paper the normal double-looping method of folding paper will not do. Paste and fold as for lining paper in concertina form.

Hanging a long length is a two-handed job as the weight of the paper below requires support. If allowed to drop, it may tear or stretch.

The papering sequence radiates out from the first length. Work towards the landing, up the stairs, across the head wall, across the stairs and along the landing wall, keeping to the vertical.

Wallpaper repairs

It is possible to effect minor repairs to wallpaper.

On ordinary wallpaper an 'invisible' patch can be applied. A piece of matching paper cut larger than the damaged paper area will be needed. To soften the edges of the repair patch tear round them.

Check to see that the patch matches the surrounding pattern exactly. Peel back about 3mm of the backing paper

from the edges of the patch. Tear off the loose damaged paper.

Paste and insert the patch, matching the pattern all round. When the paste has started to dry, use the seam roller to smooth out from the centre to the edges.

On some wall coverings, such as hessian or vinyl, it is not possible to tear a patch. A patch repair, which is less unobtrusive than the previous method, can be applied in the following way:

Cut a matching repair patch larger than the damaged area. Place this over the damaged paper and cut a square through both pieces of paper. Remove the old paper, paste and insert the repair patch. Again, use the roller.

If the paper is not damaged, but there is bubbling of the surface, caused by incomplete adhesion or the wrong type of glue, it is possible to repair isolated areas by one of the two following methods.

Cutting or injecting

This is necessary when entrapped air has left a bubble and the paper can no longer be lifted. Make horizontal and vertical cuts, with a sharp knife, at the position of the bubble. Take the cuts back a little further than the bubble area.

Ease the four corners back and repaste, allowing the paste to soak in. After soaking, press the flaps gently back into position and roll lightly.

The other method is to inject the bubble with fresh paste, using a syringe. Let the paste soak in, then roll lightly.

Uneven adhesion at joins can be remedied by peeling back the section that has failed to adhere and applying a thin film of multi-purpose adhesive. Press the edge back into place and roll lightly with the seam roller.

Wallpaper is an attractive wall covering. Modern design, colour and texture are so varied that it is often difficult to make a final choice. There are wall coverings to complement any décor scheme and finishes designed to wear well in a variety of situations.

Vinyl

Vinyl paper is a paper treated with a thin coat of PVC. The PVC coating provides toughness, durability and easy-clean properties. Vinyl papers can be lightly scrubbed, without affecting the surface.

Vinyl-coated papers are available in a wide range of colours and designs. Surface effects vary from high sheen to matt or metallic finishes.

As vinyl is such a tough paper, it is suitable for use in heavy-wear areas such as bathrooms, kitchens, hallways and children's rooms.

Vinyl covering should be hung on dry, non-porous surfaces. On porous surfaces, a suitable sealant should be applied before papering. The wall should be lined and the vinyl hung, using anti-fungicidal paste.

Some vinyl papers are pre-pasted. If using a pre-pasted covering, apply a coat of fungicidal solution to the plaster surface before starting to paper.

The method of hanging vinyl paper varies from that used to hang standard papers. As the paste is applied, the backing paper immediately soaks it up. No pre-soaking of paper is necessary and hanging can start straight away.

It is important to paste right to the edge of each length. If there is an overlap the paper cannot be stuck down with a heavy-duty-adhesive; a PVA adhesive has to be used.

A neater way is to cut away the surplus paper overlap, using a steel straight-edge and a trimming knife. Place the straight-edge over the centre of the overlap and cut through. Remove the cut paper, apply a little more paste and brush the vinyl back into position. This should give a good butt joint.

Washable wallpapers

These are coated with a thin, transparent resin and are suitable for use in kitchens and bathrooms where there is, at times, a lot of steam. Where washable papers are used in kitchens or bathrooms, they should be hung with an anti-fungicidal paste as the finish cover is impervious.

In any other situation, starch flour glue, hot- or cold-water paste, or tub glue can be used. There is a wide range of colours and designs, and the finish can be matt or gloss.

Removal

When removing vinyl or washable paper the impervious resin or vinyl surface must be scored to allow water to soak through to the backing paper.

One product consists of a vinyl coating applied to a specially constituted backing paper. The decorative coat can be peeled or stripped off, without soaking or using chemical strippers, leaving the backing paper, as lining paper, if wished, for the new decorative coat.

Embossed papers

Embossed papers provide an attractive textured effect that can also disguise minor blemishes. Walls should first be lined, with the paper hung horizontally, and a thick paste should be used to apply the final wall-covering. A thin, watery paste tends to soak into the backing paper, causing the two layers to stretch and pull apart.

Soak the paper with paste for a few minutes before hanging, so that it becomes supple. When hanging, apply even, but very gentle, pressure. Heavy pressure may flatten the embossed design and cause stretching.

The bristle end of a paperhanger's brush, tapped lightly on the surface, aids even adhesion. Cutting, for fitting round corners and so on, is best, done with a sharp knife against a straight-edge, rather than with shears or scissors.

Flock

Flock paper is of heavy quality and highly decorative, with a finish resembling the pile of velvet. Modern flock papers may have a vinyl finish; these do not need soaking and, once pasted, can be hung immediately.

Edges should be butt joined as it is not possible to stick the overlap with heavy-duty paste. Lapped joints can be dealt with in the same way as lapped edges on vinyl papers.

When cutting, use a straight edge and a really sharp knife, which will make cutting easier and minimize the risk of cutting the lining paper. Peel back the edge, remove the surplus paper, apply a little more paste and roll the edges back in. Wipe off surface adhesive with a sponge.

A roller covered with rubber, cloth, baize or chamois leather should be used on flock paper.

Ingrain or woodchip paper

Ingrain or woodchip paper is made from high-grade wood pulp. To give a woody or oatmeal effect, minute particles of wood chips are added to the pulp. This paper is very versatile and can be used to add texture to wall finishes. Some ingrain or woodchip is sold pre-decorated.

This is suitable for walls that have irregularities in the plaster. When painted, ingrain papers have an impervious surface, so should be hung using a heavy-duty, anti-fungicidal paste. Wood textured paper is useful for papering ceilings.

Fabric wall coverings

Fabric wall coverings, such as hessian, which is made from jute, should not be hung on newly plastered walls. Allow the wall to dry out for at least six months. After this, rub down the surface with medium glasspaper and apply an alkali-resistant primer.

A paint roller is a suitable medium for applying the adhesive for hessian to wall

Overlap by 25mm; use sharp blade with straight edge to cut through both layers

Edges are then peeled back and the surplus strips are simply pulled away

Before pushing edges back into place, brush fresh adhesive beneath the join

This breakfast room shows the finished surface with neat seams.

Old plaster should be washed down, starting at skirting level, allowed to dry and then roughened, to provide a good key. Any cracks should be filled.

Unbacked fabric

Before hanging an unbacked fabric, the walls should be lined. Use a lining paper of the same colour as the top cover, then if joins do pull apart, the gaps will be less noticeable.

Fabric wall coverings are best applied with the adhesive recommended by the manufacturer. Generally, backed fabrics are hung with a heavy-duty wallpaper paste, while with unbacked fabrics, a thick PVA or latex-based adhesive is used.

Paste is generally applied to the wall unless the fabric has a backing sheet.

Paper-backed hessian

Paper-backed hessian is more expensive but is easier to hang as the backing prevents stretching and wrinkling.

Paste can be applied to this but ensure that the fabric is not made too wet. Use a felt-covered roller to smooth out each length, taking care not to press too hard Heavy pressure will stretch the fabric and may cause adhesive seepage from the joins.

Hessians

Hessian coverings provide a range of coloured or neutral, textured wall effects. Backed or unbacked fabric can be painted with either gloss or emulsion paint.

Fabrics

Fabric coverings may have slight variations in the weave. Make sure that the weave matches, as well as possible, at eye level in the room.

Equipment

Tools required are the same as for normal paper-hanging, plus a foam-roller and a rubber roller.

Techniques
Fabric

Good preparation of the wall surface is needed. Lining the wall is worth the extra trouble and is essential if an unbacked fabric cover is to be used. Use scissors or a sharp knife against a steel straight-edge, to cut the fabric. Allow, in the cutting, for trimming and shrinkage.

Starting from a corner, measure the fabric width, and chalk mark on the wall a vertical line 25mm less than the width of the fabric from a corner. Do this for the entire area to be covered, marking, each time, 25mm less than the fabric width.

Next, measure and cut the first length, with a 25mm overlap at top and bottom for trimming.

Apply adhesive, section by section, to the wall, using the foam roller, to within 25mm of the marked line. Hang the first length to this line so that the fabric overlaps at both top and bottom and 25mm around the corner side.

Gently pat down the fabric and then smooth with the rubber roller. Work from the centre down and outwards to make sure that no entrapped air is left to casue blistering.

Hang the next section so that it overlaps the previous by 25mm. Hang the rest of the lengths, pasting each wall section separately, leaving the overlap edges unstuck and untrimmed.

Once the paste has dried, flatten the loose edge on the join and cut through the middle of both pieces, using a straight-edge and a handyman's knife, used at a shallow angle to avoid cutting into plaster. Paste the wall immediately beneath the join and press down the fabric. Finally, trim top and bottom edges. A seam roller can be used, very carefully, to smooth the join.

Linen

Linen is made from flax and can be either backed or unbacked. As this is a thin fabric, paper-backed linen is hung in the same way as ordinary wallpaper. Adhesive is applied to the paper backing. Unbacked linen is hung on a pre-pasted wall.

Cork

Cork wall covering consists of very thin sheets of cork or cork shavings bonded to a paper backing. The warm, textured honey tone of cork is most attractive when used in a décor scheme. A PVA adhesive should be used for hanging.

Grass cloth

Grass cloth is a textured wall covering, consisting of bark and grasses held together with thread, stuck to a paper backing. When hanging, make certain of the shading as the pieces may vary quite widely in colour. The edges should be trimmed with a sharp curved blade to prevent fraying. Grass cloth is fairly difficult to hang successfully, but the lighter types are easier to hang than the heavier.

Felt

This is an attractive wall covering. It has the décor advantage of being available in a wide range of colours and in widths of up to 700mm.

When using a wide covering, such as felt, roll the length on to a batten. The batten can be suspended between two step ladders to deal with the unwieldy size. Start positioning at the skirting level, leaving untrimmed overlaps for later butt jointing.

To butt joints, the edges of the felt should be slightly 'teased' to create a less harsh line, so helping the two lengths to blend together.

Silk

Silk is an extremely elegant, but very expensive wall covering. Paper backing is essential as the adhesive used in hanging would stain the delicate fabric. The paper also gives the silk more 'body' and makes it easier to handle.

As silk wall covering is expensive and not particularly easy to work, this may be a job for the expert.

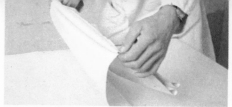

Pasted ceiling paper should be folded in concertina fashion for ease of handling

Use piece of wood or roll of paper as support, unfold and brush out the paper

Unscrew ceiling rose to facilitate the cutting in of paper; first turn off power

Brush segments of ceiling paper back around the fitting, and then refit this

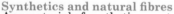

Young-set fun room or study area. Décor combines attractive, hard-wearing carpet tiles, which can be moved around, teamed with wallpaper with an aviation theme.

Synthetics and natural fibres

Any material of synthetic or natural fibres can be used to achieve a particular decorative effect. If the fabric is to be used on walls, a plastic sealant coat can be applied.

This is done commercially and has the effect of making the fabric easy to clean, yet does not alter the surface finish or affect the colour.

When using plastic-coated fabric, use an adhesive recommended by the firm that carries out the plasticizing finish.

Lincrusta

This is a heavily moulded wall-covering material composed of linseed oil and fillers, fused on to a backing paper made to simulate wood panelling, stonework, tiles, wrought iron and fabrics. Some materials are supplied coloured; others are bought plain, ready for hanging and finishing.

Lincrusta is hung in the following way: prepare the walls, size and apply lining paper with a starch glue and allow to dry; trim off the selvedge of the Lincrusta with a sharp knife against a steel straight-edge; sponge the back of the length with warm water, and allow to soak for at least 20 minutes.

Remove any excess moisture with a cloth; apply Lincrusta adhesive with a 760mm-wide brush, making sure the paste is applied right up to the edges; place in position and smooth the length into place with a rubber roller.

Work from the centre outwards towards the edges, to push out any air, and sponge off any adhesive that seeps on to the surface.

Lincrusta tiles are supplied in 11m long rolls, in 55mm² and 110mm² modules. The tiles are produced in pastel shades, and in red, black and white. They have a high gloss finish and are easily cleaned.

When fixing Lincrusta tiles, a matching border should be fixed. A small wedge or fillet of putty or paint is fixed along the top edge of the border to prevent water seeping behind the border and tiles.

Anaglypta

This is available in several weights. The papier-mâché effect is achieved by using bonded, high-quality cotton fibres in manufacture. It is an extremely durable material, highly resistant to cracking, and looks rather like plaster. It is available in high- or low-relief versions.

Low-relief, lightweight Anaglypta should be hung with a starch paste. The surface to be decorated should be clean and dust free. If there is a tendency to flaking, a sealant should be applied.

Size the wall, hang a lining paper and allow to dry. After pasting, the paper should be folded in pleats of 460mm and allowed to soak for a few minutes. Low relief is then hung in the same way as ordinary wallpaper.

Supaglypta is a very strong, high-relief version of Anaglypta. Heavier grades of Anaglypta and Supaglypta should be hung with a Dextrine paste. Soak the back of the panels until they are supple.

Dextrine paste is very firm and is best applied with a knife to the edge and contact points of the relief panels or mouldings. Panel pins may be used to secure the heavier panels until the adhesive has set.

Panels and motifs simulating plaster mouldings are available. If the Anaglypta is stuck to a firm, carefully prepared background surface, it will last for years. It can be painted with emulsion or oil-based paint.

Self-adhesive wall coverings

Self-adhesive wall coverings are more expensive than ordinary wallpaper. The adhesive is activated by putting the paper in a water tray, pasted side outwards.

Pull out the paper from the top, allowing the paper to brush against the lip of the tray; this removes excess water. Pre-pasted paper is smoothed out with a sponge and not a brush.

Other wall coverings
Cotton
Cotton wall covering can be used for badly cracked walls and ceilings.

Satin
This is a wallpaper with a highly glazed surface. When hanging, great care must be taken not to crack or scratch the surface of the paper.

Veneer
Thin wooden shavings in roll form.

Leatherette
This is a type of embossed paper, figured to give the appearance of antique leather.

Something to look up to

In many homes, the ceiling is a big 'let down'. A well-decorated ceiling provides something to look up to. You can paint or paper a ceiling. Textured finishes, panelling, polystyrene tiles or veneers are among alternatives. High ceilings can be brought into proportion with a room by means of an illuminated ceiling, which also provides a very even level of lighting.

Papering ceilings

To paper a ceiling satisfactorily, easy firm access is needed. This can be achieved by using two step ladders, linked by a long plank or scaffold board, 225mm wide, to provide a working platform.

Alternatively, adjustable trestles and suitable planks can be hired. The aim is to be able to cover the width of the room on each length, without stepping down. If properly adjusted, the platform should bring the head height to within 150mm of the ceiling.

Preparation

The ceiling surface should be prepared before papering to ensure that the surface is clean and grease free. Any cracks should be filled with a proprietary filler and smoothed down when dry.

The ceiling can be papered with a plain lining paper or a decorative embossed or woodgrain paper which will give texture and disguise any minor irregularities in the surface.

Hanging

Paper is normally hung parallel, with and away from, the main window of a room. This means that the butt-joints at each edge are in shadow and will be less obvious.

Careful appraisal of the length and width of the room should indicate the

The entire back of polystyrene tiles must be covered with a specified adhesive

Once covered with adhesive, the tiles can be easily positioned on the ceiling

A timber framework, clad with planking, enables a high ceiling to be lowered

Polystyrene ceiling veneer is rolled on once adhesive is applied to ceiling

The finished ceiling, covered with polystyrene, presents a sculptured look

best way to hang the paper for least wastage. A room 3·3m × 4·2m long will only allow two lengths to a 10m roll of paper leaving excessive wastage. Here, ignore the window as a guide line and paper along the length of the room.

It is essential to have a true right-angled guide line to work to. Using a pencil and a piece of chalked string measure one paper width, 560mm out from the corner, and make a pencil mark. Hold one end of the chalked string at this point. Mark the opposite end in the same way and 'twang' the string between the two points. The resulting chalk mark will indicate the working guide line.

Preparation of paper
Measure and cut the paper, allowing a 50mm–75mm overlap, for trimming, at each end. At this stage, cut the number of lengths that will be needed for the entire ceiling.

Start to paste the first length and fold one end over in a 300mm pleat. At the folded end, fold over a 600mm pleat and then turn back the first 300mm pleat. Continue to paste and fold in this manner until the last 600mm of paper remains. Turn this paper back 300mm to join the concertina folds.

Use a batten or a short roll of paper to support the folded paper when lifting it into position. Lay the first length of paper facing the window; subsequent lengths should face in towards the room.

Keeping the chalk line on the left side, lay the paper in the direction of movement along the platform. Unroll the first fold and position it.

Holding the concertina section close to the ceiling, brush out the first fold into final position. Move along the platform, unfolding and brushing out the paper as work progresses.

Laying each section must be completed in one continuous sequence. A commercial device for holding the folded section of paper consists of a spring-loaded pole topped with a wooden platform to hold the paper.

When the angle between ceiling and wall is reached, press the paper in firmly and score with the scissors. Gently peel the paper back and trim, leaving 6mm overlap, which is pressed back on to position on the wall.

Mark the ceiling out for the next lengths which are applied in the same way;

This illuminated ceiling consists of glass-fibre panels between a metal framework

Fix ceilingboard with plasterboard nails in staggered formation to stop cracking

Butt joints closely; then cover these with a slurry of plasterboard finish

take care to see that the edges are accurately butted and do not overlap. Work from alternate sides of the room.

When negotiating light fittings, use a similar technique as for light switches. Locate the centre of the light fitting. Make two cuts, one in the direction the paper is being laid, the other at right angles to it. Press back the flaps, score and trim, then press the paper back into position.

Frieze areas, the sections between picture rails and ceilings, are normally prepared to match the ceiling paper. Count the number of widths across the ceiling.

Measure the depth of the frieze area and add 50mm. Cut the same number of frieze pieces as widths across the ceiling. Paste and fold each section, matching the ceiling paper at the right-hand corner. Hang each piece of paper and trim the excess.

Ceiling surfaces
There are several other types of ceiling finishes. These include polystyrene tiles; veneer-sheet polystyrene in different patterns and textured effects; textured ceiling papers, wood cladding; illuminated ceilings and decorative plaster finishes.

The reasons for applying a decorative ceiling finish may be to:

● Provide a decorative surface;
● Disguise a badly cracked surface where the plaster is stable, but less than attractive;
● Conceal pipework or unattractive features;
● Reduce height in a high room;
● Add extra insulation and reduce condensation by providing a surface that is warmer to the touch;
● With illuminated ceilings or diffused recessed lighting to produce shadowless lighting or a mood lighting effect.

Illuminated ceilings
An illuminated ceiling is suitable for kitchens and bathrooms but can be used effectively in other areas of the home. It is an ideal way of lowering the height of a room and, at the same time, providing an even, shadowless light.

One system of illuminated ceiling con-

sists of a latticed framework of aluminium or plastic angle strip, inset with panels of textured translucent PVC or glass fibre.

Plastic or aluminium angle strip is obtainable in either natural finish or a variety of colours. Strip can also be painted to match a particular colour scheme.

There are three types of angle strip; 38mm × 19mm 'L' or wall angle supporting lengths, which are nailed or screwed to the walls; 38mm × 38mm main supporting tee lengths which span the width of the room and 38mm × 10mm bridging tees, which are placed at right angles to the main supporting tees.

Translucent PVC panels, 2mm thick, can be either white, or coloured to create different lighting effects. Perforated panels are made for use over cookers. All panels are easily cut with a sharp trimming knife and can be removed for easy cleaning.

Before deciding to install this type of ceiling it is important to realise that it will effectively lower the room height by at least 150mm.

This is the minimum gap required to accommodate the concealed light fittings and to allow adequate light dispersal over the area. In fact, a greater gap will allow a better light throw.

Fluorescent strip lighting is normally used with this type of ceiling as it gives an even spread of light. As the PVC panels absorb up to 50 per cent of the light produced, twice the previous light output will be needed to provide the same level of illumination.

As a rough guide, one and a half watts for each 300mm² of ceiling will give a good general light level. The level of this type of lighting effect is constant for, while it is possible to dim a fluorescent strip light, it is more expensive and more complicated to install than tungsten lighting, as a choke component and a cathode heating transformer are needed.

Before fixing the new ceiling, it is important to prepare the original ceiling area. As the light will now be reflected downwards, this area should be light reflecting.

Either paint the surface with matt white emulsion, high-gloss white paint or line it with aluminium foil. If the latter is used, an anti-fungicidal adhesive paste should be employed. A warm, still area is the ideal breeding ground for fungi.

Cover entire surface with plasterboard finish, smoothing this out thinly

Allow surface to 'go off' slightly, then dampen, using the water brush

Dampened surface is then polished smooth with flat, even sweeps of steel trowel

Estimating

To calculate the wall angle strip needed, measure the complete perimeter of the room. The length of main supporting and bridging tee angle strip depends on the size of panel used.

The main supports must be the width of the room and the number required will depend on the size of the panels and the number consequently needed to fit across the room.

The amount of bridging tee angle is calculated in the same way. These bridge either a main or a pair of supports and a wall angle along the length of the room.

To calculate the number of panels needed, establish the ceiling area and divide the panel size into this.

Before fixing the new ceiling, provision must be made for the lighting fitments. A fluorescent strip can replace a tungsten fitting.

However, as the light level needs to be even, two or more strip lights, dependent on the area to be covered, will provide better light distribution. These lights can be jointly or independently switched.

Decide on the position of the ceiling and mark this line round the walls. Use a 1m-long spirit level to ensure that the horizontal line is true. Mark round the room, a metre section at a time, to ensure complete accuracy.

Fix the 'L' or wall angle at 300mm intervals, using masonry nails, or fix by plugs and screws. Once the outside support is fixed, the rest of the ceiling can be laid into position.

Place the main supporting tee widths into position, resting, at each end, on the wall angle. Over widths greater than 3660mm, extra joining clips are used to lengthen the support strips. These clips need additional support.

Loop a piece of wire round the angle tee, at the join, securing this to a ceiling fixed hook. The bridging tees are put into position between the support tees ready to receive the panels, which slide in diagonally, and are turned and lowered into position.

Unless the panels fit exactly to the room module–which is usually not the case–the edge panels will need cutting to fit.

An attractive, but not illuminated ceiling, can be made by using acoustic ceiling tiles set in plastic angled strip with main and bridging tees used as sup-

ports as in the illuminated-ceiling system.

The framework can be set as near or as far from the original ceiling surface as required. Acoustic tiles are made from flame-resistant polystyrene. These cut down on noise level, and the brilliant white of the ceiling reflects all the available light downwards.

Ceiling tiles

There are several types of ceiling tiles such as cork, wood fibre or polystyrene, which make attractive ceiling finishes.

The ceiling surface should be prepared carefully. It should be smooth, clean and grease free. Where distemper has been used, this should be washed off thoroughly.

Large holes or any cracks should be cut back, dampened and filled with a non-shrink cellulose filler which is allowed to harden before being smoothed down.

Let's line up

The method of setting out the ceiling area is similar to that of floor tile laying. Unless you are using tiles with flanged edges, when tiling starts at one corner, fixing should start in the centre of the ceiling. Find this centre using a chalked string.

Position the chalk line from the marked points and twang the line to mark the ceiling into four sections. The point of intersection is the centre of the ceiling.

Tile adjustment

Count the number of the tiles that fit along the lines. As the tiles are unlikely to fit the module exactly, it will be necessary to cut at the outside edges of the room. If the gap is more or less than half a tile width, adjust the centre line so that there is a half-tile border.

Place a group of four tiles round the centre point, with two edges of each tile along the lines. Once these tiles are carefully aligned, further rows of tiling should be lined up accurately. Continue tiling out towards the walls.

Polystyrene

Lining a ceiling with polystyrene veneer or tiles provides a decorative surface and gives added insulation. This material, in tile form, is excellent for areas of potentially high condensation such as bathrooms and kitchens, though a wide range of textures and patterns make tiles or veneer an acceptable decorative surface for use in any room in the home.

Stick em up

When fixing polystyrene tiles apply the adhesive evenly to the back of the tile and allow it to set slightly.

Wear cotton or woollen gloves when handling polystyrene to minimise the risk of marking the surface. Position each tile and press it firmly but gently into place.

Cutting

It is unlikely that the tiles or veneer will fit the ceiling area exactly. Therefore some cutting in and trimming will be necessary at the room edges, into corners and around light fittings. Cutting round ceiling edges is done, using a scribing method similar to that for laying floor tiles.

Use a sharp trimming knife or a razor blade to cut polystyrene tiles; cut the tiles on the face side.

Flanged tiles

If flanged tiles are being used, start tiling at one corner with the flanges facing outwards. It is important to make sure that there is an even border of about 150mm around the room.

First, measure the distance across the ceiling at several points; if the distance includes an odd number of millimetres, add these equally to the border. Use a chalk line to mark the position of the border along the long and short wall.

Place the first corner tile, scribed to fit closely between the chalked marked line and the walls. Cut the tile on the scribed line, using a tenon saw. The waste side of the cut should be the grooved edge.

Veneer

Polystyrene veneer, which is supplied in rolls, is fixed in much the same way as any ceiling paper. Great care should be taken to align any pattern and ensure that the lengths are butt-jointed.

Cutting should be on the face side, using a sharp trimming knife, held against a straight edge. Veneer can also be painted to match in with decorative schemes.

Decorating

Tiles and veneer can be painted with a water-based or emulsion paint. Never use a gloss paint as this could create a potential fire hazard.

The new look for old in bathrooms

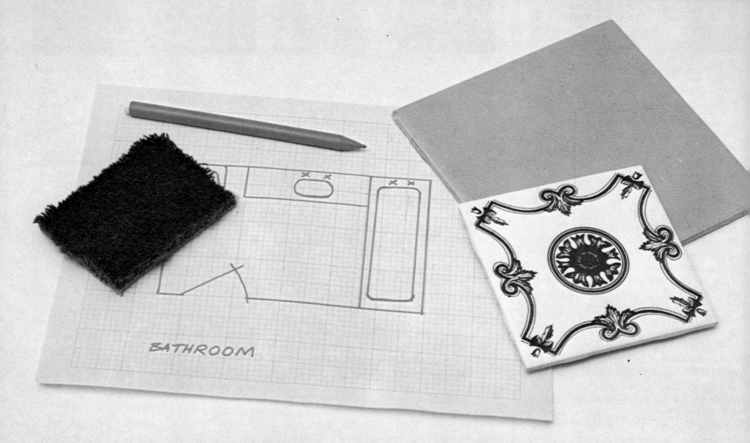

If you decide on a refit for the bathroom, careful thought is needed as to the present and future requirements of those using it. Space may be better utilized by a general rearrangement. Modern, matching colours in surfaces and appliances, and a wide range of wall and floor finishes can be used to update the bathroom and make this a décor success.

Any bathroom should be planned to suit the needs of the people using it. Requirements of, say, a young married couple, a growing family, or older and possibly infirm people, will obviously vary.

The amount of traffic, and the times of demand on hot water supplies, all need to be taken into account, for nothing disturbs the routine of a house more than a congested washing and bathing area at times of heavy demand.

The amount of equipment in an average bathroom varies but the usual minimum is a bath and a wash handbasin.

WCs may be included or be separated from the bathroom. Obviously many bathrooms are not large enough to take extra fittings such as showers, bidets or an additional wash-handbasin, but, with careful planning, a great deal can often be achieved.

The position of bathroom fitments normally depends on the siting of plumbing outlets. It may be possible to reroute pipes and waste outlets on existing systems to achieve a more workable arrangement.

Fittings are made in a wide range of colours.

Hot and cold

It is as important to take as much care when choosing taps as choosing bigger bathroom fittings. Taps should be well designed—and easy to operate and clean.

Modern taps may be made of chromed brassware, gold plated if you prefer the opulent touch, or made of tough plastic.

The upstand of the tap should stand well clear of the bath or basin. If the upstand is not high enough it is difficult to clean the tap and the area beneath.

Taps should not be mounted too near to the wall so as to pinch or bark the fingers when the tap is turned. The screw-on screw-off tap is most often used though some are foot operated.

Baths and basins

Basins are made in a wide range of shapes and sizes, in vitreous china, fireclay, enamelled sheet metal, plastic and glass-fibre. Fixings vary but basins are usually

Above: A colourful tiled arrangement in a bathroom, in which the sanitary ware, flooring and fittings all complement each other.

mounted on a matching pedestal, wall mounted, or fitted in a vanitory unit which can also provide useful storage.

A basin should fulfil certain basic requirements. It should be shaped to hold a good depth of water without wastage, enough to immerse both hands below the overflow level.

You should be able to wash your face without hitting your nose on the taps! The water should run away quickly and there should be a 'soap-sinking' deep enough to hold the soap.

Baths also vary greatly in design. They are made of enamelled cast iron, enamelled pressed steel, moulded plastics or glass-fibre. The latter materials have the advantage of being light and easy to handle.

Usually, baths are rectangular, with one end slightly sloping. Taps may be fixed at the end or the side of the bath, dependent on design. The best way to test a bath is, before buying, to lie in it and see if it is comfortable.

Most modern baths have matching side and end panels to provide a neat appearance, hide the plumbing and yet provide access where needed.

If elderly people or small children are to use the bath it is possible to fit a bath with a dipped side to allow easy access. Also an integrated hand grip is desirable. If this is not available, a wall-mounted hand grip will give safe support.

Some baths have a specially designed non-slip base. If the base is smooth, keep a rubber mat in the bath for use by the elderly or very young.

In cases where bathroom and WC are combined, it is sometimes possible to separate these two areas.

Where space is limited, the cut off could be a studded partition, decorated to match the walls, or in a bigger area a system of storage such as open shelving, cupboards or drawer units could be considered.

If the WC area is not too small, it may be possible to plumb in an additional small wash-handbasin. These can be very compact and may be recessed into the wall, surface-fixed or corner-mounted.

The 'loo'

The height of a WC is usually 410mm from the ground plus the thickness of the seat. Research has suggested that 355mm is medically a better height. In a small area, a low-level cistern may look neater and take up less head room than a high-level type.

It is desirable to locate a WC beneath a window.

You can install a slim-line cistern where space is limited. WC cisterns can be chain, lever or foot-pedal operated. On hygienic grounds, the latter is desirable.

WC pans are usually made of vitreous china or fireclay. Most seats are now made of plastic rather than wood. These are available in a wide range of colours and patterns. Padded vinyl and even heated seats are also made.

Boxing in

Pipework for baths, handbasins, showers, WCs and so on is best hidden. Try to make pipe runs neat and conceal them as much as possible. Exposed pipework can be boxed in with a simple framework and hardboard structure, but access must be left for any maintenance work that may be necessary.

Allowing for access fixing points, the covering can be painted, tiled and so on to blend with the general décor scheme.

Lighting

If the bathroom has a high ceiling, it may be possible to recess lighting above a false ceiling. Some shaving mirrors have lights incorporated. Strip lights can be concealed behind curtain pelmets or under cupboards.

All lights must be controlled by pull switches. Wall switches are illegal in bathrooms. If elderly or infirm people or small children use the bathroom, it is desirable to incorporate a low-wattage light fitting which can be left on all night.

Surfaces

All surfaces in the bathroom should be easy to clean as well as decorative. Wall surfaces are available in a choice including plain and decorative ceramic tiles, wood panelling, cork sheeting, cork tiles, washable wallpaper, laminate and paint.

Walls can be decorated with washable or waterproof wallpapers. These are hard-wearing, easily cleaned and decorative.

Cork panels or cork tiles provide attractive finishes and also possess some insulant value, are warm to the touch and help absorb sound, often a problem in the bathroom. A coating of clear polyurethane varnish will seal the cork which, particularly in panel form, may crumble and be vulnerable to small fingers.

Ceramic tiles may be plain, veined, marbled, textured or patterned, many in standard colours. It is not always necessary to use all-patterned tiles; attractive schemes can be evolved using mainly plain tiles with featured effects—such as splashbacks, bath surrounds, mosaic panels, isolated textured tiles and so on.

Laminates, plain or patterned and available in a wide range of colours, also provide pleasing and easily cleaned wall surfaces. They are also suitable for shelf coverings, cupboard facing or lining and as surrounds to vanitory units or wash handbasins.

Flooring

Bathroom floors need to satisfy a variety of conditions. They should be warm to the touch, non-slippery when wet, easily cleaned and attractive to the eye—conditions fulfilled by cork flooring. Cork tiles, sealed with polyurethane, are available in shades from dark brown to gold. Cork is easily cleaned.

Thermoplastic tiles, and vinyl sheeting

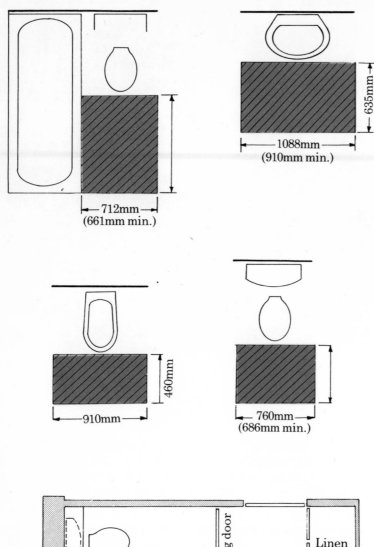

712mm
(661mm min.)

1088mm
(910mm min.)

635mm

910mm

460mm

760mm
(686mm min.)

Sliding door

Linen

Basic areas required for movement in bathroom and a compact bathroom area

are available in many colours, textures and patterns. These are also easy to clean but may be slippery when wet. Linoleum in bathrooms can also be slippery.

Nylon carpet, self-adhesive or loose-lay carpet tiles are also possible bathroom floor coverings. Loose-lay tiles have the added advantage of being easy to wash and can also be moved around to equalize wear.

Ceramic floor tiles are made to match wall tiles. The floor tiles are thicker than those for walls. Mosaic floor tiles or standard ceramic tiles should be fixed with waterproof adhesive and grouted with waterproof grouting. As ceramic tiles are cold to the touch a bathroom where they are used needs to be well heated to prevent surface condensation.

All floors should be laid on a firm, level surface. Flooring is part of the décor scheme and should complement the other fittings and furnishings.

Mirrors

Mirrors are valuable in the bathroom, particularly as an aid when shaving.

They may have plain or magnifying glass. Some mirrors have an incorporated light which helps to heat the mirror and cuts down condensation.

Lightweight mirrors, consisting of a plastic film, with a metallic coating, are not liable to condensation but scratch rather easily, and are, consequently, not suitable in bathrooms used by small children.

Mirrors can provide an added sense of dimension, particularly in the small bathroom.

Cutting condensation

As bathrooms are subject to condensation, thin polystyrene sheeting applied behind the wallpaper or panelling will help to insulate the walls, raising the touch temperature and so reduce condensation.

Emulsion paint can be used on the walls and ceilings to help prevent condensation. Ceilings may be decorated with polystyrene tiles or veneer. These materials are decorative, absorb sound and moisture and provide extra insulation.

Heating and hot water

Heating may be provided by means of a heated towel rail or clip-on rail above the radiator. Localized heating may consist of electrical radiant wall-mounted heaters.

These heaters, controlled by a pull switch, should be mounted high on the wall and well away from the bath and directed at the drying area. They must be of an enclosed pattern suitable for bathrooms.

Hot water is a vital part of the successful bathroom. This may be provided by the general domestic hot-water system or by an instantaneous hot-water heater. These heaters work by gas or electricity. When using any form of gas water heater you must have a flue outlet and adequate ventilation.

Storage

If there are children in the house cleaning materials should be kept in a locked cupboard, as should any medicines kept in the bathroom.

Bathroom cabinets may be white wood cupboards which can be painted, laminated, or supplied ready painted or finished. Cabinets may have a mirror incorporated.

Some units incorporate lighting strips, which must be of a safe pattern, and shaver points. Provision for a shaver point, of the double-insulated pattern, is desirable.

Always avoid placing shelving over baths or handbasins as heavy objects falling may cause damage.

Windows

Windows are very important. At least one fanlight window should open to allow adequate ventilation. If there is no opening window a wall or window-mounted extractor fan should be used. In a completely enclosed bathroom, a system of ducted ventilation is essential.

Windows with louvres give privacy and ventilation. Opaque decorative glass can be used. Apart from good natural lighting, adequate artificial lighting is also important. The bathroom should be evenly lit.

Finishing touches

Window furnishings may be curtaining, of possibly plastic or towelling material, venetian or roller blinds. Venetian blinds usually consist of metal slats coated with plastic, though timber slats are available. These are made in a variety of colours and offer privacy while allowing light into the room.

Roller blinds are made in a wide range of colours and patterns. Maximum light can enter the bathroom by day, by raising these fully.

Much can be done with décor finishing by choosing accessories carefully. Towels, and bathmats, in matching colours, help to give a unified look. It is in choosing these items that one can experiment and add a touch of individuality.

36

Recipe for an ideal kitchen

The kitchen has been called the hub or workshop of the home. It should be well planned, attractive, easy to clean and pleasant to work in. While this is the ideal, even the mostly unlikely and awkwardly shaped kitchen can, with careful thought, be satisfactorily redesigned as an effective work-unit.

Any kitchen redesign will be limited by the size and shape of the room and the demands on that room by a particular family situation.

Types of kitchen
There are three main types of kitchen:

The galley-type, usually in a small area where the work units are placed along one or two sides of the room, with the minimum width required for door opening between them. This provides for economy of movement and enables maximum use to be made of the storage space available.

A 'U'-shaped arrangement, usually in a larger area, consisting of storage units on three sides of a square.

The third arrangement is best in the larger kitchen. This utilizes a peninsular unit–a section of units and worktop area which may house cooking discs, placed at right angles to the main run of units.

This can act as a room divider and is useful where the room is large and is combined as a dining room and kitchen.

Scale plan
It is a good idea to make a scale plan of the kitchen on graph paper using 25mm to 300mm (1in. to the ft.) Cut out, to the same scale, pieces of paper or thin card to represent any units or appliances you may have such as washing machine, cooker or refrigerator, and any proposed new units; 'juggle' these about on the paper until you come up with a satisfactory combination.

Planning
Making the best use of your kitchen area needs careful planning. First–and this depends upon the space available–decide whether the kitchen is to be purely a work area or work and dining area combined.

A kitchen should be labour-saving, not only from the viewpoint of cleaning but also designed to cut down on unnecessary walking.

Adequate storage facilities must be incorporated in specialized work areas. The three main areas are for food preparation, cooking and washing up.

Washing up demands three working areas: one for stacking dirty dishes, the sink, and an area to receive clean dishes for drying and stacking away.

It is also essential to have a flat surface on which to place hot dishes from the oven.

These areas need to be fairly close together.

It is a good rule to have one flat area of working surface between each major appliance which does not possess a flat surface. Working surface is essential, particularly near the cooker and sink.

Ideally, doors should not face each other as this splits up the kitchen. Start

Galley

'U' shape

Basic types of kitchen
Peninsular

the layout design from the sink, to avoid, where possible, re-routing plumbing.

When planning, remember that cupboard doors need to open, cookers should not be directly under windows (because heat may crack glass) and that you must also allow for the opening of room doors.

At this stage, re-hanging doors or re-positioning windows may provide extra usable space.

Working heights

The standard height for pre-made kitchen units, from ground to working-surface level, is between 750mm and 900mm, with a depth of 535mm.

Kitchen units are available in pre-assembled whitewood, pre-finished, or as self-assembly units, which are either pre- or unfinished. Alternatively, you may prefer to make your own units, which can be tailored to fit a non-standard sized kitchen.

Unfinished units may be painted or stained, polyurethaned or laminated, to name a few treatment possibilities, to merge with your colour schemes.

Focal interest

Domestic chores are more acceptable if there is a focal point of interest outside the kitchen.

Ideally, the sink should be near or beneath a window. If the outlook is dull – for instance a drab wall – consider brightening it up with a coat of light paint. This will not only enliven the view but also reflect light back into the kitchen.

Colour

Colours are a matter of personal choice, but a useful guide is to decide the effect you want – cold and clinical or warm and homely.

Colours in the blue, green, yellow

spectrum will make the kitchen look colder than warmer colours such as brown, red and orange.

Lighting

All main working areas should be well lit. Fluorescent lighting gives shadowless working light. Spotlights can be used to provide extra light or localized light – for instance, over the cooker.

Storage

Access to storage is important, and to allow for unnecessary expenditure of energy, store the most frequently wanted items just above or below worktop level and those less needed either lower or higher than this.

Wall cupboards are best positioned about 300mm above working surface level up to a maximum of 1830mm. Open shelving is another form of storage.

Particularly in larger areas the peninsular kitchen has many advantages. This cuts down the walking distances between working areas. Built in hobs and cooker provide neat and streamlined features. A central hood over the cooking area enables effective extraction of smells.

For many homes, the U-shaped kitchen is the choice, particularly where the overall kitchen size is small. This arrangement allows a large amount of work top area. Timber panelling, stainless-steel tiles, ceramic floor tiles and laminated work-tops all provide easy-to-clean surfaces.

A space-saving concept where this is at a premium is an alcove kitchen. This has particular applications for a house

There is no advantage in having shelving that is too deep and 300mm is probably the deepest normally needed and then only suitable for storing larger items.

A shelf of between 150mm to 200mm is quite deep enough for most kitchen cartons, boxes and jars. Drawers with a depth of 150mm are useful for storing cutlery and kitchen utensils. Drawers which are very deep are only useful for storing bulk items and large cooking utensils.

Food

Storage of food safely and hygienically is important. Perishable food is best kept in a refrigerator.

Doubling up

Many kitchens double as a laundry room, with a washing machine and spin-dryer often sharing the same plumbing services. Ideally, the area used for washing clothes should be as far as possible from the cooking area. In a large kitchen you might partition off an area as a laundry.

A space as small as 1520mm × 1220mm, with a sliding door and a window, will take a front-loading washing machine, laundry basket, as well as shelves for washing powder. A slightly bigger area would also house brooms, mops and cleaning materials.

Appliances

When thinking of appliances, not only do you have to provide for the appliances, you have to try to anticipate future acquisitions. Washing machines, electric cookers and refrigerators are now considered almost standard equipment in many homes. You may add a food mixer, coffee grinder, toaster, home freezer, dishwasher, waste-eliminator, extractor fans and so on.

conversion where it can fit snugly between the chimney-breast walls and the end of a room.

Plug sockets

Plug sockets should be at working-top level, spaced roughly at 1830mm intervals round the room. No plug sockets should be within 1830mm of the sink. Sockets for 'fixed' appliances such as cookers, refrigerators and washing machines may be fixed lower down.

Before adding extra sockets, check that your wiring is able to cope with the potential extra load and renew and augment as necessary. Always remember, if you are in any doubt consult a qualified electrician.

Refuse disposal

Refuse disposal is always a problem in the kitchen. One of the most hygienic ways to dispose of food wastage is by means of a waste-eliminator.

The pedal bin with plastic liner bag, foot operated, is a less-sophisticated means of disposal. Some disposal-bag systems are designed to fit on the wall or back of base-unit doors.

Cooking smells

Unwanted cooking smells can easily permeate the house, caused by the natural convection of hot air. As it is difficult to keep a kitchen door closed at all times, an automatic door closer will help to solve the problem. Smells will be contained and steam will not spread out into the rest of the home.

A more effective way of combating cooking odours and condensation is to install a powerful extractor fan, or an air cleaner, sited near the cooker; these can either be wall or window mounted.

It is better to use a fan than to open a window as natural ventilation tends to blow the steam and smells back into the room while a fan draws them out.

It is possible to fit a cooker hood which incorporates an extractor fan. A simple

version draws up fume-laden air and the smells are neutralized by passing through a charcoal filter pad. These pads are renewable.

More complicated extractors have a powerful fan which pulls the fumes out, through a tunnel, connecting the cooker hood with an outside vent.

Condensation

Condensation occurs when steam reaches a cold surface, and turns back into droplets of water. Windows, cold spots, such as lintels over doors, and cold wall surfaces are vulnerable areas.

Adequate heating, by means of a radiator from a central-heating system, a high-level infra-red heater, or heat from a domestic boiler, will help to raise the temperature.

Polystyrene tiles or sheeting, which should be fire-retardant, can be applied to the ceiling. These are now made in many decorative effects. Not only do these help to provide thermal insulation, but they also raise the touch temperature of the ceiling surface which reduces condensation.

Wall finishes

Wall coverings vary from paint to washable vinyl kitchen wallpapers in a multitude of designs. Wood panelling, ceramic and stainless-steel tiles and cork are other possibilities.

When deciding on wall surfaces, there are two main considerations: cost and durability. If you like to change your décor scheme frequently, wallpaper or paint is probably best. Wood panelling, stainless steel or ceramic tiles are more expensive but provide a durable and virtually maintenance-free surface.

Flooring

Flooring should also be hard wearing, warm, easy to clean and attractive. The choice of flooring ranges from linoleum to thermo-plastic tiles or sheeting, vinyl, foam-backed sheeting, ceramic floor tiles, loose-lay kitchen carpet tiles to kitchen carpeting.

There is a wide range according to cost, colour, texture, design and finish required.

Final touches

The proportion of kitchen window space should be about 20 per cent of the floor area.

Finishing touches to a kitchen come in the window furnishings. Picture windows provide a good vista but limit privacy. A roller blind, either pre-made or in kit form, is a good solution. Rolled up out of sight during the day it provides privacy at night.

Roller blinds are also quite acceptable on doors. Most kitchen blinds are plasticized and only need to be wiped clean. Blinds are made in a wide variety of colours and designs.

Venetian blinds, with plain or coloured slats, have the advantage of enabling outward vision while retaining privacy. These need a little more care and cleaning.

One of the oldest decorative surface treatments, ceramic tiles are now made in vibrant colours, patterns and textured surfaces. These have many applications within and outside the home. Tiling techniques are not difficult, and the results provide an attractive durable decorative finish for floors and walls.

Glazed ceramic tiles are made in a wide range of colours and effects. These range from simple plain colours to sculptured, patterned and decorative tiles.

For use out of doors, many manufacturers can supply tiles which have been treated to make them frost-resistant. Many plain, coloured tiles can be accurately matched with bathroom fittings. Floor tiles, which are thicker than wall tiles, are also available in complementary colours.

Types of tile

There are three main types of ceramic tile. The main 'bulk' or 'field' tile usually has spacer lugs on the outer edge, which provides a neat 2mm gap between tiles. These gaps are later filled with a grout, a compressible, white material, mixed with water to a paste, which gives an overall patterned appearance.

The RE, or round-edged tile, is used for edging or for part tiling, to give a rounded-off finish, and for external corners of window reveals.

Tiles with two adjacent round edges are known as REX tiles. These are used for purposes such as splashbacks and as top corner tiles in part tiling.

Ceramic tiles are made in three main sizes – 108mm² × 4mm thick and 152mm² × 6mm thick – corresponding with the Imperial 4¼in and 6in sizes – or in panels of 50 mosaic tiles, measuring 55mm × 25mm × 4mm, mounted on a scrim backing.

Calculating the amount

When calculating the number of tiles needed, allow around five per cent of the total for breakages and waste on the tiles you have to cut. With 108mm² tiles, allow a row of three full tiles for every 430mm² of wall, and 72 tiles for every 900mm² of wall. In each case allow for two cut tiles per row. Similarly, with 152mm² tiles, allow six full tiles to the running metre or 36 tiles for an area of 900mm².

To calculate the number of RE tiles needed, measure the length of the area to be tiled, allowing three 108mm² or two 152mm² tiles for each run of 305mm.

Materials

Adhesives

This is supplied, ready constituted, in cans, or in powder form, to which you add water. Reconstituted adhesives usually have a limited life and you should mix no more than you can apply in a given time.

There are adhesives for internal and external use and for various types of surface and conditions, such as where dampness may occur.

Thick-bed adhesives are made to enable uneven surfaces to be evenly covered – though you should always prepare the surface to be as even as possible.

A can of 4·50 litres covers an area of roughly 5 m².

Grouting

This is a white powder mixed with water to a fairly stiff paste. A quantity of 1kg is sufficient for an area of 4m².

Tools

Essential tools are a notched spreader, a small trowel, pincers, a tile cutter, a spirit level or plumb bob, lath or batten, sponge or tiler's squeegee.

Additional items which may prove useful are a radius cutter, to make large holes in tiles, a tungsten-tipped drill, for small holes, and a carborundum block or carborundum file, for smoothing rough edges on cut tiles.

Notched spreader

Plastic spreaders may be supplied with the adhesive, or you can buy a notched trowel. If you have any quantity of tiling to do, the latter is a worthwhile investment. The ridges in the adhesive created by the notches in the spreader or trowel give the tile greater adhesion.

Pincers

These are used to nip out small sections of tile to fit, or to go round oddly shaped corners.

Tile cutters

These are of various types, ranging from a simple scriber with tungsten-carbide tip, to tile-cutting kits, consisting of a platform, small try-square and a wheel cutter.

Spirit level or plumb bob

Either can be used to establish an accurate vertical working line. The spirit level is used to establish the horizontal working line and to check work as you progress.

Lath or batten

This consists of a straight piece of timber, of the same length as the longest area to be tiled.

Sponge or squeegee

Either can be used to apply grout between

the tile joints; surplus is rubbed off when dry.

Surface preparation

Surfaces should be clean and free from grease. Irregularities should be smoothed down, cracks filled in and any screws, nails or other projections removed. If you are planning to tile on to new plaster, make sure that the surface is dry and free from dust. Apply a sealant to porous surfaces, to prevent the absorption of adhesive.

A painted surface, if sound, provides a good tiling surface, but gloss paint should be scored to assist adhesion. Any unstable paint should be removed by rubbing down with a medium grade of glasspaper.

Old tiles, where these present a firm,

Mark out batten into even tile widths; this avoids uneven cuts at wall ends

Fix a temporary batten to the wall at height of one tile; true with level

To support tiles above a reveal, fix a temporary batten, lined up with level

even surface, may be tiled over. These tiles are often 13mm thick, on an equally thick mortar backing. A bulky effect can be produced, particularly where the original consisted of half-wall tiling.

It is worthwhile to consider removing thick tiling. These may be chipped off with a club hammer and a bolster. Over a large area, a faster way of removal is to hire an electric rotary hammer, with a combing attachment.

Dry partition surfaces may also be tiled, provided these are rigid. It may be necessary to remove surface coverings, in order to reinforce framework or studding, to provide the necessary rigidity.

Plasterboard, plywood and chipboard should be fixed on battens of 75mm × 50mm timber, spaced at intervals of about 300mm, both horizontally and vertically.

Tile on to the 'rough' side of any board and seal the reverse side with a specified sealant for the material, though ordinary paint undercoat should prevent moisture seepage.

Expanded metal, if fixed at intervals of about 300mm, is also suitable to support rendering for tiling.

Setting out

Because floor levels vary and few corners or angles of rooms are accurate, some care is needed in setting out tiling, otherwise the results may appear uneven and irregular.

Use a plumb bob or spirit level to find true vertical, one tile in on each side

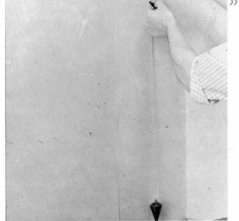

When tiling around fittings and obstructions, also use a tile-support batten

Matching tiles on sills and window reveals provide a neat 'all-over' look

First, establish an accurate working reference or datum, then take a tile and place this at your lowest tiling level – the floor or the skirting board.

Mark the height, including the spacer lug, on the wall and use the spirit level to mark a straight horizontal line. Fix the top of the lath or batten accurately along this line, over the full length of the area to be tiled. As the batten is later removed, it should be fixed with the nail heads protruding, so that these can be pulled out easily.

Check that the batten level is accurate and stand one tile on end and run it alongside the floor beside the batten, to make sure that this is neither too high nor low.

Fix temporary vertical battens one tile width in, or work to marked pencil line

After tiling, fill the joints with a grouting and polish the tiles when dry

From the centre point of the wall, mark the tile widths along the batten. This will ensure that equal cut tiles appear at the ends and help to avoid short awkward cuts. At each end, use a plumb bob or the spirit level to mark the verticals; these correspond with the point of each last full tile.

This procedure is repeated on any walls which adjoin the first. If the wall space does not allow an even number of tiles, it is better to increase the space between them slightly, to avoid having two cut pieces abutting in the same corner.

Applying adhesive

Adhesive should be applied to the surface to be covered rather than to the individual tiles, as this provides even adhesion. Spread adhesive to a thickness of about 3mm and cover only 1m² at a time.

The serrated edge of the spreader forms ridges which give good suction and adhesion. Press down firmly, so that the teeth of the spreader are in contact with the wall surface.

Tiling

Start tiling at the left-hand intersection of the batten and vertical line. Begin with the bottom row and work upwards.

Tiles should be pressed firmly into place. Never slide a tile into position as this weakens adhesion. Any adhesive left on the tile surface can be wiped off before it dries. Tiles tend to 'creep', so verticals should be checked frequently.

Constantly check that horizontal lines are also accurate and that tiles are firmly bedded and not proud of the adjacent tile surfaces. Omit, at this stage, tiling where obstructions, such as sinks and window reveals, require the cutting in of individual tiles.

Where difficult areas have to be tiled or part tiles are used, the backs of these can be individually 'buttered' with adhesive, spread to a depth of about 3mm, using a small trowel.

Allow several hours for the tiles to set, then remove the batten and fill the remaining spaces with tiles cut to fit, individually 'buttering' the backs.

Fixed objects and reveals

When tiling round a bath or hand basin, there may be less than a full tile above these items. First tile alongside the bath or basin and omit the tiling above the units.

Fix a batten above the unit to correspond with the line of the tiles on either side and tile on to the batten, which should be horizontally accurate. Once the tiles have set, remove this batten and fill in below with cut tiles.

A similar technique is used in tiling round door or window angles. RE tiles should be used on the reveal side of window and door openings – not on the face side of the wall. Tiles on the inside top of reveals should be kept in place by a long section of batten, propped up by vertical pieces of timber.

Contrast can be provided by tiling one wall plain and the other in a pattern

Bathroom accessories, such as soap dishes, are fixed in the same way as tiles. During general tiling, fix an ordinary tile loosely in the place of the soap dish.

When tiling is completed, remove the loose tile, apply a 3mm-thick layer of adhesive to the back of the accessory and press it firmly into place. While the adhesive is setting, support the accessory with adhesive tape.

Cutting tiles

A felt-tipped pen is useful for marking the line of a cut on a tile. To make a straight cut, draw a tile cutter tip firmly across the glazed face of the tile surface. There is no need to do more than just score the glaze.

Apply adhesive evenly with a notched spreader; work area of 1m² at a time

Place each tile firmly into place; never slide a tile as it may not bed properly

Walls are seldom even, so top, bottom and tiles at side must be cut in later

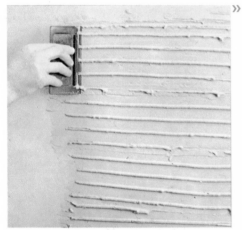

Use a straight edge when scoring tiles; press firmly with cutter to break glaze

Place matchstick beneath the cut line and press evenly on each side to snap

Awkward shapes can be cut out by carefully nibbling away tile with pliers

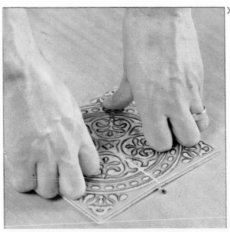

Place a small piece of wood, such as a matchstick, under the tile, and with the glazed side upwards, exert downward thumb pressure on both corners. The tile should snap evenly along the scored line. Very narrow cuts may have to be 'nibbled' away with pincers.

On a shaped cut, mark the area to be cut away and use the pincers to nibble away small sections of tile at a time. Even with care, this may lead to some false starts. For very difficult cuts, it is a good idea to cross-hatch, or score, the glazed surface of the portion to be cut away. A carborundum block or file can be used to trim up and smooth rough edges, once cut.

A round hole can be made at the edge of a tile. Place a coin on the tile and score round its outside. Next, cross-hatch a series of score marks inside the circle then carefully nibble away with pincers.

Using a slow speed, holes can be drilled in tiles with a masonry bit. The back of the tile should be firmly supported, or it may break.

An alternative to drilling a large hole with a radius hole cutter is, after marking the position of the hole, to cut the tile in half, and use pincers carefully to trim out two semi-circles. When assembled again, the join between the two pieces will scarcely show.

Grouting

Grouting should be left until the tiles are firmly set—for at least 12 hours. Using a sponge or squeegee, rub the grout firmly into the tile joints. Remove any surplus grout with a damp sponge. Once the grout has dried, rub off any powder on the tile surface with a duster and run a pointed, slightly rounded stick between the joints to give a neat joint line. Finally, polish the tile surface with a clean, dry cloth.

Mosaics

Mosaic tile sheets—roughly covering the area of five 108mm² tiles—are applied in a similar way to single tiles. Tile sheets can be regarded as a single large tile.

Check, as usual, accurate horizontal and vertical alignment and work as close as possible with each panel to the edge of the tiling surface. The backing scrim, to which the tiles are fixed, can be easily cut through with a handyman's knife; individual tiles can be detached and cut to fit.

In setting out the panels, try to avoid awkward cuts. The small size of the individual tiles will help to achieve this. The panels are simply placed on to the adhesive—and not slid into position—in the same way as a standard tile, and pressed down firmly.

The tiles are grouted similarly to standard tiles, once the adhesive has dried thoroughly. A white, plastic edge strip can be used for finishing.

An interesting application for mosaic tiles is the making of pictures or designs, by removing tiles of various colours from their backing. Unless the motif is very simple, it is best to draw the picture or design on to graph paper first, to provide an accurate design to work to.

Tiles are versatile! They can be used to provide decorative surfaces almost anywhere in the home. These examples show not only their 'conventional' use in kitchens and bathrooms, but also elsewhere in the home—as a decorative surround to a fireplace. Tiles present a clean and permanent form of wall covering

Tile style-underfoot

Ceramic and quarry tiles make attractive, hard-wearing flooring surfaces. Preparing the surface and laying is, in many ways, similar to the techniques used for wall tiling. Preparation of the floor is very important if the tiled area is to be level and present a pleasing look. Tiling can be done out of doors–though ceramics need treating, in some situations, to make them resistant to frost.

Ceramic tiles

Clay or ceramic floor tiles are made from refined natural clays fired at high temperatures.

To vitrify the surface certain additions are made to the natural clay. Fully vitrified clay tiles are frost resistant and can be used externally. They are available in a wide range of colours, patterns and textured effects. The surface can be matt or highly glazed and, in some cases, slip resistant.

Mosaic ceramic floor tiles are another way of making an attractive hard-floor finish. Made in the same way as ordinary ceramic tiles they can be either glazed or semi-glazed, semi- or fully-vitrified, in one colour or in random patterns.

Quarry tiles

Quarry tiles get their name from the French word, carré, meaning square. In addition, tiles in octagonal and hexagonal shapes are available. They are made from natural clay, unrefined, and hard burnt.

Quarry tiles are a more porous material than ceramic tiles and only top-grade 'quarries' should be used externally.

This type of flooring, as a natural material, is available in random colours: buff, natural browns, reds and blues. The random quality of the colours give the attractive decorative finished effects.

L-shaped coving tiles, are available to make internal corners. The tiles can then be taken a little way up the wall to make a skirting area.

Quarry tiles are made in a variety of thicknesses and in sizes of 102mm × 102mm to 305mm × 305mm. Generally, the larger and thicker the tile the more expensive, but also the more hardwearing it is.

These tiles are dense and hard and cutting them is not an easy job. Accurate cutting is necessary and as some tiles will crack, it is essential to buy extra tiles to allow for wastage.

To cut the tiles, a hammer, small cold chisel and a pair of pincers are needed. An abrasive disc or a carborundum stone are needed to smooth cut edges.

Screeded sub-floors

When laying a quarry-tile floor, as in all floor-laying operations, it is essential to have a level sub-floor. To level the floor, a 20mm thickness of 1:3 mortar should be laid.

Soak the quarries in clean water and then proceed to lay them in a further mortar bed 6mm thick–bedding the tiles down to a level surface.

Grouting is done with a mixture consisting of equal parts of cement and sand. When grouting, stand on a board of about 1m². This will take the weight of the body and prevent the tiles from spreading.

Once the floor is laid, the tiles should be covered with sand or sawdust, to keep the surface clean, and left for four to five days before being walked on.

Cutting

Mark the line of the cut. Using a cold chisel and a hammer, make a series of indentations along the line. Stand a brick on its side and, gripping the tile in both hands, hold it over the brick and strike it against the brick in the position of the line.

If any further trimming is necessary, use the pincers to nibble away the unwanted portion of the tile. A curved edge is indented and then the waste area is nibbled away using the pincers.

Once the edge has been cut, smooth the roughness away, using a carborundum stone or an abrasive disc.

Ceramic tiles

Tools and materials required are basically those used for wall tiling–a knotched spreader, pincers, sponge or squeegee and a cloth for polishing the tiles to remove excess grouting.

Standard ceramic floor tiles are usually matt-finished, often without spacer lugs, and made in mainly 108mm × 108mm, 150mm × 150mm or 200mm × 200mm sizes. These offer a wide range of colours and designs. Thicknesses range between 13mm and 16mm.

Mosaic tiles, individually 50mm × 25mm in size, and 6mm thick, usually come in panels of 600mm² or 300mm × 600mm on a paper backing. This is peeled off after the tiles are laid 'face' downwards.

A traditional bedding mixture for ceramic tiles is a bedding of Portland cement and sand. Modern adhesives are made in powder form or supplied in cans, each developed to suit particular situations.

Ceramic floor tiles may be laid on two main types of floors: solid floors – screeds; suspended floors – timber floors laid on joists.

Other surfaces that can be tiled include sound, previously tiled, floors, quarry floors or natural stone surfaces.

Concrete floors

Both concrete or screeded sub-floors must be allowed to dry out thoroughly before tiling starts. If this is not allowed for, concrete shrinkage may effect the bond between tiles and bedding.

Allow one month for every 25mm of depth before tiling on new concrete. There should be an effective damp-proof membrane.

If the floor appears damp or there are signs of rising damp, this should be treated at this stage.

The floor surface should be clean, level, dry and free from dust. Dusty surfaces can be sealed with an anti-dust agent. A proprietary, self-levelling compound can be used to achieve an even surface. Minor irregularities can be taken up by adjusting the depth of the bedding medium.

This is essential when using a thin-bed

adhesive method of fixing, as the tiles follow the contours of the sub-floor surface.

When laying tiles in a bedding mixture of cement and sand, some irregularities can be taken up by adjusting the thickness of the mortar.

Establish first your datum lines. These are marked on the four walls and the lines joined up. The line should allow for the thickness of the tile and the bedding adhesive. It must be level and allow for surface irregularities to be taken up.

You may have to trim doors at the bottoms and rehang them to accommodate the added floor depth.

When tiling an area with fixed units, such as a kitchen, it may be possible to remove all units and tile the complete area or to tile up to the units, using inner curved edging tiles to give a neat, hygenic edge. The level under the units might also be raised by using hardboard.

Direct bedding

On solid floors, tiles can be fixed by the direct-bedding method. This is suitable for use over stone, concrete or old quarry tiles. A clean level surface is required.

Lay a level mix of three parts sharp clean sand to one part of Portland cement. Mix a slurry of a cement-based floor adhesive, coat the back of the tiles to a depth of 3mm, position on the bedding layer, and tamp down level.

Gaps of 3mm should be left between the tile joints. Allow a drying period of 12 hours, and grout with a paste mix or 1:1 Portland cement fine-sand mix.

Another semi-dry method is to use a bedding layer of 1:4 Portland cement/coarse, dry sand mix. Add just enough water to give a crumbly mix. Spread the mix in ruled screeding bays laid on fine screed and levelled up with a spirit level, and compact down using a timber tamper. Finally, level the mix, using a straight edge drawn across the screed rules.

Mix a 1:1 Portland cement/sand slurry and, working over an area of 1m at a time, spread a 3mm layer. Lay the floor tiles 'dry'. Once the base mix has dried, use a dry mix, of the same proportions as the slurry to brush over the floor to fill the joints. Pour water over the area and compact the tile surface carefully with a tamper.

Speedy tile adjustment is necessary as the slurry sets quickly. The slurry partly fills the joints and grouting can be completed then or later. If the grouting is to be delayed, clean the floor surface.

Timber floors

It is possible to lay tiles on timber floors but the floor must be stable and strong enough to bear the extra load. As ceramic tiling will create an impervious surface, adequate ventilation of the under-floor area must be ensured.

When tiling an upstairs bathroom or shower area, it may be necessary to lay a waterproof membrane, such as 500-gauge polythene, before tiling, to protect the rooms below. In most domestic situations the floor will not need reinforcing.

Timber floors can be braced by laying sheets of tempered hardboard, spaced at 300mm centres and screwed down with rough side uppermost.

Before laying the sheets, make sure that the floor boards are free from any projecting nails. Once laid the boards should have no movement or 'whip', as this may cause the tiles to become unseated.

Adhesives

There are proprietary adhesives for fixing tiles to timber. Either a thin-bed or thick-bed method can be used, dependent on the final use of the final floor area.

An epoxy-based resinous adhesive can be used to fix tiles. Supplied in the correct

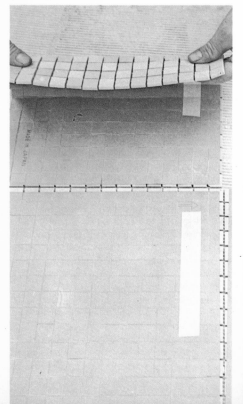

Vitreous mosaic sheets provide excellent flooring for baths and shower cubicles

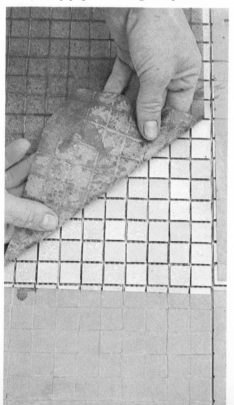

Lay sheets on adhesive face downwards; later, damp paper backing and peel off

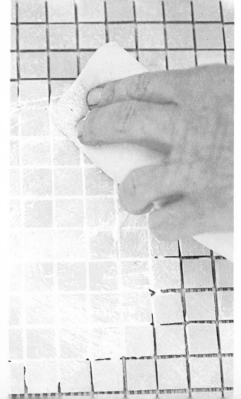

Tiles can then be grouted and the face polished with cloth when grout dries

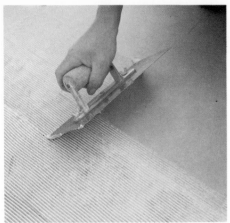

Use notched spreader to apply an even bed of adhesive to lay flooring tiles

Small pieces of card can be used where spacer lugs are not fitted to the tiles

Mark this line off in tile widths, using a marked batten. As floor tiles do not have spacer lugs, allow a 3mm gap between the tiles, using ceramic spacers or pieces of card as spacers.

Cutting in

As it is unlikely that the room will take an exact number of tiles, any cutting in can be done at the far end nearest the wall. Mark the point where the last full tile comes and nail a wooden batten across the room at the point where it finishes.

This batten must be at right angles to the centre line, even if it is not aligned with the rear wall. Nail a second batten to the left-hand corner of the first batten; this will give you a square corner.

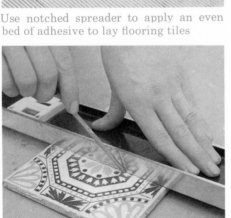

Ceramic tiles can be cut with straight edge and tungsten-tipped tile cutter

Nicobond tile cutter incorporates tip for scoring surface and pincers to break

Tiling

Start tiling at this corner. This is the keystone of the entire operation and must be correct. A slight inaccuracy here would be increasingly obvious as tiling progresses.

Apply the adhesive with a notched trowel over an area of 1m², starting at the corner where the two battens meet, pressing the tiles into the adhesive. As you work, remove any adhesive adhering to the tile surface.

Once the main body of the tiling is complete, remove the battens and fix any cut tiles in position.

Cut tiles

To cut these, place a tile upside down over the gap to be filled, and mark two points at each end, indicating the waste portion, allowing for the tile spacing. Transfer the marks to the face of the tile and score a line between the points across the surface.

Next, kneel down, and grip a spare tile between your knees, firmly hold both sides of the tile to be cut, and strike it across the score line on to the edge of the held tile. This should result in a clean break. Any rough edges can be smoothed with a carborundum stone.

'Butter' the cut tile and fix it into position with the cut edge to the wall. Allow the tiles to set for 24 hours, remove the spacers, and then grout between the joints, making sure that the grout is pressed firmly between them. Remove excess with a damp sponge and later polish with a cloth.

Shower compartment and tray, showing the vitreous ceramic mosaic flooring

A ceramic floor in a kitchen is easy to maintain and attractive in appearance

proportions, all the resin and hardner should be mixed, allowed to stand and then 'knocked up' for use. The mixture has a workable life of two hours.

Spread about 1m² at a time and use a knotched spreader or comb to score the adhesive surface. The thickness of the mix cannot be adjusted to accommodate differing levels.

A mixture of two parts adhesive to one part sand can be used to fill small hollows.

As the adhesive dries, a slight skin may form. To counteract this, twist each tile as it meets the adhesive, periodically checking to see that the tiles are in contact with the adhesive.

Tiles are fixed 'dry' and pressed firmly into position, ensuring they are evenly laid, with no raised edges. Never butt-joint tiles but allow a 3mm space all round.

Clean any adhesive from the face of the tiles, leave for at least six hours, and grout with a mixture of equal parts of Portland cement and sand or a proprietary grouting. Work grouting well into the joints.

There are various proprietary tile-fixing mediums which can be used in the thick- or thin-bed methods of tile laying, dependent on the use of the floor.

Setting out

Setting out tiles for all floor laying operations follows the same method.

Tiles should be laid to line up evenly with the doorway, running squarely away to the back of the room.

First, mark a line in the centre of the doorway and then draw a line at right angles to the first line for the length of the room.

Mosaics

Mosaic tiles are laid in a similar manner to standard floor tiles. Apply adhesive, and lay the sheets with the backing paper upwards.

Press them down firmly, so that the tiles are evenly bedded.

Remove any excess adhesive before laying the next section and make sure that the sections are accurately butted together.

Allow the adhesive to dry for 24 hours, moisten the backing paper and peel this off. The tiles can then be grouted in the conventional way.

Partial sheets or individual tiles may have to be removed and cut in at corners or around awkward or uneven places.

Putting on a new face:1

An external facelift gives a new lease of life to any home. Whether you are merely repainting woodwork or applying a decorative and protective wall surface, it is important to choose the right time of year and the correct weather conditions for working. There are numerous modern surface finishes which will add colour and texture to any home.

Exterior decorating is best carried out during spring or early autumn. External decorating work, as a rule, starts at the top and proceeds downwards. Conditions need to be dry, but not too hot.

For a complete façade facelift, start on the soffits (the boarding under the eaves), bargeboards (under the roof or gables) and fascia boards.

Next, deal with guttering and any wall cladding at the upper level that needs treatment. Whole-façade rendering should be completed, where possible, in one operation. Paint downpipes, masking the wall area behind, then tackle window frames and doors.

Where an entire façade is to be painted or rendered, particularly when using one of the highly adhesive mortar mixes, mask wood before starting.

As exterior paintwork does not usually require the fine finish of interior work, medium-quality brushes can be used. Always use a paint kettle and dispense only a workable amount of paint at a time, so that paint is not wasted through evaporation. A paint kettle is also easier to carry or attach to a ladder than a tin.

The 'colour' most often used on rendered surfaces is white. This can look most attractive, particularly in clean-air areas or near the sea, but, with a little thought, other colours can be used to great advantage. The colours used on a house can help to emphasize good features and disguise those less attractive.

Basically, house exterior decoration is a matter of taste, and care must be taken to make the best of attractive features, while minimizing the least pleasing facets. Very violent colour schemes may be exciting but rarely blend in with the surrounding area.

Each house has a particular character of its own, and this should be complemented by the external decoration.

Colour

The house is part of the environment and the colour chosen should complement the surrounding area. While your home can be painted any colour you choose, except in areas of particular natural beauty or historical interest, it is better to decorate in a way that will enhance rather than de-

tract from the general appearance of the surrounding houses.

Not only should the house match the locality and blend harmoniously with it, but the colours should also blend with the other textures and colours used in the building, particularly roof tiles and brickwork.

The use of white is necessary to add brightness to any house colour scheme. It may be used liberally, or just to highlight particular features.

When choosing a colour for rendered walls, try to see what effect a large area of the colour will give. A small sample on a colour card may present quite a different appearance over a large area.

Houses in areas that are not always bathed in sunlight can be decorated in such conservative colours as grey, cream

and beige. It is possible to branch out and use less-orthodox, darker colours, or warm shades of orange and yellow. In areas that have clear, bright natural light, pastel shades or white look most attractive.

Different areas of a house may be painted in a variety of colours. Usually, all the walls of a house are painted in the same colour but this may not be necessary on a terraced house, where the front may conform with a road scheme, while the back can be painted to complement the garden colours.

Woodwork and pipes can be made to blend in with the background by painting them in the same colour as the rendering. To make a feature of the woodwork, either use white, white framing or a tint of the background colour.

With a light paint scheme, it may be

better to paint pipes in a darker colour, as light pipe-work tends to attract dirt, particularly in heavily polluted areas.

An unattractive entrance area, if proportionately wrong for the house, can be disguised by painting the door to match the lower part of the house. A door that has unattractive proportions should be painted in a shade of the surrounding brickwork colour or rendering. Large doors, such as garage doors, might also be painted to blend with the colour used on the lower section of a house.

'Adding' width
A narrow house can be made to look wider by painting a wide band in a light colour across the front of the house. A band of decorative moulding may be suitable for this treatment. A sense of height can be suggested by painting vertical features, door architraves and window surrounds in a contrasting colour.

Features, such as porchways, decorative mouldings, and window sills may be painted white or in contrast colours, to break up the wall surfaces and add interest to the façade.

Cladding
Many modern building developments lack individuality and can be improved with the careful use of decorative external finishes. The house may lend itself to being divided into two distinct sections. The top half may be faced with white plastic or timber cladding.

Plastic cladding can be fixed vertically or horizontally to complement the proportions of the house. It requires no maintenance, other than an occasional wash down. The insulation properties of plastic cladding are good and can be further improved by laying insulant matting behind the fixing battens.

Wood cladding – matching board or shiplap – can be fixed horizontally or vertically. Wood has good insulant properties. Timber, however, requires regular maintenance. New timber needs priming, under-coating and two top coats of a suitable semi- or hard-gloss paint and will need repainting regularly, particularly if the area is white. Coloured finish coats can be used and, perhaps, picked up in window frames, door or garage colour finishes.

Natural wood cladding, such as cedar or pine, can be either treated with a protective wood preservative, which allows the natural colour and grain of the wood to show through, or a clear polyurethane varnish.

Front and side dormer areas might be clad with cedar – to match timbered panels under ground-floor windows and, perhaps, wood-finish garage doors.

Façades
Façade areas may be part pebble-dashed or treated with a textured masonry finish. Natural stone can be used to face feature areas – such as a half section of a house, a wall set at an angle to the main house area, or a chimney.

Care must be taken in adding additional decorative features, for unless the existing tile and brick colours are considered, additions may not blend in with the old.

Another way of giving a facelift to an ordinary façade might be to alter doors or windows. Again, in keeping with the character of the house, wooded doors may be replaced with glass, or a complete glass entrance area.

Windows may be enlarged, sills lowered and, possibly, picture windows fitted to replace fussy window frames with thick surrounds. A glass porch, framed in painted or preserved natural wood, may make an attractive feature, also giving an added bonus of extra storage area.

A porch should be an integrated feature of a façade and not resemble a box, stuck on without thought as to the overall effect.

Timber treatment and maintenance
External woodwork is vulnerable to weather and atmospheric pollution. The natural colour of wood is destroyed by 'leaching'–bleaching by the sun–and by the effect of pollution. Moisture and dryness also cause timber to expand and contract, loosening the surface fibres and allowing a mould to form.

These cumulative effects can be remedied by using timber preservatives, varnishes or water-repellent preparations.

Before treating the timber, first prepare the surface. Most should be brushed down to remove dirt and grit. Preparations are applied with a brush, rag or under vacuum pressure, a commercial treatment. Timber may also be dipped in preservative. Avoid using a spray, unless recommended by the manufacturer.

Preservatives

Preservatives fall into three basic types—water-borne; coal tar; and organic solvents. Some of these are poisonous, so wear protective goggles when applying and immediately wash any splashes off the skin.

Coal tar oils, such as creosote, are used for fences and sheds. It is brushed into the timber.

Water-borne preservatives, which are colourless, are normally applied commercially. Timber so treated has a high degree of protection and can be stained, painted or varnished once dry.

On a decorative timber surface, organic solvent preservatives, coloured or clear, are suitable. They can be painted over when dry.

Water repellents, which may contain preservatives, help to preserve the natural appearance of timber cladding. Dipped or applied with a brush, they can be clear or stained. To prevent moisture penetration, water repellents containing oil and wax are best but cannot be painted over.

Natural oils

Sometimes, natural oils are used on exterior woodwork. To give maximum penetration, dependent on the porosity of the wood, a mixture of boiled linseed oil and white spirit gives the best results.

However, oils do not give the effective protection of good water-repellent preservatives. The advantage of oils is that the grain and natural colour of the wood show through, but the surface, according to climatic conditions, may need treatment twice a year.

Before applying an oil-based preservative, the area should be brushed with a stiff brush and rubbed down with medium glasspaper.

Clear varnish

Exterior clear varnish gives an attractive finish and allows the natural timber to show through. Varnish is composed of alkyd, copal or phenolic resins, combined with drying oils. Four coats are needed on new timber. The first coat should be thinned.

This treatment should be renewed at the first sign of any breakdown in the surface. Remove the varnish with a solvent. Clean off with white spirit, to remove any remaining wax in the solvent and then apply two coats of varnish. On a sound but dirty surface, wash down with soapy water and finally wash again with clean water.

Use a wet-or-dry abrasive paper to rub down. Fill any holes or cracks with hard stopping, which should be coloured to match the surrounding area. Stain any bleached areas and then apply two coats of varnish. Varnish should only be applied on completely dry wood, as moisture may cause it to peel off.

Polyurethane varnish can be used externally. Again, a minimum of four coats should be applied, ideally at four-hourly intervals. Choose a dry, warm day, with a temperature of 15–25°C, and ensure that the surface is completely dry.

Polyurethane varnish tends to be brittle and peel away at the edges, and a coat of alkyd varnish may help to prevent this. If the surface has broken down, the gloss must be completely removed, the surface cleaned and new varnish applied.

If the surface colour of the wood has faded, it can be re-coloured with a stain. These are of two types. The first, in a water-repellent or organic solvent preservative, is applied initially and fades as the coat wears. These can be washed off.

The second type darkens the wood and should be used with care. This is used on timber which was originally treated with a clear water-repellent preservative, but has lost its natural colour.

External timber surfaces that might need treatment include cladding, timber window and door frames, external doors, garage doors, sills, thresholds, greenhouses, sheds, gates and fences.

Painting timber

On timber cladding to be painted, use an alkyd-resin paint in the colour of your choice. On new wood first use a suitable primer. Highly resinous woods, such as cedar and some pines, are better sealed with an aluminium primer. Use one under-

Rendering a wall: mix mortar on a dampened spot board. Turn over well with a trowel

For external angles, line up a rule, fixed some 6mm proud of the corner

The rendering coat is laid on, using upward strokes of the steel trowel

Key the floating coat, using only horizontal strokes of the comb scratcher

Use the wooden float to flatten out the burrs on the surface of floating coat

Apply the butter coat, which provides a base for the shingle, using steel float

coat and two top gloss coats for maximum protection.

When repainting, if the surface is sound, it may not be necessary to strip back and reprime. Wash down the surface, allow to dry and then rub down with abrasive paper. Wet-abrasive rubbing is easier and prevents too much dust from flying about.

Any blemishes or blisters in the paint should be rubbed down and re-primed. Knots or resinous patches should be treated with patent knotting. Holes, cracks, or joints should be filled with hard-stopping, where necessary, and rubbed down.

Badly blistered or cracked surfaces must be stripped or burnt off and the area treated as new timber. An outdoor grade of emulsion, with an appropriate primer or primer-sealer, may be used on cladding.

Aluminium cladding may be painted with an undercoat and two top coats of alkyd-resin paint. Before painting, clean the surface with white spirit and touch in any worn areas with zinc chromate primer.

Asbestos treatment
Asbestos cement can be used externally for roofing, cladding, gutters and down pipes.

It can be painted successfully, but as the material has slightly absorbent properties, paint may blister. The degree of absorbency over the surface varies and this can give a patchy finish. Another problem may be paint flaking, stickiness, discolouration

and yellow staining. This is caused by alkalis in the asbestos attacking the paint.

New sheets of asbestos should be left to dry thoroughly before painting. If the asbestos is to be used in humid conditions, it is wise to paint the back of the material with bitumen paint. Take care not to allow the paint to get on to the face of material as bitumen paint 'bleeds' through the decorative coat.

To minimize the risk of attack by alkalis, new asbestos should be allowed to weather for at least four weeks.

To prepare the surface for painting, brush off dust and any loose material. If any mould or lichen has developed, wash down with a fungicidal solution, allow to dry and then brush off the growth.

Asbestos can be painted with exterior-grade emulsion paint, oil paint, distemper, cement paint or lime wash. Before using emulsion, oil-based paint or distemper, roughen the glazed patches of asbestos which exist where the surface is more absorbent.

Apply an alkali-resistant pigmented primer before applying the top coat. Lime wash or cement paints do not need a primer but the surface should be wetted before the first coat is applied.

Alkali attack
Some paints are highly resistant to alkali attack. When using a paint that is not highly resistant, use two coats of primer to prevent the alkalis seeping through to attack the top coat.

Primer sealers can be used before

painting to counteract uneven suction but will not prevent alkali attack. When impermeable paints are used on the surface, paint, where possible, the backs of the asbestos. When not possible, use a porous alkali-resistant paint for the surface which allows the asbestos to 'breathe'.

Sheeting or soffits should be either painted with porous, alkali-resistant paint or with an impermeable paint where the sheet has previously been 'back painted'.

Down pipes and the insides of gutters should be painted with bitumen paint. Allow this to dry thoroughly before painting the outside. Applying bitumen to the insides of pipes is difficult and is usually done during production.

Roofs
Asbestos roofs are not normally painted as the cost of maintenance is high. To help asbestos roofing to blend in with surrounding roofs, the sheets can be darkened with ferrous sulphate, mixed in the proportion of 455 grammes of sulphate to five litres of water. This will give a durable brown colour, but the coverage will often be uneven.

When treating a roof, use a cat ladder, as asbestos is not safe to walk on. Flaked paintwork on asbestos should be removed with a wire brush or proprietary paint remover and washed down. Never use a paraffin or gas blow torch as the heat will crack the surface which may explode dangerously.

Do not let paint remover sink into the asbestos surface as this will crumble it.

Key the surface well with a scratcher. Make 90-degree cross diagonal strokes

'Work to rule' to ensure accurate surfaces. Brickwork is often irregular

Next, apply the floating coat, again working carefully to the timber rule

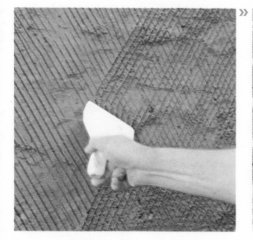

Flick the shingle systematically from a bowl or plastic bucket; avoid 'bunching'

Before the work sets hard, pat the shingle down with wood float to 'firm' surface

Keep the float dry with a piece of cloth so that cement does not coat the shingle

Even the most drab home exterior can be quickly transformed, using one of the many available decorative wall finishes. Materials which can be used to give your home a 'face lift' vary from simple exterior paints to more elaborate surface finishes, providing a wide choice of both colour and texture.

Masonry and stone paints

Rendered surfaces can be improved by the application of a paint coat. The most satisfactory type is masonry paint. This is waterproof and so is protective as well as decorative.

Some types dry to a smooth surface which facilitates easy cleaning. Before using a masonry paint, brush the surface down thoroughly with a wire brush and apply a masonry paint sealer.

Among many types of masonry paints are those reinforced with minute, short nylon fibres, which fill minor imperfections, or paints which incorporate minute particles of crushed rock. One type has a vinyl-resin base and is available in a range of colours or a two-tone mix.

Some paints are applied by brush, and others with a steel trowel.

With such surface coatings, large imperfections in external rendering must be hacked back and filled with a mix of the same consistency as the surrounding area, otherwise stress will occur between the two surfaces.

Emulsion

Exterior-grade emulsion can be used to decorate external walls. Available in a wide range of attractive colours, it provides solely a decorative finish and has no waterproofing properties.

Applied rendering

Some types of applied rendering, such as shingle dash, snowflake and Tyrolean finishes do not need painting, unless you wish to change the colour. Normally, their

Roughcast is prepared to a sloppy consistency, then flicked over the wall surface

A trowelled finish coat can be used as a basis for cement-fining or Ashlar surface

Using a wood float and slurry to prepare the surface for a cement-fining finish

Similarly, measure and mark out horizontals, again ensuring line is level

Carefully rule in the lines, using a piece of filed metal or a cut nail as scriber

Gently rub the edges of the score lines with the sponge to remove any slight burrs

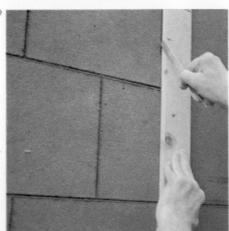

attraction lies in a two-tone colour or textured effect. Rough-textured surfaces may be difficult to cover, as the paint has to adhere to the stone and crevices of a cement mixture.

Roughcast
Roughcast, which incorporates shingle in a mortar mix, does need a decorative finish, either a waterproof paint or emulsion. If using emulsion, a colourless water-repellent sealer can be applied before the emulsion coat.

Preparation
Before starting work, mask surrounding paintwork, window frames, pipes and secondary roofs. Also, remember to protect paths as spilt paint may be difficult to remove.

A large brush or roller can be used to apply a decorative coat to rendering, other than on a roughened cement finish. Cement finishes should be applied with an expendable brush as, once used, it is impossible to clean off the hardened cement.

A stiff nylon brush must be used on a very rough textured finish to push the paint into the crevices.

External wall treatments
Cement finishes
A good way to improve the external appearance of house walls is to apply a decorative cement finish. This is not a difficult task but needs care. Cement rendering can be applied to bare brickwork, cement, stippled or shingle dash surfaces. Additional care must be taken if the surface is painted.

Three coats of sand and cement are applied to external walls. Often called rendering coats, the three layers have distinct functions.

The first coat is the rendering coat. This is 'keyed' (scratched for adhesion) and covered by the floating coat, which straightens out the surface before the application of the finish coat.

On external plastering the system used in the final coat depends on the finish to be used.

Cement fining is the coat most commonly used. This is finished with a wooden float or sponge.

Shingle dash is another finish, in which fine shingle is embedded in a fatty 'butter' coat.

Different masonry finishes, such as roughcast, Tyrolean finish, and so on, are examples of finish coats.

Tools
Laying-on trowel
It is important to buy as good a trowel as you can afford. The blade should be of thin, well-tempered steel. A banana handle will give a good grip. A full-sized trowel blade is 280mm × 115mm.

Hawk
A hawk is a flat piece of wood or metal about 300mm², with a grip fixed in the centre. A quite adequate hawk can be made from a piece of marine plywood, with a short piece of broom handle, fixed in the centre, as a grip.

Skimming float
The skimming float is usually made of white pine. The blade should be 305mm × 115mm. A wooden float produces a slightly matt surface. A steel float can be used to give a smoother surface finish.

Water brush
A water brush is essential for damping down wall areas. A 100mm or 125mm brush is suitable.

Spot board
A spot board is used for mixing up the mortar. It should be made of marine ply or strengthened plywood. The board should be 610mm × 760mm and, if made of plywood, strengthened with battens.

The spot board should be used in conjunction with a stand or an old box to keep the board off the ground. A satisfactory working height is around 810mm.

Spirit level
A builder's spirit level, which indicates both vertical and horizontal levels is necessary.

Floating rule
A floating rule is a piece of straight-edged timber about 1830mm long and 100mm to 150mm wide. It is used to level off the

Cement fining: Lightly sponge to produce sandy texture resembling natural stone

A trowelled finish coat is ruled for Ashlar; this resembles stone blockwork

Use a builder's level to ensure that the line is vertical and make working marks

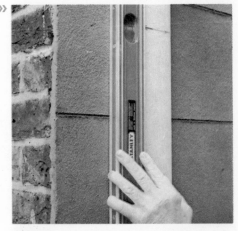

Vermiculation is a tooled finish, which looks effective with Ashlar blockwork

Tyrolean finish is applied from a machine. The 'spatter-dash' finish is attractive

Spar dash is another type of textured finish. Spar is flicked on to 'butter' coat

surface of a plaster or mortar coat, so that the surface is level with the screeds.

Feather-edged rule

A feather-edged rule is a piece of straight, tapered-edged timber, about 1m long. Where straight angles are needed, some pieces of straight-edged, planed timber 50mm × 20mm are required.

Scoop

A scoop-shaped shovel can be useful if applying a shingle-dash coat. This facilitates scooping up the gravel.

Devil float (and wood float)

This is frequently a wood float with nails partially knocked through the float face. These can be pushed through to enable the work surface to be keyed; they can then be pushed back to achieve smooth work.

Scratching to achieve a keyed surface may be also done with a commercially produced comb or one can be made by knocking some nails into a piece of wood. The comb is used to scratch diagonal criss-cross lines on the rendering coat and straight horizontal lines on the floating coat in preparation for the final coat. You can key the surface with a small trowel.

A bolster and club hammer will also be needed, for hacking back, prior to repair work. Two buckets, one to carry materials and one for water, are required.

If any material is loose it should be removed with a stiff wire brush or hacked out and the bare patches made up to the surface level with a 1:4:½ (cement: sand: lime) mixture. To give a good key, scratch the surface diagonally with criss-cross lines. Treat the base surface with a PVA primer to assist adhesion.

Brick surfaces should be brushed down

to clean off dust and dirt. Then soak the surface, allow it to dry slightly, and apply a PVA bonding coat with a brush. On a slightly doubtful surface, apply a bonding coat consisting of 25 per cent PVA bonding agent, one part of Portland cement and one part of building sand.

Mix in water until the slurry is the consistency of thickened custard. Then brush this solution well into the surface and allow to dry for 24 hours.

Ruling out

Large areas of wall surface to be plastered should be divided into sections to make for systematic working. Use 10mm battens to divide the wall area into 1·52m sections.

Fix, with masonry nails, the first batten at a corner, ensuring a true vertical by checking with the builder's level. The spaced battens will give working bays.

Start work at the bottom of the first bay. The mortar should be pushed on to the wall and spread, working upwards. Fill in each section and then level off the surface with a straight edge. Allow the mortar to set; this takes at least four hours. Then criss-cross keying marks, diagonally across the coat.

Cement paints or painted roughcast and shingle may be a little more difficult to work. If any material is loose, it should be removed, hacked out, and the bare patches made up to the level of the surface, with a 1:4:½ lime mix. Next, to give a good key, scratch the surface.

Smooth-surfaced stucco or cement work should be brushed down well with a wire brush and roughened to provide a key. A PVA slurry, consisting of one part PVA to one part sand and one part cement should be used.

A mortar plasticizer will help to spread

A colourful 'sunshine' face lift can brighten up the outside of many homes

the mixture. Lime added to the mix will facilitate the spreading power but increase suction. Suction is the rate at which the base coat absorbs water from the top coat. A high suction rate is required for some finish coats, while others need low suction.

Next apply two backing coats. The rendering coat consists of a 1:6:1 lime mix and is applied with a steel trowel. Mix these materials dry, turning well with a shovel. Make a hole in the middle of the materials and pour in water, push the inner part of the ring into the water and then add water again. Turn, until the mixture is well wetted, then mix thoroughly. If needed, a dry colourizer can be added at this stage.

Apply the mix with upward strokes, using the full length of the blade to 'lay off'. The coat should be smoothed out evenly with a floating rule and then roughened to provide a key. Comb the surface with diagonal strokes in two directions. This coat should be allowed to dry for 12 hours. The rendering coat should be 6mm thick.

The second coat, known as the floating coat, is applied to give a level surface. Lay a 275mm border round the area to be covered. This coat should be 12mm thick and is often best laid in two 6mm coats. Work each area systematically, a strip at a time, filling in the rendering as necessary and ruling off until there is an even covering. Ruling off reduces the thickness of the coat to 10mm.

The coat is then smoothed off with a wooden float. It depends on the finish coat whether or not the surface is roughened to give a key. If a roughened surface is required, use a comb to scratch horizontal lines across the surface.

Cement fining

A simple sandy-textured look with the appearance of natural stone is known as cement-fining.

Portland cement fining. This is applied to a surface with a low suction rate, so use only a little lime in the floating coat. Fining is applied to a keyed surface. The sand used should be sifted or even washed to

Looking the worse for wear, a fascia much in need of repair and redecoration

Removed flaked surfaces and make good; apply a stabilizing solution if needed

A nylon-based exterior paint is easy to apply, using a fairly stiff brush

The finished effect. The results, with correct preparation, are long lasting

remove any clay, which can cause the finish surface to craze or crack. Sand is mixed in proportion of two parts to one part of Portland cement. The cement can be white or grey, or coloured for decorative effect.

Mix the sand and cement to a firm consistency and apply on to a 6mm floating coat, which should be 'ironed' into the base coat and then rubbed over with a wood float. If there are hollows they can be filled in at this stage. Use a sponge to finish off, with light, delicate circular movements.

Blockwork

The same finish is used when a stone block, or Ashlar effect, is required. Decide on the size of block needed and then draw a master line, using a spirit level, to make sure the work lines up.

Mark out the rest of the horizontal lines, working from the master line, then mark in the vertical lines. If any of the edges are not quite accurate or have become slightly blurred, they can be smoothed off with a sponge.

An Ashlar surface, well executed, looks like a surface of stone blocks. It can be white, grey or coloured with a colourizer.

A variation of Ashlar is known as vermiculation. This is textured effect to give variety to an Ashlar surface. It is quite a lengthy process and for this reason a random effect is suggested.

Using a sharp steel object, cut out irregular shapes in the block while it is still wet. Leave a border of at least 13mm round the block and 6mm runs between each cut away area of the design.

Shingle dash

A shingle dash or roughcast finish coat can be achieved by flicking small stones or shingle on to a 'butter' coat.

The basic rendering coat should be scratched diagonally and the floating coat should be combed in horizontal lines. Smooth off any rough projections with a wooden float.

The floating coat should comprise one part cement to three parts of soft sand. A small quantity of plasticizer should be used in the mix, unless working in hot weather. In this case, a liquid water proofer should be added instead of the plasticizer.

The proportions are 25 per cent of waterproofer to 50kg of cement. After scratching in the horizontal lines, leave to dry for 24 hours.

The third coat is known as a 'butter' coat. The proportions are three parts sand to half part of cement and one part of lime. Working over a small area at a time, about 500mm², 'iron' on the coat to a depth of about 6mm.

Using clean, well-washed shingle and a laying-on trowel, flick the shingle on to the butter coat. The secret is to get the shingle applied evenly. One trowel load will cover an area one third greater than the area of the trowel.

Do not pick up too much at one time as it will be difficult to flick the wrist to apply the shingle, resulting in an uneven surface. Place a dust sheet below the work to catch shingle that does not adhere so that this can be used later. Work to within 50mm of the area being treated.

Next apply a butter coat to the next 500mm² area and apply shingle to this. When an area of about 2m² has been covered, use the wooden float to tap the shingle gently into the butter coat. The float should be used dry and wiped clean frequently.

Roughcast

Roughcasting is applied to a keyed floating coat. The mixture is made up of half a part of cement to one part of lime, to provide suction, and two parts of shingle. Pea gravel, a rounded gravel, provides a good roughcast surface. The mixture is applied directly to the surface, again using the flicking action.

The consistency should be sloppy and can be applied directly from a bucket. Many find this an easier technique than shingle dash. Gravel applied too thickly will slide down the surface.

Stipple

A variation of cement fining is a stipple finish. Lay a coat about 6mm thick on to a well-keyed float coat. Smooth down any uneven areas with a wood float and then, using a stipple brush, stipple carefully over the surface.

Another finish which offers a variation of texture is based on the same technique as cement fining. Apply a 6mm finished surface and then use a hard wire brush to make horizontal streaks on the surface. As the surface begins to harden, trowel lightly over the surface. When finished, a veining effect will be achieved.

A finish called Granosit consists of a dried material, mixed with water, and allowed to stand for 30 minutes. The float coat should be well keyed. Apply the mixture with a steel trowel to a depth of 10mm. As the surface starts to harden, using a wooden float, finish the surface with horizontal sweeps. This surface, which is water repellent, is obtainable in white and coloured finishes.

Tyrolean

This is a closely textured finish, and is applied with a special machine. A proprietary mix of Portland cement and aggregate is applied dry mixed. One bag of the mix, stirred into half a bucket of water, will give the correct consistency.

Before starting work, mask the surrounding area. Pour the mixture, a small amount at a time, into the machine. Turn the machine to the wall area and crank a handle; this will cause small blobs to be flicked on to the surface. The size of blob can be adjusted by a gauge on the side of the machine. Keep the machine moving to avoid an uneven build-up in one particular area. When working at angles, such as the corners of a building, continue to crank the machine and apply the mixture round the corners.

When re-rendering external surfaces, it is important to achieve a straight, clean edge at the outer corners of the building. The render coat can be applied, working from either side of the angled edge, with a trowel. For the floating and finish coat it is necessary to work to a wooden batten that will help to give a perfect edge.

Nail a length of a straight-edged board, using 50mm cut nails, into the brick joints. The wood should allow about 10mm thickness on one side. Fill in the lime-cement and sand floating coat, bringing this flush with the board. Use a rule made of another piece of board about 1m long. Scratch in the horizontal key lines and, when set, remove the wood and repeat the process for the other side of the angle.

Reveals

The reveals round doors and windows are treated in the following way. Fix the straight edge board to the reveals and apply the floating coat on to the main surface. When this surface is dry, remove the wood and fix to the main wall faces. Fill in the float coat in the reveals, working out towards the corner. Immediately wash off any cement splashed on to the window or door frames.

When applying a top coat of shingle or pebble-dash, use the same technique for making a good angle as the floating coat. This time, only one board is needed. Fix this, leaving it 10mm proud of the surface, and apply the finish to this board. Allow the surface to set hard and then carefully remove the board. The second side of the angle can be completed by applying the finish up the straight line already set.

Power tools: lending power to your elbow

Power tools are among the most valuable of handyman work aids. Saving time and allowing that 'professional' look to finished work, even the basic power drill, used with varied attachments, can provide great diversity in tackling a wide range of jobs around the home. When using power tools, always observe the limitations of the given piece of equipment.

Power tools of various types and suitable attachments can do much to take the hard work out of many jobs around the home, as well as often enabling them to be done more successfully.

Power tools are most popularly used for drilling, sawing and smoothing. There are two basic types of tool – the integrated tool, which is a purpose-designed unit for a given use, and the attachment, which fits to a power drill. There are also accessories, such as drill stands and sawing benches, which complement power tools.

Power saws may consist of either integrated units or attachments. Obviously, the integral saw is a better buy for major or continuous work. A variety of smoothing tools – orbital sanders, bench sanders and sanding discs – enable a range of smoothing operations to be carried out.

Jig saws are a more specialized form of power saw.

Other attachments include a paint stirrer, which ensures thorough mixing without using vast elbow power; a wire cup and discs, for removing rust from surfaces; a screwdriver attachment for repetition work, such as fixing down floor surfaces; and hedge trimmers and lawn mowers, which are either attachments or integrated tools. These use motors basically similar to those of a drill.

Devices for dowelling and mortise cutting are among the woodworking attachments which can be fitted to power tools. Special, but expensive, power planes are also made.

Extension cables, which can be wound on to reels for neat and easy stowage, are useful accessories. The maximum lengths of cable and thicknesses are related to the power of the motor and the length of the cable.

Drills

The basic power tool is the electric drill. In its simplest form it can accept a variety of attachments, to increase its versatility, but it may not always be designed for really hard work and difficult jobs. Too often, the drill is blamed because its limitations have not been observed.

It is wise to buy the best equipment you can afford and take advantage of the greater versatility and ability to tackle those jobs for which the better drill is designed.

All power drills basically consist of a compact electric motor in a shell – very

Cable length	Current (Consumption of drills in amps)				cable
	1–4	mm²	5–9	mm²	(mm²)
7·5m	6A	0·75	10A	1·0	All
15m	6A	0·75	15A	1·5	at 30°C
30m	6A	0·75	20A	2·5	ambient
42m	10A	1·0	20A	2·5	temperature

(Based on IEE recommendations).

Note: Keep cable on drum. Avoid intermediate connections in cable

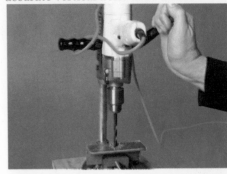

A bench stand with power tool enables accurate vertical holes to be drilled

often of high-impact plastic – with the electric motor double insulated for safety. Most drills operate on mains voltage and connect to a suitable power point with a three-pin plug.

At the 'business end' of the drill a chuck is mounted. This is opened and closed by a key, which should always be kept in a safe place or clipped to the cable of the drill. New keys can always be bought if you do lose one.

Chucks are made in a variety of sizes. The most usual are 6mm, 8mm, 10mm and 13mm. The larger, taking bigger attachments, are intended for the more powerful drills. Motors are up to ½hp (373W) in power and cooled with a fan.

The drill needs little maintenance beyond occasional replacement of motor brushes and the blowing out of any accumulated dust in the ventilation apertures at the rear. A drill with a 10mm chuck meets most domestic needs.

The less sophisticated drills run at a fixed speed – usually around 2,800 rpm. At these speeds, there is a limitation on the work the drill can do. For greater versatility invest in a twin or multi-speed drill.

Drill Speeds

Low	High
(up to 1,000 rpm)	(2,500–3,000 rpm)
drilling timber (over 10mm dia.)	drilling timber (under 10mm dia.)
drilling steel (over 6mm dia.)	drilling steel (under 6mm dia.)
Brick	sanding
Plaster	sawing
Mortar	grinding
Lime	hedge trimming
Cement	
Breeze, aggregate and cellular concrete	
glass	

Note: on hard surfaces, a hammer action is desirable; use special percussion bit. On glass, use a spear-point bit.

These run between speeds of around 900 rpm to 3,000 rpm. The slower speed is essential for drilling holes in hard surfaces. These two speeds cover most requirements. The speed is simply changed by a speed selector on the drill.

Rotary percussion

For drilling really hard surfaces, such as concrete, stone, hard brick and cement, a drill with a hammer action is needed. If you contemplate drilling hard surfaces frequently, you would be wise to buy such a drill, or obtain a percussion attachment for a standard drill. The hammer action

can be switched out and the drill then becomes an ordinary two-speed drill.

This percussive action is only used when hard masonry is being drilled. This hammer action is almost imperceptible in use; as the drill rotates it also percusses at high speed to penetrate the surface.

A special percussion bit should always be used and not an ordinary tipped drill bit, which is not designed for such work.

While a hammer attachment can be fitted to any standard power drill, if it runs at a high, fixed speed it is not suitable for drilling hard surfaces. You would need, in addition, a speed-reducing device if this is not part of the attachment.

Apart from variable-speed drills, speed reducers can turn a fixed-speed drill into a multi-speed one.

Another device which reduces speed is the right-angled speed reducer which fits into the chuck of the drill.

Using drills

A power drill should be operated with a steady, firm pressure. Excess pressure should never be applied to the work and the motor should not be under strain; it may seize up or burn out. Some motors have devices to declutch or lock out the motor when it is overstressed.

Before changing speed, make sure that the motor of the drill is stationary. Damage or wear may be caused to the gearing mechanism if you change speeds while the motor is running.

To fit attachments to some drills, the chuck has to be removed with a special spanner, supplied with the power tool. To remove the chuck, lock the spanner on the nut behind the chuck, and give the chuck a firm twist to the right. If it is tight, insert the chuck key and give this a sharp tap on the cross-bar end with a hammer.

The most common use for the power drill is to make holes. These can be made in almost any surface, provided the correct bit is used at the right speed.

When drilling in any surface, occasionally withdraw the bit from the hole to remove dust and débris which cause overheating. Masonry drills are prone to overheat, so allow the bit time to cool.

Most wood drilling can be carried out with bits similar to those used in hand drills. The only difference is that the power bit has a rounded shank.

Large holes are easier to drill if these are preceded by a small pilot hole which should be drilled very accurately.

For small drill bits (less than 5mm), use high speed; use a slow speed with larger bits if you are drilling metal. Always reduce pressure as the bit is about to break through.

If two pieces of wood are to be screwed

When hand held, the drill's vertical alignment can be checked with try-square

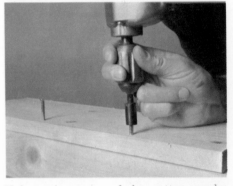

A screwdriver attachment in a drill can speed up the repetition fixing of screws

Hole-cutting saws and plug cutters can be used with drill on a variety of materials

Adjustable depth setting of a power saw should be slightly over depth of timber

Saw fence guide enables accurate lateral control of cut on a section of timber

Setting the depth carefully, a housing joint can be cut accurately with the saw

Mitres can also be produced, using the bench stand, with the saw set to an angle

Using the guide fence and protractor set to desired angle, mitres can be cut

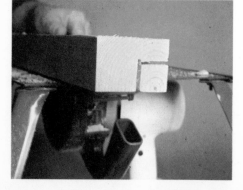
Rebates of various sizes can be cut on saw bench, using the fence as a guide

together three drilling operations are needed:

A pilot hole for the screw threads to bite into;

A clearance hole for the unthreaded screw shank;

A countersink for the screw head.

Special combination drill bits are made for drilling these three holes in one operation and are supplied with an adjustable depth stop which regulates the amount by which the head of the screw is set below the surface of the work. These combination bits are related to screw sizes.

Another bit which is available for drills is the plug cutter which produces small round plugs from the material you are using. These fit back exactly into the countersink holes to conceal the screw heads.

After use, rub down bits with steel wool and wipe with a thin oil. Any waste wood compacted into the grooves will cause the bits to clog, overheat or lose temper.

When drilling metals other than brass or cast iron, lubricate the drill bit. For steel, use a thin oil, for aluminium turpentine or paraffin, turpentine for glass and water for mirrors. The technique for drilling glass is described in the article on cutting glass.

Always mark the hole accurately and draw a cross to show the centre. To stop the drill point from slipping, either tap gently on glazed and smooth surfaces with a centre punch, just marking the glaze, to give a purchase point; or fix a piece of sticky tape on the surface and mark on it the drilling position.

Thin metal should be clamped to a piece of wood as this will reduce distortion and avoid jamming as the drill breaks through.

When drilling always carry the cable over the shoulder or clamp it in the hand. It can be dangerous if caught up in a powerful motor.

Always clamp workpieces firmly to stop them from revolving–a piece of spinning metal could be very dangerous. The drill must be at right angles to the working surface. You can use an upturned try square to check vertical alignment. However, a bench stand or a drill guide are more accurate means of ensuring accuracy.

The drill stand has many advantages, since it is adjustable for both height and radial swing. A variety of drills can be simply and quickly clamped into the stand.

Sanders

Sanders are of several types: belt, drum, orbital, finishing or disc sanders. Disc sanders are the most usual and have a rubber or flexible backing pad.

All types of these work by means of discs or belts of abrasive papers either revolving or vibrating over a surface. Abrasive papers are removable and replaceable.

The ordinary disc sander has limitations as it tends to leave swirl marks. If you are seeking finer work, it is best to use a backing bed with a knuckle joint which ensures that the pressure on the work is always even, reducing swirl marks, or the type which has a foam-rubber flexible backing.

The orbital sander consists of a vibratory attachment, or a purpose-made integrated unit capable of better work. These have a large surface pad to which an abrasive sheet can be attached.

This pad moves up and down and in small circles to impart a smoothing action to the surface.

A drum sander consists of a revolving drum of stiff foam rubber with an abrasive strip fixed around its edge.

Belt sanders consist, as the name suggests, of a continuous belt of abrasive material, enabling bigger jobs to be tackled and better results to be achieved.

Dependent on type, belts, discs and drum sanders are either tightened up on the power tool by means of screw and clamp washers or are stuck on to the abrading surfaces with a special glue or adhesive tape.

Discs, belts and sheets are made in coarse, medium and fine grades, in glass-paper or carborundum. The latter costs more but has an extended life. In addition, there are wet-and-dry and preparation papers for rubbing down paintwork.

The disc can also be used in conjunction with a lambswool pad for polishing purposes.

Bench sanders consist of a disc which is covered with an abrasive paper. It works in conjunction with a horizontal table and guide fences. The sander enables ends of timber to be sanded accurately. The guide fence can be set at 45° or 90° angles for mitreing.

A bench sander can be duplicated by a power drill, sanding-plate attachment, and a horizontal sanding stand.

Bench grinder

This enables blunted tools to be ground and honed. The best units provide a shaft on each end, with a coarse stone, for grinding, and a fine one, for honing.

Stands

Another useful attachment is the horizontal bench stand. This enables the drill to be locked into a position on a bench, and is ideal for jobs, such as sanding, polishing and grinding or wire brushing, using the appropriate attachments.

The bench stand can also be part of a lathe unit, which enables a wide range of wood-turning work to be produced. This is useful, not only as a hobby, but also for making mouldings to replace damaged ones not readily available commercially.

A drill stand permits highly accurate bench work. It can be adjusted for height and radial swing. The drill simply latches into a collar and is clamped firmly into place by a back screw. For repetition work, the drill stand enables accurate and quick location for each hole.

Attachments

Bench attachments should be screwed firmly to a stout bench, so that they do not vibrate or move during use.

The only other items of equipment you may need are a selection of 'G' cramps to hold, in some circumstances, the work.

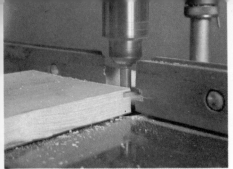
Milling attachment with drill in stand
to cut rebates. Scrap wood makes 'fence'

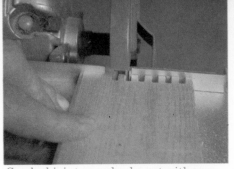
Combed joint can also be cut with saw
attachment, here using a gauge plate

Power saw in saw bench can also be used
to cut rebates by making two cut passes

Use a push stick to complete the cut
on a saw bench; keep hands well clear

Kerfing—makes a series of close cuts
two-thirds wood depth—to allow curve

Jig saw is first inserted at an angle
when penetrating material is to be cut

A choice of blades enables a variety
of materials to be cut with this unit

Removing old disc adhesive, with tip
of old screwdriver, from grinding plate

Apply new adhesive to face of plate by
pressing to surface with plate turning

Many handyman projects are made easier if a power saw is used. It is most important to buy the best equipment you can afford. There is a wide range of power attachments for such varied tasks as mitreing, planing and dowel-jointing. The best finish will only be achieved if the basic tool and the specialized attachment is used correctly.

Power saws, both as attachments to power drills and as integrated units, are among the most widely used of power tools. Saws are made in a variety of motor powers, and with various sizes of blade. The blade is circular and revolves on a spindle.

Variations on power saws are rebating attachments, which fit on to power drills and have a similar but much smaller blade and the jig saw, which has a thin serrated blade, which moves up and down to cut shapes.

The power saw is a versatile tool and can be used in conjunction with saw tables and benches to provide a permanent cutting jig, enabling a wide range of power woodworking jobs to be carried out.

Many of the jobs tackled with hand tools—such as cutting, rebating, mitreing, dowel-combed jointing—can be carried out with a power saw.

Obviously, if you intend to make a lot of use of a power saw, either use a larger drill with attachments, since small drills may not be up to the work, or buy an integrated saw. Again, choose a better one if you are going to use it very much.

Take care when using a saw that you do not strain the motor, this will be detectable by 'hunting' sounds and slowing down. Some makes of attachment have a clutch device which allows the blade to slip at a certain level of strain, to relieve motor stress.

Circular saws can be set for correct depths—just slightly more than the depth of timber—and should always work at a fast speed. Saws are fitted with a rip-saw fence to guide you accurately and can be operated at various angles for bevelling—there is a gauge on the unit to allow angles to be correctly set.

Before using the saw, remove any surface nails and screws as these will at once blunt and damage the teeth of the saw blade.

Used properly, a circular saw is perfectly safe. However, never switch it on with the hands near the blade; never make adjustments near the blade with the power plugged in; and always make sure that the retractable blade guard is in working order.

This is spring loaded and pushes back as the saw advances. Make it an automatic practice to unplug when making any adjustments at all.

The two basic attachments with the saw blade are a saw stand, on which the drill with a saw attachment is mounted, and a saw table, under which the saw drill attachment fits.

The attachment is only really suitable for light use; other than for occasional such work, it is far better to buy an integrated saw, capable of heavy duty.

When operating a power saw, start the motor before the blade touches the wood. The saw must always run at a high speed. Saws have a rip fence which keeps the blade running accurately to the line; this is set to the depth measurement of the cut.

If the blade wanders from the cutting line, never attempt an adjustment by twisting the saw, as this may jam the blade. Go back a short distance and resume cutting. If the blade binds persistently, it needs resharpening.

Blades
There are two main sizes of blade—125mm and 150mm. The smaller blade gives a depth of cut of 40mm and the larger 50mm. Circular-saw blades are available in several types and patterns.

Combination type Suitable for most purposes such as cutting thick or thin hardwoods and softwoods with or across the grain, as well as plywood, blockboard and hardboard.

Cross-cut blades possess fine teeth which cut smoothly across the grain of hardwood and softwood, and are also suitable for cutting plywood, hardboard and blockboard.

Rip blades These are used for coarse cutting with the grain.

Planer blade Has no sideways 'set' to its teeth, and relies on deep, widely spaced gullies for clearing away waste. Gives a neat cut; will saw a variety of thick or thin materials. Planer blades must be kept

If plate holes are cut in disc, correct grinding angle can be checked from back

Disc is next located on adhesive. When running, slots provide view through plate

When standing over work, angle can easily be checked from rear position

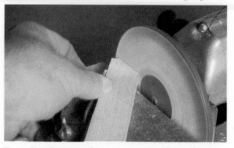

Rough edges and corners, can be taken off; angles can also be made on wood

Bevels can also be produced by using a replaceable disc on sanding unit

Bench lathe and attachments permit ambitious woodturning work to be carried out

sharp and must run at maximum revolutions, to avoid clogging, and an overheated motor.

A circular saw allows bends, mitres and grooves to be cut.

The sole plate of the saw is hinged to tilt and allows cuts to be made at any angle between 45° and 90°. Minimum depth is represented at 45° and maximum at 90°. Three basic adjustments for depth, angle and width of cut should always be made and checked before any cutting.

Bench saw

A bench saw consists of a flat table top with the saw blade projecting through it. The blade is adjustable for depth and angle of cut and protected by the sliding guard.

There are two guide fences which allow timber to be cut correctly. The rip fence parallel with the saw blade can be slid sideways up the edge of the table. Timber is guided along it into the blade for parallel straight cutting, usually along the grain.

The cross-cut guide is for cutting across the width and grain of wood at any angle and slides from front to back of the table in a slot parallel with the blade.

A protractor on the front of the guide enables angled cuts to be made.

Both fences can be removed so that large sheets of material can be cut. It is important to check the angle of the rip fence periodically, as the blade may jam if it is not exactly parallel with the blade. Some bench saws have slip clutches to disengage the motor.

Never direct short pieces of wood or

the ends of pieces into the blade with your hands. Always use a push stick to direct it. This is a simple piece of wood with a v-cut at the front end.

Wood is also likely to slip on a saw bench because the torque of the blade tends to push it aside if it is not held firmly. This may be a problem when using the cross-cut guide set at an angle.

Usually, when cross-cutting, you should hold with both hands on one side of the blade, and let the offcut fall away. Pushing from both sides closes up the cut around the blade and may cause jamming.

To cut a mitre, set the protractor on the cross-cut guide to an angle of 45° and place the wood against the guide and slide both wood and guide into the blade.

To cut a bevel along the edge of a piece of wood, again set the blade at an angle of 45°. Some saws have built-in protractors though on others the table tilts and not the blade.

Firring

Firring consists of cutting a taper on a long piece of wood so that it is narrower at one end. Firring pieces are used for rafters on flat roofs to create a slight drainage slope.

An adjustable jig is the best way of cutting these. It can be made from two battens of medium length. These are set face to face and fastened together by a hinge at one end and a slotted metal strip, secured with wingnuts, at the other.

By opening the jig to the extent desired and tightening the nuts, an accurate profile for repetition work is provided.

Kerfing

This allows a piece of timber to be bent to produce an outside curve. This is achieved by making a row of parallel cuts across the wood on the inside of the curve through half to three-quarters of the wood's thickness, all along the part to be curved. The wood can then be bent, though it is best to dampen or steam it first.

Use a cross-cut or planer blade to make the cuts as a combination blade is too coarse. Kerfing reduces the strength of wood and should not be used for load-bearing frames.

Housing joints

Housing and other grooves can be cut by setting the blade to the depth required and cutting the sides of the groove first; use the fence to keep them straight.

Next, remove the fence and cut out the wood in between by passing the wood over the blade. Mark the limit of the groove on top of the wood, to avoid cutting past the edges.

For a stopped housing, you need to cut the last distance by hand, using a chisel. This method provides for an even depth of cut all over the groove. Wood can be removed in the same way when cutting tenons.

Rebates

Rebates may be cut in two ways on a bench saw. One is to cut along one side of the rebate, using the fence, and turning the wood through 90° to cut the other side.

It is quicker to mount the blade on 'wobble washers'. These are a pair of angled washers which make the blade wobble from side to side as it spins, so that it cuts a wide groove.

The width of a rebate can be increased by making several passes. Once you have set the blade on its washers, place a section of battening against the fence to protect it.

For narrow cuts, adjust the blade to cut into the battening. The depth of cut can be adjusted in the normal way. You can adjust the width of the wobble cut by means of washers.

Jig-saws

The jig-saw and the jig-saw attachment enable curves and shapes to be cut. While safety rules should still be observed, these are far safer to use than circular saws.

The moving blade can be touched without hazard, though this is not recommended.

This attachment is limited to soft materials, up to about 50mm thick, or harder materials, such as hardwood, 25mm thick. The jig-saw can be used either as a hand-held or bench-mounted tool.

Rabbeter

The rebate attachment, or rabbeter (rabeter), can be used either free in the hand or as a bench unit with a lathe kit. The rabbeter can, with different blades, or cutters, be used to produce tongues, rebates, slots, decorative edges and grooves.

Decorating with power equipment

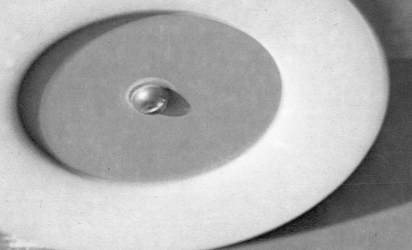

Attachment consisting of rotating foam drum with replaceable sanding sheets

Power tools or attachments can take much of the tedium from the preparation of surfaces, as well as enabling one to produce a high-grade finish. Power sprays for larger areas, and aerosols for small surfaces, also give a finish of high quality, provided they are used correctly and in the right conditions.

A spray-gun provides an excellent way of covering large surface areas with paint quickly and well. It can be used both externally and internally. Before painting it is necessary to mask all areas not to be covered.

Small objects are usually sprayed with newspaper behind them to protect the background.

When masking for interior or exterior work, take care to protect window and door areas.

Choice

The range of spray guns extends from the simple electric gun to more sophisticated units using compressors. The latter are fairly expensive and may be hired unless you plan extended considerable use of a spray unit.

Another type of gun is electrically powered, working on an airless principle. A compressor is not needed as the gun is operated by means of a self-contained pump. When using an airless pump the bounce and overspray found with some types of pump are reduced to a minimum.

The operating pressure of a spray gun should be at least 28kg/cm^2. Accessories include differing types of nozzle and a flexible extension nozzle which is useful for painting ceilings and doors.

For most home decorating jobs you will need two types of nozzle: the fishtail or fan-shaped, and the plain, round nozzle.

The fish-tail nozzle gives a wide spray and is used to spray large areas. The plain, round type gives a narrower trajectory and is used to cover narrow or restricted areas.

Never turn a spray gun upside down in use, or it will cease to operate.

All paint must be diluted to suitable consistency before it can be sprayed

Carefully mask surrounds; spray paint evenly from left to right from 200mm

Paint-stirring attachment, used in power drill, mixes brushing paints thoroughly

A variety of wire-brush attachments enable a range of jobs to be tackled

A disc sander, either fixed, flexible backed or knuckle-jointed, to smooth down

Orbital sanders work by vibratory action and produce a fine finished surface

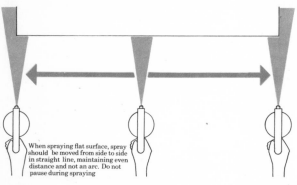

When spraying flat surface, spray should be moved from side to side in straight line, maintaining even distance and not an arc. Do not pause during spraying

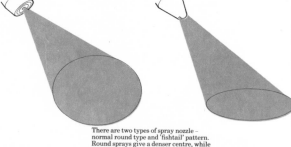

There are two types of spray nozzle – normal round type and 'fishtail' pattern. Round sprays give a denser centre, while fishtail covers wide, flat area evenly

Masking

The first task before starting to decorate is to mask, thoroughly, all areas that are not to be painted. Masking can be done quite effectively using newspaper and masking tape.

Use a tape with a low-impact adhesive backing as this can be peeled off quite easily afterwards. Anatomized paint will penetrate everywhere and it is essential to make sure that the masked areas are completely sealed.

Once the finish coat is applied, the masking tape should be left in place overnight.

When spraying large areas, such as walls and ceilings, ideally the room should be completely cleared. If this is not possible, stack furniture in the centre of the area and cover with dust sheets or sheet polythene. For extra protection, polythene sheeting can be stapled to floorboards. The area should also be well ventilated. Wear old clothes and a protective mask. Never smoke when working, or spray paint near an open fire or an appliance with a pilot light.

Externally it is not necessary to mask woodwork or rainwater goods that are to be painted at a latter stage. Stone, brickwork, tiles and any paths, patios or areas of decorative concrete will need covering as they are very difficult to clean afterwards.

Type of paint

Almost any type of paint can be sprayed provided a good-quality gun is used. Spray application is not recommended for the primer coat, as a brush will 'tease' and produce a better bond than sprayed paint, which is inclined to 'lie' on the surface.

Emulsion, oil-based, polyurethane, wood preservatives and bituminous paints can be sprayed. They should be thinned to a suitable consistency. Thinning is important as the paint has to be atomized as it is ejected.

The correct thinner will bring the paint to the consistency of thick cream. Use the type of thinner recommended by the paint manufacturer. It may need a little practice to find the right consistency. If it is too thick it will clog the nozzle; too thin and the surface coverage will be thin and inadequate.

Generally, water or oil-based paints will need thinning by a third to a half, while other paints, such as lacquer, may need equal quantities of paint and thinners.

If the nozzle of the gun becomes clogged it can usually be freed, using a thin piece of wire.

Spraying

Spraying should be carried out in clean, dry and relatively warm and still conditions. A temperature of 21°C is ideal. In colder conditions, paint takes relatively longer to dry. All surfaces should be suitably prepared and primed before being sprayed.

First, test the spray application on a spare piece of hardboard or other surface. Start at the top of the area and work, keeping the spray nozzle about 200mm from and at right angles to, the surface.

Apply using wide, horizontal strokes parallel with the surface, in a steady continuous motion. If you stop, even for a moment, the paint will run in that position. With the gun used in an arcing motion, paint will be deposited unevenly.

At the end of each stroke, release the trigger to prevent heavy overspray; overlap slightly at the end of each stroke to obtain even coverage. At least three coats will have to be applied, but this is no problem as application is quick.

Paint, such as gloss, applied too thickly, will run and look unsightly. Evenness of application is particularly important on decorative interior paint surfaces; on exterior work, such as covering stonework, slight runs will not matter.

Always allow any spray coat to dry thoroughly, or the paint may 'curtain' or run. A pimply orange-peel effect may also occur.

After use, thoroughly clean the container and mechanism with water (in the case of water-based paints) or thinners or white spirit for other paints. Remove the spray heads and clean these individually.

For spraying small areas or objects, it may be more convenient to use an aerosol can. The techniques are similar to those for spray guns. In average conditions, allow seven minutes between application of coats; longer in colder conditions.

Powered stirring

A power paint stirrer is an attachment to use in conjunction with a power drill. It provides an effective method of mixing paint, particularly large amounts, thoroughly.

Stand the can on a sheet of newspaper. Immerse the paint stirrer right into the paint, then start the drill. A high drill speed can be used. Switch off before removing the attachment, or you will distribute paint widely around the tin; clean the stirrer thoroughly after use.

Thinning chart

Type	Thinning required	Number of coats	Remarks
*Gloss paints	2–4 parts paint 1–3 parts thinner	3 light coats	10 minutes between coats 1/2; 20 minutes between coats 2/3
Gloss paints	2–3 parts paint 1 part thinner	2 or 3 light coats	20 minutes between coats
Emulsion (for absorbent surfaces, e.g. Walls/ceilings	1–2 parts paint 1–1 part water	3 light coats	20 minutes between coats
Water paints	1–2 parts paint 1–3 parts water	2 light coats	15 minutes between coats
Cellulose (paint and primer)	1 part paint 1 part thinner	As required	20 minutes between coats. Ensure ventilation
Creosote/wood dye	None	As required	
French polish	2 parts polish 1 part thinner	As required	20 minutes between coats
Insecticides	As specified by manufacturer	As required	Do not spray into the wind

*Quick-drying gloss paints are recommended

Dilution factors above are based respectively on Burgess Powerline models VS646 and VS969. Refer to manufacturers for other makes. Advice should be sought of given makers for specific paints or other liquids.

Power sanding
Drills with attachments or purpose-made tools, used with abrasive papers or metal discs, can be used to rub down surfaces. Preparing a surface can be a long job; but much of the tedium is removed by using power equipment.

Orbital sanders
These are self-contained units with a flat, elongated cushion-backed abrading surface, which rotate in small circles over the work area. Abrasive paper is stretched over the flat cushioned pad and held in place by pressure clips.

This type of sander is best used for light finishing work, such as rubbing down or keying paintwork, for further paint coats. Orbital sanders may be in the form of power-drill attachments or integrated tools.

In use, the weight of the tool will give sufficient pressure but hand guidance will be needed to prevent the pad from sliding about on the surface.

Disc sanders
The power tools more often used for heavier work are rubber or flexible-foam discs and drum sanders.

A rubber disc attachment consists of a flexible rubber backing pad to which are attached discs of abrasive paper. These are secured by means of a centre locknut and plate, or fixed with a special adhesive.

The rotary action of a fixed sanding disc may leave unsightly, scored, circular markings on the surface. The flexible type, with a knuckle joint or foam back, produces generally better work.

When using the fixed rubber disc, do not use the entire surface of the disc at one time; work with the disc tilted at an angle of 30°–this will help to minimize swirl marks.

Do not exert heavy pressure, as this may overload the drill; use light sweeping strokes. Start with a coarse paper, working through to finer paper and, for a very fine surface, use a hand-held sander to finish off.

A disc sander is not generally suitable for removing paint. The friction set up between the paper and the surface generates enough heat to melt the paint which is then driven into the surface and also clogs the paper.

Bare wood is best sanded with the grain but when using a disc sander this is not possible.

A drum sander, which is a foam rubber wheel with an outer-covering, or tyre, of abrasive paper will sand along the grain. It can be used on flat, convex or concave surfaces.

The abrasive paper is held in place with non-hardening adhesive. Where adhesive fails before the paper is worn, apply more adhesive to the non-abrasive surface.

All change
To fix an abrasive paper on to a disc with a non-hardening adhesive, rotate the backing disc, spreading the adhesive while running the drill.

Stop it and then press the abrasive disc into place; between changing the discs remove any adhering adhesive by rotating the backing disc and, at the same time, skim off the adhesive with a blunt piece of metal held against the moving disc.

Wire brushes
Wire-brush attachments, either in the form of a cup or a disc, fixed by a centre spindle into the chuck of a power drill, can be used to prepare rusted surfaces.

The choice of attachment depends on the form of the surface; a section of guttering, for example, may best be treated with the cup attachment; the inside of metal guttering may more easily be cleaned with the disc attachment, which operates end on.

Take care not to damage the surface, as a wire brush is fairly harsh in operation. It is also advisable to wear protective gloves and goggles as a guard against flying particles of rust.

Abrasive papers
The finish on sanding papers depends on the number of abrasive particles, or granules, to the mm². This is called the 'grit'. The larger the number of grits, the finer the paper.

Papers range from coarse to fine. You will only achieve a satisfactory finish if the correct paper is used. However hard you rub with a coarse paper you will not obtain a fine finish.

Start work with a coarse paper and work through the range to fine.

It is not possible successfully to rub down damp wood. Abrasive paper should always be stored in a dry place as once it is wet it is useless.

There is, in fact, now no such thing as sandpaper; the abrasive quality of various types of paper is achieved by other forms of surface coating.

These may be granules of glass, emery, garnet, silicone-carbide or flint. Glass-paper is the most common.

Each type of surface is used for different finishing jobs and can be used either with a hand-held block, a power tool sander or attachment to a power tool.

Glass or garnet paper
These are used for obtaining a fine surface finish on bare wood. Garnet paper is harder wearing, and, therefore, lasts longer and gives a cleaner cut.

Silicone-carbide paper
Is more commonly known as 'wet and dry'. It is used wet to prepare painted wood or metal surfaces. When used wet, silicone-carbide paper tends to leave a muddy deposit on the surface being prepared. This should be wiped off periodically to avoid clogging the paper. Wet paper gives a smooth finish. It is used dry for exactly the same purpose as garnet or glass paper.

Emery paper
Emery paper is used solely for preparing metal surfaces.

Tungsten carbide
Tungsten carbide discs and pads can be attached to disc or orbital sanders. These have the advantage of a very long life and do not easily clog.

Woodwork: talking timber

Timber remains the most widely used product in do-it-yourself activities; it is, perhaps, the most versatile of materials and can afford immense satisfaction in use.

It is important to choose the right wood for the right job. Basically, there are two types of timber—natural and man-made boards. Natural timbers are, basically, hardwoods and softwoods, consisting of very many types. There are many types of man-made timbers, the most common being chipboard, blockboard, hardboard and plywood.

In choosing timber you must take into account whether the wood is to be used in the house or out of doors. For outdoor use, timber must withstand all kinds of weather and should be durable and rot-resistant. These include teak, oak, sweet chestnut and western red cedar.

Teak and oak, while expensive, are the best choice for uses such as garden furniture. Sweet chestnut, cheaper and lighter in weight, may not always be so easily obtainable. Western red cedar, however, is durable, lightweight, soft and fairly cheap.

Softwood, if partially protected and used for such purposes as, for example, the framework of a shed, can be used out of doors. Softwood is widely used for making kitchen furniture, such as sink and kitchen units. Deal (redwood) is widely used and should be free from knots; it is not easy to obtain free of knots in larger sizes.

Other major softwoods are western red cedar, douglas fir, hemlock and parana pine. These are normally knot-free in most sizes but more expensive than deal.

Hardwood, such as beech or ramin, are used where two surfaces are in moving contact, such as a drawer or a folding chair. Where timber is in contact with food, such as a breadboard, it needs to be hard and close-grained, so that particles of food cannot lodge. Sycamore and beech are suitable.

Types of timber
Some of the best-known timbers, uses, properties and characteristics are as follows:

Mahogany
This is easy to work and nails, screws and glues well. Care is needed in staining, but it will varnish and polish.
Uses: high-class joinery, general utility work and furniture.

Douglas fir
Light, reddish-brown in colour and reasonably easy to work. It requires care in nailing and screwing and produces good results in finishing, though the grain tends to lift; glues well.
Uses: all types of joinery and constructional work.

European whitewood
A non-resinous wood which is white to pale-straw in colour. Nails, screws and glues well and finishes satisfactorily.
Uses: general joinery and carpentry.

Birch
This is a whitish to light board, easy to work, turns well and stains, polishes and glues.
Uses: general joinery, moulding and furniture.

Elm
Yellowish-brown in colour, variable to work but takes a good finish. Nails, screws, stains and polishes well. It needs careful selection and seasoning.
Uses: general joinery and furniture.

Oak
Moderately easy to work but requires care in nailing and screwing. Stains, polishes, varnishes and glues well. There is a liability to corrosion when in contact with metal in damp conditions.
Uses: high-class carpentry, joinery and furniture.

Parana pine
Creamy-brown in colour and easy to use. Care in selection is needed, since this has a liability to twist. This often has highly attractive graining. Finishes excellently; needs care in seasoning to avoid twisting.
Uses: interior purposes, work tops and general carpentry.

Teak
This has a greasy feel but works moderately well. Nails and screws satisfactorily with care and varnishes and polishes well.
Uses: high-class work, including draining boards and garden furniture.

Western red cedar
This is easy to use and finishes satisfactorily, though grain tends to lift. Liable to corrode metals under damp conditions; a very light wood.
Uses: exterior joinery, weatherboards, shingles, and related work.

Red Meranti-Red Seraya
Pink to reddish-brown and generally easy to work. Nails, screws, glues, stains and polishes well.
Uses: joinery and construction work.

Western Hemlock
A non-resinous, pale brown softwood. Moderately easy to saw, with fair nailing, screwing and finishing properties.
Uses: all types of general joinery.

Timber terminology
Timber may be bought sawn, planed all round (PAR), or planed both sides (PBS). Planing of timber entails a loss of about 3·5mm, so a 25mm piece of planed wood ends up at only 22mm. Similarly, a board measuring 152mm ends up at only 146mm. Unedged boards (UE) retain the shape of the tree at the edges; sawn-edged boards (SE) have unplaned edges.

When buying timber use, where possible, standard sizes; these are cheaper. Allow a little extra on lengths, in particular, for cutting and for dirty or gritty ends. A good rule is to add an extra 13mm for every 610mm. Always reject material with large knots as this would be weak. Where there is a knot, there is often a bend or twist in the wood.

Timber with traces of bark at the edges, reducing the effective width, is called waney-edged. End splits or 'shakes' are another common fault and sometimes extend a long way up the board. The other main fault is that of cupped boards—a warped curve across the width.

Timber terms and faults

Planed all round (PAR) sides and edges

Planed both sides (PBS) edges stay sawn

Unedged (UE) sides are sawn or planed. Edges show the shape of the tree

Machine planed board showing: **1** Loss of thickness at end **2** Saw marks **3** Gash in the edge caused by log carriage.

A large knot in the edge may cause weakness and a change in shape

This shows a wane or waney-edged board

End shakes – first few centimetres are useless

Cupping – heart side has become rounded

Bowing – bending along the entire grain

Board can become badly twisted

Springing – a board may bend edgeways

Sapwood on edge is lighter in colour and attracts woodworm It should therefore be inspected for bore holes

Board cut across the pith. This is liable to warp, and pith is often surrounded by very small knots

Compression shake – a common defect

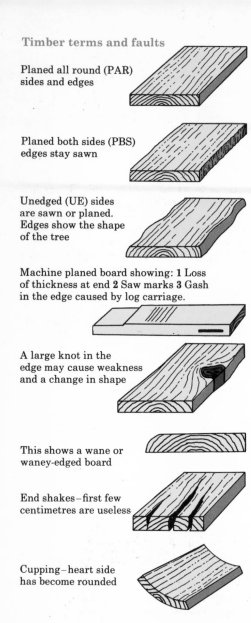

Man-made timbers

Chipboard

The most widely used of man-made boards, it is made from resin-bonded chips. Available unsurfaced, veneered and pre-finished, it does not lend itself to being worked in the same way as natural timbers but can be cut and planed at the ends. Another name for chipboard is particle board.

It is made in various grades for use as flooring and other decking surfaces. It has the advantage over natural timber of being far less subject to expansion and contraction from the effects of changes in humidity.

The four main grades of chipboard are *standard*, which is the cheapest and can be used in places where it will not be readily seen; *painting grade*, suitable for decorating; *flooring grade*, the strongest; and *exterior grade*, treated for resistance to water.

Pre-finished boards are either timber laminated or laminated in plastic. Edging strips are made to match the surface finishes.

Plywood

Widely used for woodworking jobs such as panelling and making drawer bottoms. Plywoods are veneers – thin sheets of timber glued together under pressure, with the grain at right angles to the adjacent sheets.

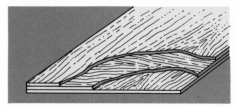

Ply always has an odd number of sheets, since an even number would be liable to warp. It ranges from two-ply, 0·8mm thick, up to 25mm for 11-ply and is made in both hardwood and softwood, such as birch and beech and West African and Gaboon mahogany.

Ordinary ply deteriorates in damp conditions, though mahogany ply will stand up to the weather if joined with a waterproof glue. A weather-proof grade is called WBP, an abbreviation for water and boil-proof.

Ply is also made with a decorative hardwood veneer on one face and is also available plastic-laminated.

Fibre building boards

These are made in several standard sizes and thicknesses and can be decorated or obtained predecorated. There are two main types – insulating board and hardboard.

Hardboard is made from softwood which has been pulped and drawn back into sheet form under heat and pressure. Standard hardboard has one smooth surface and one

rippled surface. Double-faced hardboard is made for use in situations where both sides will show. Other hardboards include oil-tempered, which has to stand up to external conditions, and enamelled and plastic-surfaced boards, for panelling and decorative uses.

Medium hardboard is made for heavier uses, such as partitioning. Hardboards range from 3mm to 6mm in thickness; medium boards are from 6mm to 13mm thick.

There is a wide variety of fibre building boards, ranging from perforated board,

known as pegboard, which has good acoustical qualities and can be used to fix light objects through the perforations, to laminated fibre wallboard, made up of thin layers of board bonded together. Insulating boards are lightly compressed in manufacture and have a textured surface. These are used to provide thermal insulation and for the reduction of sound.

Blockboard

This is made up of thin timber outer veneers with a core of solid wood and is sometimes called coreboard. Thicknesses are between 19mm and 25mm and the surface is smooth. It is stronger than chipboard and is used for heavy-duty work, such as shelving. Blockboard is very stable and unlikely to warp.

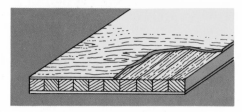

The edges of the board are not attractive, and these are filled and painted or covered with an edging strip, where the edges are likely to be seen.

Boards can be veneered, but it is usually best to have this done professionally, using specialized equipment. An alternative is laminboard – used for high-grade cabinet making – which has no edge gaps or flaws.

Cutting and finishing man-made boards

These can be cut with a panel or tenon saw. When cutting hardboard, avoid excess pressure, or you may tear the board, and always cut from the face side. Edges can be finished with a smoothing plane.

Chipboard has a tendency to 'break out' on the underside. To prevent this, mark the line of the cut right round the timber and score this with a marking knife; this will avoid splintering. Adhesive tape is an alternative. This can be applied along the line of the cut to avoi splintering or breaking out.

When cutting boards, always cut through the surface which will be seen, as this will present a clearer line.

The right way– with the right tools

The choice of hand tools today is very wide and it seems a daunting and bewildering task to choose those which are strictly essential. Why are there several types of plane and various patterns of screwdriver; what about all those other work aids and gadgets? Obviously, all have their specific or specialist applications. Proficiency and experience will provide the occasions for use of more specialized or sophisticated tools.

For home-maintenance and improvement jobs, a few basic tools should suffice. If, however, you make things or carry out more ambitious jobs around the home, you will steadily require more tools, including specialist tools or gadgets, some of which you can make.

The rule when choosing tools is to buy the best you can afford. A few good tools are better than a host of inferior ones, for these will probably not only give you poorer and discouraging results but break or wear out very quickly. Once you have bought a basic set of tools, you can always add more later.

Some people buy a tool a week or a month. Budget-plan buying such as this is a good idea and you will be surprised at how quickly your tool kit grows. A good rule is to avoid lending tools. There are more tool borrowers than buyers, and since tool borrowers may have little idea of use and maintenance, your tools can come back possibly the worse for wear.

Coupled with this is the inconvenience of not having to hand the tool you want. Tool borrowers may also be reluctant in returning tools; or in turn lend them to someone else!

The twelve basic types of tool suggested take into account the need for a number of types of chisel, screwdriver or drill bits. There is no need to invest in a full range of chisels, for example, at once. Choose only those you need for immediate use.

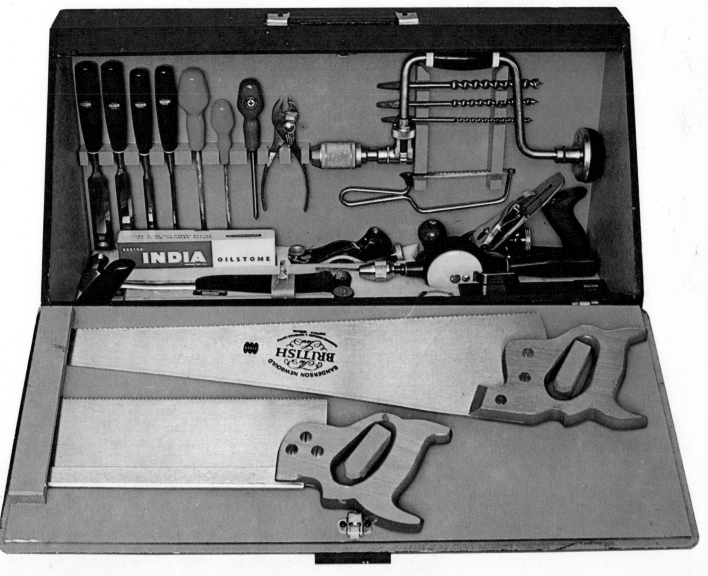

Cutting

A saw is the most-used tool in woodwork. A panel saw and a tenon, or back saw, are both useful acquisitions. You may buy these both together or one at a time. You will, however, need to invest in both at an early stage.

The tenon saw is essential for fine work. It has a stiffened backing to ensure a straight cut. A good choice is one about 305mm long with 14 points (teeth) to every 25mm.

The panel saw is designed for finished work but can be used for ripping (down the grain) or cross cutting (across the grain). Choose one about 550mm long with ten points to 25mm. Teflon-coated saws cut well through resinous or damp timber.

Drilling

A small hand drill, an assortment of twist drills and a masonry drill should cover most contingencies. The Stanley 'Yankee' Handyman push drill is a useful and easy-to-use drill, which comes with a variety of drill points. Later you will need to buy a hand or bit brace and a range of centre bits and augers.

Smoothing

A medium-sized smoothing plane abo 250mm long with a 51mm cutting edge, w enable you to tackle a wide range of jol from smoothing timber on the benc to easing doors and windows. Pla ing files can be similarly use though they are not really i tended for fine woodwork tre ment.

Holding

The vice is an essential part of wood-working and is the basic holding tool. While there are many cases in which you will later need clamps to hold timber, a portable vice is a good initial investment as it can be clamped on to many surfaces and can double as a clamp while glued and assembled work is setting. With a bench, a larger permanent vice is best.

Measuring and marking

A marking gauge is essential for any marking out of timber. This marks or scribes a line parallel with the edge of a board, by means of a small metal spike set on a wooden shaft with an adjustable crosspiece which slides up and down it. Later you will need other types of gauge, including a mortise gauge.

There are various types of measure. The retractable steel measure, in its own compact case, is a handy tool and enables you to measure longer lengths of timber than a wood or metal rule. These are very accurate, since the gradations of measurement are very fine.

However, a metal rule 610mm long is a more useful immediate acquisition for the serious woodworker and can be used to provide a straight edge. An alternative is the folding boxwood rule.

A try-square with a fixed blade is also necessary for ensuring accurate right angles – an essential in work of even limited precision. A size of 203mm or 228mm is suitable. It may be a good idea to invest in a combination try-square which enables you to mark other angles as well as right angles.

A slim marking knife is important. This marks with greater precision than a pencil. You could also use a trimming knife, which comes with a variety of blades for cutting various materials and also for cutting angles.

Joining

The two basic tools you need are the hammer and the screwdriver. Initially, you need only one hammer; the best one to choose is the claw hammer. The weight of hammer determines the work you can satisfactorily tackle. For general purposes, a 453-gramme claw hammer is suitable. You may shortly need to invest in the smaller Warrington-pattern hammer for a wider range of woodworking uses. You will also need a nail punch.

A good general screwdriver is about 254mm long. There are two basic types of screw head – the slotted and the cross-headed or 'sunburst' screw. You will need two or three general-purpose screwdrivers – a medium one and a cabinet screwdriver for screws with slotted heads.

The 'sunburst' head, usually under the trade name of 'Pozidriv', consists of a series of radial slots in the screw head. A range of four screwdrivers covers all possible types of Pozidriv head. This type of head prevents the screwdriver slipping in the slot and 'camming out'.

Sharpening

Chisels and plane irons need regular sharpening if they are to do the job for which they were made. If these become badly worn, they will need regrinding on a carborundum wheel and then sharpening and honing. To keep such tools in first-class order you will need a combination oilstone. These tools should be regularly inspected for sharpness, for poor or damaged work may otherwise result.

Wood shaping

The chisel is the basic wood-shaping tool and is made in various types to serve a variety of applications. Initially, a set of bevel-edged chisels – a 25mm, a 13mm and a 6mm chisel – should meet most or all requirements.

Optional extra

A useful additional tool which many people may want to regard as an early acquisition is the spirit level. This enables you to true up work and to make accurate fixings. A metal level is very durable and can also be used as a straight edge.

Using tools
Marking

Always mark the best-looking side of a piece of timber with a looped letter 'l' and the best edge with a small 'x'. These are carpenter's marks to show which side and edge will be exposed. These surfaces are known as the 'face side' and the 'face edge'.

Marking gauge

Hold the workpiece with three fingers and the gauge with one finger and thumb so that the stock is against the face edge of the work. Drag and not push the pin as this provides a firm, clean line for planing. Continue the line right round the work, always marking from the face edge.

To set the gauge, adjust the cross-piece with a rule to the required distance from the spike. Slide the tool up to the edge of the piece of timber to be marked.

The crosspiece maintains the spike at a constant distance from the edge, while the spike scribes a straight line.

Always work against the grain. This prevents grain from leading the point of the gauge into a non-waste section of the wood. Always mark away from the poorer edge of the timber.

When using the gauge to mark the thickness of joints, set it to half the timber thickness, minus a fraction of around 0·4mm, and gauge the setting. This should be tested by marking from both sides of the wood, which should leave just a tiny 0·8mm gap in the middle.

Marking knife

This scores more accurately than a pencil. By severing the fibres on the surface of the wood it helps to ensure a clean cut with saw or chisel. A knife with a replaceable blade will serve both as a marking knife and can be used for other jobs. The blade must remain sharp; otherwise it can slip and deface the work or provide an impositive working line. A knife with a replaceable blade ensures that you always have a sharp marking edge.

Try-square

Hold the stock of the try-square firmly on the face edge of the work with three fingers and the thumb. This forms a clamp and ensures that the work is steadily held as you mark with knife or pencil.

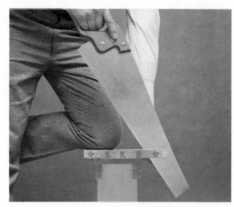

Sawing

Always saw on the waste side of the timber. As you near the end of the cut, support the timber so that it does not break off and splinter at the ends.

Panel saw

Steady the work by using three fingers and the thumb as a clamp on the saw handle. The feet should be comfortable and apart, in a boxer-like stance, and the body generally relaxed. Also, the body should not obstruct the work, as this may throw the saw off line. The arm should be free to move with a piston action, not catching the body in any way.

Start sawing at the front of the work, using the thumb as a guide and make a small backward movement of about 45° with the saw, first allowing the saw to drop on to the work across the marked cut line.

The blade should be kept vertical during sawing and the position should be such that the eye is able to sight down the cut line without contorting the body.

Maintain the saw blade vertically, gradually allowing this to drop until the handle end is on the guide line. Use an even, easy-flowing movement. Avoid short, jerky strokes which will cause the saw to move off line. Allow the saw to cut with its own weight and avoid great extra pressure.

Tenon saw

Hold this with its teeth almost parallel with the work surface. Again, use your left thumb to guide the blade for your starting cut. Draw the saw backwards, two or three times. Use as much length of saw as possible for each stroke.

Maintain your line of vision over the saw to help you to keep the line straight. When you reach the bottom of the cut, use three or four extra strokes to make sure that you do not leave a protruding fringe of fibres.

The first rule of carpentry is 'measure twice and cut once'. In using a folding rule or other measuring stick, the rule should be stood on edge on the piece of timber

being marked so that the marking graduations on the rule are actually in contact with the timber. This will avoid a marking error, as the rule will be in contact with the timber at the points where you want to mark it.

Hammers

Drive the hammer, with a short upward swing and a full follow through. To lessen the risk of hammer 'bruises' on the surface, keep the hammer parallel for the last few strokes.

Bench hooks

These are used to hold timber firm when using a tenon saw. The hook consists of a batten or lip at top and bottom of a base board, running about two thirds of the way across. When the hook is placed against the edge of a bench or working surface, the batten beneath prevents the hook from slipping.

The bench hook is simple to make. Materials required are a base board measuring about 300mm × 250mm × 25mm thick and two pieces of batten for the lips, 51mm × 25mm and 200mm long. These dimensions are not critical, but it is important to make sure that the timber is not warped in any way, or the hook will rock when used and make cutting difficult.

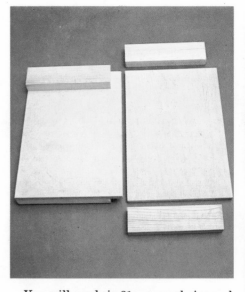

You will need six 31mm panel pins and some woodworking adhesive.

First, drive two pins just through a batten at each end and then spread woodworking adhesive on to the bottom of the batten. Align the batten accurately with the top edge of the base panel and nail the battens home. The other batten is fixed at the corresponding position on the left, below the board, so that the hook can be used either way up.

Taking care of your toolkit

Good tools need proper care and maintenance if they are to give years of reliable service. Chisels and planes are only as good as their cutting edges. Grindstones and oilstones are the basic tools used to keep a sharp edge which is essential. An oilstone box is a useful item you can make yourself to keep the edges in satisfactory condition.

There are two forms of stone–the flat stone, used for sharpening chisels or plane irons, and the wheel, also used for sharpening and for grinding badly blunted edges.

Types of stone

Grindstones are either of quarried natural sandstone, particles of sand or grit, naturally cemented together, or composition, abrasive wheels, which are hand-made stones.

Sandstones are slow-grinding substances, in which the stone may wear unevenly. They permit grinding to a good edge with little risk of burning the cutting edge of the tool, which should be lubricated with water during grinding.

The advantage of composition abrasive wheels is that, because of the fast-cutting qualities and speed at which they can be used, the grinding process is much quicker. They can also be manufactured in various grades–such as soft, medium and hard and in different degrees of coarseness and fineness.

Many grindstones consist of two wheels –a fine wheel and a coarse wheel, so that badly damaged or pitted edges can first be brought to a reasonable stage on the coarse stone and finished on the fine wheel.

The grindstone should be of a sufficient width to avoid hollow grinding of the blade edge. The grinding friction wears away worn or gapped cutting edges when the tool is held against a rotating wheel. Power grindstones are now widely used, though the older hand-turned wheels are very effective.

Where hollow or shaped-edged tools have to be ground, specially shaped stones or wheels are used, as, for example, when grinding a gouge. Tools which are ground on the convex side can, however, be ground on a flat grinding wheel.

When grinding a plane iron use a honing gauge; the iron should be ground to an angle of 25° to 30°.

Blunted or broken screwdriver tips can be reground on a grindstone.

Oilstones

Oilstones, used for honing, producing a fine edge to the cutting tool, are used after grinding. These are divided into natural oilstones, artificial oilstones and slip stones.

Natural stones are quarried and are usually obtainable in hard and soft grains. Water should be used for lubrication on coarse-grained (soft) natural oilstones and oil, of a non-drying nature, such as neats-foot oil, on the finer grades.

Artificial oilstones are manufactured by cementing together particles of carborundum and are available in fine, medium, coarse and combination grades. The combination stone consists of two grades of stone laminated together. One side is made up with a coarse grade for quickly wearing down very dull or badly nicked edges; the other consists of a fine grade for producing a keen cutting edge.

The slow-cutting natural stones produce a finer cutting edge than the fast-cutting artificial stones.

Oil is used as a medium on all artificial stones. Oils with non-drying properties should be used in sharpening, to prevent clogging of the stone, by floating off the particles of steel. Oil also prevents overheating caused by friction.

Techniques
Grindstones

To grind a badly blunted chisel or plane iron, before finishing on an oilstone, hold the chisel or plane iron at an angle of 20° to 25° to the wheel. The rotation of the grindstone should be towards the blade edge.

Take care to prevent burning at the edges of the tool during grinding as burning and overheating can affect or 'draw' the temper of the steel and cause it to soften. This will reduce the effectiveness of the cutting edge.

To avoid this, the edge should be 'quenched' frequently in water to cool it. The efficiency of edge tools depends on a hairline of sharp steel.

Move the bevel from side to side on the grindstone, keeping a light pressure. It is advisable to use a gauge, against which you can rest the tool, to obtain the correct angle. Otherwise the bevel may become convex.

There are two angles in grinding–the primary angle, or the rough edge, and the secondary angle, or sharp edge.

Oilstones

A blade is ground by moving it in a figure-of-eight motion on the stone, to produce a 'wire edge'. This is an edge of metal which can be taken off by rubbing the flat of the blade flat to the surface of an oilstone, using a few firm strokes.

Always keep oilstones clean and moist. Kerosene may be used to clean stones. If allowed to dry, they become hard and brittle and will readily become clogged or smooth. If stored in a dry place, keep them oiled and in a covered box.

Any irregularities or glaze (smoothness) may be removed by grinding on the side of a grindstone or by rubbing down with a wet sandstone.

Small, shaped oilstones, called 'slips' or 'slipstones' are used for sharpening curved cutting edges, such as gouges. Oil should be used as a lubricant.

Sharpening bits
Centre bit

This is held more or less vertically with the point on a flat surface. File the top edge of the cutter to an angle of 30°. Lightly file the inside of the scriber or spur with a file and finish using an oilstone slip.

Twist bit

This is sharpened as the centre bit. Take care not to damage the threaded point. The spurs can be filed carefully from time to time. Use a rat-tail file for the small pattern of countersink and a three-cornered file for the rose type.

Wood drills

These are ground to a 60° point; they can be filed or ground on a powered grindstone.

Care and storage

A tool box keeps tools in a place where you can find them. Tools should be kept in the dry. Lightly oil metal parts to prevent rusting. Always clean tools after use. Do not mistreat tools; always use them correctly.

Oilstone box

This oilstone box may seem, at first sight, to be rather elaborate; but proper care of tools is so often neglected and it will quickly justify itself.

The unit is lidded so it can be easily stored under a work bench when not in use. The inside of the box is laminated (Contiplas chipboard is suitable) so that oil deposits do not spoil the box, work bench

To remove plane iron, first slide back lever-cap cam and lift out through slot

Plane-iron cap assembly goes bevel side down on frog, which allows blade setting

Chisel is ground to 35-degree angle, using figure-of-eight movement, with thin oil

It is then turned over and ground flat on oilstone to remove the 'wire edge'

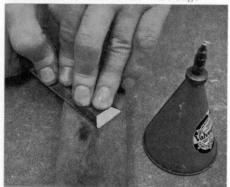

Some grindstones have both a coarse and fine wheel to sharpen badly worn tools

or work you are doing–and is easily wiped off.

By having the three oilstones, which are necessary to produce a keen edge, available in one unit and always ready for use, frequent sharpening becomes an easier operation. The oilstones are securely fixed to a base and are, as well, protected when not in use.

Start by cutting the base board to size. Contiplas provides a ready-made, easily wiped-clean surface. If 12mm birch ply is used for this instead, it should be well sealed with polyurethane.

Next, cut out to size the 12mm plywood lid, using a fine-toothed panel saw. Check your marking out in both cases and measure the diagonals of each piece to make sure that they are both true rectangles.

Cut the front and rear bearers to the given sizes from 47mm × 22mm planed softwood; one piece is 610mm and the other 590mm long.

On the base, mark out the line of the screws for securing these bearers to it at the back and front, then mark the position

of each screw hole. Dot punch these holes, drill and countersink for No. 8 countersunk screws. Clean up the prepared bearers, with a smoothing plane, glass-paper and screw into position.

Next, mark the front member of the lid frame to length, using cut lines. Measure inwards from these cut lines the thickness of the timber (15mm) and square cut lines across and down both sides (Fig. 2). Cut the two sides of the lid frame to length, plus 10mm.

Place these two pieces together in the vice, square a cut line across 5mm in from one and, from this point, measure 415mm, then square another cut line right across. Take these pieces from the vice and square all lines right round. Working to these lines, cut the pieces carefully to length with a tenon saw.

Set a marking gauge to 5mm and on both ends of the front member mark the top joint (Fig. 2). Again using a tenon saw, cut both joints.

Clean up with the smoothing plane and fine glass-paper, spread glue on the joints and pin the corners with 32mm panel pins.

Cutting list – all mm sizes

Part	Material	Qty.	Length	Width	Thickness
Base board	Contiplas	1	610	460	16
Lid	Birch ply	1	610	430	12
Front bearer	Softwood	1	590	47	22
Rear bearer	Softwood	1	610	47	22
Lid frame – front	Softwood	1	590	35	15
Lid frame – sides	Softwood	2	415	35	15
Lid hinge strip	Plywood	1	560	50	12
Box base	Birch ply	3	255	90	6
Box sides	Softwood	6	210	19	15
Box ends	Softwood	6	90	19	15
Wedges	Softwood	3	50	15	8

Hinges (2)
Screws 38mm No. 8 steel countersunk (8)
Screws 19mm No. 6 steel countersunk (for hinges) (8)
25mm No. 6 steel countersunk screws (12)
Quantity 13mm panel pins
Quantity 16mm panel pins
Quantity 31mm panel pins
Piece of leather strap 25mm wide × 170mm long
Surface-fitting screw cups + four 13mm × No. 6 screws (4)
No allowance made for waste.

Glue and pin the frame on to the plywood lid, pinning through the plywood into the frame with 25mm panel pins. Check that you maintain an even 10mm overlap on the front edge and sides, and that the ends of the side members finish flush with the back edge of the lid panel.

Glue and pin with 16mm panel pins the 12mm plywood strip inside the lid (Fig. 3). This provides extra thickness for the hinge screws. Clean up the whole assembly and screw the hinges in place.

The whole unit may now be given a coat of polyurethane varnish and left to dry while you make the small oilstone mounts. These must be made to suit the actual dimensions of the stones.

Construction details, consisting of a 6mm plywood base lipped with softwood 19mm × 15mm in section, are given in Fig. 4. These pieces are glued and pinned in position using 13mm panel pins, driven through the ply into the softwood.

The three sides should be glued and pinned. Next, place the oilstone in position and press the fourth side hard against it; first, spread glue on both surfaces. Secure the batten with panel pins.

Drill and countersink holes at each end of the box for No. 6 screws and screw the boxes into place on the base board. Put the oilstones in thin boxes and secure each with a wedge (Fig. 5).

Position the lid at 100° and secure this with a stay made from a piece of leather strap using surface-fitting screw cups and 13mm No. 6 countersunk steel screws (Fig. 6). Give the whole unit up to three coats of polyurethane varnish.

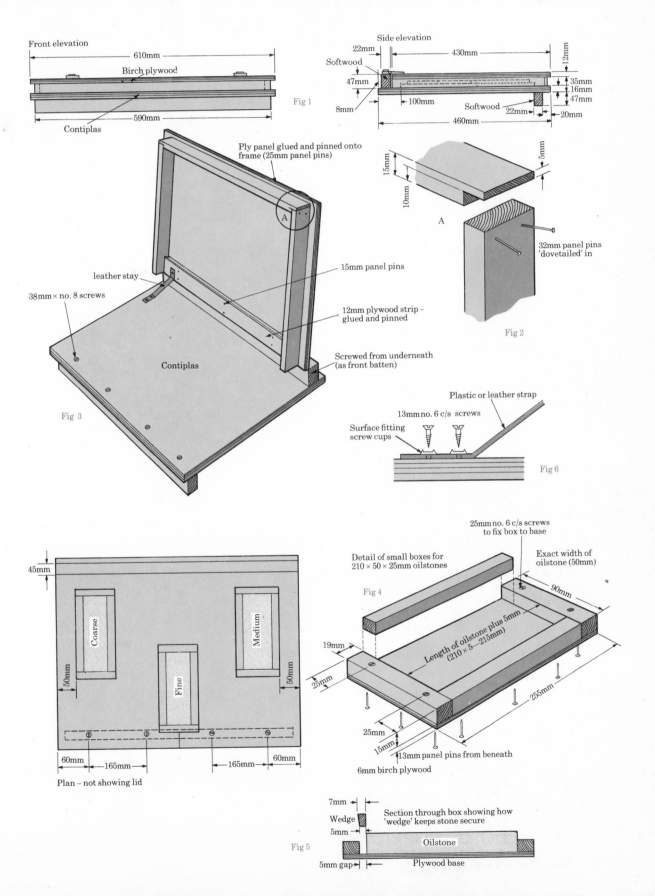

Front elevation
610mm
Birch plywood
590mm
Contiplas
Fig 1

Side elevation
22mm
430mm
12mm
Softwood
47mm
35mm
16mm
47mm
8mm
100mm
Softwood
22mm
20mm
460mm

Ply panel glued and pinned onto frame (25mm panel pins)
15mm
10mm
5mm
A
32mm panel pins 'dovetailed' in
Fig 2

leather stay
38mm × no. 8 screws
15mm panel pins
12mm plywood strip – glued and pinned
Contiplas
Screwed from underneath (as front batten)
Fig 3

Plastic or leather strap
13mm no. 6 c/s screws
Surface fitting screw cups
Fig 6

45mm
Coarse
Medium
50mm
Fine
50mm
60mm
165mm
165mm
60mm
Plan – not showing lid

Detail of small boxes for 210 × 50 × 25mm oilstones
Fig 4
25mm no. 6 c/s screws to fix box to base
Exact width of oilstone (50mm)
90mm
19mm
Length of oilstone plus 5mm (210 × 5—215mm)
255mm
25mm
15mm
13mm panel pins from beneath
6mm birch plywood
25mm

7mm
Wedge
5mm
Section through box showing how 'wedge' keeps stone secure
Oilstone
Fig 5
5mm gap
Plywood base

73

A place for tools

Looking after a tool kit properly is just as important as doing a job well. Not only should the right tool be readily to hand but it should be kept in its proper place. This purpose-designed toolbox, made largely from Finnish birch plywood, also shows you how to make the useful lap joint – one of those most commonly used in woodworking.

This tool box is designed to accommodate tools with a wide enough range to tackle almost any job around the home.

It is made largely of Finnish birch ply which requires a minimum of surface preparation and can be painted in clear polyurethane varnish.

The tool box is based upon a series of four box units; three are identical in size, and the fourth is just slightly narrower than the others.

Construction
Assembly is based on simple lap joints, one at each corner. These are glued and dovetail-pinned.

Start by cutting the long sides of the boxes to length and width. Make nine of identical length and width. Work accurately and check carefully that lengths are accurate and that the ends are at right angles to the long edges.

Mark out with try-square and marking knife and cut with a fine-toothed tenon saw.

It may help you to cut these out more quickly and with accuracy if you make up a simple box jig, with a saw-cut 680mm in from the end stop. Place the side members in this box, check that the end of the side is hard against the end stop, then, with the tenon saw in the prepared slot, cut to length. Repeat for all nine sides.

Using the same jig, cut another slot 280mm from the end stop to cut the six short sides. Cut another slot 230mm away from the end stop to cut two further short sides.

With a cutting gauge set to the exact thickness of the plywood (12mm), gauge lines across the surfaces and down the edges at each end of the long sides.

Do not gauge across the outside surface of the timber as these lines will be very difficult to clean off and will spoil the appearance of the finished box.

Re-set the marking gauge to 5mm and, from the outside face of the sides, gauge a line round the end to meet the 12mm cutting gauge line (Fig. 1).

This marks out the lap join at each end of the side. When all are marked they are ready for cutting.

With tenon saw and the wood held firmly in the vice – not too high or it will 'chatter' and cause the saw to wander off the line – cut down to the 12mm line.

Place the piece on its side on a sawing board and, working to the 12mm line, saw down to meet the first cut.

Be careful not to cut too deeply. If the corner waste does not come away easily, it may be because your first cut was not quite deep enough.

Repeat this operation on all ends, working carefully to obtain clean and accurate right-angled laps.

Cut the 6mm plywood bottom panels to size with a panel saw – allowing 4mm extra on each dimension for cleaning up with a plane. Saw these panels accurately so that all three match. Cut the narrower bottom panel to size in the same way.

Assembly
Spread woodworking adhesive evenly on each lap and on the end of each short side. Place the joint together and, making sure the ends are flush, place three panel pins through the long side into the end of the short side (Fig. 2). These pins should be slightly dovetailed.

Repeat on all four corners and then punch all nail heads slightly below the surface to give a better clamping action.

When all four corners have been pinned, go round again, putting in two more panel pins through the short sides into the ends of the long sides. Punch these slightly below the surface.

Check the diagonals; these must be identical, to make sure that the 'box' is square.

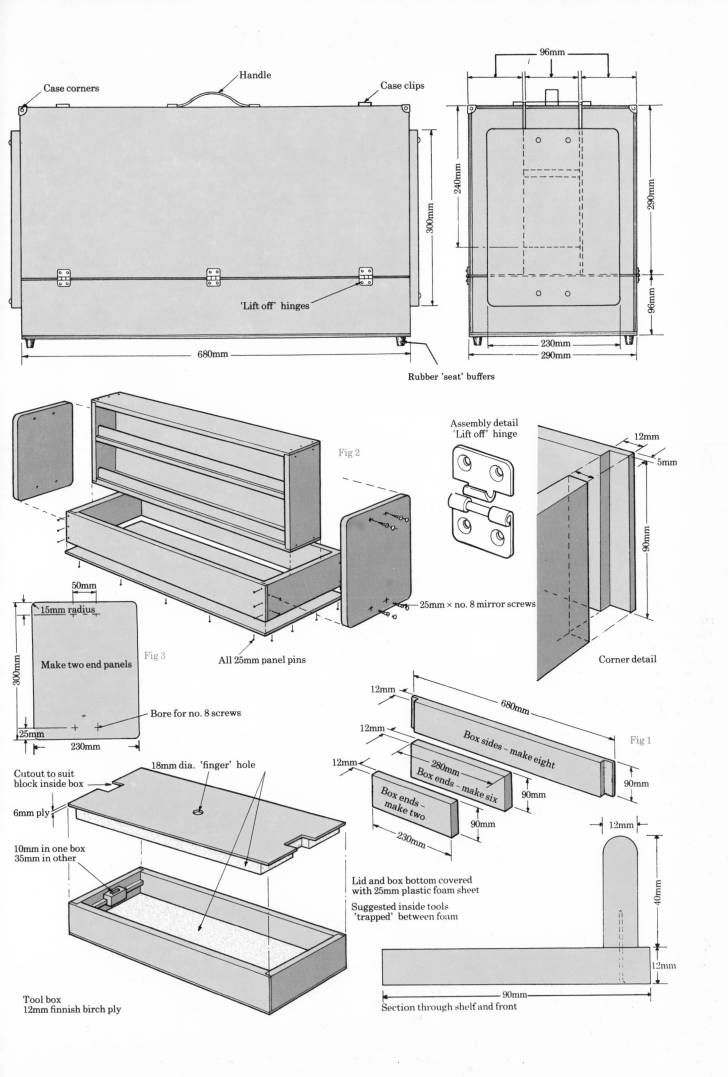

Case corners

Handle

Case clips

'Lift off' hinges

300mm

680mm

Rubber 'seat' buffers

96mm

240mm

290mm

96mm

230mm

290mm

Fig 2

Assembly detail
'Lift off' hinge

12mm

5mm

90mm

Corner detail

50mm

15mm radius

300mm

Make two end panels

Fig 3

Bore for no. 8 screws

25mm

230mm

All 25mm panel pins

25mm × no. 8 mirror screws

12mm

12mm

680mm

Box sides – make eight

Fig 1

90mm

12mm

280mm

Box ends – make six

90mm

12mm

Box ends –
make two

230mm

90mm

Cutout to suit
block inside box

18mm dia. 'finger' hole

6mm ply

10mm in one box
35mm in other

Lid and box bottom covered
with 25mm plastic foam sheet

Suggested inside tools
'trapped' between foam

12mm

40mm

12mm

Tool box
12mm finnish birch ply

90mm

Section through shelf and front

Part	Qty.	Material	Length	Width	Thickness
Bottom panels	3	Finnish birch ply	680	290	6
Bottom panels	1	Finnish birch ply	680	230	6
Box Box ends	6	Finnish birch ply	280	90	12
Box Box ends	2	Finnish birch ply	230	90	12
Box sides	8	Finnish birch ply	680	90	12
Shelf	1	Finnish birch ply	680	90	12
End panels	2	Finnish birch ply	300	230	12
Shelf fronts	2	Softwood	680	40	12

Panel pins (19mm)

No. 6 round-headed screws with Plasti-dome heads   (12)

Catches   (4)

Hinges   (6)

Handle   (1)

Rubber seat buffers or rubber headed nails (for feet)   (4)

Woodworking adhesive

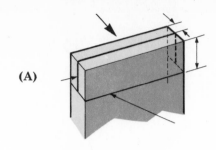

(A) Marking out details for one corner

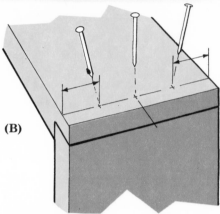

(B) Suggested spacing for the panel pins used to secure each corner

Three aspects of a versatile tool storage chest. The unit can take a lot of tools; obviously the more you load into it, the less portable it becomes. Stout end plates ensure that the unit is robust and able to take knocks. Two saws can be fitted to the fixed inside panel on one side. The side panel also provides storage, on a foam-rubber base, for a range of tools. A similar storage compartment lifts out on the other side. Both compartments have lids, enabling these sections to be used as 'satellite' tool-boxes, so that you can transport a few tools and have them ready to hand. The body of the box contains a set of drawers, providing further storage—so that most of the basic tools for jobs around the home can be kept conveniently in one place. The size can be scaled to your needs.

When you are certain that these are correct, spread glue all round the edges, place the bottom ply panel in place and, using 19mm panel pins at about 150mm intervals, pin the bottom panel.

Check the diagonals again when you have two pins in each side. If these are correct, carry on and complete the pinning operation. If not, adjust as necessary.

Repeat on all 'boxes' and leave to dry on a flat level surface, stacking one on top of another to check that they correspond.

When dry, use a smoothing plane to clean off all overlaps on the bottom of each box. Cut the centre partition in the smaller box to length. Spread adhesive, position it, then pin through the side of the box to secure it.

Round off the top edge of each of the two 40mm pieces of softwood with a smoothing plane and glasspaper. Cut these to length, and glue and pin into position.

Cut the end panels to size and mark out the radius on each corner (Fig. 3).

Saw off the waste with a coping saw and then, using a spokeshave or a shaping tool, trim these corners to the marked lines. Glasspaper well and glue and screw these on to the bottom and top centre boxes (Fig. 2).

The two outside boxes may now be placed in position and the hinges—three to each box—fitted.

Place the handle in position on the front panel, bore two holes through the panel, and insert 25mm × 3mm diameter bolts and washers to fix the handle.

Locate the catches and screw these into position.

It is inadvisable to use screws to fix the handle as these may eventually pull out when lifting the box when it is full of tools and, consequently, heavy.

Use rubber seat buffers under the base of the box as feet; screw these in place.

Coat all the outside of the box with at least two coats of clear polyurethane varnish.

The inside of the box may be fitted out to suit your particular needs; an example is shown in the main picture.

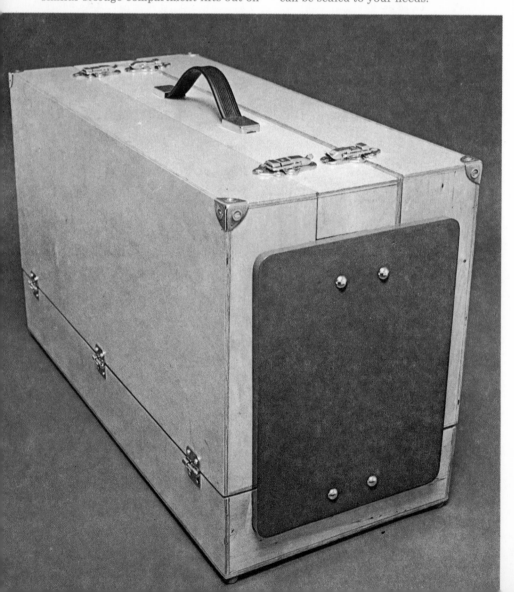

Bench of all work

With constant use, a work bench top does, in time, become very worn—chipped and unsuitable to work on. An important feature of this bench is that the top can be turned over for further use and eventually replaced, simply by removing a few screws.

The bench is strong enough to hold a large-capacity vice, and the top is big enough for tackling among the largest of home-construction jobs.

The height is 800mm—suitable for most adults. If you are taller or shorter than average, you may vary the height to suit your requirements.

All the timber widths (80mm) are the same throughout, but the legs are slightly thicker (28mm) than the rails (22mm), for strength and for extra glueing surface.

The screws are countersunk, and all surfaces which come into contact with each other are glued. Surplus glue is wiped off with a damp cloth.

Construction is based on a top and a bottom tray. Start by cutting the six cross rails, required for the trays. These must be exactly the same length (575mm), and the ends must be square.

These are marked out using the try-square and marking knife. The marking knife and a marking gauge fulfil slightly different roles. The marking knife is used to mark wood across the grain; the marking gauge is used along timber and across the end grain.

A knife gives a more positive line than a pencil and acts as a guide to the saw when cutting.

Cut six pieces 15mm longer than required from lengths of planed softwood. Place the pieces together and cramp them with a 'G' cramp or a small bar cramp.

Using a try-square and marking knife, next square a cut line across all pieces, 5mm from one end. Measure 575mm from this line and square a cut line across at the other end.

Unfasten the cramp and square the lines right round the timber with the marking knife. Using a bench hook and tenon saw, carefully cut these pieces to length, sawing on the waste side of the line. Place these pieces to one side and cramp the four front and back rails, cut to 1·05m, in two cramps.

These pieces are a little more complicated to mark out, so extra care should be taken.

The end rails are both inset 40mm. The

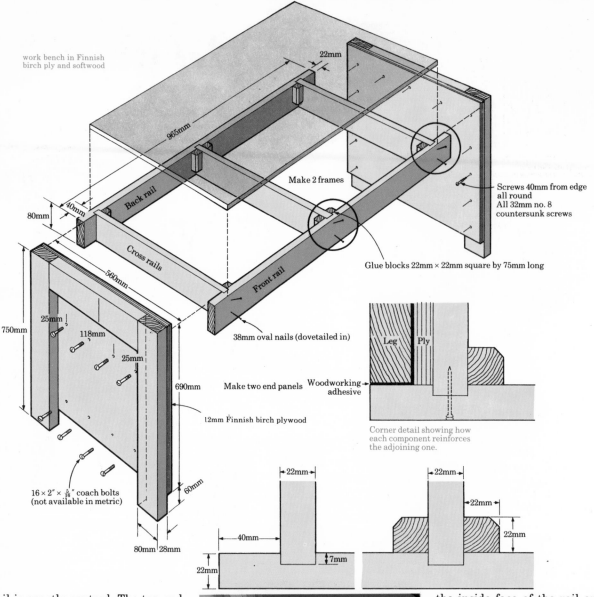

work bench in Finnish
birch ply and softwood

22mm

965mm

Make 2 frames

Screws 40mm from edge
all round
All 32mm no. 8
countersunk screws

Back rail

80mm
40mm

Cross rails

Front rail

Glue blocks 22mm × 22mm square by 75mm long

560mm

25mm

118mm

750mm

25mm

690mm

38mm oval nails (dovetailed in)

Make two end panels

12mm Finnish birch plywood

Leg   Ply

Woodworking
adhesive

Corner detail showing how
each component reinforces
the adjoining one.

60mm

16 × 2″ × ⁵⁄₁₆″ coach bolts
(not available in metric)

80mm 28mm

22mm

40mm

7mm

22mm

22mm

22mm

22mm

22mm

cross rail is exactly centred. The top and
bottom tray are made exactly the same.
Housing joints are used to secure all tray
rails.

A housing joint consists of a slot across
a piece of timber, into which the end
section of another piece fits tightly at
right-angles.

Housings are measured and marked
out with a try-square and a marking knife.
Use one of the cross rails to provide a
direct measurement, then square lines all
round the timber.

Set the marking gauge to the depth of
the housing joint and cut carefully to
depth with the tenon saw.

Check that you cut accurately; it will
assist if you keep the saw parallel as you
near the end of the cut.

Remove waste with a 25mm bevel-edged
chisel. First cut out waste on either side
of the cut, holding the chisel at an angle of
about 45°, with the bevel uppermost; do
this on each side of the slot.

This will leave a 'hill' in the centre of
the groove. With the chisel held flat,
remove the centre waste and clean up the
joint—first the corners, then the edge, and
the bed.

Use one of the cross rails to mark out
the width of the housing grooves by direct
measurement, so that the housing is made
to the exact width of the timber. Unfasten
the cramps and square the lines across on

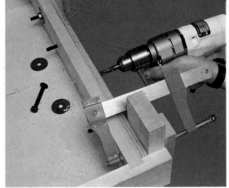

Turn bench upside down when drilling
holes for the bottom bolts

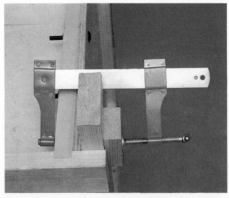

Use cramp with protective block of wood to
hold frames together when drilling holes

the inside face of the rail and down the
other edge.

Set the marking gauge to 7mm, and,
between the pairs of lines now marked,
gauge the depth of the housing. These
housings may now be cut, taking care that
cutting is to the waste side of the lines.

Saw one housing, remove the waste and
test with a cross rail for tightness of fit.
You should be able to knock the rail gently
in with a hammer and a piece of scrap wood.
If the joint is either loose or tight, make
the necessary adjustments to your sawing
when cutting the next housing.

Again, clean out the waste and test.
Repeat this for all housings, making a
tight but comfortable fit.

When all housings are cut, prepare the
glue blocks required—eight for each 'tray',
22mm² × 70mm long. Spread glue in all
housings and on the end of each rail.
Assemble the frame, using 50mm oval nails,
and secure each joint by dovetail nailing.

Spread glue in the corners of the frame
and on each glue block. Put the blocks in
place, using a 'rubbing' action, to squeeze
out as much glue as possible. This action
brings the surfaces close together. Secure
each block with 38mm panel pins.

Try each frame for squareness' by
measuring the diagonals with a steel tape
and checking that these measurements
are identical. Any slight differences can

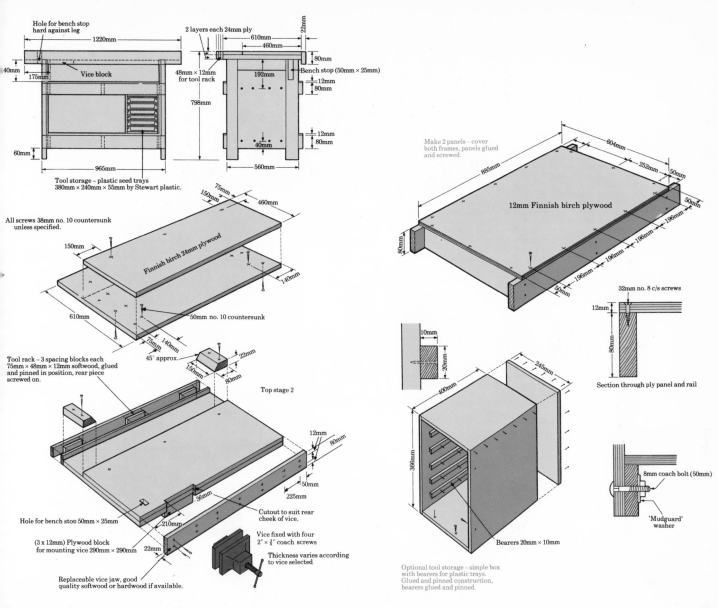

Hole for bench stop hard against leg

1220mm

40mm

175mm

Vice block

60mm

965mm

Tool storage – plastic seed trays 380mm × 240mm × 55mm by Stewart plastic.

2 layers each 24mm ply

610mm

460mm

22mm

80mm

48mm × 12mm for tool rack

Bench stop (50mm × 25mm)

192mm

12mm

80mm

798mm

12mm

80mm

40mm

560mm

Make 2 panels – cover both frames, panels glued and screwed.

885mm

604mm

252mm

50mm

12mm Finnish birch plywood

50mm

80mm

196mm

196mm

196mm

196mm

196mm

196mm

50mm

50mm

All screws 38mm no. 10 countersunk unless specified.

75mm

150mm

460mm

150mm

Finnish birch 24mm plywood

140mm

610mm

50mm no. 10 countersunk

75mm

140mm

45° approx.

22mm

150mm

80mm

Top stage 2

Tool rack – 3 spacing blocks each 75mm × 48mm × 12mm softwood, glued and pinned in position, rear piece screwed on.

12mm

80mm

50mm

225mm

36mm

Hole for bench stop 50mm × 25mm

210mm

(3 x 12mm) Plywood block for mounting vice 290mm × 290mm

22mm

Replaceable vice jaw, good quality softwood or hardwood if available.

Cutout to suit rear cheek of vice.

Vice fixed with four 2″ × ⅜″ coach screws

Thickness varies according to vice selected

10mm

20mm

400mm

245mm

366mm

Bearers 20mm × 10mm

Optional tool storage – simple box with bearers for plastic trays. Glued and pinned construction, bearers glued and pinned.

32mm no. 8 c/s screws

12mm

80mm

Section through ply panel and rail

8mm coach bolt (50mm)

'Mudguard' washer

be corrected by hand pressure. Leave the frames on a level surface to dry.

Check the overall length and width of these trays and cut panels of 12mm birch ply, 885mm × 604mm, to fit. It is important that the panels are an exact fit, so adjust the sizes slightly, to allow for any variations which may have occurred during construction.

All panels should be cut with a fine-toothed hand saw, to minimize splintering or breaking out on the underside of the panel. Trim the panels to an exact fit with a smoothing plane, mark out for the second countersunk screw holes and centrepunch the position of each.

Countersinking is the process by which a shallow depression is made in the timber, so that a screw head will finish flush with the surface. This may be done with a counter-sink or rose bit, held in a hand brace or in an electric drill.

Spread glue on the edge of the tray and on the underside of the panel. Place the panel in position and secure with four panel pins, placed on opposite sides. You may drill and countersink the holes in the conventional way, or use a tool such as the Stanley Screwmate, a small tool which drills and countersinks for matching steel screws.

The second tray is then prepared in exactly the same way. Both are set aside to dry thoroughly.

Cutting list – all mm sizes

Part	Qty.	Material	Length	Width	Thickness
Front and back rails	4	Softwood	965	80	22
Cross rails	6	Softwood	574	80	22
Legs	4	Softwood	750	80	28
Vice cheek (long)	1	Softwood	1220	80	22
Vice cheek (short)	1	Hardwood	305	100	25
Glue blocks	16	Hardwood	70	22	22
Well blocks	2	Hardwood	150	80	22
Tool racks	2	Hardwood	1220	48	12
Tool racks blocks	3	Hardwood	75	48	12
Leg panels	2	Finnish birch ply	690	560	12
Tray panels	2	Finnish birch ply	885	604	12
Top	1	Finnish birch ply	1220	610	24
Top	1	Finnish birch ply	1220	460	24
Mounting vice block	3	Finnish birch ply	290	290	12

50mm × 8mm Coach bolts (16)
8mm Mudguard washers (16)
50mm × 10mm Coach screws

32mm × No 8 steel c/s screws (64)
38mm × No 10 steel c/s screws (30)
50mm × No 10 steel c/s screws (8)

Panel pins: few 32mm
50mm oval nails
Glue

Having completed the two 'trays' and ensured that they are rigid, check the measurements between the projections at the end of each. These should be identical, but if they are not, select the largest measurement and use this for marking out the two end (leg) panels. These should be 560mm wide and 690mm long. It is, however, more important to work to the frame-work dimensions, in case of variation.

Once these end panels have been pre-pared, plane them to an exact fit. These should go tightly into the space between the tray and the rails. Mark the panels and trays for ease of identification.

Cut the four legs to an exact length–marking these all out at the same time to a length of 750mm. Glue and screw these on to the end panels, using techniques similar to those in assembling the trays.

Once the legs have been secured, cut the top rail to fit exactly between the legs, glue and screw into position, and leave these assemblies to dry.

The top of the bench consists of double layers of 24mm Finnish birch plywood, providing a very solid and flat working surface.

Two panels cut from a standard 1220mm sheet of ply allows for a 'tool well' at the

rear of the bench. Make one panel 610mm and the other 460mm wide.

These should be screwed together from beneath. There is no need, at this stage, to put in more than two screws. With the two pieces together, mark out, on the front edge, the cut out required to take the rear cheek of the vice.

All vices vary to some degree in their construction, and some are more difficult to fit than others. The vice used was from the Paramo range and was easily fitted. This vice requires a cut out 230mm long × 17mm deep. This is marked on to both

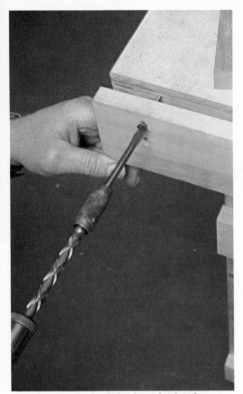

The front panel of the bench simply screws into place and is replaceable

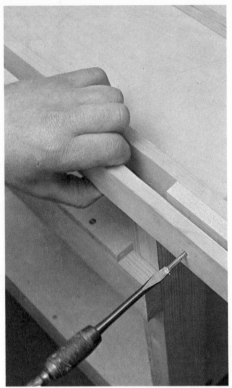

A handy rack for tool storage can be screwed on to the back of the workbench

Chopping out the slot in the bench top into which the bench stop is fitted

The serviceable vice is best fitted with coach screws; these provide a firm fixing

pieces of ply comprising the top and the cut out is gauged to depth.

Take out the screws and work on each piece individually. The cut out is best handled in the following way:

Cut down the lines marked to the gauge line. At 5mm intervals along the length of the cut, make a further series of saw cuts. This is waste material which has to be removed. Then, with a 25mm bevel-edged chisel, remove this waste.

Repeat this on the second panel and fix the vice block in position with glue and screws.

When the end panels are dry, mark out

the lines of the bolt holes. These should be 40mm from the bottom and 192mm from the top of each end assembly. Mark out the bolt holes and bore, with a twist bit, holes for $\frac{5}{16}$ in. (8mm) bolts.

Clean up the end (leg) assemblies with medium glasspaper and then similarly clean up the two trays.

Check that the leg assemblies fit into their respective positions. If not, adjust by using a smoothing plane, finely set.

Cover all contact surfaces for the bottom tray with glue and bolt the legs into position, using mudguard washers on the inside. These are extra-large washers

which help to spread the pressure when the nut is tightened.

Spread the glue and lower the top tray into position. Hold it in place with a pair of 'G' cramps on opposite corners. It will be easier to position this tray if the bench assembly so far is stood on end.

Once positioned, drill the holes and put the bolts into position. Put on the washers and tighten the nuts. Repeat this operation at the opposite ends, and check all nuts, making sure that all are really tight. Wipe off surplus glue with a damp cloth.

Rest the top on the bench assembly, with the vice block uppermost, and place the vice in position. Bore holes for the coach screws which hold the vice to the block. Use a 6mm bit in a hand brace to bore core holes for 50mm × 10mm Coach screws. Insert the screws and tighten up with a spanner.

Turn the top over and screw it into position with 50mm countersunk No. 10 screws. These screws go into the top rail of the leg assemblies and should be firmly tightened. If the top of the bench can remain a fixture, the contact surfaces may be spread with glue.

Place the top layer of ply in position and secure with screws.

A hole for the bench stop (50mm × 25mm) should be marked and cut. This hole must have its edge hard against the leg to ensure a 'frictional' fit.

Place a try-square on the front edge, with the blade protruding under the bench, to rest against the leg. Mark this position on to the front face and square this line across the front edge.

Square a line across the top surface of the bench and, from it, mark out the 25mm × 50mm rectangle of the bench stop.

Fix a piece of scrap wood with a 'G' cramp on to the leg under this position and 'chop' this hole right through, using a 25mm bevel-edged chisel.

Place the front 'cheek' of the bench in position and screw it but do not use glue. Ideally, this should be made of hardwood, but good-quality softwood will suffice.

This is the part of a bench which usually takes the most punishment and since it is easily replaceable, it can be readily renewed whenever it deteriorates too badly.

The rear tool rack is made from two pieces of 12mm softwood, 48mm wide. Cut these to length and prepare three blocks from the same timber, each 75mm long. These are the spacers.

Glue and pin the first piece in place on the rear of the bench. Position the three blocks, glue and pin, then glue and screw on the outside piece.

Make the end blocks of the trays from offcuts of the 80mm × 22mm rail material. Plane a 45° edge slope and fix these blocks with two screws each. The bevel allows dust and shavings to be swept out of the tray.

Rub down all surfaces with medium glasspaper and give the bench two coats of a clear polyurethane varnish. Similarly rub down the top, which is given a third coat of varnish. This final coat should have the gloss removed with a piece of fine steel wool, or use a matt polyurethane varnish finish.

Character walls in timber

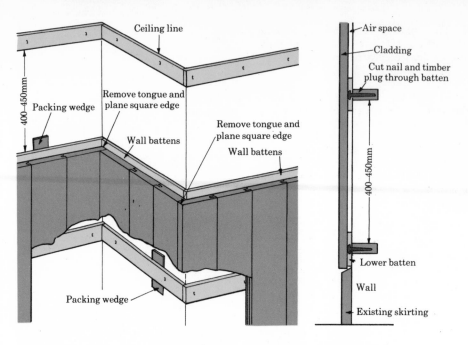

Ceiling line
Packing wedge
Remove tongue and plane square edge
Wall battens
Remove tongue and plane square edge
Wall battens
400–450mm
Packing wedge

Air space
Cladding
Cut nail and timber plug through batten
400–450mm
Lower batten
Wall
Existing skirting

Natural timber, either in plank form or sheeting, provides a durable and attractive wall surface. This can be fixed in a variety of ways–usually on battens or with adhesive on to a wall surface. The quality of the finished effect depends on the care taken in preparing the wall surfaces and during fixing.

One of the easiest to use and most attractive modern wall finishes is natural wood cladding. All the richness, variation and colour of natural timber can be used to decorate wall areas in any room in the home. Easy to fix, and virtually maintenance-free, wood cladding offers many interesting decorative possibilities.

Types of cladding
Timber cladding is available in two main forms:

● Standard-sized natural or pre-finished panels;

● Solid timber planking or boarding, either square-edged or tongued and grooved.

Both types of cladding are easy to fix, but cladding in panel form is usually quicker.

Surfaces
Wood panel cladding or timber planking can be fixed to any even, dry surface. If the wall surface is very irregular it is best to fix battens to allow for this unevenness.

The space behind also allows less pleasing visual features, such as pipes, to be concealed, yet remain accessible behind the cladding. This space can also be easily insulated.

Fixing methods vary according to the surface. Usually surfaces of concrete, brick or insulating blocks are battened. In some cases, cladding may be fixed direct to surfaces using adhesive, provided these are even. Impact or slower-setting adhesives can be used on hardboard, chipboard or plaster surfaces.

New plaster surfaces should not be directly clad for at least eight weeks, to allow the plaster time to dry out.

Damp treatment
Damp walls must be treated before fixing cladding. If there is any suspicion of this, treat the surface with a damp-resistant

coating, such as a rubber or asphalt solution, brushed over the area.

Alternative damp-prevention methods include lining the wall with 500-gauge polythene sheeting, to provide a vertical damp-proof membrane, with metallic foil, or with a heavy-duty, bitumen-impregnated paper.

The battens and the back of the cladding should be treated with a clear timber preservative to prevent attack by moisture or fungi. Avoid a coloured preservative as this might bleed through the surface.

Insulation
Insulation material, such as expanded polystyrene sheeting, mineral rock wool or glass-fibre quilt, can be inserted between the wall surface and the panelling. This will provide thermal and some sound insulation, and help to prevent condensation by raising the touch temperature of the wall surface. In warmer conditions, a layer of insulation material gives a measure of heat insulation.

Panelling
Wood panelling is available in a wide range of timber veneers and provides a quick way to cover large areas. Panels are made in thicknesses from 4mm–6mm and in sheet sizes of between 2·44m × 1·22m to 3·05m × 1·22m.

Surfaces may be pre-finished, usually with a clear coat of alkyd resin, and v-grooved to represent random planking, or simply left in a natural condition.

Wood panelling may also be treated to make it fire resistant. The grooves in panels are usually located to correspond with batten centres at 400mm.

The long edge of each board is bevelled to match the adjoining panel and form a v-groove at the joint; veneers may not be matched for grain and colour.

Natural wood, with veneers of regular width, may be matched for grain and colour.

Preparation of panels
Before fixing, panels must be conditioned to room temperatures. This is done by bringing them into the room where they are to be fixed and leaving them to stand, loosely stacked, against the wall for two days, to acclimatize them both to room temperature and humidity.

Planed 19mm × 50mm timber is best used for battening, as unplaned timber may vary in size. Space the vertical battens at 400mm centres. Horizontal battens provide additional fixing points. Add five to ten per cent of the run of battening for cutting wastage.

Close-fitting 400mm horizontal battens are used where conditions are absolutely dry. If there is any likelihood of moisture, batten widths should be reduced to 305mm to allow a free flow of air at the back of the panels.

The uprights must be truly vertical. Hollows and irregularities in the wall surface must be corrected to prevent panel surface distortion. Concave irregularities can be corrected by blocking out the recesses with small slivers of hardboard or plywood between the wall and the battening. Convex irregularities can be overcome by shaping the rear of the batten or flattening the wall.

Where gaps are not being left between horizontal battens, fix a top and bottom batten, 25mm to 50mm down from the ceiling and upwards from the floor or skirting, checking these with a spirit level. At each end of walls, fit vertical battens; those at door openings may need trimming to fit architraves.

Battens may be fixed with screws or masonry nails. Walls may have to be plugged to accommodate screws, which should be of a non-rusting type. Battens should be fixed at intervals of 380mm.

Work from one end, partly fixing each vertical batten at 400mm centres, and check that each is upright before fixing finally. Place intermediate horizontal battens at intervals of 320mm above each other.

With light fittings or power points,

first fix a square of battening around them, so that the panel can be fixed once a hole is cut out for the switch or point.

Selecting panels
Before fixing, arrange the panels along the wall to get the most pleasing effects. Where the veneer is a natural wood surface, colour may vary from sheet to sheet. At this stage, the most economical way of using the panelling can be worked out and the most attractive graduation of graining and colour chosen.

Cutting edges and bevelling
Panels should be cut with a 8–10 point hand saw with the face side upwards. First, score the panel surface with a sharp marking knife. This will prevent splitting.

Use a metal straight edge and take care not to allow the knife to slip or you will mark and mar the panel face. Hold the saw at as flat an angle as possible as this will ensure a smooth cut.

A power saw can also be used; set this so that it projects not more than 50mm below the thickness of the panel. With a hand-held power saw, cut the panel face side downwards; with a bench saw, the panel is cut face side upwards.

When cutting with either a hand or power saw, it is a good precaution to cover the cutting line with masking tape, to ensure a split-free edge.

Where a panel has to be cut and butted against another, use a sharp plane with a fine set to impart a bevelled edge. Plane away from the panel edge to prevent splintering. Colour match this edge to the next v-groove with a dye or colourizer.

Get cladding
Start cladding from one corner and fix systematically along the surface area. Allow a 3mm gap at the ceiling and floor or skirting for ventilation. Offer up the first section, position it carefully and check its accuracy with a spirit level along the edge. The remaining panels should then be true when fixed. Fix the panels using 19mm–25mm panel or lost-head pins.

Each panel edge should meet in the centre of a vertical batten. Dovetail pin at about 75mm intervals through the v-grooves and at intervals through the grooves into the battens along each panel.

Drive the pins just below the face of the panel with a nail punch. The small surface holes left can be filled with beeswax or a proprietary stopper.

A smear of woodworking adhesive can be applied to the edges of each board and the tops of battens to prevent panels from bowing between the panel-pin fixings.

Before working round switches or points, switch off the current. Unscrew and lift out the point. Locate the panel temporarily in position and drill a hole to align with the switch patrice. Pull the wires through the hole, measure the size of the switch backing, then enlarge the hole.

Use a handyman's knife or pad saw to cut out the hole. First score the surface and then carefully cut deeply until you

Cut, fit and nail battens to the wall; allow ventilation gaps at cross battens

Mark out panels accurately before you cut. Wrong cutting lines can prove costly

Fix lost-head pins through grooves into battens and punch down just below surface

Holes for fittings can be easily cut out, using a sharp handyman's knife

Establish centres are correct, so that fixings of panels can be made accurately

Cut pre-finished panels on the face side, using a fine-toothed panel saw

A sharp cutting knife and a straight edge can also be used to cut panelling

A proprietary adhesive, such as Gun-O-Prene, can be used to fix the panels

are through. Use a metal straight edge to guide the handyman's knife so that this does not slip and mark the surface. Reconnect the wires and reposition the switch.

Pin through the panel around the square batten support. Mark the fixing positions of the screws of the switch or point with a bradawl, drill holes and screw the plate of the unit back on.

Scribing
Where the ceiling line is uneven, the top of the panel should be scribed to match the contour. Cut the panel slightly oversize and hold it tightly against the ceiling. Place a piece of scrap plywood or hardboard hard to the ceiling and at right angles to the cladding.

Run this along the ceiling with a marking knife held beneath and transfer or scribe this contour on to the face of the panel. It may help to keep the panel accurately in position if it is temporarily pinned. Check the position carefully before cutting.

Ceiling cladding
A ceiling can be clad in a similar way to a wall surface. First, fix a batten framework to the ceiling. It is necessary to establish the position of ceiling joists and fix battens to these.

Panel sizes may have to be adjusted to enable joins to match the line of the battens; this may mean cutting panels and

mitreing the edges to provide a neat v-joint.

It is useful to have help when fixing ceiling panelling. Alternatively, you can make up an elongated T-shaped prop of 50mm × 25mm timber, with the upright slightly longer than the floor-to-ceiling height, to wedge the unsupported end of the panel while fixing. The cross-bar can be about 1m long. This device is sometimes called a 'dead man's hand'.

Making contact
Another way of fixing wood panels is with contact adhesive. This can be applied to any sound and level surface–though irregularities up to 6mm can be accepted.

Make sure that walls are clean and dry. Gloss or emulsion-painted surfaces should be firm and free from flaking. Papered walls should be stripped back to the bare plaster.

Apply the adhesive to both the wall surface and the back of each panel with a knotched spreader and allow to dry. When the two surfaces are brought together they will instantly bond.

Therefore, take great care to position the panels accurately, as with most contact adhesives, the panel cannot subsequently be moved once the two surfaces have made contact.

An alternative method is to bond panels directly to a wall surface using a specially formulated, gap-filling adhesive, containing synthetic rubber, called Gun-O-Prene.

For 'secret' fixings, nail pins at an angle through the tongue and punch down

Use an old chisel as a cramp to ensure each plank tightly butts to neighbour

Once inserted, the tongue of the next plank completely conceals the fixing pin

Piece of scrap wood can be used as a template to cut corner plank accurately.

This is applied with a special gun, available on loan.

The adhesive is in cartridge form; applied at the correct temperature, one covers a single standard panel. Walls must be clean and dry and stripped back.

Once the panels have been cut and arranged in order of fixing, apply the adhesive to the back of the first panel, using a steady pumping pressure on the trigger mechanism, to ensure an even extrusion of adhesive.

Draw the nozzle in a line round the outside of the panel, about 50mm in from the edge and across the width, at 460mm centres.

Next, offer the panel to the wall, check for position and press firmly into place, using hand pressure. If the wall surface is slightly uneven, the adhesive will take up gaps. Where there is no skirting board and the panel is entirely un-supported, it may be necessary to pin the panel temporarily until adhesion has taken place.

Warped panels may be fixed using this adhesive. The adhesive is applied to the panel as for a normal fixing, the panel is offered to the wall, pressed firmly into place then removed. Enough adhesive to produce a honeycombed effect will be left on the wall. Leave for 10 minutes, then reposition the panel to make the final bond.

Battens can also be fixed with adhesive. It is applied to the wall surface at 400mm centres and used in conjunction with masonry-nail fixing at high spots.

External corners
These can be mitred along the abutting edges with a plane so that they fit snugly together, but this has to be done very accurately. It is easier–and produces a successful corner–to butt the external edges of panels against a vertical strip of timber fixed at the angle.

First, batten up to the corners, so that one vertical batten overlaps the other, presenting a solid timber edge. Select the timber edge strip, which should be about 50mm wide by 6mm thick, and either match the panelling or be of a contrast wood finish, and pin this on the face edge of the angle. Punch down the heads of the pins and fill the holes.

The two panel edges can then be butted neatly against the edge strip and pinned.

Internal corners
No special treatment is involved. Place two adjacent vertical battens alongside, butt the two panels at right angles together and pin.

Timber planking
Solid, timber lining in the form of wood strips, also provides a pleasing, decorative timber finish. There is a wide range of colours obtainable in both soft and hard woods and in various profiles.

One of the most popular is tongued-and-grooved board. Usually 75mm–150mm wide and 13mm and 25mm thick, this may have v-patterned grooves at the plank edges.

Timber plank cladding can be fixed vertically, horizontally or diagonally, dependent on the situation and finished effect required. It is easier to clad a ceiling with planks of timber than with panels.

Preparation
The timber should be conditioned in a dry room, ideally where it is to be fixed, for at least seven days.

When using tongued-and-grooved or square-edged cladding, it is generally necessary to fix batten framework.

Battens may be horizontally or vertically fixed, dependent on the plane of the cladding. For vertical boarding, use horizontally fixed battens; for horizontal fixing, vertical battens.

Diagonally fixed cladding can be fixed to either type of batten fixing. Vertical battens are fixed at 460mm centres; horizontal at 610mm centres.

When cladding from ceiling to floor level, an existing skirting can be used as the lowest fixing point, so battens should not be thicker than the skirting. Alternatively, the skirting can be removed and battens fixed at floor level.

Mark out planking with a try-square and cutting knife and cut with a 8–10 point panel saw.

Fixing
Vertical cladding is started from one corner. Make sure that the first strip is level, as this acts as a datum point for the rest of the work.

Measure and cut each length slightly over size; fit the first plank the groove side of the cladding firmly into the corner. If necessary, scribe this and cut to fit if the room verticals are out of true.

Allow a 6mm gap at tops and bottoms for ventilation. Where necessary, scribe the plank tops at the ceiling, trim off excess with a sharp plane with a fine set and remove roughened edges with fine glasspaper.

Tongued-and-grooved boards allow cladding to be fixed by the 'secret' nailing method. The first strip will have to be pinned through the face of the panel, the head punched below the surface and the hole filled. Use 32mm lost-head nails.

Subsequent strips can be put in place and fixed, at an angle, with lost-head nails through the back of the groove and the heads also punched down. The tongue of the next plank slots over this, hides the pin head and holds the plank in place.

Use a chisel to cramp each board. Drive the chisel point into the batten and pull it upright to squeeze the board tightly against the adjacent board. Cramp only on the tongued side of the board. If it is damaged or bruised, it will be covered by the next groove.

Nail and cramp three boards at a time, working from the ceiling downwards, then reverse the work direction, by cramping and nailing from the floor level upwards, for the next three planks.

The last two cannot be cramped and will have to be sprung into place. You may also have to cut the last board and plane a bevel along the cut edge. Cut the boards slightly oversize and fit; they will be slightly bowed.

To achieve a tight, flush fit, spring them into position with a sharp blow of the hand. Fix these planks by nailing through the face surface of the grooves, again punching down the heads and filling the holes.

Angles
Internal corners require no special treatment. External corners may be dealt with as follows: cut off the tongue or groove from one length, to square the edge, then glue and pin this flush with the corner. Repeat with the abutting plank. This will present a neat edge. The edges can then be touched on with a dye or matching colourizer.

When fixing diagonal planking to vertical battening, it is essential to fix top and bottom horizontal battens at floor and ceiling level. The first plank fitted is the longest. This is fitted from one corner, at an angle of 45°, to the ceiling or highest point of the area to be covered.

Subsequent planks are pinned on each side of the master plank and the edges cut at a 45° angle. The planks will have to be cut slightly longer to allow for the 45° angle to be cut at each end.

Use a bevel gauge and handyman knife to mark out each angle accurately and then saw. Planks are pinned to battens in the normal way, and, when using tongued-and-grooved board, may be secured by secret nailing. The final boards will also have to be 'sprung' into place.

A point to remember is that if shelving or other support is likely to be needed later, fix support battens behind the panelling where they will be required.

Move-around storage elegance— military style

Space, or the lack of it, is a problem for many. A smart, space-saving storage unit, which is also a decorative piece of furniture, can be an ideal solution to some problems. This series on things to make using simple woodworking techniques will provide a range of useful, attractive and versatile items for the home.

This multi-purpose storage unit can be made using only simple woodworking techniques. There are no complicated joints, and the only construction skills needed are accurate measurement, cutting, hammering and simple planing.

It can be built in a variety of heights and widths, but the proportions of this unit should be maintained, to preserve its 'look'.

The unit consists of three boxes which fit together on the top of each other and are kept in place when assembled by simple bearers, pinned and glued to the bottoms. A bottom set of bearers provides the means of fitting castors or rubber feet. This provides a choice either of leaving the box in a fixed position, or being able to wheel it around.

The unit can serve as a drinks container, toy box, record-storage unit, or even a needlework box. Any box can be fitted with simple trays or containers, to serve a variety of uses.

Brass military-chest handles, which are readily available, are fitted to the front and back panels of each box unit. These are not only decorative but enable each box to be lifted off easily.

A variety of finishes is possible. The unit can be hand or spray painted, laminated, stained or varnished, papered or covered with an adhesive-backed vinyl.

Tools needed in construction are:
- Warrington-pattern hammer
- Fine-toothed 560mm panel saw
- 25mm bevel-edged chisel
- Smoothing plane
- Try-square
- Pair of pincers
- Mallet or soft-faced hammer
- Screwdriver
- Nail punch
- Bradawl
- Glasspaper block and some sheets of fine glasspaper.

Construction

Construction is entirely from 12mm Finnish birch plywood, cut from standard 2440mm × 1220mm sheets. Measure and mark out very carefully, using the try-square to ensure accurate right-angles, or the finished boxes will not 'sit' square on each other. Cut sections with the panel saw.

If you wish, a timber supplier will usually cut the panels for you on a machine for a small extra charge.

Panels should be cut slightly over-sized and then, with the smoothing plane set very finely, planed all along the long edges of the panels which form the box sides. Take off the minimum amount from the edge of each panel—just sufficiently to remove any sawing imperfections.

Smooth the inside of the panels with a piece of fine glasspaper, to achieve a fine, clean finish. Make the panels for the box fronts and backs and put these to one side.

Handles

Mark out, in pencil, the position of each brass handle. The majority of military-chest handles are recessed into the surface. The handles have a projection at the back which has to be let into the surface to which it is fixed.

Measure the length and width of this projection and accurately mark this on to the panel. Make sure, particularly, that the marking out is not crooked, for this will show up badly.

With a 25mm bevel-edged chisel, cut out the slots for the handle recess. Start in the middle by making a 'v' cut and then carefully chop out the recess. The laminations of the plywood will provide a guide as to depth.

Chop away slivers of about 3mm at a time, progressing away from the slot on one side, using the flat of the chisel so that the waste material falls back into the slot.

Work towards the edges and make the final cut a vertical one. Move back to the centre and cut the recess on the other side, again working away from the slot, so that the waste is again displaced inwards.

It is easier to cut the slots before the panels are assembled into the box unit.

Pinning

Mark a line at 13mm in from each end of the panel. This indicates the position of the 32mm panel pins used to fix the panels together. Four go into each of the narrow panels and seven into the wider panels.

These pins should be spaced evenly 13mm in from the edge, except when nailing the top box. Allowance must be made here for the narrower back and front. The pins at the top corner of this box must be 33mm in from the edge (Fig. 1).

When all the lines and positions of panel pins have been marked, these can be

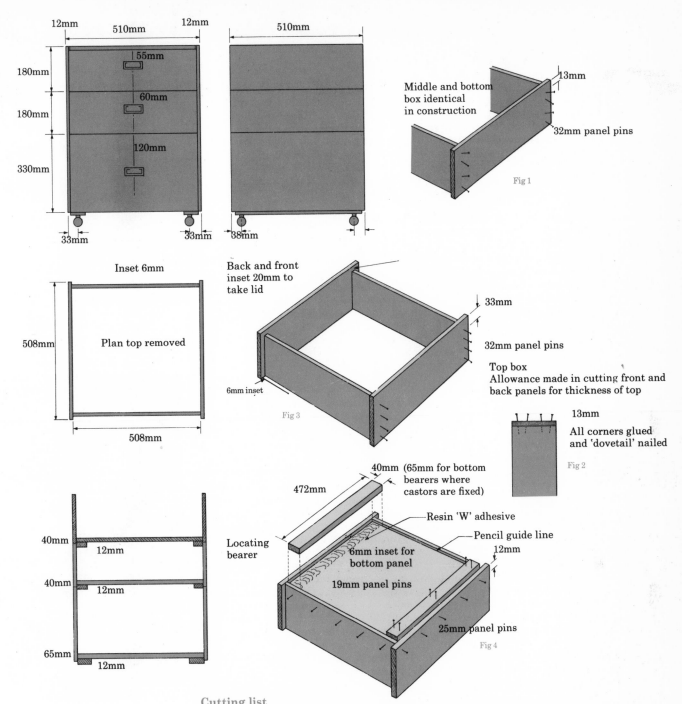

12mm 510mm 12mm

180mm 55mm

180mm 60mm

330mm 120mm

33mm 33mm 38mm

510mm

Middle and bottom
box identical
in construction

13mm

32mm panel pins

Fig 1

Inset 6mm

Plan top removed

508mm

508mm

Back and front
inset 20mm to
take lid

33mm

32mm panel pins

Top box
Allowance made in cutting front and
back panels for thickness of top

13mm

All corners glued
and 'dovetail' nailed

Fig 2

6mm inset

Fig 3

40mm

12mm

40mm

12mm

65mm

12mm

Locating
bearer

40mm (65mm for bottom
bearers where
castors are fixed)

472mm

Resin 'W' adhesive

Pencil guide line

12mm

6mm inset for
bottom panel

19mm panel pins

25mm panel pins

Fig 4

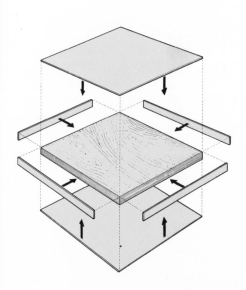

Cutting list

All in Finnish birch plywood–all mm sizes

Part	Qty.	Length	Width	Thickness
Side panels	4	510	330	12
Side panels	6	510	180	12
Side panels	2	510	160	12
Bottom panels	3	475	475	12
Top	1	510	510	12
Bearers	4	474	40	12
Bearers	2	474	65	12
Laminate (top)	2	510	510	2
Laminate (top edges)	4	510	12	2
*Laminate (bottom)	3	475	475	2

Handles	6
Castors, plate fixing	4
Round-headed 19mm screws	(16)
Brass countersunk 12mm screws	(24)
Quantity 19mm panel pins	
Quantity 25mm panel pins	
Quantity 32mm panel pins	
Woodworking adhesive	

*Optional

knocked in, in a 'dovetail' pattern, with the Warrington hammer. Allow the points of the pins to break through the surface on the other side by about 2mm, as this will help to 'locate' the panel on the end of the adjoining one (Fig. 2).

Glueing

Spread a suitable woodworking adhesive (such as Evostik) evenly on all surfaces to be mated. Allowing a 6mm overlap, locate a side on the end of a cross panel (Fig. 3). This overlap can be gauged by a 6mm piece of wood.

Tap the nails almost fully home, but leave enough showing so that you can, if necessary, pull these out with pincers. You need only do this if the pin is incorrectly located. If so, refix it about 5mm away.

Check that these pins do not break through the surface of the front or back panels and then knock them in flush with the surface of the wood.

When hammering, take care not to bruise the surface of the wood with the head of the hammer. When using a hammer on a surface which is being glued, check that the face of the hammer does not become smeared with glue and wipe it clean if necessary. Glue can cause mis-hits, damaging the wood.

Move around to each corner in turn, checking that all edges are level and line up with each other and that the 6mm overlap is maintained; knock in all nails. Punch in all the heads to 3mm below the surface while the glue is still wet.

Assembling

The punching gives a slight 'clamping' action, pulling the glued surfaces closer together and making a better joint. Finally, wipe off any surplus glue with a damp cloth.

Check the diagonals of the box by measuring with a steel tape from corner to corner; these should all measure the same if the box is square. If the box is out of true, a slight hand pressure on opposed corners should be sufficient to correct this.

Finally check for squareness and leave the unit on a level surface for the glue to dry. Repeat the process with the other two boxes. When all have dried, stack the boxes on top of each other to check that they are identical in outline.

Bottoms

Next, check the internal measurements of your boxes and cut the bottom panels to these measurements. Cut the panels slightly oversize to allow them to be planed to fit each particular box.

If the bottoms are to be laminated, this should be stuck on before the bottoms are fitted but after the panels have been planed to size. Apply the laminate slightly oversized and trim to the size of the panel.

The bottom panels are inset to a depth of 6mm. Draw a pencil line around the box 12mm from the edge, so that the panel pins used to fix the bottom can be located accurately.

Panel pins, 25mm long, in a dovetail pattern, are used to fix the bottoms. Spread glue along the edge of the panel and on the

inside of the box, then tap the panel into place, checking that the 6mm inset depth is even all round. Fix with panel pins through the box sides. These should also be punched some 3mm below the surface. Do this on all three boxes and wipe off surplus glue.

Make the pair of locating bearers from pieces of plywood. There are two to each box. Make sure that these run accurately from front to back.

The narrow (40mm) bearers are for the two top boxes, and the 65mm bearers, to which the castors are screwed, are for the bottom box. These are glued and fixed with 19mm panel pins.

The lid

Cut the lid and plane the edges. If this is to be laminated, allow for the thickness of the laminate on the edges. The top should not fit too tightly. Allow a 3mm clearance.

To locate the lid on top of the boxes, insert four rubber-headed nails, 8mm–10mm in diameter, in the underside of each lid, inset about 28mm from each corner, so that the lid fits snugly.

Finishing

Fill all nail holes with a wood filler. Choose a type which adheres to bare wood and, when dry, rub the filler down with fine glasspaper. Make up any depressions and finally smooth.

Paint magnifies any small flaw in a surface, so a good preparation job is essential. Work around the three boxes, filling in any small flaws in the edges of the plywood and, when dry, rub down with fine glasspaper.

With a bradawl, mark the screw holes on the faces of the boxes for the military-chest handles. First, drive in steel screws to cut a thread for brass screws. Brass screws complement the brass handles but break easily in hard timbers, so it is important to cut the thread. Dip each screw in a little wax polish before screwing in as this will ease entry.

Castors can now be screwed on, following manufacturer's instructions.

Test that handle fits into recess before assembling boxes. Front plate must lie flat

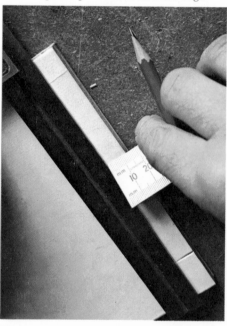
Using try-square ruler and pencil, mark line for panel pins 12mm in from edge

Make allowance for protrusion at back of handles. Chop out using bevel-edged chisel

Pinning corners together, using adhesive and 6mm offcut to gauge an even overlap

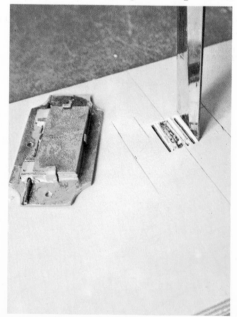

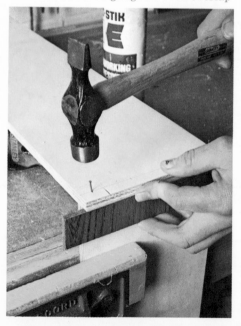

The metric module kitchen

A 'dream' kitchen of luxury quality need not be out of your reach—if you build it yourself. This complete kitchen of wall and base units can be constructed using only simple woodworking techniques. Based on 'unit' construction, each item is made up of two box structures and can be laminated or finished according to choice.

The design of this set of kitchen base units and wall cupboards is modelled on two 'box' sections–a top and a bottom box for each. On the base units, the lower box provides the plinth, while the other box supports the drawers.

A similar construction is used for the cupboards. The strength of each unit relies on the support of the 'slab' material–the sides, backs and tops. This is glued and screwed into place.

The width of any unit can be increased by enlarging the sizes of the boxes. The metric modules used here should fit an average kitchen.

Choice of materials

Finnish birch blockboard, 19mm thick × 100mm wide × 435mm deep, is used to make the plinth boxes. The top boxes are constructed of 25mm × 50mm planed softwood, 493mm deep. The overall length of single base units is 535mm and of double units 1·07m. The working height of base units is 910mm, with a front-to-back depth of 535mm.

The wall units are 352mm wide × 230mm deep × 624mm high. The tops of each are covered with a panel of hardboard, pinned to the top 'box'. Double-door units can be made by increasing the dimensions of the box sections.

All sides, backs and shelves are made of 19mm Contiplas laminated chipboard. Doors are cut from 12mm Finnish birch blockboard. Finnish blockboard, 19mm thick, is used for the worktops, which, like the doors, are surfaced with a decorative plastic laminate (Warerite). An advantage of using laminated material is that the interiors of units present a hygienic, wipe-clean surface.

You can use cheaper materials, such as standard hardboard, in place of plywood or laminated chipboard. However, a more robust job will give better service; it will still be cheaper to make the units yourself, than to buy similar factory-made furniture.

Tools needed are a coping saw, a smoothing plane, a tenon saw, a panel saw, a medium screwdriver, a carpenter's hammer and a 19mm bevel-edged chisel, or a router plane, a marking knife and a marking gauge.

Techniques

Only basic carpentry techniques are needed for construction. Joints are simple housings, 6mm deep. All other assembly is with glue, pins or screws.

Mark out and cut, at the same time, all pieces of timber of similar length; this helps to ensure accuracy.

Box-unit construction

Measure and mark out the housings, squaring the lines around the timber. Gauge the joint to a depth of 6mm and cut.

An alternative to the bevel-edged chisel, to remove waste, is the router plane. To use, set the blade of the plane to about half the depth of the groove, and pass the plane over the slot until you cut to this depth. Reset the blade slightly to deepen the groove and, finally, set to the maximum depth. The blade is held to any set depth, which ensures that the joint is both neat and accurate.

Next, mark out all cross pieces of the same length, square lines around the timber, and cut. For ease of identification, mark the narrower centre pieces with pencil.

Both top and bottom side rails are inset 19mm–the thickness of the laminated sides. The ends of the front rails slot between these panels after assembly. Panels are later secured by countersunk screws through the panels and into both faces of the side rails.

Note that the centre rail of the plinth box is raised some 13mm above the level of the end rails. This allows for any central unevenness on the floor which may cause the unit to rock.

Projections on the rear housings are left on for ease of initial marking out. These are now cut off and the ends planed smooth after assembly. The front rails should be cut slightly oversized to allow the ends to be planed smooth before assembly.

Glue blocks

Glue blocks, 19mm × 19mm × 90mm long, are used to reinforce all corners, and as you will need a considerable number, it will be helpful to make a small jig to cut these out. This consists of a three-sided open timber box with a plywood or hardwood stop across the front.

Mark on the box the length of the blocks along the sides, so that these can be cut quickly and uniformly. Once cut to length, take a corner off each block–for neatness when assembled. Remove also a small piece from the opposite corner; this enables the blocks to sit squarely in the angle of the joints, allowing for any slight irregularities and projections.

Assembling

The boxes can now be trial assembled to ensure that everything fits well. Any necessary adjustments are made at this stage.

Next, apply a glue, such as Evostik Wood-working adhesive, to the housings and at the end of all cross pieces. Spread this evenly on the mating surfaces, with a rubbing motion.

Knock the joints together, using a hammer and a piece of scrap, flat timber, or a soft-faced hammer. Secure the joints with three 38mm oval nails, in a 'dovetail' pattern. Similarly pin glue blocks and wipe off surplus glue with a piece of damp cloth.

Test the construction for squareness, by measuring the diagonals with a steel tape. Use hand pressure on opposed corners to correct any error, and leave the boxes on a level surface to dry; finally check for squareness.

End panels

Prepare the end panels for the base unit. Cut with a fine-toothed hand saw from 535mm-wide laminated chipboard. Take care to square the lines across the surface evenly, so that you cut rectangular panels. Cut to 890mm long, and gauge a line from the edge of the panel and saw to a width of 495mm.

Cut all similar panels identically, place together in a vice and mark the front edges for the drawer rails and 'kicking-space' recesses.

Square lines 22mm deep, gauge for depth and cut. Cut out the recesses with a coping saw and then pare back to the line with a bevel-edged chisel. Do this carefully, to avoid chipping the plastic facing.

Clean up the top and bottom edges of

Cutting list–all mm sizes

Part	Qty.	Material	Length	Width	Thickness
Bottom box		Planed softwood			
Front	1	or Finnish birch blockboard	1·70m	100	18*
Back	1	Finnish birch blockboard	1·70m	100	18
Sides	2	Finnish birch blockboard	406	100	18
Centre rail	1	Finnish birch blockboard	406	89	18
Glue blocks	8	Softwood	90	19	19
Top box Front	1	Planed softwood	1·70m	47	22*
Back	1	Planed softwood	1·70m	47	22
Sides	2	Planed softwood	460	47	22
Centre rail	1	Planed softwood	460	47	22
Sides	2	Conti-plas	890	495	16
Bottom	1	Conti-plas	1·38m	495	16
Shelf	1	Conti-plas	1·38m	495	16
Back (optional)	1		1·70m	890	16
Top	1	Finnish birch blockboard	1·70m	498	18*
Top-back edging	1		1·70m	38	18*
Top-front edging	1		1·70m	38	18*
Shelf support	2	Softwood	1·38m	47	22
Doors	2	Blockboard	595	530	12*
False drawer front	2	Blockboard	530	140	12
Drawer sides	2	Finnish birch ply	577	134	12
Front	1	Finnish birch ply	455	134	12
Back	1	Finnish birch ply	455	134	12
Bottom	1	Finnish birch ply	580	480	6
Guides	4	Finnish birch ply	495	16	16

Drawers should be fitted after the units are assembled. Material should not be cut till then.

*Warerite to fit

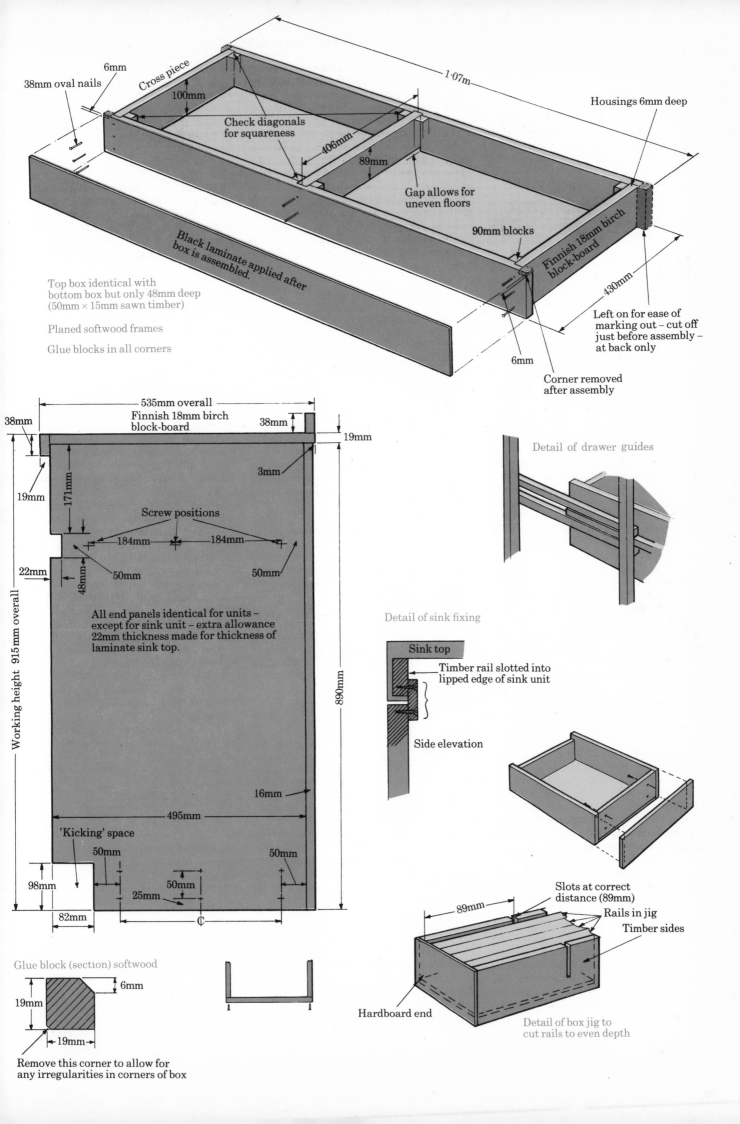

6mm

38mm oval nails

Cross piece

100mm

Check diagonals
for squareness

1·07m

Housings 6mm deep

406mm

89mm

Gap allows for
uneven floors

90mm blocks

Finnish 18mm birch
block-board

Black laminate applied after
box is assembled.

430mm

Top box identical with
bottom box but only 48mm deep
(50mm × 15mm sawn timber)

Planed softwood frames

Glue blocks in all corners

Left on for ease of
marking out – cut off
just before assembly –
at back only

6mm

Corner removed
after assembly

535mm overall

Finnish 18mm birch
block-board

38mm

38mm

19mm

3mm

171mm

19mm

Screw positions

184mm

184mm

22mm

48mm

50mm

50mm

All end panels identical for units –
except for sink unit – extra allowance
22mm thickness made for thickness of
laminate sink top.

890mm

Working height 915mm overall

16mm

495mm

'Kicking' space

50mm

50mm

98mm

50mm

25mm

₵

82mm

Detail of drawer guides

Detail of sink fixing

Sink top

Timber rail slotted into
lipped edge of sink unit

Side elevation

Slots at correct
distance (89mm)

89mm

Rails in jig

Timber sides

Hardboard end

Detail of box jig to
cut rails to even depth

Glue block (section) softwood

6mm

19mm

19mm

Remove this corner to allow for
any irregularities in corners of box

Two cleats can be fixed to the drawer, and the third to the sides of the unit

It is easier to drill holes for hinges using a power drill in a vertical stand

the boxes with the plane, then laminate the front surfaces. Mark out the position of the screw holes on the end panels, with a centre punch, drill and countersink for No. 8 wood screws.

Assemble the units, using 31mm No. 8 Pozidriv screws; where the end panels are seen, fit plastic-domed caps over the screw heads.

Finally, laminate the kicking boards. A dark-coloured laminate is best, since this does not readily show marks. The rail ends of the 'boxes', where these are seen, should be laminated with a matching colour, or carefully prepared and painted.

All exposed woodwork, other than drawer runners, should be given a coat of protective polyurethane varnish.

Worktops
Tops are cut from 19mm birch blockboard, 515mm wide and the same length as the base units. The front edge strip is also cut from blockboard but may be of solid timber, also 19mm thick. Its width should be such that it is in line with the front edge of the sink top.

This strip is pinned on and glued, and the top planed off flush with the work top. The front edge may now be laminated and trimmed. If the top edges are exposed, these should also be laminated.

The top is glued and screwed in place with 38mm No. 8 countersink screws through the top into the top edge of the cabinet sides. The top can now be laminated.

Use a 'balancer' laminate on the back of the worktop or seal the surface top with two coats of polyurethane varnish or paint to serve the same purpose.

The 38mm block upstand at the back can now be laminated on its top and front surfaces, and fixed in position by screwing it in from beneath the top box.

Cut the bottoms, shelves and backs to size and fit. The bottom panels are screwed through from beneath the plinth box. Shelves can be supported on plastic shelf bearers; there is a wide variety of these. Bearers may be surface fixed or recessed to fit holes bored into the timber sides.

Bottom and middle shelves on double base units are made from 970mm × 295mm × 19mm Contiplas. Shelves for single units are 535mm long. To prevent longer

shelves sagging, two pieces of 25mm × 50mm planed timber should be cut to the length of the shelves and fixed on edge by screws, 13mm in from the front and the back edges. The front support may be laminated or painted. The strip at the rear may be finished with a suitable polyurethane varnish.

The backs of the units are 535mm (single) and 1·07m (double units) long. These are made to the 885mm height of the end panels. For the sink-unit base, deduct 19mm from this measurement. These are drilled and countersunk then glued and screwed using 38mm No. 8 screws. Make the backs to fit the unit, in case any slight variation has occurred during construction.

Sink unit
This accommodates a single-bowl, single-drainer sink top. Merely by enlarging the size of the basic 'box' unit, a double drainer may be fitted. General construction principles are the same as for ordinary base units.

Check, first, that the sink top matches the unit measurements, since there may be slight variations between makes.

This unit is made 19mm lower than the height of worktop units, to allow for the depth of the sink top. This is located on top of the base units. Cut two pieces of softwood, 13mm × 10mm, to the depth of the lip in the sink unit edge; fit these into the lipped edges on each side of the sink top. The top is fixed with two mirror plates screwed, on each side, into this section of timber and into the sides of the base unit.

As the sink bowl occupies the space of a drawer, a false drawer front must be fitted.

Wall units
These are constructed in a manner identical with the base units. The doors of cabinets are also made up in the same way as these base units.

Doors
These are made from 12mm Finnish birch blockboard, 520mm wide × 597mm long, including the thickness of laminate, for both base units and cupboards. Where doors are to be hung in pairs, as on double units, each should be made 3mm smaller in width.

This is so that the edges of doors on units standing on uneven floors do not catch against each other. Doors may sag slightly in these circumstances, but any unevenness can largely be corrected by adjusting the hinges.

Fitting hinges
Hinges are a heavy-duty concealed type and easily fitted. First laminate door edges and fit a balancing laminate on the backs of the doors. If wished you can put on several coats of paint to act as a balancer.

Pencil mark the centre position of each hinge–400mm in from the top and bottom and 22mm in from the edge. Dot punch to mark centres and, drill to a depth of 13mm with a 35mm boring bit. It is easier to do

this if you use a power drill in a vertical stand.

After drilling the holes, the front of the doors may be laminated and trimmed to size. Tap the hinges into the holes and secure with screws provided. Screw on the carcass part of the hinge, offer the doors up to these metal blocks, and fit the doors.

Door pulls
The doors and drawers open by means of metal 'pulls', made of a standard extruded aluminium. These also act as an attractive front 'trim' to the units. A wide variety is available. This was supplied in 2m lengths and cut to length with a fine-toothed hacksaw, drilled, using standard No. 4 twist bits, countersunk, and secured with 19mm screws.

Drawers
Drawer construction uses simple, pinned-and-glued methods of assembly.

When making box-shaped drawers it is essential that the fronts and backs are cut exactly the same to ensure that the sides are parallel. Drawers for single base units measure 577mm deep × 507mm wide × 140mm high. Drawers for double units measure 577mm deep × 462mm wide. The sides and backs are made of 12mm Finnish plywood, with bottoms of 6mm plywood.

Cut the sides and check that these are identical. The front and back section are smaller by the thickness of the ply forming the sides. Assemble, check carefully for squareness, and allow to dry.

Runners, or cleats, are fixed on the side of the drawers and cupboard sides. These consist of a central cleat between two outer ones. Two cleats can be fixed to the drawer, and the third to the sides of the unit, or the other way about.

To allow for the gaps between caused by the width of the cleats, oversized false drawer fronts are fitted.

When measuring the size of drawers, allow for the thickness of the runners and add a further 5mm to allow for timber expansion.

The cleats are made from 13mm × 13mm hardwood, drilled and countersunk, and fixed with 25mm No. 8 brass screws. Cut threads with a steel screw before using the brass screw, for these snap easily if used initially in hardwood.

False fronts
All drawer fronts consist of 'over-sized' sections of blockboard, laminated to match the doors. These are glued and screwed on from the inside of the main drawer 'box' into the backs of the false fronts with four 31mm No. 8 countersunk screws; this ensures that screws do not pull out or become loose with the action of opening.

The fronts for single units measure 557mm × 140mm. Leave a 6mm gap between drawers on double units, making the widths of these fronts 508mm. Fit magnetic catches to hold the doors closed. These consist of a magnet, fitted to the depth of the door inside the unit, with a magnetic plate on the door. The catches can be adjusted slightly, to allow for door movement.

Shelving and storage —stylishly

Storage for larger items and display sections for ornaments are coupled in this multi-purpose storage system. Based on simple construction principles, it can easily be extended along or upwards; in fact, tailored exactly to the size of the room and the capacity required. Laminated chipboard shelves and doors provide an attractive wipe-clean surface, the softwood timber uprights providing a contrasting feature of the design.

This shelving and storage system is simply made, using planed softwood framework with doors and shelving of Contiplas laminated chipboard. The doors can be omitted, if wished, to make this an 'open' unit. The length can be varied to choice, and the unit even extended to ceiling height.

The cupboard sections can be moved from the bottom to the centre position, and a wider spacing could be adopted between shelves, for large books or big display items.

While the unit is capable of an infinite number of variations, the basic principles of construction remain unaltered.

Man-made boards will not take heavy loads without sagging, if the distance between supports is too large. Here, the shelves are supported at regular intervals of 710mm. The support timbers are a feature of the design.

Construction
Shelves
First, cut the four Contiplas shelves to an exact length of 2 286mm and the two end panels to 896mm, using a fine-toothed hand saw. Saw carefully and cut to a squared line. As a general rule, do not accept ends of any material as being completely square–always check for squareness and for damage, cutting the ends square if necessary.

Vertical supports
The eight vertical supports in this design are cut from standard 50mm × 25mm softwood. When planed, this reduces to 47mm × 22mm in size.

Place the eight lengths together in the vice, and secure them with a 'G' cramp. Mark out with a marking knife and square the dimensions (Fig. 2). Cut eight lengths 910mm long; this allows a little for waste at both ends.

The 'housings' or grooves must be marked out to an exact size to correspond with the thickness of the laminated chipboard. If there is any slight variation from the standard 16mm board size, make suitable allowance for this. A really tight fit between the board and the groove should be aimed at.

Choose the best side of your timber to show on the outside and square the marked lines, using a knife and try-square, across the inside face and down the other edge.

Set a marking gauge to 6mm (Fig. 2) and gauge the depth of the groove between each pair of cut lines, working from the inside face. Then, with a tenon saw, cut these grooves to depth and clean out each groove with a 12mm bevel-edged chisel, or use a router plane.

Mark the four corner supports 'back', 'front', 'left' and 'right' and put these temporarily aside. To avoid any mistakes, mark a pencil line down each one at the position of the rebate. It is very easy to cut the rebate on the wrong edge, and you will then end up with corner supports which will only fit on at the same end!

With a rebate plane, or a rabbeter attachment to an electric drill, cut the rebate (Fig. 5). These rebates are 16mm wide and as deep as the prepared housings (6mm).

Once these are cut, mark the positions of the screw holes on the vertical support. These must be in the centre of the groove and also in the centre of the support.

'Dot' punch these positions and, with a drill suitable for a No. 8 screw, bore holes, keeping the drill vertical in both directions. Countersink each hole.

With a tenon saw, cut off the surplus at the top and bottom of each support. Take care to keep the ends square and, with a smoothing plane, carefully clean up each one.

Use one of these supports to mark the positions of the shelves on to the end panels and square pencil lines across the surface.

In the centre, between the pairs of shelf lines, mark another line to indicate the positions of the screws. Set a marking gauge to 75mm and, working from both edges, mark the screw holes (Figs. 6 and 7).

'Dot' punch these positions, drill for No. 8 screw and countersink. With the gauge at the same setting, mark the corresponding screw holes on the ends of the shelves. Then reset the gauge to 8mm, half the shelf thickness, and mark a line across the first lines.

This gives the exact position for the fibre plugs which are fitted and glued into the end of each shelf to take the screws.

Next, dot punch each plug position and, with a drill suitable for a No. 8 plug, drill twice into the end of each shelf to a depth of 32mm. Fit and glue a No. 8 plug into each hole.

Clean up each support carefully with fine glasspaper and give each a coating of polyurethane. Dilute the first coat by about 20 per cent with white spirit. When dry, rub down and apply a second coat of 'neat' polyurethane and leave this to dry.

Assembly
Place the four shelves together, on edge, and secure with a 'G' cramp. With a pencil, square lines across the edges of the shelves, indicating the positions of the verticals. Work to the dimensions in Fig. 1.

Should there be any slight variation, it is important to keep the three spaces between the supports equal. When you are satisfied that the spacings are correct, square these lines across the boards and into the other edges. This will ensure that the back supports line up with the front ones.

Place the shelves on edge on the floor. It is almost essential to have help at this

stage. Place the four rear supports in position.

Drill through the holes in these supports into the edges of the shelves. Remove the supports and glue 32mm No. 8 fibre plugs into the drilled holes. Replace the supports in position and put in the four corresponding screws (Fig. 4).

Repeat this on all the supports. Turn the shelves over and repeat on the front edge. This time, insert screws which will accept decorative screw cappings.

Iron on laminate edging strip to the top of the end panels and trim this to size, following manufacturer's instructions. Place the end panels in position and screw these in place, using 'coverhead' screws (Fig. 7).

Back panels Cut the back panels from 380mm laminated chipboard to an exact fit between the vertical supports and mark these for the position of the securing screws (Fig. 8). Countersink and fix the screws in place.

Cut 50mm strips for the second shelf, and, using the same screw spacing as before, screw these backs into place (Fig. 9).

The doors are fitted using 50mm flush hinges. This type of hinge requires no complicated fitting procedure. It fits on to the surface of both the vertical support and the door.

Screws which match the countersinking in these hinges accurately are essential. Any slight screw projection will stop the door from closing properly. It may be advisable to increase the amount of countersinking on the hinge. This is simply done by using a countersink bit in a hand drill to deepen the countersinking in the hinge face.

Make allowance for both the thickness of the hinge and to allow a gap between the door (Fig. 1). Measure the distance between the supports and divide this in half. From this measurement, subtract 4mm and cut each door to this size.

Veneer the cut edges with edging strip and trim to size. Screw the hinges on to the doors, 40mm from the tops and the bottom edges, using chipboard screws. These are special screws, designed to hold well in chipboard and are readily obtainable.

Place the door on the cabinet and mark the position of the hinge. Open the door and place the leaf of the hinge against this marked position. Now put in the screws.

Glasspaper, or if necessary, plane off the tops of each vertical support and coat with polyurethane varnish.

Fix the screw-head covers into position and mark the positions of the handles on each door. Drill the required holes and fit the handles.

There is a wide variety of door catches available. Magnetic catches are among the easiest to fit. One set should be used on each door.

This pattern of concealed hinge gives a flush, 'hingeless' appearance to doors

Brass dome caps, fitted over screwheads, are neat and serve to conceal fixings

Contiplas is marked out with try square for slots to accept the unit uprights

Slot can be cut roughly to shape with a pad or keyhole saw, jig or coping saw

Finally, the joint is cleaned up with a chisel, so that upright is neatly jointed

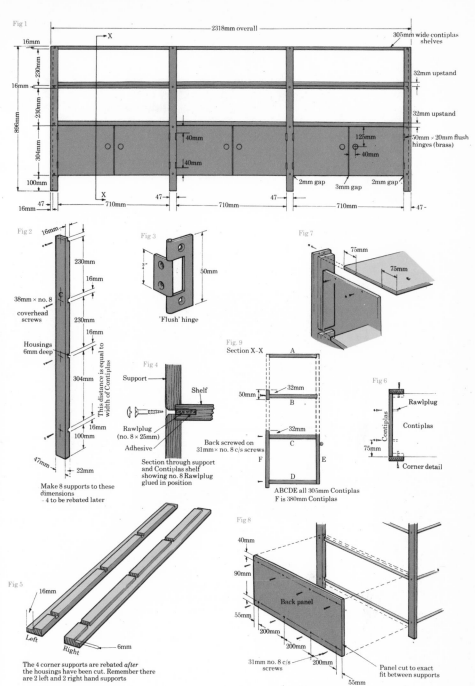

Fig 1

Fig 2

Fig 3 'Flush' hinge

Fig 4 Section through support and Contiplas shelf showing no. 8 Rawlplug glued in position

Fig 5 The 4 corner supports are rebated *after* the housings have been cut. Remember there are 2 left and 2 right hand supports

Fig 6 Corner detail

Fig 7

Fig 8

Fig. 9 Section X–X

ABCDE all 305mm Contiplas
F is 380mm Contiplas

Make 8 supports to these dimensions – 4 to be rebated later

Cutting list – all mm sizes

Part	Qty.	Material	Length*	Width	Thickness
Shelves	4	Contiplas	2·44m	300	16
Ends	2	Contiplas	896mm	300	16
Doors	6	Contiplas	From 2·44m sheet	300	16
Backs	3	Contiplas	From 2·44m sheet	380	16
Back rails	3	Contiplas	From 2·44m sheet	150	16
Supports	8	Softwood	910	47	22
Hinges	12	Brass	50	19	
Knobs	6	Brass	19 dia.		
Magnetic catch	6	—		32	
Coverhead screws	32	Steel and brass	38 × No. 8		
Steel screws	16		38 × No. 8		
Steel screws	36		31 × No. 8		
Hinge screws	48		19 × No. 4		
Fibre wall plugs	48		38 × No. 8		

* To allow for cutting

Build a set of 'separate tables'

A small occasional table is a useful item of furniture. Making this table, which is simple and functional in design, introduces the technique of making a mortise-and-tenon joint, one of the most useful in general woodworking. The table can be finished in a variety of ways – painted, stained with polyurethane varnish, tiled or laminated, to give some examples.

This type of small table can have a host of uses in the home. It can be varied in size to suit your needs, with a choice of tops – laminated, teak-veneered or tiled. Construction utilizes the mortise-and-tenon joint to give strength. It is not recommended, however, that the unit dimensions greatly exceed those given.

Additional tools needed are a 10mm mortise chisel, a mortise gauge and a mitre box.

Leg construction
All pieces of similar size are, in the normal way, marked out together in the vice. Cut four legs 32mm × 32mm and 345mm long from planed softwood and mark with a try-square and a marking knife. Square the lines lightly right across.

From one end line, measure down the thickness of the top, less about 3mm, so that the top of the leg ends slightly below the table surface. From this line, measure the width of the rail and lightly square another line across the surface of the four legs.

Mark lines 3mm in from these points

and square lines across (Fig. 2). These lines mark the length of the mortise, which will be cut later. Take the four legs out of the vice and square the top and bottom cut lines round on all surfaces.

Table top
Next, cut the top of the table. Use 18mm Finnish birch ply blockboard, or plastic or timber-veneered chipboard, such as Contiplas or Contiboard. The dimensions are 550mm × 550mm.

If the top is to be tiled, it is necessary to use a 'balancer' laminate on the underside of the blockboard to counteract the pull of the tiles, or the surface may warp. A less satisfactory alternative is to apply several coats of paint as a balancer.

Edging pieces
Cut four edging pieces 25mm × 7mm × 565mm long. These should match the timber of the table frame. These can be either cut square or mitred. If mitred, make slightly over length and cut the mitre with a sharp tenon saw in a mitre box (Fig. 3).

Mitres must be cut at a true angle of 45° so that the two angles make an accurate 90°. The work should be clamped during cutting. It can be held with a 'G' cramp, cushioned by a piece of scrap timber, so that the strip is not bruised.

Some mitre boxes incorporate a clamp to hold the material steady. Put the timber front side up in the mitre box so that you cut the mitre the right way round.

Nail one mitred strip carefully in position along one edge of the table, lining this up carefully. Knock a pin half way in at each end, so that you can make any slight adjustments by withdrawing the pins and repositioning the strip. Once this is correct, the remaining mitres should line up.

Where butt joints are used, you will have an overlap. Trim this off and plane the edges smooth with a block plane once the glue has dried.

Use the outside dimensions of this top, if different from 565mm, as the working dimensions.

If you tile the top, stick the tiles in place with resinous adhesive, which allows for movement of the wood. When set, grout the tiles in the usual way.

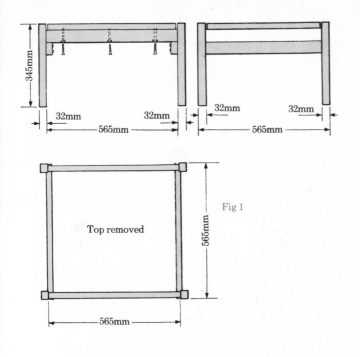

345mm

32mm   32mm   32mm   32mm

565mm   565mm

565mm

Top removed

565mm

Fig 1

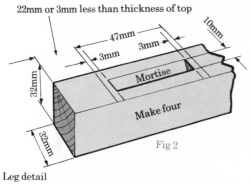

22mm or 3mm less than thickness of top

47mm   10mm

3mm   3mm

32mm

Mortise

32mm

Make four

Fig 2

Leg detail

Side rails detail

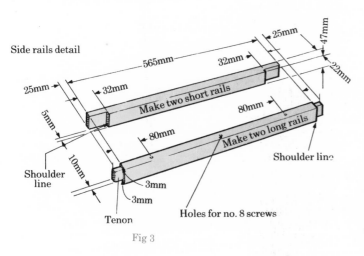

565mm   32mm   25mm   47mm

32mm   22mm

25mm   Make two short rails

5mm   80mm

Make two long rails

10mm   Shoulder line

3mm

3mm

Shoulder line   Holes for no. 8 screws

Tenon

Fig 3

Assembly detail

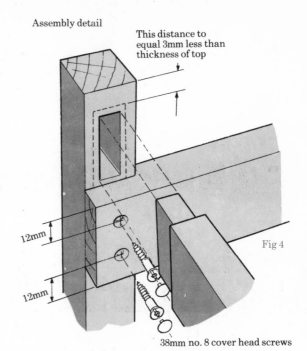

This distance to equal 3mm less than thickness of top

12mm

12mm

Fig 4

38mm no. 8 cover head screws

Top detail

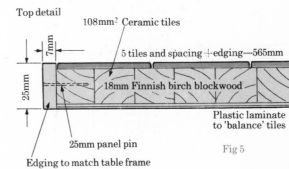

108mm² Ceramic tiles

7mm

5 tiles and spacing + edging—565mm

25mm

18mm Finnish birch blockwood

Plastic laminate to 'balance' tiles

25mm panel pin

Edging to match table frame

Fig 5

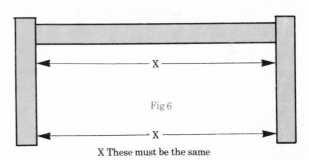

X

X

Fig 6

X These must be the same

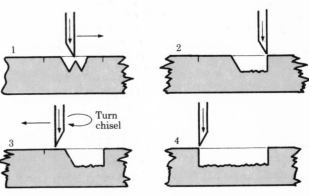

1   2

Turn chisel

3   4

Fig 7

Repeat chop another layer down to depth

5

—Depth of mortise

to the exact width of a 10mm mortise chisel (Fig. 7) by holding the chisel against the spurs.

The spurs are set to mark two lines on the legs between the prepared lines (Fig. 2). These should be the same distance from each edge of the leg. Check that they are correct by marking lightly from both edges.

If the lines coincide, the gauge is set correctly; if they do not, re-adjust the gauge and check again. When correctly set, place the timber upright in the vice and mark the lines (Fig. 2).

Without altering the set of the spurs, mark the tenons on the longer rails (Fig. 3). Once these are marked, set the gauge to 3mm, and mark the outer lines.

Cut the two shorter rails to length, plus 2mm, and reset the marking gauge to 5mm. Gauge the lines from the outside (best) surface for the recess (Fig. 4).

The four rails may now be sawn to shape. Keep the wood upright in the vice and saw so that the line to which you are working is easily visible.

The stages of cutting the tenon are shown in Fig. 8. Cut the lap joint on the end of the shorter rails in a similar manner.

Mortise cutting

Working with the mortise marking uppermost and the leg firmly cramped to the bench with a 'G' cramp, and a piece of scrap wood between to prevent bruising, cut the mortise. Work between the marked lines, starting in the centre.

Chop out a 'v' of wood about 10mm deep and follow the stages in Fig. 7. Stand behind your chisel and keep it vertical while you are chopping into the timber.

If you are anxious about going too deeply into your wood, a piece of adhesive tape round the chisel makes a good depth indicator. When all the mortises are cut, test, by trial assembly, and number each pair of joints for order of correct assembly.

Drill and countersink screw holes for No. 8 screws in the ends of the shorter rails. Drill the holes through the other two rails for securing the top. Countersink these to a depth of 10mm to accommodate the heads of 10mm No. 8 screws.

Mortise cutting can be facilitated by use of a jig, such as the Copydex Jointmaster.

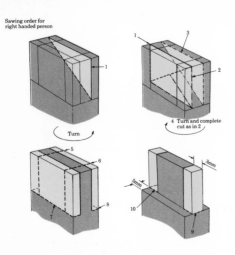

Sawing order for right handed person

Turn

4 Turn and complete cut as in 2

Marking gauge lines

gauge lines

gauge lines

Cut lines (marking knife)

Side rails

Cut the four side rails—two 565mm and two 615mm long—from 47mm × 22mm planed timber and place these on edge in the vice, keeping each pair together. The longer rails must overlap the shorter evenly at each end.

Square a line 25mm in from one end across and from this measure the overall length of the completed top and square another line across at this point. From this line, measure outwards another 25mm and square a further line (Fig. 3).

From the two inner lines at each end, measure 32mm back towards the centre and mark these points. This gives the inner shoulder lines on the two lower side rails. Take these four rails out of the vice and square the end lines on each piece right round on all four surfaces.

On the two shorter rails, square the inner shoulder lines across the outer surface and only lightly across the two edges. Avoid knife marking lines other than where they will be sawn as these will be difficult to clean off the surface.

On the two longer rails, square the shoulder lines right round the rails (Fig. 3). Always use the stock of the try-square from the face edge. You will find, if you work carefully, that the lines will join all the way round. This should be aimed at for accurate work.

Cut the two longer rails to length. Set the spurs, or points, on the marking gauge

Finishing

Clean up each piece and wax polish or polyurethane. Do not get any of these on the surfaces which are to be glued. When dry, glue up the two mortise and tenoned frames and cramp with a sash cramp.

Check that the legs are the same distance apart all the way down (Fig. 6). Sight across the legs to make sure that they are in the same plane. If not, loosen the cramp, adjust the legs, tighten again and check. Repeat until correct.

Once these frames are dry, screw and glue the lower rails in position (Fig. 4). Check diagonals for squareness.

Finally, plane off the ends level with the legs and screw the top in position from beneath.

Cutting list—all mm sizes

Planed finished sizes	Qty.	Length	Width	Thickness
Legs	4	345mm	32mm	32mm
Rails	2	565mm	47mm	22mm
Rails	2	615mm	47mm	22mm
Edging pieces	4	565mm	25mm	7mm
Top	1	550mm	550mm	18mm
Plastic laminate	1	550mm	550mm	2mm
Coverhead screws	8	32mm × No. 8		
C/S Steel screws	6	50mm × No. 8		
'Domes of silence'	4	12mm diam.		
Ceramic tiles × 108m²	25			

These are finished sizes—allow a little extra length for marking out and cutting.

Timber may be hard or softwood, dependent upon finish required.

Fixing: giving every means of support

No visible means of support

Before making a hole in any surface, first establish that it is safe to do so. Find out if there are any buried pipes, cables or other obstructions, and if you meet anything, stop and relocate the position of the hole.

With few exceptions, all fixings to hard surfaces must be made by first drilling a hole to insert a fixing device. It is important to see that the drill point is sharp and in good condition. Metals and synthetic materials are, as a rule, best drilled with an ordinary engineer's twist bit, used in a hand or power drill.

There are several basic types of fixing: masonry nails, plugs and screws (or bolts in the case of very heavy objects) are used for fixing into solid walls; and cavity-fixing devices for hollow surfaces, such as panelled walls or ceilings.

Screws and screwdrivers are main essentials in fixing. The length of screw, and its type, depends on the nature of the fixing and the load it has to carry. The intervals at which fixings are made and the load-bearing qualities of the surface have to be taken into account. If in doubt, use a larger fixing. Common sizes suitable for general use are No. 8 and No. 12 gauge screws of between 25mm, 31mm, 51mm and 64mm length.

The screwdriver is gauged or sized to the head of the screw you are turning. The best general type of screwdriver for many applications is a cabinetmaker's.

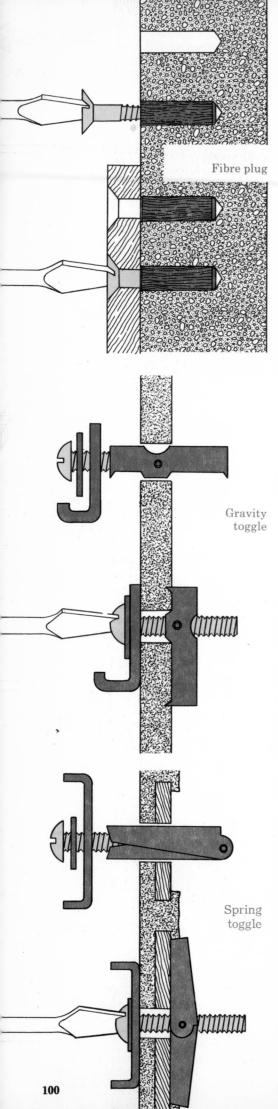

Fibre plug

Gravity
toggle

Spring
toggle

Types of surface

Solid walls are usually made of brick, concrete aggregate or lightweight cellular blocks. There are no special problems in attaching objects to brick or concrete materials. Care must be taken in making fixings in aggregate materials, since these break up more easily and have poorer load-bearing qualities than some other materials.

With very hard materials, such as solid concrete and hard brick, it may be necessary to use a percussive device–such as a percussion power drill or a 'jumper' and a heavy hammer.

Interior linings and finishings differ considerably in construction, thickness and strength. Plaster board, lath and plaster, fibre board, synthetic-resin compound panels are those most frequently used. Linings are generally fixed to a timber framework called studding. The distances separating the members of the framework are called centres. Where possible fixings should be made into these members, consisting usually of 75mm × 75mm timber, rather than into the actual lining material.

It is necessary to locate these centres, often at regular intervals of about 380mm. The best way to do this is to make small test holes through the lining until you locate the timber supports.

Where the framing cannot be used for direct fixing, only the lightest loads should be fixed to the lining. Expanding or anchor bolts can be used, but it is best to spread the load by screwing stout 'backing' boards to the timber supports and making fixings directly to the board.

Types of fixing

Wood plugs

Though largely superseded by more modern methods, the traditional hand-shaped wood plug can be useful where nail fixings have to be made. If the plugs are left proud of the brickwork they can be cut to any desired length where the brickwork is being lined or clad. Plugs should be cut with a gentle taper so that they have a tendency to twist and grip. Sharp tapers do not fill the recess and, as wood tends to shrink, become loose. Plugs should be a tight fit in the hole.

Plugs into external walls or in situations where dampness is likely should be treated with a preservative before being driven in.

If screw fixings are to be made, hardwood plugs should be used and, once inserted, a pilot hole, of slightly smaller diameter than the screw, should be drilled. Brass or bronze screws should be greased with wax or tallow before being driven home.

Preformed plugs

These are made in various materials, ranging from fibre, soft metal and synthetic resin. They require only a neat, round hole, matched to the size of the plug and a little larger than the screw to be used.

It is important that hole, plug and screws should match in size. The holding power of the plug depends upon the frictional grip obtained when the screw expands the plug.

If a small screw is used in too large a plug, the expansion will be insufficient to obtain a reliable fixing. A large screw in a small plug will be difficult to turn and may jam.

The composition of fibre and soft metal grips the hole and provides a firm fixing. Nylon plugs have teeth or ridges which grip the surrounding surface and stop the plug from turning.

Fibre plug sizes for any screw should be of the same length or slightly longer than the length of the thread, excluding the screw shank, which should never enter the plug. Fibre plug sizes are numbered to correspond with the size of screw and the drill or hole-making device used.

Plastic compounds

Sometimes, particularly in mortar or soft brickwork, a hole may become larger than desired–or a previous hole may be too large for the screw to be used. Plastic compounds, based on asbestos-fibre and cement, provide an effective and reliable fixing. However, avoid making any extra-large holes; reposition the fixing in that case. The compound is wetted with clean water, formed into a plug of the required size, and rammed into the hole; usually a tool is provided for this.

If the sides are parallel, the fixing should be secure. If the hole is wider at the face than at the back, the plug may draw out. It is then better to enlarge the hole at the back to produce a 'dovetail' shape. The tool supplied with plastic compounds is pointed at one end to form a pilot hole in the soft compound to start the screw.

The screw should be tightened into the moist filler, but where a large mass of compound is used, the final tightening should be left until the plug has hardened. These compounds should not be used in conditions where dampness exists.

Toggles

Toggles are used for fixing in hollow walls.
Gravity toggles: These have a swivel toggle which drops vertically when inserted through a pre-made hole in a hollow wall; used with bolts for heavier fixing.
Spring toggles: These have two spring-loaded gripping arms which expand after the toggle is pushed through a hole; used with bolts for heavier fixing.
Nylon toggles: Fasteners with a slotted collar which slips over a nylon strip attached to the toggle; used for screw fixing.

A selection of twist bits

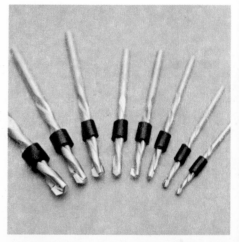

Collapsible anchors: These remain in place if the screw is removed. Insertion of the screw draws metal gripping shoulders against the inner wall of the fitting.

Rubber-sleeved anchors: Used for fixing plastic or metal sheet. These can be used in solid walls. The bolt compresses a rubber sleeve against the surface of the wall.

Nylon or plastic anchors: The action of tightening the screw draws the anchor to the wall.

Nuts and bolts

Machine bolts are used for certain fixing jobs, such as wooden framing for workbenches or light construction. These usually have square or hexagon-shaped heads.

Coach bolts are used for a variety of light or heavy applications. These have rounded heads with square collar locks to prevent the nut from turning while being tightened.

Machine screws are used for small woodworking projects or metalwork. These have countersunk round, pan or cheese heads.

Rag bolts or foundation bolts are used for general construction where framework is built on to concrete foundations. The ragged ends hold firmly in concrete, leaving the shank and thread exposed.

Masonry or anchor bolts are used for fixing to breeze or aggregate blocks, brickwork or concrete. With these a plastic anchor expands to grip the sides of holes in solid walls.

Masonry nails

These are used for jobs such as fixing shelving, battens, picture rails, skirting boards and studs for wall panelling. They are tempered to avoid bending and can be nailed straight in with a heavy hammer.

Masonry nails are in two types—one with a straight and the other a twisted shank. The latter improves penetration into hard materials.

These nails grip by compacting finely crushed material around themselves as they penetrate. This builds up a strong friction which exerts a tight grip on the nail.

The nails are made in three grades—standard, a medium and a heavy-duty pin. Standard pins are from 28mm to 70mm and will fix battens, shelving brackets and pegboard to ordinary brick or low-density concrete, aggregate or similar walls. Medium pins range in size from 22mm to 86mm and

are used for fixing into harder surfaces. Heavy-duty pins are sized from 38mm to 89mm and have spirally twisted shanks.

Fixing

Masonry pins must always penetrate a surface at right angles. A heavy hammer, such as an engineer's pattern, is needed, and firm, well-placed blows should be used.

The nail should be long enough to penetrate at least 19mm into the main surface and not less than 13mm, or it may backlash or break in the wall.

Boring and fixing tools

A hand boring tool, or 'jumper', and a heavy hammer should be turned slightly with each blow in a clockwise direction. The weight of the blow should be gauged in accordance with the hardness of the material. Light, sharp blows and frequent turning will achieve results more rapidly. A too-heavy hammer used on a tool of small diameter may cause it to snap or jam.

As a guide, the weight of the hammer should be about 340 grammes for No. 6 or No. 8 screw gauges and about 677 grammes for No. 12 gauge or heavier. If there is a danger of flying particles, wear protective goggles.

Piston-and-cylinder fixing tools

Piston-and-cylinder fixing tools take a variety of fixing pins, which are muzzle loaded into the mouth of the cylinder. The tool is then held flat to the surface and struck with hammer blows on the piston, which recoils after each strike in preparation for the next blow.

These tools can also be used for driving in masonry nails made with threaded heads to take a variety of domed or hexagon nuts.

For many jobs around the home, the ordinary tipped masonry bit, up to about 8mm diameter, can be used in hand or in power tools.

A rotary drill bit, unless diamond tipped, may jam between particles. Standard domestic electric drills can be fitted with rotary percussion attachments, and some makes of drill are dual purpose—both rotary percussion and standard.

Care must be taken to use a suitable speed when boring into brickwork or masonry, the most common surface materials.

These are the suggested speeds using standard twist bits:

Speed rpm	Cutting diameter
750–1,500	6mm, 8mm, 10mm
500–1,000	11mm, 13mm, 14mm, 16mm
300–600	22mm, 25mm, 27mm, 31mm, 35mm
400–800	19mm

To bore holes from 13mm to 38mm diameter, heavier core or trepanning bits are suggested. These are basically tubes with hardened cutting teeth set around the circumference at one end.

Speed rpm	Cutting diameter
400	13mm, 16mm, 19mm
300	22mm, 25mm, 27mm
200	31mm, 35mm, 38mm

Fixings illustrated on this page

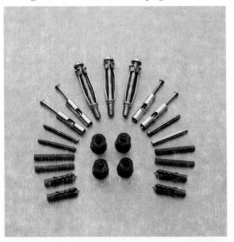

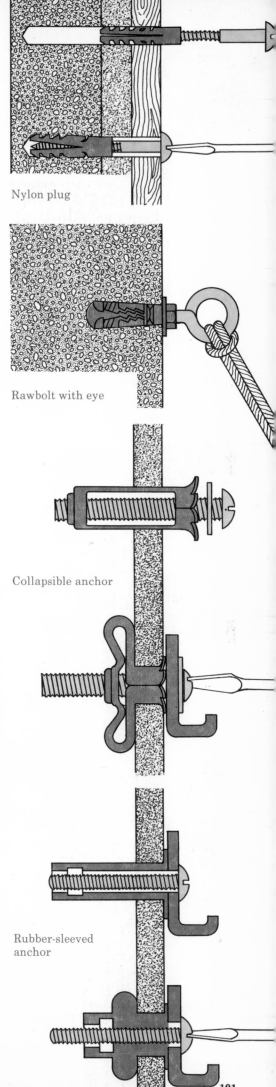

Nylon plug

Rawbolt with eye

Collapsible anchor

Rubber-sleeved anchor

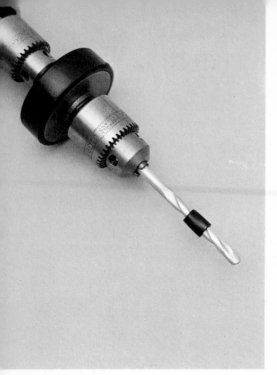

A speed reducer attached to a standard drill

Marked adhesive tape prevents the drill wandering when drilling ceramic tiles

Where you have a lot of fixing to do, such as extensive battening for putting up cladding, a cartridge hammer can be hired to speed up the work. The hammer is a type of gun which fires a hardened steel stud or pin into a surface, using a cartridge similar to that used in a ·22 rifle.

Many types of stud are made. Most have a plain flat head, like a nail, or have a threaded stem for removable fixings, the stud base remaining in position.

The penetration of the stud is governed by the material into which it is fired, the weight of the stud and the power of the cartridge.

A cartridge gun should never be used on brittle materials, such as aggregate, lath and plaster, fibre board and similar soft materials. Studs must not be driven within 50mm of the edge of brickwork, or this may break away.

Properly handled, a cartridge hammer is safe and efficient, but make sure that you are familiar with how it works; that you use the correct strength of cartridge (these are colour coded in order of power); and ensure that no one is in the line of fire.

As a rule, you should not fire a stud into a surface of less 'stopping power' than 230mm brickwork if there is a possibility of anyone beyond. Hold the gun firmly and squarely to the work to prevent ricochet.

A typical make of hammer is fired by a blow from an ordinary hand hammer on to a firing plunger on the base of the hammer. This fires the cartridge and propels the stud into the surface. With this type of hammer, firing through soft materials is virtually impossible.

A shallow hole cutter can be used for larger holes. This consists of a tungsten-carbide tipped trepanning tool with a pilot drill for accurate centring which sinks holes of up to 89mm diameter to a depth of 50mm.

For drilling very deep holes, extension pieces are available which screw into certain types of drill bit.

When working with hand or power tools, ensure that the drill bit is sharp and in good condition. Squeaking is a sign of bluntness, coupled with a drop in performance. Working with a blunt tip can overload the power drill.

If the bit tip turns blue, it means that excessive speed has been used and the temper of the steel will be ruined. Masonry bits can be resharpened at home, but this can be done professionally and many manufacturers provide for at least one free sharpening after purchase.

Two common fixing situations, a blind and a shelving system

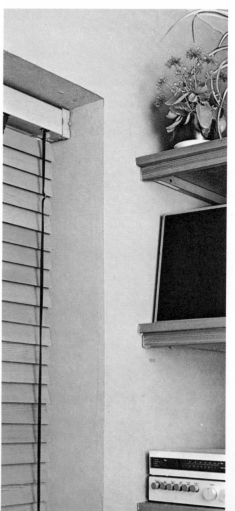

Anatomy of home repairs

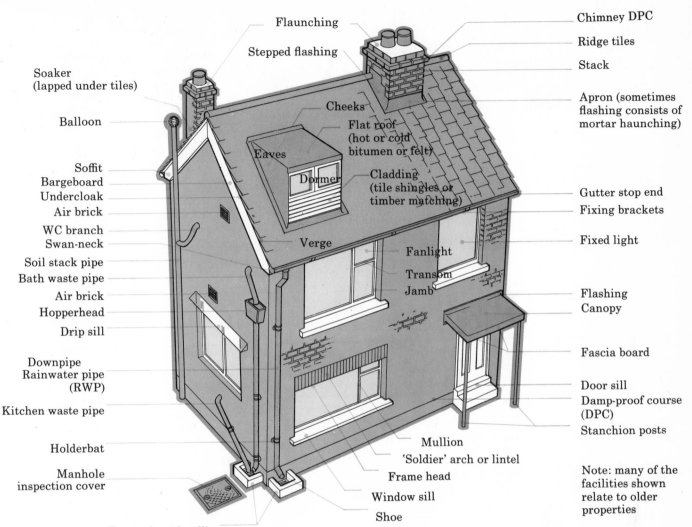

Flaunching

Stepped flashing

Chimney DPC

Ridge tiles

Stack

Apron (sometimes flashing consists of mortar haunching)

Soaker (lapped under tiles)

Balloon

Cheeks

Flat roof (hot or cold bitumen or felt)

Eaves

Dormer

Cladding (tile shingles or timber matching)

Soffit
Bargeboard
Undercloak
Air brick
WC branch
Swan-neck
Soil stack pipe
Bath waste pipe
Air brick
Hopperhead
Drip sill

Verge

Fanlight

Transom

Jamb

Gutter stop end
Fixing brackets

Fixed light

Flashing
Canopy

Downpipe
Rainwater pipe (RWP)

Kitchen waste pipe

Fascia board

Holderbat

Door sill
Damp-proof course (DPC)
Stanchion posts

Manhole
inspection cover

Mullion
'Soldier' arch or lintel
Frame head
Window sill
Shoe

Note: many of the facilities shown relate to older properties

Trapped yard gullies

Home repairs and improvements usually require a continuous round of attention. If left, the volume can quickly become overwhelming and be, at least, a chore. To keep one's home in order requires regular inspection and attention at the most likely sources of trouble and deterioration.

When carrying out work of home maintenance, start at the top and work downwards. You will need ladders and other types of access equipment. It is important to ensure that these are in good condition, suitable for the job, and anchored against movement – and used correctly. Always carefully inspect a ladder for damage. A broken rung could mean a broken back! Repair any damage or replace the ladder.

Do not be tempted into 'lash-up' arrangements when working on pitched roofs. Use a correct roof ladder; these can usually be hired.

Scaffold towers enable safe working and can be built up to various heights and moved around as work progresses. It is also easier to work from a scaffold tower than from a ladder. Two scaffold towers, with intermediate staging or decking between, enables work to be carried out over a span or distance.

Remember, however, that the rule is safety. This equally applies to people below, who could suffer injury if items fall or are dropped from above.

Start an inspection at the chimney. TV and radio aerials may be mounted either directly to these or to a mast. Fixings which secure aerials should be firm, since continual strain from winds can weaken fastenings. Brickwork must also be inspected to see that it is firm and has not suffered from supporting the aerial structure.

Chimneys

Chimney-pots, if not in use, may be clogged by birds nests. This obstruction restricts the free circulation of air and can cause damp to form in the chimney-stack. Birds often nest under eaves, guttering, in hopperheads, and where spaces have been left by fallen or displaced slates and tiles. Inspect these areas and remove any obstruction.

Eaves often harbour insects, such as carpet beetles, which can invade property through brickwork cracks and breed in carpets and furnishings.

Flaunchings (the sloped concrete on top of a chimney-stack, into which the pot is set) and haunchings (the mortar fillet be-

tween a chimney-stack and a roof) should be inspected.

Main ridge tiles are usually bedded in mortar, which may have cracked or deteriorated. Use a cold chisel to remove old mortar and remove the tile carefully.

Old, shattered concrete should be cut away and the area brushed clean of dirt. Prime the area with one part of PVA bonding agent to one part of water and make good the mortar using a stiff, 1:5 mix of cement and soft sand. A little PVA in the water will assist bonding.

Flashings

Flashings (which go over tiles) and soakers (which lap beneath them) should be inspected for soundness. Lead and zinc can be affected by atmosphere and, in time, corrosion can weaken and pit the material. Where lead has curled back, tap this back into place with a wooden mallet or a hard rubber hammer.

Damaged sections of flashing can be replaced with self-adhesive or bituminised aluminium strip. These can be stuck to almost any building material and form a waterproof seal. First, surfaces must be brushed down and be clean and dry. Porous surfaces may have to be primed – a PVA is suitable.

Slates and tiles

Slates and tiles can become displaced as a result of high winds. Remove a broken or displaced tile, push it back slightly and lift it. If the tile does not move easily, lift an adjacent tile as this will help you move the damaged or displaced tile. Tiles may be nailed at intervals to roof battens. Where a tile is nailed, lift the two above it to expose the nail, which can then be prised out easily.

Once you have substituted a new tile, slide the others back with the 'nib' of the tile over the batten. Where a new tile is difficult to engage, nibble away the edge with a pair of pincers.

Where slates have to be replaced, the nails holding them in place have to be removed before the new ones can be fixed. A ripper – a tool which can be bought or hired – is used. Again it is important to replace any broken ridge tiles or replace ridge mortar.

Gutterings and downpipes

Gutters and downpipes leak for three reasons: they are blocked up; they are cracked or holed; or they have faulty joints. These are best cleaned out with a hose, though a piece of stout timber may have to be used to clean obstructed pipes.

Broken guttering brackets should be replaced, because these weaken the support of the system, causing a likelihood of leaks at the joints. Outlets, stop ends and hoppers should be cleared of débris.

One way to prevent débris collecting is to stretch fine wire mesh over the tops of downpipes and hopperheads. Leaks at seals on cast-iron guttering and pipework can be prevented by removing surface rust and painting with a heavy bitumen paint. This can also be brushed off and neutralised, painted with a metal primer and then repainted.

Severely defective guttering should be replaced. Plastic guttering is lightweight and easy to fix. It can also be connected to existing cast-iron guttering by means of adaptors.

Proprietary sealing strips and mastics can also be used to repair seals and gaps. For severe holes, glass-fibre can be used.

Brickwork

Brickwork usually needs little maintenance. Dirty brickwork can be treated with brick paint or conditioner or scrubbed with a proprietary renovator. Normally, cleaning with a scrubbing brush and soapy water will suffice.

Damp conditions give rise to algae on roof and wall surfaces. Although proprietary chemicals can be used, scrubbing with domestic detergent is usually as good.

Efflorescence on bricks – an unsightly, chalking deposit also found on plaster and concrete – is brought about by salts in the brickwork which are drawn to the surface by evaporation, where they solidify.

While brushing will remove some of the deposit, a proprietary neutralizing solution which penetrates the surface and prevents the salts from emerging may be the answer.

Various siliconized and non-siliconized waterproofing solutions are available for use on both interior as well as exterior brickwork as a protection against pene-

Condensation stains if flue not lined

Chimney damp-proofing absent or defective

Tiles decayed, cracked or missing, underfelt not turned into gutter, gutter or downpipe blocked or faulty

White patches on new brickwork (efflorescence)

Paint failure, window putty falling out, bad joinery design

Open joints and no DPC in coping (and window sills), parapet gutter choked or defective

Cracks due to drying, shrinkage or sulphate attack

Hazards such as window obstructing footpath near wall

Surfaces easily damaged or dirtied

Damp-proof course or air bricks missing or faulty, or covered by earth or rendering

Damp-proof membrane and DPC missing or defective, decay in skirting boards

Points to watch in building and maintenance

trating damp, where bricks are old or porous or exposed to severe weather conditions. These can be applied either by brush or high-pressure spray, such as a garden insecticide spray or paint sprayer.

Crumbling pointing may have to be raked out and replaced. This can be less of a drudge if a routing head on a power drill is used. Otherwise, use a small cold chisel and a hammer.

Surface finishes

Where a house is covered with one of the standard finishes, such as cement rendering, pebble dashing, roughcast, Tyrolean effect or silicone-nylon-fibre surfaces, check carefully that the surface is in good condition.

Small defects in mortar-based finishes can be filled in with a mortar slurry, but if a large patch is faulty, or 'blown' from the surface, this should be hacked back and the section replaced. The area of treatment should first be cleaned, and an equal part of water and PVA applied to prime it.

Broken masonry, such as on the older type of window ledge and steps, can be similarly repaired, by hacking back the damaged area, cleaning and priming. You may have to use timber shuttering to hold the new mortar in place while it is 'green'.

Damp

Among causes of damp is earth, piled against walls, which may bridge the damp-proof course, letting wet penetrate the home. This can seriously damage plaster and, if not attended to at source, will leave the surface 'dead' and cause plaster to 'blow' away from the wall.

Damp can also be caused by blocked air bricks where there are suspended wooden

floors. Air bricks should never be blocked off and should be left clear. Blockages, such as leaves, can be removed easily by a piece of stick.

Blocked air bricks can lead to the emergence of wet rot and, in its wake, dry rot. All plants should be kept well clear of brickwork and all shrubs cut well back so that leaves and soil cannot silt up the area.

Scraping away lichen and moss will discourage dampness. Apply a fungicide to stop fungal growth.

Similarly, air vents in bathrooms, kitchens and so on should be inspected to make sure that these are free of birds' nests or other blockages.

Timber infestation

Dry rot is the most serious form of fungal decay in timber. It feeds on damp timber and reduces it to a dry, brittle state. Dampness and poor ventilation are the prime causes.

Wet rot starts in wood containing 20 per cent or more of moisture. The spores can spread to attack sound, dry timber. Affected timber must be hacked out and burnt.

Wood-boring insects are another menace. The first indication is the presence of tiny flight holes in timber. Insects have, by this time, taken toll of this timber and left. Damaged timber is weakened and may contain grubs, and should be removed and burnt. All sound timbers, in situations where infestation has occurred, should be thoroughly treated with a timber preservative.

Sealing gaps

Gaps between woodwork and brickwork can be sealed with a proprietary mastic.

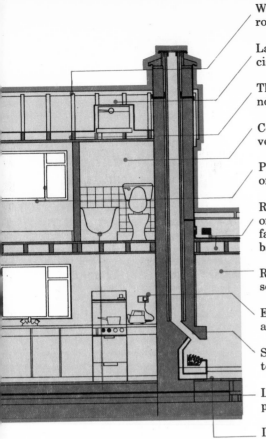

Woodworm and timber decay in roof (and floors)

Lagging inadequate on cold water cisterns and pipes in roof space

Thermal insulation inadequate, no ventilation or vapour barrier

Condensation – inadequate ventilation, heating or insulation

Paint failure on poorly prepared or damp surfaces

Roof flashings and DPC's absent or faulty, inadequate drainage falls and insulation, no vapour barrier or ventilation

Rain penetrating rendering on solid wall

Electric wiring should be tested at least once every five years

Smokey chimney or poor draught to fire

Leaky joints in copper/galvanized plumbing, timber decay

Dry rot, inadequate under-floor ventilation, woodworm

These are available in 'guns' or in applicator tubes, enabling a strip of mastic to fill the gap neatly without spillage on to surrounding brickwork.

Timber joints

Where cracks appear in the joints in window frames, doors and sills, deepen and clean any opened areas, using a two-part resin, an exterior-grade cellulose filler or a glass-fibre compound to fill the gap. Joints can be rubbed down and repainted when dry.

Where joints have become loose or broken you may have to take the frame apart, clean the joints and replace damaged tongues. In extreme cases, you may have to buy a new frame or make one. You will need a sash cramp to repair damaged frames.

After a sustained damp spell, window and door frames may have absorbed a great deal of moisture, causing the fibres to swell. Another cause of sticking is freshly applied paint.

Allow damp windows and doors a sufficient drying-out time, and open and close the door or window, inspecting carefully in order to locate the point of friction. This can then be removed with glass-paper, a block plane or a planer-file. Remove only a small section of surface at a time, and frequently test the opening and closing.

Windows and doors

All hinged windows and doors should be oiled and putty made good where necessary. Tighten all loose screws on windows and doors. Check the cords on sash windows. If they appear frayed they should be replaced. Metal windows should be checked for rust and cracked panes replaced.

Timber

External timber – particularly wood cladding – should be repainted or treated against the effects of sun and weather with a suitable preservative. Timber loses its colour by the bleaching effects of the sun and is susceptible to rain and moisture. Damp can lead to fungal growth.

Water systems

Central-heating systems and pipework should be checked. In directly heated systems, make sure that scaling of pipes, more likely in hard-water areas, is not present. It will be detectable by a loss of pressure at hot taps. Use a proprietary descaling agent to remove scale.

Check that stopcocks are free-turning, and grease them if necessary. Make sure that there are no leaks in pipes or unions. Inspect the loft cold-storage system to see that ball valves and fittings are not affected or corroded. Insulation around pipes should be checked to ensure that there is no exposure to freezing when cold weather comes.

Electrics

Electrical services should be inspected. Frayed wires should be replaced. Switches and points should be checked to see that there is no damage or fault.

Outside lighting and cable should be looked at carefully. Lighting and equipment should be suitable for outside use and checked to ensure that it is watertight and unaffected by corrosion on connections or casing.

Tiles

Wall tiles should be replaced if any have cracked. Bad tile grouting can be raked out and replaced. The sealant round the bath should be inspected and replaced if faulty.

Drains

Drain gullies collect grease and blockage can occur. There should be a grating over the gully and this should be scrubbed with a wire brush and hot water, soda and disinfectant.

Cast-iron manhole covers should be examined carefully for damage or for broken seals. If the cover is broken, buy a new one complete with metal rim. These come as a matched pair to be virtually airtight. Manhole rims should be bedded in a layer of heavy grease to make an airtight seal.

Inspect the inside of manholes. Any waste accumulation forming on the interior benching can lead to eventual blockage. This should be scrubbed with hot water and disinfectant. Damage to benching can be repaired by first cleaning and bonding with PVA, and repairing with sharp sand and cement.

Concrete

Garage floors and driveways tend to collect grease and petrol patches. Where there are no proprietary solutions available, a strong solution of detergent or domestic soda in hot water, scrubbed on to the affected areas and then rinsed, should remove grease.

Frost has a habit of cracking concrete which has been laid too thinly – usually less than 150mm. Stabilize a larger surface which you plan to reconcrete with a solution of one part PVA to five parts of water. Allow this to dry. Next, coat the area with a primer of three parts PVA to one part of water. Add one part of water to one part of PVA to the new concrete, and lay concrete when primer is tacky.

Old concrete can be refurbished with a coat of cold-laid asphalt. First, make good damaged areas and even up low levels. Clear surface dirt of grease and treat the concrete with an asphalt primer before laying and rolling.

Garden structures

Timber fences and sheds should be treated with a suitable preservative if unpainted, or repainted from time to time. Garden posts may have to be reinforced and repainted from time to time.

Sheds or garages often have corrugated asbestos roofing which may develop leaks between joint overlaps. A mastic solution can be inserted between these, or a bituminized preparation or a proprietary sealing strip can be used.

Plastic acrylic sheeting, in corrugated, flat or box-profile form, should be checked at the point where it meets the roof at the wall plate to ensure that joints are watertight. A proprietary glass-fibre or aluminium flashing strip can be used for this seal.

Flat-roof coverings should be inspected. These are usually cold-lay bituminised felt or a hot, rolled bitumen. Sections of felt can be renewed or overlapped or new bitumen applied. On some surfaces, liquid waterproofing agents can be used to bind the original surface and prolong its life. In some, minerals or fibres have been added to provide added durability.

Ladders and access: how to get safely above it all

Safety up above is all important, and to carry out the necessary jobs of home maintenance higher up needs reliable means of access. The choice of access method requires thought, as does the right way to go about putting up ladders and scaffolding. A working 'drill' aloft is vital to prevent hazard, both above and to those below.

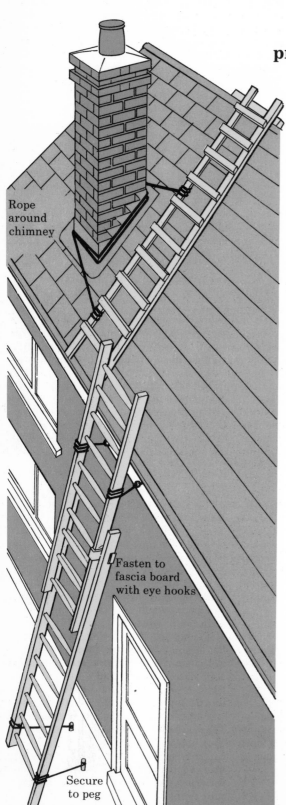

Rope around chimney

Fasten to fascia board with eye hooks

Secure to peg

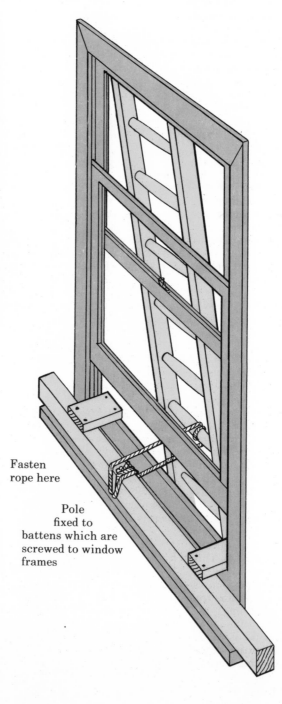

Anchor block

Fasten rope here

Pole fixed to battens which are screwed to window frames

The main, general-purpose ladder for work outside the house is the extension ladder. The uprights are known as 'strings' or 'stiles' and the cross-pieces, spaced at about 255mm intervals, are called 'rounds' or rungs. When choosing a wooden ladder, look for stiles of straight-grained fir, hemlock, pine or spruce. While spruce is the best timber, this is becoming scarce. Grain should run parallel with the edge of the stile if the ladder is of the finest quality. The best rungs are made from ash or oak.

The basic difference between a wooden and an aluminium ladder is that the latter costs more but weighs less. Aluminium ladders are also free from any tendency to warp. However, a good-quality wooden ladder, if it is well protected and not mistreated, should not warp.

Never paint a ladder, for this will serve to hide defects. Use varnish or a coat of clear wood preservative. Before use, always examine a timber ladder for cracked or rotted rungs and for any loose joints. Avoid leaving a timber ladder on the ground when not in use. Ideally, it should be stored in the rafters of a shed or garage where air can circulate around it.

Another way to store a ladder is on brackets fixed to a wall, with the ladder hung along these. Locate the ladder away from prevailing winds and cover it with a plastic sheet or tarpaulin. As a precaution against theft, it can be padlocked.

Aluminium ladders can conduct electricity but this is not usually likely to be a danger hazard. Ensure that the ladder is kept clear of any overhead domestic electricity supply. Because of the smooth construction of aluminium ladders, care must be taken to ensure that these are very firmly secured at top and bottom when erected, and are fitted with rubber feet which will exert grip and stop sliding.

Extension ladders suitable for reaching the eaves of the typical two-storey home are in two sections and called double-extension ladders. The second piece has clips to fit on to the rungs of the first section. There are various sizes of ladder. A 4·27m ladder which extends to about 7·30m is adequate for the average home.

This can be hand-operated by one man, other than in awkward situations, though assistance should be obtained where possible. If a ladder is extended over a height of 3m, someone should stand on it, or the ladder should be anchored firmly. Ladders extending higher than this are usually rope-operated.

Try to get someone to stand on the bottom when raising a ladder. However, you can prevent the ladder from slipping backwards by driving two stakes into the ground and securing to these.

Erecting

When lifting, push the foot of the ladder against the wall and work hands down the rung to push it upright. To position it, pull out the bottom until the ladder is at the correct angle.

Tie one of the lower rungs to a convenient projection on the wall or to a wooden batten passed behind a window frame if you are working on paved ground.

A full sack of cement, sand or earth behind the legs will hold the ladder safely. If the soil is soft beneath the ladder, stand it on a board to spread the weight evenly, tilting the board so that the ladder does not slide from it.

At the top of the ladder, secure an upper rung with rope to a gutter bracket or to an eye screw driven into the fascia board, to prevent side slip.

Make sure that the ladder is square to the structure and also on firm ground. Position it at an angle of about 70° or about one quarter of the ladder height.

There is no need to be apprehensive of a ladder if it whips under your weight when you climb it. If it did not do so it might snap. Never climb more than about 1800mm above the ground in a strong wind if you can possibly avoid it.

Before climbing, tie shoelaces securely and tuck your trousers in at the bottom.

Always wear shoes. Boots make it less easy to feel the rungs–and thin-soled shoes will be uncomfortable because of the rungs.

Carry cloths, brushes and abrasive papers in your pockets but any sharp items such as chisels, scrapers or paint-can hooks should be carried in the hand so that you can fling these well clear in the event of mishap.

When climbing, keep your eyes on the wall immediately in front. Never look up or down as this may cause you to become dizzy. When you get to the top, look only at the job you are doing. Always leave a minimum two-rung overlap between sections of a 4·3m extension ladder and three rungs on one 4·9m long. Do not stand on the top rungs of a ladder. The minimum safety position is about four rungs down from the top.

Never rest a ladder against a gutter

Carry upright. Grip with one hand and support above shoulder level with other

When lifting, push foot of ladder against wall. Work hands down rungs to push up

Pull out from bottom once in place. Ideal angle is one quarter of ladder height

Look straight ahead when climbing; never up or down nor lean sideways

because its weight may snap the guttering or weaken the fastenings on the brackets. If you cannot reach gutters by standing the ladder against the wall, use a ladder stay, which stands the ladder off from the wall. One end of the stay slots over the rungs, while the other end rests against the wall to hold the top of the ladder clear of the wall.

Do not lean out from either side of the ladder–keep your centre of gravity within the confines of the ladder stiles. Work on those parts which you can reach easily. Always get down and move the ladder along, rather than risk hazard.

When painting, hang the tin on a metal 'S' hook. Always hold the ladder if possible with one hand. Try to keep both hands free, and pass up tools on a line. If you are right-handed, work from right to left, and if left-handed from left to right.

Carrying

Grip the ladder with one hand and support it diagonally on the shoulder with most of the weight in front. This avoids knocking into anyone who may be behind.

Crawling boards and cat ladders

Never attempt any major roof repairs without using crawling boards or a cat ladder. Either of these may be hired for the specific job. Some crawling boards are fitted with a top section, known as a headboard, with extension lengths. Avoid working from a ladder when using a crawling board and preferably use a scaffold tower for access to these.

Cat ladders consist of a wooden ladder with an angled lip at the top which sits over the ridge tiles. These are used in conjunction with a ladder or scaffold tower. The anchor block should be securely fastened to an adjacent chimney and secured from the rear by ropes firmly fixed to a strong anchor point.

Scaffolding

Tubular scaffolding can be used to provide almost any configuration to give ready access. In the majority of situations, a scaffold tower, or a combination of towers in certain circumstances, can provide suitable access for domestic repairs at higher level.

A scaffold tower can be erected up to heights of 9·6m and has a platform size of 2400mm × 1200mm. Sectional tubes merely slot together, providing staging of various heights. Castor wheels can be fitted, which enable the tower to be moved around;

these can be locked into position. You can also fit fixed feet, which are adjustable for variations in ground height.

On any scaffold system, you should fit toe boards, an upstand of planking which prevents objects from falling over the platform edge. These should be supplied with a hired tower. The height of a tower should not exceed more than three times the dimensions of its base.

Where long areas have to be tackled, a bridge consisting of timber staging can be suspended between two towers. This will allow you to work along a dispersed area or over a surface on which it is unsafe to stand, such as glass or asbestos. Toe boards should be fitted completely along the run of staging between towers.

On very long runs you may have to introduce a third tower and an extra set of staging. Staging consists of scaffold boards. These should be in good condition and damaged ones should be rejected for safety reasons. Toe boards can be made by upright sections of scaffold board, lashed to the tower at each end.

Access to a scaffold tower can be by ladder, or you can clamber up the sections. Ladders should be firmly anchored with rope to the side of the scaffold, in the same way as for use of ladders generally.

When taking down scaffold towers, avoid throwing sections down to the ground as this can affect the temper of steel. Sections may tend to grip tightly after assembly and may have to be tapped apart with a hammer and a block of wood to disassemble them. Try to avoid damaging any protective paint on the framework. Touch-up paint should be used to make good any blemishes and prevent rusting. Some makes of tower are of galvanised steel and with these you will not face the same problems of possible rusting.

For work inside the house a good step ladder is compact and safe. A step ladder reaching to 1800mm should be adequate for most jobs around the house. These may be made of steel, aluminium or timber.

Another very useful design of ladder is the combination ladder and self-supporting steps. This type can be made into an extension ladder which can be adjusted at intermediate heights, made into self-supporting steps, or be used as two entirely separate ladders.

A combined ladder and staging system is one way of carrying out work on awkward places, such as halls or stairwells. This can be used in several ways: as a two or three section ladder, double-sided step ladder, a trestle and single section support, and as a stair scaffold. Each section can also be used as a separate ladder.

Another type of ladder is the platform steps, similar in construction to conventional step ladders but having a spacious platform at the top which allows free use of hands. This type of ladder may be collapsed so that the platform can be folded back to the rear stiles in an upright position.

The folding step stool is useful in the kitchen. Always use a firmly based means of access such as a pair of steps, since chairs can too readily topple backwards.

It is always best to pay a little more for a top-quality product, giving absolute confidence in the equipment bought.

Avoiding trouble from the top

Constituent parts of a chimney flashing

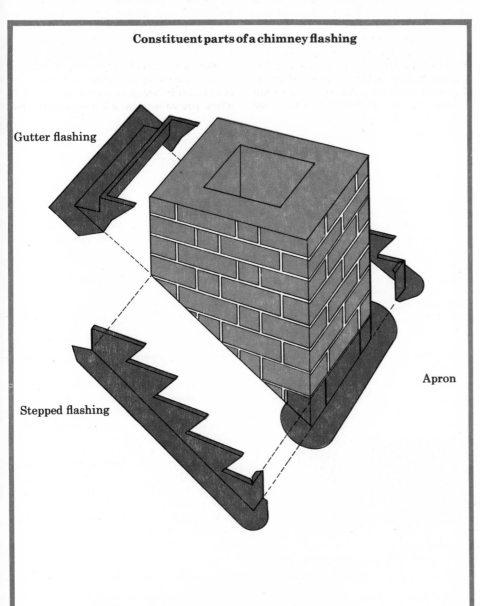

Gutter flashing

Stepped flashing

Apron

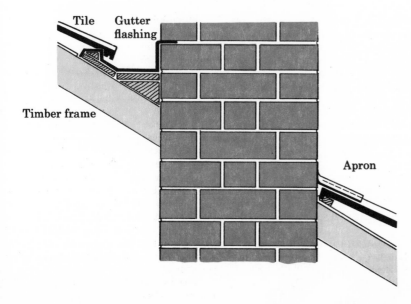

Tile   Gutter flashing

Timber frame

Apron

Moisture seems to have a capacity to get in almost anywhere, and keeping out damp can prove quite a problem in older homes in particular. However, both traditional and modern methods can often be allied to keep the home dry and free from water damage.

Flashings consist of various types of water-tight joint outside homes. These are used where chimney stacks come through roofs, where a roof abuts a wall, or around roof lights and dormer windows.

The traditional flashing materials are lead, zinc and copper. However, lead-beating is a skilled job calling for special tools. Though this is not necessarily beyond the skill of a handyman, other materials are easier to work and can usually be used. Both lead and zinc may deteriorate in time and need replacement.

Aluminium-based flashing, such as Evode Flashband, and mastics, can often be used for repair and replacement. Mastic glazing tapes and cords can also be used to effect repairs to deteriorated flashing.

Another type of flashing material is a pliable bituminous sheeting which can be softened with heat and manipulated to replace damaged areas.

The intrusion of damp into areas such as chimney breasts, the loft or an attic ceiling or bedroom is an indication that all is not well. The best time to detect the source of the trouble is during heavy rain.

In some cases, porosity of brickwork may be the cause, or a joint in zinc or other metal sheet may have lifted. Mastic or cold asphalt may be used to effect a repair.

Chimneys

A roof ladder is needed to carry out repairs to chimneys. A form of flashing around chimney pots is the sloped mortar fillet called flaunching.

This may have cracked and broken away as a result of normal expansion and contraction of the fabric of the home. While these are natural conditions in any structure, they are more intensified near sources of heat, such as chimneys.

Careful inspection may show that slight damage can be repaired with a mastic, or damage patched up with new mortar. Where patching up of damaged or de-teriorated flaunching using mortar still does not solve the problem, you may have to remove and replace the entire flashing.

In older homes, the flashing around the base of a chimney may be a mortar fillet or haunching. Modern flashings consist of stepped, side flashings, with a gutter flashing at the chimney top and an apron flashing at the bottom of the chimney. The stepped flashing is cut into steps and inserted into mortar joints down the side of the chimney.

Lead is a malleable metal and made in various weights. 1·81kg lead is needed for roof purposes. The brick joints should be raked out and the new flashing cut with

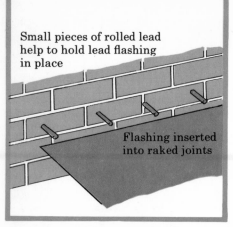

Small pieces of rolled lead help to hold lead flashing in place

Flashing inserted into raked joints

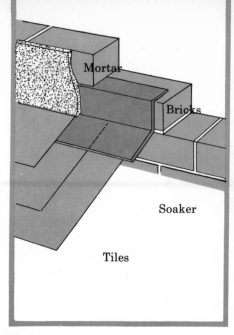

Mortar

Bricks

Soaker

Tiles

metal shears and inserted. Small pieces of rolled lead should be inserted to fix the flashing into position and the joint re-mortared with a 1:3 mortar mix.

When repairing mortar fillets use a little adhesive to bond new mortar to old. Make sure that you brush off any algae.

Cracks, however, may open up again, and some bituminous mastic or a flexible compound should be used. This can be applied with a special 'gun', so that the joint is effectively penetrated and sealed. These mastics may also be applied by trowel from a tin.

When removing old mortar from a chimney, rake out a single section of the stack at a time to a depth of 15mm–20mm. Before repointing, dampen the joints and form a weather-struck joint.

Damaged flaunching should be chipped away and replaced. Use a club hammer and chisel and work carefully, avoiding cascading large chunks of mortar down the roof. Keep a bucket handy and place the broken mortar pieces in this.

Chimney pots

It may be necessary to replace or refix the chimney pot. If you do have to remove this, seal up the fireplaces below so that dirt, dust and soot do not damage furnishings and fabrics.

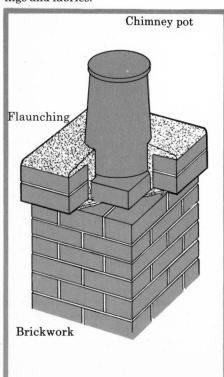

Chimney pot

Flaunching

Brickwork

Once you have removed the old flaunching, locate the chimney pot back into position, dampen the surround and apply a 1:3 mortar mix with a high-alumina cement and a little PVA adhesive to assist bonding, for new chimney flaunching.

This might be the opportunity to replace a chimney pot with a terminal if a modern heating appliance is employed, or to cap off a chimney if the fire is no longer in use. Modern terminals are usually made of a light weight material and easy to handle.

Chimney pots are usually heavier than they seem, so you may need help, if you have to lower it to the ground. If one crashes down, considerable structural damage may be caused, and someone could be injured.

Secure the pot with a stout rope, fixed round the stack. It is advisable to organize help so that you can lower the old pot to the ground.

You may have to fit pieces of slate or tile around a new pot to make it vertical. Use a spirit level to check this. Make sure that the new mortar fillet fills the gaps between the base of the pot and brickwork, and take care that mortar does not go down the flue. You can also fit a cowl to an existing chimney.

Junctions

Mortar, which seals the weatherproof junctions between a wall and chimney, frequently cannot absorb the natural movement in a structure and cracks. This is often met in older homes.

It may, however, be necessary to replace an ancient fillet. You can use lead, zinc, or felt, or remake in mortar.

Zinc is cheaper than lead and is 'dressed' similarly. You need a dresser, which is a special tool made of boxwood or hornbeam.

Any adjacent gutter outlet should be temporarily blocked off so that old mortar does not block up the stormwater drainage system.

If you are remaking the mortar fillet, apply a 1:4 mortar mixture, with a PVA additive, using a wooden float. Make a fairly stiff mix and when the mortar has dried, cross-hatch the surface with a trowel or scratcher, to provide a scratch coat for a finish coat.

Allow the mortar to go off for about a day and then apply a finish coat of about 15mm thick, with the wood float. Finally, polish this to a fine finish with a steel float.

Make sure that you maintain an even slope so that rainwater cannot collect and percolate through any point into the home.

Soakers are a flashing which go under tiles and are often covered with a sloped mortar fillet. Both the mortar and the material, frequently zinc, may have deteriorated.

Again, an aluminium bituminous-backed strip may assist to put right the trouble, but if water is percolating through surrounding roofing, usually–in older property–slates, you may have to chip away the fillet and replace the soakers.

Sometimes soakers may be in long strips, which are cut into the wall and located beneath slates and tiles, or just in small sections. A damaged section can be lifted up, once surrounding tiles or slates are removed and cut out with metal shears. A new piece can be inserted and lapped over the old by some 150mm.

Zinc must first be dressed to replace worn or damaged soakers. The joints between bricks should be raked out to about a depth of 25mm. Zinc, 305mm wide, should be cut laid on a board and dressed to provide a 20mm strip at right angles. This angled section fits into the mortar gap of the original flashing.

Establish the angle of slope, using a woodworking, adjustable bevel. Turn the strip of zinc over and lay it on a thicker board. Hammer it down, working progressively outwards from the centre, until it matches the angle of the bevel; constantly check this.

Once it is moulded to shape, dash water into the gap between brickwork to assist mortar adhesion and insert the new soaker or flashing. Provide a 150mm overlap at joints.

Fold in small wedges of zinc at each end and then gently adjust the flashing to the slope of the roof. Fill the joint with a 1:4 mortar mix with a little PVA added. Trim off surplus mortar with a small trowel.

When working on sloping roofs always work from a crawling board and scaffolding. A scaffolding tower can be used in most cases for primary access.

Damaged slates or tiles may have to be replaced and surrounding brickwork repointed where necessary.

Self-adhesive flashing

Self-adhesive, aluminium-faced sealing can be used without the need of special tools, saving a great deal of time and effort. Width must be sufficient to overlap adjoining surfaces by at least 25mm, while making sure that the sealing is 'snug' into angles and corners. On overlapping glass and other surfaces, avoid forming air pockets in the angle.

In cold weather, it should be warmed to achieve maximum initial tack. Priming of the surfaces to be sealed also assists adhesion and grows stronger with time.

At the top of a glazing bar leave enough flashing to tuck around the bar end to complete the seal.

Very rough-textured surfaces such as

Bitumen primer is applied to the area to be covered by aluminium flashing strip

The flashing is dressed down on to the primed surface. It can be cut and trimmed

Leaks on many types of roofs can be cured by applying a brush-on bitumen

pebbledash and rustic brick require an additional seal at the leading edge–such as a knifing grade of bituminous mastic.

A major product of this type is Evostik Flashband, made in 9·75m lengths and in widths of from 50mm to 610mm. A primer is available in various quantities.

Application

All surfaces must first be cleaned. Other than for smooth, non-porous surfaces, such as glass and metal, apply the primer, after removal of dust, rust and old putty. The primer dries quickly and the surface can then be treated.

The material is simply cut to length with a pair of scissors. A release paper on the back peels off and the material can be pressed and contoured into place. Warming improves the application properties.

Finishing can be with a cloth pad, roller or square-section piece of wood, first pressuring the strip firmly into any angles of the area to be waterproofed.

Brushing on

Brush-on roofing treatments for flat or pitched roofs, include Evo-Stik Supaproof, a rich bitumen-content emulsion, which can be used on roofs of concrete, asphalt, asbestos, cement, corrugated iron, zinc felt, slate or tiles. This is made in four colours–black, tile-red, slate-grey or green.

The technique of use is to brush thoroughly to remove dirt, dust and moss from all cracks.

Fill all large cracks and depressions with a filler paste, made from clean sand mixed to a trowelling consistency, using the emulsion. If reinforcement is needed to bridge the gaps in the roof, to provide a continuous surface, a sandwich of jute, hessian, linen or canvas can be laid between two coats of the product.

It should be applied when weather conditions are suitable for rapid drying.

Weatherproof tapes can be used to seal glazing bars, which must be clean and dry

Mastic sealing is a popular method of joint sealing. This can be tube applied

Do not use in frosty or damp weather or when rain appears imminent.

Apply, with a hand brush or soft broom, a good generous coat. A similar second coat should be applied when the first has dried thoroughly. A coloured finish may be used as the second coat after a first coat of black.

Brushes and brooms should be washed out immediately after use with water. Do not use paraffin or white spirit for cleaning or mixing with the emulsion.

Weatherproof tape

Weatherproof tapes are another way of sealing. The surface must be clean and dry and wiped with a cloth moistened with paraffin or petrol. All traces of the solvent should be allowed to evaporate before applying the tape.

This is pressed firmly on the surface, smoothing down the centre first, and then working outward along the length of tape, ensuring that the edges are firmly bonded and all air is excluded. On sloping surfaces, start at the top and work downwards.

Unroll as you proceed and take care not to stretch the tape, which should be pressed well down into angles, and should overlap joining surfaces by at least 6mm.

Joints are made by placing one piece over another and smoothing down. On sloping surfaces, the upper piece should always be placed over the lower.

This type of sealing does not normally need painting, but paints may be used, provided care is taken to allow the paint to flow on with the minimum of brushing. Avoid painting immediately after or during hot weather.

The compound on the tape can be cleaned from surrounding areas with a rag moistened with paraffin, white spirit or petrol. Avoid splashing the tape with solvent.

In cold weather application is improved by storing in a warm place before use.

When time on the tiles is well spent

The weather, and water in particular, has a habit of getting in where it is not wanted, more often than not through leaks in roof surfaces. Regular inspection of the roof is essential if you are to keep out the elements as an unwelcome visitor. Loose slates and tiles are not difficult to replace and flaws should be rectified quickly before damage has a chance to strike and spread.

Slates

Roof slates are laid, working upwards from the eaves. Each row, or course, overlaps the one below it, and as the vertical joints between slates are staggered in adjacent rows, any slate partly covers the two below it.

The design and slope of the roof and position of battens, to which slates are nailed, determines the size of the main slates. However, there are several sizes of slate used in slate roofing. Those on eaves are the same width as the main roof slate but are shorter. Another slate is half as wide again as the main slates; this is used at the end of alternate rows.

A narrow slate, or creasing or verge slate, is often used at the end of each course on a gable end. This type of slate is laid underneath main slates and tilts the roof edge upwards, to prevent rain from running off the roof edge and down the wall.

Since slates vary in size, shape and thickness, establish that replacements correspond with existing ones, otherwise the roof may let in water. If you cannot match a slate exactly in size, obtain the next largest size of the same thickness. The slates can then be cut to fit.

Slates can be cut to any size or shape. The tile is marked with a nail or a trowel and then laid over a board and chopped with that part of the trowel nearest the handle. Chop half way and then turn the slate round and chop from the other end.

To make holes in new slates, establish the method of fixing and position each slate, bevelled edge downwards, on a flat board and drill the holes with a brace and bit or use a hammer and nail. A good way of making sure that holes are correctly positioned is to lay an old slate over a new one and make the new holes through the holes in the old slate.

Slates are made in different colours so that you can match the roof. New slates can be bought singly or in bulk. Demolition sites are another source of supply, but check carefully that slates are in good condition. These cost only about two-thirds of the price of new slates.

One firm makes concrete tiles which resemble slates. Since these are a good deal heavier than slates you should check that the roof battens are equal to the load.

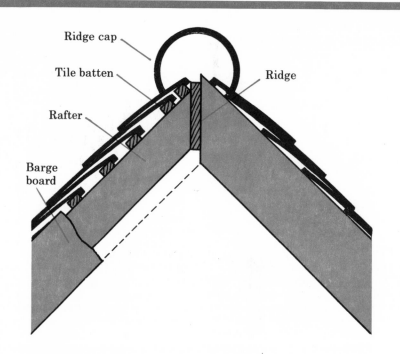

Barge boards (above) are used to face gables, fascia boards (below) support guttering

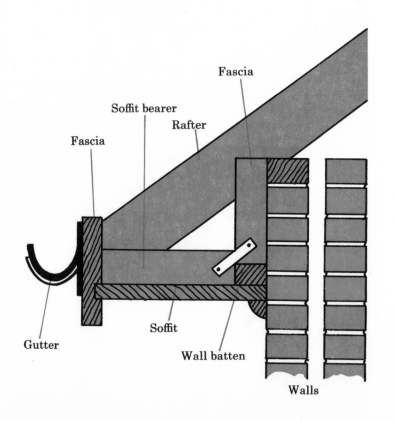

As slates age, they may flake and powder, particularly near nail holes. Hairline cracks, often difficult to see, develop along the grain. If slates have deteriorated at the edges, provided these are oversized, they can be cut down.

Slates are often referred to as bests, seconds and thirds. This has nothing to do with quality but refers to thickness and texture.

Take care when handling slates, since these are very brittle and break easily if roughly handled. Hold a slate along the longer side and tip it when lifting. Never try to lift slates from a pile, and if you are carrying several, wear canvas gloves and hold the slates on edge under an arm. Carried flat in a pile, they are likely to break or crack. Slates taken up to a roof should be stacked on edge, in a canvas or a plastic bag.

Before starting work, check the condition of the battens. If these are damaged or have deteriorated, they should be replaced. New battens should be nailed against the edges of the old ones with 50mm copper or zinc nails. Damaged timber should be cut out.

Main slates may be fixed by two edge nails or at the centre. The top and eaves courses of slates are always held along the top edge by two nails. In repairing a slate roof, always fix the new slates in the same way as the original ones.

For the first course above the eaves, short slates are used; these are covered completely by the second row. To stagger joins, nail slates either along their top edge or at centres. These are staggered in adjacent rows to make the roof watertight. For the courses at the ridge, short slates are used. These partly cover the course below, providing double thickness for weatherproofing.

Roof slates may crack or break or nails securing them may corrode. This can be caused by ageing of a house, causing movement in the roof structure, or through high winds, making the slates shear.

A tool for removing slates is called a ripper. These are not expensive to buy but can be hired. The ripper is slid under the slate directly above the one which has to be replaced. The head of the ripper is designed to hook the curved edges around the nails holding the broken slate. This 'rips' them away. It may take a little effort to remove the nails, but this must be done before the slate can be replaced.

Once the slate has been worked loose, a batten or slat will be visible and the new slate attaches to this. Slates are secured by 25mm galvanized nails. Before the nail is driven home, a length of lead 25mm × 230mm or a piece of thin copper wire, 230mm long, should be fixed to the nail. Drive the nail through the lead; wind copper wire round it before the nail is finally driven home. Line up the bottom edge of the slate with adjoining slates and bend up the end of the lead clip to secure it firmly in place.

To refit a section of slates, start work at the eaves by sliding a short slate under an adjacent, full-length slate, up to the batten centre line. As the first slate is partly covered, fix it with one nail. The others along the row are fixed with two nails.

Carefully check that each slate is on the

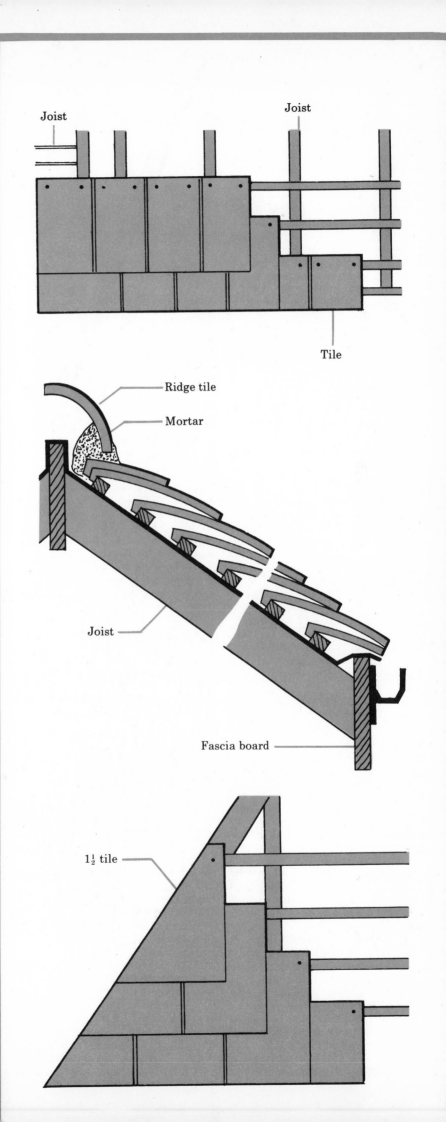

Joist

Joist

Tile

Ridge tile

Mortar

Joist

Fascia board

1½ tile

centre line, in order to allow the second row to be fixed to the same batten. Next, lift the slate in the row above and slide the first new full-length slate beneath it, making sure that the new slate aligns with the centre of the batten. Fix this with a single nail.

Lay remaining slates in the same row, so that these cover the vertical joins in the rows beneath. Carry on working up the roof and cover previous joins and securing nails with each fresh slate.

Since the nail holes are covered by the rows above, it may not be possible to nail the last few slates. Cut 25mm × 230mm lead clips to hold these slates. Fix the clips between nails securing adjacent slates. Again, fit these slates so that the bottom edges are flush with the remaining slates in the row and bend up the clips. Alternatively, you can make clips from thin copper wire.

Mortar between the ridge slates on top of the roof may fall out with age. Loose ridge slates should be lifted free and taken to the ground. Chip away old mortar from inside the slate with a trowel edge. Use care since you may crack the slate. With a club hammer and bolster, or cold chisel, remove old mortar from the roof. Apply a 1:3 cement and builder's sand mix along the ridge, roughening the surface with a trowel.

Locate the cleaned ridge slate on the mortar and tap it gently until it lines up with the height of the adjacent slates. Trowel mortar into the joints on each side and along the bottom, then smooth. Take care not to dislodge the slate before it sets.

Tiles

Laying or replacing tiles involves a similar operation, though these are heavier than slates. Tiles are again laid in courses, working from the eaves up to the roof ridge. Each course overlaps the one below, and vertical joins are staggered in adjacent rows, so that a tile partly covers two in the row beneath.

A slate ripper is helpful but not essential on tile repairs.

There are six basic types of tile: plain, pantiles, double pantiles, interlocking tiles and Roman and Spanish tiles. Unlike slate, tiles cannot be cut to size. The most common is the plain tile, measuring 265mm × 165mm × 13mm. These are slightly curved to ensure that tail ends bed evenly on the tiles below and to prevent water from creeping up, by capillary action, under the eaves.

There are three sizes of tiles – a standard tile for the main area; a tile half as wide again, called a tile and a half, at the end of alternate rows; and a shortened version of the tile and a half for the course along the eaves and along the ridge.

Tiles may be nailed to roof battens at intervals with 30mm galvanized nails; usually at every fourth course. Some have small projections called nibs, which fit over the battens. When replacing the odd tile, it is not normally necessary to use fixing nails. Nibbed tiles may be nailed, but unnibbed ones must always be nailed.

Try to match your tiles but if this is not possible, remove tiles from an inconspicuous area, using these to replace tiles in the

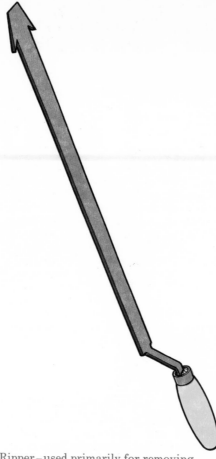

Ripper – used primarily for removing slates; can also be used for tiles

visible area, and use the new ones in the less noticeable place.

If several tiles in an area are broken, it is a good idea to strip out the entire area and retile, with new ones in one patch. Broken tiles near a verge, ridge or hip are more difficult to replace. Verges, ridges and hips are usually bedded in mortar. This bedding must be picked out with a cold chisel and tiles removed until the replacement can be effected. When reinstating the bedding do not use too strong or sloppy a mortar mix. Use a 1:3 cement/ mortar mix sufficient for a solid, watertight job.

To take out a broken tile you just push it back slightly, lift it and withdraw it. Slipping the trowel beneath an adjacent tile, and lifting this slightly, will assist the operation.

If tiles are nibbed, prise the sound ones up with a trowel and lift the damaged ones over the batten. Nailed tiles should be rocked gently from side to side to loosen them. Use a ripper, if necessary, to remove the nails. You can also use a tiler's hammer which has a head designed for knocking in tile nails and shaped on the other side for lifting tiles.

Alternatively, you can remove the two tiles above, which will expose the nails, pull out the nails and then the tile, substitute a sound one and slide the other back, over the batten then down until the nibs engage.

If the new tile is too large, nibble off an edge with pincers, a little at a time, until it is the right size. You can rub the edge smooth with a coarse carborundum stone. Allow a 12mm gap between tiles.

Tile from the eaves upwards, and to fit

the last tiles, wedge up one of the tiles and lift the others and slide in the new tiles.

The under-eaves tiles measure 165mm × 150mm, and comprise the first and lowest course. These tiles are sometimes called half tiles and may be used to form the last course beneath the ridge. Verge tiles, which measure 230mm × 255mm, are used at edges and also for cutting to the mitre angle of hips and valleys. If any of these are broken or missing, water can get behind the fascia board. This course is completely covered by the second row of tiles.

Valley junctions are shaped tiles which interlock with each other to form tiled gutters.

Tiles are usually fixed to sawn deal battens, though you may encounter feather-edged board.

On some roofs, narrower tiles, called creasing tiles, may be used at gable ends. These are laid beneath the end to tilt the edge of the roof slightly, so that rainwater does not run down the gable wall.

Pantiles, sectionally shaped like a flattened letter 's', also interlock or lap over each other. These are pointed along the verge and may have nibs or hooks and are also nailed. First, chip away pointing where necessary, lever this slightly to loosen the bed and then push and twist sideways to remove the tile. If these are nailed, a ripper may be used to remove them.

Ridge and hip tiles may deteriorate through stresses or inherent weakness, or flake and spall through combined water and frost action. This may expose the ridge timbers. A broken ridge can also slip down a roof and do a lot of damage.

Ridges are generally right-angled or semi-circular, with a 230mm diameter. The edges formed by two sloping surfaces, called hips, have semi-circular or bonnet-shaped tiles.

Chip out the old ridge and remove all bedding material. Clean the adjacent edges of ridges and try the new ones for fit. If the tile is too long, allowing a 6mm overlap on each side, mark a line, then nibble off with the pincers.

You can cut a section by bedding the ridge solidly in damp sand and chipping a groove all round with a sharp cold chisel. Concrete ridge tiles are more difficult to cut than clay ones.

A new ridge must be bedded solidly along the edges. The joints should be firm and when the cement has slightly dried, the joints should be trowelled smooth. On the end ridge, the 'open' section must be filled in with mortar and tile slips. These are small pieces of tile to reinforce the mortar.

Pieces of tile must be used to reinforce the mortar of the ridge tiles and in the tiles on the verge.

Sarking (bitumenized) felt is laid on modern roofs, primarily to keep out dust. This felt tears easily. Always fit new felt if the existing cover is torn.

Felt should be overlapped by 150mm at both horizontal and vertical joints. The bottom run of felting on a roof should be overlapped at the front to provide a drip into the gutter, while the top should always overlap the ridgeboard to form a watertight seal.

First aid for brick walls

Brickwork may occasionally need smartening up. This may mean no more than cleaning it down with a stiff broom and clean water. Mould or lichen can be removed with a mixture of one part of household bleach to four parts of clean water. Do not use detergent, as this may affect the face work of the brick. Difficult patches of dirt can be brushed down with a wire brush. Avoid rubbing too hard, however, as this may again damage the brick face.

Dull and faded brickwork can be brightened by one of the brick dyes. These lighten after a time and need renewing periodically.

Efflorescence

Efflorescence is a discolouration of white powder or feathery crystals, similar to damp salt, on the face of new brickwork or freshly plastered walls.

It forms because rainwater or water used in building a house soaks the brickwork and dissolves any soluble salts in it. The water evaporates, drawing the salt to the surface.

This does not damage brickwork but is unattractive. The walls can be brushed off periodically with a stiff-bristled broom. If you use a wire brush, avoid damaging bricks and pointing.

A neutralizing liquid can be applied to remove efflorescence. Using a 100mm brush, two or three coats of a proprietary preparation should be used, allowing about 15 minutes between applications.

Redecorating on interior walls can usually take place about a day after treatment.

You should not wash off efflorescence with tap water, since this usually contains chemicals which accelerate reappearance of salts.

Vegetable staining

Surrounding vegetation may also stain brickwork. First find the cause and remedy it, and then clean the brickwork with a stiff broom. It is wise to apply a coat of colourless fungicide. The wall should be treated in dry weather, so that the solution is not washed away by rain.

Rust

Rust is another discolouration which may appear on brickwork joints or around ironwork embedded in brickwork. Brickwork can flake and crack as a result of rust, so mortar around ironwork should be raked out. Clean the metal thoroughly and prime it. You may need to use a rust-neutralizing agent on the metal.

Rust in brick jointing occurs as a result of ironstone in the sand. The mortar will have to be raked out and repointed.

Replacing bricks

Brick is porous and takes in moisture in wet weather which evaporates when the weather is dry. On very porous bricks, water may accumulate inside and freeze. Ice expands and may cause the brick to crumble or 'spall' at the edges. The brick then ceases to offer resistance to the weather and should be replaced.

Use a club hammer and bolster to remove damaged bricks, but protect your eyes by wearing safety glasses. Cut back till you reach solid brick. Remove loose material with a wire brush and then cut back the mortar joints with a narrow cold chisel.

A matching half brick can be used to replace the damaged portion. This is called a queen closer—that is a brick cut in half along its length. You can cut a queen closer with a bolster and club hammer, working steadily around the brick until it comes apart into two halves.

Either cut the queen closer slightly undersize, or cut back to slightly more than half a brick. This allows a sufficient bed of mortar for the brick to fit flush with the existing bricks. Apply a bond of PVA adhesive to both faces, and mortar in place using a 1:3 mortar mix, plus a little PVA additive. Point finally once bricks have set.

Sometimes you may have to remove entire bricks. This is done by removing the pointing around the brick and using a narrow cold chisel to dislodge the brick.

You may also have to break out an old

Brightening the brickwork can give a new lease of life to the appearance of the home. It is, however, also important to be able to patch up or to replace damaged bricks, cure flaws and deterioration to bricks, joints and surfaces and to recognize the problems of settlement, as well as the lesser one of shrinkage.

Old pointing

A club hammer and cold chisel are the basic tools used to remove old mortar

Keyed pointing

⌃ The pointing tool enables a wide range of keyed finishes to be used on joints

⌃ **Weathered pointing**
Draw trowel down edge of brick on right

⌄ Press mortar into horizontal joints; use straight edge and trowel to trim

brick in sections in order to remove other bricks more easily.

Damaged brick at ground level or below should be removed after first being exposed by raking the soil clear.

Water repellent

It is also worthwhile treating a wall with a water repellent. This will ensure, in the case of porous bricks, that frost does not damage the brickwork again.

Once you have made good any damage, form a thin 'apron' of rendering about 150mm high along the front of the wall. Add a waterproofing liquid or powder to the mortar or a water repellent to the rendering mix.

Jointing

Before repointing badly deteriorated joints, lay a sheet of polythene down to collect mortar droppings. A plugging chisel and a club hammer are used to clear out old mortar from about 1m² of wall at a time. First clear vertical joints and then horizontal ones. Clear them to a depth of about 15mm, for any deeper may damage the wall.

Brush down the joints to remove dust and old mortar, and soak the brickwork, so that it does not absorb moisture from the new mortar.

Only mix up enough mortar for about two hours' work. Use a hawk, and first practise picking up mortar with a smooth upward sweep on the back of the trowel from the mix.

Make sure that new joints match the old. Weather-struck joints give maximum protection from damp and are advisable on chimneys and house walls.

With rough-textured bricks, recessed joints are attractive, but flush or rubbed joints look better with smooth-surfaced bricks.

With the weather-struck joint, a sloped surface allows rain to run off. The horizontal joint is recessed beneath the top brick and overhangs slightly the lower.

Push mortar into the joints, first into the uprights and then the horizontals, the top and then the bottom.

Form the slope on weather-struck joints as you go. With other joints, leave the mortar flush with the bricks. Weather-struck joints are trimmed at the horizontal joints with a pointing trowel.

Slope vertical joints to one side, matching the horizontal with the trowel. Use a small trowel or a 'Frenchman', a tool to cut off excess mortar at the bottom of the horizontal joints, in conjunction with a straight edge.

The straight edge acts as a guide while you run the Frenchman along with the angled tip pointing downwards. Once the mortar has set, brush off the area you have been working on. Repeat the process over the next square metre of working area.

To form a flush joint, let the mortar become semi-stiff and rub a piece of sacking along the joint in one direction to flush this with the brickwork. Brush off when dry.

A recessed joint is formed with a piece of metal with a pointed curved end. This can be made from a piece of metal bucket handle, using the inside bend to strike the joint. Use the pointing tool to scrape mortar from both vertical and horizontal joints to a depth of around 6mm. Rub down the joint gently with a piece of wood so that the surface is smooth and water-resistant.

In repointing you can add a vegetable dye or proprietary colourant to produce a matching or decorative effect. The colour will, however, be mutated by the texture of ordinary sand, so white sand should be used.

Settlement

This is a problem which may have been caused by imperfect foundations or movement of ground beneath the home. Common reasons are land on an unstable surface, such as an old rubbish tip, or building on clay subsoil, which moves in accordance with the amount of ground moisture.

Other reasons are rotted or decayed timber, which loses volume and causes subsidence, and tree roots affecting foundations. The roots of a tree roughly cover the spread of the branches. Roots may crack foundations or take moisture from the ground and cause soil to subside.

Subsidence is usually indicated by running cracks through brickwork joints. Gaps around door tops and window frames may be other indications, though these can be caused by natural shrinkage of timber.

There are two simple ways to check whether subsidence has ceased. Fix a piece of glass across a crack, using an epoxy-resin adhesive. Since glass has low tensile strength, any slight new movement will cause it to crack. You can bridge the gap with plaster of Paris. This will also crack if there is further subsidence.

All new structures settle and shrink and plaster cracks are not in themselves indication of subsidence.

Subsidence caused by building on clay may be apparent because cracks in inside walls may open and close with the weather. Serious settlement involves a costly and expert job of underpinning, in which hydraulic jacks may have to be employed.

Shrinkage

Shrinkage may appear as stepped cracks in the brickwork joints, and sometimes even through the bricks. These can be repaired by raking out joints and repointing, or replacing cracked bricks.

Repairs

Repairs should be carried out during dry weather, so that brickwork is dry, using a 1:2:9 mix of well-graded soft sand.

If it is difficult to point cracks you can feed a mortar grout into the fissures. Grout is a thinned mortar mixture.

The cracks should be masked with a plastic modelling or soft clay, or other impervious masking. The grout is poured into the fissure using a funnel and a piece of plastic tube. Allow the grout to dry out partially, and neatly point the cracked surface.

Bricks can be repaired with mortar containing a pigment or a matching mortar made up with powdered brick of the same type.

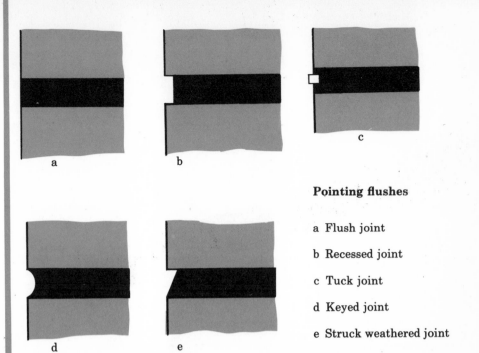

Pointing flushes

a Flush joint

b Recessed joint

c Tuck joint

d Keyed joint

e Struck weathered joint

A routing attachment in an electric drill can also be used to clean joints

Keyed pointing
Apply mortar proud of joint; rub with sacking when nearly dry, then wire brush

Damp and condensation are twin spectres, which often go hand in hand to cause damage to fabric, furniture and fittings in the home. Much can be done to relieve the problems by abating the conditions causing condensation and eliminating structural and related problems which allow damp to penetrate the structure.

Rising damp

This often occurs in older structures without a damp-proof course (DPC), or where an existing DPC has broken down. Water rises from the ground and, through capillary action, is absorbed into porous brickwork and through the plaster. The result is a band of staining, usually at skirting level, paper peeling from the walls and efflorescence-mineral salts drawn out on to the exterior brickwork surface.

Timber joists and floorboards adjacent to the failed dampcourse area may be affected by wet or dry rot.

Treatment

It is necessary either to renew, repair or insert a damp-proof course, or to use a suitable proofing alternative. DPCs should be some 150mm above exterior ground level. They can be inserted by the following methods:

Cutting out

By cutting out one section of brickwork at DPC level at a time. A chain saw is needed to cut through brickwork. Insert a layer of bituminous felt or slates encased between layers of waterproof concrete. The slates are overlapped in an under-and-over arrangement.

DPCs can be made of hard engineering bricks. Work around the building, cutting out a section at a time, mortaring the bricks in place and then making good. These bricks are impermeable and resist the passage of water. This is an involved and skilled job.

Silicone injection

Where cutting out is not a practical proposition an injected DPC can be used. Drill holes at intervals of 230mm, using 12mm or 25mm masonry drills, at an angle of 45°. Stagger the holes 100mm above floor level along the brickwork. This work can be done either internally or externally.

It may be necessary to hack back any wet plasterwork and remove skirting boards. The method of treatment varies slightly between systems. Silicone, water-resistant liquid can either be injected into the holes under pressure, a method usually carried out by specialist firms, or allowed to drip in to the wall, a method you can use yourself.

In this method, 570ml bottles, containing the silicone liquid, are inverted, placed in the holes and the liquid is allowed to permeate the wall interior. This solution will seep into the brickwork until saturation level is reached, when no more will flow from the bottle.

Bottles that empty quickly should be refilled as this indicates a natural internal cavity that must be filled.

Once a protective silicone layer is formed, the reverse of capillary action occurs. The surface tension created by the barrier forces rising dampness down.

Electro-osmosis

Where cutting out or drilling are not possible, such as with thick walls or along party walls, a process called electro-osmosis can be used. This is done by specialist companies.

Copper wiring or a ribbon of copper are inserted into the walls at DPC level. These are connected to copper earth rods set in the soil.

This method utilizes the fact that an electrical charge exists, associated with the moisture rise, between the wall and the earth. The copper ribboning and earth-rods, placed carefully, create a low-resistance circuit between the soil and building.

The electricity is discharged to earth. Damp cannot rise above this charge and the walls dry out as the moisture evaporates.

Damp-proof courses

Damp patches on the inner walls of cavity walls may appear because the DPC has been broken or bridged. Earth should not be piled up against external walls above the DPC level, as the DPC becomes ineffective and there is no barrier to prevent moisture from rising up the walls. This may need only removal of débris, piled higher than the DPC.

Problems such as a break in the DPC or a mortar-encrusted brick tie in a cavity wall require drastic treatment. Sections of brickwork in the area of damp will have to be cut out to insert a repair section of bitumen felt to a DPC or for access to a dirty brick tie.

Floors laid directly on to earth, without a damp-proof membrane, may give trouble. This can be temporarily remedied by covering the floor with a damp-inhibiting epoxy-pitch resin. If this fails, you will have to lift the old floor and lay a new floor over a bituminous, liquid membrane or a sheet of heavy-duty, 500-gauge polythene sheeting.

Whichever method is used, make sure the waterproof layer reaches at least 150mm, preferably cut into the horizontal DPC where this exists, up the walls to form an efficient seal.

Condensation

Air always contains a certain amount of water vapour, which is a true gas. Water vapour gets into the air as liquid water vaporizes. This occurs as air takes up heat by conduction, convection or radiation from its surroundings.

If, however, the heat is removed from the vapour, it condenses–that is, reverts to its liquid state.

Air can only retain a limited quantity of water vapour in its gaseous state, and this quantity depends on the temperature of the air–the warmer it gets, the more vapour it can hold. As soon as the maximum is reached, the excess water vapour turns back into liquid water, usually on cooler surfaces such as walls, windows and ceilings.

The air is said to be 'saturated' when it cannot hold any further water vapour, and the temperature at which this happens is the 'dew point'.

Condensation, therefore, results from a loss of heat by vapour, causing its temperature to fall below dew point. Its effect is simply to concentrate and make visible a quantity of dispersed and hitherto invisible water, present in the air in the form of a gas.

A simple example is the bedroom window which, on cold, damp, winter mornings, may be running with water. This happens because human breath emits a considerable quantity of moisture, so condensation forms on the window, a cold surface. This can only be cured by ventilation–opening a window or using an extractor fan.

The presence of condensation depends on three factors.

First, the amount of water vapour released into the air inside the home.

Second, the temperature of the air, of walls, ceilings and windows, because on these depends the amount of water vapour that can remain in the air.

Third, ventilation because it enables moisture-laden air to be carried away and replaced with drier air.

Many of the problems of excessive condensation are not the fault of the people in a building, but due to faulty planning and design.

Certain kinds of plaster and building materials cannot allow water vapour to pass through them, and create a build-up of vapour inside the home. The lack of effective wall or roof insulation keeps these surfaces cold, this cools the adjacent air, so condensation results. Adequate ventilation is essential to reduce the level of condensation.

Intermittent heating, as happens with some forms of thermostatically controlled central heating, can also cause condensation. Inside surfaces have no real chance to warm up, and moisture vapour, released in the warmed air, condenses on these cold surfaces.

The weather may also influence condensation. If there is a sudden rise in temperature, combined with dampness, streaming condensation on walls and windows may occur as they are slower to warm up than the surrounding air. Spasmodic or irregular heating may not warm a house fabric sufficiently, in cold conditions, to 'lift' wall surface temperatures.

Reducing condensation

Condensation can be avoided by supplying a constant level of heat, introducing ventilation and by carrying out a thorough programme of insulation in the home.

A combination of warm, inner surfaces including walls and ceilings and warm air should eradicate condensation as a persistent nuisance.

The intermittent, concentrated outbreaks that occur during activities such as cooking and running a bath, usually require some form of extra ventilation.

The easiest method is to open a window, but an extractor fan is more efficient and will quickly remove the saturated air without creating draught.

In an average-sized kitchen or bathroom, a 150mm domestic fan will probably be sufficient, but in a large room, two correctly positioned units, with the capacity to deal with the air changes required, may be more efficient.

All extractor fans should be installed as high as possible in a wall or window and as near sources of steam as possible.

Louvred windows, a series of adjustable glass slats, aid controlled ventilation. Operated similarly to Venetian blinds, they can be opened to the extent necessary to provide sufficient ventilation, while the slats can be angled to prevent cold draughts. A simple device that will often cope with 'minor' condensation problems is the plastic window grille, which is activated by air pressure.

Condensation can often be reduced by following a few basic rules:

When running a bath, or carrying out the weekly wash, keep the door closed so that steam does not disperse to other parts of the home.

Always try and minimize the 'escape' of any steam by enclosing hoses to washing machines. Trap the hose under the lid and always keep the lid in place while the machine is working.

To help prevent the formation of condensation when running a bath, first run a small amount of cold water before drawing off the hot.

To overcome condensation problems altogether, if practical to do so, fix a hose to the hot tap so that the water is fed under the layer of cold.

Surface damage

Condensation can, of course, cause both structural and surface damage, as well as being very unsightly. It often creates the conditions in which various damaging and unsightly moulds can grow.

It is possible to increase the resistance of the structure to heat loss, so that any heat generated is used effectively, fuel bills are reduced and temperatures within the home are kept steady. This greatly reduces the likelihood of condensation.

Holes are drilled at 45° angle at 200mm intervals for Wykamit DPC fluid treatment

Filled bottles are then inverted into the holes for wall to absorb DPC liquid

Exteriors of porous walls can be treated with silicone fluid applied with a spray

Electro-osmosis inverts capillary action of water through low-charged copper strip

Insulation

Insulation here means the resistance to the passage of heat from the inside of the house to the outside atmosphere. The most common ways of achieving this are roof insulation, cavity-wall insulation, double-glazing and floor lining.

There are some vital points concerning roof insulation. Many people overlook the possibility that condensation may occur in the roof area after efficient roof insulation has been completed. Because of the decrease in air temperatures in an insulated loft, and the fact that water vapour will be moving up from the house into the loft area through ceilings, ventilation is neces-

Mortar-encrusted brick tie may form a bridge, causing inner-wall damp entry

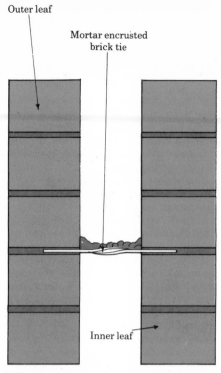

Outer leaf

Mortar encrusted brick tie

Inner leaf

A chain saw is used to cut a slot into brickwork to insert a DPC, such as slate

Strip is looped into holes in wall and electrode is earthed via a junction box

sary in the loft area. This should equal one 900th of the roof area and should be in the form of cross ventilation.

While ventilation usually exists naturally, careful consideration should be given to this point. Sometimes, air outside the house is so heavily weighted with humidity that any additional water vapour entering the loft from outside will cause an acceptable level of humidity to be exceeded, resulting in condensation forming within the loft area.

There are two solutions: Either to fix the insulation material on to the rafters so that the loft area benefits from the heat from the house, or to fix a water-vapour

barrier, such as polythene sheeting, between the joists, before laying the insulating material.

Cavity walls

The walls form about 85 per cent of the external vertical surface of a house, while 15 per cent consists of windows and door openings. Walls are vulnerable heat-loss areas.

Modern homes are built with cavity walls, consisting of either two brick leaves or a brick outer and building-block inner leaf. The cavity prevents water from reaching the inner walls, but in doing so, the free-moving air, circulating in the cavity, carries away the heat.

A cavity wall is a poor insulator. The thermal qualities can be improved by filling the cavity with a material such as mineral wool or urea foam, which is injected under pressure. These treatments are carried out by specialist firms. This type of insulation raises the 'touch temperatures' of the inner wall and helps to reduce condensation.

Solid walls

In houses with solid walls, the problem of overcoming condensation or the mould growth, often apparent in damp conditions, is more difficult.

A simple preventative method is to line the walls, before papering or finish decorating, with a polystyrene wallpaper. This layer, about 2mm thick, is supplied in rolls. Also suitable for this type of lining is aluminium foil-backed paper. Both types raise the touch temperatures.

A more substantial inner skin consists of dry lining. This is in the form of cladding with insulating material such as preformed insulating board. This type of cladding is nailed on to battens fixed to the wall. To provide extra insulation, a layer of mineral wool quilting can be fixed behind the battens.

The board used should have its own built-in vapour barrier. This is necessary because condensation can occur in the middle of a 'cold' wall; and the water will then work its own way back to the warmer inner face and appear as a damp patch.

Wood cladding is a good natural insulant and provides a decorative surface. Its insulant properties can be further increased by using mineral quilting behind battens to fix this.

Floors

Floor insulation is most easily achieved by laying carpet with the appropriate underlay. However, where thermo-plastic floors are used, problems can occur since, in any room, the lowest temperature is at floor level. Therefore, if the floor itself is cold, condensation may result because a low temperature causes the water vapour in the air to condense on its surface.

The only solution may be to relay the floor, using a material, such as cork, or foam-backed sheet flooring, both of which have higher insulant properties. These will be warmer underfoot and raise the surface temperature.

Curing woodworm and dry rot

Wood under attack is always a cause for alarm. Wet and dry rot, and woodworm, may cause fundamental damage. The signs of attack, once spotted, should be dealt with immediately, eradicating affected areas, replacing, as necessary, with new wood and treating to prevent further unseen encroachment.

Woodworm

The term, woodworm, refers to the larvae of several species of wood-boring beetles which are able to digest the substance of wood. The adult beetle lays eggs on the rough surface of unpolished wood and the grubs which hatch out bore into the timber. These leave no sign of entry, and tunnel inside the wood, for as long as up to ten years.

When ready to pupate, the larvae make a pupal chamber just below the surface of the wood. The adult beetles then bite their way out, leaving tell-tale 'flight holes'.

Piles of white wood dust, or 'frass', on horizontal surfaces, will indicate where the grubs have been active above, and close examination will reveal the flight holes, which vary from 2mm to 4mm across.

Sapwood, which is used in a high proportion of modern building, is particularly susceptible to attacks, and because of their generally small dimensions, modern rafters and joists may not readily withstand severe attack.

Treatment

Treatment of structural timbers in a house can be carried out by one of the specialist firms, which guarantees work for 20 years and offers a free survey and estimate. If, however, you decide to treat an attack yourself, remember it is no use just treating the area where you see woodworm holes; other larvae may be active but unseen in the adjacent timbers.

Thoroughness is the keynote to success in all timber treatment. For woodworm attacks in rafters, joists and flooring, apply woodworm fluid with a coarse spray using 5 litres to 18·50m² of surface area.

Estimating

To estimate the area of timber to be treated in a roof where the rafters have been boarded in under the tiles, find the area of each slope of the roof. Add the sums together and to this amount add twice the depth of a rafter, multiplied by its length and by the number of rafters.

If, however, the roof is not boarded, simply add the thickness of a rafter to twice its depth, then multiply by the rafter's length and by the number of rafters.

Use a similar procedure for the joists and purlins. A close-boarded roof of a detached house may work out as in the following example:

	m²
Two slopes each 9·15m × 3·66m	33·49
Gable end or hip-roof triangle (half base × height) 3·05m × 3·66m	11·16
50 rafters each 100mm deep × 3·66m long	18·30
50 joists each 100mm deep × 4·57m long	22·85
Total =	85·80

Allow a little more, say 90m², for purlins and gable-end rafters. At a coverage rate of 18·50m² per 5 litres, a minimum of 38 litres of fluid is needed, but if the timber is very dry, it may soak up more fluid.

Treatment may be carried out at any time of year and modern woodworm fluids, such as Rentokil, will destroy all stages of the woodworm's life cycle and prevent future attack, provided all timber surfaces are treated.

Before commencing treatment, all timbers must be thoroughly cleaned down to allow penetration of the fluids, and water cisterns should be covered throughout the entire treatment process.

Cistern lagging and roof insulation should be removed or protected from the fluid, and any exposed rubber-covered wiring cables should either be covered or coated with a polyurethane varnish before you start spraying.

Make certain any electrical wiring in the area to be sprayed is sound and well insulated. Never smoke during spraying and wear a pair of old leather or rubber gloves.

Eyes should be protected with suitable goggles and a light fume mask should be worn, to avoid the inhaling of vapour which builds up in the confined roof space.

Let us spray

The selection of a sprayer is important but the majority of garden sprayers are suitable provided they will maintain good pressure. Ideally, the unit should hold at least 5 litres and have a fairly coarse nozzle

≈ A fungal growth which shows the presence of wood rot; early attention is necessary

which will produce a 'fan' spray pattern. Suitable sprays may also be hired.

Too coarse a nozzle may result in excess fluid staining the ceiling area; on the other hand, a very fine nozzle will tend to vaporize the spray, making the work unpleasant and reducing the amount of fluid penetration into the timber. A 610mm-long extension line will also be required to reach into the roof apex, eaves and any other less-accessible areas.

If you are treating a floor against woodworm, take up every fourth or fifth floorboard, so that you can treat the joists beneath and the undersides of the boards. Replace the boards and then thoroughly treat the upper surface.

It is then necessary to cover the floor area with a large sheet of polythene if you wish to re-lay floor coverings immediately. Alternatively, you may wait seven to 14 days for the surface of the timber to dry out.

The characteristic yellow fruiting body, or sporophore, of *merulius lacrymans*

After treatment, floorboards will take at least six months to dry out completely, if they have been fully impregnated, and an impermeable floorcovering, such as vinyl tiles or sheet material, will be spoiled if laid directly on them. A temporary floorcovering should be used wherever possible.

Finally, if by accident during treatment you stain plaster with fluid, leave it for a few weeks to dry and if it still remains, apply aluminium primer and then redecorate.

Dry rot

Fungi are living plants, of which there are thousands of species, and over a dozen are known to cause deterioration of timber. Wood-decaying fungi reduce the weight of the wood, spoil its appearance and take away its strength. True dry rot is the name given to the decay of timber brought about by one particular species of wood-rotting fungi, *merulius lacrymans*.

The term 'dry' is descriptive of the dry and friable conditions to which the rotten wood is reduced. Dry rot is often a symptom of neglected maintenance or the consequence of faulty design or construction of buildings, because the fungi thrives only in conditions of dampness and poor ventilation.

Dry rot cannot develop in wood containing less than about 25 per cent moisture, and the optimum moisture content for its growth is probably between 30 and 40 per cent.

The characteristic signs of the decay by which the dry-rot fungus can be identified are:

Rust-red dust caused by gathering spores from a fruiting body indicate an advanced attack of some duration. The spores only accumulate in still, unventilated conditions.

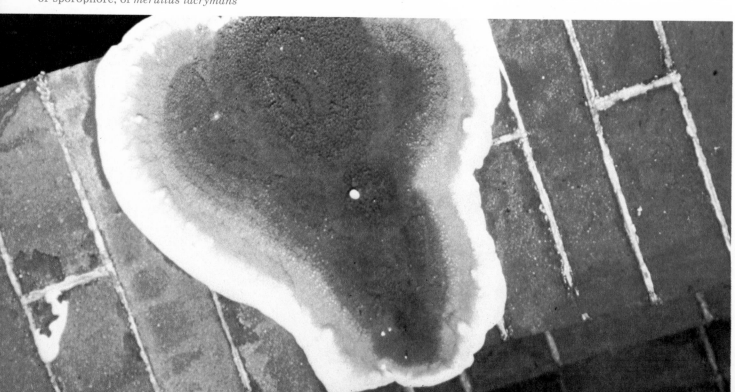

A covering of matted fungal strands external to the timber occurs as thin sheets of silvery-grey or mouse-grey appearance, tinged here and there with lilac patches; bright yellow patches may also occur. This type of fungal *hyphae* is known as *mycelium*.

In damp, humid conditions the mycelium grows rapidly. It is snowy white, rather like cotton wool, but where the edge of such *mycelium* comes into contact with drier air or exposure to light, it becomes bright yellow.

The specific name, *lacrymans*, refers to the characteristic it shows in damp conditions when in active growth. Innumerable globules of water sparkle in the light of a torch like a large number of teardrops – *lacrymans* means 'weeping'. The generic name, *merulius*, refers to the bright-yellow colouration which occurs on the mycelium, similar in colour to the beak of a male blackbird (Merula).

Wood decayed by the mycelium shows deep transverse and longitudinal fissures and the wood breaks up into cubes, sometimes of large dimensions. Such cracking is seen on the surface of the wood.

The wood becomes very light in weight, owing to the extraction of the cellulose by the fungal hyphae.

The wood becomes darker in colour, usually brown; it is friable when rubbed between the fingers; and the wood loses its characteristic fresh, resinous smell.

The appearance of a sporophore or fruiting body, which is thin and pancake-like, white round the edges, with the centre thrown into corrugation. The colour of the spores makes it rusty-red. When in active growth, the sporophore and the mycelium have a strong mushroomy smell.

A very important characteristic of *merulius lacrymans* is the ability of the fungus to produce water-carrying strands or *rhizomorphs*. These strands are formed from

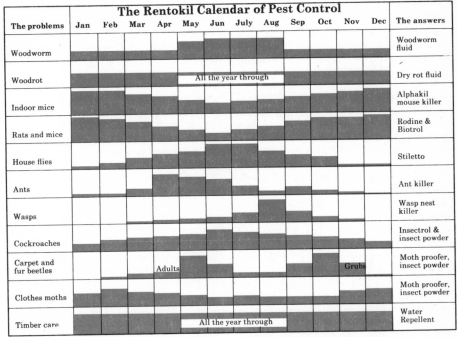

The problems	Jan	Feb	Mar	Apr	May	Jun	July	Aug	Sep	Oct	Nov	Dec	The answers
Woodworm													Woodworm fluid
Woodrot					All the year through								Dry rot fluid
Indoor mice													Alphakil mouse killer
Rats and mice													Rodine & Biotrol
House flies													Stiletto
Ants													Ant killer
Wasps													Wasp nest killer
Cockroaches													Insectrol & insect powder
Carpet and fur beetles					Adults					Grubs			Moth proofer, insect powder
Clothes moths													Moth proofer, insect powder
Timber care					All the year through								Water Repellent

The Rentokil Calendar of Pest Control

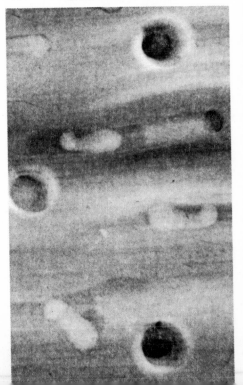

The woodworm grub feeds on the timber and leaves a pile of 'frass' behind it

hyphae and modified to form vein-like structures. They may be as large in diameter as a lead pencil.

The importance of the rhizomorph is that it conveys the water from wood, which has decayed to dry wood, elsewhere, the strands passing over brickwork, stone or metal.

It is in the hyphae constituting the rhizomorphs that food reserves are stored, so that even if the affected wood is taken away, the rhizomorph is still capable of further growth and infecting new wood. The rhizomorphs are also able to penetrate soft brickwork and mortar.

Wet rot

Outbreaks of wet rot, known generally as cellar fungus, or *coniophora cerebella*, are almost twice as frequent as those of dry rot, but are seldom as difficult to treat. Wet rot requires moister conditions than does dry rot, and the optimum water content for growth is between 50 and 60 per cent—hence its name. It is, therefore, sensitive to drying and all activity ceases when the source of moisture is removed.

The special characteristics by which cellar fungus, and the decay caused by it, can be identified are:

The fungal strands are never so thick as those of dry rot, seldom exceeding the diameter of thin string or twine. These strands are brownish or black, but when freshly produced, are yellowish-brown. The fungal strands, when growing on the surface of the wood or over damp plaster, often develop a dark fern-like shape. They are vein-like in appearance and are said to be similar to the blood-vessels of the cerebellum (part of the brain); hence the specific name. They do not penetrate into brickwork.

White mycelium is never produced by this species, either in the cottonwool or in the sheet form. The sporophore is rarely found in buildings, although it may be common out of doors. It consists of a thin plate, olive-brown in colour, of indefinite shape, covered with small tubercules.

The spores are rarely found indoors in any accumulation, but are so light that they are present almost everywhere in the air, consequently any timber in buildings with a sufficiently high moisture content is likely to be attacked by this species.

Other species of fungus also causing wet rot in buildings are the white pore fungus or mine fungus, *poria voillantii*, and *paxillus panuoides*, both of which attack only softwood.

Treatments
Dry rot

Any outbreak of dry rot needs prompt, thorough treatment. Defective plumbing, faulty damp-proof courses and blocked air bricks or similar faults must first be rectified. Also, replace any broken air bricks and clear blocked ones. If the house has been flooded, or burst pipes have soaked timbers, check that the wood has dried out thoroughly.

Even if the location of any outbreak may seem obvious, make a systematic inspection inside the house. Look for signs of surface buckling of the timber and test with a sharp knife or tool.

Inspect beneath the floorboards for the signs of decay listed earlier. If evidence of an attack is found, consider that point as being the centre of a sphere, having a radius of about 1m, and make an extremely close examination in every direction within this area.

Whenever continued evidence of decay is found, extend the 'sphere' principle of investigation until the limits of the attack have been found and the causes traced.

All timber in the affected area and 1m beyond the last visible evidence of decay must be cut away, provided this does not weaken the structure. If there is such a risk, seek expert advice. Any plasterwork or rendering coats which have been penetrated by the fungal strands should be removed.

The whole area of attack should be opened up, thoroughly cleaned down with a wire brush and the decayed material removed from the building by the shortest possible route.

All affected timber should be burned immediately and any plaster sprayed with a fungicide such as Rentokil Dry Rot Fluid. These measures are vital to avoid further infection spreading to other areas of the building.

If masonry is affected, drill a series of holes covering the contaminated parts at staggered centres to allow dry-rot fluid to saturate the affected area. It will then reach all possible mycelium within the masonry. Working from the highest level downwards, apply a good proprietary fungicidal fluid to all brick, block concrete and earth surfaces until they are saturated; 5 litres of fluid to 4·64m, for surface treatment, is normally adequate when applied with a coarse spray.

If the fungal strands have penetrated the brickwork or masonry, then both sides of the wall should be treated by the hole-drilling process.

All replacement timbers must be thoroughly treated with a fungicidal wood preservative, and the sawn ends steeped in the fluid for at least five minutes before installation. Any joist ends are best protected with fungicide, plus a coat of bituminous paint, before setting these into a wall.

Apply two liberal coats of fungicidal fluid to all timber surfaces adjacent to the area of cutting away, to a distance of 1·52m from the furthest extent of the cutaway timber. Allow the first coat to be absorbed before applying the second. Five litres per 18·58m² should be applied.

Allow any brickwork or masonry to dry out completely before redecoration or rerendering. It is advisable to apply a 6mm thick coat of zinc-oxychloride plaster over the rendering coat before applying the finishing coat of plaster.

This zinc-oxychloride coat should extend 300mm beyond the limits of the attack to inhibit fungal growth. Any areas not to be replastered, can also be treated with two coats of zinc-oxychloride paint.

Wet rot

The treatment of wet rot is less drastic than that required for dry rot, and as long as the cause of dampness is removed and the timber allowed to dry out, no further growth of the fungus will occur.

Test all the timbers in the area of fungal attack with a strong, pointed instrument to determine the extent of sub-surface breakdown. Cut out and burn all timber which has suffered surface or sub-surface breakdown due to fungal attack, together with any dust, dirt and general débris.

Select thoroughly dry, well-seasoned timber for replacement. Cut it to size and apply two liberal coats of dry-rot fluid on all the surfaces and also over the adjacent existing timbers, and on brick, block and concrete areas before replacement timbers are fitted. This pre-treatment of new timber is a vital part of any remedial work and must be carried out after the timbers have been cut to size.

If an extensive outbreak of rot is suspected—especially with dry rot—it is wise to consult a reliable specialist timber preservation company, which will conduct a free survey, submit an estimate and report without obligation, and issue a 20-year guarantee on completion of any work.

Plastering: what you need to know

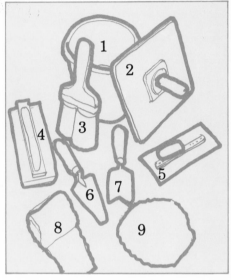

Tool and materials in plastering
1 Plastic bucket 2 Metal hawk 3 Two knot damping brush 4 Wood float
5 Finishing trowel 6 Gauging trowel
7 Angle tool 8 Scrim 9 Plaster.

To achieve a smooth, well-plastered surface needs care and patience. Sometimes, the remedy for a badly cracked wall or ceiling area is to hack off the old plaster and start again. Alternatively, the surface may only need simple patching. Textured finishes can present an attractive 'face' and make a pleasant ceiling surface.

Ceiling repairs

Repairing larger cracks is slightly more involved than repairing minor cracks. To repair larger cracks in walls or ceilings, you need a proprietary filler, medium-grade glasspaper, a glasspaper block, a filling knife or scraper, an old paint brush and a spot board or hawk.

Use the scraper or filling knife to scrape out the old plaster then brush out the dust. Open out the crack, making an under or V-cut, which will help to key the new plaster in place. Brush out any further dust.

The replacement filler can be a proprietary type; use a cellulose-based filler for large cracks that have to withstand stress or heat. Mix the filler on the plasterer's hawk with a little water to a workable consistency. If the mix is too wet, it will not stay in place. Mix enough for only an hour's work.

Use the brush to dampen the area around the crack and, with a pliable filling knife, press the plaster into the crack, leaving it slightly proud of the sound surface. This can be rubbed down when dry.

On deep cracks, apply the filler in layers, allowing each layer to harden before the next is applied. Level off the final layer with a broad filling knife.

On an emulsioned ceiling, mix a little of the colour with the filler. This will help to make the crack disappear when the area is repainted.

A filled surface crack can also be painted with a dilute coat of the emulsion before the area is repainted.

Where damage is extensive, the filler should be mixed with equal parts of clean sand. Fill in a layer at a time, allowing each layer to harden and dry out before the next is applied. Only the surface layer should consist of proprietary filler.

Shrinkage cracks

Small, shrinkage cracks often appear in the angle between the walls and ceiling of new buildings. This type of shrinkage is not normally serious but is unsightly.

Use a scraper to open up the crack to 2mm wide. Dampen the plaster along the crack with clean water. Mix the filler to a creamy consistency and use the finger to press the mix into the gap. Allow this to set slightly and then, using a damp brush

clean off the excess. Do not paint for at least 24 hours.

Plastic surfaces

Where the ceiling is plastic surfaced, use a filler formulated for use with this for repair. Use a sharp cutting knife to cut back all the loose surface paper. If the plaster core of the plasterboard is exposed, dampen this and then apply a thin layer of a cold-water mix formulated for use on plastic surfaces.

Special scrim paper tape should be soaked, and then laid, using a paint scraper, in strips over the damaged area. Allow to dry for at least 12 hours. Next, apply a second coat of filler evenly.

Use an applicator, which may be a proprietary type or simply made from a piece of laminate 200mm × 115mm in size secured between two pieces of softwood 40mm × 13mm and 200mm long.

Damp round the repair area and apply, with a brush, an even coat of filler. To match the textured surface of the surrounding area, use a texturing tool.

This is a block of plywood, about 150mm × 100mm with a handle. A sponge is fitted to the block and covered with polythene sheet secured round the handle with an elastic band. The pad, which is textured, is then applied to the ceiling to match in the new surface with the old. Excess can be removed with a damp brush.

Work to a timber rule when plastering reveals and corners; remove, then polish

Wall rendering coat is 'devilled' with scratcher to provide key for finish coat

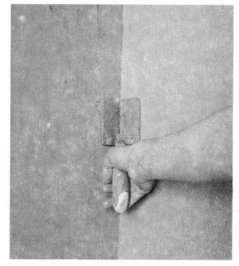
Edging tools are made to provide smooth finish to either inner or outer reveals

Vertical timber rule is fixed slightly proud of surface and plastered flush

Lining paper

It is possible to disguise hair line cracks particularly on ceilings. The simplest and cheapest way is to cover the area with a lining paper and then paint the surface. If the surface is particularly uneven, embossed, chipwood or pebble-dash paper might be used, their textures camouflaging any irregularities.

More permanent finishes are the plastic type of textured finish. These are applied with special tools but are quite within the scope of the home handyman.

Polystyrene, either in veneer or tile form, also makes an attractive cladding material. It also has the added bonus of raising the surface temperature and helping in the battle against condensation.

Replastering

For replastering walls or ceilings you will need the following tools:
● Hawk,
● Spot board and suitable support; for this an old firm box of convenient height will do,
● Metal float,
● Angled trowel,
● Gauging trowel,
● Wooden float,
● Two-knot stock or a distemper brush,
● Scratcher; one can be simply made from nails, with their heads removed, driven into a piece of wood.

Prepare the wall by removing any loose materials and lightly brush down with a wet brush.

When patching, there is the benefit of surrounding plaster which limits the area covered and, at the same time, acts as a guide for plaster thickness when ruling off.

When plastering a whole wall there is no such guide and the first operation is to make one.

Mix up a small quantity of backing coat and apply a 150mm² 'dot' of this about 150mm from a side wall and the same distance from the ceiling. Make the dot about 12mm thick and keep it as even as possible.

Repeat with another dot 1·3m below this, using a rule and spirit level to check that the surfaces are vertical. Repeat once more just above floor level.

Check with a line–help will be needed here–that the three dots are in the same plane and amend them as necessary. Now repeat this whole process at the other end of the wall.

This done, place dots intermediately at about 1·3m centres across the wall.

Once you have checked that the surfaces of the dots are in the same plane the next step is to join them up with screeds, first vertically and then horizontally.

Mix up a quantity of backing coat and, with the steel laying on trowel, screed between the dots from the floor right up to the ceiling. This done, rule off, preferably using a straight-edge rule about 1·8m long, and again check for verticals.

Repeat this process across and then up the wall so that the wall is divided up into convenient working areas.

The remaining areas of brickwork can now be treated in exactly the way as for applying a floating coat on a patched area.

Go over the whole wall with the devil float, wash down any adjacent surfaces and leave to dry out.

If a sanded floating coat is being used, allow at least 24 hours, but if a lightweight plaster is used, four to six hours is sufficient.

Before applying the finish plaster, test the surface for suction. This is extremely important if the floating coat has been left for longer than the times given. Brush water on to the surface; if it is sucked straight in there is too much suction which can not only weaken the final coat, but make it difficult to apply.

Dampening the wall well should overcome this problem, but if this fails, brush

Paint is well rolled out in the tray and then evenly applied to the ceiling

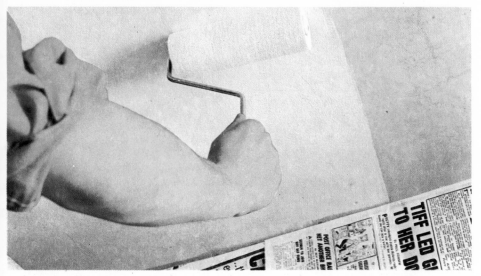

Finishing touches to plastered ceiling can be with emulsion paint from roller

on a bonding coat of PVA or wood adhesive (one part PVA to six parts water by volume). This should be done immediately before laying up the finish plaster.

Mix up the finish and skim on another coat with the laying trowel. Start with a band, about trowel width, immediately below the ceiling, then continue, with a vertical movement, over the whole wall, working from left to right if you are right handed or from the other direction if left handed.

Once the wall is covered, repeat the process with the wooden float. Then with the wooden float, apply a third thin coat horizontally. Make sure that any seams are well consolidated.

Apply the final coat of finish plaster with the steel trowel using long, firm, vertical strokes. Finally, polish the plaster using a sprinkling of water as a lubricant.

The angle trowel (or twitcher) should be used between operations to consolidate the corners.

After polishing, clean up adjacent walls and floor before the plaster sets hard.

Ceilings and walls, in older properties, may consist of lath and plaster. Once a ceiling has deteriorated badly it may be necessary to remove it completely rather than trying to do a patch-up job.

Stripping a ceiling is never a clean job, so before starting clear the room completely. Hang dust sheets over the doors to prevent dust travelling to other rooms, and cover the floor.

Use a club hammer and chisel to remove the old ceiling, taking care to clean the joists thoroughly. Punch down, or remove any projecting nails.

Modern ceilings usually consist of decorative plasterboard or plasterboard covered with a finish plaster coat. Plasterboard is composed of a gypsum core, sandwiched between paper lining.

It is available in various-sized sheets, but for most purposes 1·2m × 2·4m is a convenient size. There are two thicknesses – 10mm which should be used at standard 450mm centres – and 13mm for more widely spaced joists.

Plasterboard

Plasterboard is heavy and care must be taken to support edges where they abut the wall. Two methods are suitable for this job. The more satisfactory and stronger method is to plaster the board into the wall plaster surface.

Before starting to plaster the ceiling, cut back a 50mm wide strip along the top of the wall edge where it joins the ceiling. Butt the board tightly up to the unplastered wall surface. Strengthen the joint with scrim. Fill in the gap when applying the finish plaster coat.

The other method, which is not so strong, is to abut the board edge to the plaster surface of the wall and reinforce the right-angled joint between wall and ceiling with scrim.

At all times, use jute scrim unless the boards are not to be plastered. In this case, use cotton scrim.

Cutting

Plasterboard can be cut by scoring the face side, using a sharp knife held against a straight edge. Lay the board, face side upwards, on a bench or table, the cut edge aligning with the edge of the support surface.

The core is snapped by pressing down sharply on the overhanging edge. The board is turned over and the paper backing is cut through with a knife.

Plasterboards are nailed either across or along the joists, using either 30mm or 40mm galvanized plasterboard nails, dependent on the thickness of the board. Boards should be put up in both directions, particularly over a large area. This will avoid long joins which may cause later cracking of the finish coat.

Nailing should be at least at 150mm intervals and nails should be positioned no less than 13mm in from the edges. Nailing any closer will cause the boards to split at the edges. Drive the nails in firmly but without damaging the paper covering.

A 3mm gap should be left between the boards. This allows for scrimming, with 90mm-wide jute scrim, before plastering.

If you are working single handed, a device called a 'dead man's hand' will be necessary. This is a pole, or piece of straight-edged timber with a platform 600mm wide fixed to the top. The pole or timber support stands on the floor, with the platform resting beneath the ceiling supporting the plasterboard, leaving both hands free for working.

Measure out and cut the required lengths of scrim. Mix about half a bucketful of finish plaster. Transfer this to the hawk and, using a laying-on trowel, work along the joins between the boards. Press the plaster well into the gaps.

Position the scrim at one end of the joint and guide it into position over the gap, using the trowel to press it firmly into the plaster. Leave the joints between the ceiling and wall until last.

After scrimming, start laying on the plaster coat, treating each board as a separate area. Scrim a thin layer of plaster, using the steel trowel, up to but not over, the scrimmed joints.

Use the wood float to apply further plaster until the ceiling surface is covered to a depth of 5mm. With the steel trowel, lay on a small amount of fresh plaster to fill in gaps, and even off where necessary.

The strip between the wall and ceiling, if the plasterboard abuts the unplastered surface, is next filled in, using an angled trowel. It is smoothed off with a steel trowel.

Once the ceiling has started to set, smooth over the plaster with a clean trowel. A small amount of water, 'flicked' on from the brush, aids this process but do not make the surface too wet.

An angled trowel is used to smooth the corner between the walls and ceiling. Plaster is a quick-drying compound so the job, once started, must be finished rapidly.

What to do if your plaster cracks up

Cracks and holes not only look unsightly, but are signs of deterioration in the fabric of the home–and should be quickly put right. Plastering techniques are a matter of some practice, with the careful and systematic application of the methods involved. Choice of plaster materials is also important in relation to the type of surface, in order to achieve good results.

Plaster cracks are usually caused by slight settlement or traffic vibration, a heavy knock or, sometimes, by damp penetration or even impurities in the original plaster mix. There are two types of crack: check cracking, due to shrinkage of plaster which is usually slight and of minor importance, and map cracking, which is deeper and wider and may be due to settlement of a building or possibly caused by timber shrinkage.

Plaster types
Plaster is applied basically to two types of surface–those to which some type of key is attached, such as wooden laths or expanded metal, and solid surfaces, such as brick, building blocks or concrete.

On solid surfaces two coats of rendering, known as the floating coat and the setting or finishing coat, are usually applied. When almost hard, the floating coat is keyed by scratching the surface; this ensures a good grip for the finishing coat.

When plaster is applied to lathing an extra coat, known as a backing coat (or pricking-up coat, when applied to metal lath) may be necessary.

Plaster may be bought ready mixed in bags; only the addition of water is required to make it workable–or traditional mixtures of sand, lime and Portland cement or plaster of Paris may be prepared.

The type of plaster you decide to use will largely depend upon the existing surface you are making good. If it is a soft finish, such as lime-hair plaster, found in many old houses, then a proprietary ready-mix, soft plaster, called a retarded hemi-hydrate, will best suit the work.

If, however, the surface is hard and grey in colour then a slow-setting hard plaster over a backing coat of cement:sand:lime is preferable.

There are different types of soft plaster, for various background surfaces: solid, with normal absorption, a grade for high absorption, and grades containing anti-rust agents and bonding fibres for applying to metal lath, wood-wool slabs and expanded polystyrene. There is a bonding coat for hard, low-absorption surfaces, a grade for heavier surfaces, and a setting coat, suitable for all backing coats.

The harder, anhydrous plasters, which are grey, pink or white in colour, should not be applied over a soft, hemi-hydrate backing coat or to patch soft plaster; either will produce cracking.

A suitable backing coat for anhydrous plasters is white hydrated lime (obtainable in 25kg and 50kg bags), Portland cement (obtainable in 50kg bags), and good-quality fine building sand in the proportions 1:1:6 by volume.

For filling cracks and small abrasions, use one of the cellulose-based fillers. Cellulose fillers have the advantage over the older gypsum-based fillers that they do not shrink.

Setting times
Anhydrous plasters have a gradual and continuous setting time of two to three hours; towards the latter end of this time they may be softened with water and any irregularities polished out with a steel finishing trowel.

Retarded hemi-hydrates have a 'final-set' time of about $1\frac{1}{2}$ hours. Only during the first 60 to 70 minutes can the plaster be worked, and it is not possible to soften it once the hardening process starts, although a little water, as a lubricant for the trowel, may be used during the final polish.

You may find, due to the short setting time, that hemi-hydrate plasters are difficult to work over large areas; on the other hand, they are ready mixed, lighter and cleaner to work with. It is worthwhile persevering as, once the technique is mastered, they are in fact easier to use than anhydrous plasters.

If you do use ready-mixed plaster only mix up the quantity you need and do not 'over-mix'–that is do not add more plaster to water than recommended.

Mixing
The way in which plaster is mixed is critical to achieving a good finish. When-

ever possible, follow manufacturers' instructions exactly. When mixing up sanded mixes, make sure that the gauge box (or measuring container) is kept clean, and that the quantities are exact. Turn the dry materials over thoroughly until an even colour is produced.

Finishing plasters can most easily be mixed in a bucket. Fill a clean bucket half-full with clean water and sprinkle the plaster into this until plaster settles on the surface, then stir briskly until a creamy mixture is obtained.

Should you wish to use lime plaster, rather than a lightweight mix to repair an existing surface, first make a lime putty, by mixing hydrated lime to water until a creamy mix is achieved. Let this stand for 24 hours, then tip some on to the spotboard in the form of a ring.

Pour some water into the ring and into this pour plaster of Paris (casting plaster) until all the water is soaked up. Mix thoroughly with a gauging trowel. Always use clean water and tools, otherwise the plaster may be weakened.

Estimating quantities
For general gap filling with cellulose fillers, a large carton will usually be more than enough for a room. For estimating the coverage of soft plaster allow, dependent upon background, the following:

Backing coats:
Normal absorption
11mm thick $6.5m^2$ to $7.4m^2$ per 50kg.

High absorption
11mm thick $6.5m^2$ to $7.5m^2$ per 50kg

Metal lath (metal)
8mm thick $6.5m^2$ to $7.8m^2$ per 50kg

Metal lath (wood wool, polystyrene)
11mm thick $3.3m^2$ to $5.0m^2$ per 50kg

Bonding grade: Hard surfaces
11mm thick $5.3m^2$ to $8.3m^2$ per 50kg

Heavier surfaces
8mm thick $7.0m^2$ to $7.5m^2$ per 50kg

Finish
2mm thick $20.5m^2$ to $24.7m^2$ per 50kg

When estimating a sanded floating-coat mix, calculate according to the quantity of sand needed. Roughly 380mm³ of sand mixed with lime and cement to proportion 1:1:6 by volume will cover a 30m² wall. The 380mm³ of sand should be mixed with 100kg cement and 50kg lime. Pink cement 3mm thick will cover 11·5m² per 50kg. Grey cement 3mm thick will cover 13m² per 50kg.

Include about 10 per cent for wastage on all calculations.

Tools for the job

Preparation:
- **Putty knife** or old **screwdriver.** Used for scraping loose plaster from cracks.
- **Bolster, cold chisel** and **club hammer** for cutting out patches and trimming old plaster.
- **Paint brush** for damping backgrounds.

Mixing:
- **Two buckets,** preferably rubber or polythene, for mixing up plaster and holding water; it is important to clean these out thoroughly after each mix.
- **Spot board** This can be a piece of ply, preferably marine, about 270mm², to contain plaster. Plaster can also be placed in a light metal bath.
- **Gauging trowel** available in various sizes, but one of 15mm length will be most convenient; it is used for measuring (gauging) small quantities of materials and working small areas of plaster.

Application:
- **Laying-on trowel** has a steel blade of about 280mm × 120mm, reinforced by a steel or alloy tong attached to a handle. The banana shape is easier to hold as straight-turned handles are liable to slip.
- **Skimming (or hand) float;** made of wood measuring about 300mm by 115mm.
- **Angle trowel (or twitcher).** These can be for internal or external angles. The latter is more for convenience than necessity.
- **Small tools;** various shapes and sizes, the most common of which is the leaf and square. They are usually made of steel.
- **Scratcher;** used for keying backing coats. It can be made from a piece of ply through which nails are driven.

- **Devil float;** has a similar use to the scratcher, but is better on large areas as it smooths burrs as it keys.
- **Feather-edge rule.** A straight piece of wood with one edge chamfered to 6mm thick. Made from 125mm × 25mm timber about 1·5m long, it is used for working down backing coats and working angles.
- **Filling knife;** used for filling cracks. It should have a thin, springy blade.
- **Hawk.** Made of metal or wood, it has a working surface of about 300mm² and is for holding plaster up to the working area. Other general tools you need are a saw, a spirit level, a plumb line, a measuring rule, a claw hammer and, for mixing large quantities of cement, lime or plaster, a shovel.

Patching cracks and blemishes
First of all clear the crack of dust and loose plaster by scraping with a putty knife or old screwdriver. Where possible, undercut the edges to give better keying. Run a damp brush down the crack; this will help the filler to bond to the wall and, at the same time, clear the crack of dust. Some manufacturers of cellulose filler specifically tell you to omit this procedure, in which case brush the crack with a dry brush.

If the crack is more than 6mm deep, using a steel small tool, fill it with proprietary filler, mixed to manufacturer's instructions, to within 3mm of the surface. When this has set, damp down and fill to the surface with more fresh filler, flushing it off level with the surrounding surface using either a small tool or steel finishing float.

If gypsum, as opposed to cellulose-based fillers are used, they are liable to shrinkage, so fill the crack proud of the surface and smooth down when it has dried out.

Medium-sized holes in plasterboard
Where the holes are more than 13mm across, use anhydrous plaster and scrim cloth to fill the hole. First, enlarge the area round the hole with a cutting knife, by a further 13mm wide and 6mm deep. Cut a piece of scrim cloth to the size of the enlarged hole. If the hole is very large, two pieces may be overlapped.

Dampen the recessed area round the hole and place small blobs of plaster round the edge. Locate the scrim over the hole. The blobs of plaster will hold the scrim while the entire area is covered with a thin plaster coat. Once the surface begins to set, apply one or two more coats to bring the repair up to the level of the surrounding area. When the plaster coat has almost set, dampen with a brush and polish with a metal float.

Power sockets
Resiting a power socket may necessitate a minor replastering job, using a cellulose filler. Before starting work, switch off the power to the socket and remove the fixing-plate screws. Clean out the cavity and dampen the surrounding plaster before applying the first coat of filler with a pointed trowel.

If there is a gap at skirting level, crumple some chicken wire or use expanded metal to plug the hole, plaster over this, and allow the coat to set. Before applying the second and final coat, dampen the area, screw back the face-plate and polish the final coat with a metal float. Do not reconnect the power until the plaster is quite dry.

Lath-and-plaster repairs
Large holes in lath-and-plaster walls can be repaired, using expanded metal to support the repair area. Hack back loose plaster, undercut, and cut the mesh to size. Either nail it to existing timber uprights or bend it over the laths. Apply plaster with a pointed trowel, a little at a time, building up the surface with thin layers. Leave the first coat for at least 24 hours before damping down for the finish coat. Smooth and polish this with a metal float, damping down with a little water.

Smaller holes in lath and plaster can be repaired with a cellulose filler, provided the laths are intact, to support the new filler. Clean up the area by pulling away torn paper. Where the laths are broken, prepare a plug of paper, of roughly the size of the hole, soaked in plaster. Push this carefully into the hole below the surface, and cover with a thin coat of filler to within 2mm of the surface.

Once dry, dampen and apply a thin finish coat to bring the repair area level

On hair-line cracks, enlarge with a v-cut, or undercut with sharp implement

Damp down the crack with a paint brush to aid actions of suction and bonding

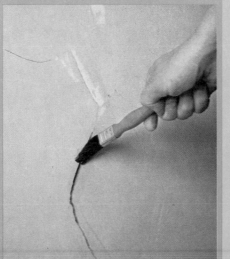

It is useful to mix a dilute water-PVA solution to aid bonding on shallow cracks

with the sound surface. To assist the repaired area to blend in with surrounding surfaces, go over the area with a damp brush to fuse the edges of the repair.

Patching large areas (solid walls)

Before decorating a room some filling will usually have to be done, but sometimes it is easier and better to put in a large patch, rather than to fill a lot of individual cracks. There are also hollow patches where the plaster has 'blown', that is, it is no longer bonded to the wall.

You can recognize 'blown' areas by tapping the wall gently; it will sound hollow. Unless these hollow spots are cut out, they will soon craze and, under extreme circumstances, cause wallpaper covering to split.

To prepare a large area for patching, the whole of the damaged plaster must be removed with a bolster, cold chisel and hammer.

First, cut a line around the extremities of the damage with the bolster, then remove the plaster within this area right back to the brickwork.

Then clean up the edge by cutting back a further 25mm; this edge may then be undercut with the corner of the bolster. Clean the area with a damp brush and apply the backing coat of plaster. To do this, mix up the plaster or sand base on the spot board; when it is ready, scrape a convenient amount on to the hawk; hold the hawk against the working area and, with the laying on trowel held at 35° to the horizontal, scrape the plaster from the hawk on to and up the wall. Work from the bottom to the top of the patch.

If the patch is 10mm deep or less, fill the hole level with the surrounding plaster. If more than 10mm, fill to half the depth and, when almost set, scratch the surface to give it a key. When dry, apply another (floating or straightening) coat up to the surrounding level.

Using the feather edge, rule off the plaster to the surrounding level, working from the bottom to the top and operating the board with a side-to-side scraping motion. If there are any hollows, fill them and rule off once more.

Where hemi-hydrate plaster is used, cut back the edges of the patch to about 3mm below the surface before it sets; this can be done with the corner of the trowel.

If a sand-based floating coat has been applied, then the whole of the new surface must be cut back to a depth of 2mm to 4mm. This is to allow for the finishing coat. This job is best done with a short rule, narrower than the patch, and it is for this reason that the initial cutting out must be done cleanly. Having cut back, go over the surface lightly with the scratcher, then smooth off the burrs with the wooden hand float.

Mix up the finishing coat and pour it on to the spot board; clean out the bucket ready for further use. Put some finishing plaster on to the hawk and, with the wooden float, skim the plaster over the surface of the work, keeping the strokes as vertical and as even as possible. When the surface is covered, repeat the procedure, this time with horizontal movements, pressing firmly.

Check this coat with the feather edge and, if too much plaster has been applied, rule it off to the required level. Wash the float and work over the plaster in a continuous circular motion, consolidating the plaster, particularly any seams.

Now, using the steel trowel with a little plaster slurry, work over the surface with a vertical pressing motion. During this operation the plaster might tend to drag slightly; if so, apply a little water with the brush to act as a lubricant.

Finally, as the plaster sets, polish it with the steel trowel and wash off the surrounding edges with a sponge.

Repairing corners

There are a number of ways of repairing damaged external corners; the method used depends on the degree of damage.

Small chips can merely be refilled with a cellulose filler, while larger, jagged edges may need reinforcing below the plaster coat. This can be done in one of two ways. The first, using aluminium or nylon strip, is best when the surface is to be papered, as the strips fit flush with the plaster. A stronger reinforcement is a round-nosed expanded metal corner piece, which can be plastered over.

To make good small chips, first remove any loose plaster and dust. Mix the filler to a fairly stiff consistency and apply to the corner, proud of the surface area. As the filler starts to set, use a finger to round the corner slightly. Wear rubber gloves. Once

the filler is dry, rub down with medium glasspaper to match the surrounding corner angle.

An expanded metal angle bead is fitted in the following way. Hack back about 125mm of plaster, using a bolster and club hammer, on both sides of the corner. Place blobs of plaster at 610mm intervals down both surfaces. Fix the expanded metal corner round the wall angle, checking the true vertical with a straight edge and spirit level, before pressing the edges of the metal into the plaster.

The straight edge is used to adjust the reinforcement, allowing 2mm for the thickness of the finish coat. Render both vertical surfaces to within 2mm for the final finish coat, applying this thinly over the corner nosing, slightly proud of the bead.

Another way involves using battens, but this type of repair will not give extra reinforcement. First, trim back the plaster and nail a batten to the brickwork, so that it protrudes by the thickness of the plaster. With a plumb line or spirit level, ensure that it is vertical. Use galvanized plaster nails to fix the batten and place them into the mortar between the bricks; remember to leave the heads proud for easy withdrawal.

Apply a floating coat between the plaster and the batten, rule off, cut back and key as necessary. When the plaster is dry, remove the batten, tapping it lightly to free it from the plaster before withdrawing the nails.

Next, fix it to the adjoining plane and apply a floating coat as before. When this coat is dry, remove the batten and, with a steel trowel, arris the corner. The finishing coat may then be applied.

In the case of hemi-hydrate finish, this may be applied to both sides simultaneously, taking care to apply the slurry evenly. With anhydrous plaster it will be advantageous to use the batten. Fix the batten to overlap one corner of the floating coat, by the amount it was cut back (2mm to 4mm). This time, the batten should be packed out with thin ply, stout card or hardboard, by the amount that it projects.

The finishing coat can then be applied to the corner. When this is polished and set, the batten may be removed, and the other side finished in the same way.

Leave for 24 hours and then round off the corner using fine glasspaper.

Fill using a broad filling knife. Finish proud with some fillers, flush with others

When dry, carefully rub down the filled crack, using a fine grade of glasspaper

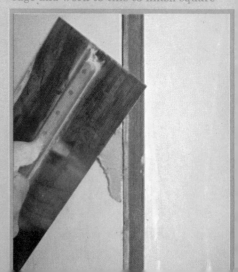

With damaged corners, fix batten to one edge and work to this to finish square

Repairs to rickety stairs

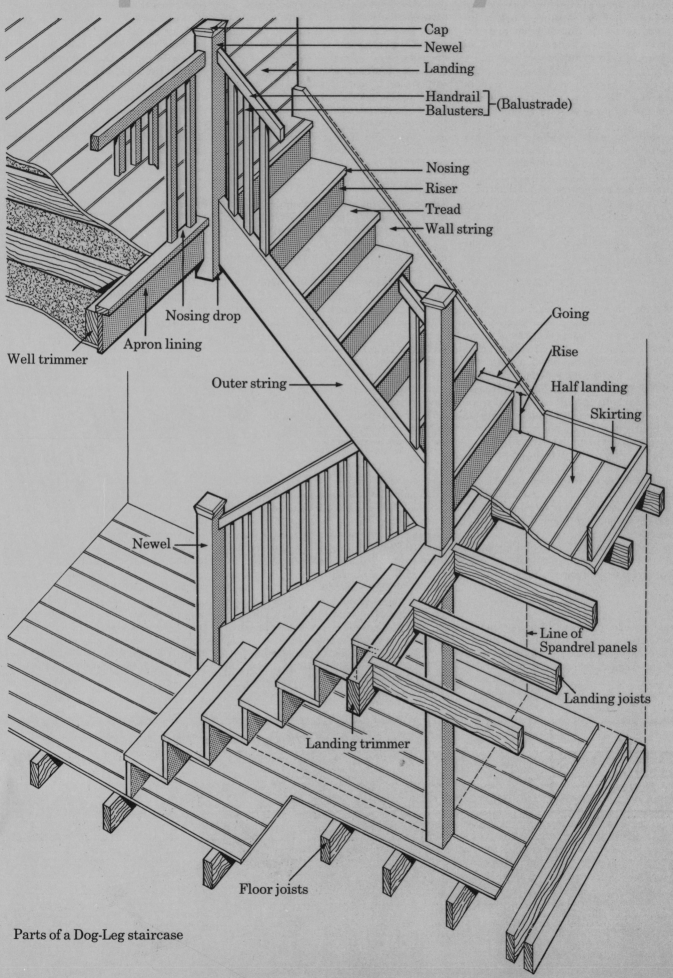

Cap
Newel
Landing
Handrail
Balusters — (Balustrade)
Nosing
Riser
Tread
Wall string
Going
Rise
Half landing
Skirting
Nosing drop
Apron lining
Well trimmer
Outer string
Newel
Line of
Spandrel panels
Landing joists
Landing trimmer
Floor joists

Parts of a Dog-Leg staircase

131

Among the most annoying faults in the home are squeaky or loose stairs and floorboards. More often than not either can be quickly put right with hammer and nails or screwdriver, screws and glue; in other cases more work is involved. Gaps in floorboards are not only unsightly but may cause loss of heat and let in draughts.

Gaps in floorboards may be treated in three ways. They can be filled or caulked, taken up and recramped or covered over. Before starting work, first switch off the electricity mains to avoid any possibility of getting a shock if you should accidentally cut through wires beneath floorboards. Wires usually run lengthways – across the joists – under the centre of floorboards.

The position of joists can be found easily by the nail positions. Joists are usually located apart at centres or distances of 400mm and are about 50mm–75mm wide.

Holes and cracks

Holes and small cracks can be repaired with a proprietary filler. This can be rubbed smooth after it has set. If the floor is uncovered, a small amount of stain can be added to the filler material so that the repair matches the floor surface.

Wide cracks between floorboards can be filled by cutting slightly tapered wood strips. These should be coated with glue and lightly tapped in place with a soft-headed hammer or mallet. Any projections can be planed smooth after the glue has set.

First, establish the thickness of the gap, and then mark this on a section of oversized timber. Transfer this measurement, slightly oversized, to a marking gauge, mark the timber and then cut with a panel saw.

Slightly taper with a smoothing plane and knock this into place. Secure to joists, at intervals, with 40mm panel pins.

Gaps

Gaps can be filled with papier mâché when these are under 6mm in width. To make, tear newspaper up into pieces of postage-stamp size and mix in a bucket with boiling water, a little at a time; pound the paper with a piece of timber until this becomes a thick paste.

Allow to cool for an hour and pour in a glue size. Once the mixture is cold it can be trowelled between boards with a scraper; push this well down. The floor can be rubbed smooth with an abrasive paper once dry.

If the floor surface is not covered, a soft, white, unprinted paper can be used, since newspaper papier mâché is greyish in colour. Prepare as before but bind to a thick paste using a cellulose-based wallpaper adhesive. The mixture can be coloured with a liquid dye to match floorboards.

Shrinkage

Timber flooring may shrink and gap considerably. Where there are serious gaps, the floorboards may be lifted and recramped to close up the gap. A pair of flooring cramps may be hired for this job.

First, loosen the boards and recramp and nail them in sequence. When you reach the last board, the gaps will have built up and be fairly wide. A wide strip of timber may be needed to finish off.

It is good practice not to lay strips of less than 75mm in width, since narrower ones may break under 'point' loading from heavy furniture.

To overcome this, the last board may have to be reduced in width so that a suitably dimensioned strip of timber flooring can be inserted. An alternative is to use a wider board to close the gap.

Cramping

You can make your own floor cramps and use the following technique to relay floorboards. Start lifting boards close to the skirting at one side but leave the board beneath the skirting in place. Plane off any tongue on the first board you take out.

Next, cut four softwood wedges from timber slightly thicker than the floorboards; these should be at least 455mm long, 50mm deep and taper to a point. A pair of these wedges must be placed at intervals of five floorboards.

Place the wedges together and temporarily fix, by half nailing, a piece of scrap board tightly against the wedges as a support.

With two hammers, knock the wedges together, hammering from alternate ends: this forces the boards evenly together. You can now nail down the boards, using cut nails or screws.

Once you come to the skirting, use a chisel to lever the final board tightly against the others and nail down.

The gap between the board beneath the skirting and the final board may then be filled with a piece of matched boarding, cut to size. If you wish you may use a piece of tongued board, first cutting away the top of the tongue.

Patching up

Sometimes, a worn section of flooring cannot be patched up and must be replaced. This may be a simple matter of prising up and taking out a complete section of flooring; however, if only a short section is affected or it is easier to replace a small rather than a larger piece, it is best if you can cut through the board in the centre of a joist.

Check carefully that new sections of board are of the same width and thickness as the old. If the boards are merely butted together, the new section is simply nailed back in.

If you need access beneath the board to any services, the section should be screwed back. Drill and countersink the hole, so that the screw head is not proud of the surface.

Cutting out

Cutting is most easily done with a power saw. The depth of the cut should be carefully set to that of the thickness of the floorboards. Avoid cutting into the joist. First, pull out any nails so that the blade of the saw is not damaged.

It is better to make a bevelled joint, so set the blade to an angle of 45° for cutting out the old section and make sure that the new piece is also bevelled so that it fits snugly against the existing floorboard.

A faulty section may also be cut out by drilling a hole through the board close to the joist and then, using a pad saw or saw

Tap tapered strips of wood, cut slightly oversize, to fill gaps in floorboards

Section of floorboards can be lifted, supported on piece of wood then easily cut

Short length of board can be cut at angle with floorboard saw, padsaw or a jigsaw

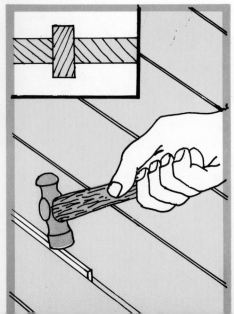

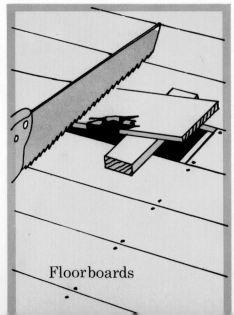

Floorboards

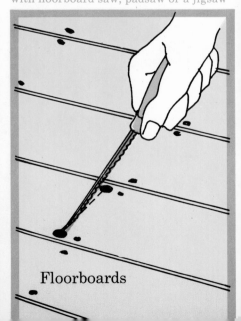

Floorboards

knife, sawing obliquely through to each edge of the board. This operation is repeated at the other end of the damaged section.

Tongued and grooved

Where the board is tongued and grooved, it is necessary to cut down one edge with a thin, broad chisel or a saw knife along a tongued section, which leaves the boards on either side with a tongue and groove respectively.

The bottom wall of the groove must be removed so that the top one rests on the tongue of the adjacent board. Make a cutting line on the outside of this wall, using a marking gauge.

Noggings

The replaced board and the original sound sections butting to it must be supported on either side with a fillet or 'nogging' nailed or screwed to the relevant joists.

These fillets must be at least 38mm thick and fixed with 64mm long nails. Fix each nogging with two nails into each joist.

Another method of lifting floorboards is with a cold chisel, bolster, or crowbar. These can be used to prise up the end of the board after punching in the nails. Take care, however, that you do not cause damage to adjacent boards. Once the board is raised sufficiently, slip a thick piece of wood beneath it to keep it up. The board can then be cut through beside the joist.

The claw of a hammer is intended to enable you to lever up floorboards. Insert the claw beneath the board to be lifted and tilt the handle, using the head of the hammer as a fulcrum on the joist.

Floor sanding

A proprietary floor sander can be hired and is an effective way to smooth an uneven floor, once boards are fixed down and nails and screws are punched below the surface. Remove layers of paint or varnish.

Use a coarse grade of paper; this fixes to a drum. Start at one corner of the room and work diagonally across; pull the machine backwards then re-sand along the same line.

Overlap each by about 75mm until the floor is sanded. If necessary, repeat in the opposite diagonal direction.

Change to a medium or fine paper and sand in one direction, along the boards, pull back and work over each strip twice.

Since you cannot get completely into corners, use a smaller rotary sander, orbital sander or sanding disc to finish these areas, with a fine grade of paper.

A safety tip: The fine sawdust becomes energized by the action of sanding and may flare up dangerously if burned afterwards.

Squeaky or loose treads

A loose or squeaky tread may be irritating but indicates little other than that a wedge beneath the stair tread has worked slightly loose. Wedges hold treads and risers firmly in place.

Another cause may be that glue blocks reinforcing the joint between treads and risers may be a little loose and need refixing. These are triangular in shape and are held in place by glue and screws, usually 75mm long.

The trouble is only serious if you can feel the tread move physically beneath your feet; it is time to cure the problem or serious trouble may occur, since wedges or blocks, or both, have become seriously loosened.

Access to wedges and glue blocks is beneath the stairs. If the underside of the stair is open, this is simply a matter of reglueing and refixing where necessary.

Wedges should be removed one at a time and then refitted. Any warped or broken ones must be discarded and new ones made. The original slope of the wedge should be exactly followed in the new.

Loose glue blocks should be reglued and screwed back firmly. Take care that all surfaces are first clean and dry or a poor joint may be the result.

Cracked treads should be reinforced with blocks of wood or corner-screwed steel angle brackets.

On older staircases, you may find that the underside is covered with a lath-and-plaster skin. This will first have to be removed, so you can obtain access.

It is unavoidably a dirty job and you should mask off, with dust sheets or poly-

thene sheet, as much of the surrounding area as you can.

Wear protective clothing and cover your head, then hack out the plaster work with as little dust as possible.

It is a good idea to replace the plaster with boarding or some other removable surface for easy future access.

Newel posts

Newel posts can become loosened – usually at the floor joist to which these are fixed. Usually, these only need rescrewing, but you will need to take up floorboards to do this.

If either the joist or post is damaged or split, use steel angle reinforcing brackets to make the repair.

These should be firmly screwed into place; glue or fit back damaged sections and support these with reinforcing blocks if needed.

Another problem is where the joint between the newel post and the outer strings becomes loosened, for this also loosens all the treads and risers. The post must be braced with woodblocks, 32mm square, which are glued and screwed into the inside corner.

Worn nosings

The rounded front part of a tread, the nosing, on conventional staircases, projects slightly and may become worn or damaged. This may happen on uncarpeted stairs, where the wear is usually in the middle of the nosing.

To replace a tread involves considerable work, but the nosing can be easily replaced with new timber. Make sure surfaces are clean and dry. Measure the amount of nosing to be removed and cut a section of hardwood to the corresponding width and thickness.

Mark the section accurately so that you cut it off completely flat. Next, cut away the worn section, just slightly forward of the riser, using a small saw.

Do not go completely back to the riser, as the joint, particularly if it is a tongued-and-grooved one, may be weakened.

The new section should be pinned and glued into place and allowed to dry thoroughly. Fixing pins should be punched below the surface of the wood and the small hole filled with a proprietary filler.

The nosing can be rounded with the spokeshave to correspond with the nosings on the staircase.

Worn steps

It is a simpler matter, on many staircases, to replace a worn bottom step; however, it is important to preserve both the height and width of the old one, since the 'going' or slope of the staircase should not be altered. This could be hazardous and cause someone to trip.

Squeaking can be caused by side friction between boards. The way to cure this is to dust the joints with a talcum powder or French chalk. Warped boards tend to lift nails slightly, allowing the boards to creak. These can be reinforced with countersunk screws, fixed at intervals.

Bearers nailed or screwed to joist give support for the boarding when replaced

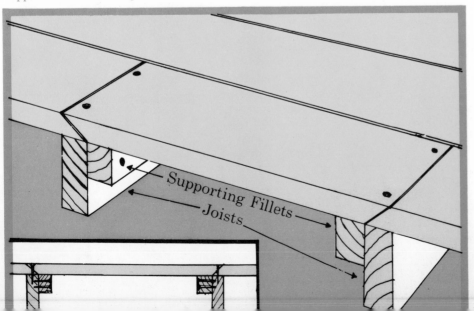

Supporting Fillets

Joists

Hang that door!

Doors that creak and do not hang properly can be the subject of much irritation. Whether rehanging an existing door or hanging a new one, a careful scheme of operation is necessary, or the door may not hang properly, catch and be difficult to close. A door should fit correctly, with the minimum of gap, particularly if it is an outside door.

Doors are usually hung so that when they open they screen the room from both view and draught. A door must have a clear, all-round allowance for expansion in wet weather.

For an outside door, leave a clearance around the top three sides and at least 3mm at the bottom. For an inside door, the average clearance is about 2mm at the top three sides and 6mm at the bottom.

Panelled, solid doors have more movement than doors using man-made boards, which are more inert. Leave a new door in a room for about 48 hours to adjust to humidity.

Cutting to size

To protect a door in storage and transit, the stiles, the long rails, are made over-length and project beyond the end of the door at top and bottom. These extension pieces are called 'horns' or 'joggles' and have to be cut off.

It is best to leave these on, to protect the door from damage, until you are ready to hang it. Lay the door across trestles and cut these off flush with a hacksaw, finishing with a block plane.

Most doors have to be adjusted to fit the door frame. This is done by planing or 'shooting' the door. A home-made support can be made up to hold the door while the edges are being planed, consisting of a piece of 75mm × 50mm timber about 510mm long with an angled notch about 40mm deep and 50mm wide in it. A large wedge, about 255mm long, secures the door when placed in the support.

An alternative to using trestles and the support is a unit such as the Workmate portable bench, which can double for both and provides lateral support when planing, since the bench contains an integral vice along its length.

When shooting the stiles and rails, use a long plane, such as a jack plane; shoot from either end, as this will ensure an accurate line, free from hollows.

If the frame is out of true when the door is offered up, the door may have to be scribed to fit. You may have to wedge the door up into position with plugs at the bottom while you are checking the fit.

Once the hanging stile is a good fit against the jamb, the opposed stile should be planed. This edge must have a slight bevel on the inside edge of the non-hinged or lock stile to fit properly. A door about 50mm thick requires a bevel of about 2mm.

Next, fit the head of the door, testing the fit with the hanging (hinged) stile in position. Allow a little less clearance above the lock stile than the hanging stile, since the doors tend to drop in time, partly because of wear on hinges.

Fitting at the bottom on an outside door depends on the type of step or whether draught extruders or weather seals are being fitted.

Exterior doors are best hung with what is called a 'kick'. This means that the door, when opened, is slightly out of vertical, which increases the clearance at the bottom.

This is often necessary for porch floors, which may have a slight fall in the direction of the door. The kick is achieved by slightly varying the amount by which the hinges are recessed.

Hinges

Most doors are hung on cast-iron butt hinges. These are made in a range of sizes; the best average size for doors is 400mm. For heavy doors, it is advisable to use three hinges. This also helps to prevent warping and spreads the load. Where three hinges are fitted on standard doors, slightly smaller hinges can be used.

Pressed-steel butts are less strong than cast-iron ones and are more likely to give trouble through rusting.

The top and bottom hinges should be fitted to line up visually with the edges of the rails.

Prop the door into the frame, again on wedges, to hold it steady. Make a mark on both the door and the frame 150mm from the top and 230mm from the bottom. These will then line up with standard top and bottom rails. If an intermediate hinge is being used, mark a position halfway between these points.

Remove the door, take a hinge and draw round one leaf with a marking knife, in turn on the stile and on the door frame. Position the hinges inside the marked pencil lines. Set the position so that the hinge knuckle just clears the door and the frame.

Next, set a marking gauge to the thickness of the hinge flap and mark the front surface of the door and the frame for depth.

Hinges are always hung on the door first, so first cut the slot for this recess. To fit a hinge, chisel along the marked lines on the door. Make a series of cuts across the grain, to the depth of the gauge line, then pare, with the grain, to remove the waste. Turn the chisel bevel-side downwards to chop diagonally, which makes it easier to remove waste wood.

The leaves of cast-iron butts are normally made to taper slightly. When the outer surfaces of the leaves are held parallel, there is a clearance space between them.

The bottom of the recess should slope slightly to correspond with any taper of the leaf of the hinge, so that this fits flush with the surface of the wood

The door should be placed in the opening so that the loose part of the hinge is on the inner surface of the frame. Position a wedge beneath the door and a piece of packing, just under 3mm, above the top rail. This brings the door up to its correct position.

Saw the protective horns or 'joggles' from the end of the door and then plane

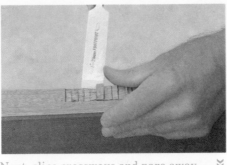

Next, slice crossways and pare away waste timber to the depth of the hinge

The hole is then squared and cleaned up with a wood chisel to accept the lock

Try the door for fit. There should be clearance of about 2mm at top and sides

The joint is finally cleaned up to the correct depth, using flat of the chisel

The recess for the lock plate is cut out of the door edge, using a chisel

Plane the door so that it fits snugly. A hand or power plane can be used here

The hinge should fit neatly into the slot. Screw holes can now be drilled

The holes for the screws to secure the lock in position can then be drilled out

Use the hinge as a template to mark out. Cut out the profile with the chisel edge

A marking gauge can be used to square across the width of the lock shoulders

Marking gauge is again used to mark out the depth of the latch and the spindle

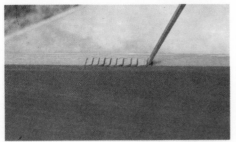

Make a series of wedged cuts to the depth of the hinge; keep within profile

The lock itself can be used to mark out the width of the body of the lock

This is drilled out, again using a twist bit. Check carefully that hole is accurate

A suitable twist bit may be used to drill to the depth of the lock body

Latch position is marked on door jamb from position of latch and chopped out

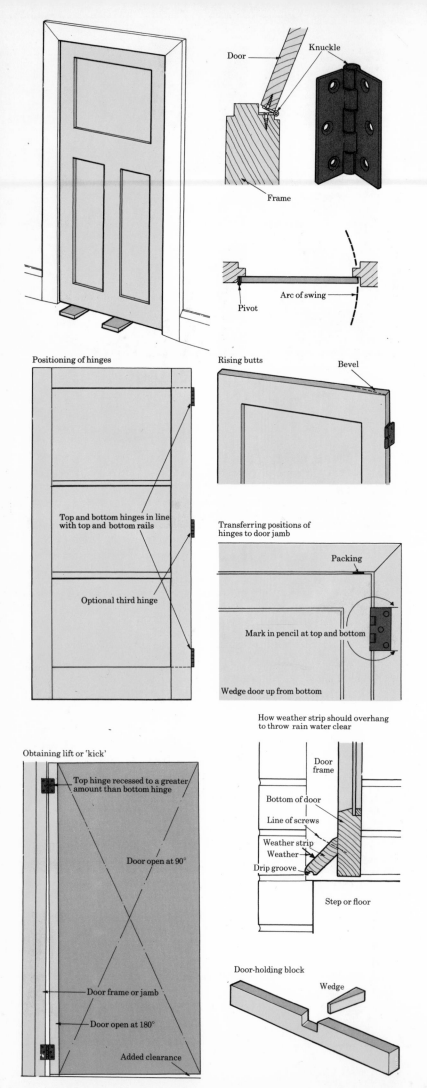

Door

Knuckle

Frame

Arc of swing

Pivot

Bevel

Rising butts

Positioning of hinges

Top and bottom hinges in line with top and bottom rails

Optional third hinge

Transferring positions of hinges to door jamb

Packing

Mark in pencil at top and bottom

Wedge door up from bottom

Obtaining lift or 'kick'

Top hinge recessed to a greater amount than bottom hinge

Door open at 90°

Door frame or jamb

Door open at 180°

Added clearance

How weather strip should overhang to throw rain water clear

Door frame

Bottom of door

Line of screws

Weather strip

Weather

Drip groove

Step or floor

Door-holding block

Wedge

Hang it!

Hang the door by inserting only one screw into the sides of each hinge. Make fixing position holes with a bradawl. Check the swing of the door and establish uniformity of clearance, then insert a second screw into each hinge and check again.

If adjustments are needed, these can be made by removing the door and chiselling the recesses as needed. If a recess is too deep, a packing piece made of thin card can be used to correct this. Make sure that the heads of screws are fully countersunk and offer no projections which affect the closing of the door.

If the door catches on the hinge side—because the hinge knuckle projects and causes it to swing wide—impart a slight bevel.

Rising butts are hinges which swing the door clear over carpets, by lifting progressively as it is opened. To provide initial clearance at the top of the door, the first 75mm or so of the top or head rail should be bevelled slightly on the inside edge.

A door should stay open in any position. If it does not, the screws are wrongly placed. To correct this fault, take off the door and adjust the screw positions slightly. If the door is badly out of true, you may have to reposition the leaf of the hinge; the existing screw holes should be plugged and new holes made.

Door furniture

Door furniture is fitted next. A wide variety is available in the general category of mortise locks and latches, rim and cylinder locks—the latter is a form of rim lock.

The height at which a door handle is fitted is a matter of choice, though it will look better if it has a definite relationship with any glazing bars. A midway position between two bars presents a neat appearance.

To fit a latch, square a line round the stile at the required height and gauge the distance of the latch on the stile face. With a bit and brace, bore a 15mm hole at this point to accept the spindle of the latch.

Next bore and chisel a slot in the edge of the door to accept the body or barrel of the lock. The size of this depends on the size and shape of the barrel; square the lines with a try-square and marking gauge. Use this as a template for accurate marking.

Drill a series of holes corresponding with, but slightly less than, the width of the body of the barrel of the lock and to the depth of the body; chisel these out squarely.

Insert the lock body and screw the end plate to the face of the stile through its fixing holes at the top and bottom. Attach the spindle and the door handle.

Determine the position of the striking plate by direct transfer from the latch when the door is closed. A small mortise can then be chopped through the hole in the plate with a chisel to accept the latch.

The action of the latch will be made smoother if the lead-in part of the striking plate is bent back slightly, into a small recess in the door frame.

Restoring and refitting sash windows

Windows and doors are parts of the home where deterioration can set in very quickly. It is important to give these regular attention, to avoid the considerable expense of replacement and the damage which neglect can cause to the fabric of the home. Painting regularly is always the first line of defence against wear and weather.

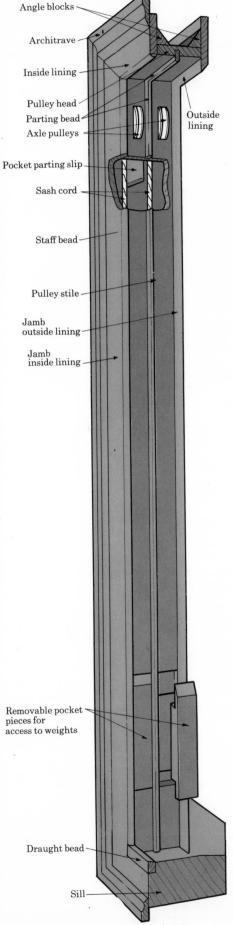

- Angle blocks
- Architrave
- Inside lining
- Pulley head
- Parting bead
- Axle pulleys
- Outside lining
- Pocket parting slip
- Sash cord
- Staff bead
- Pulley stile
- Jamb outside lining
- Jamb inside lining
- Removable pocket pieces for access to weights
- Draught bead
- Sill

Sash-window repairs

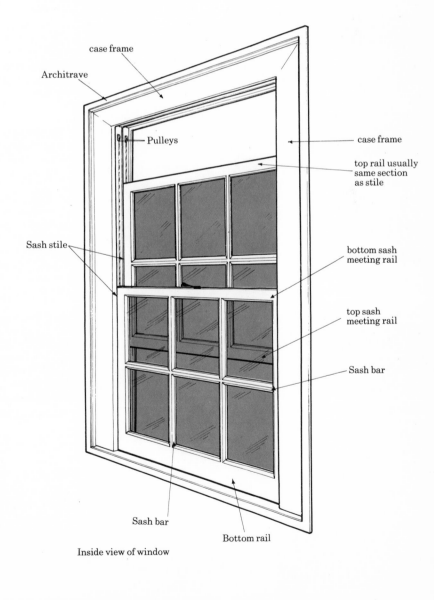

- case frame
- Architrave
- Pulleys
- case frame
- top rail usually same section as stile
- Sash stile
- bottom sash meeting rail
- top sash meeting rail
- Sash bar
- Sash bar
- Bottom rail

Inside view of window

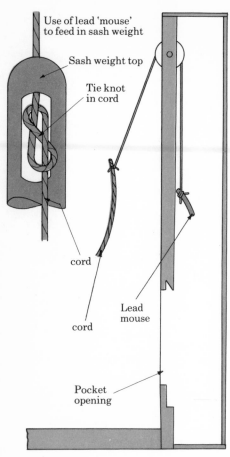

Use of lead 'mouse' to feed in sash weight

Sash weight top

Tie knot in cord

cord

cord

Lead mouse

Pocket opening

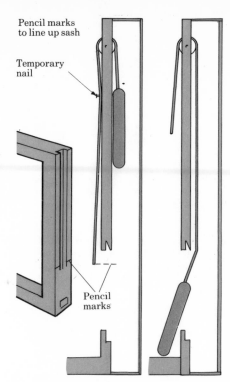

Pencil marks to line up sash

Temporary nail

Pencil marks

The lead mouse is used to weight the new sash cord and is later removed
Before taking out the lower sash mark the place where the ends of the sash cords come on the cord and on the frame

Properly maintained, windows and doors, both wood and metal, are unlikely to cause much trouble. Lack of or poor maintenance is the usual cause of deterioration. Frames may jam and not open properly; warping may occur, and glass crack or become loose; tenons may rot and break or glue joints come apart. Metal windows may rust and warp. In either case, the expensive solution may be new frames.

Paint fulfils a vital protective function. If it is not kept up to standard, it will deteriorate, flake away and allow timber to become saturated, causing it to swell up in wet weather. Wet rot may irreparably damage the fibre of timber.

Because damp is an all-pervading problem, repairs should ideally be tackled during dry weather. Apart from the inconvenience of removing doors and windows during cold and wet weather, timber remains swollen and problems are not easy to rectify.

If you have a number of doors and windows to repair, take out only one at a time. It is a good idea to tack a piece of 500-gauge polythene in place over the opening, fixing this to battening, so that it stays securely in place.

Windows and doors

There are two basic types of window – the casement and the double-hung sash. However, the movable part of any window's called a sash. There are various types of door – solid, panelled, ledged and braced, glazed, part-glazed, and doors with fixed or opening lights.

The principle of repairs is much the same for both doors and windows. However, it is the latter that tend to demand

the greater attention, so reference is largely to repairs of windows.

A casement window that will not close properly is a problem. Sash windows may stick and be difficult to slide. Look, at this stage, at the sash cords, for these may have frayed and need to be replaced.

Order of repair

The main operations involved in repair and maintenance are: removal of windows; taking out glass; dismantling the frames; cleaning up joints; glueing and repegging joints; checking for squareness and alignment; removing old paint; repriming and repainting; reglazing; and, finally, rehanging. Broken or rotted tenons may also have to be replaced.

When removing an upstairs window without help, use a strong line to support the window before you loosen the hinges. This should prevent hazards such as a window falling out and being wrecked and, perhaps, injuring someone below.

If you are working alone, place an improvised pallette of straw, sacks or other soft material below the window and lower it out on to this. Where possible, get help, for windows may prove heavier than they look.

First, remove the screws fixing the windows to the window frame. It is easier to remove screws on the actual frame once it is taken out of the surrounds.

Before attempting to take out screws, remove all paint from the screw slots, so that the screwdriver gets a good purchase and does not break out the screw head. Clearing a paint-clogged screw head is best done with a spiked tool such as a sharpened nail.

If screws prove stubborn, first try to tighten them slightly since this will help

to loosen the threads. You can also give the end of the screwdriver a few sharp but careful taps with the hammer as this often frees a stubborn screw.

Penetrating oil can be left to soak in on rusted screws. If all else fails, you may have to drill out the screws.

Sash windows

Sash windows are correctly called double-hung sashes or box windows and operate with cords, pulleys and weights; these counter-balance both the inner and outer sash, while sliding up and down. One end of the cord is nailed to a groove in the side of the sash, while the other attaches to a weight, in a hidden shaft within the frame.

The pulley wheels attach to pulley stiles – the upright sides of the frame which hide the weights. Part of each pulley stile consists of a removable section of timber known as a 'pocket', which fits flush with the stiles and provides an access hatch to the weights. These pockets are usually screwed into place.

Remove the fixing bead round the inside edge of the window frame carefully. Start in the middle of a long bead by gently prising it away from the main frame by around 25mm. Use an old chisel. Now tap the bead smartly back into place. The pins securing it should pop up through the surface of the wood and can then be removed with pliers.

If this does not prove effective, you can drive a wedge in the middle and use a chisel to lever progressively towards the ends of the bead. Next, remove the parting bead between the sashes, using the chisel to ease it out of its groove.

The lower sash can be taken out and rested on the window sill. Before removing it, mark in pencil on the front of the sash the place where the ends of the sash cords come, and make a corresponding mark on the frame.

Remove the nails with a pair of pincers, while holding the sash cords. This prevents the weights at the other end from falling behind the stile boards. The inner sash can be removed next and stood aside. Repeat the marking procedure.

Finally, unscrew or lever out the pocket covers. Take out the weights by pulling them through the pocket openings.

Once the frames are removed, old glass can be taken out, following the techniques in the chapter on window glazing. All window and door furniture, such as catches, should also be removed.

On tenon joints, remove the wedges in the middle of the joints by drilling a hole in the middle and prise these out with a slim chisel. With dowelled joints, remove the dowels, using a drill of the same diameter as the dowels.

Once the window is taken apart it may appear to be something of a jigsaw. Mark, on each side of each joint, a letter or a number in sequence to make it easy to identify the correct piece when you reassemble the sections.

The joints can be taken apart by holding a piece of timber against the frame and tapping with a mallet. Take care to avoid damaging them. Once apart, use the chisel or a scraper to remove old glue, or brush the joint with boiling water to soften the glue. Finally, clean the joint with fine wire wool.

New tenons

Often, a tenon is broken or damaged and needs replacing. This is best cut off and replaced with a new tongue. A hardwood fillet provides the new tenon, half of which is inset into the horizontal member of the window sash, the rail.

To make this, cut a piece of hardwood to the same depth and thickness of the old tongue but twice the length, and add 6mm. The extra length allows the new tongue to project through the mortise so it can be sawn almost flush and planed smooth.

The new tenon slots into the rail, and may be drilled and pinned with dowels. First, cut off the old tenon flush with the end of the rail. Put the rail in a vice, mark out with a try-square the distance of the tongue back along the rail. Cut a slot for the section of hardwood to fit into, using a coping saw.

Next, drill three pilot holes in the form of a triangle through the rail so that the hardwood is just marked and remove the piece of hardwood. Make a mark with a nail punch at a distance of 1mm on the outside of these three points and then drill 10mm holes. These off-line holes pull the joint tight when it is later dowel fixed.

Drill 10mm holes through the rail and assemble the rail and hardwood fillet. Coat the concealed part of the fillet with glue, slightly point three 10mm dowel pieces, cut slightly over-size for trimming. Coat these with an exterior grade glue and tap home; allow the joint to set.

The joint can then be planed smooth. Finally, the tongues can be haunched back to fit the mortise slots.

Reassembly

After new tongues have been fitted, reassemble the sashes. Coat the tenons with adhesive and slide these into the mortises. Sashes must be quite square; check this by placing the inside of a try-square on the outside corners of the frame; these should be square at all points. Another way is to measure the diagonals; if these are equal in length, the frame is true.

Once the sashes are assembled, you need to drive in hardwood wedges to consolidate the mortise-and-tenon joints. These are the same thickness as the tenon and should be glued with an exterior grade of adhesive, then driven in from the outside at the edges, using a mallet or rubber-headed hammer.

Cramping

It is important to hold the work steady while doing this as the frame may go out of square or the tongues of the tenons might become stressed and damaged. It is best to use sash cramps; if you do not possess these, they may be hired.

An improvised wedge can be made up by nailing blocks of wood to a surface, and supporting the frame between these. In this method, the blocks are set at a distance slightly greater than the length of the frame. The frame is tightened

Stages in the repair of window tenons

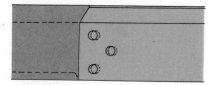

Detail of new tenon

Holes displaced to pull joint tightly together

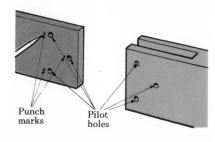

Punch marks Pilot holes

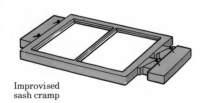

Improvised sash cramp

between the blocks by driving in four small wedges between the block and the frame at one end.

Another way is to make up a tourniquet of rope, tightened with a piece of wood, to cramp tightly round the outside edges of the assembled sash.

Before the adhesive dries check carefully that the frame is true and wipe off any excess glue.

Sash cords

On sash windows, if attention is needed to repair the frames, it is probable that sash cords may also need replacing. You can obtain pre-stressed wax cords, or allow for stretching in use.

The lead mouse

You also need a length of string and a small, flat piece of lead called a 'mouse'. This is used to weight the new sash cord and is later removed.

The mouse is rolled round the end of a 150mm or 180mm length of string. It is about the thickness and half the length of a cigarette. The mouse should be bent slightly in the middle and fed over the groove of the outer pulley wheel until it falls down behind the stile.

Next, tie the new sash cord to the other end of the string, and pull this over the wheel and out through the pocket opening. The mouse can now be removed.

Tie the sash cords to the top of the weights. Use either a flat-finish knot, or bind the loose end of cord so that no knot or lump can interfere with the action of the window opening.

Pull the weights up about 50mm from the bottom and partly nail through each cord into the pulley stile. This is to hold

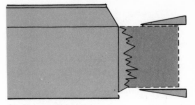

Wedges used to consolidate joints

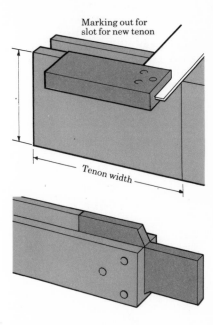

Marking out for slot for new tenon

Tenon width

the weights temporarily in position. Next, cut each cord level with the pencil marks made earlier on the stile.

The outer sash should be positioned so that you can fit a cord into its groove. Line up the end of the cord with the pencil mark on the edge of the sash, fixing it with four or five clout nails, starting at this mark.

Once both cords have been fastened, the temporary nails can be taken out of the cords and stiles and the sash can be lifted into place. Test the sash operation by sliding it vertically.

The weights for the inner (lower) sash are similarly fitted—except that these should be pulled up almost to the pulleys.

Finally, replace the pockets, spring back the parting bead, and lift back the inner sash. To ensure that the sash slides smoothly, put candle wax in the two channels and on the edges of both staff and parting beads.

Another problem is tightness of sashes. This may be caused by excess paint on the outer surfaces. Strip any build-up of paint and prepare and repaint the surface.

Reglazing

Reglazing of sashes follows the techniques of glazing casement windows. However, beware of old or weathered glass. This may be brittle and break easily. You may wish to contemplate replacement with a decorative, patterned glass. Similarly, casement or sash windows of various types may be removed and replaced with proprietary, aluminium-framed louvres.

You may also wish to extend and reinforce frames, so that you can fit one of the forms of double glazing.

Stop that drip!

Plumbing equipment in the home is rarely noticed or appreciated until something goes wrong. Regular routine maintenance is needed where there are moving parts such as taps, stopcocks, flushing and cut-off valves. The dripping tap and the faulty overflow are two common problems; repair is normally straightforward with no major domestic disruption.

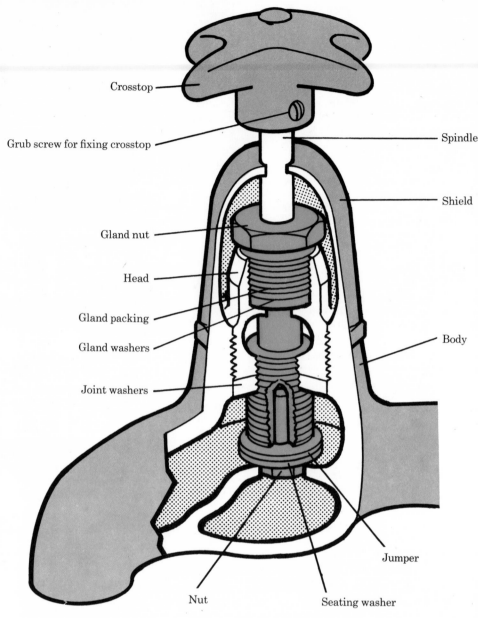

Crosstop

Grub screw for fixing crosstop

Spindle

Shield

Gland nut

Head

Gland packing

Gland washers

Body

Joint washers

Bib tap

Jumper

Nut

Seating washer

Plumbing maintenance may have to be carried out from time to time, particularly on those sections of a system which consist of moving parts, such as taps and the mechanism of cisterns. It is desirable to inspect these moving parts periodically to ensure that they are running efficiently.

Taps and stopcocks

The most common and irritating fault is that of the dripping tap. Taps are highly efficient, but are put to constant use and remain one of the most vulnerable parts of any system.

There are two basic types of tap–the bib tap, which has a horizontal water inlet, and the pillar tap, with a vertical inlet.

Both work on the same principle. A resilient washer is pressed down over the valve seat when the tap is turned down, preventing water from flowing from inlet to outlet.

This washer sits loosely at the base of the spindle; the handle attaches to the

spindle. When the handle is turned, the spindle rises, allowing the water pressure to lift the jumper and water to flow.

One type of jumper does not, in fact, 'jump', since it is attached to the spindle by a press fit. This is used in situations where water is at low pressure and would not raise a conventional jumper.

This washer is the weak part of the system. It may become worn, or the valve seat become partially obstructed as a result of foreign particles preventing the washer from correctly seating, leading to the familiar drip.

Before you dismantle a dripping tap, first turn it on fully, as the sudden force of water may dislodge an obstruction. If this fails, you will have to turn off the water main and dismantle the tap.

Before starting, assemble all the tools and materials you may need, so as to minimize domestic dislocation. Where a kitchen tap is concerned, you should turn off the main stopcock.

This stopcock also should be inspected occasionally. Never leave it fully opened, or it may jam. Grease the stem periodically to ensure that it can be operated quickly and smoothly in the case of an emergency.

Draining down

Though the kitchen tap is the most used and the one most likely to need attention, where hot or cold taps are supplied from a storage cistern, it is best to shut down the supply between taps and supply to avoid draining down the storage cistern.

Hot taps can normally be isolated by shutting down the valve in the cold feed to the hot-water cylinder. If, however, there is no valve, the hot cylinder will only have to be partly drained, by drawing off the 'crown' of water in the cylinder.

To isolate cold storage supply, either shut down the main stopcock or tie up the ball-valve in the cistern and open all taps.

One type of tap where it is not necessary

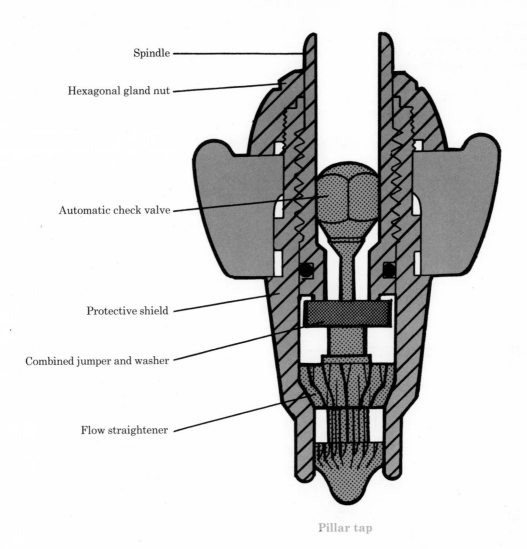

Spindle

Hexagonal gland nut

Automatic check valve

Protective shield

Combined jumper and washer

Flow straightener

Pillar tap

to turn off the water supply to repair the tap, is the 'Supatap'.

Dismantling the tap
Once the system is drained, remove the tap cover. This should only need hand pressure, but if you have to use a wrench or a spanner first wrap a cloth round it to protect the surface of the tap from damage or marking.

If the cover is difficult to remove, clean the threads and smear lightly with petroleum jelly.

Beneath the cover is the headgear. Its hexagonal nut should be loosened to expose the washer on the valve seat. If the jumper is of the low-pressure pattern, it will come off with the spindle.

Jumpers are usually made of brass and the washer secured to this with a brass nut. This can seize up, and as it may distort as as you try to free it, have a spare jumper and washer set handy.

Grease the threads of the nut when screwing down the new washer, and this will give ease of movement. Not all washers are suitable for both hot and cold taps, so check that the washer is correct. However, synthetic rubber washers are suitable for both, and an oversized washer can be easily trimmed to fit.

If water is by-passing the washer, the valve seat, on inspection, may be found to be worn and pitted and have to be reground. Usually, this is a specialist job requiring special tools. You can, however, use a nylon washer and seat set which fits over the existing valve seat to effect a repair.

Where water trickles over the top of the tap cover, this suggests that a leak has developed through the gland. The tap handle may then have to be removed.

Take out the small grub screw which holds the handle to the spindle and put it safely on one side. Insert a piece of wedged hardwood between the handle and the cover to free a sticking handle.

Unlock the gland screw and remove old packing, replacing this with wool, cotton wool or string soaked in grease, such as petroleum jelly or tallow.

Compress this into the stuffing box, leaving enough room to enable the gland screw to be tightened securely on to its thread.

Avoid overpacking the stuffing box as this will make the tap difficult to turn. To stop future leaks, give one or two extra turns on the gland screw.

Cisterns
The modern toilet cistern is piston actuated; older patterns used a bell-type mechanism which did not normally require attention, other than possible adjustment to the ball valve. This pattern is easily recognised by its belled central dome.

If a ball float becomes perforated or the washer on the outlet is faulty, both patterns of cistern may overflow.

The piston siphon is more efficient. When the flushing lever is depressed or

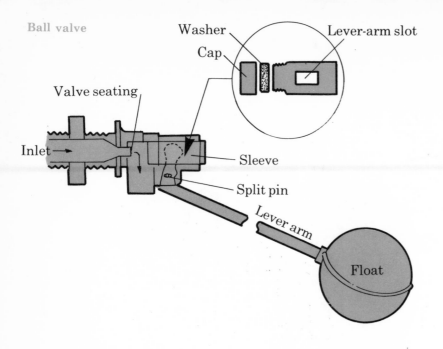

Washer
Cap
Lever-arm slot
Valve seating
Inlet →
Sleeve
Split pin
Lever arm
Float

WC cistern

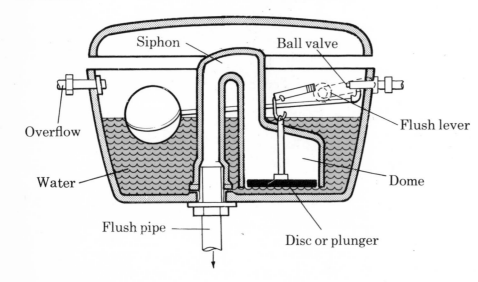

Siphon
Ball valve
Overflow
Flush lever
Water
Dome
Flush pipe
Disc or plunger

the chain pulled, a disc or plunger in the siphon enclosure rises, forcing the water above it and down the flush pipe to the toilet pan.

In the flush pipe, a partial vacuum is created which is sufficient to siphon off the water in the cistern. The disc is perforated, allowing water to flow through it from the cistern.

It is closed by a plastic flap or washer on the initial up-stroke. The flap acts as a non-return valve and if distorted or punctured, the flushing section may fail or be impaired.

To change the washer on a piston cistern, first flush the cistern and tie up the ball float arm to shut off the flow of water. Bale out or mop up with a cloth any residue of water remaining.

Unlock the nut beneath the cistern which secures the flush pipe to the siphon. On some plastic cisterns this nut is only hand tight. If a spanner is needed, this can be used to uncouple the larger nut holding the siphon to the base of the cistern.

Check when replacing the siphon that

the joint between it and the cistern is in sound condition.

Replace any worn washers and apply a smear of non-toxic jointing compound to ensure a watertight joint.

Remove the flush-lever linkage; normally, it can be lifted out bodily. Take out the siphon and remove the plunger disc from the base of the dome; take off the small retaining washer which holds the valve washer in place. Replace this with one of an equivalent size. If a replacement is not available, you can make one by cutting a disc of heavy PVC sheeting, using the old washer as a template.

Now the unit can be reassembled, once you have checked that the connections at the base of the cistern are satisfactory. Release the valve arm and allow the cistern to refill.

Ball valves

The method of replacing or repairing a faulty ball valve, or 'float', is the same for both a cold-storage cistern or a WC.

Usually, worn washers, perforated floats, eroded seatings, lime deposits or grit on moving parts are the causes of trouble and correction does not involve physical removal of the cistern connections.

If replacement of the mechanism does become necessary, check that a similar inlet valve is used in replacement–high, low or medium pressure, in accordance with the water supply.

Supply to the cistern must be shut off when maintenance or replacement is carried out. If the ball float is perforated it will become waterlogged and sink and the cistern will overflow continuously.

A new ball float is simply screwed on to the threaded spindle at the end of the float arm. A perforated ball can be temporarily repaired by first tying up the arm, removing and draining it. The ball can then be encased in a polythene bag, with the neck of the bag tied over the lever arm.

Washers

A faulty valve washer may also cause a continuous overflow. Worn valve seatings can be reground, as with a tap, but capping with a nylon seat or replacement of the unit is not expensive.

Replacing a faulty washer entails removing the cistern lid or cover and extracting the split pin securing the lever of the piston, enabling the piston to be removed. On some types you may first have to remove the cap on the end of the cylinder.

To do this use a wrench to uncouple the washer retaining cap; the piston will then detach into two halves. If there is grit behind the valve seating flush this clear before replacing the valve.

Air locks

Air locks in modern plumbing systems are rare. These are most likely to occur after refilling following repair-and-maintenance work. The most common problem is the air lock, caused when a volume of air is trapped between two bodies of water in a pipe–usually where it changes direction from up to down.

The mains pressure is usually sufficient to force the entrapped air bubble to the nearest tap or valve where it is easily released. –

A more difficult type of air lock to clear is one where the pipe is fed from the cold-storage cistern. This is because of its much lower head of pressure. To clear such an air lock, connect the low-pressure storage side to the high-pressure mains.

Join the appropriate taps with a piece of hose. Leave a tap or ball valve open on the blocked side to allow the air to escape when the two taps are turned on.

Where the air lock is on the hot-water side, temporarily block off the vent pipe above the cold cistern–but remember to unblock the vent once the lock is cleared.

Where there are frequent air locks, check the routing of pipes with a view to modifying them to eliminate possible tortuous runs of pipework. It may be necessary to fit air-release valves at points where air locks persistently occur.

Clearing blocked drains and gullies

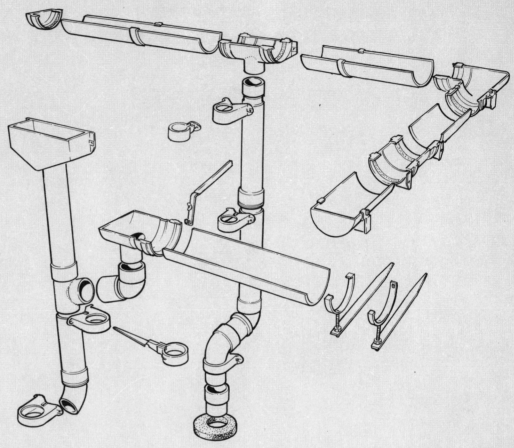

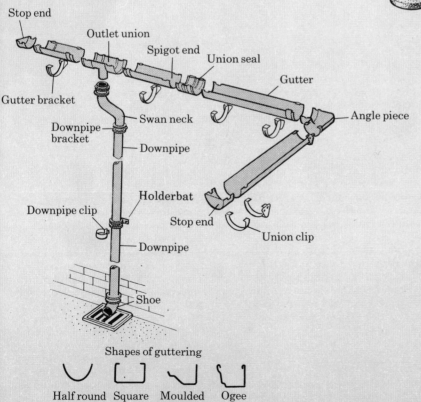

Stop end

Outlet union

Spigot end

Gutter bracket

Union seal

Gutter

Swan neck

Angle piece

Downpipe bracket

Downpipe

Holderbat

Downpipe clip

Stop end

Downpipe

Union clip

Shoe

Shapes of guttering

Half round Square Moulded Ogee

When domestic waste systems go wrong, speedy correction is most important. The entire system, from taps to flushing and storage cistern mechanisms, should be inspected from time to time to keep them trouble free. Below ground, manholes and pipework should also be inspected periodically. Traps and gullies are the remaining areas of possible trouble.

Waste systems do not generally require a great deal of attention but it is important to ensure that, during the winter, any external services are free of residual water – such as may happen in runs of horizontal pipe-work or if a waste pipe should sag.

Types of drainage pipe-joint

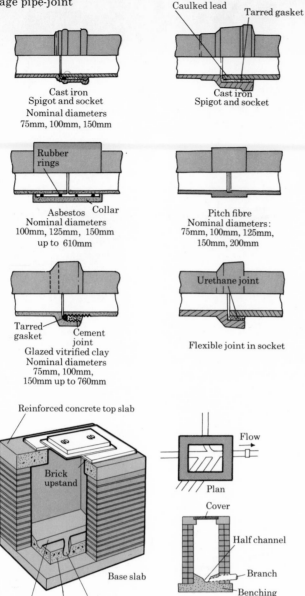

Cast iron
Spigot and socket
Nominal diameters
75mm, 100mm, 150mm

Caulked lead   Tarred gasket

Cast iron
Spigot and socket

Rubber
rings

Asbestos Collar
Nominal diameters
100mm, 125mm, 150mm
up to 610mm

Pitch fibre
Nominal diameters:
75mm, 100mm, 125mm,
150mm, 200mm

Tarred   Cement
gasket   joint
Glazed vitrified clay
Nominal diameters
75mm, 100mm,
150mm up to 760mm

Urethane joint

Flexible joint in socket

Reinforced concrete top slab

Brick
upstand

Base slab

Main
channel   Branch
      Haunching

Flow

Plan

Cover

Half channel

Branch

Benching

Section

Drainage inspection chamber

One way of helping to prevent large blockages is the routine inspection and clearing of waste traps, gullies and manholes. A blocked waste trap can usually be cleared with a rubber plunger cup.

When using this, half fill the sink or basin with water. Block, temporarily, any overflows and then work the plunger up and down over the drain exit, with a vigorous, jabbing motion.

Waste traps

If the blockage persists, this will necessitate access to the trap which provides the water seal. This entails removing a plug in the side or bottom of the trap. First, place a container of sufficient size beneath to collect débris and water when the plug is unscrewed.

Traps may be made of copper, lead or plastic. Do not impose excess strain on the trap or you may fracture it. Support it while you are undoing the plug and then hook out any débris with a piece of wire.

WC pans

A blocked WC pan may respond to treatment with a plunger but this should be used with great care to avoid stress on the pan which may cause it to break. It is, however, unusual for blockages to occur or persist in the soil system.

Manholes

Blockages may occur in manhole inspection chambers at point of entry or outflow for a variety of reasons. The main causes are roughened surfaces or fractures, permitting débris to adhere, or benching which is inadequate–perhaps too low, allowing an obstruction to build up.

Fractures or other damage should be speedily rectified, since these would represent a public-health infringement and health danger. Flaws in benching should also be corrected; the benching should be smooth, and gently sloped on either side of the outflow pipe.

Drain rods

Sometimes, a blockage may occur through no fault of the system. Normally, this can be cleared easily by prodding free with a stick. In other cases, you may need a set of drainage rods, together with fittings, to deal with a variety of circumstances.

Rods screw together and are each about 1m long. These provide reasonable flexibility, allowing them to be fed along a blocked pipe from within the manhole or along the pipe from outside, in the case of shallow manholes.

The main attachments, which screw on to the head, are a rubber plunger, corkscrew head, hook, scraper and brush head. The brush set resembles those used by chimney sweeps. The corkscrew is intended for lifting plugs in manholes but can also be used to clear blockages. Rods can be bought or hired.

To find a blockage, start at the house and open up each inspection chamber in turn. When you locate an empty one, this indicates that the blockage is between this and the previous one.

Place a temporary barrier over the mouth of the outflow in the empty chamber. A piece of chicken wire rolled into a ball is suitable and allows water to pass but stops solid matter. Take care, however, that the wire does not enter the pipe and further block it.

Next, attach the rubber plunger and insert this at the blocked-up chamber. Turn the rods in a clockwise direction as you insert them as this ensures that they do not unscrew. You should, in most cases, be able to push the obstruction clear. If this fails, you will have to try the hook. Use the scraper to remove débris adhering to surfaces.

Once the blockage is dislodged, remove it, or break it down, and finally flush with water to disperse. Then use a hose to flush out the length of drain. Use the brush to clean off any encaked débris as this may cause a blockage to recur, then sprinkle disinfectant.

Once the blockage is cleared, check the cause as a flaw or deterioration may need to be remedied. Inspect carefully before replacing the inspection cover on the manhole.

Manhole covers

Where a manhole cover is broken and needs replacing it is generally necessary to buy a new rim as well as the lid, since these are made as a matched pair to ensure a good fit.

Although a matched rim and lid should fit together tightly, they will not provide a totally airtight seal. It is necessary to apply manhole grease liberally to the rim before putting on the lid.

Where the lid is removed for inspection, it is advisable to remove all old grease and repack the seal, which also prevents dirt and foreign matter from getting into the manhole and, possibly, causing a blockage.

Rims are usually set in concrete surrounds, so are relatively simply to replace. To take out an old rim, chip away the surrounding concrete, using a club hammer and small cold chisel. Any deterioration in mortar and brickwork should also be made good.

Care should be taken not to damage brickwork below the rim. Bed this rim or cover frame in a 1:3 cement: sand mix over the entire area to ensure an even bearing for the frame.

Place the lid in position to avoid twisting the frame; make sure that the cover is evenly in place and will not rock. Check that alignment is accurate with a spirit level

Benching should be shaped so that it slopes from the channel in the centre to the sides of the manhole at a gradient of about 25mm : 152mm.

It should be made of a mixture of 1:4 cement: sharp sand and finished with a steel trowel. It must be kept clean, and if any cracks appear, these should be at once repaired.

When remaking benching, take care not to allow mortar to fall into the gulley—if any does, remove before putting the drain back into commission.

When repairing cracks, a PVA adhesive should be used to bond new mortar. The existing surface should first be cleaned thoroughly with a wire brush.

Brickwork should also be inspected at fairly regular intervals, and if any rendering or faulty pointing is noted, this should be repaired.

Testing manholes
If a manhole defect leads to a loss of water, the fault should be traced, rectified and the manhole loaded and tested continually for an hour, during which there should be no significant water loss.

A fall of more than 25mm in this time would be excessive and not accounted for by absorption within the chamber walls or by dissipation.

The section of drain adjacent to the suspect manhole should first be isolated and charged with water. This is done by means of drain plugs, which have rubber walls, expanded by means of a screw on the centre of the plug body, to fit into the entry point of the channel.

By unscrewing a centre nut, the section can be drained slowly. Always reduce the pressure of water by first releasing this nut, as the pressure of water might drag the plug into the pipe and be difficult to extricate.

Types of manhole
If you have to carry out a substantial repair of an inspection chamber, it might be as well to consider replacement with one of the newer prefabricated units—plastic, concrete or pitch-fibre.

Channels in the base of a manhole can be pre-cast, half-round self-glazed or of pitch-fibre pipe, or formed in a concrete base with a smooth object, such as a tin. These must consist of a 1:4 cement: sharp sand composition.

Sharp angles should be avoided in channels as this could lead to blockages.

Manhole sides must be constructed of dense and non-porous bricks, such as engineering bricks, which are able to withstand constant conditions of damp. These should be laid using an English bond.

Where conventional bricks are used, these should be 'parged' or rendered to provide the same protection as engineer-

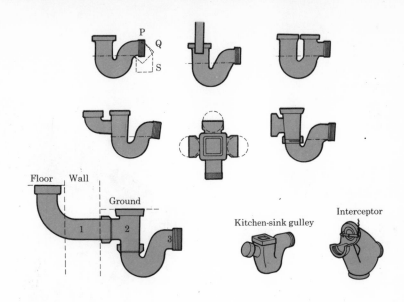

Types of trap

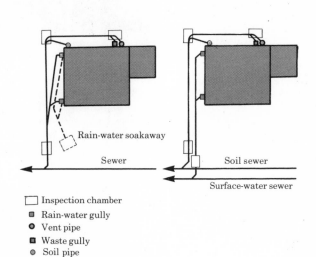

☐ Inspection chamber
▧ Rain-water gully
◉ Vent pipe
▣ Waste gully
● Soil pipe

Left: new one-pipe system
Right: older two-pipe system

ing bricks. Not all local authorities will permit the use of ordinary bricks.

Burst pipes
The burst pipe, of which the first indication is usually the ominous drip of water following a thaw, is becoming a thing of the past. This is partly because of new, versatile materials, which are less prone to burst, and higher standards of lagging and loft insulation.

Before the onset of cold weather, check all lagging. Bursts are more likely to occur in lead pipe than copper, stainless steel or plastic.

Burst pipes are caused by the formation of ice, which expands, distends, and then bursts the pipe. Sections of most modern pipes are often connected using compression-type fittings and the effect of ice formation in the pipe will usually be to push the fitting off the pipe.

Provided this is noticed before the thaw, it is easily rectified by reconnecting the joint, saving yourself from possible flooding.

If a burst is detected, first shut off the water supply. Using a blow torch, gently

heat the area of the burst—keeping a receptacle handy to take the thawed water. It is simple to cut out a damaged or distended section and place a new piece of pipework in position, joining this with a capillary or compression connector.

If the pipe is in leadwork, cut out the damaged section and replace it with a piece of of copper or stainless-steel pipe. The jointing technique is the same as that for connecting a stopcock on lead supply pipe—the only difference being that you will finish up with a pair of joints.

Alternatively, you can hammer the split closed, clean and prepare the pipe and wipe plumber's metal around it to repair it.

The same procedures apply if a hole is knocked in a pipe.

Lagging
Prevention is better than cure and periodic inspection of vulnerable pipes should take place during cold weather. Exposed pipes should be carefully lagged with bandage, polystyrene or foam lagging. Pipes above loft insulation should also be lagged.

145

Joining the plastic rain drain

A string line is used to establish the fall; clips are fixed at 1m intervals

Ensure a slight but even guttering fall; this prevents collection of rainwater

Rainwater goods is a general term used to cover guttering and down pipes. Once usually made of cast-iron, rainwater goods are now widely available in plastic, which is light, easy to handle and needs little or no maintenance. Guttering is made in a variety of profiles. Connection of the new rainwater system is usually a reasonably straightforward job.

Guttering, or rainwater goods, is an essential part of the fabric of the home. The modern tendency is to fit or replace existing guttering with PVC plastic.

At one time, most guttering was made of cast iron. Zinc and asbestos are other types of guttering but much less used. Asbestos tends to become brittle with age and zinc deteriorates.

Less used is pressed-steel guttering, usually supplied galvanized or primed, and vitreous enamel, made in a range of colours.

Access
Erection of new guttering, though not difficult, may call for assistance – particularly if you are using traditional cast iron.

Over porches and the like, guttering can be put up with access provided by trestles and scaffold boards. It is most important to be on a level with the gutter position, or you will find it difficult to sight it so that you can line it up accurately.

At main roof level, you will need scaffolding. A portable scaffold tower is best; this is easily erected and can be fitted with wheels, enabling the tower to be moved around at will. Wheels can be locked once the tower is in position.

Where you are working over the full width of a house, you may have to use two scaffold towers, with scaffold staging between, to bridge the working area. Special staging, of substantial planks, can be hired for this.

Choosing
Plastics have every advantage. They are cheap, lightweight, do not deteriorate and need no painting. They are also easy to handle and assemble, and to remove if necessary.

Plastic guttering is made in either half-round or square sections. The latter has a greater water capacity than the half-round type.

Plastic guttering is normally available in grey, white or black.

Two other types of guttering are the cast-iron 'ogee' pipe, a cross between half-round and square section, and the moulded section.

Rainwater goods consist of a range of components, which are put together rather like a kit. The main terminology of individual sections is:

Gutter Section collecting storm water

Down pipe The means of draining away accumulated water

Stop end Section at the end of a run of guttering

Running outlet Intermediate terminate with spigot to connect gutter and down pipe

Hopper head Connector fed into by individual pipes and connected to down pipe

Swan neck (or swanneck) Angled section which provides a stand off or offset, where the fascia, to which the guttering fixes, is forward of the wall line

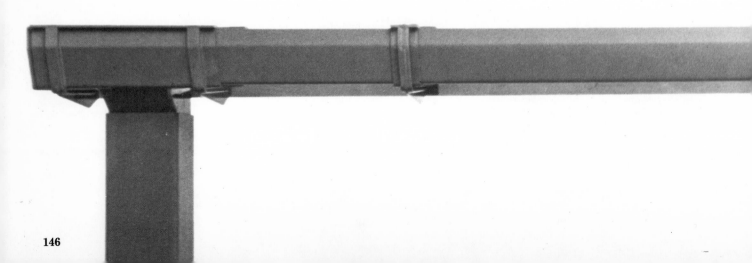

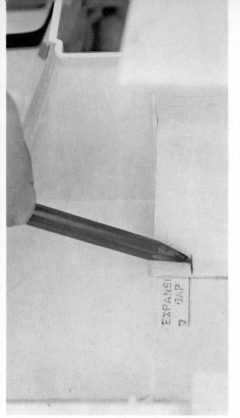

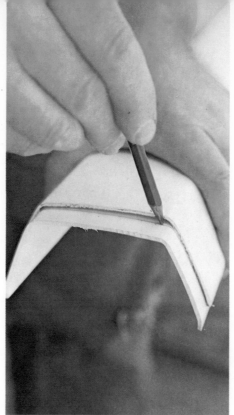

Allow for the expansion gap; mark the guttering against the fitting and cut

A scrap piece of guttering can be used as a template, to cut this squarely

One type of fine-toothed saw which can be used to cut PVC material easily

Shoe An angled outlet at the bottom of the down pipe; used where water discharges over a trapped yard gulley

Angles Sections, like a short letter 'L', for inside and outside angles, in 90°, 120° and 135°, dependent on make.

Note
Stop ends can be combined with outlets. There are also long and short stop ends. Other specialized fittings and connectors include PVC to cast-iron connectors. Always refer to manufacturer's instructions.

Estimating and measuring
First, estimate your guttering needs. PVC guttering is available in lengths of 4m and made in sizes from 2·5m to 4m. You need to work out where outlets and down pipes must be fitted in relation to the drainage arrangements.

Next, measure for the run of guttering and down pipe and then fill in the requirements for connectors, stop ends, shoes and swan necks.

Jointing
Most guttering laps together, using neoprene seals secured with clips, forming what is called a 'dry' joint.

Some makes use a union, which is a short section with neoprene seals at each end. The gutter sections are located in these. Other systems use a variety of methods to secure sections of both guttering and down pipes.

Where neoprene seals have deteriorated on existing guttering—usually as a result of grit being swept beneath them by water—these can be easily replaced. Some forms of plastic guttering, but not down pipes, are joined together by the cement-welded technique.

Cutting
Guttering and down pipes are easily cut, using a fine-toothed saw. Cuts should be made squarely, otherwise you may get problems of leaking if joints do not seat squarely.

With square sections, it is simple to cut pipe and guttering accurately, using a try-square to mark the line of the cut.

Where half-round guttering is used, wrap a piece of newspaper round the pipe or guttering, line up the corners of the paper and mark the cut line in pencil. A section of guttering can also serve as a template.

Measurements must be taken carefully before cutting—and then carefully re-checked. Errors can be a costly business.

It is helpful to set out sections of the guttering on the ground before fixing to make sure that you have all the parts and that everything fits together. The first stage in fixing is to fit the fixing brackets to which the guttering is attached.

If there is any dip, as a result of a misplaced bracket, water will collect at a particular point. Use a string line to set up the brackets.

Setting the fall
Guttering should be fitted with a slight fall. This is to ensure that there is no possibility of overflow during a period of heavy rain.

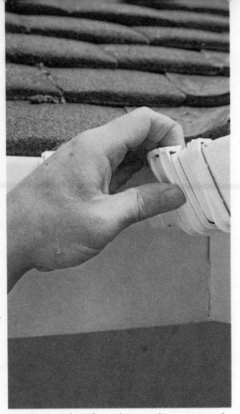

Angles used to form internal or external corners can be fitted either way round

To establish correct alignment of down pipe, use a plumb bob or a spirit level

Assemble the downpipe section 'dry'; chalk-mark the position for fixing

To establish the fall–a ratio of about 1:120–that is about 25mm per 3m run–temporarily fix a nail into the fascia at one end and attach a length of string as long as the guttering.

Line up the string so that it is level, using a spirit level, and mark this point. Measure off the fall ratio beneath this and put in another nail and attach the string to this. The string should be taut and not sag; a nylon string is best as it is not affected by humidity.

Guttering should be secured at a maximum of 3m centres. Screw the first bracket in place and work progressively along, accurately to the string, fixing with non-rusting screws.

Fixing

When joining guttering sections together, allow 13mm for expansion of joints. An expansion mark is usually indicated on neoprene seals.

Once sections are in place, joints are usually secured by snap-fix clips which clamp the seal joint for a leak-free union.

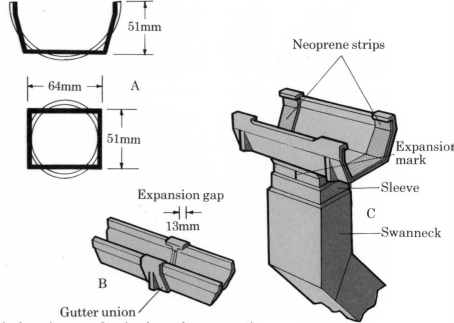

Equivalent pipe areas for circular and square sections and expansion allowance for joints in plastic

51mm

64mm   A

51mm

Neoprene strips

Expansion mark

Sleeve

C

Swanneck

Expansion gap

13mm

B

Gutter union

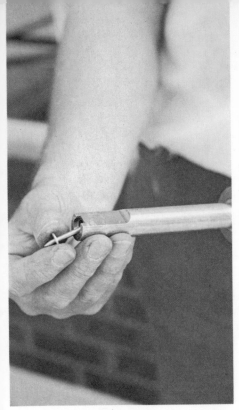

A special tool can be used to fix the downpipe securing clips with drive pins

Use a heavy hammer on the head of the fixing tool in order to drive the pins

A finished section of guttering which effectively shows the use of the parts

Some makes of guttering require a notching tool to cut a recess out of the guttering in which to notch the clip. These can be hired or bought.

Brackets should not normally be located more than 150mm away from a socket. Stop ends, which may incorporate the socket outlets, can be put on later.

Angled sections are simply used either way round to produce an inside or an outside angle. Most angle pieces are of 90°. It is a good idea to check the actual angle by making up a template of card or hardboard.

Downpipes must be fixed at a maximum of 2m centres and joined by a socket spigot.

Chalk on the wall, at intervals, the vertical alignment, in order to establish the fixing points for the down-pipe brackets. The chalk will easily brush off.

Try, where possible, to make fixings into the mortar joints. Use a masonry drill to make the holes and plug to take screws which should be galvanized or sheradized.

Masonry nails can be used for fixings.

When connecting down pipes to ground-level outlets, make sure that alignments are correct, and adjust if necessary, since distortion of the pipe must be avoided.

Check alignments carefully as you proceed. Use a spirit level or a plumb bob to ensure that the bracket and pipe outlets line up.

A shoe may be fitted to discharge into a trapped yard gulley.

Connections to services below ground are made in accordance with the existing system salt-glazed pipe, pitch-fibre or plastic pipe. Where the service discharges over a gulley, the shoe fitting is merely attached.

Finally, check that all joints are able to expand to the extent necessary. Plastic has a high rate of expansion, and sections may distend or come apart if this is not correctly allowed for.

Soakaways

Drainage may be to a sump or soakaway, into main soil systems or highway stormwater sewers. Drainage into main sewers is not usually permitted and most storm-water is now taken to garden soakaways, to avoid overloading stormwater services during periods of heavy rainfall.

The soakaway is eventually tapped by the water authority, as the water falls to a level or district 'table' where it can be pumped out and stored.

The soakaway-pit size is related to the amount of stormwater capacity of the drainage system. An average domestic-sized pit measures some 1130m³, located about 460mm below the ground level.

This may be a rectangular pit, lined with selected clean hardcore, to disperse the water. Where the ground is soft and friable, it may be necessary to build a brick chamber or line the walls of the pit with concrete.

An alternative filling is a random honeycomb of bricks. The soakaway should be capped with a concrete lid, about 150mm below ground level.

A pipe leading from the stormwater drainage should be taken into the soakaway at about one third of depth from the top and about one third of the width in, and should maintain a slight downward fall.

Repairs to gates and fences

A post-hole borer enables these holes to be made with precision to required depth

Set first post in hardcore to about half its depth; tamp down with scrap timber

Posts should be lined up accurately with string line between the furthest points

Use scrap wood as a marker and measure carefully for distances between posts

Check horizontals. Posts are bedded half-way in soft soil till cant rails are in

Fix the rails through the tenons into the uprights, using aluminium nails

Establish correct space between fence posts when fitting a ready-made gate

All posts and cant rails are fixed and fencing carried out as single operations

If fences and gates are regularly maintained and treated with suitable preservatives there is no reason why they should not last for a very long time. It may be, however, that neglect or damage necessitates repair; in most cases, this may be done with little effort.

Fence posts

Fence posts will most likely be damaged at their base, usually where rot and damp have caused them to deteriorate. The post may either be completely replaced or supported on a concrete spur.

To replace a post, first cut the post away at each mortise, trying not to damage the tenons. Remove the post from the ground, preferably in one piece. If it is embedded in concrete a large iron bar may be used as a lever.

The old post may now be used as a guide for marking out the new. The new post should be the same dimensions as the old one. Its length must be one and a half times the above-ground height.

Once the post is marked out the new mortises may be cut with an auger bit, brace, chisel and mallet.

The post should now be treated with preservative. This is best done by soaking the base for 24 hours and periodically brushing the rest of the post with the solution. Ensure the mortises are well soaked.

Set the post in the hole and 'joggle' the tenons into place; there is usually enough play to enable this to be done quite easily. Ensure the post is vertical and the arris rails horizontal, then backfill with hardcore and earth or fresh concrete, and tamp well down.

Finally, drill 13mm holes through the post and arris-rail tenons and insert dowels to hold the tenons rigidly in place.

If only the bottom of the post is rotten, then a concrete spur may be used to support the good upper section. Concrete spurs may be bought from builders' merchants and it is as well to know the dimensions of the old post, so that bolts and washers of the correct length can be supplied.

Fitting a concrete spur

First support the fence on either side of the old post (bricks and 50mm × 50mm batten braces are most suitable for this). Saw through the post, above the rot level, and then dig out the old stump.

Set the spur into the hole and pack out the base until the post and the spur fit snugly, then mark the positions of the bolt holes.

Withdraw the spur and, using an auger bit of the right size, drill through the post. The spur may then be replaced and bolted to the post. Place large washers between the nuts, or boltheads, and the timber.

Check that the post and spur are vertical, then fill in the holes with well-tamped concrete.

The temporary fence supports may be removed when the concrete has fully set, in four to five days.

Use scrap-wood crosspieces to hold posts in position during fixing; check verticals

Insert cant rails, bottom one first. Put these in for full length of posts

Gravel boards can now be nailed to the cleats on the post, once holes are filled

Where a fence is erected on a sloping site, fence sections should be stepped

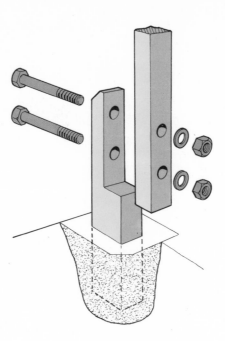
Fence posts may be revitalized by removing the rotten base and bolting the good section to a concrete spur.

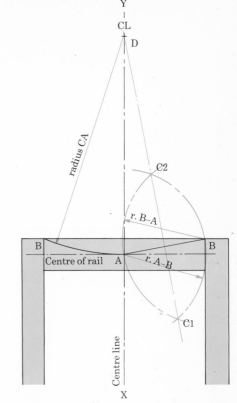
The radius for a curve passing through three pre-determined points can be resolved by using this simple geometry.

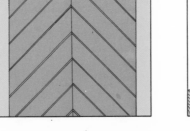 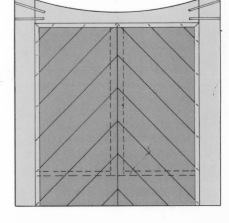
Using through dowels and rebates it has a sturdy construction and is easy to make.

Boards rotted at the base

Sometimes fences are erected without a gravel board. This omission leads to rotting of the fence boards at the bottom. With a line pinned between two posts, and parallel with the bottom rail, as a guide, cut away the entire damaged portion of the fence.

The ensuing gap may be filled, either by inserting a gravel board, which may be fixed to short battens nailed to the posts, or by laying a concrete foundation and building up an infill wall of bricks or screen blocks.

If the latter method is used, the fences should be treated with preservative before the wall is built.

Broken arris-rail tenons

Where the arris-rail tenon is broken, clean off the end and remove any damaged pieces from the mortise. Give the whole area a good soaking with preservative and then fix the rail back in position, using a proprietary metal arris-rail bracket.

They are made to fit over the arris-rail to which they are nailed or screwed. Similar fixings are employed to hold them to the post.

Mending gates

The first sign that a gate needs repair is that it will not close properly. This may be symptomatic of either a displaced support post or broken or loosened joints in the gate itself.

If the trouble lies with the post, then the gate must be removed from its hinges and the post either replaced or realigned and, where possible, tied in with an adjoin-ing fence or wall. The gate should not be rehung until any concrete has completely set.

Where the gate is in need of repair, then the most likely cause is one or more broken joints. The gate may be carefully taken apart and new pieces of timber inserted to make new joints. The old, good joints may then be cleaned up and the whole glued up and reassembled.

Sometimes, a quick, simple repair may be carried out by using angle brackets or plates screwed to sound timber. This may work very well and, though unsightly, can increase the gate's life by some years.

Making a gate

If a gate is too badly damaged it is probably easier to buy or make a new one. The following describes how to make a simply constructed gate. A chevron-pattern gate looks attractive and is not difficult to make.

The tools for the job
The tools required to make this gate are:

- rule
- marking knife
- try-square and adjustable bevel or combination square
- tenon saw
- bench plane
- shooting board
- 32mm bevel-edged chisel
- mallet
- brace and 12mm Jennings-pattern auger bit
- hammer and punch
- two 200mm 'G' cramps
- two 1·2m sash cramps
- bow saw
- internal spokeshave
- wheel brace and bits
- screwdriver.

Other more sophisticated tools may be used if available, such as power saws and drills.

Suitable timbers
The timber used to make the chevron pattern is standard tongued, grooved and V-jointed (TG and VJ) board which is readily available in various forms of pine and slightly less available and more expensive, in red cedar. The latter timber has many qualities and is easy to work, which makes it ideal for exterior use.

Other timbers, particularly hardwoods such as oak or padauk, are excellent for exterior use, but are expensive and TGVJ boards would have to be milled to special order.

The main framework of the gate is made from the same timber as the TGVJ.

Timber sizes
For a single gate, the stiles, the vertical side members of the frame, are 100mm × 32mm.

The centre stile is 50mm × 22mm.

The rails, the horizontal frame members, are 125mm × 32mm for the top rail and 150mm × 25mm for the bottom.
The TGVJ is 100mm × 16mm.

The TGVJ supports are cut from 25mm × 22mm timber.
All timber is planed all round (PAR). Double gates require the centre stiles to be of 100mm × 25mm.

Any shaping to the top rail is carried out after the frame is assembled.

Preparing the Timber
The actual size of the gate depends upon individual tastes, also the width of existing openings for which the gate is to be made. Using a try-square, marking knife and a rule, the stiles are first marked to length

and cut square, allowing 6mm waste at either end.

The rails are then similarly marked but cut with only a finger-nail thickness of waste. This is then planed off, using a shooting board and a finely set bench plane. When doing this, the board must be 'shot' from both edges; this will obviate splitting the corners of the timber.

Centre stile and rail lengths
The length of the rails is the overall width of the gate, less the combined stile widths. The centre stile length is the actual outer stile length, less the combined rail widths, plus 25mm. This stile should be cut and shot in the same way as the rails.

The centre stile is held in position by means of a half-lap at its top end and a notched half-lap at the lower end. To make the lower joint, take the bottom rail and on the face, side and edge, mark the centre of its length with a pencil.

Next, measure, on either side of the centre line, half the width of centre stile and pencil round this. Now set a marking gauge to half the thickness of the rail and mark across the last two lines drawn on the face edge.

The gauge may now be set to a depth of 25mm and a line marked across the two outer lines in the centre of the face side.

Clamp the board, face side up and face edge forward, to the bench and, with a tenon saw, make a series of cuts through the corner of the timber, just short of both gauged lines. The waste may now be removed with a bevel-edged chisel.

Holding the chisel upright and at right-angles to the grain, make a series of cuts across the grain and again remove the waste. This operation is repeated until the cavity is neatly cleaned out.

Halved joints may now be cut at either end of the centre stile. The bottom joint is 25mm long and the top joint, cut to half lap the TGVJ support, attached to the top rail, should be slightly smaller to allow for machining of the timber.

Marking out the top rail
It is important to mark out the top rail before assembly in order to know where the upper edge will be. The easiest way to do this is to prepare a drawing of the gate to a scale of 1:5 or larger and scribe the curve.

Draw the centre line X–Y and, on this, mark point A in the rail centre. Join up the points A and B and, using these points as centres, scribe arcs through the opposite points. The arcs cross at points C1 and C2.

Project a line through these points until it crosses the line X–Y at D. This point will be the centre of the radius of an arc passing through B–A–B.

Once this drawing is complete, it can be squared up and the arc may be enlarged to full size on a piece of card, which may then be cut out and used as a template for the curve on the finished rail.

Jointing the main frame
The joints used to hold the stiles to the rails are simple through-dowels. Each joint will require three dowels 150mm long by

12mm thick for the top rail and 9mm thick for the bottom rail.

After the dowels have been cut to length and the ends chamfered, they should be clamped in a vice and shallow grooves cut down their length with a fine tenon saw. Five or six grooves per dowel will be sufficient. These grooves will let any air escape from the dowel holes, stopping any tendency to hydraulic action.

To position the dowels, line a rail and a stile up on the corner of a bench against two battens previously tacked to the bench at right-angles to each other. Once they are in position, cramp them firmly to the bench. Place a piece of scrap timber between the cramps and the work piece to protect it.

Using a brace or electric drill and appropriately sized bit, the dowel holes may be bored to a depth of 135mm–150mm. The important thing to remember is to keep the holes within the width and thickness of the rails; holding the bit dead horizontal will help to facilitate this.

Once the holes are drilled, take the frame members apart and, with a chisel held flat on each piece of timber, clean up any swarf round the edges of the holes.

When all the joints are drilled, the whole frame may be cramped together, after exterior-grade resin glue has been applied to all meeting surfaces. Once the frame is cramped up and is square, squeeze some glue into the holes and on to the dowels, then tap these into their respective holes. Clean off any surplus glue and leave to set.

While the glue is setting, the TGVJ supports may be cut to length and a half lap cut into the centre of the top support, to take the centre stile. The supports may now be drilled and countersunk at 200mm centres.

When the dowel joints have set, these should be glued and screwed to the inside of the frame, lining up with the bottom rail. The centre rail may now be pinned and glued into place.

All screws and pins used should preferably be either sheradized or brass.

Once the main frame is assembled and cleaned up, including the removal of protruding dowel ends, the top curve may be cut out with a bow saw or electric jig saw. The resulting curve may be cleaned up with a spokeshave.

Stand the frame on the ground with its top uppermost and supported in a vice or, if a jig saw is used, it may be supported on trestles or a portable bench (such as the Workmate).

All that remains to do is cut the TGVJ boards. These are best cut individually, either using a mitre box and tenon saw or a circular saw with a fine blade and the T-rest set to 45°.

The boards are fitted with their tongues uppermost; after they have been cleaned up on a 45° mitred shooting board they may be glued and secret-nailed to the frame.

The gate may now be cleaned up with glass-paper and given a good coat of exterior-grade preservative.

It is now ready for hanging and the simplest method for this is to use cross-T (or garnett) hinges which should be fixed to the top and bottom rail.

Home electrics: switch on to safety

Electricity is probably the most significant single force in modern life. It provides light, warmth and power from a whole range of modern appliances, from the domestic household appliance to TV and radio.

All matter contains tiny molecules of electrons, or electricity, both negative and positive. The generation of electrical forces by power stations causes these electrons in wire to move along at incredible speeds, rather like a train shunting wagons. These atoms are harnessed in the home to provide the essentials of modern life.

The turbines move the negative particles along wires and build up an excess of negative atoms at one end. These are drawn back to the generating source, creating a flow of atoms or electrons along the supply wire.

Electricity is commonly regarded as a fuel. It should properly be regarded as energy, generated by large turbines at power stations, operated by steam, atomic energy or hydro-electric water power. Water power provides half the daily electricity of the world.

Electricity is never consumed; it flows back to the power station along the wire. All that happens is that its energy is harnessed.

Electricity is generated at 11,000 volts and transmitted from the power station at 132,000 volts, 275,000 volts or 400,000 volts, and at a fairly low current or amperage.

It is transformed down to a lower voltage by local sub-stations or transformers, and fed into homes at 240V. In many countries the voltage is lower–110V. This is safer but needs heavier cable to be able to provide higher amperages for heating appliances.

Types of current

There are two types of current–direct current, (DC) and alternating current, (AC). Electricity cannot be stored easily and has to be generated to meet the needs of a community or industry as it is needed.

The turbines at the power stations, rotating at some 3,000 revolutions a minute, create a flow of electrons first in one direction and then in the other, some 50 times or cycles per second, providing alternating current.

Flow of electrons

The flow of electricity may be compared with the flow of water from the tap. When the tap is closed, flow ceases. Opening the tap is comparable with switching on elec-

tricity. Similarly, with electricity, water pressure may be compared with voltage.

The rate of water flow, similar to the flow of current, is determined partly by pressure and partly by the size of outlet. A narrow pipe allows less water to flow than a wide one; a thin wire restricts or resists the flow of electricity.

Electricity flows through water, earth or air. It flows best through metal. Copper, and, to a lesser extent, aluminium are common conductors of electricity. Materials which resist electrical flow are called insulators. The most common insulators are rubber, PVC and porcelain.

Good earths

The earth wire is a 'safety' wire, designed to take current safely to earth in the event of a short circuit.

Earth connections are traditionally made to water pipes or to other metal fixtures. With the growth of plastics in domestic plumbing, connection to metal surfaces may be distinctly dangerous, for plastic is a good insulator. Very often, a device called an earth-leak circuit breaker is fitted between the electricity company's fuse box and the meter, which records electrical consumption.

This detects the presence of voltage on the domestic earth circuit, or unbalanced or earth-leakage current, and automatically switches off supply. With this method, all the domestic earth wires are connected to an earth terminal on the circuit breaker.

Ohms Law

Electrical values are worked out by a formula called Ohms Law. The ohm is the unit of electrical resistance encountered in a circuit. Some examples of Ohms Law are given as follows.

The higher the electrical resistance, the lower the amperage. To find the strength of electricity required, divide voltage of the household supply by the resistance of the equipment. If an appliance has a re-

sistance of 16 ohms and the voltage is 240V, the amperage is 15A.

The rate at which a piece of equipment uses electricity is calculated in watts. The rating of equipment is in amperes or amps. To find amperage divide the wattage by the supply voltage. A 2000W fire, divided by 240V, gives 8·3 amps. The nearest standard fuse is 13A. Up to 750W you can use a 3A fuse and between 750 and 3000W 13A fuses.

To determine watts, multiply amps by voltage. An appliance rated at 12·5A multiplied by 240V will have a consumption of 3000W or 3kW. It is usual to use the kilowatt (kW), which is 1000W, as the unit for higher wattages.

To find out the current needed by a 2·5kW heater, divide wattage (2500W) by 240V, giving 10·4A. Therefore, use a 13A or 15A circuit and fuse.

The number of amps depends on the resistance or ohms. To find wattage, multiply amps by volts to obtain the power; the answer is in watts.

A light bulb with a resistance of 1000 ohms will have a current of $\frac{1}{4}$A, found by dividing 240V by 1000 ohms.

Light, heat and power

Electricity is converted into light or heat by being directed along a wire too small for the flow of electrons. This gets hot and glows. The intensity of light or heat depends on the wire or element.

To provide power, an electric motor rotates. Motors are of two basic types–the brush motor and the induction motor. The brush motor is made up of two sets of electro-magnets, an outer set, called the stator or field coil, and the inner, which revolves, called the armature. The shaft which works the appliance is connected to the armature, and revolves when this spins.

When electricity is switched on, the coils of the stator and those of the armature become poles–north and south. North poles attract south and a motion is set up. This type of motor can be used with either AC or DC current.

Induction motors work on AC, which

Electrical symbols

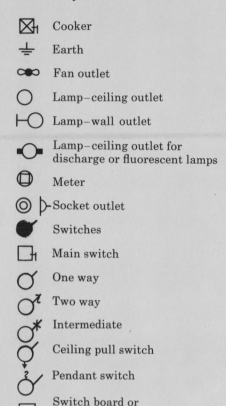

⊠⊢ Cooker

⏚ Earth

∞● Fan outlet

○ Lamp–ceiling outlet

⊢○ Lamp–wall outlet

●○ Lamp–ceiling outlet for discharge or fluorescent lamps

⊡ Meter

◎ ▷ Socket outlet

● Switches

☐⌐ Main switch

○⟍ One way

○⟍² Two way

○⟍⊁ Intermediate

○⟍↑ Ceiling pull switch

○⟍? Pendant switch

☐ Switch board or fuse board

Basic ring main system in the home

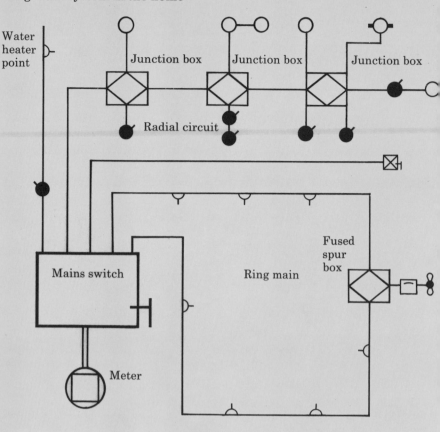

Water heater point

Junction box   Junction box   Junction box

Radial circuit

Mains switch

Ring main

Fused spur box

Meter

---

automatically reverse flow many times a second, reversing the current flow when a north and south pole come together.

Electricity enters the home by means of a service cable terminating at a sealed company fuse box. This cable has three conductors–two plastic-sheathed ones–red for live and black for neutral–and a bare, or earth, wire. Electricity flows along the red wire and returns along the black. All fuses should be placed in the live side of a line or cable.

The electricity company's fuse box contains a fuse of high amperage, 60 amps, and is designed to protect its supply cables and the local transformer from damage.

This box should never be tampered with. The electricity board alone must deal with faults at the company fuse box and back from it.

Some homes have an additional meter. This is coloured white and records the consumption of off-peak electricity, used with electrical storage heaters and immersion heaters.

Fuses

The fuse box or consumer unit, fulfils two purposes. It is a safety as well as a control point for the household electricity. It enables the electricity, entirely or in part, to be shut down, and it provides master fuses.

The fuse is a vital part of the electrical system. It is usually housed in porcelain or bakelite 'carriers' on fuse boxes. It contains a piece of wire thinner than the rest of the circuit wiring, which melts and breaks the circuit if the circuit becomes overloaded or a short circuit develops.

On modern fuse boxes there is usually one fuse for each circuit, rated in accordance with the load it has to carry.

Another type of unit is called a miniature circuit breaker. This does not carry fuses, but if a fault develops the unit shuts off and cannot be switched back on until the fault has been corrected. The domestic fuse box is connected to the company's equipment by means of heavy-duty cable, called 'tails'.

On fused plugs the fuse is in the form of a ceramic cartridge.

In early days of electricity fires were common, caused by overloaded wiring, because fuses were not generally used.

In older installations, the mains switch may be separate from the fuse box. If the switch is part of the fuse box, this points to the fact that modern wiring is probably installed.

Domestic needs

Supply needs to the home are generally grouped as follows:

● Upstairs lighting
● Downstairs lighting (including porches)
● Upstairs power points
● Downstairs power points
● Cooker (where fitted)
● Garage and workshop

Sometimes upstairs and downstairs lighting are grouped on one circuit and the domestic power on another. With larger properties, it is usually desirable to use the separate circuits. Lighting circuits are rated at 5A. Many houses have more than one circuit, since the maximum current is 1·2kW at 240V.

Modern lighting is either of the junction

Basic terms

*A **Conductor** is any material which will allow the passage of electricity. In domestic installations this is usually cable or wire.*

*An **Insulator** is the opposite of a conductor–it blocks the passage of electricity. The rubber or PVC sheathing around cable or wires is a simple example of insulation.*

*A **Circuit** is a loop of conductor wires from the source of electrical power, through the various appliances and back to the source.*

***Volts** are a measure of electrical 'tension' or 'pressure'. An analogy can be drawn with water pressure which varies with the height of the storage cistern or reservoir from the outlet or tap.*

***Amps** are a measure of the speed at which an electrical current flows.*

***Watts** are a measure of how much electricity passes a given point during a given period of time and are the basis of the kilowatt-hour 'unit'.*

*A **Short Circuit** occurs when resistances fail by insulation breaking down or bare conductor wires touching. A very fast current flows which could melt the conductors. To avoid this a deliberate weak spot, called a fuse, is*

included in the circuit.

*A **Pole** is an electrical terminal point. A single-pole switch consists of a straight, on-off switch, where the circuit is either opened or closed. A double-pole circuit allows current to flow in two directions, in accordance with the switch position (as on two-way circuits). A single-pole switch can have one or two ways; it is connected to the live wire to make or break the circuit. A double-pole switch breaks both the live and the neutral wires. These are used for outside lighting and on water heaters.*

*The term **Gang** indicates the number of switch connections or terminal points in a plate. Two switches or two outlets are double-ganged. One switch is single-ganged. The maximum number of switches on a plate is four.*

*An **Open Circuit** is one in which electrical current is stopped by opening a switch, unplugging an appliance or 'blowing' a fuse.*

***Resistance** could be called the 'friction' encountered by electricity as it passes through a conductor. The by-products of this friction are harnessed to produce heat, light or power in electrical appliances. Resistance is measured in ohms.*

Safety first

Safety is of paramount importance when carrying out electrical work. These are the rules you should observe:

1 Always disconnect plugs from sockets before interfering with the attached appliance.

2 Always turn off the consumer unit when doing jobs concerned with any particular circuit in the house.

3 Isolate the individual circuit you are working on by removing the fuse carrier from the consumer unit.

4 Always remove the plugs from the socket by the housing; never by pulling the flex.

5 Remember, when dusting or cleaning, never touch plugs, sockets or light fittings with damp hands or wet dusters.

TABLE 1

Cable	Rating I	Rating II	Use
1/·044	11A	13A	Lighting
3/·029	13A	16A	Lighting
3/·036	16A	20A	Small power
7/·029	21A	25A	Ring (30A)
7/·036	28A	33A	Power
7/·044	34A	41A	Cookers
7/·052	43A	52A	Cookers
7/·064	56A	67A	Cookers

TABLE 2

Cable	Rating I	Rating II	Use
0·5mm² (flex only)	3A		Lighting
1·0mm²	11A	13A	Lighting
1·5mm²	13A	16A	Small power
2·5mm²	18A	23A	Ring
4mm²	24A	30A	Power
6mm²	31A	38A	Cookers
10mm²	42A	51A	Cookers
16mm²	56A	68A	Cookers

box or loop-in variety. The junction box is used as a connector to feed various lights individually. The loop-in principle takes electricity from light to light in turn.

Older power circuits consisted of radial wiring, each fed back to the fuse box and individually fused, usually at 15A. Modern practice is to use a ring main.

As the name suggests, all the points are linked as one circuit or ring; this spreads the electrical load over the whole circuit. The rating is 30A and the maximum load for a ring is 7·2kW. Fuses may not blow, however, until twice this load has been attained.

Spur points, individually fused, can be taken from a ring circuit. These should not exceed 50 per cent of the total number of outlets. Fused, flat, three-pin plugs and matching sockets are used on ring circuits. These can, if chosen, be individually switched off, though this does not affect the circuit operation.

Many homes have too few power points and rely on a single centre light for each room. It is a good rule to have points distributed at intervals of about 1830mm; this reduces the amount of running flex when appliances are plugged in.

Rooms are better and more pleasingly lit by a variety of lights: wall lights, standard or table lamps and more than one ceiling light.

These can also be coupled with dimmer switches to control light intensity. This not only conserves the life of the lamp but cuts the electricity bill.

Electrical wiring falls into two categories – fixed and flexible. Fixed wiring consists of three conductors, two sheathed and coloured red (live) and black (neutral) with an unsheathed earth. Flexible wiring is brown (live), blue (neutral) and green and yellow (earth).

Modern cable is sheathed in PVC and has an indefinite life. In the course of any rewiring you may have to connect metric cable to existing imperial cable. This will set no problem, provided the slight difference in amperage rating is borne in mind and the new wiring is still within the current-carrying capacity of the circuit.

Imperial sizes are given in Table 1. In the first column, the number and size of wires forming a conductor are given. For instance, imperial 3/·029 cable has three wires, each of 0·029in. in diameter, for each conductor.

Rating I indicates a twin cable, with or without earth, enclosed in metal or non-metal conduit. Where such cable is not enclosed or clipped to a surface, its rating is slightly higher than enclosed cable (Rating II).

Ratings for metric cables are given in Table 2. Low-load circuits, including ring mains, consist of single-strand conductors, while power cables use conductors of seven strands.

These are not identified, as were imperial cables by the number and thickness of conductors, but by the diameter of the cable in millimetres.

House wiring, for example, contains one strand of 1·13mm wire for each conductor; ring mains consist of single strands each of 1·78mm diameter wire; and the average cooker wire consists of seven strands each of 1·04mm wire.

Tools

You will need a basic number of tools. These should include at least two sizes of screwdriver, both with insulated handles and one with a small blade and the other a larger blade, a small pair of pliers for

nipping the wires of cables and a cable stripper.

A power drill, for drilling into walls, a hammer and bolster for chasing out walls would also be useful.

New for old

Old lighting and wiring usually has to be stripped out completely. This is because older cables are usually covered in rubber and cotton which perishes after about 25 years. Such wiring can be very dangerous, since the wires may become exposed in metal conduit, which may be earthed to pipes. A serious electrical shock is possible.

Ancient lighting flexes are another source of danger. Old switches may wear and insulation break down. This can be dangerous on metal switches.

Radial power wiring is limited and encourages the use or connection of a number of appliances with multi-adaptors – a bad practice which can lead to overloading of the circuit.

Practices no longer sanctioned include conventional light switches in places where moisture is present, such as bathrooms. These should be marked down for substitution by a pull switch. Bathroom light fittings should also be of an enclosed pattern, for safety.

Older fuse boxes, which so often sprout further sub-boxes, should be changed. A modern consumer unit provides a neat assembly of all the circuits safely in one box.

Remember, it is possible to run new wiring and fit a new fuse box without electrical disruption to the household. Once everything is installed and checked, the electricity authority will connect the 'tails' to its main fuse box to bring your new electrical installation alive.

When it's time for an electrical refit

Wiring up plugs and changing fuses are among the simplest tasks in electrical work. However, the rules of safety are all-important. Electricity, the great unseen, should be the servant and not the master. The basics of fuses, plugs and sockets and the electrical ratings–the safe working limits–are described.

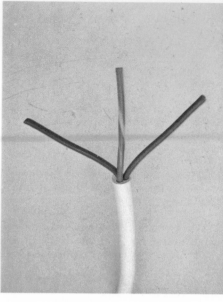

Standard colours for flexible cables are brown (L), blue (N) and green-yellow (E)

Safety

In the interests of safety it is essential that certain rules are followed when wiring up electrical equipment. Properly wired equipment also gives more reliable service.

Electricity should be your 'slave'. Just at the flick of a switch you can command instant light, heat, sound and vision. Improperly used it can also be a deadly enemy.

Plugs and sockets

Equipment to be used is connected into the house supply using plugs and sockets. Sockets must always be on the supply side.

This system may be a ring main which uses square-pin plugs rated at 13A, or the older, round-pin plugs rated at 2A, 5A and 15A. These use unfused plugs, unlike the ring-main system, which makes the former more complex and less safe. For these reasons it is no longer used; all new houses employ the ring-main system.

Fuse boxes and fuses

It was once common practice to have separate main switches and fuse boxes for each circuit–lighting, the cooker, the water heater, and, probably, several for power outlets. When extra circuits were added, a jumble of ill-assorted fittings and circuitry would result, producing the likelihood of hazard, since it was no longer clear which circuit was which and what electrical load was, consequently, being borne.

In modern practice, a consumer's power-supply control unit, or consumer's unit, is generally used. This is a compact fuse-box unit with fuse holders of the correct amperage for the appliance or circuit.

Permanent connection between switches and fuses is made by a solid bus-bar, made of copper, which is a broad metal strip able to handle a high current. A short bus-bar connects to a heavy neutral block; this is provided with a number of screw holes and climbing screws for the neutral wires of each circuit. For the earth connections, a similar brass block is used.

It is most important to use a fuse of the correct rating, since the fuse is the deliberate 'weak link' in a circuit. Keep a supply of fuse wire near the consumer unit, or, in the case of cartridge fuses, an accessible box of these.

Another type of fuse box is called the miniature circuit breaker, or MCB. This has an automatic switch to control and to protect the installation. If too many appliances are switched on and overload the circuit, it automatically breaks contact and switches off. It is not then possible to re-engage the circuit until the fault is corrected or the circuit load is reduced to safe level.

The MCB can also be used to switch circuits in an installation, which enables these to be isolated at will.

The consumer's unit should be located close to the electricity authority's own meter. It is best mounted on a board to protect it from damp.

Cables are fed through into the consumer's unit usually through 'knock-outs', which, as the name suggests, are easily pushed-out sections. The wires should be insulated by rubber grommets located in these holes to prevent chafing. One entry hole is used for the circuit wiring and the other for the meter 'tails' which are connected to the company meter.

To connect up a consumer's unit, cut back the sheath on the wires and connect the red cables to one side of the fuse. Firmly twist the wires with a pair of pliers, and then tighten these securely in place so that no dangerous stray wires, which could cause short circuiting, stick out.

There are several categories of fuse rating and these are colour coded on the front of the fuse holder. The colours are white, lighting; blue, electric fire; yellow, water heater; red, ring main; and green, cooker. Make sure also that the correct grade of cable is used and that this corresponds with these fuse values.

When connecting the ring main, note that you have two sets of wires–the beginning and the end of the ring circuit.

It is a good idea to fix a label on to the consumer's unit–these are often provided –to identify the individual circuits.

Finally, connect the main earth wire and meter tails. You need a length of about 1m of green-covered 2·5mm² single-strand cable for the earth lead, and also 1m each of red and black insulated 16mm² seven-strand cable for the tails.

Connect the green wire to the earthing block on the consumer's unit and the red

How a flat, three-pin 13A plug is wired. Note the live side is connected via fuse

Loop-in wiring used on a four-plate ceiling rose. Each is connected in turn

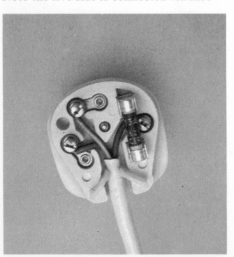

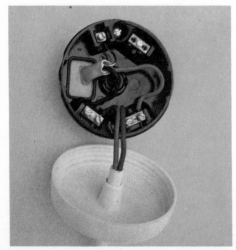

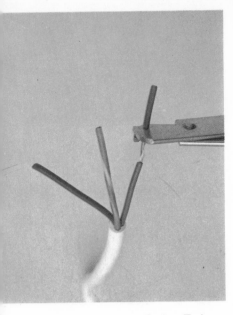

Strip back short sections of wire. Twist the individual strands firmly together

and the black wires into the bottom of the main switch. Take care to see that the polarity is correct; red = live and black = neutral. The tails and earth are then connected by the electricity authority into the company's fuse box.

All wiring circuits in the house are fused. This includes a ring-main system which has a main circuit fuse for each ring as well as fused plugs. Fuse ratings are always given in amps. This indicates the maximum current it can sustain without failure.

New fuse systems use unpluggable, rewirable fuse carriers, or cartridge fuse carriers. Some employ earth-leakage detector, main-circuit breakers.

Older systems have wall-mounted rewireable fuses with unscrewable safety covers. With the old system it is possible to get at the fuse without switching off the supply, so great care must be exercised when replacing fuse wire, to make sure that the mains supply is switched off at the main fuse box.

With the new system the mains has to be switched off before the fuse cover can be removed.

There are three ratings of fuse wire used for rewiring fuses, and these can often be bought with the three types on one card. The thicker the wire, the higher its rating; these are always clearly marked.

The three types are:

● 5 amp, for lighting circuits;
● 15 amp, for heating circuits and
● 30 amp, for power circuits. The last is the one used for ring-main systems.

Always use the correct rating when rewiring a fuse. If a fuse persistently fails, then do not try rewiring with a higher rating. This condition indicates a fault in the circuit which must be corrected.

In a house which has a ring-main system, this only applies to the circuits carrying the three-pin wall-mounted sockets.

The lighting circuits are not part of the ring main, and are rewired using the 5A rating fuse wire.

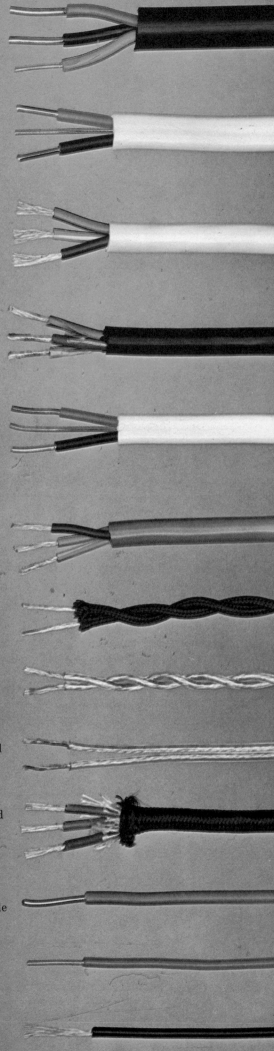

Hituf cable; power use. May be buried in the ground or beneath surfaces without conduiting

Power cable 2·5mm² twin-with-earth PVC: 600–1000V. Ring mains, power circuits

Heat-resisting PVC insulated and sheathed flexible cord; 300–500V. Immersion heaters and electric fires; check current rating

Rubber insulated and sheathed flexible cord; 300–500V. Portable appliances, power tools

Flat PVC insulated and sheathed wiring 1·5mm². Domestic lighting

PVC insulated and sheathed flexible cord; 300–500V. Portable appliances

Rubber insulated rayon-braided twisted flexible cord; 300–500 V. Light fittings

PVC insulated twin-twisted unsheathed flexible cord; 300–500V. Light fittings

PVC insulated parallel-twin unsheathed flexible cord. Rating and use as above

Rubber insulated circular rayon-braided flexible cord; 300–500V. Domestic appliances, standard lamps

PVC insulated unsheathed single-cord 2·5mm² cable; 600–1000V. Earthing cable

As above 1mm² domestic wiring (L)

As above ·75mm² domestic wiring (N)

A dimmer switch is neat and allows the light intensity to be reduced at will

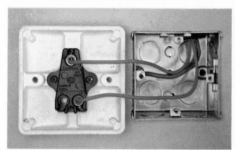

Detail wiring of a single-gang switch. An earth connection is made to metal box

A miniature circuit breaker (MCB). Below left are fuses for garage sub-circuit

The procedure for rewiring a fuse is as follows:

● Turn off the mains supply at the main switch. Turning off the switches which control the appliances does not isolate the mains at the fuse.

● Pull out the fuse carriers in turn to find the faulty one. This is indicated by broken or fused wire.

● Remove the broken wires, and clean the carrier. Often it is blackened by the burnt wire; these are carbon products which must be removed. Also make sure the screws that clamp the wire are clean.

● Rewire the carrier, using wire of the correct rating.

● Replace the fuse and close the fuse box before re-connecting the supply.

Standard fuse box with the fuse holders colour coded to show circuit loadings

You may notice that there is a fuse box in the mains supply before the meter. This is called the company fuse box which is sealed. It must not be opened.

If the fuses in this box go then someone from the electricity board must be called in to replace them. Opening the box yourself will incur a penalty.

Three-pin 13 amp plugs are available in 3A, 7A and 13A ratings. Thirteen-amp fuses are used for heating, 7A for electric drills and 3A for standard lamps and other lighting. Appliances to be wired in have literature indicating the fuse rating used with them. Food mixers and TV sets, for example, generally use 3A fuses.

TVs and amplifiers usually have their own fuses as well. Amplifier fuses can blow if speakers are short circuited. Also they blow because of switch-on surge. If an amplifier is fitted with anti-surge or

slow-blow fuses then they must be replaced with the same type. If the correct fuse is not used to replace a blown one, then it may not adequately protect an amplifier.

Wiring plugs

Leads fitted to equipment must now comply with modern colour coding system: brown-live, blue-neutral, green/yellow stripe-earth. This replaces the old system which was red-live, black-neutral, and green-earth.

On a three-pin plug with the cover removed, the earth pin is the larger of the three pins. The live is on the right-hand side of the plug, the neutral is the pin located on the left-hand side.

On a fused plug one of the fuse clips is on top of the live pin, the other carries the screw terminal to clamp the wire.

Do not use an old plug with a cracked plastic base or cover. When the wire has been fixed in, it must be clamped using the clamp and screws provided with the plug. This prevents strain on the wire at the terminals.

Some equipment is supplied with moulded two-pin plugs. This can be connected into a two-pin adaptor. First, make sure that the equipment has its own fuse. If not, remove the two-pin plug and wire it into a three-pin plug with a 3A fuse. In this case, the earth pin will not be used.

Do not overload a supply point by having a 'Christmas tree' of plugs, or connect equipment by poking wires into the socket.

If a three-pin system is used, heating appliances must be connected to the 15A plugs, and so on, lights to the 2A or 5A plugs.

When stripping wire prior to fixing a plug only remove enough insulation to fit in the terminal. Ideally a pair of wire strippers should be used. Make sure that the wire does not become nicked.

Wires should never be knotted to prevent them from pulling. This places undue strain on the insulation which can crack. Use the plug's cable clamp. If in doubt, buy a new plug.

Light in the home is usually taken for granted. The basic types of house lighting, using modern long-life cables, are the loop-in and junction box methods. The number of house-wiring circuits is partly a matter of convenience but also a question of load. Lighting circuits can offer convenience and versatility, with two- or multi-way switching arrangements.

Lighting wiring circuits follow two general patterns: the loop-in system, where power is taken in turn to ceiling roses, or by 5A junction boxes, from which each ceiling rose and wall switch is individually connected.

Let light into your life

Loading

Twin-with-earth 1mm² cable with a 6A rating should be used. This can be loaded up to 1400W. If heavier loads are used, then they must be sub-divided into smaller units and run from separate circuits. Normally, one circuit on each floor of an average house is sufficient.

Assuming an average consumption of 100W for every lighting outlet, the maximum number of lighting points for each 5A circuit is 11.

Earthing

The most important safety consideration is correct earthing–so that electricity, if a short circuit occurs, will direct itself safely to earth.

An earth-continuity conductor (ECC) in the cable should be run to all terminal points in a lighting circuit–ceiling roses and switches–whether these are insulated or not.

This ensures that an earthing point, which must be used for metal switch or lighting fittings, is available if later needed.

Earthing is essential to provide protection from faults, and all protective metal parts in a circuit must be earthed.

When a live part of the circuit comes into contact with an earthed part, the electricity is conducted away. This causes a fuse to blow, which indicates a fault.

The term 'consumer's earth terminal', indicates that connections are to a direct earthing point or an earth leakage circuit-breaker. This should be tested at intervals and also when any new wiring is carried out.

A simple circuit tester can be made using a torch battery and a bulb. Do not use this on live wires or on equipment which is plugged into the power supply; always switch off the supply before testing.

You need a panel of wood a little longer and wider than a standard torch battery. The battery can be clamped around this with rubber bands. Fit a bulb holder and bulb on to the panel and solder the live terminal of the battery to one side of the holder.

Attach a length of wire, with a probe or a crocodile clip at the end, to the other side of the holder. Similarly, attach a terminal to the other plate of the battery.

If the bulb lights when the probes are connected across the neutral and earth

points, this indicates an earth leak which must be corrected.

There is either a breakdown in cable insulation, causing wires to touch or a loose or incorrect connection at a switch or other terminal.

Conductors

House circuits have two supply conductors and an earth conductor. Of the supply conductors one is live (L). All fuses, switches or circuit breakers are placed in this lead. The other, neutral (N), is at, or near, earth potential. The third is the earth (E) lead.

No switches, fuses or circuit breakers should be placed in the neutral and earth leads Flexible cables are colour coded as follows:

 Brown–Live (L)
Blue–Neutral (N)
 Green/Yellow–Earth (E)

Fixed cables are coded:

Red–Live
Black–Neutral
Earth–Green or unsheathed

Always follow this code when wiring electrical circuits.

Fuses

All plugs must be protected by fuses which should be fitted into the live (brown flexible cable) side of the circuit. In fixed cables, the fuse is in the red cable.

You must use fuses of the correct current rating in the consumer unit as well as in plugs. Each lighting circuit must have its own fuse.

There are two types of fuse: the cart-

ridge and the re-wirable types. In some cases, fuses may be replaced by miniature circuit breakers (MCB) in the consumer units. The fuses must then be installed in control or distribution units.

Planning

Any re-wiring, or the extension of existing wiring, should be carefully planned so as to make the job as straightforward as possible.

Use twin-socket outlets and multiple switches where possible. This will make wiring and cable routing simpler.

In bathrooms, use only pull-cord switches. This is in the interest of safety. A wall switch may be fitted for the bathroom, provided it is outside the door.

Skirted lamp holders must be used where condensation is present, such as in bathrooms or kitchens.

Rose junctions

Rose junctions are used for both loop-in and junction box wiring. For loop-in wiring they must have four terminals.

In this case the switch wiring, the mains supply, and the bulb wiring all go directly to the rose junction. This means that all but the switch drop runs above the ceiling.

Junction boxes

A junction box (JB) is used for joining circuits, and is useful when extending existing wiring. It provides take-off points for the next light instead of the ceiling rose. This is also used for junction box wiring in conjunction with three-terminal ceiling roses. When planning wiring, it should become apparent which circuit is most suitable.

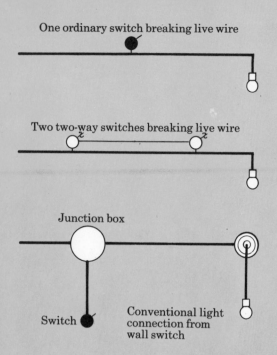

One ordinary switch breaking live wire

Two two-way switches breaking live wire

Junction box

Switch

Conventional light connection from wall switch

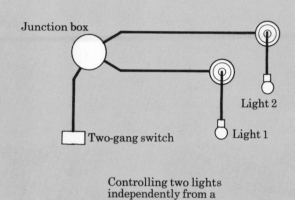

Junction box

Two-gang switch

Light 2

Light 1

Controlling two lights independently from a single two-way switch

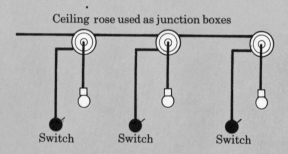

Ceiling rose used as junction boxes

Switch   Switch   Switch

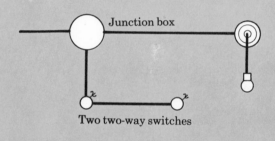

Junction box

Two two-way switches

Cables

There are several main methods of fixing cable: surface wiring, fixed with clips at short intervals; concealed wiring, through conduit tubing.

This tubing may be metal or nylon. When fitted inside metal conduit it must be earthed. The rating of cable when run through conduit is reduced. For the 6A cable it should be rated at 5A in conduit.

Cables which are to run across plaster surfaces may be concealed. This can be done by 'chasing' out the plaster with hammer and cold chisel to take the cable which must be conduited, unless it is a reinforced type such as Hituf. Once positioned the conduiting can be plastered over.

Cables may run freely in the roof space as long as they are slack and are resting on the roof surface or run along the sides of joists.

Wires must never be laid so that they are under tension, and in no circumstances should they be knotted.

The plastic insulation and sheathing on cables can be attacked by some wood preservatives. This may cause an electrical insulation failure leading to fire hazard. Always check that a preservative will not affect new or existing cables.

Surface wiring

Where cables are to be fixed to a surface, they may be secured with tinned copper or purpose-made plastic clips. Clips are available in various sizes and should be of a suitable diameter to enable easy fixing. These are fixed with brass pins or gimp pins.

Non-corroding clips must be used in damp conditions and clips of different metals should not touch each other, as this may cause electrolytic corrosion.

An example is where chrome and steel come in contact; the steel soon corrodes, as can often be seen on cars.

When fixing on brickwork, a wooden batten can be screwed to the wall, using wall-plugs. The wire is then secured to the batten with clips.

Alternatively, the wire can be fixed, using specially shaped PVC clips, with hardened steel fixing pins.

The batten need not necessarily be used on good brickwork as clips can be fixed in line with the mortar between courses.

PVC cable can be fixed at regular intervals with clips, to avoid loose sections of running cable. Plastic clips are neat and quick to use.

Bends in cables should not be less than three times the radius of the diameter.

If a shaped support is made for the bend the cable can be clipped to the support and allowed to hang freely from it. This is convenient when wiring in cavity walls.

Under-floor cables

When cables run under floorboards at right angles to the joists, holes should be drilled in the joists to route the cable. These must be fixed at a minimum of 50mm below the floorboards.

Cables running across the line of joists should never be laid in notches as these are too vulnerable in this position to accidental damage. It is better to keep holes through joists within the outer third of the joist span.

When wiring parallel with, or through joists, ensure that the fittings to be wired can be easily reached.

Raising floorboards

This presents no problem if the flooring is simple planks and an end is visible. Nails can be drawn out or punched down and the end of the board simply levered up.

The boards can then be supported and raised in turn.

If no board end is free, the position of a joist can be established by seeing where boards are nailed down. A hole can be

1 Junction box (one light)

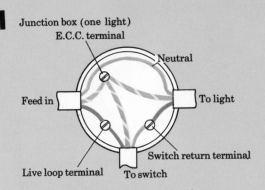

E.C.C. terminal
Neutral
Feed in
To light
Live loop terminal
To switch
Switch return terminal

2 Junction box (more than one light, individual switches)

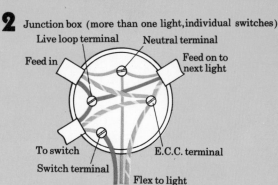

Live loop terminal
Neutral terminal
Feed in
Feed on to next light
To switch
E.C.C. terminal
Switch terminal
Flex to light

3 Junction box (two lights, one two-way switch)

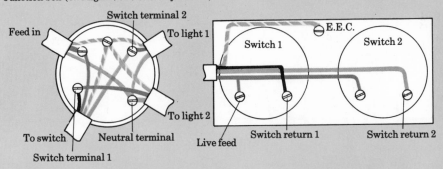

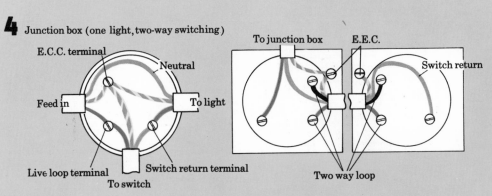

Switch terminal 2
Feed in
To light 1
E.E.C.
Switch 1
Switch 2
To light 2
To switch
Neutral terminal
Live feed
Switch return 1
Switch return 2
Switch terminal 1

Code

	Live conductor
	Neutral conductor
	Second neutral conductor in four-core wire
	Earth continuity conductor (E.C.C.)

4 Junction box (one light, two-way switching)

E.C.C. terminal
Neutral
Feed in
To light
Live loop terminal
Switch return terminal
To switch

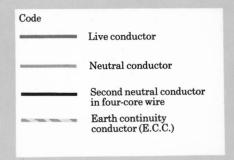

To junction box
E.E.C.
Switch return
Two way loop

---

drilled in the board and a key-hole saw inserted to cut through the board beside the joist.

When the board is replaced the cut end should be supported by a timber nogging.

With tongued-and-grooved boards the tongue may have to be sawn off so that the board can be raised.

If junction boxes or other fittings have been used under floorboards, ensure that future access is possible.

Wiring a switch

Twin-with-earth cable must be used from the junction box or rose junction. The red wire goes to live (L), the black (N) to the switched side of the lamp and the green or bare to earth (E). This cable is taken to the switch through the knock-out hole in the metal switch box.

Cable should be protected from sharp edges at entry to the metal box by means of a rubber bush.

The red and black wires are connected to each side of the switch, and the earth wire is clamped to the metal box with a screw.

For a two-way switch, a fourth wire is necessary. Ensure that all wires are double insulated, possessing both an inner cover and a sheath. Three-core-and-earth cable can be used.

Methods of wiring lights
Lamps in parallel

These may be fitted in large rooms or long passages where more than one light is wired on the same circuit. In this case, a rose junction can be used, so that the lamp terminals of one fitting can be connected to the next.

Two-way switching

This facility is one where a single lamp can be independently controlled from two different points. Single-pole, two-way switches, have to be used. Two-way switching is most commonly used for landing lights, exterior lights, and bedroom lights where one switch is over the bed.

Wiring circuit is shown in Fig. 4. All other wiring necessary usually already exists.

To add this facility to a bedroom, a cord-operated, two-way ceiling-mounted, pull-cord switch can be installed above a bed. This greatly reduces the amount of re-wiring necessary.

Intermediate switching

Intermediate two-way switching is useful for houses having two landings, for long corridors, or rooms having three entrance doors and so on.

The circuit is an extension of that shown in Fig. 4.

The intermediate switch has four connections. Two of these are poles and switch alternately between the other two connections. A normal two-way switch will not work in this position.

An indefinite number of intermediate switches can be used in this way. Take care to wire these switches correctly.

Dimming lights

The intensity of a light or lights may be reduced by means of a dimmer switch. These must be mounted in a metal wall box to avoid possible interference with radio and TV equipment.

Dimmer switches use solid-state (transistorized) circuitry to provide progressive dimming by rotating the switch. They are very efficient – and the light level selected is also related to the cost of running. In addition, dimmers may reduce the initial surge on bulbs and extend their life.

Drill speed controllers work on a different principle and will not provide a graduated dimming of light. Conversely, lamp dimmers will not work effectively as drill speed controllers.

The amperage rating given for the dimmer must never be exceeded or the unit may be damaged.

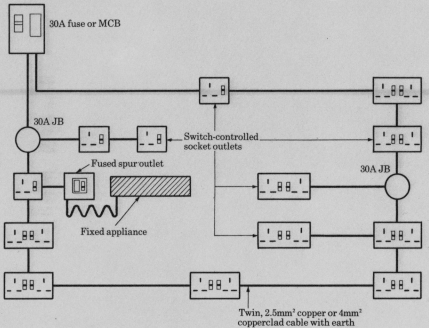

30A fuse or MCB

30A JB

Switch-controlled
socket outlets

Fused spur outlet

30A JB

Fixed appliance

Twin, 2.5mm² copper or 4mm²
copperclad cable with earth

Ring circuit with non-fused spurs
supplying an area of not more than 100m²

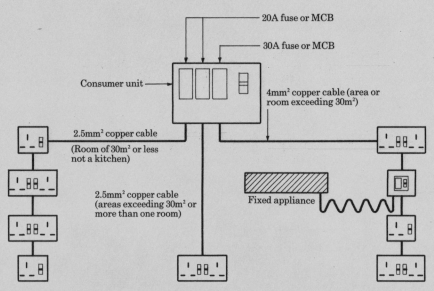

20A fuse or MCB

30A fuse or MCB

Consumer unit

4mm² copper cable (area or
room exceeding 30m²)

2.5mm² copper cable

(Room of 30m² or less
not a kitchen)

2.5mm² copper cable
(areas exceeding 30m² or
more than one room)

Fixed appliance

Radial circuits may be used where the demand is
either unusually high or unusually consistent.
They may be used for extensions and conversions,
or you may run a spur from a ring main.

**Power can be used indoors and out-
doors. The modern ring-main circuit
distributes the load on an electrical
circuit at any one time. For the average household, two circuits provide a
convenient arrangement. Outdoor
lighting and power can serve garage or
greenhouse, as well as garden lighting
and pumps for garden pools.**

Outdoor lighting
For an outdoor light, such as a porch,
wire to any fitting on the house wall
should consist of 1·0mm², twin-with-earth
cable. The earth, neutral and live points
should be connected up at a convenient
junction box or ceiling rose.

While in older circuits there may be
no earth wire, the outside lamp must be
earthed, and a separate earth continuity
conductor may be used.

The lamp fitting should be a fully
weatherproof type if it is to be in an exposed
position. If so, it must be enclosed in a
globe which seals on to a rubber gasket.
The neutral and live are taken to the
bulb holder, in the normal way, and the
lamp frame is earthed.

Outdoor wiring
A grade of cable with an approved plastic
insulated covering, such as PVC, PCP or
CSP, must be used for outdoor wiring.

Non-corrosive cable clips should be
used. If possible, avoid clipping cables to
render or similar surfaces. Wiring to a
detached garage or shed may be routed
underground or overhead.

Cables should not be run along fencing
or railings.

Overhead wiring
The cable may be run in conduit or suspended from a wire which takes its weight.

Heights should be 5·2m above the
ground if any vehicles pass beneath,
3·5m for suspended wiring and 3·0m for
conduit wiring.

Conduit can be used for spans of up to

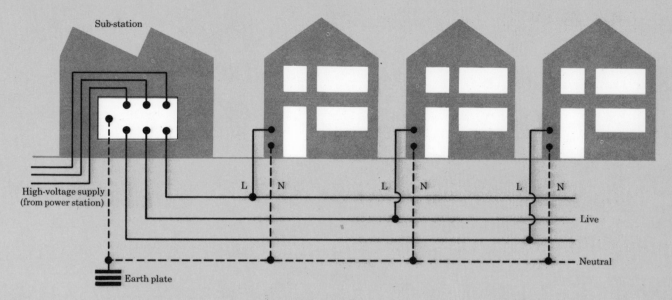

Sub-station

High-voltage supply
(from power station)

Earth plate

L N   L N   L N

Live

Neutral

How electricity is distributed

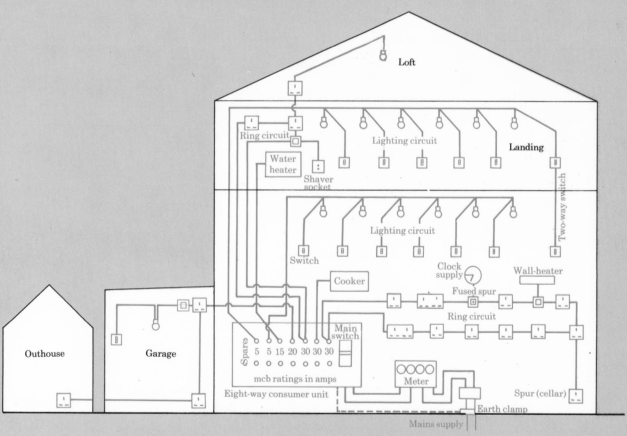

Loft

Ring circuit

Water
heater

Shaver
socket

Lighting circuit

Landing

Two-way switch

Lighting circuit

Switch

Cooker

Clock
supply

Wall-heater

Fused spur

Ring circuit

Main
switch

Outhouse

Garage

Spare

5 5 15 20 30 30 30

mcb ratings in amps

Eight-way consumer unit

Meter

Spur (cellar)

Earth clamp

Mains supply

Typical house-wiring

3·0m; for longer spans a supporting wire should be used.

Holes should be replugged with mortar to minimize the risk of fire spreading and to keep out rain. Similarly, where wire emerges from the conduit, if outside, this should be plugged with a proprietary weather-proof sealing compound.

Where a supporting wire is to be used, it should be 'strained' between strong fixing points, The cable is then fixed by clips to the wire. Clips can be spaced at 460mm centres. In this way no strain is imposed on the cable.

Where cables are led round at angles, the inner radius must be at least eight times the cable diameter.

Underground wiring
Underground wiring is often more convenient when wiring a greenhouse or an outhouse some distance from the main building. Mineral-insulated copper-covered cable, Hituf cable or armoured cable are generally used, though PVC is suitable in many cases.

The cable should be laid in a trench 500mm deep so that it will not be disturbed when digging. The soil that covers it should be free from flints. To make sure of this, the first 75mm depth of soil cover should be sifted to remove all the stones. Cable should have a protective cover of stout tiles or be run buried in galvanized-steel conduit.

The supply must not connect directly to the mains in the house but must go through its own switched fuse box. This is because you must be able to isolate external circuits independently of the house circuits.

The use of 4·0mm² cable is advisable on long runs carrying high loads, to minimize voltage drop. A 2·5mm rating can be used if loadings are only to be small.

In the greenhouse the cable must be connected to a mains switch and fuse unit, mounted about 1500mm above the ground. Greenhouse and garden circuits can be wired from this.

For outhouses and garages a ring circuit can be used.

Garden equipment

Pumps for fountains or waterfall effects are run from the standard mains supply. These units are fully protected against corrosion. Cables supplying these should be of the armoured or Hituf variety connected to the pump's lead with a weatherproof cable connector.

Pumps that are immersed in water should be of low voltage. These are run from a double-wound transformer to isolate the mains and provide the lower safer voltage. The transformer may be in an outhouse under cover.

Pumps should not be operated unless water is in the pumping system to prevent possible damage.

Garden lamps should be of the fully weatherproof variety which are supplied with a mounting spike (which also earths them) and a length of three-core double-insulated cable.

The number of lamps which can run off a connection to a lighting circuit or a 2A socket outlet is three.

Where lamps are required to be submerged in pools, then a 12V or 24V waterproof type with the appropriate transformer should be used.

If permanent lighting is required, avoid continuous operation, which can lead to overheating.

Where temporary leads are run outside the home for drills, lawn mowers and other appliances, all cable fittings, such as plugs and sockets, should be of a weatherproof pattern. However, use, where possible, a long lead with no joints.

Ring mains

Many houses have electrical circuits which are inadequate for present-day demands. Many older homes were designed when electrical appliances that are in wide use today were not available.

If your power wiring is overloaded and inadequate, rather than trying to modify it, it is better to rip the whole lot out and install a ring main, now the standard method of wiring domestic power circuits.

A ring main is a circuit which starts and finishes at the consumer unit. Flat three-pin 13A plugs and sockets are used.

Planning

Before installation, the siting of sockets should be planned. First, you can have a ring circuit supplying up to 100m² of floor area. This gives a combined wattage of 7·2kW. Using the 'T in a saucer' diagram this gives:

$$\frac{\text{Watts} \qquad 6500}{\text{mains voltage} \quad 240} \quad \text{about 28A.}$$

If the floor area of your home is, say, 170m² you will need at least two ring circuits.

Each circuit will need its own 30A fuse, so a new consumer unit will have to be fitted, preferably on a new board.

When siting two ring-main circuits, the loading should be equally distributed on both. While you can have an unlimited number of sockets on a ring main, what is important is the loading of appliances actually plugged in at one time.

Wattage can be calculated by multiplying voltage by current. Since AC mains are about 240V, if an appliance draws 10A, then its wattage is 240 × 10 = 2400 watts or 2·4kW.

Conversely, if an appliance is rated at 2·4kW, you know that it will draw 10A, and, therefore, must have a 13A fuse to protect it.

Using this formula you can calculate what loading will be expected on a circuit,

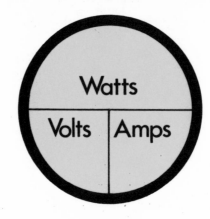

and the fuse that should be used to protect the appliance. Lamps drawing about 150W need a 3A fuse. TV sets, and, particularly, colour receivers, should be fitted with 13A fuses.

Toasters, irons and single bar fires draw about 1kW and need a 13A fuse; three-bar heaters and high-speed kettles draw about 3kW and need 13A fuses.

When planning a ring main, do not skimp on the number of sockets you install; it is easier to put them in when you do the job, and parts are not costly.

Fused spurs

Sometimes it will be inconvenient to run a ring circuit to some points, for example, a socket in the loft for a lead lamp. For these applications, a fused spur can be used.

Each spur can have up to two sockets on it and two separate sockets or a double one can be used.

The number of spur sockets must not exceed the number of sockets on a ring circuit.

Waste eliminators

Some items, like waste eliminators, are permanently fixed into position, and, therefore, do not need a plug and a socket.

In this case, a fused spur is used to connect them into the ring main. The fuse rating can be calculated from the formula. Only one appliance may be connected to one spur.

An electric clock is a low-current device and is wired in using a special 1A fused clock connector.

Other appliances

Electric cookers and immersion heaters

are not wired into the ring main if they exceed 3kW, the maximum load that can be connected to a fused spur.

A cooker is usually about 8kW and, thus, is wired independently to a 45A fuse at the consumer unit. The appliance is also wired through a control switch outlet situated near the appliance. Heat-resistant cable should be used when connecting cookers or immersion heaters to their outlets.

Cable

The cable used for wiring a ring main must be of a rating suitable for the loading to be imposed on it, otherwise it may overheat. The type used is 2·5mm² twin-conductor-with-earth insulated-and-sheathed cable.

Some types have a red live wire, a black neutral wire and a green or unsheathed earth wire.

New cable, consisting of a live, sheathed wire and two unsheathed wires, the negative and the earth, called combined negative earth, (CNE), is coming into use. The unsheathed wires are bonded (joined) at switch and appliance. Wires are sheathed in PVC.

Cable supplying the consumer unit from the meter should be 16mm².

You may mount a wall radiant heater in a bathroom as long as it is out of reach and is operated by a pull cord switch. No portable electrical appliance should ever be used in a bathroom.

Socket outlets

Socket outlets should be placed to avoid trailing flexes and use of multiple adaptors. A suggested minimum number of positions is: Kitchen, four; living area, three; dining area, two; bedroom, two; hall and landing, garage (where integrated with the house), store or workroom, one each.

Use switched outlet sockets with indicator neons for preference, particularly where there are children.

Radial circuits

A radial circuit is a single-cable, installation, independent of the ring main, taken from the consumer unit or through a fuse.

This may serve one room of less than 30m² in area, and supply up to six single or three double 13A outlets. It may not be used in a kitchen, which may contain high-wattage appliances.

The circuit, in twin 2·5mm² cable, with earth, must be protected by a 20A fuse or MCB, is limited to two single, one double, or to two fused spurs for fixed appliances.

With a room of more than 30m² in area, 4mm² cable should be used, protected by a 30A fuse or MCB. Up to six 13A outlets may be used for fixed appliances.

Installation

All installation wiring is the same as described for lighting. Surface wiring and underfloor cabling follow the same rules, and earthed metal wall boxes must be used to mount the sockets.

Sockets should be fitted at least 180mm above the floor.

Plumbing: the domestic scene

Much domestic plumbing work is a matter of improvement and updating – the removal of festoons of ancient lead or iron pipework and its replacement by neat copper, stainless-steel or plastic piping.

Modernizing a plumbing system may suggest improvements in the layouts of the bathroom and kitchen, or the provision of extra facilities, such as a downstairs cloakroom.

Major additions, such as a utility room, may also fit in with updating and call for extension to the plumbing and domestic hot-water systems.

Labour-saving devices in the kitchen, such as a washing machine, water heater, waste-disposal unit or dishwasher; or, in the bathroom, water heaters, showers or bidets, all require various degrees of adaption to existing plumbing.

Before you carry out any major re-plumbing work, it is necessary to get approval from your local authority. This does not apply to routine jobs such as replacing a cracked wash hand basin or replacing or rewashering taps.

With major replumbing work, it is necessary to submit a drawing of the proposed changes, together with details of the existing layout. This must show all the detail, down to stopcocks and valves.

In the case of a bungalow, you need only provide a simple plan drawing, but, for a house, the full elevations must be shown. It is not necessary to produce these drawings to high architectural standards – the rule is that they must be accurate, clear and intelligible.

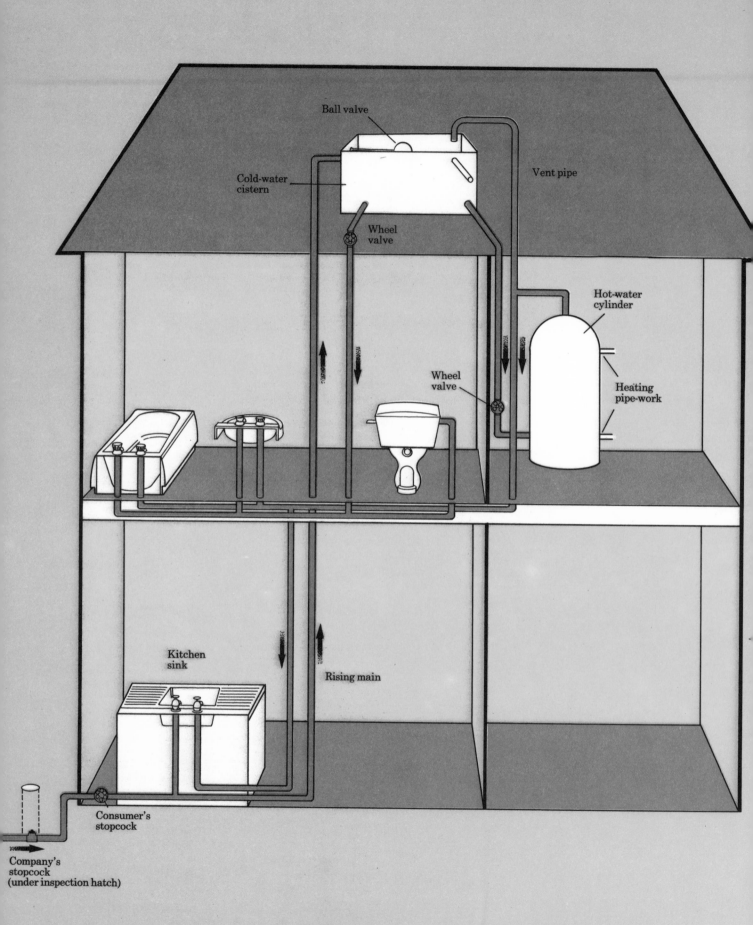

Ball valve

Cold-water
cistern

Vent pipe

Wheel
valve

Hot-water
cylinder

Wheel
valve

Heating
pipe-work

Kitchen
sink

Rising main

Consumer's
stopcock

Company's
stopcock
(under inspection hatch)

A typical indirect water
supply to a house.
There is one direct tap
—the cold tap at the kitchen sink

Approval

One also needs to comply with the byelaws of the local water authority. These will meet model water-board requirements, subject to local circumstances, and a copy of the local water authority's rules should also be carefully studied. It is also a good plan to have a word with the local council to get advice on its requirements.

Once you have received the go-ahead to do the work, plan your work programme carefully. In particular, take care to ensure that any work you do does not rob the household of water for a long period of time. Where possible, carry out the work in definite, planned stages, and make as much advanced preparation as possible, by cutting and pre-assembling pipework and fittings.

Our dependence on water is very great and illustrated by the amount of daily consumption. In an average town, each person uses an estimated 910 litres. A bath takes around 90 litres, washing uses 25 litres, and even washing of hands accounts for seven litres. If we take industrial use into account, there is an enormous consumption of thousands of millions of litres each day.

It, therefore, makes sense that plumbing services should be well installed and not lead to waste. Faulty overflows and dripping taps cumulatively mean waste losses.

Domestic storage

Modern domestic water services are based on provision of a cold-water storage cistern, usually placed in the loft. The size of cistern, usually of between 230 litres to 365 litres capacity, depends on the needs of the household. A family of four requires a minimum capacity of 230 litres.

The storage cistern is there to balance, at any one time, the load on the mains supply in the district. For example, if a group of households were together to draw off a large amount of water, this could lead to a possible loss of mains pressure. As the storage cistern can only recharge at an even rate, and serves most of the household needs, this ensures that there can be no excess burden on the mains.

This system utilising loft storage is known as the 'indirect system'. Older, direct-to-tap systems, known as the 'direct system' are not now usual.

The main advantage of the indirect system is that it provides a reservoir of water, even if there is a break in supply, or the water has to be shut off. Also, mains supply comes in at a very high pressure and causes more wear on pipe bores and fittings and is more likely to produce 'water hammer', a noisy vibration of pipework.

As nearly all the internal services are served from the storage cistern at low pressure, there is little likelihood of noise or wear. The main basic service which may be supplied directly from the rising main is the kitchen, providing a source of fresh, non-storage water at the cold-water tap.

The consumer's responsibility for the domestic service starts beyond the company stopcock, usually located in the pavement outside the home. Because the access points can get covered in during pavement resurfacing or other work, it is a good idea to provide your own stop-cock just inside the premises if it is at any time necessary to shut down the supply to the home.

Rising main

The supply pipe to the house from the company stopcock should be buried deeply enough in the ground to be clear of damage from garden implements and also be below what is called the 'frost line'–a depth of 460mm. The supply in the home is called the 'rising main' and is usually provided by a pipe of 15mm bore, unless the house is rather larger than average or if you live in a low-pressure area, where a 22mm-bore pipe may be needed.

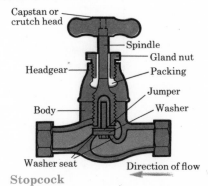

Capstan or crutch head — Spindle — Gland nut — Packing — Jumper — Washer

Headgear

Body

Washer seat — Direction of flow

Stopcock

A stopcock should also be fitted into the rising main just inside the home. A common position is beneath the kitchen sink. Wherever it is fitted, it should be accessible so that water can be turned off quickly in an emergency.

The stopcock is known as a non-return valve, which means that water can flow in only one direction; this is marked on the body of the stopcock with an arrow. It is important to fit this in the correct position, or water will not flow.

To avoid any possibility of pollution, there must be no prospect of back-flow to the mains from the domestic system, hence the non-return function of the stopcock.

After supplying the kitchen sink, the rising main should be taken by the most direct route possible to supply the storage cistern. In most modern plumbing systems, domestic hot-water needs are met from a hot-water cylinder, which may be heated in a variety of ways. Draw-off hot water is replenished from the storage cistern in the loft.

This cistern must be capable of being drained down faster than it can be filled, so that it can in no circumstances overflow. Supply to the cistern and to toilets is controlled by a ball valve, in which a plastic or copper airtight ball floats on the water (called a float) and rises with the water to lift an arm controlling an inlet valve. The arm is capable of some adjustment to set the level of water.

Cisterns must also be fitted with overflows, the outlets of which should be located in a prominent position outside the house to give an 'early warning' of trouble.

Shut-off or gate valves should be incorporated into the plumbing circuit so that, in particular, the cistern and the supply to the hot cylinder can be isolated where necessary.

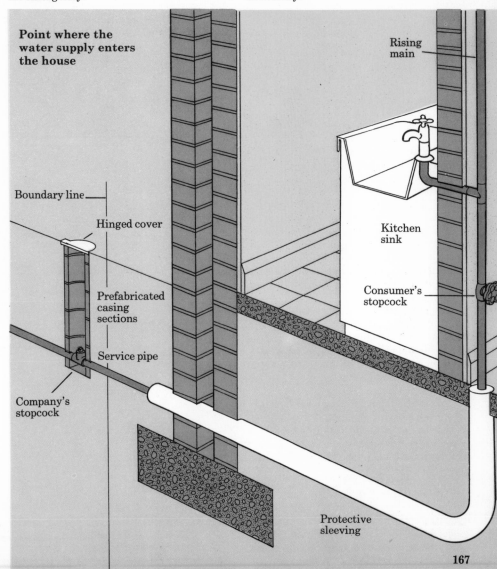

Point where the water supply enters the house

Rising main

Boundary line

Hinged cover

Kitchen sink

Consumer's stopcock

Prefabricated casing sections

Service pipe

Company's stopcock

Protective sleeving

Drainage

The other essential half of the plumbing system is drainage. This falls into two categories–that above and that below ground. The system above ground consists of pipework from sinks, WC's, baths and gutters. Below ground, the services are known collectively as 'drains'.

Traps, which act as water seals, are fitted to outlets going into the drainage system; these prevent foul sewage air from percolating the home. Traps consist of two types–tubular and bottle; these are made in shallow-seal and deep-seal versions for differing circumstances. Traps have a tubular plug or a detachable bottle to facilitate the removal of any blockages.

WC pans have one or two types of trap–the 'p' or the 's' trap, roughly resembling these letters. The type used depends on whether the outlet connection is through the floor or goes through a wall. Left-hand and right-hand wall and back-wall exits are made.

Traps known as trapped yard gullies are used to connect kitchen and bath waste outlets to the main drainage and have a 'u' bend to provide the water seal.

Under modern building regulations main pipes, normally with a diameter of 102mm, which connect baths, toilets and basins, to the drains must be located inside the house structure. This presents a less unsightly exterior appearance but was introduced as a safeguard against freezing up in cold weather.

As water seals prevent noxious gases from entering the home, they have to be vented to the atmosphere. This is provided through a vent pipe positioned about 1m above the highest window in the home or where there is no likelihood of permeation of smells.

One-pipe and two-pipe systems

In older homes, a two-pipe drainage system, consisting of separate disposal for foul water and waste water, is common. Waste water is usually drained into a hopper and then to a trapped yard gulley into the main drainage.

Modern systems use a single pipe and nearly all services of waste and foul water are directly connected to this stack pipe by means of branch fittings. Exceptions are for the kitchen waste, draining to a trapped yard gulley, and in the case, for example, of a cloakroom on the other side of the house, which would have separate branch drainage.

One-pipe, single-stack systems reduce the amount of pipework used, saving both time and money. One possible problem is that of siphonage, where the use of one appliance sucks the water seal from the trap of another, allowing foul air to penetrate the home.

This can be caused if two services are connected to a single outlet joined, in turn, to the stack in a one-pipe system. This, however, is a practice to be avoided; each connection should be made separately and directly to the stack.

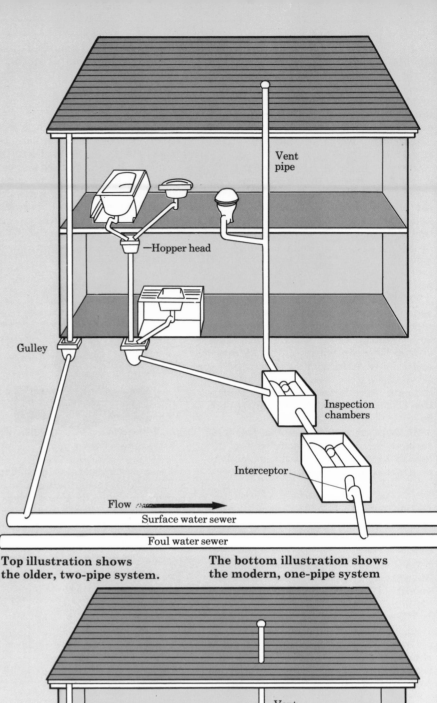

Vent pipe

Hopper head

Gulley

Inspection chambers

Interceptor

Flow

Surface water sewer

Foul water sewer

Top illustration shows the older, two-pipe system.

The bottom illustration shows the modern, one-pipe system

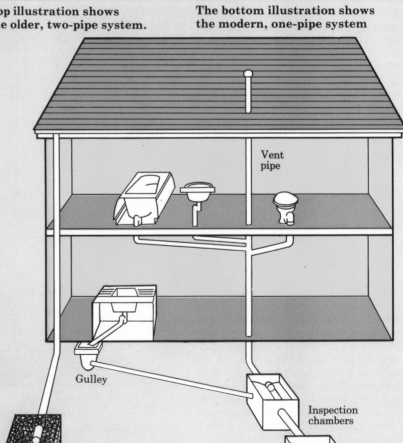

Vent pipe

Gulley

Soakaway

Inspection chambers

Flow

Sewer

New look for old systems

Old plumbing may not only be in-efficient–it can also be dangerous. Constricted and heavily scaled hot-water circuitry could burst, causing possible injury from very hot water, or vast damage could result from a cas-cade of water, spoiling the fabric and furnishings of the home. Plan carefully any updating of your plumbing to limit dislocation of the household.

Aesthetically, festoons of leaded pipe-work in bathroom or kitchen are in no way attractive. This pipework may also have deteriorated and be in need of replace-ment. However, even old lead has a capital value and can be sold.

Where there are old direct heating systems, fired by a kitchen boiler, pipe-work is heavily scaled internally and the flow of water is, consequently, constricted. This can be dangerous, for very hot water can be under great pressure in old pipe-work which may easily fracture and cause scalding.

Heating arrangements, in older systems, may be linked with an outdated galvanised hot-water tank. Greater reli-ability and efficiency will be achieved by replacing this with a modern copper cylinder.

In fact, plans for modernising heating may well run parallel with the full re-plumbing of a home.

The materials available in modern plumbing provide a wide choice and give scope for improvement. Also the life cycle of modern materials is greatly in excess of many older ones.

The main materials used in modern domestic plumbing are copper, stainless steel and various plastics, including glass-reinforced plastics (GRP), otherwise glass fibre.

Copper is now widely used in place of lead and galvanized mild steel in plumbing work. Plastics are rapidly gaining ground in the situations where these are accept-able, and can be simpler and cheaper to fit than traditional metal plumbing. Plastic pipe, however, cannot be used for hot-water supply.

Tools
There are a small number of tools and items of equipment needed for any plumbing work.

Hacksaws and rotary cutters
Pipes can be cut either with a hacksaw or a rotary pipe cutter. The standard hacksaw is either 255mm or 305mm long. Some can be adjusted up or down in size.

When cutting soft copper, low-tungsten steel blades can be used. With stainless steel, more durable but more expensive high-speed steel blades are used. For pipe over 15mm, a blade with 22 or, preferably, 32 teeth to each 25mm should be used. A junior hacksaw can be employed for most pipe cutting and has the advantage that it can cut in awkward places more readily than can larger hacksaws.

Blades should be fitted with the teeth pointing away from the handle. An arrow on the blade indicates the direction of fitting. Adjust the wing nut to take up the slack in the blade and then apply just three full turns.

Pipe should be firmly secured. When cutting, use a long, steady stroke at a rate of about one stroke per second for low-tungsten blades and about 70 per minute for high-speed steel. Release pressure on the return stroke. Never start a new blade in an old cut, or this may fracture the blade. Cut the tube straight across, and never at an angle, for this would produce an inadequate joint.

Support the pipe adequately on either side when cutting tube, to avoid distortion.

A rotary pipe cutter cuts both fast and

accurately. If any large amount of cutting has to be done, this is a good investment. There are two main types of rotary cutter–one with two rollers and a cutter and the other with three cutters. Rotary cutters possess three toughened wheels, one of them the cutting wheel, mounted on a frame, forming a triangle.

These can be used on various sizes of pipe. The cutting wheel is mounted on a threaded spindle to provide adjustment to suit the pipe. The cutting is performed by rotating and gradually tightening the spindle to deepen the cut until the pipe is cut through.

Files
A flat and a round file are needed, depend-ent on whether or not you are using a hacksaw or a rotary pipe cutter. The pipe cutter also possesses a device at the end to remove burrs from the pipe. If left, these could cause turbulence and impede the flow of water in the pipe.

After using a hacksaw to cut pipe, run the flat file across the face of the cut, to remove any irregularities and then slightly chamfer the outer pipe ends; this will make it easier to connect fittings.

The pipe cutter puts a slight bevel on the cut, so there is no need to apply a bevel where this has been used. Use the round file to remove burrs from inside the mouth of the pipe after cutting with a hacksaw.

Spanners
Two adjustable spanners are needed to tighten fittings. The most suitable general sizes are either 255mm or 350mm long. Where heavily rusted iron pipe fittings

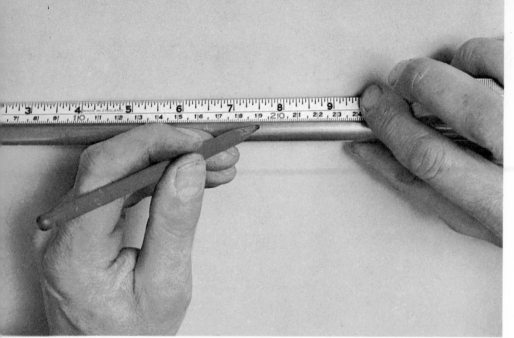

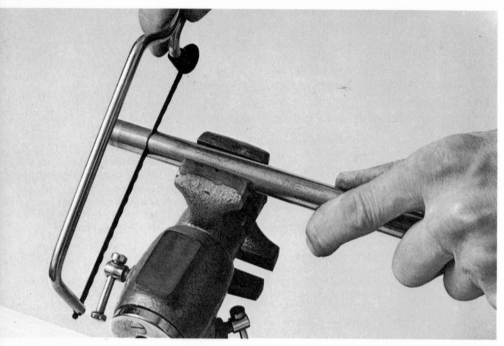

Measure carefully the length of pipe; allow extra tube for entry to fitting

Pipe should be cut squarely with fine-toothed hacksaw. Use protective vice jaws

A wheel cutter is another way of cutting tube. This is rotated around the pipe

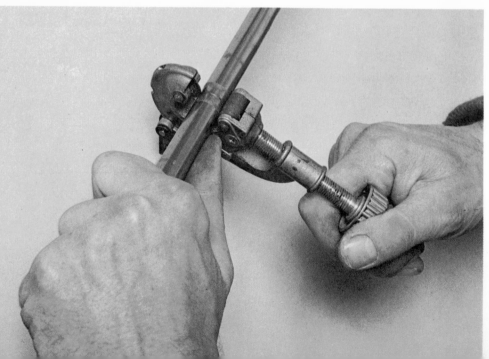

have to be removed, a pair of Stillson wrenches might be needed.

These enable you to clamp securely on one side of the pipe, while manipulating the other section of pipe with the other spanner.

Bending springs and pipe benders

Bending springs, or a bending machine, which can be bought or hired, are the best methods of bending pipe. Small fittings, such as 15mm elbows, should be used sparingly, as water turbulence and pressure loss can result at such joints.

Bending springs consist of a piece of tough coiled spring steel which is inserted into the pipe, with the middle of the spring roughly corresponding with the point of bend.

An eye is provided at the top of the spring to which a piece of wire or nylon cord can be attached to facilitate its removal. A screwdriver can be inserted into the eye and turned, in order to 'unscrew' a tight spring.

To bend pipe, insert the spring into the tube and bend the pipe against the knee with an even pressure. If you over-bend the pipe slightly and then unbend it, the spring should then be easy to remove.

A bending machine makes bending pipe even easier, and tighter and more precise bends are possible. These do not employ springs, but use formers, called 'slippers', or shoes. These shoes are half rounded and, when in position, encircle one half of the tube. The former is also half rounded, so that the tube is encircled during bending, to prevent it from kinking.

The action of bending is achieved by a handle which pulls the shoe around the appropriate former – 15mm, 22mm or 28mm – to form the bend. This former is in the form of a radius bend.

A useful device you can make for a spring is an extension which eliminates waste of tube. It is difficult to contain a short end to less than 150mm or 200mm because anything below this leaves little hand hold. Where a short tail is required, wastage of up to 150mm of tube can occur.

To make this, obtain a 300mm length of tube of the same diameter as that being used and a straight connector compression fitting, from which you file out the centre ridge or stop. Attach the fitting securely to one end of the tube.

This extension bar enables a bend with a tail of only 75mm to 100mm. Slide the spring through the bar and fitting and then into the tube awaiting bending. Lightly tighten the loose end of the straight connector and it will then be rigid enough to make the small-tailed bend.

Other items you may need, which depend on the types of fitting used, are a blow torch, plumbing lead, a 'mole', tallow, solder, flux and fine wire wool.

Lightweight vice

A lightweight portable engineering vice with fibre jaws or a pipe vice would be useful. You can hold lengths of pipe in its jaws, without damage, during cutting. Never overtighten the jaws of vices as this may distort the pipe.

Blow torch

A blow torch, such as a butane-gas one,

is needed for any soldering work. There are two types of blow torch–those with an exchange cannister, for which you obtain a refill, and the throw-away replaceable type. Professional blow torches have large cannisters, connecting the torch head by a piece of flexible pipe. These are a worthwhile investment if you have any volume of work.

Other pipework

Lead and galvanized-steel pipework, found in older houses, needs special skills to join and manipulate. Joining the old to modern metals may not produce altogether satisfactory results.

Where galvanized pipe is connected to copper pipework, corrosion problems can arise. This is likely to occur in hard-water areas, where there is danger of electrolytic corrosion taking place if these two metals are joined, as this sets up a chemical re-action. A special fitting has to be used to separate galvanised and copper pipes.

Old pipework is often heavily scaled or calcinated which impedes the flow of water.

Heat or penetrating oil may be needed to remove stubborn fittings, but heat will only be effective where water has been fully drained from the pipes.

An easier way, with stubborn joints, is to saw through the pipe on either side of old fittings.

Steel barrel pipework is still used in some cases but requires the use of stocks and dies in order to join sections together. A set of dies is relatively costly to buy but can be hired. Barrel pipe is relatively cheap compared with copper or stainless steel, and is sometimes used to provide gas services to domestic appliances.

To manipulate steel barrel pipe, you need a firm bench, with a heavily anchored pipe vice or an engineer's vice with fibre jaws. It also needs a fair amount of physical strength to cut threads on this type of pipe. A metal lubricant should be used to ease the cutting operation.

Copper and stainless-steel tube

Copper plumbing tube is of the light-gauge hard-temper type, known as Table III tube. Bending springs used have to correspond with the gauge of tube. A thicker tube called Table I, while of the same inner diameter, can only be bent using a Table I spring. For stainless-steel pipe use a Table III spring.

These are the metric equivalents of pipe of imperial gauge, with measurements shown for the outside diameter (OD) of the pipe.

$\frac{3}{8}$in $\frac{1}{2}$in $\frac{3}{4}$in 1in 1$\frac{1}{4}$in 1$\frac{1}{2}$in 2in
10mm 15mm 22mm 28mm 35mm 42mm 54mm

The following sizes are interchangeable without modification:

$\frac{3}{8}$in $\frac{1}{2}$in 1in 2in
10mm 15mm 28mm 54mm

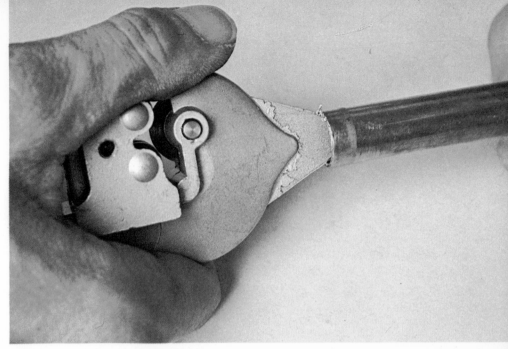
Burrs can be removed with the pipe-trimming blade at the end of some makes

Where pipe is cut with a hacksaw, remove burrs from the inside with a round file

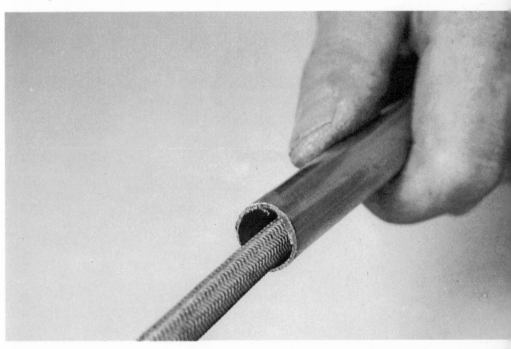
The outside of the tube should also be cleaned with a file and the ends squared

The way to make good connections

Top left: end feed fitting
Top right: capillary fitting
Bottom: compression fitting

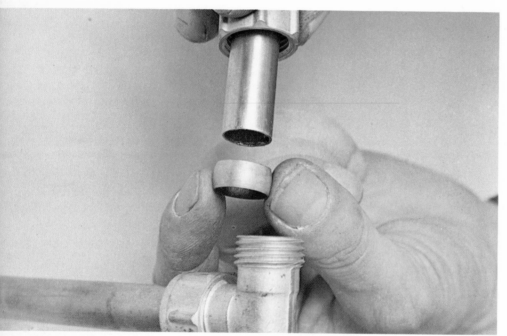

Brass cone or olive is used to seal joint on compression fitting when tightened

A smear of jointing compound may be used to consolidate a compression joint

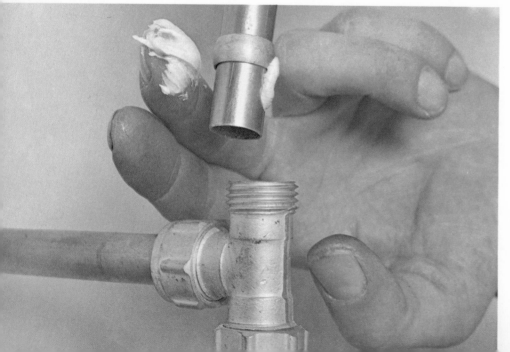

'Making the right connections' is vital where plumbing is concerned. There is a wide range of fittings to meet every situation likely to be encountered in fitting domestic pipework–though there are cases where it may be advisable to bend the pipe mechanically. Modern fittings are simple to use.

There are five situations where you may need to use a plumbing fitting. These are where it is necessary to join two lengths of pipe in a straight line; to allow the introduction of a branch connection; to facilitate a change of direction; to control the flow of water, either mechanically or automatically; and to release air or drain-off water.

Because of the high cost of fittings, and since these are a possible source of flow resistance and turbulence, use of fittings should be avoided if a mechanical bend–either using a spring or pipe-bending machine–can produce the same result.

A change of direction may also influence the water-flow characteristics. A tight bend may disrupt the smooth, forward impetus of water. For this reason, sharp changes of direction should be avoided.

In some cases a bent coupling or elbow may have to be used in tight spaces. It is always advisable to use, where possible, the slow-bend type of fitting. This fitting, with its larger radius, reduces the breaking force which is exerted in changes of flow.

Other larger-radius fittings which help to maintain this uninterrupted flow pattern are the sweep tee and the curved tee.

Flow resistance can be created by the careless use of jointing materials, such as non-toxic plumbing compound, used to consolidate joints, hemp and PTFE tape. The latter has tended to supersede hemp and jointing compound as a means of sealing threaded joints against leaks.

Such materials can easily creep past the pipe ends and form an obstruction and cause turbulence. The removal of burrs from pipe ends is equally important.

Choice of connectors

There are two types of pipe connectors: the compression fitting and the capillary fitting. These break down into two further types, the manipulative and non-manipulative compression fitting. Solder fittings are either pre-soldered or of the unsoldered, end-feed type.

The choice is governed by various factors. In some cases, access may not allow the use of a spanner to tighten compression fittings, and a soldered one may have to be used. Aesthetically, a solder fitting is neater than a compression one and is also cheaper.

For the inexperienced person, the compression fitting is more reliable, for a leaking soldered joint is more difficult to correct, and some skill is needed to make these joints.

A leaking compression joint can usually be corrected by slightly tightening the locking unit on the fitting; however, overtightening can distort the tube and cause leaking which may be difficult to cure.

The manipulative fitting is seldom used in domestic plumbing or heating. Using this entails 'belling' out the mouth of the tube with a special tool, the mouth of which is then compressed about the body of the fitting. The union is completed by tightening locking nuts.

Compression fittings

Compression fittings rely on the compression of a metal cone or ferrule, usually made of anealed brass or copper and commonly called an olive, against the external wall of the pipe. When the nuts of the fittings are tightened, the olive effects a watertight seal.

If the tube is not pushed fully home to an internal stop or shoulder and held in position when the lock nuts at each end are tightened, a poor joint may result. A machine-moulded ridge within the fitting prevents the tube from travelling further than the correct depth.

Equally, the pipe should be cut squarely; if it is not, it may be a potential source of leaking. Check finally that there are no flow-inhibiting burrs before connecting the tube.

Although compression fittings are made to a general pattern, it is important to use the type of olive made for the fitting. Some olives have a longer chamfer on one side than the other, and this long chamfer should be inserted to enter the body of the fitting.

It is a wise provision to apply a little jointing compound over the olive. This is not specified by manufacturers but helps to ensure a watertight joint.

Modern thin-wall copper tube is easily distorted out of shape. Some three-quarters of a turn, after tightening the fitting by hand, is usually adequate for joints on fittings of up to 28mm. Use the second spanner to hold the body of the fitting while you tighten each nut.

If you are making a number of connections, either complete each before proceeding to the next, or mark each after

Push the pipe firmly up to the internal stop and tighten the back nut by hand

Lock with a spanner. Tighten firmly but do not overtighten or the joint may leak

Before making a capillary joint, clean the tube ends thoroughly with wire wool

connecting so that none is overlooked for subsequent tightening. It is surprisingly easy to forget to tighten a fitting.

Capillary connectors

Before making a capillary joint, careful preparation is necessary. You must first ensure that you do not set the surrounding area alight. To avoid this, use a piece of asbestos mat placed at the back of the work. A butane-gas torch is easier to use than a petrol or paraffin torch. Set the torch, after igniting, to a hard, medium blue flame. Butane produces a very hot flame, so take care to keep your hands well clear.

The soldered fitting contains a reservoir of solder in a ring within the fitting. The end-feed pattern does not contain solder and this has to be introduced into the mouth of the fitting during connection. Some unsoldered fittings are pre-tinned to facilitate the jointing process.

Check that ends are cleanly cut and free from burrs. It is then necessary to clean both the tube ends and the inside of the fitting; this can be done using fine wire wool.

Next, apply a smear of flux to the mating surfaces. This helps to prevent an oxidizing process from occurring which may nullify the solder bond.

A special 'aggressive' flux is necessary for jointing stainless-steel tube. This removes the oxide film, which forms more quickly on stainless steel than on other metals. Several types of such fluxes are available, in both liquid and paste form, most containing an acid base. All excess flux must be wiped clean from the surface after jointing.

Techniques for jointing both copper and stainless steel are similar. Insert the pipe into the fitting up to the stop end. You can join a section of pipe at one end only, by standing the unjoined end of the fitting in a lid of water to prevent solder from melting. However, it is best to complete all joints and solder all connections as one operation.

Wipe off any excess flux and apply heat evenly to the mouth of the fitting. Do not concentrate heat at any one point and avoid applying heat after the union is complete, or the solder will blacken and break down. Choose a cored solder as this is easier to use.

The joint is complete when a ring of solder appears completely around the mouth of the fitting. An added precaution is to touch a piece of cored solder around the mouth, while the fitting is still hot, to consolidate it.

End-feed fittings are heated evenly with the blow torch and the solder wire is applied to the mouth of the fitting and slowly rotated until the mouth will accept no more. Leave a ring of solder around the edge.

Do not disturb newly made joints; allow them a minute or so to cool.

Similarly, clean the insides of fittings. A special brush can be used to do this

Coat the ends of pipe with flux and then push pipes into fittings up to the stop

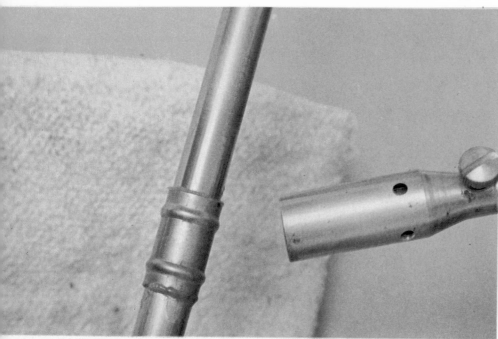

Apply heat evenly around the pipe with blow torch until ring of solder appears

Fittings

There are three main types of fitting:

● *The straight coupling*
● *The bent coupling, or elbow*
● *The branch fitting.*

Straight threaded couplings used to join iron pipework are known as nipples or unions.

The bent coupling may be right-angled or obtuse, swept or 'slow'. Similarly, a branch fitting may be right-angled or obtuse. The most common branch fitting is the tee-piece, so described because of its resemblance to the letter 't'. This is used where a connection or branch has to be made in a section of pipework.

Where a smaller-bore pipe has to be connected to a larger outlet, reducing sets can be used. Both capillary and compression adaptors are available to reduce the diameter of the pipe bore.

Another situation which may be encountered is the matching of tubes of metric and imperial gauge. In some sizes, these measurements do not exactly correspond. Sets are available to match metric and imperial pipework and fittings. There are special devices made to reduce or expand tube to metric or imperial dimensions.

Where a pipe or branch has to be terminated either permanently or temporarily, stop ends can be used in conjunction with fittings. These are available for use with both compression and capillary fittings. Where the termination is only temporary, a compression stop-end fitting may be used, as this is easily removed.

The terminations of fittings are described in a specific order. For example, a tee-piece fitting, which is one with more than two outlets, with two equal 15mm outlets and a 22mm branch is described as a 15mm × 15mm × 22mm tee. In other words, each end dimension is given first, followed by the size of any branch.

Fitting outlets are equal or unequal. An equal tee, for example, is one where all outlets are of the same diameter.

Threaded fittings

Some threaded fittings are known as male-iron or female-iron fittings and traditionally connect to threaded iron connections. The other ends of the fitting may terminate with either compression or capillary ends.

These fittings are usually used on boilers, hot-water cylinders or storage appliances, such as cisterns, and have to be sealed with either PTFE tape or hemp and non-toxic jointing compound. The hemp is 'teased' into a thin string, smeared lightly with a plumbing compound and wrapped round the joint.

PTFE tape is a white plastic which is wound round the threads of the fitting in an anti-clockwise direction for about one and a half turns. The fitting is tightened in the normal way, with a spanner.

Clipping pipes

Pipes should be clipped to walls at short intervals. Various types of clip are made. With some the clip is fitted in place first; in others, clips are fitted over the pipe, which is positioned first. Where pipe is taken through walls, sleeving (one pipe size larger than the pipe) should be used, so that pipes are not pinched and to allow for expansion of hot water.

Feed solder into the mouth of fitting. Joint is made when it accepts no more

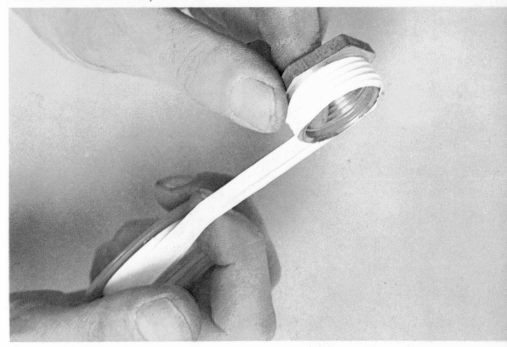

PTFE tape is wound three times in an anti-clockwise direction

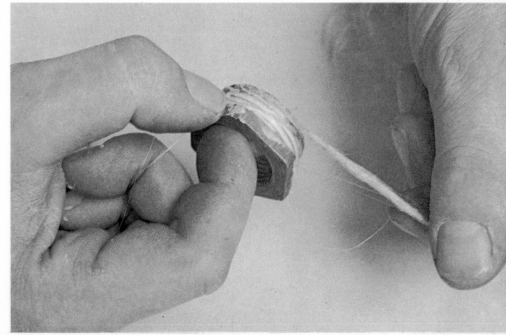

Strands of hemp coated with a non-toxic plumbing compound also seals pipe threads

Plastics used in plumbing have many advantages, but supply services must be limited to providing cold water and not connected in any way to the domestic hot water. Plastics are light to handle, easy to use, reliable in operation and virtually imperishable. Also, they are often less obtrusive than metal tube, where the pipework is exposed.

Plastics have an application for practically every purpose in plumbing. The exception is for the distribution of hot water, though plastics which are suitable for use with hot water have been produced. The two obstacles here are the high cost of plastic

Components and materials in a cold-water plastic-plumbing system:

1 Stop cock
2 Gate valve connected in circuit
3 Solvent-weld fluid
4 Cleaning fluid
5 Tee-piece connector, 15mm
6 Tee-piece connector, 22mm
7 Straight swivel coupling
8 Angled swivel coupling
9 Straight connector, 15mm
10 Reduced connector
11 Angled connector
12 Straight connector, 22mm
13 Key Terrain taps
14 PVC cold-water tubing
15 Tubing fixing clips

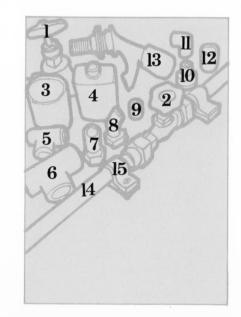

materials able to handle hot water, and design considerations. Plastics expand considerably at higher temperatures. Very careful design and installation would be necessary to allow for this high expansion factor or 'coefficient'.

Plastics are lighter to handle than metal and have a predictably longer life and greater reliability than some metals.

Another advance is that electrolytic corrosion, which can occur in hard-water areas, particularly if copper and galvanized steel are used together, cannot occur where plastics are used.

PVC also has better insulation characteristics than metal and creates virtually no problems of condensation on pipe. As PVC is a good thermal insulator, water in pipes will not readily freeze. However, normal insulation practice should be followed in exposed situations, and pipework below the ground should be installed below the frost line.

There are no bore restrictions from build-up of hardness of scale. PVC also has excellent noise-absorption qualities.

PVC pipes must not, however, be used for cold down services, to hot-water cylinders or calorifiers or for cold-feed services for heating systems.

PVC pipe is widely used in domestic plumbing. Its high rate of thermal expansion, in common with all plastics, has to be carefully and adequately accommodated.

Up to about 30m of pipe is needed to pro-vide cold-water services for an average house. These services can be used in conjunction with other plastics – soil and waste service and plastic storage cisterns.

Fittings used with plastic are about half the cost of those used for copper or stainless steel, but comparatively more are needed. Bends cannot reliably be formed in plastic as they can with metal pipe, and elbow fittings are needed. Plastic pipe can be bent, using a blow torch or hot-air gun, but some degree of skill is needed to do this successfully.

It is cheaper to plumb with plastic and in many ways simpler. Because of the correspondingly greater pipe bores, compared with the internal sizes of copper and stainless steel, smaller pipe can be used,

Measure and cut the pipe squarely with fine-toothed hacksaw; hold pipe firmly

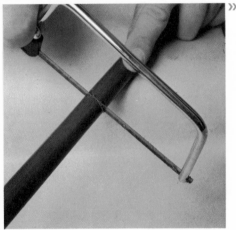

Burrs left on the inside of the pipe are best removed, using a rounded file

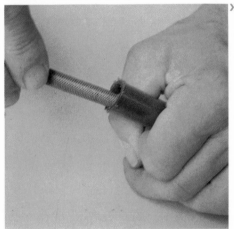

Flat file is used to clean off outside burrs and ensure pipe ends are square

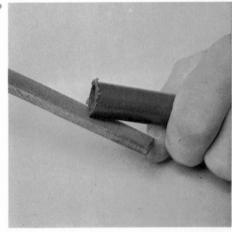

Abrade inside of fittings and spigot with glasspaper to facilitate the join

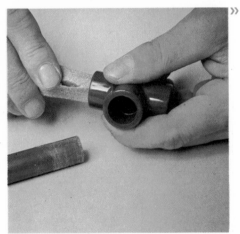

Use cleaning and degreasing fluid on mating surfaces to ensure a sound joint

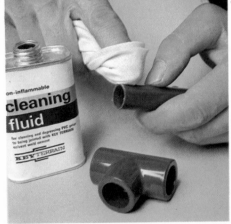

Apply solvent-weld fluid evenly on both surfaces. Avoid using excessive amounts

The joint can be made by pushing parts firmly together. Leave to set firmly

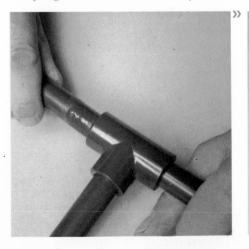

Standard fittings, such as a brass stop-cock, can be connected into plastics

Standard gate valve fitted in plastic pipe run, with supporting pipe clips

These are the most widely used plastics for making plumbing components.

PVC *This is an abbreviation for poly-vinyl chloride. The most widely used of plastics and capable of handling moderately hot water (20°C), is unplasticised PVC, or uPVC. Another type, with similar properties, is cPVC, or chlorinated PVC.*

Polythene *This is made in both high-density and low-density (HD and LD) forms and widely used for loft storage cisterns. In pipework, the rigid HD is used for pipes above 50mm diameter. It is also known as Alkathene, a proprietary name used by ICI.*

Polypropylene *This is another plastic suitable for use with water temperatures of around 20°C.*

GRP *This is often called fibreglass, but correctly it is glass-reinforced plastic, the base of which is glass-fibre mat, bonded by polyester or epoxide resins. It is used largely for cold-storage cisterns but some hot-water cylinders are made from GRP.*

ABS *This abbreviation stands for acronitrile butadiene styrene and is a plastic widely used to make waste and soil systems.*

which reduces comparative costs still further.

Where 13mm pipe is needed in copper, 10mm uPVC pipe can normally be used, as PVC also provides greater flow rates, with lower frictional resistance, than metal pipework, because of its smoother bore.

PTFE
PTFE tape, wound three times in an anticlockwise direction round the thread, both seals and lubricates the joint.

Where it is necessary to connect plastic pipes to metal fittings—such as taps, ball valves and adaptors, these are joined by components which are an integral part of the adapting fitting or with PVC fittings reinforced with metal bands.

Tools
A fine-toothed hacksaw, a sharp cutting knife, a flat file and some fine wire wool are needed. For fixing pipe clips, a hand drill, screwdriver, screws and wall plugs are required.

For jointing pipes of up to 50mm, a spigot and socket-weld method of jointing is used. The socket fittings are designed to provide an efficient and reliable joint and are used in conjunction with a proprietary solvent cement.

The working methods are as follows:

● Cut the pipe to the required length with a fine-toothed hacksaw, ensuring that the spigot end is cut square. Mark the position of the cut, double checking that this is correct, and wrap a piece of paper round the pipe, bringing its edges together on the line of the cut. This template should ensure an accurate square cut.

When cutting, never force the hacksaw. Draw it rhythmically back and forth across the pipe, using only moderate pressure;

● Degrease the mating surfaces of both pipe and fitting with cleaning fluid;

● Slightly chamfer the outer edge of the pipe;

● Roughen the mating surfaces with an abrasive paper or cloth;

● Apply an even coat of cement to the fitting socket and to the pipe: brush with an axial movement and immediately push the fitting on to the pipe. Hold it in position for a few seconds and remove surplus cement. Never dip the pipe into the tin and always apply the cement with a brush;

● Do not disturb the joint for about five minutes and only then handle with care.

Although solvent welded joints achieve setting in minutes, the weld does not reach its full strength until 24 hours after jointing. One hour drying time should be allowed for every 1·055kgf/cm² (15psi) before testing.

The tin of cement must be closed immediately after use, as the solvent evaporates quickly. It is also highly inflammable, so avoid smoking or the presence of naked flame.

Brackets
In common with other plastics, PVC has a high rate of thermal expansion. The correct position of pipe brackets to allow for thermal movement is essential. Pipe clips must not be secured immediately adjacent to the fitting, in order to ensure longitudinal movement of the pipe.

Unless each fitting and expansion point is anchored firmly, there can be accumulated movement or escalation, making the installation dimensionally unstable.

In some cases, particularly on horizontal pipe runs, this could lead to the pulling apart of joints. Clips must be carefully aligned to ensure longitudinal freedom.

Brackets should be fitted at the following maximum centres:

	Horizontal installation	Vertical installation
10mm	750mm	1·50m
13mm	900mm	1·80m
19mm	1·05m	2·10m
25mm	1·05m	2·10m

Pipes must not be rigidly fixed by any form of grouting where they pass through walls or floors. Fittings should not constitute any form of obstruction.

Where pipes pass through walls the use of sleeves is recommended. There should be a minimum air space of 75mm between PVC pipes and high-temperature heating mains.

The recommended number of joints per 0·454kg (1lb) is as follows:

10mm – 175
13mm – 140
19mm – 110
25mm – 75

Wiping a leaded joint
The traditional leaded joint is a plumbing skill which at one time was essential in any basic plumbing. New, simpler materials, and the disappearance of lead pipework have reduced the need for this skill. A wiped solder joint may still be needed where the domestic cold-water supply comes into the house in lead pipe. A wiped joint may be needed where a stopcock has to be joined to such pipework. Pipework can be continued beyond the stopcock within the house in copper, stainless steel or plastic.

To make a wiped joint, the lead pipe must be cleaned and then belled out to accept a section of pipe or fitting. A smooth, thick, tapered fillet of solder is then built up over the joined ends. Tools needed to bell out the pipe are a hardwood cone or metal 'dolly' and a 'mole' cloth, for wiping the joint.

Materials needed are: tinning solder, a 450 gramme stick of plumber's metal, flux, a tin of plumber's black, and tallow. The latter is used when wiping the joint with the mole.

Before making any connection, turn off the water at the company's stopcock in the road, or at your own main outside stopcock if there is one.

A hacksaw may be used to cut and trim the lead pipe. The cone or dolly is then inserted. The hardwood cone is tapped in with a hammer. As it is driven in, it should be twisted between blows to prevent it from sticking. The metal dolly, resembling a screwdriver with a rounded tip, is inserted in the pipe and rotated with outward pressure and motion.

Bell out the pipe to a depth of about 38mm. Next apply plumber's black some 50mm back along the pipe, to stop solder from spreading beyond the limits of the joint. The completed joint should be about 75mm long. A section of either tinned copper or stainless-steel pipe or the spigot of the fitting, also tinned, can be inserted into the belled end of lead pipe. These ends should be similarly treated with plumber's black, some 50mm back along the tube.

With a shavehook or a penknife, clean both the end of and the inside of the pipe. The outside should be scraped until the metal is bright, back to the line of the plumber's black. Clean the spigot or the end of the pipe with fine wire wool. The end of the fitting or pipe should be slightly bevelled with a file to facilitate a good fit into the lead pipe.

Next, coat both mating surfaces evenly with flux, tin the surfaces and then bring the two ends firmly together, heating the entire area of the joint with a blow torch. Keep the flame moving to ensure an even distribution of heat and apply only enough heat to melt the tinning solder. Next, apply the plumber's metal to the joint. Fill up the rim of the belled portion. Apply

sufficient heat to melt the solder to a plastic state, so that it does not run off the joint.

Use about a quarter of a stick and then heat the mole in the blow lamp flame and dip it in tallow. To spread the solder around the joint, use a circular wiping action and taper the ends of the joint. You will need to reheat the solder from time to time to keep it workable.

Build up the solder until you have used about 20mm of the stick, then reheat and wipe the joint smooth until the edges are neatly faired.

Do not disturb the joint until it has cooled thoroughly. Take particular care to avoid manipulating the pipework while making the joint or you may fracture it.

Using a wooden 'dolly' to bell out the end of a lead pipe to take copper spigot

Apply lamp black about 50mm back along cleaned tube to restrict spread of metal

Tube is tinned with plumber's metal before insertion into the lead pipe

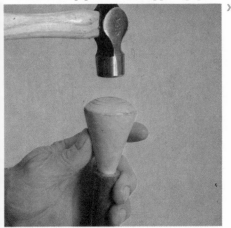

The inside of the lead pipe should be thoroughly cleaned with a shavehook

Simple wire spring is tool to facilitate tube insertion and hold parts together

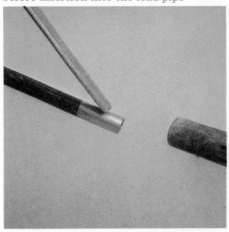

The joint is wiped using tallow which facilitates the flow of plumber's metal

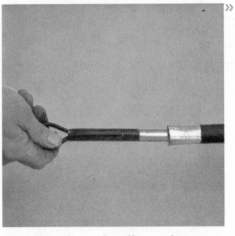

Metal is built up evenly around the joint; keep the flame moving steadily

Heat the mole, apply tallow and sweep it around the joint to provide neat union

Completed joint; connections can be made in copper, stainless steel or plastic

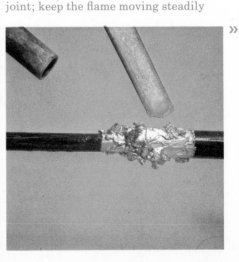

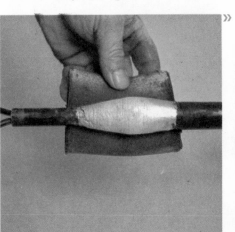

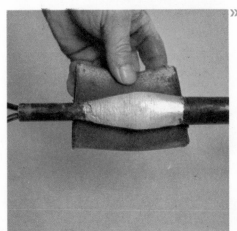

When it's old cisterns go

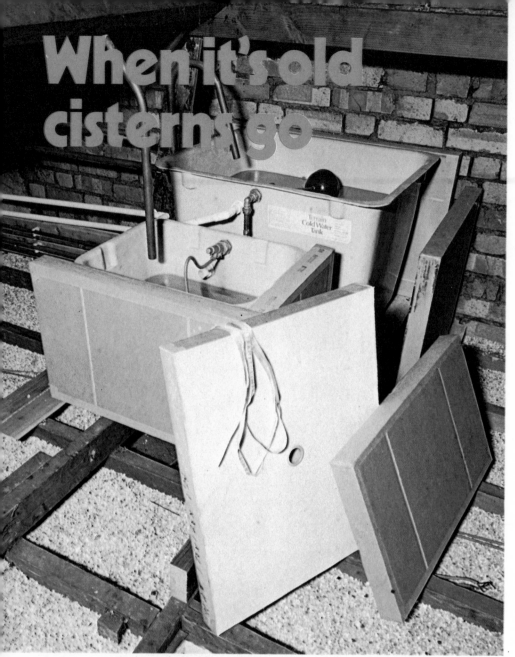

Storage and heating make-up cistern.   Strawboard insulation is partly fitted

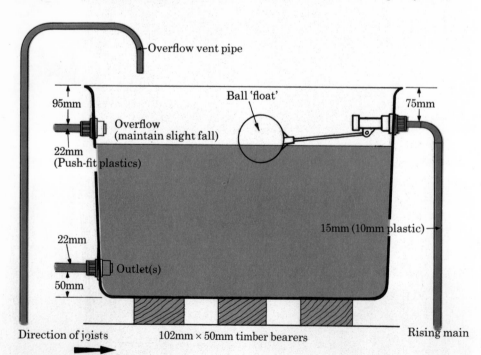

Overflow vent pipe

95mm

Overflow
(maintain slight fall)

22mm
(Push-fit plastics)

Ball 'float'

75mm

22mm

15mm (10mm plastic)

Outlet(s)

50mm

Direction of joists   102mm × 50mm timber bearers   Rising main

Connecting and supporting
a PVC storage cistern.
Continuous base support required
for GRP cisterns

Cold-water storage, within the home, usually situated in the loft, provides a reservoir of water which equalizes the 'pull' on the mains and provides against any reduction or shut down of the main supply. Modern cisterns are made of lightweight materials, and are easy to handle and fit. Different households needs are met by a variation in size of cistern.

Storage cold water (known as potable water) enables a reservoir of water to be stored in the home against the shut down, for any reason, of the mains supply. It also reduces the mains demand, at any given time, by meeting most of the domestic water needs at a constant rate from a storage source.

Traditionally, cold cisterns consisted of galvanized metal, a material likely to corrode. Electrolytic action–a chemical re-action in hard-water conditions–and the build up of lime scale may lead to the con-striction of outlet pipes and deterioration of the actual storage vessel.

PVC and GRP

The modern approach is to replace old storage cisterns with either PVC or glass-fibre (GRP) cisterns. Some types of PVC cistern can be folded up and trussed with rope to permit access to a fairly small loft opening. All plastic cisterns have the advantage of being light to handle.

The cold storage cistern is usually placed in the loft. Because it is fairly bulky, it is not easily situated elsewhere in the home. Also, the noise of running water, as the cistern fills, becomes less of an annoyance. The loft, in addition, provides a high point to create static head or pressure, necessary to ensure a strong flow at outlets.

Storage capacities

Storage cisterns usually have a capacity of between 230 litres and 365 litres. This depends, of course, on the demand for water of the particular home. A typical, three-bedroomed household, with a family of four, normally requires a minimum water-storage capacity of 230 litres.

An old metal cistern can sometimes present a problem of disposal. It may originally have been put in before the roof was completed–or slates or tiles may have had to be removed to install it. If you have to take out the old cistern, you may have to cut it up with a metal sheet saw. Often, the best solution is to disconnect it, drain it down and move it into the corner of the loft, where space allows, and forget it!

Ancient galvanized or lead piping, often corroded or scaled, may require replacement, and the opportunity can then be taken to replan the plumbing layout, if need be. The cistern can be repositioned if this improves the pipework arrangements.

The modern cistern is often, and wrongly, called a 'tank'. A tank is a vessel sealed from pressure of the atmosphere, though this is the form of older storage vessels.

Storage cisterns are supplied from the rising main, usually by copper or stainless-steel pipe of 15mm nominal bore or 10mm-bore pipe if in uPVC plastic.

Always measure height and position of a fitting carefully before cutting the hole

Hole cutters are made in various sizes and can be used in hand or power tools

A fitting can be used as a template to mark the size of the hole to be cut out

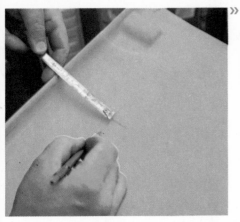

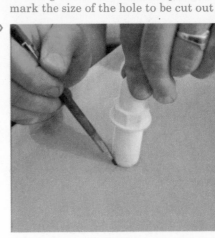

A series of small holes can be made with a drill around the perimeter of circle

The holes are joined up and the opening trimmed to size using a half-round file

Polypropylene washers, on each side of the fitting, provide satisfactory seal

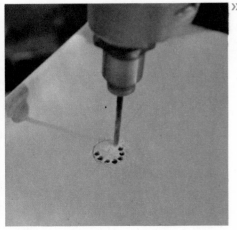
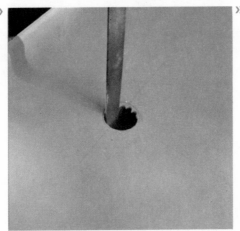
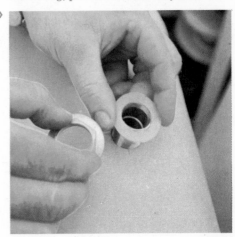

Connections should be tightened firmly; do not overtighten or subject to stress

A gate valve on the outlet pipe enables the cistern to be isolated if necessary

Connector for the ball valve is similarly fitted with polypropylene sealing washers

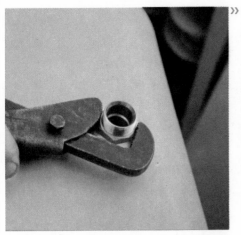

View of a plumbed-in cistern; cold supply is connected with angled or swivel union

Plastic overflows are fitted and then tightened similarly to metal pipework

Overflow pipe in plastic is joined either by push-fit or solvent-weld connection

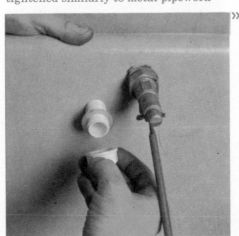
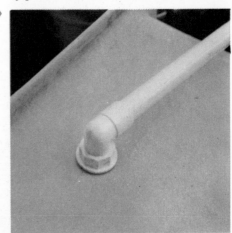

Inlet supply

Inlet supply is controlled by a ball valve, which shuts off water by means of an arm operated by a plastic or copper ball, called a 'float'. This lies on the surface of the water and rises as the water flows in, raising a lever arm, which closes the inlet valve at a determined level.

There are two types of ball valve–high pressure, and low pressure. The high-pressure valve has a smaller water outlet than the low-pressure type. If you use a high-pressure valve where supply is from a storage outlet, filling a cistern may take an indeterminate length of time. Mains supply is always at high pressure.

The low-pressure valve is similar to the high-pressure type but with a larger outlet. This is used on toilet cisterns, which are fed from the outlet or low-pressure side of the storage cistern.

A useful refinement is a gate valve in the rising-main supply to the cistern. If the cistern has to be isolated for any reason it can be shut off without affecting supply of fresh water at the kitchen sink.

Feed pipes

Dependent on household needs, one or two feed pipes may be taken from the cistern. One may serve the cold make-up supply to the hot-water cylinder, while the other meets the needs of wash handbasins, baths and bidets.

These outlet pipes are normally adequate if plumbed in 22mm pipe. However, if there is a continuing high demand for hot water, a 28mm pipe can be provided to supply the hot cylinder.

The other essential pipe is the overflow. This has to be a size larger than the inlet supply and usually has a diameter of 22mm.

Expansion

The storage cistern is also used as a form of safety valve for the hot cylinder. Heated water expands, so an expansion pipe must be fitted to the cylinder to accommodate this. Hot water must not be contained, for this could be dangerous.

The expansion pipe is taken from the crown of the cylinder via an off-set fitting and curved over just above the cold cistern to provide the necessary hot-water vent.

The pipe should never be allowed to dip into the cistern, for this would set up a siphonage circulation and pump hot water through nearly every tap in the home!

Changing the old cistern involves a major shut down in domestic water services, so plan carefully for the minimum dislocation and make sure that you are equipped with all the materials and tools needed.

Shut down the supply stopcock and open taps and any drain cocks, to drain away most of the water. As outlets are usually located at about 75mm above the bottom of the cistern, this means that the residue of water will have to be baled out.

Fittings

Fittings are usually easily unlocked, with adjustable spanners, where these are of the conventional compression type. Some fittings, used with iron pipework, may be heavily corroded and may have to be heated with a blow torch to expand them before removal with a large wrench.

One component which is frequently reusable is the ball-valve assembly. Sometimes the float ball becomes punctured, waterlogged and, therefore, ineffectual. The ball can be simply unscrewed and replaced.

It is sound practice to complete as much as possible of the replumbing of a new cistern before fitting it. If this can be done before putting it in the loft, it will make things a lot easier from a working point of view.

If a metal cistern is used, with consequent risk of corrosive electrolytic action, a suitable copper-to-galvanized metal connection should be used to separate the two metals.

The hole to fit the ball-valve assembly should be about 75mm below the top of the cistern and be slightly larger than the threaded valve stem. The hole for the overflow should be about 20mm below this point. Outlet connections are located at about 75mm up from the cistern bottom.

Cutting holes

Holes are made by marking the position with a centre punch and then using a hole cutter or a large auger bit to make the hole, centring on the punch mark to prevent the cutter from slipping.

There are two types of hole cutter–one has a number of interchangeable blades of various sizes and the other an adjustable cutter on a bar. Both have a twist-drill centre, which makes the pilot hole and, at the same time, provides a pivot point.

A hand drill is better to use than a power drill, since plastic heats up and becomes difficult to drill at speed. Use a file to remove any burrs left by drilling.

Holes can be made more laboriously by marking the circumference of the hole and drilling round, at intervals, with a small drill bit, until the hole is cut. The segments left can be trimmed off with a sharp knife or keyhole saw and the hole then cleaned up with a file.

Ball valves

Ball valves have two loose nuts on the stem; these go on either side of the wall of the cistern and allow adjustments to be made to the amount of projection of the stem. Another type has a single nut fixed on the outside cistern wall.

Plastic or fibre washers are fitted on either side of the cistern wall, before the fitting is tightened up, to ensure a leak-proof joint–though water cannot usually rise to this height.

Once the ball valve is in place, a swivel compression 'tap' connector, containing a loose fibre washer, should be fitted to the stem. This ensures a water-tight joint when tightened. The outlet from the connection is joined to the rising-main inlet.

Tap connectors can be either straight or angled, to suit the nature of your pipework.

The type of valve with a silencer pipe which projects into the water is no longer approved, because of the risk of siphonage back into the mains in certain circumstances. Some types have an outlet at the top, allowing water to flow gently into the cistern, via a discharge chamber.

Overflows

Overflows are another form of safety valve; if they are working, they fulfil a vital function–preventing a fault from causing possible considerable damage to the fabric of your home.

Overflow fittings can be made in either plastic or metal. The easiest to use is the plastic 'push-fit' variety, where a piece of pipe simply slots into a socket-ended section.

The overflow must be fitted to allow a slight continuous fall. The outlet point should be located so that it is clear of obstructions and where you can quickly spot it. Avoid positioning it where it can saturate any part of the fabric of the house.

Filling up

The cistern, once plumbed in, should be adequately supported beneath before it is filled. PVC cisterns can be placed on two or three sections of 100mm × 50mm timber, set across the joists. GRP cisterns should be supported by a continuous piece of material, such as 19mm blockboard.

Where capillary fittings are used for making connections near the cistern, take great care to protect the sides from the effect of heat.

Before filling the cistern, check carefully that all joints and connections are properly made. Check carefully for leaks during filling. If these occur, shut off the water and drain down the cistern. Never try to tighten up joints with water in the cistern; you may rupture it and cause a flood!

The ball valve is adjusted when the cistern is almost full. This is set to ensure that the water level is at least 25mm below the overflow pipe. You may have to bend–very carefully–the float arm to get the setting correct. With some patterns of valve, you merely adjust an alignment screw.

Test the operation of the ball valve, by drawing off a small quantity of water, and then observe the refilling and supply cut off.

After about a day, check the system carefully to establish that no joints are 'weeping'.

Clean water

In modern building practice, roofs under tiles are felted to keep out dust. In many older homes, the loft becomes a dust trap. It is wise to make a lid for the storage cistern if one is not supplied.

This may be made from blockboard, chipboard or from various types of building board. If water is likely to affect the material, paint it. Make a hole in the lid to admit the hot-water vent pipe.

Lofts should be insulated against loss of heat, which makes a cistern vulnerable to freezing. This, and all related pipework, should be lagged.

No loft insulation material should be placed beneath the cistern. This is to allow heat from the house to rise and keep the storage water from freezing.

Domestic hot water is an essential amenity in any home. Its provision may be linked with a central-heating system, or heat may be provided by an independent source, such as immersion heater. There are several types of hot-water cylinders and of immersion heaters, which can meet every situation. Once installed, lag a cylinder to prevent unnecessary loss of heat.

Hot water in store

In older houses, hot-water facilities are often provided by a square galvanized storage tank, heated by a solid-fuel boiler in the kitchen, possibly supplemented by an immersion heater. These arrangements rarely include satisfactory heating and are relatively costly to run.

Modern practice is to heat water through a hot-water cylinder, usually made of copper, though glass-fibre and stainless-steel cylinders can be used. The cylinder water is usually heated by the house central-heating system or by means of an immersion heater.

A standard cylinder is 915 × 450mm in circumference. The bottom of the cylinder is concaved or 'dished' to give strength. The top is domed or 'crowned' to help to prevent air locks. The capacity of such a cylinder is usually adequate for the domestic hot-water needs of a three-bedroomed home. For bigger homes and families, and situations where there is a greater demand for hot water, larger cylinders can be used.

Direct and indirect
There are two main forms of cylinder – the direct and the indirect. In the direct cylinder, the circulating hot water is heated, drawn off and then replenished by fresh storage water. The indirect cylinder has an inner jacket, called a calorifier, through which hot water circulates to heat the surrounding draw-off water. These two waters do not co-mingle.

Another version of the indirect cylinder is the self-priming type. The primary and secondary waters are separated by an air bubble. The water in the cylinder must be kept below boiling point, or the bubble will disperse, and the waters merge. It will then be necessary to allow the water to cool and contract so that the bubble can re-form.

The circulating hot water, when it is part of a central-heating system, is purged of air which lowers the risk of scaling and corrosion. 'Live' water contains a high proportion of oxygen. When this is purged of air, the 'dead' water is unlikely to give problems.

Circulating hot water can be distributed by what is called natural or gravity circulation or it can be pumped. Gravity circulation works on the principle that molecules of hot water expand, allowing expansion and distribution of hot water to take place. This requires pipework possessing a minimum bore of between 22mm and 28mm.

In the process of circulation, the molecules of the cooling water contract and return to the heating source, where the water is reheated and re-cycled.

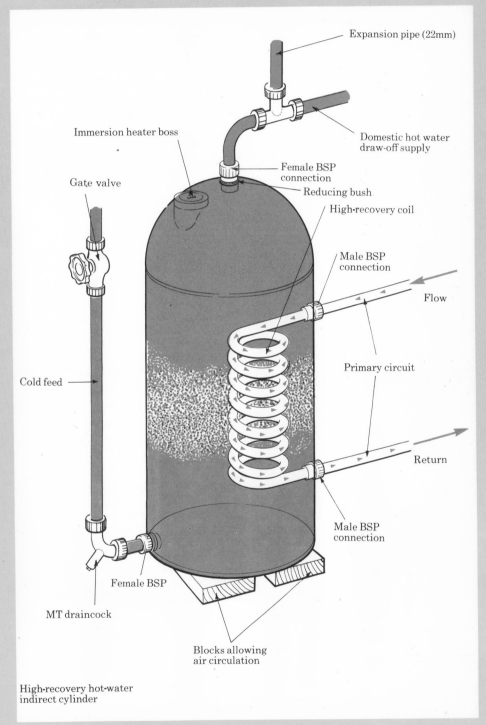

High-recovery hot-water indirect cylinder

Labels: Expansion pipe (22mm); Domestic hot water draw-off supply; Immersion heater boss; Female BSP connection; Reducing bush; High-recovery coil; Gate valve; Male BSP connection; Flow; Cold feed; Primary circuit; Return; Male BSP connection; Female BSP; MT draincock; Blocks allowing air circulation

Pumped primaries
When a pumped system is employed to circulate the hot water, 15mm or 22mm pipe can be used, dependent on the capacity of the hot cylinder. This method is called a pumped primary. It is essentially part of a central-heating system and to allow this to work most effectively and economically, a special type of indirect cylinder is needed.

This is called a high-recovery cylinder, which heats and reheats water very quickly. A conventional cylinder will heat and recycle water from cold in about an hour; the high-recovery version takes only about half this time.

A self-priming cistern may not be used on a pumped-primary system, as the pump action would release the separating air bubble.

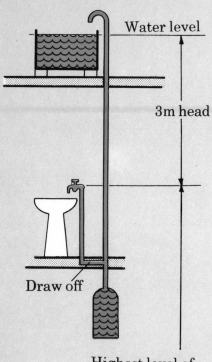

3m head

Water level

Draw off

Highest level of
draw-off system –
in this instance
the tap fitting is
on hand basin

Two examples, of how to estimate the
'pressure head' of water at the taps.
The head is that between the level of
the water supply and the draw-off point
–either the branch supply or the tap.

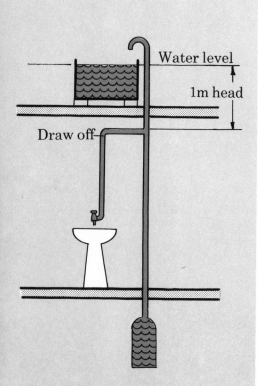

Water level

1m head

Draw off

A direct cylinder can be adapted by a special element, to convert it to a high-recovery unit. It is then suitable for use on hot-water pumped primary circuits. The element fits in the immersion-heater boss.

Immersion heaters

With electric central heating or when solid-fuel heating is not operating, hot water can be provided by an immersion heater which screws into this boss.

A direct cylinder is used where the immersion heater alone provides hot water. Some solid-fuel appliances use a direct cylinder only when the heating system, which provides hot water as part of its function, is not in use.

This may be operated, using a time clock, to heat water at chosen periods.

Ratings

Immersion heaters are now nearly always 3kW wattage rating. Because of the high current rating, these should be connected via a separate power circuit, using a cable of 4mm². Immersion heaters have thermostatic devices allowing temperature settings to be between 49°C and 82°C. For domestic purposes a satisfactory setting is around 60°C.

Types

There are two types of heater–the dual and the single-stage coil. Hot water stratifies and rises and the water at the crown of the cylinder is always hotter than that lower down.

Water stratifies to the extent that there can be a marked difference in temperature over a very small distance.

The two-stage heater will either heat the water in the crown for light draw-off use, such as washing up and washing, or heat the bulk of the water for major use, such as baths.

The immersion heater length should be about two-thirds of the depth of the cylinder. The heater screws into the boss. The threads are sealed by winding PTFE tape round the thread against direction of turn, or by using hemp string and plumbing non-toxic compound.

Next, unscrew the sealing plate from the boss, and insert the heater. Then, tighten this against its sealing washers using a large wrench. Do not overtighten as this might rupture the cylinder. These are usually made from thin copper which, though overall structurally strong, are vulnerable at connection points.

Where hot-water is part of an oil or gas-fired heating system, function controls are usually used to operate switching of heating and hot water.

Electric storage heating systems, operating on off-peak electricity, can be used to heat the domestic water overnight on this cheaper tariff; heat loss can be boosted at full rate where necessary.

Good connections

Cylinder connections are all of similar, male-iron thread type. These consist of the hot-water draw off, taken from the crown of the cylinder, and the cold feed from the

cold-water storage cistern, made to a connection about a quarter of the way up the cylinder.

The primary hot-water connections are located on the opposite side of the cylinder. The flow circuit connection is about a quarter of the way down from the top of the cylinder and the return one an equivalent distance from the bottom.

Cold supply is usually provided by 15mm tube. The draw-off water needs are usually met by a 22mm tube but sometimes 28mm pipe is required where there is greater hot-water demand.

Room for expansion

To allow for hot-water expansion, a 22mm vent pipe is taken by an offset fitting from the crown of the cylinder and brought up to and curved over the loft cold-water cistern, above the water.

This pipe is a safety precaution, for though hot water normally expands up the vent pipe for about 1–1·5m, it seldom vents into the cistern, unless excessively high temperatures are inadvertently attained.

Keeping hot

Sometimes taps are some distance from the cylinder, leaving a large amount of cold water in the pipes, which first has to be drawn off. This can be avoided by means of a system of secondary installation. A normal draw-off connection is fitted, with an added supply circuit positioned above this and returning below it. When water is drawn from the distant hot tap it breaks the secondary circulation system.

Location

The cylinder is most usually and best placed in an airing cupboard, where heat dissipated is put to use. However, excess loss of heat is expensive and the cylinder should be insulated. This is best done with one of the proprietary jackets–made of foam, glass-fibre or mineral wool. These jackets are 'tailored' to fit the size of cylinder and normally are fitted, quickly and simply, with straps, around the cylinder body.

Once the cylinder is filled with water, it will be very heavy. It should be stood on stout pieces of timber, set across the direction of the floor joists. Allow space beneath, for air to circulate, otherwise condensation may occur under the dished base.

A gate valve should be incorporated in the cold-water feed near the cylinder and a drain cock fitted to enable the cylinder to be drained down if necessary.

A terminal on some cylinders enables a drain cock to be screwed in. Otherwise, the cold-feed pipe to the cylinder is a good position. An MT pattern angle coupling can be fitted at the point where the pipe enters the cylinder.

Where the cylinder makes provision for a drain cock, the small sealing plate must be removed.

It is important that drain points are fitted where they can be quickly and conveniently reached. Taps in supply or draw-off pipework may be either compression or capillary ended. These are connected in the same way as other fittings.

A draincock should be fitted at lowest points – as here on the cold-feed inlet

Flow connection for indirect cylinder. Threaded joints are sealed with PTFE tape

Compression joints are used to provide connections for boiler flow and return

Threaded, reduced connector is screwed into the crown of the hot-water cylinder

Male-iron coupling with compression outlet is screwed into the reduced fitting

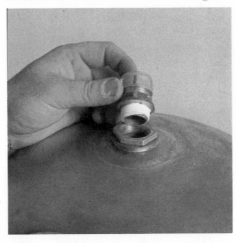

A smear of non-toxic plumbing compound is used to consolidate compression joints

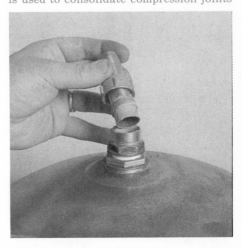

Hot draw-off connection. Avoid overtightening fittings or cylinder may rupture

Seal ring of immersion-heater boss cap is consolidated with non-toxic compound

If immersion or microbore element are not used, the blanking cap is fitted to boss

Wednesbury Micra version heating element screws into the immersion-heater opening

The twin-pipe unit fitted into place. The flow and return connect to the stems

Plumbed-in cylinder should be stood on a platform to permit air to circulate

A pipework crossover arrangement behind pedestal unit permits 'invisible' supply

Taps may be bedded in plumbing mastic – do not overtighten as surround may crack

Give your bathroom a boost

Tubular trap fitted to a bidet, using an 'o' ring to effect the water seal

Overflow connection to a cistern can be plastic push-fit or solvent-welded type

Tubular and bottle traps, normal and deep seal, permit 'p' or 's' outlet connections

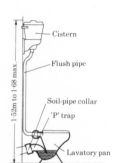

Plastic pan connector provides a push-fit seal and enables easy removal later

Close-coupled cistern slots into place. Pan is floor-fixed using brass screws

Pan extension piece

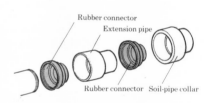

Swivel connector is used to join up the water supply to the inlet of the cistern

Bath screw-in overflow assembly with 'o' ring. This is coupled to the waste outlet

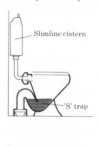

Pan with 'S' trap

Pan with 'P' trap

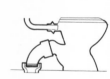

Waste outlet seal is consolidated with bedding ring of non-toxic plumbing mastic

Tails from taps or mixer unit are joined to hot and cold using swivel connectors

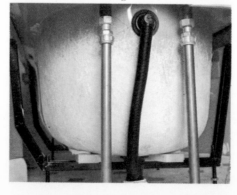

Bathroom waste traps

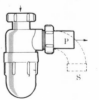

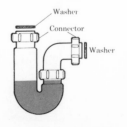
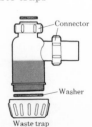

186

Unfortunately, the bathroom is often the 'Cinderella' of an otherwise well-decorated and equipped home. Updating the bathroom provides an opportunity to rethink the general layout and appearance. Showers and bidets can often be accommodated in a small bathroom by careful replanning. Modern methods and techniques can enable you to achieve a quick turn-round with the minimum of upheaval.

Modernizing the bathroom may involve a total turn round in plumbing and replacement of existing bathroom appliances. In any new scheme you might consider the inclusion of refinements such as bidets, heaters, and showers.

Many modern bathroom fitments are made of plastic or other new materials less likely to deteriorate with age or use than some items of older equipment.

As usual, before replacing any fitting or appliance, turn off the water supply, but try to minimize domestic dislocation. Storage cisterns should be emptied, stopcocks shut down or loft-cistern ball valves tied up, to shut off water.

Where you are replacing sanitaryware, try, where possible, to use new equipment which corresponds in size and the position of fittings being changed with the old, to eliminate unnecessary re-routing of pipework.

Sanitaryware is generally supplied with gummed paper edging. This is to provide protection during transit and fixing. Never remove the paper until the equipment is finally fixed and do not attempt to scrape it off, as this could damage the surfaces. Always soak off protective paper.

Wash handbasins
There are three categories of wash handbasin – the pedestal, which rests on a vitreous-china centre column; the wall-hung basin, which is fixed to the wall by a mounting bracket; and the inset, or built-in basin, for use in vanitory units. Fittings to fix these depend on the maker's design.

To take out an old wash basin, shut off the water supply and unscrew the locking nut at the top of the waste trap; this allows the trap to fall clear of the basin.

Unscrew the connecting nuts beneath the taps; a basin wrench will make the job easier. This tool is angled to facilitate unscrewing basin fittings. Next, unscrew the old basin from the wall and unscrew the base screws of any pedestal unit.

On sanitaryware, it is important to avoid direct connection of metal to china. Washers made of plastic, leather, cork or rubber should be used, as tension may cause the appliance to crack.

Taps, wastes and overflows should be set in a thin rim of mastic, such as a metal-glazing or proprietary plumbing putty. This never fully hardens and allows for expansion and contraction between pipe fittings and basin. Excess mastic will be pressed out by the action of tightening the fittings and is easily trimmed off.

Once taps are fitted, place a washer and backnut on to the tap 'tails' and tighten up with a basin wrench or spanner.

On wastes, putty is applied around the flange; the fitting is then inserted into the outlet, with a rubber washer beneath this.

On a bracket-mounted basin, fix the bracket to the wall, taking care to line this up carefully with a spirit level; make sure that fixings are firm. Locate the basin, so that the fitting projects through the centre hole of the bracket, then fit a leather washer and a flanged backnut over the waste. Tighten the nut by hand and then lock it firmly with a spanner.

Locating pins fit through the rear of the bracket on the basin. Place a rubber and a metal washer on to these and then tighten up the wing nuts.

The inlet pipes can then be connected to the taps and tightened with the wrench or spanner. Next, connect the trap to the waste fitting and tighten its locking nut.

Water can then be turned on to allow the system to be checked for leaks. Any slight 'weeping' can normally be corrected by tightening up connections.

Pedestal basins are fixed by screws to the wall; the pedestal is screwed to the floor through fixing holes in the basin and pedestal unit. The union between basin and pedestal is usually completed by wing nuts.

To avoid a series of acute bends, it is generally best to cross over the pipework inside the pedestal, to help avoid turbulence and constriction of water flow. The pedestal provides the facility of concealing pipework.

So that the installation of pipework can be 'tried for size', the pipework with taps, waste and related fittings should be assembled and checked before the pedestal is finally screwed to the floor, so that any adjustments can be made.

Swivel 15mm connectors are used to join the supply pipes to basins. One end of the fitting is threaded and screws on to the tap tails. Usually, a fibre washer completes the union. If the fitting is not of this type, PTFE tape is wrapped round the thread.

Waste outlets on basins are generally built into the body of the basin and, once fitted, connect to the waste outlet.

Bidets
Though in many bathrooms one may be difficult to fit for reasons of space, the bidet is a desirable item of sanitaryware. It is plumbed in a similar way to a wash basin and has comparable plumbing requirements. A hot and cold supply is required for a mixer tap. Waste connections are made in 35mm diameter pipe. The unit is usually screwed to the floor in the same way as a WC pan.

WC systems
There are three main types of domestic WC suites. These basically differ in the type of cistern – the high-level, the mid-level and the low-level cistern.

There are two main types of low-flush suite – the low-level wash-down pan and the close-coupled suite. A further low-flush WC, known as a corbel closet, has a wall-attached pan.

Modern cisterns are usually made of plastic or vitreous china. Many older types

of high-level pattern had a body of cast iron, though increasingly these are made in plastic.

The average capacity of a cistern is 10 litres or 12 litres. Cisterns are usually reversible, so that water supply can be connected on either side. When assembling the internal mechanism of any cistern, take account of the side to which supply is to be made.

High and low
Both high-flush and low-flush cisterns are joined in a similar manner to WC pans. A 22mm plastic flush pipe is connected to the cistern with a nut and washer. One end of this pipe has a preformed curve which allows connection into the back of the pan. This is covered by a rubber cone which slots over the stem at the point of pan entry.

Flush pipes can be cut to length and are so made that sections can simply slot together. Always, when fitting a low-level cistern, adhere to the manufacturer's recommended length of flush pipe, or you may not achieve a sufficient head of water for efficient flushing.

A high-level cistern of the older pattern can normally be removed and replaced by a modern, low-flush cistern to update the appearance of a WC suite.

Siphonic suites
Siphonic close-coupled suites are usually assembled by placing the siphonic cistern in position over the pan and joining it to the pan with two locking screws. These tighten a rubber gasket around the joint which provides the water seal.

Ball valves
Ball valves, in conventional cisterns, are fitted in the same way as those in storage cisterns. To assemble the ball valve and associated mechanisms, first fit the siphon which 'sits' in the cistern, with the dome or piston housing on the same side as the ball valve. These are either 100mm or 115mm in diameter.

The ball is located on the opposite side to the dome. Take care that the siphon housing is centred when tightening the large nut which fixes it. Supply to cisterns is made in either 15mm diameter copper or stainless-steel tube or 10mm diameter plastic tube.

When assembling the ball-valve, make sure that the float and arm have adequate clearance between the cistern wall and internal mechanism. This arm may need to be bent slightly to give clearance and to set the level of water required.

Check that the valve is of the low-pressure (storage supply) pattern. To cut down filling noise, a silencer pipe should be fitted.

Straight or angled compression connections are made to the bulkhead fitting housing the ball-valve assembly and must be of the female-threaded 'tap' type.

Fittings should contain a fibre washer, which provide a water seal. The other end of the fitting connects to the supply from the storage cistern.

Wall fixings for cisterns vary from

Secondary, hot-water system which
eliminates cold 'dead-legs', allowing
instant hot-water supply at taps

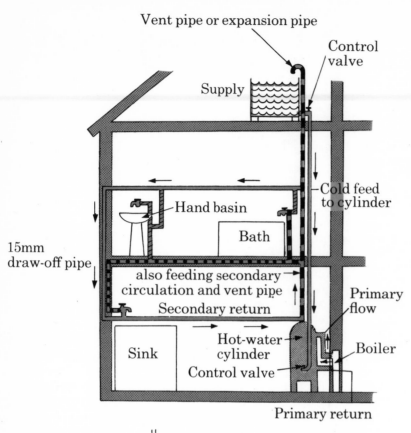

Vent pipe or expansion pipe

Control valve

Supply

Cold feed to cylinder

Hand basin

Bath

15mm draw-off pipe

also feeding secondary circulation and vent pipe

Secondary return

Primary flow

Sink

Hot-water cylinder

Control valve

Boiler

Primary return

▮ 22mm draw-off pipes   ‖ 22mm secondary circulation pipes

▮ 15mm draw-off pipes   ▦ 22mm draw-off secondary circulation pipes

screw holes in the top part of the casing to vertical suspension brackets. It is essential that fixings are firmly made, since a displaced cistern could release a torrent of water! It is a good idea to fix a backing board and to anchor the cistern to this.

Overflows must be one size greater in diameter than the supply pipe. These fix in place with a washer and a nut, attached to a bulkhead fixing. Use of plastic elbows enable the overflow to be taken out behind the toilet.

WC pans

WC pans terminate with a water-trap bend, known either as a 'P' or as an 'S' bend. The 'P' trap is used to provide an outlet through a wall, while the 'S' trap generally provides a floor outlet.

Some types of pan are supplied with a choice of 'P' or 'S' trap, have provision for outlet connection on either side of the pan, and do not need any extra connecting pieces.

A damaged and leaking WC pan should never be patched up, since the leakage could provide a serious threat to health and hygiene.

Where an "S" bend pan connects to a vitreous, glazed pipe, take care to avoid damaging this outlet if the pan is removed. It is safer to break out an old pan at the

bend, to avoid undue stress on the collar of the soil pipe.

Place rag into the collar to prevent débris from falling in when the pan is removed, and then carefully chip away the segments of the pan at the collar joint.

Such joints are usually consolidated and sealed with tarred hemp, called gaskin, which is wrapped together between the socket and spiggot. The joint may be finished with a mortar fillet, usually consisting of fast-setting cement.

When the joint for the new pan is to be made in a similar fashion, wrap the tarred hemp tightly round the pipe and push this well home. Do not allow loose ends to intrude into the pipe as this may cause blockages.

Where a type of suite brings the position of the pan forward of the one replaced, extension pieces, either in plastic, vitreous, glazed pipe or china, can be mortared in or, in the case of plastic, connected with rubber sealing rings. Modern plastic, push-fit rubber connectors are simple to fit and have the advantage of being easy to remove and put back.

There are various types of plastic connector which enable quick-fit connections to be made between the pan outlet and the soil-pipe. These have a screw-in stem and a rubber outlet seal and provide flexibility

in movement, as well as facilitating removal of pans, without the tedious need to break out mortar collars.

When fitting a WC pan or bidet on solid floors, bed these on to a thick screed of mortar. First check that the pan is level and allow the mortar to dry before checking and testing for firmness.

Alignment of a new pan can be made using a spirit level. On uneven solid floors, small timber wedges can be slid beneath the pan to level it.

Never screw directly into the fixing holes through the WC base or you may crack it. Use brass fixing screws, set into rubber grommets. Brass will not corrode or rust. Tighten the screws down evenly but avoid overtightening.

Check that the pan is firm and free from movement. It must never rock, or joints might crack and the pan become unseated.

The only tools needed to change a toilet seat are a spanner and a screwdriver. There are three basic types of fixing, all through pre-made holes in the back of the pan. Differences are only of detail and instructions should be supplied with a replacement seat.

Fitting baths

Enamelled cast-iron baths are still the most widely used, with enamelled pressed-steel baths, next in popularity. The latter are much lighter and, consequently, easier to transport and fit. Cast-iron has, however, far greater heat-retention properties.

Acrylic-plastic baths, while gaining in popularity, have the rather unfair reputation that they easily scratch and mark. Scratches can be fairly easily removed with fine wire wool, and finished off with metal polish. Do not, however, use abrasives as a cleaning medium.

Plastic and steel baths are generally fitted with a cradle support, though some plastic baths, with ribbed supports, do not require cradling.

Modern baths possess levelling devices to enable the bath to 'sit' correctly on the floor. Old baths may need wedges under the feet if the floor is uneven.

Taps, waste outlets and overflows are fitted similarly to wash handbasins. Mixer taps have separate stems for hot and cold inlets; the actual mixing is done in the body of the tap.

With both pressed steel and plastic baths, because of their thin structure, spacing pieces between the tap and the underside of the bath are needed to accommodate the square shoulders or lugs under the tap body. These help the tap to lock into the correct position.

Combination wastes and overflows, now widely used, generally have a flexible hose between overflow and the slotted waste outlet. These are simply fixed, using jointing compound and plastic washers.

Once the bath is installed check, with a spirit level, that it is level. This automatically provides the correct fall for draining the bath, since the floor of a bath slopes.

The rim should be kept as close as possible to the wall, so that edge sealing, with trim or with mastic, can finally be carried out.

Lime scale, a sediment which builds up and restricts the bore of pipework, can be a problem. A water softener, which can be a portable device or plumbed into the mains, can cure the difficulty. Gas and electric water heaters, the installation of which are also described, are prone to scale in hardwater areas. Used in conjunction with a water softener, the problems of scaling are eliminated.

There are four basic types of low-pressure electric water and storage heater. These usually consist of a copper cylinder inside an enamelled steel case.

Free-outlet

'Free-outlet' or single-point heaters supply hot water to one particular place. It is possible to serve two adjacent points by means of a swivel-arm arrangement. The most usual sizes have a capacity of around seven litres or 14 litres.

The main use is at kitchen sinks or wash basins where there is no alternative hot-water supply or, the hot-water source is a long way from a storage system and water would be wasted. Some free-outlet heaters are made in sizes of up to about 90 litres

Cold water may be drawn from the mains, where the appliance is fitted over a kitchen sink, though supply can be taken from the storage cistern.

The local water authority should be informed if you want to supply the heater direct from the mains.

The heater works by drawing in cold water at the base of the cylinder, causing hot water at the top to spill out over a weir-type outlet. The design allows for the expansion of hot water.

Another type of low-pressure water heater possesses a pipe layout similar to that of a standard hot-water cylinder. Cold water from the storage cistern is heated by an immersion heater and vented back to the storage system by means of a draw-off pipe. Several draw-off points can be taken from the pipe run.

Low-pressure heaters must be connected to the cold storage cistern and not to the mains.

Some types have two immersion heaters, one in the upper section, for hand-basins, and the other in the lower section, working with the first, to supply hot water at times of greater demand; then both heat the entire heater water content.

Heaters can be both floor- or wall-mounted.

Combined operations

Where there is no other hot-water system, or where there is a limitation on head room which prevents the use of an independent storage cistern, a combination system can be used. As these incorporate their own cold-storage arrangements, these are usually more economic to install than a conventional water heater.

This pattern of heater must be placed above the highest draw-off point, otherwise it will not have the necessary head of water. The combination unit is a dual-purpose appliance, with an upper cold-water cistern and a lower hot-water sec-

This type of gas instantaneous hot-water heater can be stowed away out of sight beneath a kitchen unit. It incorporates a flue to the outside.

Water softener can be fitted beneath a kitchen unit, out of sight yet accessible

Connections are inlet and outlet; the smaller, centre outlet is the salt drain

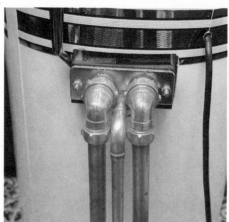

Water softener, together with its salt container, located beneath kitchen unit

Connections can be with compression or capillary fittings; or in a combination

Wall-mounted (hot-water) heater provides instant hot water at various taps in home.

tion, connected by a supply pipe at the bottom of the hot-water section.

A vent pipe, taken from the base of the top section, provides for hot-water expansion. Fitted with a conventional overflow connection from the cold-water section, the self-contained combination unit is completed with a cold feed which enters a ball valve from either mains or storage.

Where a combination unit is fitted, ensure that it has an adequate capacity, otherwise the low-capacity cold-water section may be emptied when demand is heavy.

A remedy is to reduce the flow of hot water, allowing the cold feed to keep pace, or increase the size of the unit, taking care to leave a safety margin. Combination units may be used in conjunction with indirect hot-water systems.

Cistern pattern
The cistern type of electric water heater works on the same principle as a combination unit. These are intended to be seen and usually encased in enamelled steel jackets.

The hot-water section in some models is insulated, as is also the division between the hot and cold sections. Heating is by means of an immersion heater and the hot water may be drawn off anywhere in the house. A wide choice of models is made.

Instantaneous heaters
The instantaneous water heater does not use storage arrangements. Incoming cold water flows over plates which contain electrical elements, heating the water.

Flow is regulated by the temperature of the water required. These heaters are not able to provide the full supply of a storage heater but are effective in providing localized hot water at a given point.

These have many advantages where used as heaters for showers or handbasins, and most models can be run directly from the mains or from a storage cistern, provided a sufficient head of water exists. Only a single supply pipe is needed, which makes installation cheaper.

Since you only heat water you are going to use and are not subject to the heat losses of a storage heater this type of water heating is competitive in running costs. There is no great difference in initial cost between a direct heater and a storage heater.

Electrical considerations
A 13A power supply is needed to serve electrical water heaters. This may be in the form of a fused spur from a ring-main circuit or an independent power circuit.

Gas
Gas-fired heaters fall into two types—storage and instantaneous. The storage heater has a circulatory boiler connected to a hot-water cylinder; this heats the water which is then transferred to the storage cylinder through a circulating pipe.

Another pipe draws cooler water from the base of the cylinder back to the boiler for reheating, similar to normal domestic hot-water arrangements.

Since gas appliances emit fumes, some means of removing these must be provided;

this is generally achieved by means of an asbestos flue pipe taken through an exterior wall or a metal flue grill.

Gas circulators may be directly coupled to a hot-water cylinder and the flue taken out through a rear wall. Most of these types have their temperatures thermostatically controlled.

Instantaneous gas water heaters can possess either single- or multi-point outlets, and subject to approval, may be run off the mains or from the storage cistern. The latter should provide the minimum 1m head of water. There are a wide range of gas appliances to meet all domestic needs.

A single-point instantaneous gas heater is a good choice at a kitchen sink or wash basin. Where connected to mains, the hot water can be used for cooking—water from a hot cylinder cannot be used for this.

One type of unit is able to supply water at temperatures varying from warm, hot to boiling; this is achieved by fitting hot and cold taps and a three position temperature selector.

Some gas-fired heaters supply hot water at several points in the home. The water flow opens the main gas supply when a hot tap is turned on.

The supply is lit by the pilot light. A safety device prevents the main gas supply from operating when the pilot light is not ignited.

Some heaters can be partially recessed into the wall. Fresh air, for combustion, is drawn in through a room-sealed duct from the outside, which allows the working parts of the unit to be let into the wall. Some project as little as 130mm from the face.

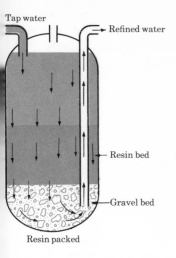

Tap water → Refined water

Resin bed

Gravel bed

Resin packed

Cycle 1 Downflow conditioning

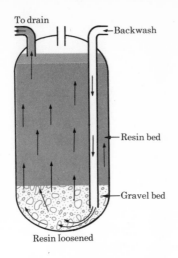

To drain — Backwash

Resin bed

Gravel bed

Resin loosened

Cycle 2 Upflow backwash

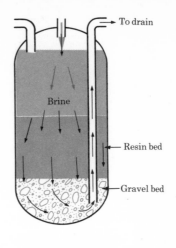

To drain

Brine

Resin bed

Gravel bed

Cycle 3 Downflow brining

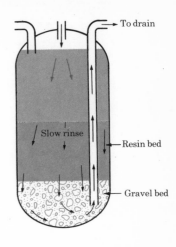

To drain

Slow rinse

Resin bed

Gravel bed

Cycle 4 Downflow slow rinse

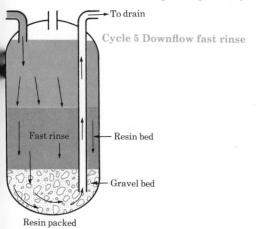

To drain

Cycle 5 Downflow fast rinse

Fast rinse

Resin bed

Gravel bed

Resin packed

Sofnol five-cycle water softening process

Air-break valve

Hard-water supply to kitchen tap, Garden use

By-pass assembly

Cold storage cistern

Drain

Rising main

Water softeners

Hard water is a common problem. Elements, such as calcium and magnesium, present in tiny particles in water, cause deposits of lime scale to form on the inside of pipes, reducing the bore and the efficiency of water flow.

Flow can become so constricted that it may eventually fail; on some heating systems, this can also present hazard from burst pipes containing scalding water.

In hard-water areas, up to 75 per cent more soap has to be used to produce a satisfactory lather, compared with soft-water areas, such as where water supplies are from mountain streams.

Electrical and gas water heaters, kettles and other appliances are all prone to scaling in hard-water districts. Clothes, when washed, can present less than a 'shining-white' look; skin and hair textures are also improved by using soft water. Crockery may also be less smeary and have 'sparkle' where soft water is used.

A water softener extracts the 'hardening' particles chemically. A unit can be fitted to filtrate the entire domestic supply, or just to condition the cold storage water. 'Hard' water then remains at the kitchen sink, for drinking, and for the garden tap.

The unit is plumbed into the rising main. The installation position is very much a question of choice. Hot storage water, mixed with hard water, will, obviously, be semi-hard. A car washed with 'soft' water will, however, be easier to clean and less prone to leave 'water rings'.

A water softener consists of a cylinder with an inlet and an outlet, connected across the rising-main cold-feed. The softening process is carried out by the flow of incoming water through a resin bed, which removes particles that cause water hardness. The resin bed is cleansed or rejuvenated by salt from a reservoir, which is afterwards flushed out at a third, drain, connection.

The entire action of the unit, which is electrically controlled, is automatic but may be overriden manually. Running costs for an average unit are minimal.

A typical unit works on a multi-cycle phase. The resin ion-exchange bed exchanges the hard-water elements, such as calcium and magnesium, for sodium, which is soft and does not leave a deposit. The full process takes about 35 minutes.

Units are made in various shapes and forms and provide for the needs of households of various sizes. Units can be fitted in a kitchen, utility room, bathroom, or wherever there is reasonable space. Under-sink versions are also made. Some models incorporate the salt reservoir; on larger models, this is a separate unit.

Some units are complete with a special by-pass kit, which allows the unit to be switched out at will.

Where there is unusually heavy demand for soft water, a manual button enables this to be reset outside the normal phase of operation.

The unit is simply connected using standard fittings. This means first shutting down the mains stopcock and cutting into the cold-water feed.

If it is not possible to fit the unit directly into the cold feed, it may be necessary to re-route this to the position chosen to locate the water softener.

A typical unit, such as the Sofnol water softener, works on a five-cycle principle.

These are:

Cycle 1: Downflow conditioning. The flow of tap water keeps the resin bed tightly packed so that, as it conditions, it also filters out rust, iron and other suspended solids.

Cycle 2: Upflow backwash. The upward flow of water loosens the resin and washes away the iron, rust and other minute particles trapped during the first cycle. A controlled flow rate ensures the proper cleansing of the resin.

The backwash must be properly controlled by the unit so that the solids are effectively flushed away. This could otherwise result in clogged controls or a fouled resin bed.

Cycle 3: Downflow brining. Brine next flows in at the top of the resin tank and is separately controlled to ensure optimum salt effectiveness. Some makes combine the backwash and brining functions.

Too slow a backwash function, and a brining phase which is too fast, can waste salt and water and not condition the resin bed properly.

Cycle 4: Downflow slow rinse. This phase removes minute particles.

Cycle 5: Downflow fast rinse. This flushes away any pockets and concentrations of salt and iron left in the resin bed after the slow rinse. The unit is now regenerated and ready to perform a fresh cycle.

Where the unit supplies the cold-storage cistern, the demands on this will control the operation of the water softener, within the capacity of a given model.

Outlook indoors: showery

A shower cubicle can be accommodated in a relatively small place in bathroom

A 'showery outlook' indoors may point to one of the most invigorating ways of bathing–taking a shower. This may consist of a separate unit or an attachment to a bath. Shower cubicles can be fitted in various otherwise-unused corners of the home; you can make up a shower tray from glass fibre or from concrete.

The choice, when considering fitting a shower, is broadly between the independent shower head or the flexible shower attachment. The former can be either a fixed-height attachment on a wall or a flexible arm which can hang on a wall attachment. The flexible attachment connects to a mixer tap set.

The former requires a separate shower cubicle; the latter requires no extra facilities, beyond making provision against any splashing which may occur.

A shower can be provided in a space of only about 760mm². Many bathrooms have a space where a shower facility could be sited–either by constructing a separate cubicle or fitting a ready-made one.

Frequently, apparently wasted space, such as deep cupboards or recesses beneath stairs or space on landings, can be adapted for shower cubicles. You should, of course, take into account the position of supply services, to ensure the most favourable routing of water supply and drain outlets.

Showers have many advantages over the 'sit-down' bath. Used in place of a bath, a shower takes less space and uses less water. It also provides a continual flow of clean water. It is quicker to take a shower than a conventional bath, and there is not the same risk of slipping as when getting out of a bath.

A purpose-made shower attachment fitted to a bath mixing set allows the flow of water to be directed either into the bath or to come from the shower head.

To restrict the spray to the bath, the area around the shower attachment should be enclosed. Frames from aluminium section can be cut to fit and screens of plastic or glass fitted. You can make up your own sections and screens.

The shower cubicle consists of three fixed sides, with, usually, a curtain at the fourth. On some expensive, factory-made units, the fourth side may consist of an opening glass door.

The interior walls of a shower cubicle must be of materials which are waterproof. Surfaces can be made water repellant by waterproof surfacings or by tiles–ceramic, plastic or stainless steel. The adhesives and any grouting used must be waterproof or water will get behind the tiles and cause the surface to lift and crack.

Waterproof adhesive is also desirable, especially for floor tiling, which can consist of standard ceramic tiles, stone, or mosaic.

It is necessary to include a tray or upstand to receive the water. A precast

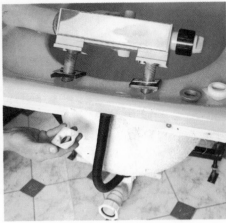
Bath shower assembly fits in place of conventional set of hot and cold taps

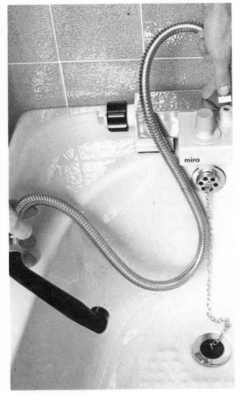
Shower fitting is by simple screw connection; mixer also serves bath tap

High-level point for shower fitting. Plastic curtains prevent water splash

tray of plastic or fireclay can be used. Ready-made trays incorporate a waste outlet, which is connected to a trap.

A shower has to have two sources of supply –hot and cold water. These are mixed either manually or thermostatically to provide a spray at comfortable temperature.

One method of intermingling the flow is with a mixing set. This allows the flow of hot and cold water through two valves or screw-down taps. It is advisable to set the water flow to the pressure and temperature required before entering the cubicle.

Open the cold supply and then turn on the hot service until the required temperature and spray force is reached. A fluctuation of pressure on the supply could affect the mixture setting and produce dangerously hot water.

Thermostatic mixing valves, though far safer, are much more expensive. While not dependent on separate supplies, they

are best given 'first-pull' call on the system. Temperature settings are maintained regardless of fluctuations of pressure. Most mixing valves have a separate control which allows the spray force to be varied.

To provide the correct pressure, there should be a minimum 'head' of water of 900mm, though 1220mm to 1520mm provides a more forceful spray.

The 'head' is the point from the base of the cistern to the top or head of the spray, to provide pressure for the most common type of spray, the rose. An 'atomized' spray, which is much finer, needs a minimum head of 2450mm. If the distances are reduced, the water may flow inefficiently.

Most shower units require cold supplies using pipes of 15mm bore (10mm in plastic), though some may need 22mm supply to maintain an adequate water force. If bends in pipework are likely to hamper supply, the larger size will be needed.

Mixing valves operate in a similar fashion to mixing sets and thermostatic mixing valves–except that the water-mixing and temperature settings are controlled through a single regulator.

The dangers from fluctuating pressure also apply to mixing valves and sets. Only a thermostatic valve can overcome this problem.

Showers should be connected to the low-pressure side of the domestic system–the storage cistern–and the pressure of both hot and cold water should be as even as possible.

Connection to the mains is forbidden in the UK but this is not the case in certain other countries. Where mains connection is made, there is no corresponding problem of maintaining pressure, since the rising main is usually of a high pressure.

In the atomized units, the water droplets are atomized by centrifugal force. The rose-type head breaks up the main body of water and distributes it in a maze of tiny droplets. It is pleasant and invigorat-

Where only a low 'head' of water can be obtained, accelerator pump can be fitted

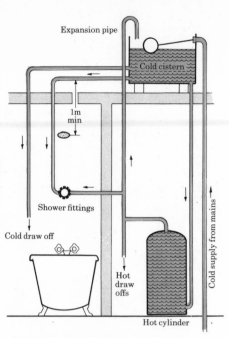

Expansion pipe

Cold cistern

1m min

Shower fittings

Cold draw off

Hot draw offs

Cold supply from mains

Hot cylinder

A minimum 'head' of 1 metre is needed for successful operation of a shower

also be advisable to increase the height from the minimum to compensate for possible pressure loss.

Waste outlets should be taken into a waste trap which has a minimum diameter of 38mm. There must be access to the trap for cleaning and a tubular trap is preferable to a bottle trap, since the latter may block up more readily on shower installations.

A slight drainage fall (1:80) must be maintained to connect up with the plumbing services, which, in modern practice, should be to the main soil system. In older systems, the water may discharge into a hopper head.

Wastes can be plumbed in copper or plastic but the latter is quicker, cheaper and simpler.

The fitting of the waste outlet follows the same technique to that of a bath or sink waste.

Lighting in showers must be of the enclosed pattern. Any internal lighting should be controlled by a pull switch. If using a light switch it should be located safely outside the bathroom.

Wires and light bulbs should not be exposed: light bulbs can explode if subjected to splashing.

Making a shower tray

A shower tray can be built of concrete, using an inner and outer mould composed of timber shuttering. To give strength, a reinforcing basket of 6mm steel rods or mesh can be made up, corresponding with the shape of the tray.

The mould is a reversed one and some 100mm of concrete, of a 1:2:3 stiff mix, is suitable. Where the drain plug is to be located, cut a 40mm wood plug, wrap this in paper or wax the plug and insert it in the mould in the appropriate place.

Allow the concrete some days to harden and then gently tap away and dismantle the shuttering. Continue to take care, since the concrete will be brittle for some two weeks, and turn it over.

The mould can be tiled once the tray is located in position. It may be necessary to raise this up on brick or wall blocks to give clearance for the waste and related trap and pipework beneath.

A similar mould of timber or plaster of Paris can be used for a glass-fibre tray. Glass fibre presents a surface which will show every blemish, so aim for a very smooth surface. Rub down the mould and treat with a proprietary filler where there are blemishes.

It is necessary to apply a mould sealer over all porous surfaces and then a wax emulsion to non-porous surfaces, such as metal glass or laminate. Various proprietary glass-fibre kits are available. Detailed descriptions of working techniques are supplied with a number of kits.

Surfaces should be treated with a release agent, to prevent the glass fibre from sticking to the mould. First, apply a coat of resin called the gel coat, which contains any additives to provide colouring.

This is followed by successive layers of glass-fibre mat and resin, with mixed-in catalyst. Finally, a sealer completes the job.

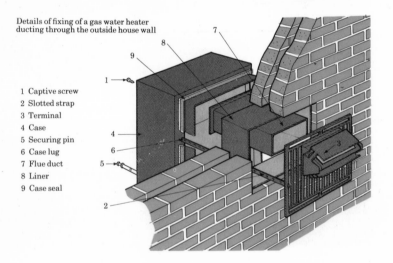

Details of fixing of a gas water heater ducting through the outside house wall

1 Captive screw
2 Slotted strap
3 Terminal
4 Case
5 Securing pin
6 Case lug
7 Flue duct
8 Liner
9 Case seal

ing and is achieved by forcing the flow of water through many small holes in the headplate.

Connecting

To connect up a shower arrangement to the existing plumbing system, you must empty existing pipes. Turn off any cistern stopcock, or tie up the ball valve and drain the cistern down. Open all the hot-water taps; this will drain off the water in the crown of the cistern, which will be sufficient.

Usually, the system can be connected most easily by means of tee-piece connectors. If there is a heavy storage-water demand or the pipework follows a long and tortuous route, it may be advisable to fit a separate supply pipe from the cistern. This will require complete emptying of the cistern, and a new connection will have to be made about 50mm up from the bottom.

It is possible to chase out wall surfaces and sink in pipes, or they can be boxed in behind the shower walling. It is essential

that these should be accessible for maintenance and this is best done by fitting removable panels or tiled sections on to panelling which can be removed. Tiled panels can be drilled and fixings made by cupped chrome-headed screws.

Where pipework has to show, it can be painted to disguise it or stainless-steel tubing may be left exposed; this can look quite attractive.

Testing all installations before final concealment or boxing in of pipes is important. Where possible, it is much better to conceal all pipework, and many shower fitments provide for hidden supplies, taken in at the back.

Where you contemplate installing a shower in an upstairs room, it may be difficult to provide the desired water head. This may be achieved by raising the height of the storage cistern by placing it on a stout platform. This, of course, means draining down the system, extending and, possibly, re-routing loft pipework.

If the pipe run to the shower is long and there are a number of bends, it may

Revamp your kitchen plumbing

you decide to update your kitchen, ou will find that renewing, re-routing extending plumbing services is usu-y needed. While basically hot and old water is needed at the kitchen nk, you may want to provide services r permanently plumbed-in appli-nces such as waste eliminators, dish-ashers and washing machines.

itchen re-plumbing, more often than ot, is needed as a result of updating ser-ces and fitting new sink units. This may ean re-routing of existing plumbing and e replacement of old lead-work or iron pe.

For example, an existing set of taps may e of the 'bib' or wall-mounted type, which ed routing through the base of a ainless-steel sink unit. These are nor-ally fitted with fixing holes to admit llar taps.

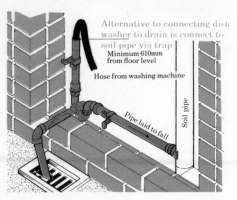
Alternative to connecting dish washer to drain is connect to soil pipe via trap
Minimum 610mm from floor level
Hose from washing machine
Soil pipe
Pipe laid to fall

Waste outlet with bedding ring of mastic is fitted into outlet hole in the sink

Overflow connection fits on to the waste. This connects over polypropylene washer

Next, a lock nut is tightened and the bottle trap, with 'o' ring seal, screws on

Key Terrain mixer tap slots into openings in top of sink. Single taps can be used

After assembly of tap, swivel connectors containing fibre washer seals fit to stems

Standard connectors are used to join the supply pipes. Stop cock is in rising main

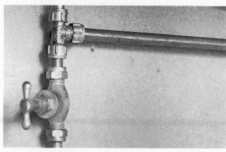

Sink assembly, with fitted waste and key-hole plate assembly of waste eliminator

Tubular wastes are used on eliminators. These are less prone to sedimentation

Main body of Parkamatic Eliminator slots into keyhole housing fitted to sink waste

Unit motor clips on to main body; 'o' ring completes seal. Finally, connect mains

A double-bowl arrangement in a Carron sink, with separate bowl for eliminator

Sinks

Modern sinks are usually made of stainless steel, vitreous enamel, plastic or plasticized steel. These may consist of single- or double-drainer units. Single drainer tops can be either left or right handed. Tops can also have single or double bowls.

The waste outlet on a modern sink is usually of 35mm diameter. If, however, a kitchen-waste eliminator is to be fitted beneath, the hole must be capable of enlargement to a diameter of 90mm. This also almost certainly dictates the use of a stainless-steel sink, as other types are not normally capable of having the outlet enlarged.

Modern sinks are supported on a base cabinet by brackets and fixing rails. Fixing may vary slightly with differing makes.

Taps

Taps may be single or mixer. Holes are usually cut in the top of the unit, at the rear, to admit the taps. Taps are bedded in the sink unit in either a thin rim of non-hardening mastic or the joint is sealed with polypropylene washers. A plastic 'top hat' connector then screws on to the tail of the taps from beneath; lock nuts are tightened over these.

Next, 'tap' or swivel connectors, either straight or angled to meet the pipework arrangement, are screwed on to the tail and tightened. These can be either capillary or compression ended, and may contain a fibre washer to provide a seal, or PTFE sealing tape is wound around the threads to effect a seal.

Mixers are fixed in basically the same way as individual taps, with hot and cold connections made to the appropriate stems, since the mixing function is performed within the body of the tap.

Service

In the kitchen, service connection normally comes direct from the rising main using a 'tee-piece' branch connection; the service is carried on to supply the cold storage cistern. Cold-water pipe-work is usually of 15mm diameter but can be 10mm if the service is in plastic tube.

Once the sink top is lined up and taps and terminals are fitted, check that the outlets meet the supply pipes. It may be necessary to angle pipework to facilitate connections. It is best to use a pipe spring or bender rather than small fittings as this will reduce water turbulence although there may be cases where the very-tight angle afforded by a fitting is necessary. Pipes should be clipped to the walls at intervals to cut stress and vibration.

Outlets and traps

The waste outlet is next fitted. The waste is either bedded in non-hardening mastic or set into a rubber washer. The waste grill is fixed by a centre bolt. A washer fits over the waste connector which, in turn, is screwed to the threaded sink outlet.

Before screwing the trap on to the outlet stem, check that it is in line with the waste outlet. The kitchen trap should be

5mm deep. You can use either a tubular or bottle trap. These can be made of lead, copper or plastic. The plastic type, screwed together with a rubber 'o'-ring seal, is quick and reliable to fit and needs no special skills.

Overflows

Some overflows have a flexible tube connected to the overflow grill and then to a screwed boss on the waste trap. The trap should be readily accessible, in case of possible blockage. The waste-outlet pipe can be in plastic tube, fed into a trapped yard gulley. A slight fall should be maintained on pipework for waste services.

Plastic pipework cannot readily be bent, so fixed or variable elbow bends are used to provide an angle or change of direction. Most plastic pipework and bends are connected by the solvent-weld method. Plastic tube is easily cut with a fine-toothed hacksaw blade.

Washing machines

These may require both hot and cold supply, though some work on a single hot or cold supply. The principles of connection are similar for most makes.

Connection to water supply is provided by flexible pipes which fit to the back of the machine. These are usually longer than needed for permanent connection, since a washing machine can be connected for temporary supply to the taps.

These pipes can be easily cut with a sharp knife, though take care to cut squarely and allow sufficient flexibility for the unit to be pulled out for access. The pipes are connected with hose clips and unions to the supply.

Hot water can be supplied by an independent source or by a back boiler. This can be from either a gas or an electric storage system, including an immersion heater, or a multi-outlet instantaneous gas heater, provided this has sufficient hot-water pressure. Single-outlet heaters of any type should not be used.

A minimum head of 2·44m (·28 bar) is generally needed for both hot and cold supply.

Connections can be made from existing pipework by extensions or branches, joined by 'tee' connections. You should incorporate a shut-down valve in the pipework, so that supply can be cut off for ease of removal of the machine.

All fixed pipework must be clipped to wall surfaces and can usually be run unobtrusively at the rear of kitchen units. Once pipe stems are prepared, the flexible hoses can be pushed over the pipes and the hose clips tightened up.

Smear soap over the pipe-connecting 'tails'; this enables pipes to be pushed well home to ensure a leak-proof union.

It may be necessary, to avoid water siphoning, to incorporate, into the permanent waste pipe, an airbreak or vent to the atmosphere. This should be at least 455mm above the level on which the machine stands.

To achieve this, use a 'stand' pipe with a minimum diameter of 35mm, into the top of which the crooked end of the drain hose of the machine is fitted. This should be mounted so that the top end is 790mm above the level of the floor.

The gap between the rubber crooked hose and the bore of the standpipe provides the necessary airbreak to avoid siphonage. The lower end of the standpipe should be taken to the drain, maintaining a gentle, even fall.

Fix the plastic stand and drainage pipe to the wall with plastic clips. A hole through the house wall can be cut with a bolster and cold chisel, or by using a hired rotary hammer drill with a plug-cutting attachment.

On the outside wall, the waste pipe should be fitted at a slight slope to the drain and fixed at intervals with clips to the wall. Pipework can be of the plastic, solvent-weld type or push-fit connectors.

Electrical supply can be from 13A ring main or use a separate point of the same rating, with a three-pin plug. Once the unit is connected at all points, open the shut-down valves to supply water to the machine.

Machines can be located beneath working surfaces; in the case of top-loading units, these should have sufficient pipework to pull the machine forward to an accessible loading position.

Dish washers

The supply arrangement for a dish washer and installation are similar to those of a washing machine. It can usually be operated as a permanently plumbed-in unit or temporarily connected.

The most convenient position in the kitchen should be chosen, since it is in daily use. This is probably under a working top, between kitchen units, on a working top or fixed to the wall. Non-standard-height units can be mounted on a simple timber plinth to bring them up to the height of other appliances.

Connections for a dish washer usually consist of a 15mm hot supply and a 22mm drainage outlet. Usually, connection can be made to the kitchen hot-water supply with a 'tee' branch end, fitted with a stopcock or gate valve, to shut down supply if the unit has to be removed. Connections are made using a hose ferrule fitted on to a branch pipe stem.

The outlet pipe should incorporate a water-seal dip. This can be made by bending the pipe with a spring or bending machine. The pipe slides into the drain hose and fixes with a hose clip.

The drain-pipe connector should be at a maximum height in the highest part of the drain line, but no higher than 900mm.

The 22mm pipe, which can be of copper, stainless steel or plastic, should be taken out through the wall. It must be clipped to the outside wall, drain into the trapped yard gulley, and maintain a gentle fall.

Like washing machines, dish washers should be provided with separate power point or connected to a standard 13A ring main with a three-pin plug.

Kitchen-waste eliminators

These turn waste into paste and have considerable hygienic advantage since practically all perishable waste can be speedily and effectively disposed of. Exceptions are plastics, aluminium milk-bottle tops, glass and fibrous materials, such as banana skins, which can wrap round the blades of the unit.

Waste-disposal units are operated by an electric motor driving an impeller and shredder blades. These reduce the waste to a paste or slurry which is disposed of as normal sink drainage.

A standard 13A electrical supply is needed, but it is desirable to provide either a pull switch or a wall switch fitted well away from the sink, to avoid operation with wet hands.

To fit a unit, the standard sink outlet requires enlargement. Some sinks can be supplied with the enlarged hole. A standard sink outlet is 38mm; an opening of 90mm is usually needed for eliminator outlets. Enamelled, cast-iron or fireclay sinks cannot be enlarged and have to be replaced.

Hole-cutting saws and, where necessary, recessing equipment can be hired to cut the hole. Usually, sinks are recessed, and all that is necessary is enlargement of the hole.

The hole can, however, usually be cut by a simple metal saw, resembling a junior hacksaw, or provided the blade steel is of sufficiently high-tensile strength, a junior hacksaw can be used.

First, carefully mark the position of the hole, cut a starter hole, with a small-diameter drill, then carefully cut out to the diameter of the outlet. Once cut, trim the opening with a round file.

While the hole should be cut with reasonable accuracy, there is usually tolerance of a few millimetres.

Certain techniques are basic to all units, but the maker's instructions should be studied and followed carefully.

The existing sink outlet and waste trap must first be disconnected. A new waste-outlet assembly fits into the enlarged hole, then a clamping device connects to a sink bush, which is coated with mastic sealing. A top housing is fitted and lined up for the position of the outlet pipe.

The outlet bend should have a minimum fall of 7½° but a 15° fall is better; this is connected to the trap. A tubular trap is usually specified for waste units since this is shallower, and, consequently, less liable to retain sediment.

On a variety of models, a reversing switch is fitted, which allows any jams to be freed. On some makes of machine, a dummy plate is provided which fits in place of the body of the unit. If a fault develops in the mechanism, and the unit has to be removed, the sink can remain in use by fixing this plate.

Where plastic outlet pipes are used, the body of the unit should be separately earthed.

An 'o'-ring seal joints the top housing and leaks are unlikely. Slight adjustments can be made to reset seals if there is any seepage of water.

The sink should be firmly fixed at all points to minimize vibration of the unit, which may cause fixings to work loose.

A 38mm waste pipe should be taken into a trapped yard gulley and below the gulley water level, to avoid leaving deposits. If discharge is into a septic tank, this must have a capacity of at least 5,000 litres.

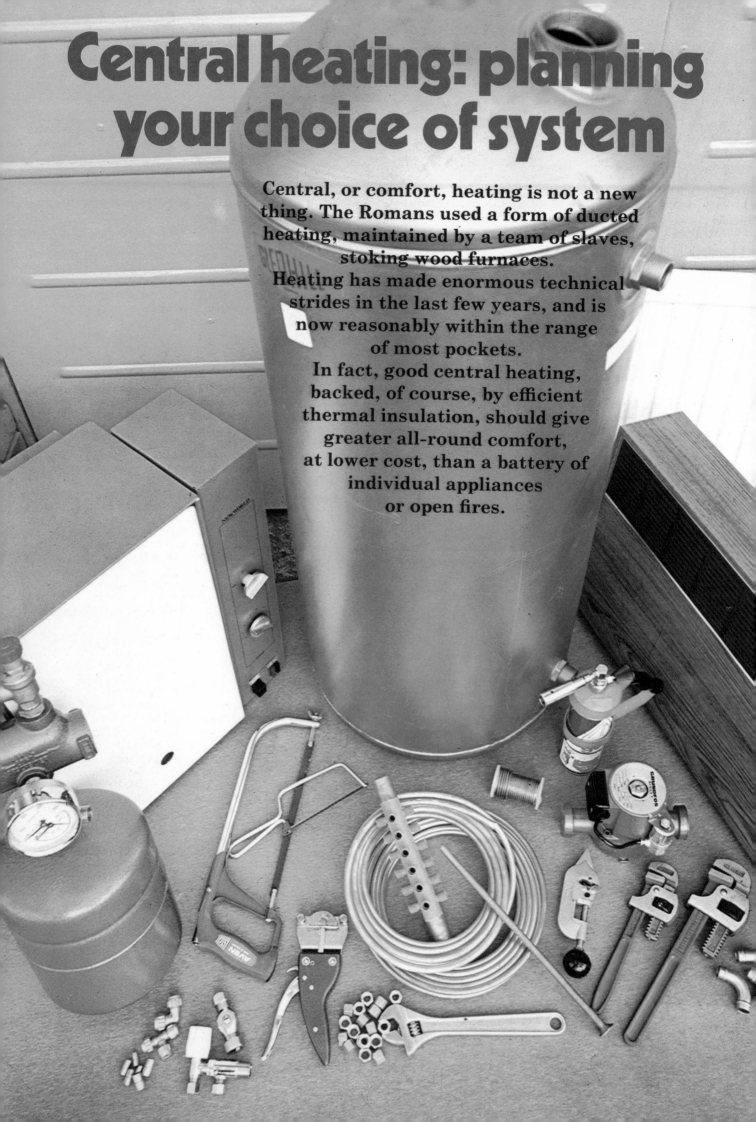

Central heating: planning your choice of system

Central, or comfort, heating is not a new thing. The Romans used a form of ducted heating, maintained by a team of slaves, stoking wood furnaces.

Heating has made enormous technical strides in the last few years, and is now reasonably within the range of most pockets.

In fact, good central heating, backed, of course, by efficient thermal insulation, should give greater all-round comfort, at lower cost, than a battery of individual appliances or open fires.

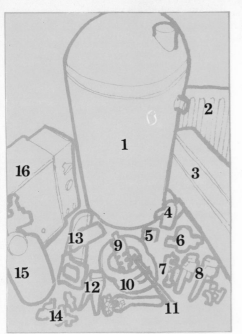

1 Gledhill high recovery hot water cylinder

2 Myson Hullrad

3 Myson fan convector

4 Blowtorch

5 Solder

6 Grundfoss Series 4 pump

7 Pipe cutter

8 Stillson wrenches

9 Wednesbury manifold

10 10mm microbore copper tube

11 15mm bending spring

12 Hand pipe bender

13 Junior and standard hacksaw

14 Radiator valves

15 Pressure vessel with related equipment

16 New World 502 boiler

Modern heating utilizes a range of fuels efficiently, and scientifically directs heat where it is wanted to the best advantage.

Central heating is so called because the source of heat is from one point–though the heat is directed around the home. In one or two cases, central heating is provided by warm-air units which emit heat from a central position and circulate this through wall ducts into each room. However, this may also spread stale air and cooking smells.

Which system?

There is a wide choice of heating appliances–gas, oil, solid fuel or electricity. Radiators, or other heat-emitting units, also offer a wide choice.

Heating systems are either 'wet' or 'dry'. The wet system, the most common, derives heat from heated water circulated along pipes from a boiler to various heat exchangers–panel radiators, skirting or fan convectors or ducts. The water finally returns to the boiler along return pipework, where it is reheated and recycled.

In modern smallbore and microbore systems–the term relates to the pipe sizing–a pump is used to accelerate the water flow.

Modern heating systems also allow the provision of domestic hot water, called the 'primary' circuit. In some designs, hot water is pumped for the primary. In other cases, 'gravity', or natural circulation, is set up by the expansion of hot water.

The microbore principle, which has many technical and physical advantages and may give lower running costs, in some respects is an extension of the smallbore system.

Many early piped heating systems relied totally on the effect of gravity circulation by using large bore pipes; this was neither economic nor efficient.

Open smallbore and microbore systems utilize a feed-and-expansion cistern, located at a high point, such as the loft. This provides for the thermal expansion of hot water, which discharges into this cistern if the water reaches a high temperature.

Evaporation loss is also made up from this cistern, which is simply a smaller version of a cold storage cistern, fitted with a ball valve to regulate the supply of water.

Sealed systems are completely isolated from atmosphere and are pressurized and able to operate at much higher operating temperatures than open systems.

Another arrangement is the loop system, providing a form of heating 'ring main'. Loop systems are a development found largely with linear heaters (skirting convectors). Installing these can cut down dislocation to house fabric. The skirting radiator is part of a continuous smallbore pipework loop. Power convectors may usually be used on loop systems.

The first smallbore heating systems utilized a single pipe. Pipes were run along the skirting boards, to avoid lifting floorboards. This did not always present the most attractive appearance aesthetically. The grave disadvantage of this arrangement is that water temperature falls as heat is transmitted, and further along the system the size of radiators have to be increased to give the desired heat output.

Smallbore and microbore systems utilize separate flow and return circuits, enabling an even temperature of flow water to be maintained.

Electrical

Electrical systems are normally 'dry', though there are electric storage systems which heat hot water and circulate this around pipework.

The most common form is the storage unit. This runs off cheap electricity, stored at night, which heats up refractory blocks, with electric elements.

These are, in effect, electrical radiators, which emit the stored heat throughout the day and can be switched over to full-price electricity by day if a boost is needed. Some are fan-assisted to give a higher heat output. Such systems do not, however, provide instantaneous heat.

Ducted systems can be operated by any kind of heating source. The heat exchange is effected by air circulating and fan assisted through an electrically heated element, or through grills with circulating hot water. Ducts or 'registers' of appropriate sizes are placed to provide the desired comfort levels.

Ducted systems, with few exceptions, are installed during house building because of the trunking or ducting needed to circulate the warm air.

What cost?

There is no completely 'cheap' system of heating. All heating systems cost money to run, but a well-designed system can provide comfort and fair economy. As a rough indication, electrical systems are the most costly to operate, though careful use of off-peak services can bring costs appreciably below costs in situations where electrical appliances are casually used on full-price electricity.

Solid fuel is generally the cheapest, followed by oil and by gas. However, divisions can never be clear cut, and costs for a smaller home may be marginal between the various types of fuel.

Solid fuel

Solid fuels are divided into two main classes: natural, mined fuels, which are cleaned and sized, and processed fuels, made from natural fuels. These are in two forms–carbonization and briquetting. Natural fuels consist of house coal anthracite and Welsh dry steam coal, which are smokeless. House coal may be used with open fires and some types of room heater; dry steam coal is suitable for openable room heaters and boilers.

Both open and closed solid-fuel room heaters can provide hot-water central heating as well as domestic hot water. However, the output of such appliances will not always heat the larger house, and a system of 'zoning' to direct heat into rooms of maximum occupation–living rooms by day and bedrooms by night–may be necessary.

Solid-fuel boilers are usually thermostatically controlled and can provide very high levels of heat output.

Where solid-fuel room heaters are used, it is necessary to have independent hot-water heating during summer when the room heater or fire is not in use. This is best provided by an immersion heater, which screws into a boss in the hot-water cylinder.

Redfyre thermostatic solid-fuel room heater provides full heating and hot water »

Low-water content boiler, by Radiation Ltd, provides whole-house heating and hot water

Open room heaters heat by direct, radiant heat and through a convector grill at the top of the fire. Closed heaters mostly have hoppers which feed fuel by gravity on to the fire. A room heater is normally kept alight through the winter and may need refuelling up to three times in 24 hours. Many high-output heaters have a secondary combustion chamber which effectively 'consumes' the smoke products and enables a wider range of fuels to be burnt.

There are three types of solid-fuel boilers – the section, gravity-feed and pot-type boiler. The first is made of cast iron and consists of a number of sections bolted together in relation to the heat output. Fuel is normally fed by hand.

The gravity-feed unit has a steel boiler, is rather more sophisticated and is fed by a hopper. These are usually thermostatically controlled and use an electric fan which produces a heat intense enough to melt the ash into easily removed clinker. Such boilers have a very high utilization of heat – 75 to 80 per cent.

The pot-type boiler is usually thermostatically controlled and consists of a square or circular firebox, surrounded by a cast-iron or welded-steel boiler. This has an efficiency of between 60 and 70 per cent.

Oil
Oil-fired boilers fall into three types – the wallflame, the pressure-jet and vapouriz-ing boiler, of which the best-known is the wallflame boiler.

Standard pressure-jet boilers burn a gas oil and are inherently noisy and should be fitted in a boiler house away from the home.

Down-firing pressure-jet boilers can operate on kerosene or gas oil. The kerosene-burning versions are relatively quiet and can be used inside the home. Vapourising boilers use domestic paraffin and are quieter still.

For all oil-fired systems, a large-capacity storage tank is needed which has to be accessible to the supply source. Because of this extra equipment, oil-fired systems are the most expensive to install.

Gas
Gas-fired systems merely have the fuel piped into the home from the main supply and have this advantage of convenience. Gas is not always available in rural areas where oil may be the best all-round choice of fuel.

Gas boilers offer a choice of balanced, room-sealed or conventional-flue arrangements. This allows a choice of installation position in the home.

Place for the boiler
Boilers have tended to occupy a traditional position in the kitchen, taking up valuable floor space. Some modern gas boilers are very small, hold very small quantities of water and can be hung on walls, fitted in cupboards or even fitted on outside walls.

All heating systems require some form of controls. The small low-water content gas boiler usually requires a moderately sophisticated control system, which provides considerable efficiency and economy in operation.

Full or part?
Central heating may be said to fall into four general categories – full, partial, background and zoned heating. Full central heating means that desired comfort levels are maintained when the ambient (all-round) temperature outside the home is 1°C. In both partial and background heating, other appliances must be used to maintain the required levels of comfort.

Background heating, though supplying some level of comfort in various parts of the home, assumes that topping up is needed at various times of the year and in certain rooms. This level is usually around 12·8°C.

Partial central heating includes background heating but is not restricted to this. It may mean that all rooms are partially heated to a standard lower than that for full central heating or background heating, or it may mean that some rooms have no heating at all. This also assumes that some leakage of heat from one room to another takes place.

Background heating applies to the standard of heating provided, while partial heating may refer either to the standard of heating or to the fact that only certain rooms are heated at all.

Both partial and background heating, provided there is sufficient capacity to meet extra demand, may later be extended to provide full central heating.

Zoning
Zoned or selected central heating falls between the two previous definitions. Here the boiler or heat-producing appliance lacks the capacity to heat the entire house at one time and the heat must be 'zoned' to those rooms of maximum occupation at a given time, such as living rooms by day.

Controls are frequently employed to perform this zoning function, which can either be automatic or carried out manually, by switching in or out various radiators or convectors.

While all systems take account of the transfer of heat between various parts of the home, methods other than full central heating have limitations, since the essence of effective central heating is to heat adequately both the space and the fabric of a structure.

Topping up
Making up lost heat uses less energy than to restore a considerable loss of fabric and space temperature, as a result of switching the system out completely for periods during the day and at night. It is best to operate the heating system at a lower temperature during such times, as it will prove cheaper to top up the system to the optimum temperatures than heating completely from 'cold'.

Designing the heating system you need

Establishing the heat requirements for a satisfactory level of comfort in the home cannot be arrived at haphazardly. This does not, however, need advanced mathematical skills, for by careful and simple calculation you will be able to work out your requirements to provide comfort with reasonable economy.

Finding the comfort levels you need in the home is basically a matter of simple arithmetic. Even if you are not mathematically minded, it should not be difficult to work out your heat requirements systematically, using a simple formula.

Heating values are expressed in kilowatts per hour (kW/h). Also still used is the Btu/h, or British Thermal Unit/h. This unit of heat measurement will eventually give way fully to the kW/h measure of heat.

An apparently astronomical number of Btu's are needed to heat a home. This is because each unit represents only roughly the heat from one lighted match.

One Btu is the degree of heat needed to raise 1lb of water by 1°F in temperature. Its relevance in a metric system is clearly limited.

One watt per square metre (w/m² °C) is the heat required to raise 1kg of water by a temperature of 1°C. A watt equals 3·4 Btu. One kilowatt/h is 3412 Btu/h.

Metric and Imperial

Imperial heating terminology, though still in parallel use, is being phased out. Fittings and pipework have all been metricated, but some terminology and measurement terms in Imperial will still be encountered.

These are the principal terms:

Pressure The Imperial values are given in inches water gauge (in.wg) or pounds force per square inch (lbf/psi), or lbf/in.². The metric equivalents are the millibar (mbar) for in.wg and the bar for lbf/in².

Temperature Formerly expressed in degrees Fahrenheit (°F), Celsius (formerly called Centigrade) is now used. Example: 60°F (15°C).

Pressure 30in mercury (30″ Hg)–1013·25 mbar. This relates to the setting of gas input pressure and is usually carried out by the gas authority.

Sales unit Therm–100 megajoules (MJ).

Calorific value British Thermal Units/h is expressed in Megajoules per cubic metre (MJ/m³).

Heat rate Btu/h is expressed in kW/h. This relates to consumption and not to effective output. Where information may be required to calculate running costs, megajoules per hour may be used in addition to kilowatts–kW(MJ/h).

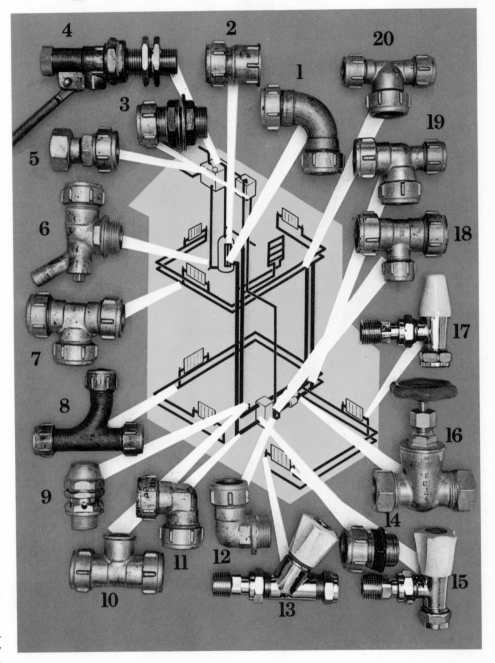

This shows typical central heating and hot water systems, making use of a universal range of plumber's fittings. Those seen are:

1 Slow bend, which gives minimal resistance to water
2 Reduced coupling, usually seen on side of cylinder
3 Copper-to-male iron fitting
4 Valve assembly for cold cistern
5 Tap-swivel connector
6 Slow bend
7 Equal-tee coupling
8 Sweep tee, reduces turbulence where separate currents meet or divide
9 Automatic release valve, used to make sure that pressure in circuit does not become too great
10 Copper-to-copper tee with female iron branch
11 Slow copper-to-copper bend
12 Slow bend, copper-to-male-iron
13 Straight radiator valve, often used in drop-circuit installations
14 Copper-to-male-iron straight coupling
15 Angled valve from radiator
16 Wheel valve used for isolating part of the circuit
17 Lockshield valve, reduces flow of water to balance radiators
18, 19, and 20 are all reducing tees for right-angle joints

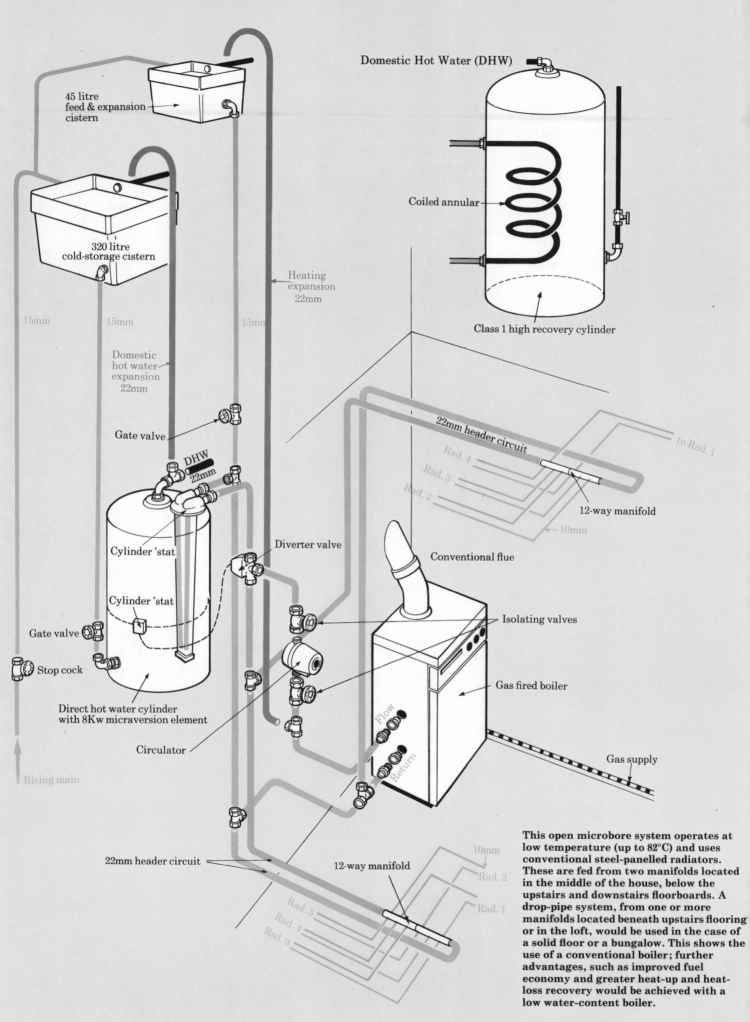

45 litre feed & expansion cistern

320 litre cold-storage cistern

Domestic Hot Water (DHW)

Coiled annular

Class 1 high recovery cylinder

Heating expansion 22mm

15mm 15mm 15mm

Domestic hot water expansion 22mm

Gate valve

DHW 22mm

22mm header circuit

to Rad. 1

Rad. 4
Rad. 3
Rad. 2

12-way manifold

10mm

Cylinder 'stat

Cylinder 'stat

Diverter valve

Conventional flue

Isolating valves

Gate valve

Gas fired boiler

Stop cock

Flow

Return

Direct hot water cylinder with 8Kw micraversion element

Circulator

Gas supply

Rising main

10mm

Rad. 2

Rad. 1

22mm header circuit

12-way manifold

Rad. 5
Rad. 4
Rad. 3

This open microbore system operates at low temperature (up to 82°C) and uses conventional steel-panelled radiators. These are fed from two manifolds located in the middle of the house, below the upstairs and downstairs floorboards. A drop-pipe system, from one or more manifolds located beneath upstairs flooring or in the loft, would be used in the case of a solid floor or a bungalow. This shows the use of a conventional boiler; further advantages, such as improved fuel economy and greater heat-up and heat-loss recovery would be achieved with a low water-content boiler.

'U' values

Heat passes through different substances at different rates. This is called the heat-transference factor, or 'u' value and is expressed in terms of watts per square metre in °C (w/m² °C).

The lower the 'U' value, the better the heat-retaining qualities of a substance. This is measured by the rate in watts passing through a square metre (m²) of a substance for a fall of 1°C in temperature.

You have to establish the 'U' values of the materials used in constructing the home to arrive at given heating needs. Into consideration you need to take the required comfort levels and allow for a number of air changes per hour. It is not entirely a contradiction to insulate a house well and then ventilate it, for damp and stale air must be changed.

In living rooms, the number of air changes per hour should be two; for bedrooms and non-living areas, the factor is 1·5 per each hour.

The 'U' values you need are for windows, walls, floors and roofs. Windows possess the highest rate of heat loss, but this can be halved by double glazing.

Heat losses

Heat is lost in varying amounts through the house fabric, and air must be changed to retain freshness. Stale breath contains a high proportion of moisture, which is why people often complain of damp and running water on windows or other 'cold' surfaces.

Ensure that you are not losing excessive amounts of heat. The loft, in particular, should be insulated with a minimum thickness of 50mm of glass-fibre wrap or its equivalent.

Assuming a sensible level of thermal insulation and the elimination of wasteful heat losses through doors and windows, the following are suggested room temperatures and number of air changes, generally accepted as providing suitable comfort levels, allowing for temperatures outside of —1°C.

Room	Temperature	Air changes
Kitchen	16°C	1·5–2
Toilet, hall, staircase, cloakroom	16°C	1·5–2
Bathroom	19°C	2
Living room, dining room	22°C	2
Bedroom	13°C	1–1·5
Bed-sitting room	22°C	1–1·5

With these figures, conduction of heat from one room to another is ignored. Social habits of a household come strongly into finding the amount of heat needed, and thus the size of fuel bills.

In arriving at the amount of heat required for any home, factors such as the amount of hot water needed and variation in comfort levels likely to be desired have to be considered.

For example, the comfort levels of a bedroom should consider possible future use. While 13°C is acceptable for a bedroom where this may have to serve the dual function of a study, advance provision should be made for extra heat when needed.

Calculating

Single-glazed windows have a factor of 5·68w/m² °C; double glazing reduces the 'u' factor to 2·84; cavity walls have a factor of 1·65; solid walls 2·33; suspended floors a factor of 2·16; solid floors 3·58; tiled-and-felted roofs, 3·18, reduced by good roof insulation; and a plaster ceiling a value of 1·65.

It is usually taken that comfort levels are provided by an internal temperature of 22°C in living rooms, in halls and 13°C in bedrooms. These calculations are based on an ambient (outside) temperature of 0°C, or freezing point.

This example of how to assess your needs for heat is based on a living room 3·66m × 4·57m × 2·44m high, with a 2·44m × 1·22m window and a solid floor. You have to establish the area for both the inside and exterior walls, the temperature requirements of adjacent rooms, and the areas of the ceiling, floor and glass.

First, establish the volume of the room by multiplying length × breadth × height. This provides a figure of 40·83m³ (3·66 × 4·57 × 4 × 2·44).

Work out the area of the outside wall: 3·66 × 2·44 + 4·57 × 2·44 = 20·09m². Take away the area of the glass (2·44 × 1·22 = 2·98), leaving a figure of 17·11.

Establish the area of the inside wall: 3·66 × 2·44 + 4·57 × 2·44 = 20·09.

Next, calculate the area of the floor: 4·57 × 3·66 =16·72m².

For final calculation establish the difference between the ambient —18°C 0°F and the desired internal temperature (22) and the temperature difference between this and the adjacent room temperature, the hall, (6).

Then multiply the number of air changes per hour × cubic capacity of the room by ·37, which is the nominal 'U' factor for heat loss in w/m³ °C on air changes × temperature difference.

Next, multiply the area of the wall by the 'U' factor × the temperature difference between the inside and the outside. Follow the same procedure for the floor and other surface areas. The totals, when added, provide the units of heat in watts you need for comfort.

You will reach high totals by simple multiplication. Divide each of these by a thousand to obtain the figure in kilowatts.

Figures are arrived at as follows:

Room volume 40·83 × 2 (air changes) × ·37 (air-change 'u' factor) × 21 (temperature) = ·668
Outside wall: 20·09 × 1·65 ('u') value of wall × 21 = ·694
Inside wall: 20·09 × 3·80 × 5 = ·382
Floor (solid): 16·72 × 3·58 × 21 = 1·256
Heat loss through glass 2·98 (area) × 5·67 ('u' value) × 21 = 3·55
Total 3·355 kW/hr

This is in the order of 3⅓kW per hour.

No allowance is usual for downstairs ceilings. The final total would be correspondingly reduced by double glazing ('u' 2·83w/m² °C).

These factors are based on average conditions and exposure. In excessively exposed or in sheltered conditions, you will need to make corresponding adjustments.

Sizing of radiators ensures that correct temperatures are derived at a flow temperature of 82°C on conventional small-bore systems, with a return temperature of 71·°C.

The amount of radiator surface needed

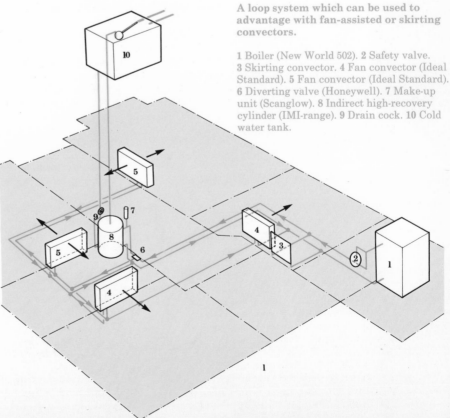

A loop system which can be used to advantage with fan-assisted or skirting convectors.

1 Boiler (New World 502). 2 Safety valve. 3 Skirting convector. 4 Fan convector (Ideal Standard). 5 Fan convector (Ideal Standard). 6 Diverting valve (Honeywell). 7 Make-up unit (Scanglow). 8 Indirect high-recovery cylinder (IMI-range). 9 Drain cock. 10 Cold water tank.

can be readily arrived at from manufacturers' data. For temperatures above 82°C, exposed steel-panelled radiators are not advisable and skirting or fan convectors, thermal or other enclosed radiator units, should be used.

Skirting radiators emit ·123kW at a temperature of 82°C and ·180kW at 96°C. Steel-panelled radiators may be used at elevated (up to 96°C) temperatures or high temperatures (above 96°C), provided these are enclosed and cannot be directly touched.

A rule-of-thumb method of determining heat output requirements at standard temperatures is to allow 2·60m² of radiator surface for every 28·31m³ of space; for double radiators allow 3·15m².

Another practical rule, which can be very accurate in average conditions, is to measure the room volume and, for a desired temperature of 21°C, multiply volume by 83. For a temperature of 16°C, this is multiplied by 63 and for a temperature of 13°C, multiply by 49. This gives the figure in watts. Divide this by 1,000 to obtain the kW/h rating.

Design considerations

Gravity circulation is created as a result of pressure difference between two columns of water having unequal temperatures. The hotter water, as it expands, has less density than cooler columns of water which displace it and start up a circulation.

This circulation will continue while a temperature difference – and, therefore, a pressure difference – exists between the two columns.

This principle of pressure variation applies to systems relying on a pump to create the circulation. Pressure differences are caused by the pump action, the pushing action on the outlet side creating a positive pressure (P) while a negative pressure suction (S) is present on the inlet side. From this it is evident that at some point (P) must merge with (S). This is called the 'neutral point'.

Positive and negative

Whether the circuit water works under negative or positive pressure relies on where the pump is positioned in the circuit. If it is fitted in the return pipe, the circuit will be under negative pressure: if in the flow circuit it is under positive pressure. In many cases, it makes little difference which method is chosen. A situation where it is important, however, is where pipework is taken through a roof space.

Should the pump be fitted in the return, and the circuit placed under suction, it may suck air into the circuit through the vent pipe. This is because of the limited static head available under these conditions, such as in bungalows with solid floors, where overhead circuitry may be necessary.

Avoid placing a pump at the lowest part of the system, as this encourages the collection of sediment.

With many modern pumps, the 'heads' are adjustable between 1·52m and 4·87m, and there is no problem in adjusting the

circulator to provide the desired system output and response.

Pipework sizing

As the pump, or circulator, provides a definite motive force, sizing for any small-pipe or loop system using conventional pipework circuitry presents little problem.

For an average three-bedroomed house of about 100m² area of floor, the following guide can be used to find the correct size of the forced-circulation pipework for a given radiator load.

Up to 5kW (15,000 Btu)	15mm pipe
5kW to 11·5kW (40,000 Btu)	22mm pipe
11·5kW to 22kW (70,000 Btu)	28mm pipe

It is assumed that the layout is conventional and closer to a square than long and thin and has a ground and a first floor. Actual runs of pipe should not be excessive – a 25m long run of 15mm pipe, for example, should be avoided. Water always takes the easiest path, following through the circuit or radiator offering the least resistance.

Index circuit

The capacity of a heating circuit is based on that part of the circuit which contains the greatest load; this is called the index circuit, and may be the longest pipe circuit or that which carries the greatest heat load. As long as the pump is capable of meeting the demands of this circuit, it follows that it will also be able to satisfy the resistance of all other circuits.

The index circuit may try to rob other circuits of heat. This is adjusted by restricting the flow of water to this circuit to the extent necessary to allow remaining circuit requirements to be met, and is called 'balancing' the system.

Both a lockshield and handwheel valve should be fitted to conventional radiators. The handwheel allows radiators to be shut down individually or the temperature of the radiator to be reduced by restricting the flow of water; the lockshield is used to balance radiators.

It is used in conjunction with clip-on thermostats, one of which is attached to the flow pipe and the other to the return pipe. The lockshield is adjusted until the correct mean temperature of the supply pipework on each radiator is achieved.

The mean temperature is that halfway between the flow and the return temperature – 82°C flow, 71°C – mean temperature 77°C.

Static head

Static head in inches, feet or metres is the height of a column of water above the point of measurement, and static pressure, psi or bar, is the pressure exerted by a column of water on an area of 645mm² (1sq.in). There is relationship between static head and static pressure. Because the density of water varies with temperature, all pressure calculations in hot water are based on an arbitrary water temperature of 16·7°C (62°F).

Where the millibar (or lbf/in²) unit of pressure is too large a unit for calculation, the bar (or in.wg) is used. This is the pres-

sure exerted at the base of a column of water 25mm (1in.) high when the water temperature is 16·7°C.

Boiler output

A boiler should be slightly higher in output than the capacity required. The heat output for all the radiators should be calculated plus about 3kW, other than for pumped primary circuits, with about 25 per cent allowance for exceptionally cold weather.

In a single-pipe system, the radiators are connected in series, and there is a by-pass pipe beneath each radiator. Water flowing from the first radiator is fed into the second, and so on.

By the time the water reaches the last radiator, it may have cooled by about 10·5°C. Heat output from this radiator is, therefore, reduced by about 20 per cent. With two-pipe systems, however, all the radiators receive the water at more or less the same temperature, allowing for some heat loss in transmission.

Though it may appear that twice as much pipe is required with this system, it is not so. There is, in fact, very little more needed than in a single-pipe system, and it certainly is more satisfactory in operation.

Humidification

Central heating can dry out the atmosphere and cause physical discomfort.

An over-dry atmosphere can damage woodwork, furniture, pianos, pictures and soft furnishings. Natural moisture is drawn from timber and fittings, causing warping and other damage.

Air humidity is measured as relative humidity (rH). This is defined as the 'percentage of moisture or water vapour in the air by weight at any given temperature to the weight of water vapour required to saturate the air at the same temperature'.

If the rH factor is too low the atmosphere appears stuffy. If it is too high we suffer what might be called the 'tropical' effect. While the degree of comfort required by people differs, a level of 50 per cent rH is suggested for rooms of 21°C.

About 430 millitre at 0°C = 100 per cent
rH very high
10°C = 50 per cent
medium correct
21°C = 25 per cent
very low

Though you can open windows to reduce any imbalance, this is negative and the best solution is a humidifier.

These are basically water containers which allow moisture to evaporate and rectify the moisture loss. The most usual is the radiator-hung version. The best types have an absorbent pad which holds the water and, as heat builds up, allows water to evaporate through the pad. Effectively, an efficient 3·5 litre humidifier will evaporate its contents in 24 hours.

Electric, fan-assisted humidifiers are also made. Another type converts water into micro-atomised particles which are ejected into the atmosphere by an atomisation humidifier.

Installing central heating: your 20-point plan

Installing a central-heating system is a job which can cause major domestic upheaval if not tackled carefully and systematically. Work to a definite plan, have everything to hand, and complete each stage before proceeding to the next. Provided you work to these 'rules', you should quickly have a more comfortable–and valuable–home.

Installation of central heating means following the rules of good basic plumbing–but with a few small differences. The first rule is to assemble everything you need, for at some stage you will be interrupting the domestic water system to make connections.

Fit as much as possible before you shut off the water supply, to minimize dislocation, and work in easy stages–then things will not tend to get out of control!

Tools and equipment

These are broadly those used for general plumbing. You need a pipe cutter or hacksaw, with a fine-toothed high-tensile blade; bending springs (probably both 15mm and 22mm); two spanners, either 200mm or 305mm; a hammer; a cold chisel; a blow torch; a case opener, for lifting floorboards; a handbrace and 19mm auger bit; 38mm No. 12 screws and wall plugs when hanging radiators; an Allen-key set, to fit stems of radiator valves; a power saw; a spirit level, used to align boilers and radiators; and a lead light, for use in dark corners.

Among materials you may need are solder or solder paste; flux; non-toxic plumbing compound; PTFE pipe-thread jointing tape or hemp and jointing compound; fine wire wool; and asbestos cloth, for protecting behind fittings when using a blow torch.

You only need solder or solder paste where you use capillary fittings.

It is best to avoid using standard 15mm fittings, of either compression or capillary type, for bends unless a tight bend is necessary, since this may lead to water turbulence and frictional loss. Use a 'slow' bend–either a fitting or a bend made using a bending spring.

Fittings are largely the same as those used in general plumbing. Boiler fittings, radiator valves and manifolds, on microbore systems, require similar fitting techniques to other plumbing components.

Capillary fittings are neater and cheaper than compression fittings–but need a little more skill to make the joints. If one leaks, it is not so easily patched up as a compression fitting, which usually only needs tightening. The system, or part of it, may have to be drained down to repair a leaky capillary joint, since the presence of water prevents solder from taking.

Workplan

It is best to work to a systematic plan. This is a suggested 20-point programme of work:

1
Assemble all the materials and fittings needed;

2
Plan all pipe runs so that there is the minimum domestic dislocation; lift floorboards and fit them back loosely, so that you can work quickly and without impedance;

3
Thoroughly flush out radiators;

4
Fit all radiator and lockshield valves, plugs and air vents;

5
Hang all radiators or fit convectors;

6
Put in heating pipe runs and connect up the radiator pipework;

7
Install the expansion cistern (where fitted), together with the pipework of the ball valve to the mains supply, and connect the overflow pipe;

8
Install the cylinder and pipework for the domestic hot-water supply and any immersion heater. The latter allows for hot water while the boiler is being installed. It is only likely that you will install an immersion heater permanently with some solid-fuel systems.

Where a self-priming cylinder is fitted an immersion heater cannot be used, for design reasons;

9
Install the boiler and the flue pipe, where the latter is required;

10
Fit the gas supply or oil line, where appropriate. The gas supply can usually be taken from a branch fitting, made on the outlet side of the meter–but check with the gas authority that the supply is adequate to meet heating needs;

11
Connect up any primary (hot-water) circuit;

12
Connect up the pipework circuitry to the boiler;

13
Fill the system and check for leaks. Vent the radiators, making sure that all the lockshield valves are fully open;

14
Flush out the system completely–at least twice:

15
Fit the pump into circuit and circulate hot water, again checking for leaks;

16
Wire in all thermostats and other electrical equipment;

17
Switch on the heating and balance the system. Use clip-on thermostats to adjust lockshields or other balancing valves;

18
Check that the control system is working satisfactorily;

19
After the system has operated for about two weeks, disconnect the pump and flush out again;

20
Check finally for leaks and loss of pressure, particularly with sealed systems operating at elevated or higher temperatures. As air is expelled from the system, water levels have to be topped up.

The pump is not fitted initially and is removed when the circuit is flushed out so that it does not collect harmful sediment.

Slight variations in technique are needed for microbore installation. This may involve fitting pressurised equipment and manifold distributors. Microbore piping is usually easier to run than small bore, because it is more malleable and can often just be threaded beneath floorboards.

Take account of the line of your joists when installing pipe runs. Joists run at right angles below floorboards. If it is necessary to run pipework across the joists, these must be notched to accept the pipes.

Pipes must have sufficient clearance to allow for thermal expansion, otherwise odd creaks may occur. Pipes of 15mm, 22mm and 28mm are usually fixed at intervals with pipe clips.

Never build pipes in or allow them to be gripped between floorboards or joists in such a way that movement, caused by the expansion and contraction of the pipe, produces noise.

A power saw can be used in lifting tongued-and-grooved floorboards, by running the saw along the tongue of one board, allowing the remaining boards to be simply lifted out.

Special floorboard saws are made which enable individual boards to be cut. If you have to cut through a floorboard, go through it at an angle, or directly across it, beside the joist. In the latter case, a timber noggin can be nailed to the joist to support the board.

Floorboarding over pipe circuitry should, if possible, be screwed back and not nailed. This provides for ease of access.

Pump

The pump, or circulator, should be fitted with isolating valves on each side. These can then be simply shut down to isolate the water and allow the pump to be removed without having to drain off circuit water.

It does not greatly matter if the pump is installed in the flow or in the return line of the circuit. A pump mounted upstairs, in a conventional system with a feed-and-expansion cistern, might, in some cases, when first started, surge water into the storage or make-up cistern.

This will not happen if it is fitted in the return pipe.

Do not install the pump in the lowest part of the circuit as this can encourage the formation of sediment. To avoid a situation where the pump again may discharge water via the safety pipe into a cistern, the cold-feed connection and safety pipe should both be on the same side of the pump.

Sometimes, and usually initially when live air is still present in the water, there can be considerable noise from the pump. Most pumps have a vent button, which, when operated, should reduce or cure this.

Expansion cisterns

Expansion cisterns should be located about 1m higher than the main cold-feed cistern and should be connected either close to the boiler heating return connection or into the primary return pipe of the gravity system. Expansion, or safety pipes should be in 22mm-bore pipe and taken over the cistern in a gentle curve–but clear of the water.

Hot cylinders

Provided the water content of a thermostatically controlled small-bore system does not exceed about 135 litres, a self-priming hot-water cylinder can be used. However, these must not be used on solid-fuel systems without thermostatic control, either on the cylinder or on the boiler, since if the water boils, the two waters will mix. The system operates on the principle of an air bubble which separates the primary (heating) and secondary (draw-off) waters. If used on a pumped-primary circuit, the separating air bubble would be pumped out. A special high-recovery cylinder or one accepting a microbore element (direct cylinder) should be used in the latter case.

Valves

A lockshield and a handwheel valve are usually fitted at either end of a radiator. Aesthetically, these look best at the bottom, but if it is physically easier to fit them to the inlets at the top of the radiator, such as on a drop-pipe system, you can do so.

Some types of radiators have the valves built in. Valves may not be necessary at every point on skirting convectors, beyond a balancing valve for the circuit, where a single-pipe series-loop arrangement is used.

A radiator can be easily removed, simply by shutting down both the valves and uncoupling the lock nuts. With care, the water displaced can be collected in a strategically placed bucket.

Radiators

The tops of radiators (or the bottoms in the case of top-entry pipework) are blanked off. An air-release valve is usually fitted at one end of the radiator, though in the case of top-entry connections, the air release valve may be found in pipework in the loft.

Blanking fittings and air-release valves are threaded. These are wrapped with PTFE tape and screwed in with a spanner.

The air vents are simply opened with a key to allow the release of entrapped air, which collects at highest points in systems.

Conventional steel-panelled radiators are hung on brackets fixed securely to the wall. Since radiators are fairly heavy once charged with water, ensure that the fittings, and the fixings are adequate.

Some radiators possess more than two brackets, but this depends on the size.

To fix, mark and check the position of the brackets carefully. Radiators are usually located about 150mm from the floor at the base. Some makes allow slight adjustment on the fixing brackets to enable accurate horizontal alignment.

Where possible, fit radiators below windows, some 75mm below the sill, because these are the room cold spots. Windows are areas which cool surrounding air and create turbulence or draughts.

However, convenience of installation should govern your final decision on the position of radiators. Convected dust above wall-hung radiators may tend to discolour the wall surface. This can be remedied by fitting a shelf about 75mm above the radiator and projecting 25mm to 50mm forward. Where you have uneven walls, a piece of foam rubber can be mounted on the wall face of the shelf.

The effect on transmission of heat when radiators are painted with ordinary paint is very small. Special radiator paint can be used. However, metal paints, such as aluminium or bronze, may reduce the overall emission of heat by up to 15 per cent.

Special points

Install boilers strictly in accordance with the maker's instructions, allowing, for conventional-flue boilers, an adequate air supply. Boilers should stand on a level and fireproof surface, and special care should be taken to conform with local fire and safety requirements.

Make sure that the gravity return pipe to the boiler does not return below the boiler base. This is because the effective resistance of a gravity return pipe can be as much as six times more than that of a rising gravity pipe and could mean a loss of natural circulation.

Never combine the cold-feed and expansion pipes, as this could entrap air in the boiler, with damaging results. Where connection is made to the lower part of the boiler pipework, air is pushed up the safety pipe as the system fills.

Locate draincocks at lowest points in the circuit and at the base of both the boiler and the hot-water cylinder. This will enable the circuit to be drained down partly or fully when necessary.

Filling up

After filling the system with water, all radiators and air cocks should be open to ensure that air is expelled. The water temperature may be raised to half the working temperature for about half an hour and the pump switched off.

Re-vent the system and the pump to clear air collected by the rise in temperature. During the first few weeks of operation, the system should be vented from time to time, to ensure that all air has been expelled.

With a microbore or other system fitted with automatic air venting, this process is carried out automatically.

Pipe bores should be clean and boilers should be flushed out at least twice before starting the pump. It is sound practice to flush the system again after it has been operating for some weeks.

Oil-storage tanks

The size of an oil-storage tank depends on the boiler loading and, therefore, the amount of fuel consumed, plus the space available. The tank should be large enough to hold at least an eight-week fuel supply, calculated at a maximum rate of consumption.

Fuel is also cheaper when bought in larger quantities. Tanks are best sited in the open and above ground. There may be local requirements to be met if it is installed within a building, such as a garage.

A storage tank needs substantial supports, either brick piers or steel framing. The latter is best and usually comes with the tank.

With brick piers, great care is needed when fitting the tank on the top, so that you do not topple the brickwork. A waterproof membrane must be placed between the tank base and the top of the pier.

A concrete raft should be built to accommodate the tank support and should consist of 150mm of concrete on well-tamped hardcore, overlapping the edge of the construction slightly all round.

The tank is connected to the boiler by a flexible oil line, which can be either above or below ground and should be run in the most direct manner.

This line can be either of black metal or copper, and encased in a proprietary tape to prevent corrosion, or in a bituminous solution. A line should have a minimum diameter of 6mm and a maximum length of 9·15m. Over this distance, 10mm pipe should be used to a maximum of twice the length.

Joints should be of the manipulative type, belled with a small tool, if copper, and should use threaded joints, with a petroleum jointing compound, on black metal.

The feed line should contain a filter. A fire safety valve must be located in the pipe at an accessible point. If you fit a tee-piece in the line, this enables a flow-rate gauge to be fitted. A sensing element to operate the fire valve should be fitted above the boiler burner.

The pipe outlet from the tank should be not less than 300mm high and the top of the tank not more than 3·05m above the level of the burner of the boiler.

A draw-off valve should be fitted directly or close to the tank in the oil-feed line. If put on the tank, it must be some 50mm above the bottom, to prevent the intake of sediment.

Other fittings are a fill or offset fill pipe, a 50mm vent, isolating valve, drain valve and contents gauge. The fill valve must be extended to the edge of the tank and be in such a position that the delivery hose is easily connected. This pipe should terminate in a 50mm male-thread hose-coupling connection, with a non-ferrous screw-on cap.

Where the tank has to be located at some distance from a roadway, an offset fill line may have to be provided. This is usually of 38mm diameter and in black steel, terminating in a 50mm male connection.

If this line is over 24·40m long, the diameter should be increased to 50mm. A valve to prevent oil spillage while the hose connection is being made should be fitted. The valve gland packing or diaphragm must be of a pattern suitable for use with fuel oil.

An isolating valve, for connecting the oil supply to the burner, should be fitted in an accessible position. Again, the gland packing, or diaphragm, should be compatible for use with fuel oil.

Tanks must be fitted with a vent pipe, taken from the highest point and be as short as possible. The vent must terminate in the open air and should be fitted with an open-mesh wire balloon.

A drain valve should be fitted in the lowest part of the tank, to remove sludge. The contents gauge should be of an unbreakable type and fitted on to the side of the tank. These are of two basic types. The simplest consists of a sight-level tube, which allows the contents level to be read in the same way as a thermometer.

A gate valve should be fitted to the underside of the tank, to remove any small quantities of water which may have condensed in the internal walls of the tank and collected at the bottom.

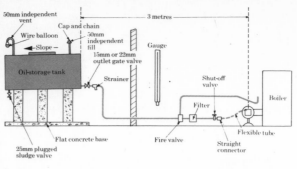

One-pipe system

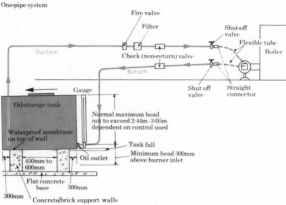

Two-pipe system

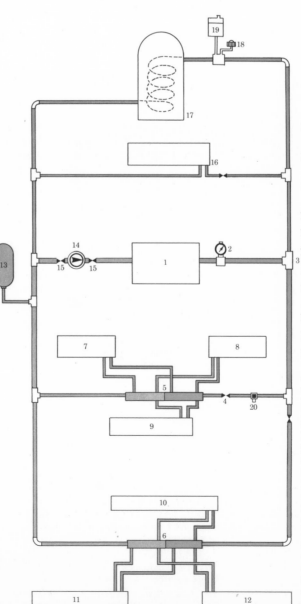

A two-pipe system removes any air sucked into the oil-feed line. This may occur if the oil tank is below the burner; the bottom of the tank is less than 150mm above the level of the burner; or if the tank is buried.

If the oil tank is below the burner level, the pump must be powerful enough to lift the oil to this height. The oil line should have a general inclination up to the burner, to avoid air pockets. Where a high point is unavoidable, a tree-piece and vent fitting should be fitted.

To enable the burner to be removed from the boiler, 1·5m to 3m of oil line near the burner should be of reinforced clear plastic tube, which indicates air bubbles, a source of boiler failure.

Schematic diagram with check-list of components

1 Boiler (New World 502)

2 Safety valve (Scanglo)

3 Diverting valve (Honeywell)

4 Balancing valve (Balofix)

5 Lower manifold (SMC)

6 Upper manifold (SMC)

7 Fan convector (Ideal Standard)

8 Fan convector (Ideal Standard)

9 Fan convector (Ideal Standard)

10 Skirting convector (Ideal Standard)

11 Skirting convector (Ideal Standard)

12 Skirting convector (Ideal Standard)

13 Pressure vessel (Scanglo)

14 Pump (SMC)

15 Lockshield valves (Scanglo)

16 Bathroom radiator (Hullrad)

17 Indirect, high-recovery cylinder (IMI-Range)

18 Auto air vent (Scanglo)

19 Make-up unit (Scanglo)

20 Drain cock (Wednesbury)

An arrangement for a sealed microbore system, utilizing pressurized equipment. A twin manifold system is used. Conventional radiators cannot be used where a system is intended to operate at elevated (around 105°C) or medium (around 110°C) temperatures. Enclosed radiators, skirting convectors or fan convectors must be used, since conventional radiators would be too hot to touch and could cause burns. Various patterns of high-efficiency thermal radiators are made which are suitable for use with systems operating at medium or elevated temperatures.

Microbore heating: open or sealed systems?

Redfyre Centrajet 18/28 down-firing Hydronics' pressure vessel, gauge and pressure-jet boiler, with Perrymatic release valve. Pump: Grundfos 4/35

Among the great strides taken in heating in recent times, the most spectacular development has been that of microbore central heating. In many situations, this is not only quicker to install than conventional, small-bore heating, but more efficient, more economical to run–and less likely to give trouble. The choice is between open and sealed systems–at a range of operating temperatures.

Microbore

Microbore central heating is an extension of the small-bore system, which is sometimes called minibore. It also utilizes two-pipe, flow-and-return arrangements, using small-gauge pipework.

Technically, the advantages of using microbore pipes are: low pipework heat loss, good response and running economy of low thermal-capacity boilers, a reduced number of fittings, and simpler to install.

There is also less disturbance to the fabric of the home during installation, easier balancing of the circuit and less chance of 'hydraulic' noises within the pipes, once in operation.

Manifolds

The heart of the system is a manifold, usually located somewhere in the centre of the house. Pipes to radiators–a flow and return in each case–usually run radially from it.

Where a home has a solid floor, a central manifold may serve radiators or convectors on a drop-pipe principle. The radial arrangement of the manifold system ensures a high degree of circuit self-balancing. With suspended floors, both an upstairs and a downstairs manifold may be used.

The manifolds are fed by main flow-and-return 'header' pipes from the boiler. On a larger heating installation, several manifolds may be used.

Microbore pipe is made in gauges of 6mm, 8mm or 10mm and supplied on reels of 20m or more. The pipe is malleable and, therefore, easy to manipulate. This greatly lessens the number of components and reduces the need to cut and manipulate sections of tube.

The distance from a manifold to a radiator or convector should, ideally, be no more than 7·5m, with a total combined pipework run of 15m.

Microbore can be further divided into open and sealed systems, though sealed systems can also be used on standard small-bore circuits.

Low-water content

Microbore systems work on a principle of circuit low-water content and may use modern, low water-content (low thermal-capacity) boilers. The heat exchange units of these boilers are usually made of copper or stainless steel. This means that as there is little residual heat retained by the boiler, system controls can react swiftly and accurately to precise temperature conditions.

High thermal-capacity boilers are those with cast-iron heat-exchange units. These hold a much larger quantity of water and the jackets ensure the maximum local heat retention.

Residual thermal retention makes such boilers less accurate in response to actual circuit conditions, and these are less satisfactory in performance when used on microbore systems.

Pipework

Heat dissipation below floorboards on microbore pipes is very low. Unless the system is likely to be shut down in cold weather for a protracted period, it is unnecessary to lag these tubes; this would be necessary with small-bore or larger pipework.

Since microbore pipework is almost invisible when painted, and because of its relatively low heat emission, it can be concealed, if necessary, in plasterwork without likely problems of cracking.

It can be bent by hand or over the knee, but with proprietary hand-held pipe-benders, neat, even bends can be produced.

This type of system has, in most cases, definite advantages over small-bore circuitry and is usually cheaper and easier to install, assuming, of course, that the layout design is good.

Pumped primary

Microbore circuits also use the pumped-primary method of heating hot water. For this reason, a high-recovery cylinder or a microbore heating element, which fits into the immersion heater boss, on a direct cylinder, is necessary to maintain the fast response and high heat recovery associated with the system.

Sealed systems

The feed-and-expansion, or 'header' cistern, as with conventional small-bore systems, is incorporated at the highest point in the installation. It serves various roles: it absorbs expansion of heated water, maintains a constant pressure within the system, and provides a source of replenishment for evaporative loss.

Sealed or closed systems differ from the common 'open' system, which employs a feed-and-expansion cistern for venting. Sealed systems should not be permitted access to the atmosphere, so expansion has to be catered for in another way.

Generally, open systems are those working at a flow temperature of 82°C, while sealed systems work at temperatures of 93°C and above.

When a system is sealed many advantages are gained. The feed, or 'header' system is eliminated, together with the associated components and circuitry. This makes the system suitable for bungalows where solid floors dictate a drop-pipe arrangement. The problem of low static head, causing water to be induced over the

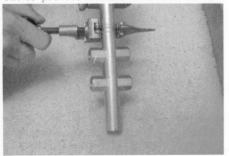

Perrymatic Hydronics' manifold can be cut to provide number of outlets needed

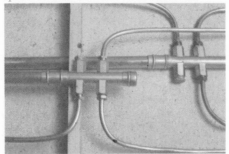

Blanking pieces are fitted to one end; spare outlets can also be blanked off

Aga 48 gas boiler in position. Note the pressure-release valve on flow circuit

With twin-entry valves, an 'inner tube' is fitted two thirds length of radiator

A flexible connector is used to make final connections for radiator valve

Twin connections at one end provide a neat appearance to the radiator pipework

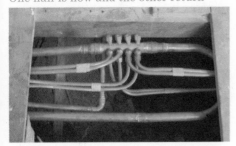

Wednesbury Microfold is a 'split' unit. One half is flow and the other return

Ideal Standard Concord w 10/15 wall-hung low-water content boiler with SMC pump

Balanced-flue duct is fitted into hole cut in wall and outer casing is assembled

The complete skirting convector is fitted on to studs which are screwed into wall

Neat, in-line Balofix valves enable the fitted convectors to be correctly balanced

Ideal Standard skirting convectors can be fitted to wall with screws or masonry nails

Connections for pipework return neatly over the top of finned heating element

Finally, the cover plate snaps on neatly. The adjustable damper is located above

Myson fan convector which services two rooms–with an outlet grill at the rear

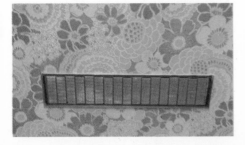

View of rear grill. Output on either side of wall can be separately controlled

Fan convectors are neat and give a high performance for the space they occupy

Golf Slim-Line radiator has low touch temperature and finned waterway

vent pipe or air to be drawn in, are eliminated. However, certain additional control circuitry is needed.

Sealed systems rely on the fact that much higher temperatures can be utilized. With open systems, the upper temperature limit is dictated by the boiling point of water. Allowing a safety margin, this temperature limit is placed at 82°C; and no such system should work at higher temperatures.

Because sealed systems are shielded from the atmosphere and pressurised by the molecular expansion of water during heating, much higher temperatures can be attained without boiling.

Temperatures of up to 110°C (medium temperature) can be used, provided system components are capable of working at this heat level. In practice, 99°C (elevated temperature) is rarely exceeded in the domestic field, largely because of psychological fears than to any other factor!

Air in open systems causes noise and may produce air locks. Once initial venting of a sealed system is complete, by allowing it to run at design temperature for several hours, these problems should not arise.

Absence of air in a sealed system reduces the likelihood of corrosion. Air is a retarding factor as far as heat transference is concerned, and its absence increases the efficiency of transmittance between water and the heat-emitting appliances.

The freedom from air locks allows certain types of layout which would be avoided when designing small-bore systems. For instance, in the two-storey house, two distribution manifolds could be placed at each end of the building on the first floor only, with inverted loops of pipe serving the ground-floor radiators.

Good microbore design is, therefore, a compromise of the 'radial' ideal and small-bore design practice, without the same concern of possible air locks.

Expansion vessel

Though no feed-and-expansion cistern is required in a sealed system, it is necessary to provide for the molecular expansion of heated water, since this cannot be compressed. This requirement is met by a component called a diaphragm expansion vessel or tank, filled with air or nitrogen and directly connected to the system water, against which the expanded volume can 'flex' and be absorbed. The diaphragm is usually of a rubber composition.

While the expansion vessel can be placed anywhere in the system, it is usually located near the boiler. This vessel must, for systems of up to 24kW rating, be connected by 15mm pipe and above this by 22mm pipe.

Pressurisation of the system is governed by the size and capacity of the vessel, its given pressure, the static head available, and the water content of the system. These are taken into consideration when sizing the expansion vessel. These vessels are factory pre-pressurised from between 0·5 bar to 2 bar. Under expansion, pressure increases to between 2 bar and 3 bar. Two bar is equivalent to about 21·3m water 'head'.

Safety valve

A safety valve should always be incorporated into the circuit. The pressure vessel should be sized to be at 0·5 bar (9·15m head) below this. The valve is usually set at 2½–3 bar, representing, at 3 bar, a 25·9m head.

The vessel takes up the thermal expansion of about 1/20th of the water content in an average circuit. For normal installation, the water content of a system using radiators is about 30 litres for every kW and around 15 litres per 3kW for convectors.

The pressure vessel should contain no water at all when the circuit is filled. Once the water becomes hot, this gradually overcomes the pressure behind the membrane. Once the system cools, the membrane will force out the contracting water.

Manufacturers' data enables the size of vessels to be easily established. A good working formula is:
for homes with a heat requirement of 14·5kW (50,000 Btu/h) a 4-litre vessel is needed;
between 14·5kW and 29·3kW (100,000 Btu/h), a 7·5 litre vessel is adequate, and over 34kW (150,000 Btu/h), a 12-litre vessel is necessary.

The two basic domestic temperatures are:

● low – up to 82°C;
● elevated: 82°C–99°C;

Automatic air vent

Regardless of how well a system is vented during filling and after initial heating, a certain amount of air will be released in subsequent heating and cooling cycles. In conventional systems, this air is released by the vent pipe.

An automatic air vent is used in sealed systems. Most of these operate on a float principle which relies on the tendency of air to rise above the body of water. The lowering of a float within a collection chamber triggers off a trip mechanism which releases collected air.

High-limit thermostat

The other basic safety device, needed on elevated and medium-temperature equipment, is the high-limit thermostat. This is designed to shut down the boiler in the event of failure of the main boiler thermostat and the pressure-release valve. Controls on boilers are designed on a fail-safe principle, for added security.

Venting and make-up unit

An automatic venting and make-up unit consists of a non-return valve, to prevent backflow of water to its supply reservoir. It is fitted at the highest point in the system; the automatic air vent is attached to the body of the non-return valve.

Air separator

This enables speedy removal of entrapped air from the system. The inlet and outlet of the unit are set at a tangent, creating a vortex which starts a centrifugal action

and forces water to the head of the chamber and air to the centre. Centrifugal action is effective even at high-water velocities. This unit should be mounted on the suction (S) side of a pump, since air in water is more finely dispersed after passing through the pump.

Pressure

It is sometimes suggested that sealed systems are, in some way, dangerous, largely as a result of the pressure element. The pressure element is a source of misconception. In fact, this is a good deal lower than in many larger open central-heating systems.

An important aspect of diminishing pressure is the effect of leakage from badly made joints. Leaks will mean a loss of pressure, as well as water, and if the loss is allowed to continue, a condition, in some installations, could occur where the pressure becomes less than that of the atmosphere.

A steam 'flashpoint' could be reached at temperatures below boiling, and temperature-actuated high-limit controls are designed to deal with this should it occur.

Pressure gauge

It is desirable that a sealed system is fitted with a temperature and a pressure gauge which may be a combined type.

Always ensure that the pressure within a sealed system, when cold, is not allowed to fall below 0·5 bar and regularly check the pressure-gauge reading.

Regular checking of readings is no more involved than checking the setting on a room thermostat. If leaks occur, they will usually show up during the first few weeks that the system is in operation.

Radiators and convectors

While many advantages are gained by using higher water temperatures, these eliminate the use of the conventional steel-panel radiator. Water flowing at these temperature levels would cause severe burning if the surface were touched. This also applies to exposed pipework which must either be covered with a protective coating or boxed in.

Care should be taken when choosing fan convectors that the components, particularly the fan and blades, are able to withstand higher temperatures.

System choice

The size of the system helps to decide whether to use small-bore or microbore. If this is to consist of a small back boiler serving a hot-water cylinder by gravity circulation, with only two or three radiators, using only the minimum of controls, then a small-bore installation may be cheaper to install.

A single-pipe loop could be used as opposed to a two-pipe design needed on microbore systems. The rule is that the greater the number of radiators, the cheaper a microbore system tends to become, compared with a small-bore system.

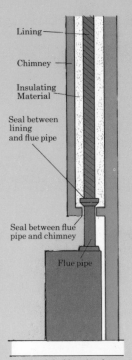

Lining

Chimney

Insulating Material

Seal between lining and flue pipe

Seal between flue pipe and chimney

Flue pipe

It is advisable to insulate the lining. An infill with lightweight granular material is suggested

Chimney brickwork

Flue liners note sockets uppermost

Insulated infill

Door for cleaning and inspection

Condensate collecting vessel

Asbestos rope seal

Access cover

Appliance

Floor level

d.p.c.

Collecting condensate from a chimney

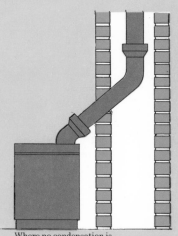

Where no condensation is anticipated, connect the lining directly to the flue pipe from the appliance.

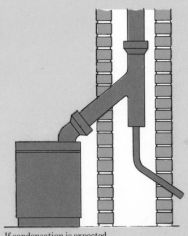

If condensation is expected then a drain should be fitted.

Let the boiler breathe out

Nearly every type of heating system emits the results of combustion – waste gases, which produce corrosive fumes and condensation. It is, therefore, essential to have a flue to take away these gases, without harming the fabric or penetrating the home. A flue is also necessary for the correct combustion of heating appliances. Insulating both the flue and the appliance may also be necessary.

All fuels produce gases and water vapour when burnt. With solid-fuel open fires, these harmful by-products are greatly diluted with warm air which enters the flue above the fire and carries them away. Unfortunately, this also results in a great deal of wasted heat escaping up the chimney.

While modern gas and oil-fired boilers are able to make rather more efficient use of the fuel consumed, if they are to perform satisfactorily, without risk of damage from the effects of condensation, special attention must be paid to the flue.

A chimney not only provides a safe means of carrying away the products of combustion but also provides the 'draw' which pulls in air for efficient combustion of the fuel being burnt.

The effective draw of a chimney can be reduced by a number of factors. A 'cold' chimney on an outside wall will slow down the escape of flue gases. The number of bends should be as few as possible, since these also tend to hinder the flow of the flue gas. If the flue is too large, this may cause the chimney to smoke.

Design considerations
One effect of a badly designed chimney is to increase the amount of condensation (condensate) inside it.

Whenever a fuel is burnt in contact with air, a small amount of water vapour is produced with the products of combustion. With the modern high-efficiency appliance, the majority of the heat produced is converted into useful heat. The gases which pass out up the flue are, therefore, at a lower temperature than those from the traditional open fire.

When these low-temperature gases meet the cool walls of an uninsulated chimney, the water vapour which is held in suspension in the flue gas condenses on to the walls of the flue.

This condensation will then absorb other combustion by-products to form an acid solution which, over a period of time, will attack and damage the brickwork of the flue.

If allowed to continue, this attack can lead to instability of the chimney and bad staining of internal wall decorations. The highest concentration of vapour in a flue occurs when gas is being burnt and the lowest occurs when solid fuel is burnt.

Therefore, if condensation is to be avoided, the chimney serving a gas appliance must be well insulated.

To eliminate this problem a chimney must be:

● Insulated to reduce heat losses from the flue gas;

● Lined with a smooth and non-absorbent impervious material, so that condensate does not cause damage;

● Only of sufficient size to convey the full output of gases away from the appliance;

● As straight as possible, since bends tend to increase the possibility of condensation. If bends are necessary, the minimum angle of the flue to the horizontal should not be less than 45°.

The size of the cross-sectional area of a flue liner depends to a large extent on the type of fuel being burnt and the input rating of the appliance.

Whenever possible, the size of the flue recommended by the manufacturer of the appliance should be used.

Check the size of the flue on the appliance outlet so that you can arrive at the correct size of the flue lining.

As gas appliances tend to produce more condensate than other fuels, provision should be made to collect any which may occur.

A flexible flue lining can be fed into the chimney–or pulled up from below

A clamp plate fixes to the top and any excess pipe is cut off with a hacksaw

Finally, the chimney cowl is clamped and mortared in position on the plate

The incoming end of the flue lining is clamped to a section of vitreous pipe

The back plate of the flue outlet is sealed with length of asbestos string

The flue pipe is located in the socket outlet and also sealed with asbestos string

The space between the tube and the flue brickwork is then filled, under pressure, with a liquid vermiculite composition. After about a day, to allow for setting, the tube is deflated and removed.

The resulting flue is then at the correct diameter and also thermally insulated in one operation. This method of lining, called 'Insuflu', is suitable for flues of up to 230mm diameter and up to 26m high.

Hearth conditions

All Class I appliances must have a constructional hearth at least 125mm thick. This hearth must extend the full depth of the recess and project a minimum of 310mm in front of the face of the recess and at least 150mm on either side of it.

Any Class I appliance not set in a recess must stand on or over a constructional hearth at least 840mm² × 125mm thick.

Timber or combustible material must not be placed under a constructional hearth within a vertical distance of 255mm from the hearth surface, unless there is a 50mm clear air space between it and the base of the hearth. Timber supporting a floor at the edge of a hearth is excluded from this.

The following Class II appliances are not required to discharge into a flue; a gas cooker, a room-sealed appliance with a special intake and outlet terminal, a gas heater in a drying cabinet or airing cupboard.

A Class II appliance must be placed over a non-combustible hearth at least 15mm thick. It must extend at least 125mm beyond the back and sides of the appliance and extend forward at least 230mm horizontally in front of any frame.

If the flame of the appliance is more than 230mm above the floor, then a non-combustible hearth is not required.

The appliance must be isolated at the back, top and sides from any combustible part of the building, except the floor or hearth, by a shield of non-combustible material at least 25mm thick and separated by an air space at least 75mm wide.

Some makes of boiler incorporate a drip tray at the base of the flue. Water which collects quickly evaporates as a result of the local heat from the boiler.

Terminology

The main descriptions used in connection with chimneys, flues and appliances are as follows:

Appliance *a heat-producing appliance (including a cooker) which is designed to burn either solid fuel, oil or gas.*

Chimney *includes any part of the structure of a building forming any part of a flue other than a flue pipe.*

Flue pipe *a pipe forming a flue, which does not include a pipe built as a lining into either a chimney or an appliance ventilation duct.*

Class I appliance *a solid-fuel or oil-burning appliance having in either case rating not exceeding 37·6kW/h (150,000 Btu/h).*

Class II appliance *a gas appliance having rating not exceeding 37·6kW.*

Class distinctions

Any chimney serving a Class I appliance should be lined with either one of the following materials:

Rebated or socketed clay flue linings; rebated or socketed flue linings made from kiln-burnt aggregate and high-alumina cement; glazed clay pipes and fittings which comply with an approved standard; or round or square-section asbestos-cement pipe.

On solid-fuel boilers, the first 1m–1·5m of pipe should be of vitreous enamel. The flue can be continued in asbestos-cement pipe.

A flexible liner may be used on oil-fired appliances, together with one of the above materials, or it may be used on its own.

These linings must be jointed and pointed with high-alumina cement mortar or asbestos string and fireclay cement. The linings must be built into the chimney with their socket ends uppermost.

A chimney serving a Class II appliance may be lined with any of the following materials:

Round or square-sectioned asbestos-cement pipe; stainless-steel flexible flue lining, on its own or with other materials; acid-resistant tiles embedded in and pointed with high-alumina cement mortar; or glazed clay pipes and fittings which are jointed and pointed with high-alumina cement mortar.

These linings must also be built into the chimney with the sockets uppermost.

Work to rule

There are eight rules you should follow before installing any flue lining.

- Always make sure that you are using the correct diameter lining for the appliance. If you have any doubts, check with the manufacturers.

- Sweep the chimney thoroughly before installing the lining.

- Use a tapered nose plug to protect the lining during installation.

- Seal the top and bottom connections and other inlets to the space between lining and chimney.

- Insulate clearance between lining and chimney where this exceeds 25mm all round.

- Always fit a flue terminal.

- Never use a flexible flue lining as an exposed flue pipe.

- Never use a flexible flue lining with solid-fuel appliances.

212

Solid-fuel Smoke Gobbler (Parkray heater). Smoke is consumed in secondary chamber

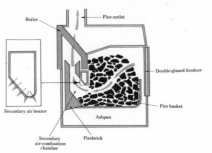

Solid-fuel Smoke Gobbler (Parkray heater). Smoke is consumed in secondary chamber

Joint is then firmly sealed with a bed of fireclay cement around the rim

Lining existing chimneys

Although it is possible to line an existing chimney with pipes or tiles, in some cases this would entail a considerable amount of alteration – possibly rebuilding the entire chimney. In most cases a flexible steel liner can be used, other than with solid-fuel appliances.

Ideal flue conditions can easily be created by connecting the boiler to a flexible metal liner installed in the chimney space. This has two advantages: the flue can be matched exactly to the boiler's requirements; and it protects the chimney itself from the harmful products of condensation.

Be flexible

Stainless-steel linings are also light-weight and flexible. These are produced in a wide variety of diameters and the one grade is suitable for many types of gas or oil appliance. These tubes consist of laminated metal strips, spirally wound to form a tube of great flexibility.

They must not, under any circumstance, be used in conjunction with fires burning solid fuel. This is because some solid fuels produce hydrochloric or sulphuric acids which attack the liner.

Installation of a flexible flue is quick and simple. The following materials are all that are required:

● A clamp seal matched to the size of the lining and the flue to be lined. This item locates the lining firmly at the top of the chimney.

● A tapered plug – or nose cone – to suit the diameter of the lining. This protects the lining and guides it round bends.

● A length of rope about 9m longer than the flue to be lined.

● Condensate drain (if required) for connection at the bottom of the lining.

● Thermal insulation is needed if the clearance between the lining and the chimney exceeds 25mm all round. This gap between the brickwork and the lining should be insulated with a loose infill, such as vermiculite or mineral wool.

● Flue terminal or cowling, for connection to the top of the lining.

Installation

To install the lining, remove the chimney-pot and cement flaunching which supports it. After the flue has been swept, test for internal obstructions by passing the tapered plug through the chimney on the end of the rope.

A nose cone with a rope is usually provided to enable the lining to be pulled down by a rope; this is later detached.

Connect the tapered plug to the lining and lower the lining down from the top of the chimney. Get help at the bottom to pull the rope, easing the lining round bends. Alternatively, the lining may be fitted by pulling it up from the bottom of the flue.

The bottom end of the lining should seat on the shoulder of the socket on the appliance primary flue. If condensation is anticipated, the lining should be connected to a condensate drain – and the annular space formed between them should be partially filled with firmly caulked asbestos string.

Fill the joint with a cold caulking compound of plastic asbestos fibre, mixed to a suitable consistency, and finished with a chamfered edge to make the joint waterproof.

Flexible lining is expensive, so calculate carefully; allow for bends a little more generously than the actual bend, so that the curve can be as gentle as possible. Leave also sufficient liner for connection to the flue outlet at the appliance.

Avoid stretching or otherwise distending the liner as this may pull the steel lamination apart. Steel flue lining is easily cut with a hacksaw, but take similar care to avoid unravelling.

Another way to avoid unravelling of the lining is to wrap a piece of sticky tape around it before cutting.

Sections of stainless-steel lining can be joined with a special connector.

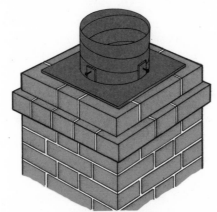

Fit the clamp-seal over the lining to rest squarely on the chimney. Firmly tighten the knurled screws to bite into the lining without actually breaking through.

At the chimney top, remove all flaunching and seat a clamp plate and ring firmly on the centre of the chimney opening and clamp the flue pipe. Trim off excess. Remake the flaunching, using a 1:5 high-alumina cement mix. Neatly slope the new flaunching to take away rainwater. Make

sure that the connections and flaunching are not disturbed until this sets.

Fit a cowl of suitable pattern. Usually, a 'straight' cowl is used for gas appliances, and a coned type for appliances using oil.

Terminal point

The outlet from a Class II gas appliance must allow free discharge, prevent down draughts and entry of any matter which might restrict the flue.

The terminal must be positioned so that a current of free air may pass over it at all times: it must be at least 610mm from any opening window, skylight, ventilator or inlet to a ventilating system.

It is very important to seal the space between the lining and the chimney at the top and bottom. If necessary, add loose infill, such as mineral wool, for insulation and seal the seating of inspection and soot doors.

Asbestos

Where a flue is fitted outside the home, asbestos is commonly used. This is available in various lengths, with a socket at each end. Asbestos cement is either round or square sectioned and easily cut. The pipe is, however, brittle and care should be taken not to crack it. Use a newspaper 'template' completely wrapped round the pipe, so that the cut ends are square; if these ends are not square a poor joint may result.

Pipe is always cut at the spigot end. It is fixed to walls at intervals by brackets, which should be plugged and screwed.

If possible, insulate the pipe, to reduce the likely effect of condensation.

Where sulphur content in flue gases can cause erosion, lead-aluminium tube should be used for gas and aluminium lining for oil-fired appliances.

Vitreous enamel

This is similarly supplied in various lengths, with a socket at one end. Vitreous pipe can be cut with a sharp saw but care should be taken to cut cleanly and avoid splintering the enamelled surface.

A flexible carborundum wheel can also be used on a power drill to cut vitreous-enamel pipe. Wear protective goggles as a safeguard against splinters when cutting.

The bends

Angled bends, usually of 135° radius, are made in asbestos and vitreous enamelled pipe. Bends have a socket at one end and a spigot at the other. Enamelled pipe bends may be supplied with an inspection plate.

Insuflu

Another method of lining an existing chimney, developed by Rentokil Laboratories, uses an inflatable rubber tube which is placed in the flue.

Each end of the flue is then sealed and the tube inflated until its diameter corresponds to the size of the flue required. Metal spacers are attached to the tube where a bend occurs to keep the tube in the centre of the flue.

Your heating: when it's all 'under control'

Central heating can be a waste of money – if effective controls are not fitted to the system. There is a wide range of controls, ranging from thermostatic radiator valves to sophisticated multi-programme controls. System controls ensure that unnecessary heat is not expended – and will help to keep your heating bills down.

Controls on heating systems are desirable for reasons both of economy and comfort. They cannot normally be fitted to 'uncontrolled' solid fuel appliances, where restriction imposed by controls could be dangerous.

Controls which restrict the gravity circulation from non-thermostatic solid-fuel appliances, where this pipework acts as a 'heat leak', should not be used.

Control systems enable you to conserve heat, for a single degree of heat greater than that needed–undetectable from a comfort aspect–could add up to five per cent to fuel bills, building up to a sizeable amount. Manual controls on a boiler alone may vary by a swing of as much as 6°C or more in temperature.

Primary and secondary

There are two types of controls–primary and secondary, or 'comfort' controls. The primary controls are fitted to a fuel-monitoring appliance; these also provide a combustion safeguard. The primary controls concerned with the basic appliance function are fitted during manufacture.

Secondary controls are intended to meet the comfort requirements of the home, consistent with the lowest possible running costs.

Heating controls should be of the 'fail-safe' variety–that is designed to shut off automatically in the event of a fault. Most boiler controls are of this type.

There is a wide range of secondary controls, from simple time clocks and more sophisticated programmers, to thermostatic valves, room, cylinder and frost-sensing thermostats.

Control methods

The simplest controls are the handwheel and lockshield valves on radiators. The handwheel provides full local control, so that a radiator or other heat-emitting appliance can be either fully or partly shut down. The lockshield should be set during the balancing of a circuit; further adjustment is not normally needed.

There are two basic ways of controlling the temperature of the radiators which, in turn, govern the room temperature. First, a centrally mounted room thermostat, which senses the temperature of the air, and switches the pump on and off; and, second, thermostatic radiator valves, used in conjunction with a constantly running pump.

Using an air thermostat, the entire system is governed by the actual air temperature in the thermostat. It is, therefore important to pay attention to:

● Correct sizing and balancing of radiators;

● Correct choice of room thermostat;

● Its correct siting;

● Its correct wiring.

A more economic and efficient service can usually be provided by operating the heating and hot water services at different temperatures. Hot water is normally fed to the radiators at a much higher temperature than that of the domestic hot water.

By controlling the water temperature solely from the boiler thermostat, boiler 'short cycling' will occur. The boiler will keep firing at frequent intervals, merely to replenish its own heat losses, not to provide any useful heat. This is obviously a highly wasteful and uneconomic state of affairs.

The boiler thermostat's function is to maintain the temperature of the heat exchanger at a predetermined level and also to act as a top-temperature limit.

As long as the air temperature in the flue is higher than the incoming air temperature, air flow will occur and this will cool the heat exchanger to the point where the boiler thermostat will call for heat again.

Similarly, water circulation by gravity in the primary circuit will result in cooler water entering the boiler and this will also cause the boiler thermostat to call for heat.

With modern, low-water content boilers, this cycling occurs more frequently than with boilers employing large, cast-iron heat exchangers with a high thermal mass.

The solution is to control the boiler from where there is a genuine demand for heat–the cylinder and the room. The boiler thermostat should be set at its maximum temperature to act merely as a top limit.

Scanflex air vent and Scanflo non-return valve used in a sealed heating system

Honeywell or Drayton roomstat, used with «any conventional pattern of programmer

The efficiency of a boiler falls rapidly as the boiler thermostat setting is reduced. Below 60°C the risk of condensation increases; this can have a serious effect on the life of the heat exchanger.

Thermostatic radiator valves

Thermostatic radiator valves are individually fitted to radiators and enable selective control to be achieved over given parts of the heating layout. These automatically control the amount of water flowing through each radiator, by sensing the local temperature of the air. With the exception of a single make, these are not suitable for use on single-pipe systems.

While this may appear to be a desirable arrangement, there are two drawbacks:

As no electrical signal is involved, the operation of these valves cannot be linked to the boiler firing or time control. Temperature sensing is arbitrary and does not reflect the true air temperature in the room.

An air thermostat is best, because of its ability to be wired as an integral part of the whole control.

Programmers

A programmer is the most common main heating control. This consists of a time clock which enables, over a period of 24 hours, a choice of heating and hot water. Most programmers provide some five 'programmes' related to the clock setting.

These are: central heating off and hot water on twice a day; central heating and hot water twice; central heating twice with hot water all day; central heating and hot water all day; and constant central heating and hot water.

Some programmers have an over-ride switch to enable hot water to be switched in outside programme times, without having to reset the tappets on the dial. An off position enables the system to be shut down.

With gravity-feed hot-water systems, the programmer switches on the supply of fuel and ignition, allowing the hot-water circuit to operate by gravity action; with central heating, it also switches on the pump.

The arrangements are slightly more complicated on miniaturized and sealed pumped-primary circuits, since a relay box may be needed to permit the operation of motorized control valves. These open and close, in order to control the appropriate heating and hot-water circuits.

There are more sophisticated types of programmer, enabling control of independent twin-circuit systems, providing up to as many as 16 separate programmes on a multi-function separator with a motorized valve. Without a valve controlling the pumped-primary circuit, there is a choice of ten programmes, achieved by, in effect, combining two time switches operated by the same dial.

Motorized and mechanical valves

Motorized valves are fitted into the pipe-work circuits and open and close in accordance with programme settings. The motorized valve can be of the three-port type, swinging between hot water and central heating, in accordance with demands, or the in-line motorized valve. Two of the latter are normally needed, one in the heating pipework and the other in the hot-water supply pipe.

In a pumped-primary circuit, for example, where hot water is in circuit with heating circulation, only heating needs isolating when hot water alone is needed.

A relay box is sometimes used to co-ordinate various controls–room thermostat, boiler thermostat and controls, programmer, motorized valves and cylinder thermostat–the electrically controlled and the independent mechanical, bellows type.

Honeywell Controls cylinder stat with its associated three-port diverter valve

Drayton three-port 'flow-share' valve does not need choice of service priority

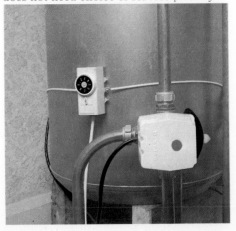

Cylinder thermostats

The electrical thermostat fits on the body of a cylinder to sense temperature. This can be set to various temperatures and is usually attached by means of a metal band around the cylinder, located about a third of the way up. The usual acceptable hot-water setting is 60°C.

This type of thermostat can be used to control a motorized valve to shut off supply when heat requirements are met.

The mechanical type of valve fits into the cylinder; a sensor phial reacts to temperature and opens or closes an inlet valve.

However, with a pumped-primary circuit a motorized valve must be used, since the isolation of hot water from heating is still necessary.

Diverter valves

Diverter (or diverting) valves, usually mounted on or near the boiler, are used on pumped-primary circuits. The use of these enables the usual allowance in boiler capacity for hot water, necessary on gravity circuits, to be disregarded.

A diverter valve works by satisfying, in turn, either the heat requirements of domestic hot water or heating. This has advantages where used with low-water content systems and high-recovery cylinders. Usually, the domestic hot-water demand is set to take priority over that of central heating.

Other than on exceptionally cold days, it is seldom necessary to accept slightly cooler central heating–and then only if there has been an exceptional demand on domestic hot water.

Similar three-port diverter valve and cylinder stat by Satchwell Controls

Honeywell system may be completed by Chronotherm or Day-Nite Round controls

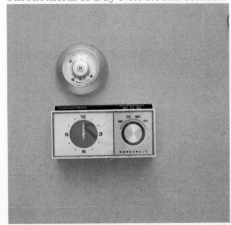

Horstman programmer can, for example, complement Drayton system, using a relay

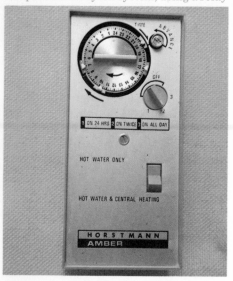

Satchwell Libra, multi-programme clock, can be used with motorized valves

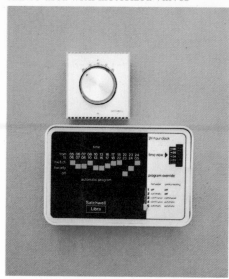

provide 'zoned' heating control. This works by switching in or out a group of radiators or similar appliances. Zone control can also be effected by means of thermostatic radiator valves.

Room thermostats

A room or air thermostat enables master control of house temperatures to be achieved. This operates on the principle that, with a balanced whole-house heating system, if the temperature is correct in a given room, it should be correct in all the others.

A thermostat should be mounted clear of draughts, or radiators and not in rooms of major occupation, and at about a height of 1·52m above the floor. For convenience, the thermostat should be in an accessible place, so that changes in setting can be made in comfort levels.

Why rooms of major occupation, such as lounges or kitchens, should be avoided as sites for an air thermostat, is because extra heat is generated by people, or by kitchen appliances, all of which raise the temperature artificially.

This means that other rooms would be cold, since the thermometer would react to the highest temperature.

Set the room thermostat for the desired optimum domestic temperature. When the chosen levels of comfort are reached, the heating will shut down, switching on again when the heat demands require topping up.

Thermostats can be either mains or low-voltage operated. The low-voltage models are claimed to be more accurate than those on mains voltage.

It is important to maintain even overall comfort levels, since the home should be regarded as a unit. It is a false economy to shut off heating in little-used rooms, since this will serve only to 'raid' heat from a warm to a cold zone.

Satchwell motorized valves enable full control of heating and hot-water circuits

Thermostatic Honeywell valve provides mechanical control of individual radiators

Night cut-back

The night cut-back type of control works on the basis that it is more economic to keep a reasonable level of temperature in the home throughout the heating season, rather than to shut down the circuit during any period.

This is a sound theory, for considerable energy may be needed to restore lost space and fabric temperatures.

GEC Xpelair humidifier prevents dry air. Control by Honeywell

This Randall multi-programme control and room stat complement each other

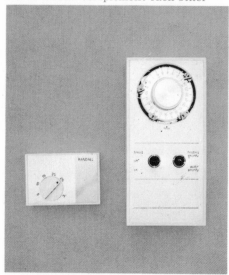

Frost-sensing thermostats

The frost-sensing thermostat is a control which can be located outside the house. This works in conjunction with the internal room thermostat and enables fine control to be maintained over indoor temperatures. These are, however, among the more expensive of heating controls.

Control equipment is usually supplied with simple wiring diagrams, enabling connections to be made without the need for specialised electrical knowledge.

With older, high-thermal (cast-iron) capacity boilers, a thermostatic mixing valve can be fitted. This filters back hot water into the heating pipework, by-passing the boiler and saves fuel when the heat demand is small.

This does not necessarily mean a cold home, for the hot water is heated very quickly on pumped primaries, particularly with low-water content systems, used in conjunction with high-recovery cylinders.

The system switches over to provide domestic heating once domestic hot water needs are satisfied.

If hot water is drawn off, or cools, the diverter valve swings back to satisfy the cylinder thermostat's call for heat, before reverting to the heating position, once this is met.

Some diverter valves have a switch to vary the priority. A newer type, the 'proportional' diverter valve, 'shares' the call for heat between cylinder and central heating.

Motorized valves can also be used to

Thermal insulation: making your room cosy

Heating the home is a relatively costly matter, so it is important not to waste heat through poorly insulated structures. Up to 75 per cent of the heat produced can be lost through roofs, walls, floors and window areas in poorly insulated homes. This article tells you how to keep down costs by using correct insulation materials.

Thermal insulation

To achieve comfort in the home and keep heating costs down, warmth must be retained for as long as possible. Good insulation helps to keep the home warm in winter and cool in summer. In many homes, huge heat losses occur as a result of poor thermal insulation.

In homes that are empty all day, then heated when the family returns home, internal linings with good thermal-insulaation qualities reduce the time taken for the temperature to reach an acceptable level. The fabric of the home will also more readily retain heat.

Of all money spent on heating, up to 75 per cent is lost through the fabric of the house, largely through chinks, gaps and poor insulation. Heat is lost in two ways—by conduction via the exterior structure and ventilation through air changes.

The major points where heat is lost are through the walls (25 per cent), roofs, windows, flues and doors (all 20 per cent) and through floors (10 per cent).

The thermal efficiency of a material is expressed by what is known as its 'U' value, or thermal transmittance co-efficient. This is the amount of heat lost from one side of a structure to the other, per m² per hour and per degree difference on each side.

This is usually expressed by the formula: 'U'w/m²°C. This means transmittance of heat in watts at °Celcius per m². A high 'U' value means a high heat loss and poor insulation. The lower the value, the better the insulant qualities of the structure.

For example, a roof with simply tiles on battens has a 'U' value as high as 3·17, while tiles laid on felt and with ceiling insulation consisting of 25mm quilt or 50mm of loose fill, has a low 'U' value of 0·85.

Walls

Wall structure may be one of three types: solid walls of brick or stone; cavity walls with one brick wall and an inner leaf, either of brick, building or aggregate block; or an outer brick leaf with an inner 'dry' plasterboard or similar lining. This latter type of construction is often found in frame houses.

The method of insulating a solid wall is by fixing the insulant materials to the inner skin. Heat loss will be cut and cold surfaces on which condensation forms will be warmer.

Materials

Polystyrene This resembles wallpaper, is barely 2mm thick and is hung with a special adhesive. Quite fragile, it dents easily but insulates the wall and raises the surface 'touch' temperature.

Aluminium foil-back paper can be used in the same way. These materials are applied in a similar manner to ordinary wallpaper—cut with scissors or a trimming knife and the rolls butt-jointed and fixed with an adhesive.

Polystyrene tiles can also be used but they are more commonly fixed to ceilings. Polystyrene tiles should never be painted with gloss paint as thus treated they represent a fire hazard.

They are best painted with an emulsion or fire-retardant paint. Many of these tiles are now of the self-extinguishing, fire-resistant type. Special adhesives are made for fixing polystyrene tiles. It should be applied evenly over the backs to inhibit the spread of flame.

Insulating boards These consist of polyurethane or polystyrene sandwiched between a variety of materials and may be backed with aluminium foil.

Wood cladding This is a natural insulator, makes not only a good insulant surface but also provides an attractive decorative appearance. The method of fixing is to nail the board to battens screwed to the wall. Added protection would be provided by a layer of **mineral-wool quilting** fixed behind the battens.

Fitted units, particularly in bedrooms, provide good insulation but if these are on the inside of exposed walls it is sensible to line the backs with expanded polystyrene sheets or slabs which also help to reduce condensation. These cupboards should be ventilated by drilling holes at the top and bottom of the doors.

Cavity filling Cavity walls can be filled with 'liquid' insulating material. This may be mineral wool, urea-formaldehyde, polyurethane or other insulating products. The material is injected into the wall, under high pressure, using special machines.

Holes are first drilled at intervals in the structure, to remove a core from the brick. The nozzle of a high-pressure pumping machine is inserted into the hole and the material forced into the cavity.

Once the nozzle is removed the brick plug is replaced and remortared to blend in with the original surface.

This work is carried out by specialist firms. This method is increased in its effectiveness if the inner wall is of cellular building blocks which have high thermal properties.

A 75mm thick cellular building block has the same insulating value as a 325mm thickness of ordinary bricks.

Thermal plaster also adds to the heat-retaining qualities of a wall.

Floors

Floors are of two types: suspended floors, timber-boarded floors laid on joists, or solid concrete laid on to a waterproof membrane. In some very old properties the floor may be laid directly on to subsoil.

A suspended floor has a 'U' value as high as 2·71 and can be a considerable area of heat loss. There must, of course, be underfloor ventilation to combat timber decay, but draughts blow up through badly fitting floorboards and gaps between the skirting and floorboards.

If you have to lift floorboards to fit central-heating pipe runs or electrical wiring, a quilt of 13mm insulating material or aluminium foil-backed paper can be laid across the joists to provide an insulant layer.

The entire floor may be covered with hardboard if floorboards are unlikely to be

Micafil vermiculite is raked to depth of 50mm–75mm, using home made gauge

Glass-fibre wrap is unrolled between joists. Wear protective gloves to handle

A hot-water cylinder should be lagged. This jacket has glass-fibre filling

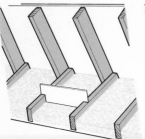
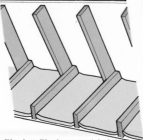
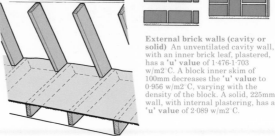

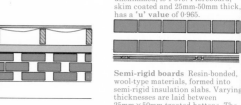

External brick walls (cavity or solid) An unventilated cavity wall, with an inner brick leaf, plastered, has a **'u' value** of 1·476-1·703 w/m2˚C. A block inner skim of 100mm decreases the **'u' value** to 0·956 w/m2˚C, varying with the density of the block. A solid, 225mm wall, with internal plastering, has a **'u' value** of 2·089 w/m2˚C.

Insulation fixed to the wall Rigid insulation board or polystyrene can be fixed either directly to wall surfaces and plastered over or to sound plaster. Skim-coated polystyrene, of 25mm-50mm, has a **'u' value** of 1·079. Fixed to a 225mm wall, the **'u' value** is 1·306. Fibreboard, 25mm-50mm thick, has a **'u' value** of 1·192.

Loose fill Loose-fill material, polystyrene, cork, vermiculite or Rockwool are ideal for infilling between joists with irregular centres. Pour material to a depth of 50mm–75mm, levelling and raking it. **Value** 0·567–0·852

Blanket Blanket material of glass, mineral or Rockwool material laid between joists. Material from 25mm-100mm thick. **Values:** 25mm 0·908 100mm 0·454.

Blanket Glass, mineral, slag or Rockwool or eel-grass quilt, a 25mm thick blanket laid loosely across the joists. Lap by about 25mm and tuck down carefully at eaves. Does away with need to insulate pipes separately beneath blanket. **Value:** 0·795.

Boards fixed to battens Insulating board fixed to 25mm × 50mm battens give a cavity of still air which is a good insulator. The **'u' value** of foil-backed plasterboard, 6mm thick unskimmed, is 1·079. Fibreboard, skim coated and 25mm-50mm thick, has a **'u' value** of 0·965.

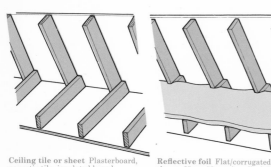

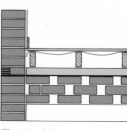
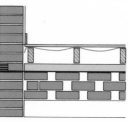
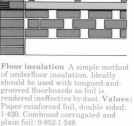

Ceiling tile or sheet Plasterboard, acoustic tile, insulated board, polystyrene, urethane, cork or asbestos, in tile or sheet form. Decorative or finished surface can be glued or pinned to existing roof. Useful on flat roofs or where loft is difficult to insulate.

Reflective foil Flat/corrugated sheets, 25mm-50mm, in rolls, laid over joists. Allow an overlap and staple foil to joists. Secure at eaves. Where laid, allow slight droop. **Value:** 1·192.

Board materials Insulating boards, 25mm, capable of supporting floor loads, can be laid over joists. This involves re-fixing skirtings, doors, fitted furniture. A better method is to cut the board to fit between joists, supported on treated battens. **Value:** 0·965-1·079.

Floor insulation A simple method of underfloor insulation. Ideally should be used with tongued-and-grooved floorboards as foil is rendered ineffective by dust. **Values:** Paper-reinforced foil, double sided: 1·420. Combined corrugated and plain foil: 0·852-1·249.

Semi-rigid boards Resin-bonded, wool-type materials, formed into semi-rigid insulation slabs. Varying thicknesses are laid between 25mm × 50mm treated battens. The slabs are then covered with plasterboard. Slab 25mm thick has a **'u' value** of 0·795.

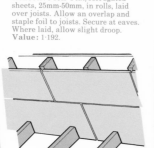

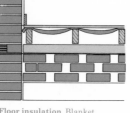

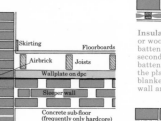

Reflective aluminium foil Reinforced foil used to insulate whole roof space. Should be pinned or stapled. **Value:** 1·306. Value can be reduced to 1·022 by fixing plasterboards on battens over foil.

Board Whole roof-space insulation achieved by fixing insulation board, cork, foil-backed plasterboard, asbestos, urethane, polystyrene to rafters. Example: 25mm polystyrene gives a **value** of 0·908.

Floor insulation Blanket insulation should be draped over joists. Adjacent lengths should be butted. Nail down floorboards to compress material over joists. Board may need chamfering to fit under skirtings or doors. **Value:** 0·852-1·022, dependent on blanket thickness.

Solid floors A solid-concrete ground floor in contact with the earth or subfloor has a **'u' value** of 1·13. A wood-block surface decreases this to 0·85. Ventilated wood floor. The traditional timber floor on sleeper walls has a **'u' value** of between 2·71 and 1·42. Do not block up ventilation grilles or air bricks

Skirting — Floorboards — Airbrick — Joists — Wallplate on dpc — Sleeper wall — Concrete sub-floor (frequently only hardcore)

Insulation blankets Insulation or wool blankets fixed over wall battens 25mm × 50mm thick. A second layer of 25mm × 50mm battens are fixed for application of the plasterboard. 75mm-100mm blanket has a **value** of 0·738; 225mm wall and reinforced foil: 0·852.

Cavity-insulation foam Granulated Rockwool or urea-formaldehyde foam, injected under pressure through holes drilled in external walls. Improved **'u' value** about 0·567.

---

lifted frequently. This not only excludes draughts but provides the necessary first base needed for many floor coverings.

Any gap between skirting and floorboards may be filled with a piece of quadrant fixed firmly to the floor–not to the skirting board as there may be floor movement.

Large gaps between boards can be filled with thin pieces of wood or with a proprietary cellulose filler mixed with a little PVA adhesive. This can be rubbed down when dry and stained to match the boards.

Even folded pieces of newspaper pushed between gaps in floorboards will cut draughts and improve insulation.

Solid floors have a lower 'U' value– 0·20. Additional comfort can be gained by careful choice of carpeting. Use the best-quality underlay and the thickest carpet you can afford or, possibly, one of the newer foam-backed vinyl floor coverings.

'U' values

These are the 'U' values of various types of floors:

● Wood floors on joists: 2·71 to 1·42

● Parquet or lino over floorboards on joists: 1·42
● Thermoplastic tiles on concrete: 1·13
● Wood blocks on concrete: 0·85

Roof space

There are two ways of insulating the loft space. You can either insulate between the joists on the floor of the roof space or between the rafters on the ceiling of the area.

Unless you wish to use the loft space as a work room or it is to be converted for extra living space, the easier method is to lay insulant material between the joists.

Polystyrene, slab or granulated, vermiculite fill, eel-grass, mineral wool, glass fibre, felted wool or vegetable fibre and cork, compressed in slab form or in particles can be used.

Glass fibre

Where joists run at even widths, glass-fibre matting can be laid between or over the joists. This can be cut with household scissors. Protective gloves should be worn as minute glass-fibre particles may irritate the skin.

Rolls of insulant matting are made in various lengths and, when laid, should be 25mm at least wider than the space between joists so that no part of the ceiling is left exposed.

When laying the matting over joists, use 1m wide matting and overlap the edges by at least 75mm. Drape the matting over the end of the joists to prevent draughts getting underneath.

Loose fill

Expanded polystyrene, mineral wool, vermiculite and cork are obtainable as loose-fill materials in particle or in pellet form.

These are poured between joists to a depth of about 50mm. As the material is poured, it should be raked level with a timber template cut to the depth and width of the joist space. Do not compress the material.

The ends of the joists can be sealed with building paper but do not block any air vents as this may cause condensation. Once laid, loose-fill material is quite stable.

Mineral wool

Mineral wool is available in semi-rigid slabs which can be laid between joists. The depth of insulation depends on the type of home heating you have.

The more heat produced in the house, the more is lost through the roof space, and, therefore, the greater depth of insulation needed.

Foil-backed lining

The second method is to insulate the gaps between rafters. Attach foil-backed insulating felt or bitumen-backed paper between the rafters. Apart from cutting down on heat loss, this will help to keep the roof area clean. Slabs of expanded polystyrene can be placed between the rafters.

Lagging

It is important to realize that if you insulate the floor of the roof space you then create a much colder roof area. The warm air from the house is no longer rising to fill the space.

Therefore, it is important to lag all pipework and plumbing services located in the loft. Pipe coverings are made to fit standard pipe sizes.

They are either rigid, of glass fibre, cork, mineral wool or expanded plastic, or flexible, of synthetic rubber, expanded polystyrene or foamed polyurethane. These 'sleeves' fit round the pipework.

Each section should be overlapped, taking care that joints and entry points to the storage cistern are covered.

Such lagging materials can be cut with scissors and secured at intervals with tape or string.

Cisterns and hot-water cylinders should be insulated. Lagging sets consist of panels of expanded polystyrene, compressed insulant board or glass-fibre jackets.

Another method of insulating a cistern is to construct a case of chipboard, leaving a 50mm–70mm gap round the sides and at the top, filling the space with loose-fill insulant material.

Do not put insulant materials under the cold-water storage cistern. The trickle of heat from below will avoid freezing when the outside temperatures fall.

Any pipes positioned between the joists can be covered with loose-fill material or matting.

Draughts

Draughts can cause needless discomfort but can be greatly reduced. A completely air-tight home, though almost impossible to achieve, would be very uncomfortable. There have to be regular air changes to remove stale air.

Movement of air within a building is caused by outside wind pressure and warm air, which rises, filling the colder areas.

Doors and windows

The main sources of draught are from ill-fitting windows and doors and, in homes with open fires, the chimney. A fire must have air in order to burn but a great deal of heat can be saved by fitting a chimney throat restrictor.

It is very important to realize that insulation does not mean no ventilation, as all solid fuel and gas appliances need a balanced free flow of air. An electric fire should be placed in front of the chimney opening to prevent loss of heat up the chimney.

Draught excluders

The gap round a door through which heat is lost and draughts come in can be very large indeed. Under-door draughts can be cured by a draught excluder.

There are two basic types: the coupled draught excluder, which is fitted to the door, and the threshold type, fitted to the floor or door frame.

The coupled draught excluder works on a drop-bar principle, in which a bar of metal, wood felt or plastic adjusts to different floor levels, forming an effective seal when the door is closed. The bar rises as the door is opened, clearing the carpet.

An excluder made of felt rides more easily over uneven surfaces. Some draught excluders can be fitted into a groove made under the door but this is a longer job as the door must be removed first.

Threshold excluders are made of metal, wood or plastic. They are fixed with screws, panel pins or adhesive. This type of excluder is usually chamfered or shaped to prevent the hazard of tripping.

Coupled excluders suitable for either internal or external doors are available. For external doors a metal extruder with a water bar should be used.

Metal stripping

Another method of insulating the door surround is to use sprung metal strips, made of either aluminium or bronze. These are fixed around the door frame and then 'sprung' outwards so that the metal strip presses against the door when it closes to form a seal. A metal threshold seal on the door sill is also needed.

It is possible to fit 'sprung' metal strip windows, but it can be an expensive business. Some cheaper and effective methods of stopping draughts include foam rubber or plastic which is fixed to the frame usually with adhesive.

Some foam rubber strip has self-adhesive backing; you merely peel off a strip of protective paper and press the foam rubber into place. The surface must be grease-free and dry to ensure good adhesion.

Type and description	Use
Expanded polystyrene Thicknesses vary from 6mm to 75mm or more. Normally supplied in slab form and is a spongy, plastic material. Breaks or damages easily; needs handling with care. Usually flame resistant. Available in sheet or tile form; supplied also in thin form in rolls.	Lagging cold-water cisterns; insulating ceilings; as underlay for wallpaper (thin version).
Mineral wool and glass fibre Available in several forms–loose, fill, in bags; in matting, semi-rigid slabs, and as quilting. Can cause irritation to skin; is rot-proof. In slab form, fibres are held together with bonding agent.	Insulating attic floors (loose fill and mat); fixing to joists before putting up cladding (quilt); lagging cisterns (semi-rigid). Used for hot-water cylinder jackets.
Fibre building board In rigid sections and normally made from felted wool or other vegetable fibre. Can be nailed, screwed or glued and may be painted.	Fixing to joists, rafters and battens.
Felting Supplied in rolls; impervious to fungicidal attack, although jute felt is susceptible under damp conditions; generally combustible.	Nailing to battens before fixing cladding; fixing to rafters and joists.
Compressed straw A natural insulator; susceptible to fungus in damp; may be treated to give flame resistance; easy to cut; can be pinned or nailed.	Lagging cold-water cisterns; fixing to battens and rafters.
Cork Available in loose fill or in slab form; can be plastered or painted and used between two sheets of plywood or plasterboard.	Insulating attic floors (granulated); slab form is suitable for insulating walls or attics.
Gypsum Intended for inside use; can be painted or plastered. Obtainable in loose-fill form; possess only moderately good insulation properties.	Used for insulating roof slope, ceilings and so on; loose-fill suitable for attic floors.

Glazing: glass with care!

Choosing glass

Glass is made in a variety of thicknesses. The choice depends on the size of sheet and the degree of exposure to wind and consequent suction loads on the surface. Most domestic glazing uses glass 4mm thick.

Glass is now sold by thickness; it was formerly sold by weight. The main basic thicknesses are: 2mm, 3mm, 4mm, 5mm, 5·5mm and 6mm. Special glass is required for greenhouses, the 3mm grade being most suitable.

Types

There are two basic types of clear glass—sheet and float.

Sheet glass is made in three grades: OQ—ordinary quality; SQ—selected quality; SSQ—special selected quality. For general glazing purposes, the OQ grade is suitable.

Sheet glass used for normal glazing work is a clear drawn glass. Since the opposite sides of a pane are never perfectly flat and parallel, some degree of distortion is inevitable. Sheet glass is commonly used for domestic glazing and is available in thicknesses from 3mm to 6mm.

Float glass is made by floating the liquid glass over a surface of molten tin. This produces a glass similar to plate glass, which it has replaced. Float glasses are made in thicknesses from 5mm to 25mm. As this glass is free from distortion and is strong, it has many applications, including those of glazing large picture windows and for such things as glass table tops.

Float glass is also produced in plain or tinted decorative forms by using various processes, including acid etching, electro-floating and sandblasting. Additional dec-

orative effects are obtained by the introduction of certain materials into the molten glass mix, to alter its light and heat-transmission characteristics.

Patterned glass includes glasses with several different decorative finishes and is frequently used for 'modesty' glazing in bathrooms and toilets.

A typical example is rough-cast glass, which is smooth on one side and obscured on the other. These glasses are usually produced by passing molten liquid glass through rollers, to produce patterns in plain and tinted versions. Thicknesses are generally between 3mm and 5mm. The degree of transparency and light diffusion depends largely on the type of pattern used.

Wired glass has a metal mesh embedded in it. This mesh helps to hold the glass together and reduces the risk of injury from falling glass.

It is also accepted as a fire-retardant material. The mesh may be square (Georgian) or diamond pattern. Such glass is often used in porches and garage roofs, but as it is difficult to cut if re-used it is best bought ready cut to size. It is made in 6mm thicknesses only.

Toughened glass Float, sheet and even some patterned glasses can be toughened by a special process which can increase the strength of the glass by four or five times. It is suitable for doors and similar areas where there is a danger of impact, since it shatters into granules instead of sharp splinters if broken.

Another type of glass is a strong, translucent glass used mainly outdoors for car-ports and the like, though it can be used indoors.

Solar-control glass reduces the transmission of heat, light and glare from sunlight. It is available in a range of colours in float, laminated, rough-cast and patterned form.

Mirrors are also made from float glass of SQ grade. This is moisture-proofed, silvered and edged in a variety of ways, by machine and by hand grinding.

Ordering

When you order figured glass, always give the height first and the width next. This is critical, for instance, in the case of ribbed glass, since the pattern should run from top to bottom. If you give the width first, the pane would end up with the ribs running from side to side.

In measuring up irregular openings, such as arched window frames, it is always safer to make up a template in hardboard or plywood. If the opening is to be glazed with figured glass, mark the side which is going to be towards the outside of the house 'face'. If this is not done, the 'wrong' side of the cut pane may become a dirt trap and be difficult to clean.

Storing

Glass should be stored vertically at an angle of 25° in a dry place. Lean the panes on two wooden slats propped against the wall and place rag or newspaper pads under the top edge of the panes to stop them from coming into direct contact with the wall. The surface of glass is easily spoiled by dust and moisture, before or after glass is fitted, so protection or regular cleaning is desirable if glass is to remain in the best condition.

Tools: T-square; tape; felt-pen; glass cutter; pliers; circle-arm cutter; oil box

Double check measurements and mark the position on glass with felt-tipped pen

Press evenly with cutter to score; use a single stroke and do not back track

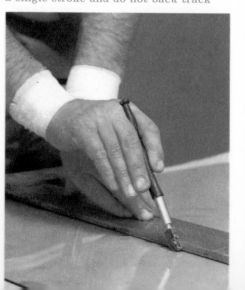

Choosing the right glass for your needs is as important as using the correct techniques to cut it. Glass comes in various grades and thicknesses, types and designs. It is both decorative and functional, since a window is an integral part of the structure of the home.

Handling and carrying

Gloves should always be worn when handling glass. These should not be too stiff, since it is important to be able to feel the glass to handle it safely. You can use folded newspapers or old pieces of inner tube as improvised 'laps' when carrying glass. Wrist bands are a further safety recommendation.

Always handle glass gently but firmly and never grip it tightly. To reduce dangers of breakage, carry glass vertically and not at the horizontal and never balanced on the head. When negotiating sharp corners or winding staircases, allow plenty of room for the glass behind you.

Small sheets of glass may be held under the arm, supported from beneath by the hand at the centre of balance. If the pane is too large to fit under the arm, hold the centre of the bottom edge with one hand and tilt the pane forward, holding the leading edge near the top corner with the other hand. Rest the upper portion of the sheet against the forearm and shoulder.

Large sheets should be carried by two people. The one in front should adopt the same position as a single person handling a large sheet. The one at the back should support the glass with one hand cupped around the lower corner holding the bottom edge, with the back edge against the shoulder. The top edge should be held with the other hand. Where people are carrying glass care must be taken to walk in step at a slow pace, particularly at any change of level and when turning corners.

Glass can be carried up ladders—supported by a second person for larger sheets, but this practice should be avoided as it can be very dangerous in the event of a gust of wind or if one slips.

Transporting glass

Smaller panes can be carried on the back seat of a car, but protect the upholstery with a blanket, lay the glass flat on the seat, and turn the blanket over the edges to prevent damage to the glass and to the car.

If you are carrying two or more panes, interleave these with newspaper. Glass carried in the boot should also be wrapped in a blanket, so that there is no direct contact with the car body.

Larger panes may be carried on a roof rack. First, lay a sheet of 19mm blockboard on the roof and cover this with a blanket, place the glass on the blanket and then fold it over the glass. The whole assembly should be lashed to the rack with a sash cord or a clothes line. Remember that sharp braking may throw the glass forward.

Tools for cutting glass

A steel glass cutter is adequate for most work and cheaper than the traditional glass cutter's diamond. If you can, choose a cutter on which the wheel is clearly visible when the tool is in use, as this promotes greater accuracy.

The back of a glass cutter has small notches cut out. These are not, as sometimes supposed, devices for notching off protrusions and edges but are gauges, so that you can gauge the thickness of glass correctly for the job in hand.

If you are doing any quantity of glass cutting, it is worth the trouble to make up or buy a T-square, to guide the cutter during its stroke. A 1220mm length of 76mm × 6mm ramin or oak, preferably chamfered at one edge, with a 305mm length of 51mm × 13mm placed at right-angles across one end, is satisfactory.

A notch should be let into the cross arm, adjacent to the chamfered edge on the long arm, to allow the cutter to run cleanly off the edge of the glass at the end of its stroke.

A pair of pliers, for trimming narrow strips of glass and uneven edges, a ruler or steel tape for measuring and a felt-tipped pen, or Chinagraph crayon, are other tools. A small empty tin, filled with felt and soaked with light machine oil enables you to lubricate the cutter.

Cutting

Preparation: Professional glass cutters wear protective wrist bands, since a splinter of glass could cause serious injury. It is advisable, then, either to wear wrist bands or to wrap your wrists with household bandages or something of that sort.

You will need a large, flat working surface to lay the glass on, such as a bench, kitchen or dining table. Place a blanket on the table to protect it and the surface of the glass from being scratched.

Where odd shapes must be cut, always make a template first from stiff card, carefully checking its accuracy. Make this about 3mm smaller all round than the actual measurements, to allow for the distance between the edge of the cutter and the cutting wheel.

Before cutting, clean the surface of the glass by wiping it with a proprietary glass cleaner or with methylated spirits. Mark the cutting line on the surface and re-check dimensions before cutting.

Lubricate the glass cutter before use by wiping it on the felt in the tin container. Hold the cutter so that the handle rests between the first and second fingers and

Place glass cutter under glass at the score line; press down evenly to break

Wear protective gloves when carrying glass; support it firmly as illustrated

Stand pane at angle on soft base, with front timber 'stop'; lean on soft 'laps'

the bottom of the hand remains clear of the glass.

With the straight edge held 3mm from the marking line, to allow for the thickness of the wheel, score the surface of the glass along the line with the cutter, using a firm, smooth stroke. Draw your arm back while keeping the rest of the body stiff. Never back-track, as the glass may break at a point other than where you want.

Scoring should be completed as one operation. This is so as to score the glass evenly, enabling the piece to be snapped apart easily. Once the score mark is made, lift the glass and tap it gently from underneath along the length of the mark. Then position the edge of a small batten, about 50mm wide, directly under the cutting line or use the cutter as a fulcrum.

Place your hands on either side of the glass surface of the line and as close to it as possible, and press down slowly and firmly with your fingertips until you get a clean break along the cutting line.

Where it is necessary to remove small strips or pieces of glass, score the line as before and then, using the jaws of a pair of pliers, break off the waste pieces in small bits.

Curves and angles can also be cut by scoring the glass to the shape required by means of card templates. Once the glass has been scored to shape, tap it carefully from the underside and then, gripping the piece firmly on each side of the score marks, snap evenly downwards to break the glass.

Removing rough edges

After completion of cutting, rough edges can be smoothed away by using a carborundum stone. You will need two—a 121 fine and a 122 medium. You will also need a natural pumice stone, some pumice powder and a wood block. Both the carborundum and pumice should be kept wet at all times when being used.

The first stage is called arrising and is to remove the sharp edge. Use the medium stone at an angle of 45° and rub downwards in one direction. Once the edges have been arrised, the flat part of the edge can be ground with the face of the medium stone.

Rub it up and down, keeping it in contact with the glass at all times. Follow with the fine stone to produce a sheen.

Basic polishing can now be done with the pumice stone, but to get a really fine finish, use a wood block dressed with pumice powder.

Glass chart

Application	Suggested type of glass	Normal thickness	Other information
Windows			
Single glazing			
up to 2 m2	Float or drawn sheet glass	4mm	Windows must withstand wind
between 2 m2 and 3·3 m2	for clear vision	5mm or 6mm	pressure, therefore in exposed
over 3·3 m2		6mm, 10mm or 12mm	sites thicker glass may be
up to 750 m2	Patterned glass for privacy	3mm	necessary.
between 750 m2 and 1·8 m2		5mm	
Double glazing	Two panes float glass for clear vision	Hermetically sealed units vacuum or air spaces varying from	All types of double glazing keep heat in during cold weather, reduce condensation and 'cold
	One flat and one patterned for privacy	4mm to 12mm, or secondary sashed	zones' near windows
	One solar-control glass (tinted) and one float glass for protection from sun's heat	(fitted to existing windows)	
Doors			
External			
All-glass	Toughened glass	12mm	Glass at low level might present a
Framed	Float or patterned	5mm or 6mm	hazard, particularly to children.
Internal			It is suggested that toughened
All-glass	Toughened glass or patterned	10mm	glass be used. Framed doors, including patio doors, can be double glazed
Framed	Float or patterned	5mm or 6mm	
Partitions, room dividers	Patterned glass	5mm or 6mm	See above
Sliding doors for serving hatches, cupboards etc	Float or patterned glass	3mm, 5mm or 6mm	Large selection of patterns, including amber, blue and green tints
Table tops			
Large	Float glass	12mm, 15mm, 19mm or 25mm according to size	
Coffee tables	Float (clear, grey, green, bronze) or rough cast	10mm or 12mm	
Shelves	Float or rough cast	6mm, 10mm or 12mm	
Mirrors	Silvered float	6mm Verity range standard sizes or mirrors 'made to measure'	
Pictures	Diffuse reflection	2mm	Use on water-colours, prints and so on, to eliminate dazzle from lighting
Greenhouses, cold frames, cloches	Horticultural sheet glass	3mm or 4mm	A cheaper-quality glass with good light transmission necessary for growth
Windbreaks	Toughened glass, such as (Pilkington) Armourplate or Armourcast	6mm or 10mm	Ideal for terraces and swimming pools; no maintenance required
Fire-resistant glazing	Polished or rough-cast wired glass	6mm	Suitable for fire doors and partitions where up to one hour fire resistance is needed

The glazed look for doors and windows

A broken window is probably one of the most inconvenient things which can happen at home. It can also be dangerous because of broken and jagged pieces of glass, so should be quickly repaired; this is not a difficult task. Updating your glazing can bring more light into your home and give an opportunity to make use of some of the many interesting coloured and textured glasses which are made.

Glazing work is best carried out in warmer weather, as at lower temperatures glass becomes brittle. Avoid using old glass; this turns brittle with age, is difficult to cut satisfactorily and will tend to break.

Situations requiring glazing attention are door or window repairs or replacement, improvements where an ordinary clear glass is replaced by a patterned or textured glass, or where a timber door is replaced by complete glass or glass-panelled door, to let in more light.

In some cases it is advisable to remove frames, when glazing or reglazing, for safety or access reasons.

Wood frames

Glass is held in a channel called a rebate, usually with putty and special pins, called sprigs, but sometimes with panel pins. When handling glass, always wear thick protective gloves. Apart from the danger of injury from slivers of broken glass, new glass may have sharp edges.

Tools

You will need a glazier's hacking knife, or an old screwdriver, to remove the existing glass, a pair of pincers, to pull out glazing sprigs, and a Warrington-pattern hammer with a cross-pein head.

Techniques

An intact pane can, with care, be removed undamaged, though this is more difficult to do in cold weather or when glass is old.

Work from the top of the frame down-wards when removing glass. First, loosen all the putty around the outside edge of the glass with the hacking knife. This will expose the sprigs or pins; these can be carefully pulled out with the pincers. Eventually the pane, or remnants, can be lifted out. Take care, however, that the glass does not fall out and shatter.

Old, hardened putty may have to be hacked out with a hammer and chisel. Any segments of glass remaining in the rebate can be prised out with pliers.

Next, remove all old putty down to the bare wood. Clean the rebate with medium glasspaper, apply a coat of wood primer and allow to dry. Drying takes about four hours.

Measure the rebate with a steel tape, from the inside edge of each rebate, taking each side top and bottom separately and then measure across the two diagonals. These measurements should be equal if the frame is square.

Glass must be cut slightly undersize to allow for expansion. For sheets of average size, allow around 1·5mm, but twice this where the pane is more than 370mm² in area.

Once you have cut the glass, it is wise to remove sharp edges with an oilstone lubricated with water, oil, turpentine or white spirit. So that the glass fits accurately in the frame, mark the outer face side; a wax pencil or crayon can be used.

Standard putty is used for glazing timber frames. A non-hardening mastic should be used when fitting sealed double-glazed units or glazing metal frames.

Putty

Roll the putty in the hands until it is soft and easy to work. If putty is too oily, it can be wrapped in newspaper to absorb the oil. Linseed oil can be added to standard glazing putty to soften it. Once the consistency is correct, lay a 3mm thick strip of putty, called the bedding putty, into the back of the rebate with the thumb.

Place the glass in the rebate. Set this in from the bottom, leaving an equal space on each side, and press the glass, firmly at the sides, into position against the putty; never press glass from the centre.

Press evenly around the edges until all surplus putty is squeezed out, leaving about 1·5mm between the back of the glass and rebate. Cut off excess putty with the putty knife.

Fix the glass into place by tacking the sprigs or pins into the frame, parallel with the face of the glass. Start the pins with the cross-pein head of the hammer. Keep the side of the hammer parallel with the face of the glass and on it while fixing; this will avoid hitting the glass and, possibly, cracking it. Space the sprigs at intervals of about 150mm.

A strip of weathering putty should now be evenly applied at an angle on the outside of the rebate.

Smooth the putty with the putty knife, keeping this lubricated with water to prevent putty from sticking to the blade. Hold the blade in one corner against the rebate, with the tip resting at an angle of about 45° on the glass, and draw the blade smoothly downwards.

This angle is important as it allows rain to run off and not collect. Trim away excess putty with an even pressure of the knife. Trim each area with one stroke to ensure a clean surface line. Make a neat mitre at each corner. Finally, go over all the putty surfaces with a damp, soft brush

Allow two or three weeks to elapse and then paint over the putty with an oil undercoat and then a finishing coat to match surrounding paintwork. Allow paint slightly to encroach, by about 3mm, on to the surface of the glass, to seal the join.

Wood beads

These can be used in place of weathering putty, but the glass should be set in bedding putty. Bead can be square, splayed or quarter-round softwood. It is fixed with 19mm–25mm panel pins and glazing felt. When using wood beads, a slightly thinner glass can be used.

Measure the sides and tops of the rebates and check the diagonals for squareness. The four beads should be cut slightly over size; mark these in pencil to show the respective positions. Mitre the ends, using a mitre box and dovetail saw. Paint the backs of the beads with a primer.

Lay the beads flat and gently tap two panel pins part of the way into the centre of the bead at about 25mm from the face of each mitre. This will establish the angle of entry for fixing into the frames. Remove the nails and drill holes; this prevents the beads from splitting. Drill further holes at about 15mm distances along each piece.

Put the beads into position and gently tap down the pins, just to the face of the beads.

These are not fixed permanently until all four are in position. Fix first the upright, next, the opposed bead and then top and bottom beads; check also that the glass remains accurately in position.

With a centre punch, tap the pins below the surface. The holes can then be filled with putty or a filler, and any inconsistencies in the mitres made good. Then the bead can be rubbed down, prepared and painted.

Glass vibration, which can be noisy and even cause glass to break, can be avoided by using adhesive glazing felt in place of bedding putty. This is cut to length and set into the rebate before fitting the glass.

Use stout protective gloves to remove segments of glass from a broken window

An old chisel or steel blade can be used to hack out old putty and glass

Next, carefully pull out old glazing sprigs or pins with a pair of pliers

Measure the rebate, both horizontally and vertically; double check

Check for squareness by measuring the diagonals; these should be equal

Hole for metal glazing clip; remove these carefully for reuse.

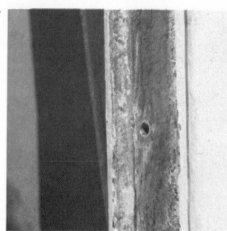

Locate pane of glass in the bedding putty and lever it gently into place

Place the hands on either side of the pane and press it evenly and firmly in

Fix glazing sprigs and then trim off surplus putty on inside of the rebate

With thicker glass or in larger areas, cups and screws can be used in place of panel pins. If made of brass or white metal these can look attractive, particularly on natural or varnished timber.

If cups are not used, the screw pilot must be recessed with a countersinking bit. First drill the pilot hole; this is unnecessary where cups are used.

Countersunk heads should be recessed below the surface of the beads. To fix, position one of the side beads and make a hole through the pilot hole into the frame with a bradawl, and fix in the order used for pinned beads.

Brass screws fixed through hardwood should first be lubricated with candlewax to prevent them from snapping off.

Metal frames

Though the procedure for glazing metal frames is largely the same as for wooden frames, a mastic glazing medium has to be used and added provision must be made for expansion.

Sprigs are not used; glass is held in place by spring clips, resembling a bent letter 's' which hook into the rebate. These press on to the glass face. When reglazing, carefully remove existing clips for re-use.

Metal frames require small plastic expansion pieces in the bottom frame rebate. These are set into the bedding mastic and their thickness must be allowed for when cutting glass.

Two causes of glass in metal frames cracking are rust and distortion. In some cases you may have to contemplate fitting a new frame, if deterioration is considerable or the distortion cannot be corrected.

Any rust should be removed by cleaning the affected area with wire wool. It should then be treated with a rust inhibitor and primed.

In some cases, metal glazing beads are fixed to the outside of steel and aluminium windows with grub screws. Before removing these, first lubricate with a drop of penetrating oil; this facilitates removal.

In cases where, with any window or door, only surface putty needs renewing, simply remove the deteriorated putty and re-putty the rebate with new weathering putty.

Once the rebate is free of débris, next clean up the rebate with a dusting brush

On metal frames, the rebate should be prepared with a coat of metal priming

It is a sound idea to protect the eyes with protective goggles during glazing

Clip seen in place, holding glass firmly against facing putty

Bedding putty is applied evenly into the rebate and the pane of glass is inserted

Expansion pieces in the bottom rebate are necessary with metal window frames

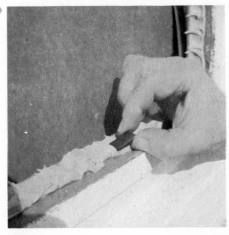

Ball putty in the hand and evenly apply the facing putty to glass and the rebate

Use putty knife at angle. Keep putty moist so that knife does not make it drag

Finally, trim off surplus and mitre the corners; later apply protective paint

Be your own master glazier

Cutting holes or circles in glass, or drilling holes in mirrors, need not be a job only for the expert. With care, the right tools and some patience, the handyman is quite able to cope successfully with such tasks. Leaded window lights may, from time to time, need replacement of panes, or the frames may need repairing. If tackled systematically, this is no more difficult than other types of glazing.

Cutting holes and circles

To cut circles or holes you need a tool called a radius or circle-arm cutter. This is a cutting wheel, mounted on an adjustable arm, which revolves on a central pivot and suction cup.

The length of the arm can be adjusted to vary the radius of the circle. This tool is much easier to use on glass in a flat position, though it is possible, with care, to cut a circle from a fixed pane of glass.

To find the centre point, mark diagonals on the piece from corner to corner, with a felt-tipped pen or crayon. The intersection of the diagonals gives the centre.

If the circle is not to be cut in the middle of the glass, mark out a rectangle in the chosen area and work accordingly. Measure off, along one diagonal, the exact radius of the circle to be cut, from the point where the diagonals cross.

Fix the suction pad on the cutter on this central point and set the arm so that the cutting edge just reaches the length of the radius. Now scribe the circle, holding the cutter firmly and applying even pressure all round.

The pivot must be held down firmly on the glass while the cutter wheel is revolved.

Safety circle

Once this is completed, move the cutting edge about 20mm inwards and scribe a second circle. This is known as the 'safety circle', because it helps to keep the edges of the glass from splintering.

With the metal tip of the glass cutter, tap the underside of the glass upwards towards the cuts. Work slowly and carefully around both circles. The object is to 'open up' the cuts so that the removal of the waste glass is both clean and neat, without splintered edges. Tapping out could take 10 or 20 minutes—and there is no advantage in rushing it.

Next, divide the safety circle into wedge sections, using the ordinary glass cutter. Cross-hatch these wedges and, with the head of the glass cutter, tap out one small piece of glass from beneath, then carefully break out the glass in the safety circle with pliers.

Next, make radial v-cuts to the line of the outer circle. Take care not to mark over this line, or the glass may shatter. These score marks should be at intervals of about 25mm and are broken out with pliers. First tap and then break out glass until the whole of the opening is cleared.

Drilling

Drilling should be done using spade or spearpoint bits, which are made specially for glass drilling. A power drill can be used at a slow speed, but a more reliable method of drilling is by using a bit and brace. The speed of drilling should not exceed 350 revolutions per minute.

Holes should not be drilled closer than 13mm from the edge of a glazed surface and, if possible, keep this to 25mm. Where a masonry drill is not available, a tapered triangular piece of file may be used, with care, in a brace. The turning motion should be slow, steady and with even pressure.

The glass should be laid on an absolutely flat surface. Mark the drilling position by pressing the tip of the bit on to the glass. This is to fracture the surface, to prevent the bit from wandering while drilling.

When drilling a mirror, start on the non-reflective side, to prevent damage to the silvering. To find the drilling position, cross measure from the outside edge of the glass. Avoid too much downward pressure as this may fracture the glass.

Make a small well of putty around the drill hole and fill this with turpentine or white spirit; with mirrors use water as oils will cause staining beneath the glaze. When you begin drilling, the spirit will turn white with powdered glass; when this happens add more spirit.

Just before the hole breaks through the glass, stop for a moment and clean away débris. Proceed carefully as the bit nears the other side. Do not stop turning or you will run the risk of splintering the glass around the edge.

There is a danger that the drill may 'break out' a large sliver from the face side of the mirror if you drill only from one side.

It is a good idea to finish off by drilling from the face side just before the bit breaks through from the back. Again, mark accurately from the edges and drill with great care.

To find its centre point, mark out the diagonals of the area of the circle

Radius-arm cutter has central suction cap and adjustable glass-cutting head

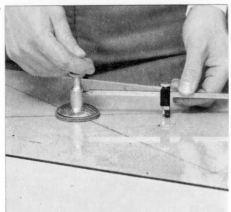

Scribe outer circle and inner 'safety' circle; tap with cutter to spread out

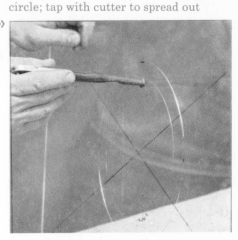

Score between inner and outer circle at intervals to safeguard pane from breaking

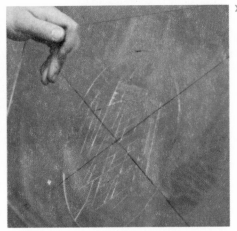

Carefully tap out the criss-crossed section, using the head of the cutter

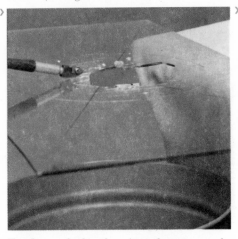

Tap cross cuts to 'spread' these and remove safety circle with pliers

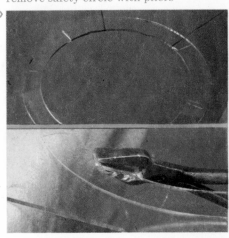

Cutting a circle is cutting a hole in reverse. Score safety lines from edge

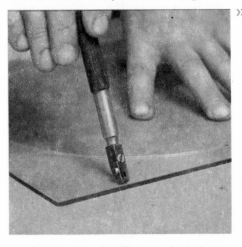

Tap beneath the glass in order to spread the score marks made by the glass cutter

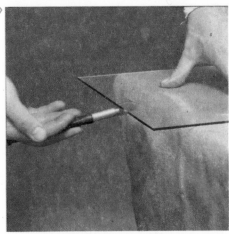

Using the pliers, gently break off the outer segments to leave circle of glass

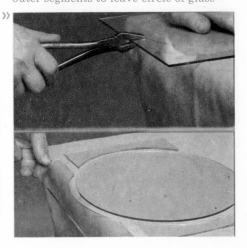

Mark the point of drilling, make a ring of putty and pour the lubricant

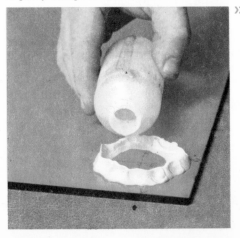

Mark starting point with tip of spade drill; drill slowly and keep lubricated

Arris edges with carborundum block; this is used at angle of 45° in one direction

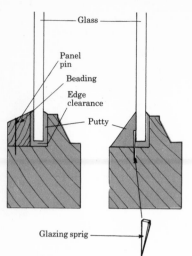

Glass

Panel
pin

Beading

Edge
clearance

Putty

Glazing sprig →

The finishing touches in window glazing:
facing putty or wood beading

Repairing leaded lights

In the traditional leaded light, separate pieces of glass are held in a framework of specially shaped lead extrusions called 'cames'. The whole framework, called the light, is then inserted in the rebate of the window casement like a single pane of glass.

Tools needed are a glass cutter, a 6mm wood chisel, a soft brush, a putty knife, a hammer and a soldering iron.

Materials: gold-size putty cement, plumber's black, solder, flux and wire wool. Gold size is an addition to the putty which prevents cracking and should be mixed well into the putty. Gold size accelerates drying.

Even if only one or two pieces of glass are broken in a leaded light, it is likely that you will have to remove the whole light to replace them.

If you can repair the window in situ, do so. Leaded lights are easily distorted when removed from their frames. Where a window has bulged badly, however, take it out carefully.

Always work on the outside of a window so that any disfigurement of the cames cannot be seen from the inside.

Start by carefully cutting away the putty, avoiding damage to the outer lead cames. Remove the sprigs or oval brads – there are normally two to each edge of the frame.

Insert a wide chisel behind the light and ease it gently out of the rebate, working progressively along each of the edges in turn.

Lay the light on a flat surface and, with a knife, cut through the top of the cames, cutting diagonally into the corners to enable the edge of the lead to be prised up. Slip the blade between the lead and the glass and draw it along the came.

Repeat the process with the blade of a screwdriver until the lead is gradually lifted and bent back.

Continue until the glass is loose enough to draw out. Tap out the glass from the inside of the window. Collect the pieces and dispose of them. Clean out the grooves in the cames with a chisel, taking extra care to ensure that there is no débris left in the corners.

Brush round all the empty cames and then fill these with a soft, gold-size putty cement, pressed well down into the came. Cut the new glass carefully to size and insert this.

Support the light on a flat surface, such as a piece of hardboard, and press down the cames firmly with a putty knife, handle of a screwdriver or a wallpaper roller to ensure that they are all flat on the glass. Carefully trim off surplus putty from both sides of the glass with the putty knife.

Burnish the broken joints with an abrasive pad or medium-grade glasspaper or with fine wire wool.

The conventional way of sealing the corners is to solder them. Plumber's black is applied beyond the corner of each joint to limit the spread of solder. Check that the surface is clean, or the solder will not adhere.

Soft soldering is carried out at temperatures of between 120°C and 240°. An electric soldering iron is the best choice. Soft soldering is a relatively low-temperature process for joints which do not have to take a lot of weight or heat.

Apply flux and place a little solder on each broken joint with a moderately hot iron. To finish the joint neatly, to match the others, rub with the soldering iron, in a circular motion.

Alternatively, you can seal the corners with plastic repair materials. Clean the joints, knife the plastic into them and allow it to set hard.

Where leaking is caused by a fault in the putty, mark the leaking points with a wax crayon during wet weather.

When the weather is dry, open the cames up slightly, and scrape out the old putty. Replace it with new and press the cames firmly back into place. Check again during wet weather.

Use oyster knife to raise lead came to 90° angle; cut to lift at solder joints

Take rubbing on piece of paper in order to establish size of glass needed

Mark outline in pencil; use as template to cut glass. Nick off pane corners

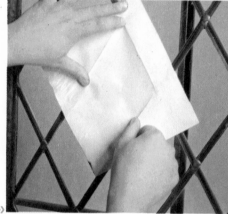

Insert new pane using putty knife. Hold knife under came when pressing this back

Press on top surface with shaped piece of boxwood, keeping putty knife beneath

Finally, fork putty into the came. This is special soft putty for leaded lights

Glass décor in the home

Thoughtful use of mirrors can add new dimensions to small spaces and lighten dull areas in the home. At one time, regarded largely as looking glasses, high-quality mirrors are now recognised as important in decorative schemes. There are various types of conventional mirror, mirror tiles and light-weight mirrors with many home applications.

The best-quality mirror is made of float glass covered with silver coating to give a true reflection. Before coating, the glass is selected to make sure it is flawless.

The surface is washed to remove any contamination. To prevent tarnishing, it is coated with a layer of copper and several layers of water-resistant paint and resin, before silvering.

Reflective quality depends, to a certain extent, on the quality of the mirror. A mirror used to lighten or create a feeling of space need not have such highly reflective qualities as a mirror, for example, in a bathroom, where its use is functional as well as decorative.

Float glass gives the highest-quality reflection but, used in large areas, can be costly. The standard thickness of float glass used in mirrors is 6mm, though mirrors of 3mm and 4mm are available. Float glass is also fragile and should only be used where it can be fixed securely.

Fixing

There are five ways of fixing mirrors:

● Hanging;

● With screws and plugs;

● With mirror clips or corner screws and wall plugs;

● On narrow ledges or aluminium angled brackets;

● With self-adhesive pads (used only for light-weight mirrors or mirror tiles).

The traditional hanging mirror is drilled to or fixed with clips to a timber backing, usually suspended by chains from a No. 8 chrome-headed screw (31mm/38mm). This is fixed into the wall or hung by a picture hook on a picture rail.

Though satisfactory when hung this way, mirrors look best when mounted flat to a surface, as this avoids the demarcation line between the mirror edge and the wall and gives a better reflection.

Heavier glass should be mounted directly on the wall. If the wall surface is smooth, direct fixing is quite easy. On a bumpy, irregular wall, mount the mirror on a piece of 19mm blockboard, which should be sealed on both sides and along the edges to prevent warping.

When fixing mirrors to walls it is important to leave a small gap, of around 3mm, to allow free circulation of air. This is important in areas of high condensation such as bathrooms and kitchens. The space can be achieved by using nylon washers on the fixing screws.

A laminated lead backing provides added protection, though a coat of varnish helps. Nylon sleeves, spacers and so on are desirable on all fixings, as rubber and some plastics may react chemically with the mirror finish, causing damage to the surface.

Mirror screws can be used to fix small and medium-sized mirrors. A mirror bigger than 1220mm × 910mm is too heavy for screws, as weight and stress may cause cracking at the corners.

Mirrors may be supplied with pre-drilled holes and suitable chrome-headed mirror screws and caps. The screw heads have counter-sunk screw holes. The mirror can be drilled with a spear-point drill.

With ordinary screws, use a screw with a slightly rounded top and a nylon mirror washer.

Plug the wall to take the fixing screw. If the hole is drilled slightly larger than the shank of the screw, but not its head, there is no need to countersink the hole.

When fixed, the screw head will partly sink into the hole and the chrome head will cover the rest of the projection.

Screw holes at each corner should not be less than 25mm from the edge of the mirror. On larger mirrors, screws are needed at 300mm intervals along each side. Small mirrors may only need two fixing points.

Small mirrors of 3mm or 4mm glass may be fixed on a flat, non-porous surface with self-adhesive pads. Large, heavy mirrors can be fixed by using plugs, screws, washers, clips or mirror corners.

Mirror corners, plated to match the mirror, are used to support the corners and are screwed through two eyelets into a wall plug.

To fit these, place one at each corner of the mirror and mark the position of the eyelet holes on the wall.

The corner is then screwed into position in the wall plug. In this system, the screw heads show.

Mirror clips have the advantage of fixings that are concealed behind the mirror. These clips hook round the edge of the mirror. A round clip is used at the bottom to hold the mirror rigidly and prevent it from slipping. The top clip has a long slot to allow for adjustment of the mirror.

To fix, offer the mirror to the wall.

Draw round it to mark the position it will occupy and plug and screw the non-sliding bottom clips. These should be set at 300mm intervals along the length of the mirror. The part that clips round the mirror should be level with the pencil mark. Fix the top clip so that, at its fullest extension, the hook at the front of the clip just touches the pencil line.

A mirror longer than 600mm should be secured with side clips of the type used at the top of the mirror. Rest the mirror in the bottom clips and then press it against the wall, hooking the top and side clips over the glass.

Clips or corners can be used for large mirrors. If the mirror is quite large and heavy, a system of mirror corners and fixing clips might be used along the bottom of the mirror. The disadvantage of this is that the arrangement may look ugly.

The weight of 6mm float glass is about 4·50kg/m². A mirror of 300mm² requires two fixing points; a 1·5m² mirror needs four fixing points.

A really heavy mirror is best fitted on a narrow ledge. The base can be supported by a j-shaped strip of aluminium fixed with plugs and 'invisible' fixing screws.

These fixing techniques are used on solid walls, brick, concrete, building blocks and so on. If the masonry is crumbly use a plastic plugging material. Similar techniques are used on solid doors and heavy wood partitions, but in this case, plugging is not necessary.

Fixing on hollow walls follows the same methods as for solid walls, except that toggle-bolts or other fixings are used. The mirror is still attached with screws, mirror corners or clips.

Mirrors are fixed on hollow doors and flush doors using techniques as for hollow walls.

Mirror tiles and lightweight mirrors

Mirror tiles are cheaper than sheet mirrors. To the quantity required add five per cent for cutting and breakages. Use an ordinary glass cutter to cut the tiles.

Fixing is with self-adhesive pads. These are pressure sensitive on each side and are placed at each corner on the back of the tile. There are usually four pads to the standard small tile. Larger tiles may have more fixing pads.

Remove the backing paper from the pads and press the tile firmly, but gently, on to the surface. The surface should be gloss painted as the tiles adhere more firmly to this type of surface. The slight resilience of the foam pads provides a degree of safety, since the tiles are not under tension once in position.

Mirror tiles are ideal for use in situations where a broken reflection does not matter and, in some cases, may give an unusual effect. As they can be easily cut, mirror tiles are useful where there are irregular areas.

There are several types of lightweight mirror. These are made of silvered acrylic sheeting. Available in thicknesses of 3mm and 6mm, the sheeting is unbreakable but scratches easily. For use as a mirror the 6mm grade is most useful as the 3mm sheet is really only strong enough for use as a

Black, vitreous glass as mirror surround. Second mirror reflection gives 'infinity'

A mirrored hall can reflect light and provide an illusion of greater size

Tiles combined with glass shelving, backed by a mirror

decorative covering and not as a functional mirror.

Lightweight mirrors are useful in bathrooms as condensation does not form on the surface. It is also an advantage to use a lightweight mirror where the mirror is to be mounted on a door.

This type of mirror can be mounted on to 13mm chipboard and fastened with a double-sided tape or special acrylic sheet adhesive. The mirror is either fixed with mirror screws, the holes being drilled carefully with a blunt twist drill, or secured using impact adhesive. If the mirror is small, light self-adhesive pads can be used.

Mirror effects

The interior glass most often found inside the home is a mirror. Convention has tended to confine these largely to the utilitarian bathroom cabinet and the small, wall-hung mirror.

Large mirrors reflect light and give added dimensions to a room. For that reason, mirrored halls and galleries are to be found in many stately homes.

The trend today towards 'compact' modern living means that mirrors can be used to open out areas and create the feeling of dimension that is lacking in reality.

A dark, narrow hallway, decorated in light, receding colours, can be made to look much wider if one wall is covered with mirrors. Either sheet mirror or mirror tiles can be used. Not only will an extra sense of space be added, but all available light will be reflected, making the area brighter.

Small bathrooms can be made to look twice as large if one wall is a complete mirror. This gives a further illusion of space if the mirror is fitted flush between the joints of the ceramic tiles, or at right angles into the corners. Modern bathroom cabinets may have a mirror on one or on both doors. This idea may be extended to an entire wall of storage units, faced with mirrors.

A window alcove with a dull outlook may be made more interesting if blocked in and backed with a mirror or mirror tiles. Well-lit, it will provide a three-dimensional display area for attractive ornaments, glassware or plants.

An interesting feature can be made of alcoves, backed with a mirror, if lit with concealed lighting.

Mirrors can be placed between wall-mounted book shelves or behind shelving used for books and storage.

In the kitchen, especially in the small kitchen, a breakfast-bar area can be given added width by using a mirror-tile surround. This might extend the vista and prevent the 'shut-in' feeling of sitting close to a wall.

A mirror placed at the end of a dark hall will reflect light and increase the sense of width. The area under a stairway might be opened out, cleared of any clutter of cupboards, and turned into a mini-office and telephone area.

Mirror tiles used to face the wall area would help to reflect light and make an interesting feature of an otherwise dead area.

An alcove mirror with built-in dressing table also helps to give vista to a room

Double glazing: an extra layer of comfort

Double glazing is a comfort medium, and may, if the gap between the two panes of glass is deep enough, provide effective sound insulation. Fixed pre-made double-glazed panes can be used, or one of the many types of applied or coupled glazed sashes, which offer a choice of system suitable for use with any type of existing single glazing

Double glazing is one of the ways of preventing heat loss through the fabric of a building. It has been estimated that up to 20 per cent of heat waste through the fabric is lost through windows and around gaps in badly fitting frames.

It is important to look at double glazing as part of whole-house insulation. Potentially, out of money spent on heating an uninsulated house, 75 per cent is wasted. Loss occurs through walls, roofs, doors and windows, floors and flues.

Opinion varies on the question of how much money is saved by double glazing. Basically, it increases the comfort level but does not usually greatly cut heating costs.

A single sheet of glass is a poor insulator. If used in an exposed condition it can have as high a 'U' value as 5·67w/m² °C or 6·24.

The area around a window is a cold 'zone'; the nearer you get to the window the colder you find it. When expanding warm air reaches this cold surface, it cools and contracts, causing turbulence which creates a draught. A vacuum, a 'sandwich' of air or inert gas entrapped between two sheets of glass, raises the face temperature of the inner pane, so that warm air is no longer dramatically cooled.

Though double glazing a window area can save up to 80 per cent of the heat lost through the glass, as this usually represents only a small area of the total house fabric, the actual saving, in heat terms, may be as little as 10 per cent.

The amount of thermal insulation provided by double glazing depends on the gap between the two sheets of glass. Basically, the greater the gap, the greater the degree of insulation. A double-glazed unit with a gap of 5mm would have a 'U' value of 3·40, while a 13mm gap would improve the value to 2·96.

Before fixing double glazing, it is important to check that heat is not escaping through badly fitting window frames. It is pointless to fit double glazing if heat is escaping and you are prey to draughts from outside.

There are various methods of dealing with the problem. If the frame is badly distorted and the wood rotted or warped it may be better to repair or replace the entire frame.

A variety of window draught excluders are available, ranging from sprung-metal stripping, to go around door and window frames, adhesive-backed foam-rubber strip to a type in a tube which is squeezed out along the opening and allowed to dry. Before applying an adhesive-backed or plastic extruder, first make sure that surfaces are free from grease and dry.

As an aid to sound insulation, double-glazed units do not have very high sound-insulation properties. Domestic glazing units have a gap varying between 5mm and 13mm, but to provide an effective sound barrier this gap needs to be 100mm or more.

A unit like this could not be fitted easily to most domestic windows and would need specially modified window fittings.

Factory-made units

The pre-sealed, factory-made unit consists of a double sheet of glass, vacuum sealed or filled with inert gas. This type presents the appearance of conventional glazing and requires no further attention once fitted. With such units problems of condensation on the inner surfaces of the glass are virtually eliminated.

Factory-made units are heavy and may implode if dropped, so get help in handling these. Careful, correct measurement is most important. A rebate at least 13mm deep will be required if the unit is to be glazed into an existing wood or metal frame.

This allows for a 5mm gap between the sheets of glass. Units are made with smaller gaps. Check that the frames are in good condition and adequate to carry the weight of a factory-sealed unit, as this weighs at least twice that of a single sheet of glass.

When fixing pre-sealed units to existing window frames the most satisfactory method of fixing is to use beading, tacked and then painted to match the rest of the framework.

Alternatively, the unit can be glazed, in the conventional way, using a non-hardening glazing mastic.

Pre-sealed units have the added advantage of providing only two surfaces to clean and are neat in appearance.

There are no summer storage problems which apply to other types of glazing units and no ventilation problems. Most suppliers of double-glazed units will supply and fix, or measure for you and then supply for you to fix.

Sealed units are available in over 100 standard sizes but most firms will meet a 'one-off' order. As this may take some time, try to anticipate your needs in advance.

Applied and coupled sashes

Applied-sash or coupled-sash units are popular forms of double glazing. These come in a variety of kits or you can evolve your own system. An applied sash is fitted to the rebate of the window or other window surround, while the coupled sash is fitted to the window frame.

It is possible to have coupled sash sliding units. Sliding-sash units usually consist of a head track, side member and sill track. The fixing position of the head track decides the final position of the window.

In deciding the position of the track, make sure there is room for any projecting window furniture between the existing window and the track. Some kits include a sealing strip to stop draughts.

For sliding windows to slide easily it is essential to have a true frame. The lack of this does not preclude this form of double glazing.

Most firms supply packing pieces which can be used to ensure a 'true' frame, allowing windows to slide easily. As the distance between the sashes is normally 100mm, it provides some acoustical advantage.

Coupled sash

This is simple to install and involves the fixing of a removable glazed panel, to the existing window frame. In summer this panel can be taken down and stored.

When making up a coupled-sash unit, the frame of the glazing unit should normally be 19mm less than the dimensions of the window opening and the glass 8mm less than the dimensions of the frame.

Cut the main frame channel to size and fit the glazing strips round the glass. This should be first laid flat. The basic components of the majority of systems are usually four main channels and four corner hinges, locking nuts and screws and neoprene sealing strips.

To assemble, the four main channels and corner hinges are placed roughly in position. The locking nuts and screws are fixed loosely to the corners.

Cut the neoprene sealing strips to the correct length, mitre the corners (some kits include a mitre block) and then insert the strips into the channels. After fitting the corner hinges to the main frame, the glass is fitted into the frame.

Usually, a sliding foot is provided for the window stay. This is fitted into the groove of the bottom channel. The unit is then tightened and offered up to the window frame. Mark the position of the hinges and set these so that the frame hinges accurately into place.

In detail, coupled sash units may vary but this is the method used to fix most units. For further insulation, a neoprene strip can be fixed to seal the joint between the unit and the window frame.

Before positioning any made-up double-glazing unit, remember to clean both sheets of glass thoroughly on both sides. Condensation between the sheets may prove a problem.

There are two methods of combating this. One is to drill a series of small holes upwards in the base of the frame to provide ventilation. The other is to use silica-gell crystals. These are placed along the bottom of the unit where they act as blotting paper to absorb the moisture. These may become saturated in time and need to be removed and dried out. Coupled-sash glazing frames can also be applied externally to window frames.

Kits, consisting of plastic framing, into which you fit your own glass, are available. Some types consist of a coupled sash which unclips completely, while others have an adhesive-fixed plastic head, into which the glass is fitted when needed.

Applied sash lifts into place, is fixed by clips, and can be removed in summer

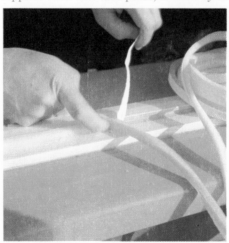

Foam draught excluder has sticky back – but clean surface before pressing down

Sprung metal excluder provides a close seal around the edges of an outside door

The frames for applied or coupled sash units can be made of plastic, wood or aluminium.

Moisture is drawn through the fibre of timbers, even when painted. A strip of aluminium foil – which is available in an adhesive-backed form – can be used to seal the reveal between the glass to keep out moisture.

When using applied or coupled-sash units, it is important to realize that provision should be made for adequate ventilation without draughts. A completely sealed atmosphere with no air changes is neither healthy nor desirable.

An adequate form of double glazing can be provided by using double-sided tape and acetate sheeting. The double-sided tape is placed round the window surround to hold the acetate sheeting in place.

A good basis to start from

The surface quality of a finished floor is only as good as that of the sub-floor beneath. There are various types of floor surface and a variety of ways to renew or merely reinforce these. Whether you renew worn areas or provide a base for a decorative surface, an even and properly prepared sub-floor is important.

Sub-floors consist of two types:
Solid—concrete tiles or stone floor and
Suspended—timber boards or sheets fixed
to timber joists.

Solid floors

Solid floors provide an excellent base for
any type of wood flooring but must be dry
and level. Any problems of dampness must
be cured, at source, before a new floor is
laid. An uneven surface may need rescreeding.

Minor irregularities in level can be
rectified by using a proprietary self-
levelling compound.

Suspended floors

Suspended floors may present more problems than solid floors. Even a sound surface will tend to move, as wood expands
and contracts with the fluctuation of the
moisture content in the air. Normally,
this movement can be offset by laying a
covering floor skin, such as hardboard.

Chipboard

If the floorboards are in a poor state of
repair they may need completely renewing.
New tongued-and-grooved or square-edged
boards can be laid, but a flooring grade of
chipboard, 19mm thick, is worth considering. Chipboard consists of wood chips,
bonded and consolidated with resin, under
heat and pressure. The result is a hard-
wearing surface which is quick to lay and
can appear attractive when sealed with a
clear polyurethane varnish which provides a hard, durable finish.

First, remove old, worn floorboards.
Check the condition of joists and replace
damaged sections as necessary. Measure
the centres of the joists, as the width will
determine the size of chipboard sheet you
use. The edge of each chipboard section
must fit along the joist centres.

To fix down the ends, you may have to
insert cross pieces, or noggins, between
the joists. These are angle nailed through
the joists with 75mm wire nails. At the
end of a wall, the nails are driven in at an
angle through the noggins into the joists.

Careful measurement of a room is
needed to establish how many whole and
part sheets are needed to ensure the most
economical floor coverage.

Before laying chipboard, any projecting screw heads or brads should be removed or knocked down and the top of
the joists cleaned, so that the new board
will fit evenly. At the borders of rooms,
chip back plaster projections with a
bolster and a club hammer.

Chipboard is fixed with 50mm countersunk screws at 300mm intervals along the
board edges. At adjacent edges, stagger
the position of the screws to even stress.
Work round each section, partly driving
in each screw. Go round again and finally
screw down. This ensures that boards go
down evenly.

Flooring-grade chipboard can also be
laid over badly worn and uneven floorboards. Prepare the floorboards, using a
rotary sanding machine if necessary and
nail the chipboard to the flooring with
75mm wire nails.

Hardboard

Hardboard also provides a firm base over
worn floorboards. The boards must be
fixed securely and smoothed down to
remove any ridges or irregularities. Before
securing a hardboard surface to a floor,
ensure that wiring or pipe runs remain
accessible.

Flooring-grade hardboard 5mm–6mm
thick, should be used. Where floors are
subjected to humid or damp conditions,
oil-tempered hardboard should be used.
Standard hardboard can be tempered by
sponging or brushing the mesh side of the
surface with water to allow the boards to
expand to their fullest extent.

Place the sheets back to back, and
leave them for 48 hours before fixing.
Boards should be fixed with 13mm hardboard nails at 150mm centres.

If there is likely to be any movement on
the sub-floor, nail it down securely before
fixing the hardboard. Make sure the joints
between the hardboard sheets do not
coincide with those between underlying
floorboards.

Hardboard can be nailed down or
screwed. If it is to be screw fixed, pre-drill
for the screws but do not counter-sink.

Another method of fixing is to use a
suitable grade of flooring adhesive to
stick down the hardboard to the sub-floor
which must be clean and free from dust
or grease.

Before fixing hardboard to a concrete
screed, again ensure that the surface is
clean and free from dust and grease. Worn
areas can be built up with a self-levelling
compound or a filler consisting of a 1:3
cement: fine sand mix with one part of
PVA adhesive, diluted with three parts of
water. Trowel on the mixture and feather
off the edges.

Apply adhesive to the backs of the hardboard sheets, taking care to cover edges
and corners. It is not essential to cover
the back of the sheet entirely. Once in
position, the sheet should be weighted
down until adhesion is complete.

On new concrete screeds, hardboard
may be laid after allowing two to three
weeks for drying out. Ensure that the surface is free from dust, apply adhesive and
then position the hardboard.

Floorboards in good condition can be
rubbed down and treated with polyure-

thane varnish, to provide an attractive
floor finish. First, nail boards down securely and fill small gaps with papier
mâché filler.

Sanding machines

A large area can be smoothed down with
a hired sanding machine. The machine has
a bag to collect the dust and various
grades of sanding sheets are supplied
with it.

Preparation of the area before sanding
is important; check that all the floorboards are secure, and punch down any
nail heads and remove tacks or remnants
of floor covering.

A floor sander will remove varnish, old
paint, stains, grease and dirt from any
type of wood.

If, however, the floor has a very thick
paint covering, remove this with a proprietary stripper and scraper. Thick paint
will clog the sanding discs and be rubbed
back into the wood.

Using a coarse abrasive sheet on the
sanding drum, first work diagonally one
way across the room, and in both directions, if necessary. Change to a medium or
fine abrasive sheet and smooth the floor
in the direction of the floorboards.
Between each sanding operation, sweep
the floor clean.

Use an orbital sander, a drill attachment with a sanding disc or a hired edge
sander for awkward corners and near
skirtings. Rub down small difficult areas
with medium glass-paper wrapped over a
block of wood. Once the surface is completely stripped and dust free, apply clear
polyurethane varnish, stain or a sealant
to choice.

Sometimes it may be necessary to lay
a screed where a suspended floor has been
removed or where an old screed has been
hacked out. When laying a screed in place
of a suspended floor, ensure that there is
adequate underfloor ventilation for remaining rooms with suspended floors.

Damp-proof membranes

Before rescreeding, lay either a bituminous liquid or 500-gauge polythene
damp-proof membrane. In plastered rooms
chip away the bottom few millimetres to
expose the damp-course. The membrane

Self-levelling screed, such as Evode
levelling compound, used on solid floors

Floor sander enables uneven wood floors
to be smoothed. First use this diagonally

This is trowelled out to find its own
level. Surfaces should first be cleaned

The sander is next used down the centre
of floor boards; dust is collected in bag

An edge finisher can be used to smooth and to clean up the corners of a room

To finish off in tight corners, an orbital sander can be used for light sanding

Royalboard floor-grade hardboard is put down in staggered formation

When laying tiles, work outwards from centre points from crossed diagonals

Apply self-adhesive tiles, such as Halstead on to a clean surface

Overlap a tile on a tile and mark cut position with another tile when edging

must join or be cut into this.

A bituminous membrane is usually applied in two coats with a stiff broom. The first coat is diluted by some 25 per cent water, to make it easier to spread and ensure that the liquid flows in to all corners and crevices. Sweep the coating up the wall so that it finishes above the level of the DPC. Splashes can be wiped off plaster.

Allow the first coat to dry and apply a neat coat about 24 hours later and leave the floor for several days. Any traffic at this stage should be over temporary boards as the bitumen coat will lift if walked on.

Screeding

Prepare a 1:3 cement:sharp sand mix, using only a little water, until it is of the consistency of brown sugar. First, mix the sand and cement dry thoroughly, make a hole in the middle of the heap and add water sparingly.

You need some sections of straight timber, 1850mm long × 50mm × 25mm to provide screed rules. These are used to set out the screeding area in bays or sections, and are laid at intervals of about 1850mm. Place one rule along one wall, at your working height, or datum point; mark the height of this point, so that all levels are the same, around the room.

The rules should represent the height of the screed, so pack screed beneath the first to bring it to the correct height. Do the same with the second rule and check, with a spirit level, that this is level with the adjacent rule. If the level is short, rest this across a straight edge.

Next, fill up the bay with screed and, with a section of straight-edged timber, plane the screed smooth, using a to-and-fro action, with the timber rested on the rules. Work, section by section, towards a door

or window, so that you do not find yourself trapped at the wrong end of a newly screeded floor! Use a plank at least 1850mm wide, laid across the screed rules, to work from.

Work over short distances of about 1850mm. After finally checking levels, lift out each screed rule in turn and fill the holes left with screed.

Plane the screed surface overall with a wood float and finally polish smooth with a steel plasterer's or screeding trowel. Keep the blade damp to stop the surface from dragging, but take care not to make it too wet. The secret of a good finish is to keep the screed just damp.

Work across the room, returning to the starting wall for next and subsequent rows, completing the final section from outside a door or French window.

Allow at least a week before allowing light traffic. The surface may be dusted with sharp sand, which prevents the surface pulling up if it is walked on while still slightly tacky.

Choosing flooring

When choosing a vinyl or linoleum flooring, there are two considerations to keep in mind—the suitability of the flooring for the area to be covered, and the décor effect that will be achieved.

Suitability means that the flooring should be chosen with regard to the amount of wear to which it will be subjected. With so many qualities available, this is basically a matter of common sense. The greater the wear, the better the quality of product that should be used.

Soft floor furnishings, both sheet and tiles, come in various thicknesses, graded to give satisfactory wear in all areas of the home.

There are two basic types of smooth-surfaced flooring—**linoleum** and **vinyl.**

Linoleum

This is produced by blending together a number of natural products—cork, linseed oil, gum, resin, woodflour and colour pigments—which are rolled on to a compressed felt or canvas backing. The product is then left to mature.

The most basic material is felt base. The felt is saturated, treated, coated, printed and sealed. Felt base is economical to buy, but will not stand heavy wear.

A pattern that will not wear off is found in inlaid linoleum. Chips of linoleum are compressed into the material under great pressure. This flooring is very hard-wearing.

Another hard-wearing surface is pattern-inlaid linoleum. The pattern is made by cutting coloured linoleum shapes and placing them in various patterns on to the backing material. The design is then welded together, on to the backing material, with heated rollers. A three-dimensional textured effect can be imparted by embossing a basic inlaid linoleum.

Lino tiles

There are two types of lino tiles, both consisting of inlaid linoleum. Lino tiles can be used to create a variety of designs. The basic lino tile is loose laid; self-adhesive tiles have an adhesive bonded in to the backing and are stuck down after being dipped into hot water, to activate the adhesive, or peeling off a protective backing paper.

Vinyl

Vinyl is made of PVC (a resinous substance called polyvinyl-chloride) which is combined with a mixture of colour pigments, fillers and plasticizers.

This can be divided into two main types, according to method of manufacture. In one, the pattern is printed on to the vinyl and sealed by a layer of pure PVC. The second method is to inlay the pattern into the material.

An inexpensive vinyl floor covering is felt-backed vinyl. The pattern is printed on to the felt backing and covered with a coat of PVC. Patterned vinyl gives a strong, flexible floor covering. The pattern is printed on and covered with PVC. This is a hard-wearing surface for use in heavy traffic areas, such as kitchens and bathrooms.

Particles of contrasting vinyl, are pressed, under heavy rollers, into vinyl sheet to give the marbled effects of vinyl sheeting.

A resilient, vinyl flooring is produced by backing vinyl sheeting with a latex foam or thick wool-felt backing. This gives a comfortable, quiet and resilient floor covering.

Vinyl is also used in tile form. Flexible vinyl tiles, some of which can be cut with scissors, are made in a range of thicknesses and qualities.

Rigid vinyl tiles, also known as vinyl-asbestos tiles, are very tough, hard and durable. These are made of vinyl, reinforced with a mineral filler. They are suitable in areas subjected to very heavy wear.

Flooring: providing a touch of underfoot luxury

Personal preferences for colour and pattern are
main considerations when choosing carpets.
The problem is usually how to select the right
carpet from the bewildering range which is
made. This article tells you about quality,
fibre content and wearability, so that you can
choose to fit your budget.

Wilton

Tufted

Axminster

Blend

Cord

The choice of carpet is wide enough to cover every contingency. There are woven and tufted carpets, all wool, man-made fibres, or a combination of wool and artificial fibres as in this selection

Top right: A good underlay extends the carpet's life and feels soft underfoot

Wool

Polypropylene

Man-made

Carpeting the home can be the most expensive aspect of furnishing. Modern materials no longer make this necessarily the very expensive operation it once was; you can now buy soft floorings that are both cheap and tough, and easy to lay. Many were originally developed for the office or for contract use. These cheaper carpets are non-woven and made from such synthetics as nylon and polypropylene – the bulk of them are synthetic cord carpets. Where budget is the main consideration, alternatives to carpeting include sisals and rush matting, which though in the lowest price brackets are worth considering.

Colour and design

Most people have particular colour preferences, so personal choice must play an important role in selection; but it is wise to keep the options open where choice of colour for a carpet is concerned. The carpets dictates the choice of the remainder of the furnishings and this should be strongly borne in mind: a carpet goes on after the remainder of the furnishings have been replaced and it is the dominant if not the key factor in the room scheme.

When choosing a pattern, remember to keep strong patterns to one surface only – the floor – or the walls, or furnishings such as curtains. Too many patterns can cancel each other out, so if your selection is a bold flowing pattern, make sure that the rest of your patterns are small but complementary.

How to avoid confusion

When shopping for a carpet you will be faced with a vast choice of textures, constructions and fibres, in addition to a wide range of colour and design. Before a carpet can be selected with any degree of confidence, it is necessary to know something about how they are made. Never be in a hurry – it is always worth shopping around and finding out about carpets.

Construction

Domestic carpets are generally made in one of three constructions, Axminster, Wilton or Tufted. These terms describe the method of manufacture; they are not necessarily an indication of quality or fibre content. Neither is Wilton nor Axminster a brand name; these are generic terms used to describe the method of construction.

Axminster is a woven carpet using up to 35 colours in the design, and each fibre is dyed before weaving. The majority of patterned carpets are produced by this method, for it gives an even pile and a huge pattern selection.

Wilton is again woven but mainly in plain colours, giving a velvet pile finish. But there are some patterned Wiltons, using up to five colours in a design. Many Wiltons are textured, carved and sculptured, effects being predominantly in either one or two tones.

The difference between the two types is the method of weaving, but from a wearability viewpoint there is little difference between them.

Tufted. This is manufactured by an entirely different process to the traditional centuries-old weaving method of the Axminsters and Wiltons. Each tuft is inserted into a pre-woven backing and then covered with latex, while a second backing is added to increase the stability of the tufts. The method is a modern one, and is faster in production than traditional weaving.

The majority of the tufted carpets are in the lower qualities and price ranges. However, there are now a number of better grades, including several with luxurious long-wool pile, so that the tufted carpet is gradually being up-graded. Most tufted carpets are plain or mottled, but a few have simple designs. Some have a five-colour design printed on the pile surface.

Non-woven. These are a newer type of carpeting and, as the name implies, it is made on a different machine in which a mass of fibres are interlocked by a needling process which compresses the fibre into a close, flat surface which is very tough. This type of carpet has a flat non-pile surface. Loose-laid carpet tiles which are made in the same way often have a single-directional pile.

Wearability – What is the best?

When buying a carpet the most important thought apart from the price is: how will it wear? As significant as wearability and the length of service is its appearance: will it remain good looking? There is nothing more distressing than a carpet which loses its good appearance while it still has a long life span, for there is little advantage in a carpet that will last indefinitely if it looks awful.

The carpet's appearance will depend very much on the fibre content. Carpet pile and surface fibres fall into five main categories: natural fibres, such as wool, cotton and silk; acrylics; cellulosics; nylons and polypropylenes. In the main, the man-mades and synthetics generally are used for the tufted qualities, while the pure, natural materials are used in the medium to best-quality carpets. Some carpets, however, are composed of mixtures of these fibres, the mixtures containing some of the benefits and disadvantages of each individual component.

Natural fibres

Of these, wool is the most important and the most widely used, either blended or as a 100 per cent wool-content carpet.

Wool has unequalled resilience to crushing and does not soil as readily as most other fibres. Neither is it prone, under normal conditions, to static as are most of the synthetics. Its other advantages include flame resistance and the greater choice of colour design and texture, making it the most widely used carpet fibre.

The quality of wool varies, dependent on the type of sheep from which the wool has been taken and the conditions under which they are bred. The best-quality wool comes from sheep which live in hilly and mountainous country, the pelts invariably being thicker and of better quality, because of the hard conditions under which they live.

All wool and wool-mixture carpets keep their appearance well and will offer years of hard wear if properly looked after. For this reason and because the price of raw wool fluctuates, all-wool carpets are generally to be found in the higher-price brackets.

Other natural fibres which make carpets are cotton, which is used for bathroom rugs, and specially woven cotton carpeting, for use in bathrooms and bedrooms. Cotton is absorbent, dries quickly and is washable. The pile flattens, however, and it soils easily.

Silk has been used for centuries for superb Oriental and Chinese carpets and rugs which are in the top luxury class.

At the other end of the scale are sisals and jute. Sisal is coarse and tends to be stiff, but can be dyed to strong colours, is hard-wearing, inexpensive and mostly used for mattings and rugs, with a bouclé or flat surface. It does stain easily and provides, in this respect, a slight maintenance problem.

Jute is mainly used for carpet backing or underlays, but it is occasionally used with viscose rayons to make inexpensive cord carpeting.

Cord carpeting was originally made from the hair of animals and apart from the synthetic varieties still is. Haircord makes a tough, durable floor covering, rather harsh to the touch, which is sometimes blended with wool or viscose yarns to make it softer.

Synthetics

Of all the man-made fibres acrylics have the nearest appearance to wool, for this looks and feels similar but soils quicker and burns readily.

Acrylics are less prone to static electricity, however, than some of the other synthetics and because they do not absorb liquids, acrylic carpets can be cleaned more easily.

Modacrylics are claimed to be less in-

flammable than the acrylics and are often blended with them.

Nylon is used mainly in the cheaper tufted carpets and is very hard-wearing, although it does not keep its good appearance which is why it has not proved very popular.

Nylon fibre reflects and magnifies the dirt lodged in it so that a nylon carpet may appear dirty when it is not. A modern nylon with improved properties has been developed to overcome this difficulty. This fibre has been constructed in such a way that the light no longer shines directly through it, magnifying the dirt, but is refracted away from the eye. Despite this tendency to show soiling very easily, nylon can be simply and easily cleaned.

Its other disadvantage is that it is prone to static electricity which can impart shocks, when, for example you touch metal or a wall when standing on nylon. This can be kept down by occasionally spraying lightly with water. When exposed to flame, nylon melts into a mass.

Man-made fibres

These are cellulosics and are produced from wood pulp or cotton linters and include viscose and rayons. Rayon (brand name Evlan) in its pure form is definitely a spare-bedroom carpet. These are bulky fibres which, if used on their own, flatten easily, but add bulkiness to blends of other fibres. A mixture of cellulosics are sometimes added to a nylon carpet to combat static electricity. The greatest advantage is its cheapness.

Polypropylene

This is one of the newer synthetic fibres and is used in a variety of forms. Polypropylene is making headway in the cheaper ranges and is used widely for cheaper cord carpets, which are proving to be one of the most popular of the inexpensive carpetings. This can provide a cheap form of wall-to-wall carpeting. Carpets made from polypropylene are durable and generate little static and generally are easily cleanable. Polyester offers a lush pile construction which is both soft to the touch and hard-wearing.

Blends

Many carpets are blends of synthetics or synthetics blended with pure wool. Though purists may claim that nothing can approach worsted wool for softness of touch, the price often puts it out of reach. Blended with synthetics it becomes reliable but a cheaper purchase. The most popular blend is 80 per cent wool and 20 per cent nylon, which gives all the advantages of wool with the tried durability of nylon and produces a hard-wearing pile.

Inexpensive carpets blend viscose with nylon to produce a pile with a good resistance to flattening which also gives a reasonable performance in use. There are many blends.

What carpets to put where

Carpet manufacturers claim that the majority of complaints they receive are from customers who have used a carpet in the wrong area.

When the time actually comes to purchase a carpet the advice of a good retailer is helpful, to round off your own analysis of the situation. Look also at the manufacturer's label when choosing; this gives definite instructions on where the carpet should be used. Carpets labelled for heavy domestic use should be laid in areas of heavy traffic such as halls, staircases and living rooms, which are in constant use.

General domestic and, in some cases, medium domestic carpets can be used throughout the house, except for stairs and halls, provided there is not a lot of traffic–so look at your family's way of life before deciding on the correct grade.

A carpet labelled 'light domestic' should be used in a bedroom, but 'medium domestic' in a bed-sitter. Bedrooms get light traffic and the carpets do not soil easily, so a cheaper carpet can be used. A bed-sitter, on the other hand, gets heavier wear.

Buying for the living room needs a lot of care and consideration, for this is the hub of the home and if you have pets as well as children your carpet will come in for a lot of wear, so a heavy domestic carpet is indicated. A couple with no children or pets could lay a carpet of medium quality.

Stair carpet is in a class by itself and needs choosing with care–for not only does it get hard wear, but the wrong sort of pile will 'grin' or separate on the stair nosing.

In choosing stair carpet look for a close, tightly woven pile, a curly pile (short twist), a looped pile or a cord type.

Top left: Carpet can be extended over surfaces to make a decorative feature
Left: A strong colour can appear striking in room décor. Both are heavy-domestic tufted, ruffle-top carpets by Georgian
Bottom right: A patterned carpet, such as this County Down broadloom, gives a splash of floral colour to a room scheme

Getting down to basics in carpet laying

Choosing a carpet is one thing, and laying it is another. A carpet is a costly item, so it is important to follow the rules of laying correctly—recognising that great care is needed where an expensive carpet is concerned. Looking after a carpet, once laid, is essential, as is the careful selection of a suitable underlay, to add years of life to the carpeting of your choice.

When decorating from scratch, never leave the carpet until last—select it first. If you are only re-carpeting and wish to keep existing furnishings, try to make sure that the carpet links up well with the existing materials, for the carpet is the most dominating factor in your room scheme.

Do not be afraid to use colour. Think of colour as important, and then think of a theme. Take into consideration the aspect of the room. If it is facing north and 'cold', a brown, red, orange or yellow carpet will make it appear warmer and give sparkle. A warm, south-facing room can take a carpet in the cool colours of the spectrum, such as blues and cool greens.

A dark room can be made to look quite different by using a light carpet, and a formal room less formal with a deep, shaggy pile carpet. Bright modern designs can overcome old-fashioned proportions if you live in a Victorian house, and a traditional-style carpet can make a room which has functional, modern furniture look softer and more welcoming.

Carpet can also do a lot to make a room larger or smaller. A long, narrow room can be made wider by using a boldly striped carpet; if you cannot find a good striped design, stick stripes of alternating coloured 'body' carpet, such as Wilton, to form the desired effect. A light and dark tone of one colour can be successful or, for a striking effect, try bright, primary colours or use loose-lay carpet tiles.

A closely fitted carpet in a small room will have a broadening effect, since this does not break up the lines of the floor area. A small flat looks better carpeted throughout in the same carpet, making it appear more spacious. Each room can be given individuality by using distinctive furnishings. Large designs have the effect of making the floor area look smaller.

Unlimited schemes can be built around carpets, whether your choice is plain or patterned, textured or shaggy pile, modern or traditional. A lot of the fun of choosing a carpet comes when deciding on the colour and the pattern.

Long life for carpets

It is no use purchasing an expensive carpet or even a cheap one, if you do not look after it properly from the start. A strategi-

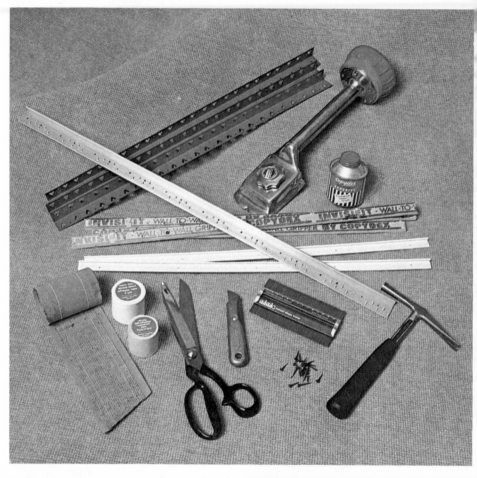

1 Seaming tape
2 Double-sided and single-sided tapes
3 Carpet shears
4 Handyman's knife
5 Profile former
6 Carpet hammer
7 Foamgrip for foam-backed carpets on stairs
8 Doorway edging strip
9 Tackless gripper
10 Stair carpet gripper (blue)
11 Carpet stretcher and knee kicker
12 Carpet adhesive

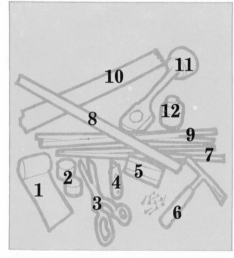

cally placed rug will help with the problems of areas in rooms that get extra wear, such as around the fireplace, inside doorways and beside a bed.

Before attempting to lay any carpet, thoroughly inspect the floor for any unevenness, such as old nails or other protrusions. Unevenness beneath a carpet will cause a patch of wear. Loose and uneven floor boards, protruding nail heads, electric flex, or even small pieces of string or paper, will, over the years, cause expensive damage.

Underlays

Having done all this you must think about an underlay. This is an absolutely essential item and is part of the cost of carpeting on which you cannot economize, unless you are laying rush or sisal carpeting. The principal function of underlay is to act as a shock absorber between the carpet and the floor. It takes the brunt of the hard pressure from above and compensates for unevenness beneath, as well as acting as a sound-deadening agent.

A layer of brown paper between the

floor and the underlay will keep the carpet free from dust rising from the floor boards and will also take up some of the unevenness.

There are three classes of underlay: paper felt, underfelt and rubber. Paper felt is a thick, grey paper, sold in widths of 1830mm or 910mm. It is inexpensive and is suitable only for rooms with low traffic volume, such as bedrooms.

The very best underfelt is called 'needle-loom' hair felt and is available in 1370mm widths. Some types of underfelt consist of felt layers bonded together with latex to give a cushioned effect.

Rubber underlays can be made of foam rubber or natural rubber. They are usually 1370mm wide and the better qualities represent the best of underlays, although they do not absorb underfloor dust as well as felt.

Many modern houses have underfloor heating and rubber underlay should not be used in these circumstances, as foam rubber tends to smell after long exposure to dry heat. Rubber does not conduct heat as efficiently as felt.

The only types of carpet that do not need any underlay are carpets with a built-in underlay or carpet tiles, perhaps the easiest form of soft floor covering for the amateur to tackle. Although well known in the contract carpet trade, carpet tiles are relatively new on the consumer market. They fall roughly into three categories: velvet or shag piles; directional piles; and the flat-surfaced needle-punched variety.

The first two are normally loose-laid and are easy to fit, and the latter is bonded to the floor with an adhesive or double-sided adhesive tape. In all cases it is necessary to ensure that the sub-floor is even, clean and dry.

Tiles are then laid out in the main body of the room, in the desired pattern, butted up well together. The edges of the room are then fitted with tiles, cut to fit with a handyman's knife, from the back. Fit a metal edging at doorways, for neatness and safety.

Preparing the floors

Wooden floors
These should be thoroughly inspected for any protrusions, such as old nailheads which should be removed or punched flat. All old tacks should be taken out. Loose floorboards should be nailed down and any high ridges, such as occur on warped boards, should be planed down. Wide cracks should be filled with strips of wood or papier-mâché.

If the floor is so badly warped that it cannot be repaired easily, cover with a sub-floor of hardboard or plywood before laying the underfelt and carpet.

Concrete floors
These are common in modern housing and the same applies to stone floors, found in older dwellings. If the surface is badly cracked or ridged, to reduce the wear on the carpet the floor must be screeded with a self-levelling flooring compound. If the floor is dusty or powdery, the same screeding compounds can be used by floating a thick layer over the floor, to prevent the dust from working into the underlay and the carpet.

Thermoplastic tiles
These are very commonplace in newly-built houses and before laying a carpet on this type of flooring, make sure that the room is well ventilated and free of condensation.

Carpet laying
Acquiring a carpet is an investment and a costly process. The cost of having a fitted carpet laid professionally is small compared with its value. If, however, you are contemplating laying a cheaper carpet such as a tufted quality in a low-traffic area, or a sisal carpeting, you can tackle the job yourself. But remember that a badly laid carpet will be difficult to clean, unsafe to walk on and will wear badly.

Tools required
A hammer, a large pair of scissors, a linoleum or handyman's knife, a 1m rule, chalk and a chalk line, latex adhesive and carpet tape. You also need a carpet stretcher or 'knee-kicker'. These can be purchased, or hired.

Measuring and estimating
Measure the room in which the carpet is to be laid in the direction in which the carpet will lay. For rooms which are rectangular, measure lengthwise. Include the full width of the door frames, so that new carpeting extends slightly into the adjoining room. Broadloom is the easiest carpet for the non-professional to lay, especially in rectangular or square rooms with no alcoves. It can be bought in several standard widths: 4·57m, 4·11m, 3·91m, 1·60m, 2·20m and 1·83m.

Body carpeting, such as Wilton, is more economic, particularly in an irregularly shaped room, but requires seaming, takes more time to lay, and should be done professionally. It normally comes in 685mm and 910mm widths.

When ordering patterned carpet it is as well to allow 1·52m to 1·83m extra for matching the design when laying the carpet.

Method of fixing
Most wall-to-wall carpets can be fastened with tacks or by any of the makes of carpet grippers. Carpets can also be loosely laid, with only a few fixing tacks at doorways.

There are two lengths of carpet tack: 19mm and 25mm. The first is used on the carpet hem—when it is folded at the edge—and the second for corners where the folds of the hem make three thicknesses.

Hemming is not necessary on tufted carpets.

Carpet grippers can be used by the home handyman and should be selected according to the backing of the carpet. These consist of wooden or metal battens with numerous spikes projecting at a 60° angle. The all-metal versions have teeth projecting from the main body.

Nail the fittings to the floor, round the room, end to end, 6mm from the wall, with the spikes facing the skirting. The spikes grip the backing threads of the carpet and hold it in place. These systems can be used on stone or concrete floors. The fittings are glued or nailed into place with a strong contact adhesive.

Cutting carpet
If you intend to cut the carpet yourself, spread it out on the floor and chalk the exact pattern of the room on to the pile surface, but not on the back. Use a pair of scissors or a sharp handyman's knife to cut out the shape.

To join, place the two widths together so that the pile surfaces meet face to face, matching any pattern very carefully. Make sure that the piles of both pieces are running in the same direction: this is particularly important with plain carpet.

Seam the two widths together with carpet seaming tape and adhesive, pulling the carpet tight to take up fullness, tucking any protruding fibres back into the pile. Or you can sew it by hand.

Laying the carpet
When laying the carpet, empty the room of all furniture and, if possible, take off any doors that swing into the room. Open the carpet to room length and position it before putting down the underlay. The pile should sweep away from the window—this avoids shading in daylight. Fold one half of the carpet back on itself about halfway, then put down the underlay on the floor thus exposed.

Repeat the procedure the other end, having laid the carpet loosely over the underlay. This will prevent wrinkles in the carpet which are caused through the movement of the underlay.

If using rubber underlay, join the seams with adhesive tape. With felt underlay, stitch the seams before laying.

If you are planning to tack the carpet down, start at the corner of the room where there are two plain walls, that is, with as few abutments as possible. Butt the carpet up against the wall, leaving about 40mm up the skirting for the hem. Fix the carpet temporarily with tacks about 150mm out from the skirting along these two walls.

To fit traditional carpet, fix gripper strip 3mm away from walls around room

To butt seams in rubber underlay, use a single-sided 50mm tape on the top

Butt underlay to the gripper strip and trim to fit with handyman's knife

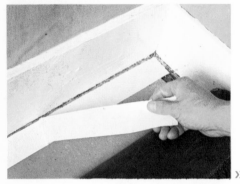

Lay double-sided self-adhesive tape in gap, remove back, fix carpet and trim

To protect carpet in doorways, use edging strip. Measure and trim bar to size

Nail down bar. Bars can be single or double sided, cut to fit where necessary

Join with seaming tape and adhesive; put half tape under edge when tacky

Next, place the piece to be joined on to tape, making sure edges butt closely

A template former can be used to trace profile shape around difficult corners

Use your knee-kicker to stretch the carpet along the length–then the width. This is very important, for if a carpet is stretched in the wrong way it can, of course, be ruined as it will wrinkle and pull out of shape.

Start from the centre of the wall, stretching alternately towards both corners. Fasten the stretched area with tacks as a temporary fixing.

Where there are projections such as pipes and fire-places, first trim back the underlay about 50mm from the wall to leave a channel for the hem. Fold the hem, tacking through the fold every 130mm, to hold the edge firmly.

When using tackless systems, position the carpet in the room and put down the underlay as described. Trim the underlay so that it meets the edge of the batten that is furthest from the wall. Fix the carpet along two walls, as described above, and use the knee-kicker to stretch it over the spikes of the tackless fittings. Remove the temporary tacks and restretch the carpet, allowing 10mm overlap. Turn down the overlap and press it firmly into the channel between the wall and the fittings.

A carpet can be protected at the doorways by using a metal bar which is nailed

to the floor, the carpet being slipped under the clip and stretched into place. If the carpet is merely tacked, bind the edge in the doorway with binder tape to prevent fraying if the selvedge has been trimmed off. Non-woven or latex-backed carpet will not fray, of course, but the tape will help to give the carpet strength at an area where it is exposed to hard wear.

Before refitting the doors, measure the thickness of the carpet pile and underlay to make sure that the door will swing short over the carpet; the end can be planed off if it is too low to move with ease over the pile.

Carpeting the staircase
Close-fitting carpet on a staircase gives a look of luxury, and planning and laying may be left to the expert. Strip carpets, which do not fit in the stairs, can be more easily laid as they are easier to handle and cost less then close-fitted carpets.

Maintenance
To prevent undue wear and tear, a stair carpet should be shifted periodically. Allow for this in the original measurements by adding an extra 460mm to the length. Shift the carpet up each stair tread

75mm to 100mm every nine months until the 460mm has been used. After that, return the carpet to its original position and continue to move up as before.

Runners for stairways come in standard widths of 460mm, 700mm, 985mm and 910mm.

Measuring
To find the length, measure in millimetres the depth of one tread and the height of one riser; add the two measurements together and multiply by the number of stairs, dividing the resulting figures by 910 to determine the length required.

If the staircase has bends, first calculate the total carpet length as above, then measure each winding tread separately at the widest point which will be covered by the carpet, and again the height of each riser. Add these figures to the length required and divide by 910 to find the total required length.

Underlay
As with carpeting for a room, a good-quality underlay is important. This can be used as a complete runner or in the form of pads, which must be tacked individually. A stair

Position carpet to cover gripper and stretch the carpet on to gripper pins

Cut carpet about 6mm oversize and tuck edge down between gripper and skirting

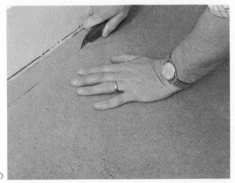
Foam-backed carpets should be fitted on felt paper, cut 50mm from skirting

On a double binder bar, hook carpet on both sides; trim with handyman's knife

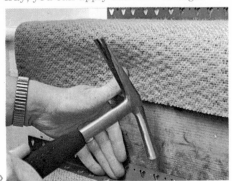
To seal the edges of carpets which may fray, you can apply adhesive to edges

Tuck carpet under edge of bar. Hammer down, using protective block of wood

Cut extra 25mm on carpets which fray when fitting by tacking and hemming

A metal stair strip can be nailed down when fixing stair carpets invisibly

For safety, landing carpet should cover nosing, to obviate join at top of stairs

carpet and runner underlay can be fixed with rod and eyelet fittings, being tacked only at top and bottom. Pads are best used with staircarpet grippers, as these hold the back of the carpet in position for the pads. The stair pads should be large enough to butt against the riser and extend over the tread-nosing to meet the top of the gripper on the stair below. Special grippers are available for fixing foam-backed carpets to stairs.

Laying stair carpet
For maximum wear resistance, lay the carpet with the pile facing down the stairs. Check the sweep of the pile by stroking it back and forth lengthwise–the smoother stroke is the lay of the pile.

If you are using stair rods, fit the rod in position before putting down the underlay. Reverse the carpet so that its pile lays on the bottom stair tread, butt the end of the carpet against the riser of the second stair and tack in place. Let the carpet drop over the first tread-nosing to the floor and slide a stair rod through the eyelets at the foot of the stairs and over the backing threads of the carpet.

Lift the carpet over the nosings of the first two stair treads and tuck into the

stair where tread and riser meet, pulling the carpet tightly. Continue laying, using the same method for each stair.

If tackless fittings are used, the method is slightly different. Nail the angled strip into the angle formed by tread and riser of each stair, except the bottom one, then fit underlay pads. Fix the end of the carpet, pile facing down, to back of the bottom tread with an angled strip and to the top of the first stair riser, which should have a flat metal strip.

Keeping the carpet taut, stretch it over the tread-nosing of the two bottom stairs. Keeping it taut, press the centre into the first angled strip and smooth the carpet into the teeth.

For staircases with a bend, known as 'winders' a series of folds are required in the carpet to take up the 'slack' which occurs at the narrowest point of the stair.

For carpets held with stair rods, you make folds in the carpet, starting at the bottom winder, pulling the carpet taut from the tread and swinging it round, following the bend in the stairs. Fold the slack down towards the lower stair and tack through the doubled carpet, across the width of the fold, pull the carpet taut and repeat on each stair.

The procedure is different with tackless systems. Nail a gripper to the tread of the first winder, stretching the carpet over the tread and swing it round to follow the turn of the stairway as above. The slack is folded downwards to meet the flat strip. Mark the back of the carpet at the base of the fold on both sides.

Turn back the carpet, holding the two marks well into the angle where tread and riser meet. Secure the fold with a second flat strip, nailed into the riser through a double thickness of the carpet. Pull tight, cover the next winder and repeat.

Carpet care
Finally, when the carpet is laid, look after it. New carpets tend to shed their pile during the first few weeks of wear–so during this period do not use a vacuum cleaner. Remove loose pile with a hand brush or carpet cleaner only. When moving furniture lift it–pushing the furniture across a carpet only damages the fibres.

Most carpets are automatically moth-proofed; the label on the carpet will give you details.

A fitted carpet can be cleaned with a carpet shampoo. Take care not to soak the carpet or it may shrink.

Cork or wood?

Cork flooring provides a durable, easy-to-maintain surface. These cork tiles, made by Wicanders, have been presealed and are simply stuck down with a contact adhesive. They are made in colours and here have been used in a hall.

A presealed wood flooring, by Point One Products, is also durable and hardwearing. This has a self-adhesive contact backing. Wallcovering: lightly textured Anaglypta, finished in Crown cream paint; curtains by Sanderson. This shows flooring in a lounge.

The natural colours and richness of timber provide, in the form of wood floors, both a decorative and hardwearing flooring surface. Wood flooring may consist of hard or soft wood, laid in strips, or a woodblock or parquet flooring. Techniques of fixing and treatment depend on the type of floor and the finished effect required.

Woodblock flooring, available in a variety of thicknesses and sizes, is usually kiln dried which means that the moisture content is stable and the wood will not continue to dry out and warp or shrink when laid.

This type of flooring usually consists of solid wood blocks or wood veneer bonded to thinner plywood blocks. Some blocks are tongued and grooved, while others are loose-laid or bedded in adhesive.

Hardwood solid blocks are best in areas of heavy wear. Softwood is not durable enough to stand heavy traffic, except when used in block form. A softwood block floor will give good wear.

Suitable hardwood timbers are maple, oak, afromosia, sapele and teak. These are used for both block and strip flooring and are supplied pre-sealed or machine sanded ready for final sealing. Hardwood block is best laid on a solid sub-floor.

Block parquet and mosaics are made of solid blocks of wood, in the form of a panel which is stuck down to a rigid sub-floor. Mosaic panels are normally arranged in a herringbone or basket-weave pattern. Some are backed with felt or paper. Felt-backed blocks are stuck with the felt side downwards.

Paper-backed mosaics are fixed with the paper upwards. This paper is removed with a rotary sanding machine, as part of the finishing process. Work along the grain of the wood.

One high-quality, durable, woodblock floor is called end-grain. These blocks are cut from timber $25mm^2$ to expose the end grain. End-grain parquet is laid on a timber sub-floor.

Plywood parquet resembles block parquet but is less suitable for heavy-wear areas. It can be used to form basket-weave or herringbone patterns. The durability of the flooring is only as good as the top layer of plywood which may be finished in one of many timber effects.

Acclimatize
There are various methods of fixing wood flooring, dependent on the sub-floor and the type of flooring to be used. All wood blocks or strips should be acclimatized at room temperature for at least a week before laying.

Underfloor heating should be turned off for at least 48 hours before work starts. Always check first that the flooring material is suitable for use with underfloor heating.

Woodblocks for strip flooring can be laid on concrete or timber sub-floors.

Sub-floor treatments
Timber floors must be level and smooth before work starts. Plywood or hardboard sheeting may be laid to provide a level, stable surface. Before laying a sheet flooring, remove the skirtings.

On concrete, a bituminous adhesive will prevent blocks from the effects of damp. When fixing on concrete floors only use adhesive. Panel pins are not necessary, except at the threshold of doors.

Laying out
The room should be divided exactly in half. Use a chalk line to mark the centre position. It is important that this is true, for floor laying starts from this point and works outwards towards the walls. A 10mm expansion gap should be allowed at the wall edges which is later covered with the skirting or a piece of moulding.

A simple pattern consists of squares made up of four strips of wood, laid in a chequer-board pattern, with the grain of the wood alternating within each section. A herringbone pattern can be laid in the same way, starting at the centre marked line.

Here, a straight border is used at each wall edge. Small pieces of block, to complete sections of the pattern, may be cut and fitted before the border is laid.

As woodblocks tend to expand and contract slightly, use an adhesive that allows for this, such as a bituminous adhesive. Each block should be glued down and then secured with a 25mm panel pin at each end. These are punched in and the holes filled with a suitable filler.

Loose-laid
Tongued-and-grooved interlocking panels of strip wood can be loose-laid. Some makes of loose-lay tiles are supplied with a cork or polythene backing sheet which is laid on the sub-floor before fixing the panels. This is important on a concrete sub-floor.

Lay the sheet, with the cork or polythene sheeting face downwards, allowing a 13mm expansion gap between each length and at the edges.

Start work at the corner of the room with the longest, uninterrupted run of wall. Make up a square section using nine or 12 strips, sawing off the tongued-and-grooved edges on the wall side.

Square the panel up to the long wall, ignoring the shorter wall. Any gaps along the short length can be covered later

Using a hammer against a block of hardwood, to protect the edge of the panels, tap the rest of the strips into position. Each strip is positioned so that the wood grain is at right-angles to the last one laid.

A profile or template can be cut out of stiff paper, to give the outline of any projections. Transfer this outline to the wood strip and cut out the waste area with a fine-toothed panel saw. You can also use a proprietary template former.

Any strips that have to be cut should be fitted before the previously laid section is tapped into final position. Cut pieces at the edges should be fitted as each row is laid. Apply PVA adhesive to the cut edge, before laying, to prevent blocks from pulling apart.

An edging tool may be necessary to tap the final pieces home at the skirting edge.

It is wise to remove doors before laying woodblock flooring, as the new floor level will be higher than the old and may not allow for easy opening. The bottom of the door may need planing to overcome this.

When laying floors in adjoining areas treat each area as an entity. The block should finish halfway under the door when in the closed position.

If the floor levels between two rooms vary, a diminishing strip will need to be fitted. This is a length of wood that is tapered and grooved on one side to take the tongued edge of the last panel laid.

At the threshold of a door, the panels will need to be cut and fixed to the sub-floor, either with a PVA adhesive or 25mm panel pins, punched below the surface, and the holes filled with plastic wood.

The diminishing strip is then butted up to the threshold panels. It can be fixed with an adhesive or pre-drilled and screwed down with wood screws. Direct fixing is possible into a wood sub-floor.

A concrete floor should be plugged before the screws are fixed, but take care not to penetrate the damp-proof membrane. Small gaps round the edges will be covered by the skirting. A larger gap may be filled by covering with moulding.

Point One Products' self-adhesive hard-board is covered by protective membrane

The method of laying a herring-bone pattern with Point One woodblock floor

Strip has self-adhesive backing to bond flooring. Gentle hammering consolidates

Use piece of floor to conform with the skirting profile when laying edge strip

A good straight edge is provided by metal spirit level; cut strip on inside of line

Finished edge strip will fit snugly and give a neat appearance to the floor

With tiles, such as Wicander's Cork-o-Plast, apply contact adhesive to floor

Next, apply adhesive to the back of the cork tile and allow to become touch dry

Tiles should be laid carefully, since touch-dry surfaces instantly form bond

Once the floor is laid, allow time for the wood to settle and then sand down using a rotary sanding machine. The flooring can then be wax-polished or sealed with a polyurethane varnish. On veneered blocks, a polyurethane sealant coat will protect the wood and give longer wear.

Cork flooring
Cork flooring consists of cork chippings or granules bonded together with resin to make a warm, resilient natural floor covering. Available in a range of wood tones, cork wears well and has good insulant properties.

A popular form of cork flooring is the cork tile, which is available in several thicknesses. Cork tiles may be unsealed, wax-coated or sealed with a clear poly-urethane varnish. The tiles are either 250mm² or 300mm² in size.

Estimating
Estimating the number of tiles needed is done in the same way as for vinyl tiles, allowing five per cent for cutting and wastage. A patterned floor can be planned on paper first to enable the correct number of tiles of each type to be bought.

Before starting to lay unsealed cork tiles, these should be conditioned.

Spread the tiles out in the room where they are to be laid for 24 hours before use. Sealed or waxed tiles do not need this conditioning. Cork tiles should not be laid directly on a concrete sub-floor that has no damp-proof membrane.

Setting out the room is done in the same way as for laying vinyl tiles. Start tiling at the centre right-angle where the guidelines cross.

Adhesive
Neoprene-based adhesive is used to fix unsealed tiles; sealed tiles are fixed with an adhesive recommended by the manu-facturers.

Laying
Start at the centre guideline and spread about 1m² of adhesive, using a notched spreader to make a ridged keying surface. Work up to, but not over, the chalked line.

Place the first tile at one of the four angles made by the guidelines and press into place. Continue tiling the area, butt-ing the tiles up carefully. Avoid allowing adhesive to get on to the face of the tiles.

Unsealed tiles are particularly difficult to clean. On sealed or waxed tiles, im-mediately wipe off any spillage with a damp cloth.

At edges, scribe and cut a tile to fit, using a tile-width piece of hardboard or card to mark the line to be cut, and cut with a sharp knife. Cork tiles should al-ways be cut on the smooth side with a very sharp blade.

Continue to tile the entire room area, laying an area of 1m² at a time. As each section of tiling is completed, use a rubber roller to smooth them down.

Cutting in round awkward shapes or projections is best achieved by cutting out a template, or by using a template former to transfer the outline to the tile to be cut.

Cork, in common with other forms of floor tiling, should finish under the door when in a closed position. Once laid, a cork floor should be left to settle for 24 to 48 hours.

Care and maintenance
Cork tiles are easy to maintain. Sealed tiles merely require wiping over with a damp cloth or mop. Waxed tiles require mopping and re-waxing occasionally.

When the choice is vinyl

Measure floor to scale, marking each tile on to piece of scaled graph paper

Draw an outline and count number of full and part squares falling within this

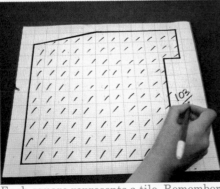

Each square represents a tile. Remember to count each segment as a complete tile

For patterned floors, shade in design and colours till you get desired scheme

An important part of any home-decoration scheme is the choice of flooring. Modern, easy-to-clean and lay, smooth-surfaced floorings provide a wide range of colours and designs which are attractive, versatile and hard-wearing. Choosing, calculating and laying techniques are described in this article.

When choosing plastic tiles or sheeting for your floor covering, the first step is to find out the amount of material you need to cover the area.

Calculating Tiles

To calculate the number of tiles needed, draw a scale plan of the floor to be covered, on graph paper.

First, measure the floor area of the room. Next, draw the outline, to scale, on the graph paper.

Count the number of squares and part squares within the outline. Each square or part of a square, represents a tile and this gives the number of tiles needed.

If a pattern is required, plan out the design on the graph paper, using a different colour for the motif tiles. These can be counted separately or deducted from the total number of tiles for the area.

Lay sheet vinyl flooring along longest wall edge with 50mm overlap; mark wall

Take 150mm block. Pull flooring back so block equals distance between two points

Use a sharp knife or scissors to cut vinyl, such as Nairn Cushionflor, to shape

The marks should be a wood block apart. Use this block to trace outline on wall

To trim seams for butt joints, match, overlap 25mm, and cut through middle

Sections are butted over joining strip with 50mm self-adhesive linen tape

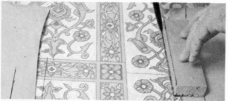
Transfer outline to inside thickness of block, matching the angles of contours

Outline can also be marked by measuring. Place sheeting some 50mm from the wall

Mark distances at intervals from architrave; join up points and cut to fit

Sheet flooring

The amount of sheet flooring or linoleum can be calculated quite easily. It is normally made in widths of 1220mm, 1520mm or 1830mm and in lengths of up to 27·45m.

Measure the total floor area. Multiply the length by the width to obtain the area in square metres. Where a patterned covering, with repeats at 230mm, 300mm or 460mm, is to be used, allow for the pattern repeat on each strip of flooring.

Generally, the sheet is laid so that the pattern appears to recede from the room entrance, unless a pattern is laid across a room specifically to give an illusion of width.

Soft flooring
Sub-floors

However good the floor covering, the finished result will not be perfect unless the sub-floor is prepared properly. Soft-floor furnishings can be laid on timber, concrete, hardboard and chipboard.

Sub-floors should be dry and clean, free from grease, oil, dirt and dust. Sheet flooring should not be laid on a damp sub-floor. Some types of flooring have damp-resistant properties, but if these are used they should only be loose laid.

Floorings wear well and look best if they are stuck to the sub-floor.

On a concrete sub-floor, all holes and cracks should be filled. If the surface is uneven, a layer of self-levelling compound may first be floated across the floor and allowed to dry.

Timber sub-floors make a perfectly satisfactory surface for soft-flooring finishes but they must be firm and level. Wood expands and contracts, with the moisture content in the air, so these floors tend to move slightly.

Hardboard will provide a rigid, smooth floor. When using hardboard, ensure that the wooden sub-floor is as level as possible.

A floor that has been treated with any type of timber preservative should be covered with non-porous foil lining paper before the hardboard is laid.

Any projecting nails should be removed or knocked into the floor. Use serrated nails at 100mm intervals and stagger the joints when fixing hardboard.

Equipment

The equipment needed to lay sheets flooring and tiles is basically the same, varying in one or two items. For laying sheet flooring you need a ruler, a pencil, a block of wood about 150mm long, for scribing, a handyman's knife, a lino-cutting tool or scissors. A roll of self-adhesive tape 50mm wide may be needed.

Tile laying requires marking and cutting equipment, plus a piece of chalk, a length of string, an adhesive spreader and the adhesive.

Sheet flooring

Some time before laying sheet flooring, it is a good idea to bring the material into a warm room. This helps to make it more pliable and easier to handle.

Scribing

It is usually necessary to scribe sheeting to fit closely to walls or skirtings, since these are often not true. Lay the first strip of flooring along the longest wall edge in the room; allow an overlap of 50mm at each end. With a pencil, draw a line on the skirting board and flooring 300mm from the end wall.

Pull the flooring back slowly until the distance between the mark on the skirting and that on the floor is 150mm long, the length of the block of wood.

Leave the flooring in that position, and, using the block of wood, run one end of it along the wall and mark, on the flooring, the line it takes.

Cut along this line with the handyman's knife. This removes the overlap at the end wall and the flooring can be pushed back into the corner. The two pencil marks will line up again to provide a perfect fit.

When vinyl or linoleum is laid in doorways, it should be trimmed so that it reaches exactly half way under the door when shut, so that any join is not visible from either side.

Do not attempt to lay flooring widths of different sizes together. In some of the cheaper vinyls the pattern is not designed to match edge to edge. When loose laying these, allow an overlap of 13mm on the seam and 25mm on all outside edges. Leave the overlap for about two days to settle before cutting in exactly to fit the walls.

If laying a product that has an edge-matched pattern, stick the joins down firmly with a 75mm band of adhesive or on to self-adhesive tape. Do not stick down the outer edges of the flooring.

Patterned flooring looks better if the pattern matches, both across the width and along the length of the room. Lay the first strip along the length of the wall. Place the second length beside it, so that the pattern matches, allowing a small overlap on the end walls.

Mark a pencil line 300mm from the wall across both pieces of flooring. Pull back the second sheet of flooring from the wall until the two pencil marks are the length of the block of wood, 150mm, apart. Use the block of wood held against the end wall skirting to scribe a line on to the flooring. Cut along this line and slide the material up to the wall. This will ensure that the patterns match.

Fitting at the final wall is done by overlapping the last sheet a convenient number or 'repeats' and trimming off, on the wall side, the distance of the overlap.

To fit the flooring round awkward shapes, use a proprietary former or a template made of stiff paper or card. Cut out to fit, roughly, round the shape. Take a ruler and position it against the object to be fitted around. On the template draw a line round a ruler's width away from the projection—that is on the outside of the ruler.

Lift the template from the floor and lay it on top of the flooring material. With the ruler, draw another corresponding

Fit flooring to wall. Line up the pencil marks to ensure perfect edge to end walls.

To match pattern, lay first strip, match, and allow small overlap at end walls

Mark a line on both pieces at about 300mm from walls, then pull back overlap

A scriber – a piece of wood with pin through it – used to mark contours

Using a paper template to cut roughly around projection; trace with wood block

Finally, cut to shape; flooring fits neatly around the door architrave

Copydex template former also enables the accurate cutting of a profile shape

This consists of metal pins, clamped in plate; these contour to profile shape

outline on the flooring, a ruler's width inside the outline drawn on the template. Cut the flooring along this line and fit the flooring into position round the object.

Self-adhesive tape, 50mm wide, can be used to stick down seams if the floor is loose laid. Joins tend to curl up and can be dangerous and unhygienic. Stick the tape halfway under one side of the join; line up the other seam, checking first any matching pattern. Position it over the other half of the tape, then lower it and press down firmly along the join.

Floor tiles
Preparation
Vinyl or lino tiles can be laid on either concrete or timber sub-floors. Preparation of the sub-floor is as for laying sheet flooring. The same considerations apply; the floor must be clean, dry, level and grease free.

When laying on old synthetic or rubber floor tiles, check first that these are free of wax and that any damaged tiles are replaced. Some types of tile may have constituents that might react chemically with new tiles.

If there is any doubt, remove the old tiles. These can be heated with a blow torch to facilitate removal. The residue of old adhesive should be cleaned off the floor before laying new tiles. Slightly irregular wood surfaces can be corrected by laying a saturated felt underlay.

Certain types of tiles, such as vinyl asbestos tiles, will be more pliable and less brittle to work with if kept at room temperature for some time before laying. If the tiles are self adhesive the sticking agent is activated with hot water or exposed by removing a protective backing sheet of waxed paper.

Guide lines
Tiling starts from the centre of the room. First, mark out the guide lines. As the walls of a room are rarely true, the exact centre is found in the following way.

Establish and mark the exact centres of

the two end walls; rub chalk over the length of string; position the string between the marked points and snap it against the floor. Establish the side wall centres and position a second chalk line. The room will then be marked out in four sections.

Laying
To find out how wide the gap will be between the last whole tile and the wall, put down a line of tiles loosely along the chalk lines; do not stick these. The space left at the edge should not be less than half a tile. If you are left with a gap of less than half a tile, adjust the chalk line by moving it half the width of a tile further away from that wall.

Using a notched spreader apply up to, but not over the chalk lines, about 1m² of adhesive; do not make this too thick.

First, apply adhesive to the under edge of the tiles which butt the chalk line, so that these do not lift along that edge. Starting at the point where the chalk lines cross, lay the first row of tiles.

Position the first tile at the point where the lines intersect. Press the tile down firmly round the outside and then in the centre. Work outwards until you reach the gap between the wall and the last complete tile.

Cutting in
Fitting in tiles at the edge can be done in two ways:

If the gap is the same along the length of the wall, take the tile to be cut and place it over the corresponding tile in the last complete row from the wall.

Butt a square tile against the skirting and over the tile to be cut. Mark the line of the overlap on the bottom tile. Cut the tile and fit it into position.

After the complete row has been trimmed, stick the tiles down, taking care not to force them into position.

Where the gap between the last row of complete tiles and the wall is not even, use a spare tile as a marker to indicate the variations in distance.

Place the tile to be trimmed on the last corresponding complete tile. Join the two marks with a ruled line, cut the tile and fit into position.

Vinyl tiles can be scored with a cutting knife and snapped cleanly. Lino tiles must be cut through.

Cutting round corners, door architraves and so on can be done by using a template or with a spare tile, a pencil – and care.

Place the tile to be cut on top of the corresponding tile in the row laid last. Use the spare tile, held vertically and parallel with the run of the floor, to mark off the shape of the corner point by point. Join up these points together and the shape of the corner will be reproduced on the tile, which can then be cut.

Self-adhesive tiles
Tiles that have self-adhesive backing are easy to lay. Mark out the floor as before. Dip the self-adhesive tile into a bowl of hot water for 5–10 seconds to allow the glue to soften.

Shake the tile to remove excess water and press the tile into position. As the tiles are laid, remove any water on the surface. If the tiles have to be trimmed, use the same techniques as for non-adhesive tiles but before immersing in hot water.

Other self-adhesive tiles have a layer of adhesive material on the back protected by waxed paper. This is peeled off after any cutting necessary, before the tile is placed in position.

Floor care
Both vinyl and linoleum floors, well cared for, will give years of easy-care use. Most linoleum can be polished. After laying, wash over with warm water and mild detergent and then use a suitable wax or resinous polish.

Adhesive, on the face of vinyl tiles, should be cleaned off with a little white spirit. Wash the tiles with warm water and a mild detergent, then apply two coats of a suitable liquid vinyl polish.

Furniture finishing:

There is an infinite range of treatments and finishes you can apply to furniture. Older items can be given a new lease of life; but it is important as in most things, to prepare the surface correctly, so that the finished result is worth while. Damage to furniture can often be repaired to be indistinguishable from new, using simple restoration techniques.

new life for old furniture

Stripping pine chest in steel tank or with bucket; soak in tank for two hours

Use 1/30th caustic soda: 5-litres water; add soda to water; scrub with fine wire wool

Wear rubber gloves and protective clothes. Immediately wash off splashes on skin

Item stripped by hand can be left to dry for about a day, dependent on the weather

Brush stripped item with cold water and leave tank item for two days to dry out

Chest can then be finished with clear polyurethane varnish or with wax polish.

The main two areas of furniture-finishing are painting new whitewood and the restoration of older pieces, already finished, but looking the worse for wear.

Whenever finishing furniture, make sure that the working conditions are clean. Never work in a dusty garage; protect the floor with newspapers or dust sheets.

It is important, with nursery furniture, to see that any paint materials you use do not contain lead.

Whitewood

Furniture that has not been finished by the manufacturer, generally known as whitewood, varies considerably in quality – from well-made products to those that are rather roughly knocked together.

Because the new wood may not have been adequately seasoned – the ideal moisture content is 12 to 15 per cent – there is risk of warping and twisting. Shrinking may also take place, and this is twice as great across the grain than along it.

So, before applying any type of finish, stand the piece where it will eventually be housed, for several weeks if possible, to allow its humidity to adapt to that of the room. This is important where the home is centrally heated.

Do not buy whitewood furniture showing blue streaks. This indicates the use of sapwood, and the blue will often 'bleed' through the subsequent finishing coats.

Preparation

Before applying any type of finish, smooth the entire surface with flour-grade abrasive paper, preferably garnet as it has a fine cutting action, wrapped around a wood block of a size you can conveniently hold in the hand.

Quirks and enrichments will have to be tackled by wrapping the abrasive paper round your index finger or by using a blunt, pointed piece of wood. You could also use a fine nail file.

Gaps may have to be filled with wood filler, or with a cellulose powder filler. Knife this well in and finish slightly proud, so that it can be rubbed down level when hard. As shrinkage of the stopping material will occur, several applications are better than one, leaving time for each to harden, before applying the next.

In addition to stopping up obvious gaps, the surface may need filling – that is, making good the cellular construction of softwoods and the pores of some hardwoods.

Do this with a cellulose filler as for gaps but, instead of knifing it on in a thick consistency, mix to a cream and brush on in the direction of the grain. Leave for a few minutes and wipe off across the grain. When hard, smooth in the direction of the grain.

Whenever you are rubbing down timber, follow the direction of the grain. If you rub across, the hard portions will show scratch marks.

Some cheap plywoods are so furry that, however much smoothing is done, it is difficult to get rid of 'hairy' bits. Give the surface a coat of wood primer, thinned with the same quantity of white spirit and leave for several days to harden; then rub down and the hairs will snap off.

Touch over the exact area of exposed knots with patent knotting. Leave to dry for a few minutes and touch in again, this time extending the area slightly. Do not go too far, as paint does not adhere all that well to the shellac content of the knotting. This 'staggered' application will help to 'feather off' the edges of the knotting, so that a bulge is not obvious.

Leave for some hours before painting or the paint film will entrap solvents and cause blistering.

If a knot looks particularly resinous or is loose, cut it out. Stop up the hole with wood slightly thinner than the thickness of the piece you are treating. Glue it in position, fill proud with filler and sand level when dry.

Knots that are only moderately bad can often be made less virulent by warming them with a blow lamp and wiping off exuding resin with acetone or white spirit.

Where paint fails to adhere over patent knotting, touch in with a thin finishing coat. This will have far better inherent stickiness than either primer or undercoat. When dry, prime and undercoat all over.

Undercoats fill minor imperfections and give 'body' to the finish. Since these are highly pigmented, they tend to look 'ribby' – and this will appear through the finishing coat. To obviate this, apply the undercoat with a foam roller, leaving the brush for twists, twirls and corners.

Painting

The choice of finishing coats varies between alkyd resins which give the widest colour range, polyurethanes, which are harder, and one of the so-called plastic coatings which are harder still. These may or may not be based on polyurethane. The last two are suitable for furniture in the kitchen and bathroom which is subject to more than usually severe wear.

Always 'lay off' every coat of paint in direction of the grain of the wood and not across it. You can spray on colour; the most convenient way of doing this is with an aerosol pack. These are available in small sizes so there is no need to buy a litre to do a small job.

Experiment first on an off-cut of wood. Overspray half way on to a previous lap and release the press button momentarily at the end of each sweep; this will give a coating of even thickness.

Aerosols are useful for wicker furniture, or you can apply the paint with a sponge or with a paint pad. These penetrate the interstices of awkward surfaces more thoroughly than a brush, and without the same risk of blobs and runs. Alternatives to paint are waxes and polishes, stains and varnishes.

Staining and varnishing

Staining can be carried out when the making good of cheap wood does not necessitate too much patching. Even then, parts treated with filler will present a surface which is less absorbent than the wood itself; these areas will show through as light patches.

Touch in these parts with stain several times if necessary, after the first application has soaked in and dried. Then brush on a final coat of stain all over to even up the colour. If these applications are likely to produce a darker colour than you want, start off with a lighter stain.

Waxing or polishing a surface means you have to keep the surface similarly treated. Wax also holds dust. It is better to apply several coats of varnish. Polyurethane, like paint, is harder than ordinary wood varnish and is available in either glossy or matt finish.

You can also get coloured plastic coatings and transparent polyurethane varnishes. With these, there is no need to stain the wood first. Such varnishes are almost indistinguishable from French polish and much harder wearing.

Real French polish is beautiful when new, but its soft surface readily marks. It requires a great deal of skill to ensure successful application. Never use wax on it – just clean it with a chamois leather. If signs of 'bloom' appear, add a little vinegar to water and apply with a cloth, using the chamois afterwards.

Graining

Hand graining also requires special skills, knowledge of woods, and specific tools to achieve a finish which is indistinguishable from the real thing and was once the pride of traditional craftsmen.

However, you can get a pretty good match by using Gransorbian, which is a kind of relief papier mâché, moulded in patterns of different kinds of timber. The relief is printed on to the wood. You can also get a fair imitation of a pine surface by using a dry-brush process.

For this you need ground coats and scumbles – best obtained from builders' merchants, supplying professional decorators.

Select the ground coat of colour similar to that of the lightest parts of the wood being imitated and brush this all over the prepared surface. When dry, dab on the scumble, which should match the darkest parts in colour, with a brush. While this is still wet, draw a dry brush along in the direction of the grain of the wood with a 'wiggling' motion.

Any imperfections can be made to look like knots by wrapping a cloth round your thumb and twisting it on the surface. Examine a piece of pine to see how the grain lines run round a knot, and the effect will look more natural. Leave to dry and then protect the surface with two or three coats of varnish.

To simulate a join in the surface, apply masking tape where you require the join to show and draw the brush diagonally away from it. Peel off the tape, leave to dry and apply the tape to the other side.

To effect a matching design for a quartered panel, divide the panel in half downwards and across with a pencil. Draw just the main features of the top left-hand panel on a sheet of paper and make three tracings of them.

Perforate here and there along the lines of the tracings. Turn one tracing over and, laying it over the top right-hand quarter, 'pounce' coloured pigment or chalk through a pad, or apply a dryish

Rag-wool buff in power tool takes the hard work out of polishing a chest

Rollwood veneer, in teak or mahogany, is neatly applied using contact adhesive

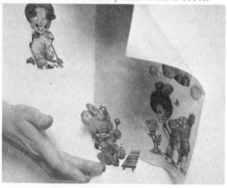
Old, 1910 whitewood chest, repainted and updated with modern handles and transfers

Wet-and-dry paper used to cut back old paint to smooth surface before undercoat

Decorette transfers slide off with water and are dabbed into place with a cloth

Undercoat applied with a medium-sized brush. Rub down then apply top coat

colour with a cloth to show the main lines of the design in reverse.

Turn the second tracing upside down for the bottom left-hand quarter, and the third tracing over and upside down for the bottom right-hand quarter. Now you will have guide lines for brushing out the scumble.

Laminboard, blockboard and chipboard are treated in the same way as wood, but some chipboards need considerable filling and sealing to present a smooth surface. As hardboard is extremely porous, do not use ordinary wood primer because too much oil will be soaked up. Apply hardboard primer or well-thinned emulsion paint before finishing with oil paint.

Garden furniture is best treated with teak oil or with a varnish which resists the effects of ultra-violet rays.

Special effects
Various timber effects can also be achieved by the use of self-adhesive vinyl sheeting which, since it is resistant to chemical spillages, is ideal for horizontal surfaces in kitchens and bathrooms. Contact plastic sheeting is easy to cut and stick on. You can buy these materials plain or in designs. Ordinary vinyl wall covering can

be used, though it tends to accentuate the least unevenness in the substrate.

Stick-on transfers can be used for brightening up nursery furniture, and for a wide range of furniture applications.

Refinishing old furniture
Take off the existing polish with white spirit, turning the cloth and renewing it frequently so that the wax is not spread. Provided the scratches are not too deep, you can now disguise them with scratch-cover polish, 'painting' a little with a fine brush into the scratches.

Leave this to soak in, then apply the polish over the entire surface, and the defect should be virtually undetectable.

Deep dents can be made good by dripping a little boiling water into the crevice to swell the grain of the wood and restore it to its proper level, or you can drip wax, matched in colour, using the tip of a soldering iron to melt it. Scrape the surface level with a sharp knife, and when dry, provided the dent is not too deep, fill it with wax polish.

Chipped veneers present a problem. You will have to match this, as nearly as possible, with a similar veneer from a timber shop. Lay the new piece over the

damaged part with the grain running in the same direction and cut through both new and old veneers with a sharp knife. Lever off the edges of the old, clean off any residue of existing adhesive, and glue on the patch.

In some cases, you will need to experiment to find out what materials were used on old furniture.

First, try dry scraping with a proprietary timber scraper; some nitrocellulose finishes chip off fairly easily. If this does not work, use a non-caustic paint stripper. When the old surface coat has been removed, by whatever is the best means of removing it, rub down the surface thoroughly and revarnish or paint as for new wood.

Paint stripper will not lighten a darkly stained wood; and there is a danger that the stain will become activated by the solvents in the new finish and 'bleed' through it. Aluminium primer sealer will stop this from happening, but the surface will then have to be painted, because the sealer is silvery in colour.

Apply two or three finishing coats; undercoating is not necessary because the sealer has considerable filling action.

If, on the other hand, you merely wish to lighten the stain, apply a wood bleach after removing the varnish. This may produce patchiness; in this case, after the first bleaching, go over the dark parts again. You may then have to rebleach the entire surface to make it uniform.

Relief ornamentation is generally in the form of moulding, which is pinned and glued into position. If this has become broken, the quickest way to put it right is to take off the damaged section and match up, as nearly as possible, with fresh moulding.

If this is not feasible, patch up using cellulose filler or fireclay or by mixing cabinet maker's cement with white shellac to a consistency of a thick cream.

Leave the mixture to stand for 12 hours, then brush or knife it on. Use a modelling knife carefully to trim the repair. Work is best done on a horizontal surface, so tip the furniture on its side or back.

Cigarette burns can be removed from a painted surface by digging out the charred wood with a sharp penknife, filling the hole proud with a cellulose filler, smoothing level when dry and touching in with paint. Then with fine abrasive paper, lightly etch the remainder of the surface and recoat the entire top.

Other finishes
A two-tone effect enhances a relief surface and can be quickly carried out by using a dryish brush with a second colour and dragging it over the high-relief first colour when dry.

Another way is to coat the entire surface with one colour. Leave to dry and overcoat with another colour. Wipe off this colour from the high parts while it is still wet.

By using an advancing hue (something with a little red or yellow in it) on the high parts, and a receding hue (with a little blue in it) in the valleys, a flattish relief can be made to look more pronounced.

How to become an expert upholsterer

Yesterday's furniture, often discarded and mouldering, may be today's bargain. Much Victorian furniture is now at a premium; Edwardian is less so, but becoming increasingly sought after.

A chaise longue is an example of a piece of furniture which can be restored to gain a new lease of life; it may also prove to be a valuable investment once restoration is carried out.

The techniques described to re-upholster this item are valid for similar pieces, though some adjustments may have to be made, dependent on the type of construction and finish.

Old furniture, filling, usually consists of horsehair. This is expensive and now often fairly difficult to obtain. Modern fillings usually consist of foam-rubber latex and reconstituted polyether on a base of rubber webbing and hessian.

Button backing is a technique which generally requires a fair degree of skill and practice to achieve a successful result. The technique evolved for button-backing this unit is less complicated and should be within the capabilities of most.

It should be noted that when re-upholstering old furniture it may first be necessary to carry out repairs to the frame and, perhaps, to restore damaged woodwork. Often older furniture, as in this

Shabby, leather-covered chaise longue badly in need of total restoration

Prise off old cover with ripping tool and mallet; remove hessian and stuffing

Similarly, using the same tools, prise out the tacks from the old webbings

The webbing is interwoven, in order to provide overall tension and strength

Hessian is then fitted over the webbing and tacked in place, at short intervals

The headrest and back seen completely hessianed, for polyether and latex foam

Stick a piece of 50mm latex the length and width of the backrest to pad out the top

The headrest and the backrest are seen completely covered with the latex sheet

The rear of the backrest, with both padded top and the final latex sheet stuck down

Reverse of cover is marked in chalked diamond pattern; make allowance for pleats

Button tied with slip knot; form pleats before it is pulled down and tied off

Buttoning tied off; cut ends carefully with scissors to avoid nicking material

case, has been patched up or imperfectly repaired at some earlier point.

The answer is to start from scratch: remove and discard the old upholstery and restore, as closely as possible, to the original.

Tools required:
- Ripping chisel
- Upholsterer's mallet
- Upholsterer's needle (long, straight)
- Sharp knife
- Felt-tipped pen.

Materials:
- Nylon tufting twine
- webbing
- 50mm rubber and jute webbing
- 340-gramme hessian
- 50mm reconstituted polyether
- 25mm latex pin-core foam block
- finishing fabric
- 100mm calico strip
- Buttons, suitable braid
- Tacks: 13mm, 16mm.

Stripping the unit
Start at the bottom
Place the sofa upside down on a pair of trestles. Remove the bottom cover, using a ripping chisel and mallet. Place the blade of the chisel against the side of the head of the tack in the direction of the grain, with the chisel pointed slightly downwards.

Give the chisel a sharp blow with the mallet to drive the blade under the tack head to knock it clear. Work in the direction of the wood grain to avoid splitting the timber. Once the bottom cover is removed, the webbing will be exposed.

Where the top cover of the seat is tacked off under the rail, these tacks should next be removed. Where the top cover is tacked to the rebate on the timber side rails, as in this case, the next stage is to remove the old webbing.

Removing webbing tacks
The webbing tacks are removed by again using the chisel under the head of the tack. Knock all the tacks clear but do not bother to remove the webbing from the old springs.

Headrest
Remove the outside cover of the headrest. This is usually sewn down each side, tacked along the bottom under the rail and back-tacked at the top. The tacks holding the headrest cover will be exposed and can be levered out.

On this sofa it was tacked on the back edge and across the top of the back; the front edge was finished off in a rebate on the polished wood scroll.

Seat cover removal
Next, remove the seat cover. This is always removed after the headrest cover, because the cover is tacked on top of it. To facilitate removal of the seat cover, place the sofa on its back, covering the floor to avoid damaging the polished wood.

Remove all the tacks along the front edge, including the tacks holding the various canvasses, which are exposed as the seat cover is loosened. Then remove any tacks holding laid cord that has been used to lash the springs in place.

Proceed all round the sofa in this manner, repositioning the sofa as needed for access. The webbings, springs and stuffing of the seat should drop out in one piece on completion.

Carry out a similar operation on the inside back canvasses and webbings. When all has been removed check the frame for any odd tacks that may have been missed.

Restoration
At this stage examine the frame for any loose joints and repair, regluing or remaking as necessary.

Once the unit is stripped, any repairs or renovations can be made to the frame

To improve corner line, shaped piece of wood was inserted, using dowel rods

New rubber webbing is tacked at close intervals over frame, back and headrest

Polyether and latex stuck together. Calico strips are stuck in place before tacking

Calico strip is stuck to headrest latex, pleated round headrest and then tacked

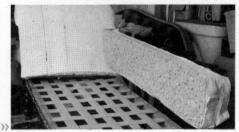

Backrest-rail polyether is fastened with calico strips, then tacked to backrest

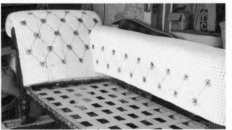

Mark even diamond pattern in chalk, so buttoning holes can be cut out with knife

Next, a piece of hessian is fitted into the back loop of the nylon tufted twine

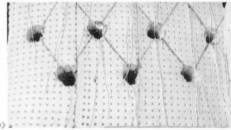

Twines are threaded through with needle and buttons are threaded on to these

Head and back rest completely diamond buttoned and pleated; seat is next covered

Tack seat cover beneath headrest and pull down and tack to frame along bottom

Finally, the decorative edging braid is stuck on around edges over line of tacks

This sofa was re-upholstered using a filling of reconstituted polyether and latex rubber. The rail and polished spindles were foam-padded and these, with the backrest, diamond-buttoned.

Re-upholstery
Webbing-up
The first stage is to web-up the seat, using rubber webbing. This webbing gives a little more spring than the jute webbing which was used with coiled springs.

Seat
The webs are tacked on the top of the rail, not on the bottom as would have been originally the case. The first webs are stretched from the back rail of the seat to the front rail. Take an end of 50mm webbing and locate it in the centre of the back rail.

Tack it down using four 16mm improved tacks (tacks with large heads) in a spaced line, across the width of the webbing, and 13mm in from the end of the webbing.

Stretch the webbing over the centre of the front rail, giving about a 25mm stretch for every 455mm of webbing. Tack off along the front rail as for the back rail. Cut the web, allowing an extra 13mm from the tacks. Proceed along the seat in this

manner, leaving a 50mm space between each webbing.

The webs running the length of the sofa should be inter-woven with the webs from back to front. Take the end of the web and, starting at the foot of the sofa, interweave this for the full length and tack it in the centre of the rail at the head.

Take the loose end of the webbing at the foot of the sofa and, giving it the appropriate stretch, tack off and cut. Continue to interweave webs, allowing a 50mm space between them and making sure that you have an alternating weave on each web.

Headrest webbing
Web-up the headrest in a similar manner – with this exception: in the case of a plain finished back use rubber webs; but when diamond buttoning is to be used, jute webbing is best for the headrest and back rail.

For diamond buttoning, the next stage is to cover the webbed area of the headrest with hessian, turned in 25mm to give double thickness for tacking. Use 13mm improved tacks, spaced at intervals of about 25mm.

With a scroll headrest, tension the hessian from side to side, and stretch evenly from top to bottom. Avoid excessive

tension on a small headrest as this will cause it to dip in the centre, and the shape of the scroll will be lost.

Cover the back rail in a similar manner. This is a flat surface, so equal tension can be exerted all round. If the seat is not to be diamond buttoned, there is no need to use hessian.

Cutting polyether and calico
Measure the width and length of the head-rest, adding 13mm to the width and 50mm to the length. Cut, with a sharp knife, a piece of reconstituted polyether foam to size. Next, cut two strips of 100mm calico the length of the polyether. Use a suitable latex adhesive to stick the calico to the long face sides, leaving a 50mm overlap at the bottom.

On the top surface of the foam block, mark a 50mm margin in from one of the short edges. Apply adhesive within this margin. Cut a 100mm calico strip the width of the block. Stick this to the treated surface area, allowing a 50mm overlap at the edge.

Positioning of polyether
Place the foam block on top of the hessian. Allow the calico on the short end to hang over the top of the scroll, with the bottom of the foam level with the backing rail.

Home upholstery can produce this finished result. A more ambitious example is shown below. Button-backing is a technique which greatly enhances the finished look.

Starting at the bottom of the headrest, tack the calico on the side of the frame; on the front edge, the calico must finish in the rebate of polished-wood facing.

Forming round the scroll

When the curve of the scroll is reached pleat the calico to form the foam round the curve. Finish off by tacking the calico on the top end, underneath the scroll, undercutting the foam as required to shape it in.

Cutting the latex foam

Next, cut a piece of 25mm-thick latex pincore foam block the same size as the reconstituted polyether foam fitted to the headrest. Using a latex adhesive, stick the rubber on top of the foam. An alternative method shown is to fit the polyether and the foam block as a single operation. Position the calico strips, tacking and pleating these round the head rest. Undercut the top back edge shaping this into the scroll.

Diamond buttoning

With a piece of chalk, mark the position of the diamond buttoning on the latex foam block. The diamonds can be as large or small as desired; 190mm × 140mm is a good, average size.

Measure carefully to find the centre and

subsequent positions. Mark out the centre diamond first and work out to the sides, top and bottom.

Try to get an even balance, keeping the end rows of buttoning half a diamond width from the edges. Make a 25mm diameter hole on the four points of each diamond, cutting through the rubber and foam, exposing the hessian underneath. Use a long, sharp penknife for this job.

Securing the holes

Take a 380mm length of nylon tufting twine and, using an upholsterer's long, straight needle, pass the twine down the hole in the rubber and polyether and through the bottom hessian, then back again up through the hole, taking up a 13mm long piece of hessian, to anchor the twine.

Even out the twine and leave the two strands hanging loose from the top of the hole; these are used later to secure the buttons. Repeat for all button holes.

Cut a piece of finishing cover the width and length of the headrest. Add an extra 125mm to each side, for overlapping, plus 38mm for each hole, to allow for pleating. Allow 75mm at each end to the length, measured from the bottom backing rail to the back of the scroll; again, add 38mm for each pleating hole.

Marking out diamond pattern

On the reverse side of the cover, mark out the diamond design you have made on the rubber, making the diamond size on the material 38mm longer and wider than the diamond measurement on the rubber. This also allows for the fold of the pleat.

Starting with the centre diamond, thread two strands of tufting twine and pass the upholsterer's needle through the corresponding mark on the cover, working from the 'wrong' to the right side of the material.

Securing the buttons

Remove the twine from the needle and thread one end of the twine through the button loop, make a slip knot and pull the button down into the foam. Do not finally tie these yet.

Repeat this operation at all points of the centre diamond, adjusting the button tensions as required. Form the pleats of the diamond as you go. All pleats should fold down towards the bottom of the headrest; repeat this on all the diamonds.

When all the diamonds are positioned satisfactorily, tie off the buttons with a further slip knot.

Finish the cover over the sides of the headrest by tacking this to the sides with 13mm tacks. Take up the fullness in pleats in line with the edge buttons.

The top and bottom of the headrest are finished in a similar manner. At the polished-wood rebate edge, trim the cover neatly up to the tacks with a sharp knife, as this edge will be braided.

Webbing up the back rail is similar to that of the seat and headrest. Cover the webbing with 340-gramme hessian. Cut a piece of reconstituted foam, large enough to cover the whole back rail, finishing level with the top of the rail.

Fasten with calico strips, tacked to the frame of the headrest. Cut another piece of reconstituted foam the length and width of the back rail, plus 50mm, to overlap the foam already positioned on the front of the rail.

Stick this to the front piece of foam. Fasten with calico strips to the frame at the back. Cut a piece of latex pin-core foam block the length of the back rail and wide enough to cover the foam-bottom front edge and to form over the top back edge. This is stuck to the bottom of the front foam pad and taken over the back of the top rail

As this back pad is only 255mm deep, there will only be one row of diamond pleating along the length of the pad. Mark out the rubber and cut holes, as for the headrest. Cut out the finishing cover

to fit the length of the back rail, plus a 38mm allowance for each button hole.

Allow sufficient spare to tack off on the back of the rail at each end and deep enough to tack on the bottom rail of the seat and the top back edge of the back rail. Allow 38mm for each hole. Mark out the cover on the reverse side, as for the headrest, and button. Pleat out the fullness opposite each button at the top and bottom and tack off.

Seat

Cut a piece of reconstituted foam, 100mm thick supplied in 50mm thickness, two layers will have to be stuck together. Cut the pieces the length and width of the seat, adding 13mm to each measurement. Cut the corners to the shape of the frame and fasten to the frame with calico strips as for the headrest.

Cut a piece of 25mm latex pin-core foam block to the same size and shape as the reconstituted foam. Stick pin-core rubber on top of the foam and cut a piece of finishing cover the length and width of the seat. Allow sufficient to cover the edges and to tack on to the side, back and front rails.

Tack off, using sufficient tension to even

out the cover, and round off the edges. Pleat out the fullness around the corner.

Trim off the cover into the polished wood rebate on the front of the sofa with a sharp knife. This edge is now ready for braiding. This is later stuck in place with a latex adhesive.

Outside back covers

Cut a piece of finishing cover long enough to cover the outside back rail, plus 50mm for turnings, and deep enough to finish off under the seat. Cut a piece of pin-core foam block to the length of the back rail and wide enough to cover both the bottom and front edge and to form over the top back rail. This should be turned in 25mm all round and sewn by hand, with a needle and matching thread, then tacked off under the seat.

The outside back of the headrest is covered in the same way as the outside back of the rail.

To make a dust cover, which is tacked to the underside of the seat, cut a piece of hessian to the length and width of the seat frame. Turn in the edges 13mm and tack the hessian to the base of the seat, using 13mm tacks.

Finally, stick the braid on with the latex adhesive.

Laminates: the smooth touch

Laminates, which are available in a wide range of exciting colours and designs provide a modern, durable, stain resistant and easily cleaned surface. Once applied a laminate surface needs no further attention. In addition to plain colours, laminates are made in simulated wood and marbled effects, tile patterns and random designs. These provide a wide choice to fit in with any décor scheme.

Decorative laminates are made from several sheets of compressed paper, a core of heavy brown kraft paper applied to a decorative surface paper, resin–bonded under great pressure and heat, to produce a single sheet of dense, hard material.

Laminated surfaces can be used anywhere in the home where a hard-wearing and easy-to-clean surface is required. Modern laminates are made in both plain colours and a wide range of decorative designs. They are produced in three sizes of 1220mm wide sheets: 2440mm, 2740mm and 3050mm, and an extra-wide 4120mm × 1520mm sheet. There are two thicknesses: 1·5mm for surfaces which have to take hard wear and 1mm for lighter uses, such as shelf linings and the inside of doors.

Planning your needs saves money. Work out the sections you want and buy sheets accordingly. It is possible to buy offcuts quite cheaply for small areas. Laminate can also be bought ready cut to size but this usually costs around 50 per cent more.

Some types of household cleaners, such as bleach and fruit juice, may stain laminates. A good rule is to avoid putting very hot objects on to a laminated surface and to wipe up spillage quickly.

Always store laminate flat and away from damp surfaces. Before using, keep it indoors for at least 48 hours, so that it adjusts to room temperature. Though inert, laminate is subject to slight expansion and contraction from temperature variation.

Before fixing laminate to any surface, ensure that this is clean, dry and free from grease. It should also be rigid. If the surface has been painted or varnished, this should be taken down to bare wood. The best surfaces are those consisting of blockboard, plywood and chipboard. These provide continuous surfaces without joints which could pull away with fluctuations in humidity.

Unsupported surfaces, such as the insides of cupboard doors, should be lined with a thin, cheap (1mm thick) laminate, to prevent warping caused by the outside sheet of laminate.

Tools

Cutting knife. *One of the various handyman's knives, fitted with a special laminate-cutting blade, is best used to score deep lines into the laminate surface. A piece of steel file, sharpened to a point, is also an effective cutting tool.*

Laminate cutter. *A tungsten-tipped tool which can also be used to cut deep lines in the laminate.*

Fine-toothed tenon saw or veneer saw. *These are useful for small jobs that do not involve too much cutting. Any large amount of work will blunt the teeth of the saw.*

Special cutters. *There are purpose-designed hand tools, one popular one resembling a pair of scissors, designed for cutting laminates.*

Power tools. *A jig saw, either an attachment to a power drill or an integrated unit, can be used to cut laminate. This is particularly useful for cutting out shapes or circles. Carborundum discs attached to power drills require care in use for cutting laminate.*

Another attachment is a combined milling cutter and laminate edge trimmer. This has a base platform to enable it to run accurately along the surface.

Notched spreader. *This is used to distribute adhesive over the surface to be laminated. The teeth or notches produce ridges which give grip evenly over the surface.*

Preparation

Before cutting your laminate, plan the layout to ensure the minimum of wastage. Measure carefully before cutting, double checking always. Lay the sheet, decorative side upwards, on to a flat surface, such as a large table or the floor. Allow 3mm oversize for trimming. To mark out rectangular shapes, use a pencil and a steel rule or a piece of straight timber at least 6mm thick.

Measure round the shape to be cut, allowing the extra 3mm all round to allow for trimming. A try-square, used with a straight edge, will enable you to mark accurate right angles.

For irregular shapes use a template. The best one, if possible, is the surface which is to be faced. Place the template right way up on the facing laminate. If marking the backing laminate place the template upside down.

It is best to use the surface to be laminated as a template but if this is not possible make an accurate template of a rigid material such as stiff card. A paper template can be used but this is best fixed to the surface with adhesive tape and the outline transferred on to the surface.

A felt-tipped pen can be used for marking. Where a template is used for a lining laminate, mark the shape on the back of the sheet.

Cutting
Scoring

Cut laminate face side up to avoid edge flaking. First, set a straight edge along the cutting line, steadying this with one hand.

To avoid making costly mistakes, check twice when measuring and marking

Use a straight edge to guide the blade. Score until dark line appears in laminate

Once the line is scored, snap laminate upwards, evenly and firmly, along line

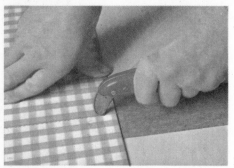

To protect surfaces beneath the work, put a smooth piece of timber underneath

Use knotched spreader to apply contact adhesive evenly to each bonding surface

Locate timber battens on the surface and position the sheet of laminate on top

Block plane used to trim laminate flush with edge; use also file or metal scraper

To remove entrapped air, tap over surface with hammer and smooth wood block

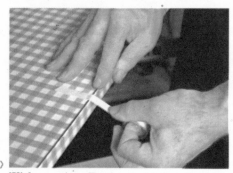

With a resin adhesive, hold the edge in place with several pieces of sticky tape

Take the handyman's knife or laminate cutter and score gently the full length of the sheet from one end. Hold the cutting tool tightly against the straight edge and score firmly and accurately along the line, using three or four even strokes. Use increasing pressure until the under surface of the laminate shows in a clean unbroken line. Do not rush this part of the scoring. Take care that the cutter does not slip, as this will make an unsightly mark· on the face of the laminate.

Once the under surface shows, remove the straight edge and continue scoring until the piece is cut through. You can also score partly through the surface, and, with the straight edge held in place, 'snap' off the waste piece, by bending upwards. This works well over a short length but over a longer piece the waste piece may break off unevenly unless the sheet is well supported. The sheet may be clamped to a surface, using G-cramps with pieces of timber to protect the laminate.

Sawing

Place the sheet of laminate, decorative side upwards, on a firm table, work bench or trestle. Position it so that the pencil line indicating the cut projects slightly over the edge.

Use a further support, such as a trestle or table, if the overhang is more than 75mm

in width, or clamp the sheet. Score along the pencil line using a cutter. Use the saw 'flat', at no more than an angle of 20°. If you hold it at a greater angle the sheet will vibrate and cause edge flaking.

Saw gently to avoid damage to the surface finish. When you have almost cut to the end of the sheet, hold the off-cut piece as you complete the sawing and straighten the angle of the saw.

Take particular care as you near the end, as this is where the corner of the sheet is most likely to snap off. Any rough edges can be smoothed with a file.

Power tools

These should not be forced through the laminate. The jig saw cuts on an upstroke and to avoid flaking of the laminate surface, this is best used to cut laminate placed face downwards. When using carborundum discs, wear protective goggles or stand well clear of the disc, since tiny flying splinters will be thrown up.

Because of the vibration of power tools, it is desirable to clamp the sheets so that there will be no movement.

Cutting irregular shapes

When cutting irregular shapes, curves or circles, you can use one of two methods. First, cut a template to include the wastage

area of 3mm. Place the template on the face of the laminate (the reverse for backing) and fix it in place with adhesive tape, double-sided or folded over to achieve this. Score round the shape, using the cutter or blade vertically until the under surface shows.

Once the line is scored, remove the template and continue scoring until the shape comes away cleanly. You can also use a

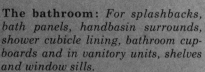

Where to use laminate

The bathroom: *For splashbacks, bath panels, handbasin surrounds, shower cubicle lining, bathroom cupboards and in vanitory units, shelves and window sills.*
The kitchen: *Working surfaces, cupboard linings and facings, sink and cooker splashbacks, kickboards, shelves and window sills.*
Other rooms: *Shelves, window sills, bedroom furniture, table and desk tops, cupboards and wardrobe doors.*

Fine-toothed panel saw can also be used to cut laminate; support work carefully

Goscut tool can also be used for cutting – rather like using a pair of scissors

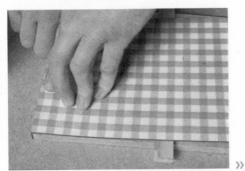

Once the sheet is in place, with a slight overhang, slide out battens and roll down

Locate drawing pins at edges, so that laminate can be accurately positioned

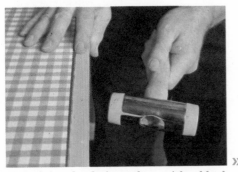

Tap edging firmly into place with a block of wood when using a contact adhesive

Trim edge strips with a file or a small block plane, to produce neat black bevel

drill to make a series of small holes round the shape to perforate the edge. Then, using a fine-toothed keyhole saw or jigsaw, cut round the shape. The rough edges will need smoothing with wire wool and polishing with light lubricating oil.

Fixing

Many adhesives are used for fixing household laminates. These may be divided into three types: impact or contact adhesives; synthetic resins; and epoxy-based resins. Impact adhesives demand accurate initial positioning.

Before starting make sure that you have the materials and tools to hand. You will need a large notched spreader if you are dealing with a big area. A suitable spreader can be made of any firm material, with serrated 'teeth' cut out. A piece of laminate is ideal.

It is a good idea to carry out a 'dry' check of the position of the laminate. This you can do by marking the corner angle of the surface to be laminated, and then partly knocking in locating pins. The laminate can then be aligned against these guide markers to check accuracy.

It is important that adhesives are applied evenly over the whole surface, otherwise air pockets may form, causing the laminate to 'lift'.

Since contact adhesives allow no latitude once the laminate is in contact with the surface, lay a series of thin wooden battens across the surface of the board and position the laminate over the battens. Position the sheet so that there is a 3mm overhang all round and then withdraw the lath at one edge and stick down about 50mm of sheet. Slide out the laths one by one and roll the laminate on to the surface. This action prevents air from being trapped.

Another way is to position drawing pins in a corner to ensure alignment. Greaseproof paper can also be laid on the surface and the sheet positioned as before. The paper is withdrawn with one hand, and the other is used to roll the laminate on to the surface.

Keep a tin of an adhesive solvent near in case you spill any adhesive on the laminate.

Contact or *impact adhesives* demand quick accurate work. First coat both contact surfaces with adhesive. Allow the adhesive to become 'touch dry' before contact is made. You must ensure complete accuracy since adhesion is positive and virtually irremovable once the surfaces touch. The time the adhesive takes to become touch dry may vary from 30 minutes in cold weather to only four to six minutes in warmer weather.

These adhesives are highly flammable and should be used only in well-ventilated conditions.

Pour adhesive on to the centre of the back of the laminate. Using a notched spreader, pull the adhesive evenly across the surface to the edges. Use the same method to apply adhesive to the base surface. Allow the adhesive to become 'touch dry', with no damp patches, since these will not adhere. Bring the laminate reverse into contact with the board surface. Press the laminate down to ensure firm contact and no air bubbles.

One type of contact adhesive possesses a thixotropic agent which allows some movement of the laminate sheet after contact.

Synthetic resin: This allows plenty of time for setting. Apply adhesive with the notched spreader in the same way as for contact adhesive. Spread the adhesive until it runs out at the edges when you use pressure. Constant pressure should be applied over the entire surface, preferably placing weights–such as books–on it till the adhesive sets. A guide is when droplets at the edge dry. These can then be trimmed off with a knife.

Epoxy resins: These are waterproof, 'two-part' adhesives, using a base and hardener, which you mix together. Use the same technique for this adhesive as for synthetic resin. It is important that the surface is clean, free from grease and is dry. If the surface is not clean, the adhesive will not stick. Mix to maker's instructions.

Trimming

Once the adhesive has dried, the spare edge can be trimmed off. Use a small sharp block plane, with the blade set to a fine trim, using firm, sweeping strokes, and working from the outside to the middle. You can also use a flat file. To achieve a very smooth finish you can rub down the edge with fine wire wool and a fine-grade oil. Alternatively you can also use a fine glass-paper to finish the edge.

Edging

Edgings give a finished look to your work. If you are using a laminate strip cut the strip slightly over size. Stick the edging with adhesive using the same method as for sheets. These edges can be bevelled, producing a neat, dark line of the laminate core paper. The block plane is run along the edge at an angle to produce the bevelled finish.

Some edgings are in contrast plain colours such as black, and overlap the edge of the laminate. Wood and metal trims can also be used. A bevelled finish can impart a neat look to laminated edge.

Some people prefer to fix edgings first, and then laminate the main surface. This shows less of the brown core and there is less chance that the edge veneer may be pulled away.

Over short runs, using non-contact adhesive, you can hold the strip in place with adhesive tape until the adhesive sets. For longer runs it will be necessary to use cramps placed at about 150mm intervals. Place a piece of protective timber between the laminate and the cramps.

Ornamental bricklaying

Successful outdoor building is a combination of careful design and the correct construction techniques. A patio combines bricklaying and related skills, to construct a variety of walls, as well as the methods of laying decorative patio slabs, for modern outdoor living.

After a few days, once foundations have hardened off, the site can be set out for bricklaying. Set up a profile string in line with the brickwork outside edge. Put down, at intervals, 'spot' boards, each measuring about 600mm × 600mm, made from scrap wood, to hold the mortar. Stack bricks neatly between them, but far enough away to avoid getting splashed by mortar. A total of 25 standard bricks covers an area of about one metre square.

Tools needed are a spirit level and straight-edge, a 255mm or 280mm bricklayer's trowel, a small pointing or 'dotter' trowel, a club hammer, bolster or cold chisel, a wire brush, a shovel, a pair of bricklayer's pins, and a few metres of cord.

Mortar for bricklaying consists of a 1:8 cement/soft sand mix, with one part of lime or plasticiser. This makes the mixture 'fatty' and more easily workable. Use slightly less sand in cold weather.

Mortar and concrete

Generally, it is either the coarse or 'hungry' sands which need either lime or plasticiser. The colour of a mortar can be controlled or adjusted by choosing suitable sands and altering the proportion in which they are added to the mortar mix.

Only mix as much mortar as you need at a given time and try to avoid adding water to a mortar already mixed. In hot weather it may be necessary to dampen the bricks to control excessive suction.

First spread a thin bedding course of mortar screed along the foundations, and draw a 'course line' along this. The first course of bricks is laid to this line. To establish the course line, place the spirit level vertically downwards on to the mortar, with its edge against the profile line. Make sure that you do not lean the level against the line, for this may cause error.

Mark the vertical line on the screed with the trowel. Repeat this at short intervals and then, with level or straight edge, join up the marks by scratching a trowel line along the mortar. Take care not to cover the line when laying the first course of bricks, as this may cause error.

Bricklaying

The brick trowel is the most important tool used in bricklaying. Its main use is to pick up the mortar from the spot board and to spread it to an even thickness, in preparation for bricklaying.

It may also be used for the rough cutting and trimming of a brick. In the latter case, it is important to keep the fingers well clear when chopping bricks.

The choice of a trowel is an individual one, with considerations of weight, size and 'lift'. For a beginner, a small, lightweight trowel is probably best, for a larger trowel may be more difficult to handle.

Mortar should never be allowed to harden on the blade of the trowel, for this creates a rough surface and prevents free-and-easy movement when picking up and spreading.

When a trowel handle wears smooth, it should be roughened up with glasspaper. The blade should be thoroughly cleaned after use, by washing then rubbing its surfaces with a piece of soft brick. Take care to wipe the blade well with a dry cloth to prevent rusting, and store in a damp-free place.

The first thing to acquire is the art of handling mortar with the trowel. One edge of the trowel is curved, and the other has a straight edge for 'drawing' the mortar off the board.

Keep the side of the mortar 'spot' board nearest to you clear. When drawing off mortar, the trowel is always kept at right

Place mortar on spot board near working site; stack bricks fairly near the work

Position string line for line of wall and lay a thin screed of mortar beneath

With a straight edge, scratch the course line in the screed with the trowel tip

With trowel parallel over work, tilt edge down and then run furrow in mortar

Remove excess mortar by running the edge of the trowel along the edge of brick

Place brick in position, tap it down lightly and evenly with trowel handle

Slice off the excess mortar from the brick ends with the edge of the trowel

Constantly check verticals with a spirit level; check from two angles at 45°

Also constantly check horizontal alignment in order to ensure even brickwork

angles to the board, with the straight edge downwards.

Cut some mortar from the heap at the back of the board and draw it towards you, maintaining a to-and-fro slicing action. This shapes the mortar into a neat, pear-shaped roll, which is taken up on the flat of the trowel.

To do this, sweep the trowel towards you, with the leading edge scraping the board clean and the trailing edge raised slightly to trap the mortar. This should provide a fully loaded and evenly balanced trowel.

Hold the loaded trowel parallel with, and about 75mm to 100mm above the course of bricks, tilt one edge downwards, while pulling the trowel towards you with a sharp backward movement which helps to stretch out the roll of mortar on top of the bricks.

Level out the mortar with the back of the trowel, using the top 100mm from the tip. Make alternate side-to-side strokes, lifting the leading edge of the trowel slightly in each case and pushing lightly away from the body.

When the bed of mortar is about 20mm thick, tilt the tip of the trowel downwards and make a continuous furrow, parallel with and about 75mm back from the face of the brickwork. This helps to make a firm facing joint and allows the bricks to settle down evenly.

Where there is to be a corner in brickwork, mark out another screed line, at right angles to the first, again using the stretched lines as a guide. Now put down the first strip of bedding mortar over the marked screed. Mortar for cross joints can either be 'buttered' on to both meeting corners of each brick before it is laid or put on when the brick is bedded down.

Corners

Form corners by laying bricks alternately on each other at right angles and build up by 'racking back'–laying one brick less in each succeeding course.

In 115mm-thick brickwork, the cross joints should be filled completely, but in 230mm-brickwork, only the first 50mm at each end need to be filled as the laying action on the next course takes care of this. Try to maintain a uniform 6mm gap between bricks.

Use and care of line and pins

A line and pins are used to keep the bricks straight and level along each course of a wall. All brick walls over a metre long should be built with their aid. The line should be of good quality hemp and should not be too thick.

If the line breaks during use, it should not be tied together with a knot but the ends should be neatly spliced. The pins should be of good-quality steel and stoutly bladed, so as to prevent them from bending when in use.

Damage to the blade usually occurs when the pin has to be hammered into a hard mortar joint. This can be prevented by first driving a stout cut nail into the joint to a depth of about 20mm, and then withdrawing the nail, leaving a hole into which the blade of the pin is easily inserted.

When erecting a corner or stopped end of a wall, it is useful to leave 'pin holes' in the face of the brickwork, in preparation for the building of the wall using the line.

The pin holes are formed by inserting the point of the brick trowel into the one vertical cross joint of each course, before the mortar sets hard. The small slot formed

by this takes the blade of the pin.

Before winding a new line on to the pins, suspend it over a hook and attach a weight to the end. This ensures that the line is well stretched and prevents it from becoming twisted during use.

A layer of insulation tape should be wound round the shanks of the pins before winding up to prevent the line from being affected by rust.

The ends of walls are always built up first and the builder's line pins are tucked into mortar joints between each corner. The line is then 'snagged' over to the top edges of the quoin bricks and tightened by winding the slack on to the spade ends.

If you are building up to any height it is a good idea to make a gauge rod from straight timber marked with saw cuts at 75mm intervals. This is used to check that courses are going up evenly.

The spirit level is used to check that bricks are level, plumb and flush. Adjustments to the level of bricks is made by tapping these down lightly with the handle of the trowel then striking off with the trowel and returning to the spot board any excess mortar which is squeezed out.

Minor adjustments can be made by adjusting the thickness of mortar in vertical joints. If bricks have to be cut, it is best to use a club hammer and bolster, and steadily chop around the brick with even blows until it comes apart.

Jointing

As walls are built, the joints must be pointed or finished while the mortar is still fairly soft. A flush joint is achieved by scraping horizontal joints with the edge of the bricklayer's trowel and vertical joints

Draw mortar forward with slicing action in order to make neat, pear-shaped roll

Sweep up mortar by drawing trowel forward with edge scraping board

With the trailing edge slightly raised, finally pick up the pear of mortar

Strike off surplus mortar flush with the brick, using the edge of the trowel

When mortaring the ends of bricks for cross joints do this near the spot board

Pick up mortar and 'butter' the end of the brick for cross joints at each corner

Build up the end quoins and snag a string line across run of bricks and lay to this

When the mortar has dried slightly, point the joints. Use a pointing tool for this

Bricks can be cut with the trowel edge; it is easier to use club hammer and bolster

Brickwork Glossary

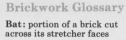

Bat: portion of a brick cut across its stretcher faces

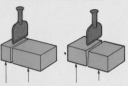

Bed joint: horizontal mortar joint

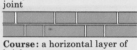

Course: a horizontal layer of bricks

Cross joint (or Perpend): a vertical mortar joint

Header: A brick laid with its 115mm × 75mm face parallel to the face of the wall

Lap: the horizontal distance between any cross joint and the nearest one to it on the next course up

Queen closer: A half brick cut lengthways

Quoin: The external corner of a wall

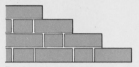

Racking back: The step pattern formed during the construction of a quoin

Stretcher: A brick laid with its 200mm × 75mm face parallel to the face of the wall

Toothing: The 57mm projection of alternate courses to leave a bond when the wall is continued at a later date

---

with the 'dotter' trowel. Once the surface is dry, blemishes can be removed with a wire brush.

Capping

Tops of walls may be finished in a variety of ways. The most common is with capping or coping pieces. Coping, either half weathered (sloped one way) or weathered (sloped both ways), can be used on tops of walls. These are mortared in place, using ordinary bricklaying trowel techniques.

Screen walls

Screen walls require a similar bricklaying technique but must be supported at intervals, usually of eight screen blocks, by brick or concrete piers. These blocks, made of concrete, are bedded in mortar and built up to a string line, but without the need to 'rack back'.

The pillars can either be built from brick or consist of pilasters – hollow blocks which when filled with concrete provide strength and reinforcement. Over longer sections of wall, some manufacturers suggest reinforcement with mild steel rods, inserted into the concrete.

To tie in the blocks to the pillars, 'butterfly' brick ties or expanded metal strip can be used. These are located halfway into the joints between bricks and halfway into the joints of pilasters or walls.

Some blocks are laid with galvanized wire bedded between the joints, to give strength.

Walls of up to 910mm in height and of any length should have piers at the ends and also at 3050mm intervals. Walls up to 1850mm high and of any length need piers at each end and at 2150mm intervals. Screen-block walls over this height need to be of double thickness.

Joints can be pointed and brushed in the same way as conventional bricks. Avoid building above three to four courses in height without allowing the mortar to 'go off', or the blocks may bulge and topple.

Stepped walls

An ornamental wall can look most effective when advantage is taken of a sloped site to stagger or 'step' this at varying levels. Double hollow walls can be filled with earth – but allow drainage holes in the base. Such walls can be very attractive when planted.

The extent to which a wall is stepped is partially a matter of its looks, or aesthetics, and making an economic use of materials. A greater number of 'steps' on a steep slope will economise on the use of bricks.

It may be necessary to make use of a number of half bricks to ensure the continuity of bond on a stepped wall, but this will be apparent during setting out of the brickwork.

The footings must be correctly stepped, or you will have difficulty in building the wall accurately. To decide on the number of steps, first establish the angle of the site and transfer this to a sheet of graph paper.

To establish the fall, set up a post at the front of the site, at least as high as the highest point of the slope. Fix a peg at ground level at the rear of the slope, across to the front post. Tie a string between these two points and align this horizontally with a spirit level.

Measure the height of the line at the front and the length of the site. This will give you the fall ratio. If, for example, the length of the area is 10m and the height of the string on the front pole is 3m, you have a 3m in 10m fall.

You will be able easily to transfer this ratio and dimensions to graph paper, using a tenth scale, marking the angle of fall accordingly. This enables you to decide, as much as anything, on the 'look' of the proposed wall.

Once you have decided on the number of steps, measure these out and put in pegs to correspond with the front of each step.

The post at the front of the site is then marked with the height of each step, by taking a string line from each marker back to this post. Check that the line is truly horizontal in each case. You now have the measurements of the height of each stepped section.

Footings can now be excavated. These are dug in further short steps, between the markers for the main wall steps. Each step in the footings corresponds with the length and the height of the bricks used for the walls.

Each step, therefore, goes up in increments of the height of a brick. Using a brick 305mm long and 75mm high, the first step would be 75mm high, the second 150mm above that, the third 225mm, and so on. Stepped footings enable considerable economy to be made in materials.

To lay the footings, you will need short pieces of timber, to contain the concrete at each step level, or alternatively build the front of each step up with a brick. The latter provides an accurate module for height. When pouring the concrete, check carefully for accuracy of each stepped section. Make sure, also, that at no point does the front of stepped footings rise above ground. The front should be at about the depth of half a brick.

A steel tape is used to measure out the position of the stepped wall sections. Until brickwork is above ground level you will not be able to work to a string line, so use a straight edge initially.

Paving

When buying patio slabs, allow about five per cent for breakages and waste when cutting. Slabs should be cut on a bed of soft sand, using a sharp bolster. Score a shallow line completely round the slab, gently tapping and deepening the cut as you proceed, until it breaks.

The slab will emit a ringing note which will deaden after a while, indicating that it is about to crack apart. Slight irregularities can then be chiselled off the cut edges. You may be able to use any broken slabs elsewhere, cut to a smaller size.

Paving needs firm basing. On soft ground it is advisable to provide foundations of well-consolidated hardcore. Use a straight edge, level and pegs to ensure that the base is even, allowing the correct fall for rainwater to run off.

Always lay slabs with the textured, non-slip surface upwards. It is a good idea to set out a few slabs 'dry' to see where cutting is needed and how the arrangement will work out.

A nylon line stretched across the ground will help you to line up your first row. Actual laying techniques will depend on the density of the subsoil, local weather and the amount of 'traffic'.

Where greater surface stability is needed on sifted soil or sand, place a trowel-full of mortar under the corner of each slab.

Where heavy traffic is expected, prepare a fairly stiff 1:5 cement:soft-sand mix, and spread this over the surface, covering just sufficient area for one slab at a time. Slabs should never be pummelled into place to correct any unevenness or to align a slab with its neighbour.

Tap the surface of each slab gently at each corner, with the handle of a club hammer. Use a straight edge and a spirit level to ensure that adjoining slabs are flush.

Slabs may be close laid or left with small gaps between them. Adjusting these gaps may often obviate the need to cut slabs. Gaps can be grouted with a dry mortar mix, brushed into the joints, or left open.

Grass, plants and other foliage may be allowed to grow through these gaps, imparting, in time, an established look to the patio.

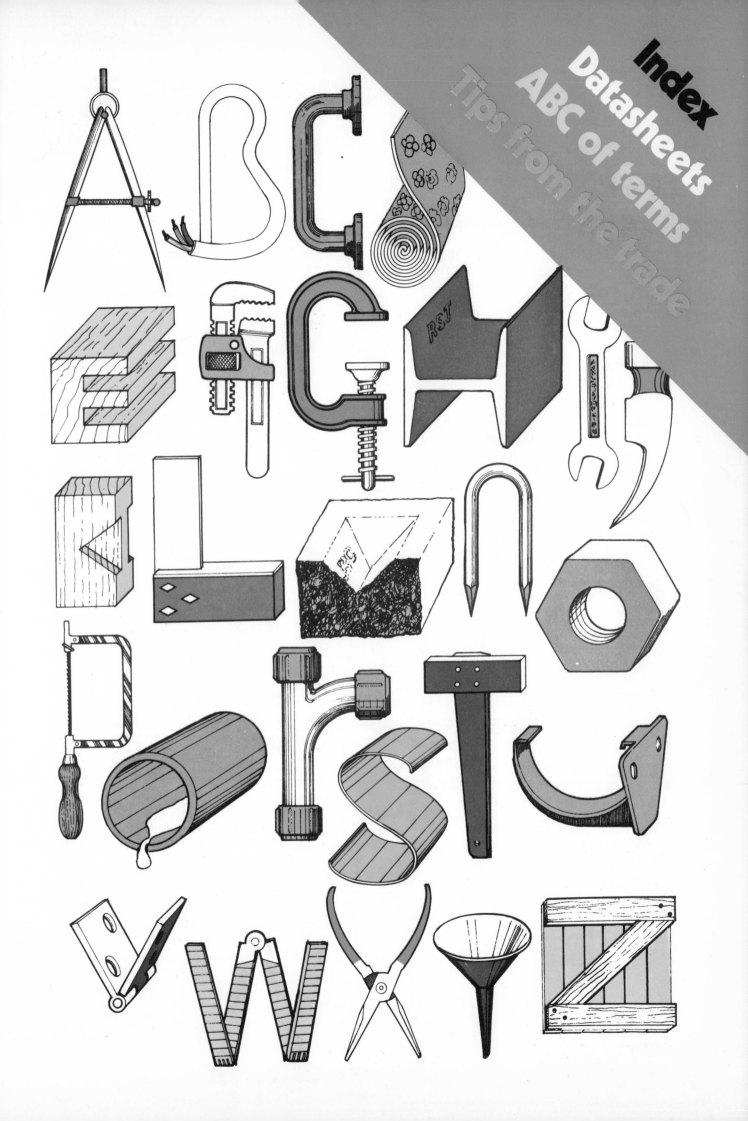

The metric unit is merely the unit of 10. In many cases, calculations are arrived at simply by moving a decimal point one or two places. In practice, the metric system simplifies the process of arithmetic. Britain has been 'going metric' voluntarily since 1965. There is an international co-ordinating body called the International Standards Organisation (ISO). Britain is a member of this body and metrication in Britain accords broadly with its proposals.

Britain is at the moment still undergoing the process of metrication. Most world trade, it is calculated, will be metric by 1980. Every major world country is in the process of going over to the metric system.

There are some similarities between imperial and metric measurements. For example, timber closely follows metric sizing (2in × 1in = 50mm × 25mm).

LENGTH

Imperial	Metric
1 inch	25·4 millimetres
1 foot	305mm
1 yard	0·914 metre
1 mile	1·609 kilometres

Metric	Imperial
1mm	0·039in
10mm (1cm)	0·394in
1 metre	1·094yd
1 kilometre	0·6214 mile

Approximate guide:
4in = 100mm
11yd = 10 metres
6 miles = 10 kilometres

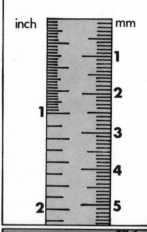

COVERAGE

yd²/gal	m²/ltr	m²/5ltr
1	0·18	0·90
2	0·37	1·85
3	0·55	2·75
4	0·74	3·70
5	0·92	4·60
6	1·10	5·50
7	1·29	6·45
8	1·47	7·35
9	1·66	8·30
10	1·84	9·20

CAPACITY

Imperial	Metric
1cu yd³	0·7646m³

Metric	Imperial
1m³	1·308yd³

Approximate guide:
4yd³ = 3m³

METRIC PAINT CONTAINERS

¼ pt	100ml = 0·022 gal
½ pt	250ml = 0·055 gal
1 pt	500ml = 0·11 gal
quart	1 litre = 0·22 gal
gallon	5 litres = 1·1 gal

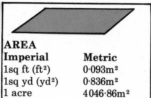

AREA

Imperial	Metric
1sq ft (ft²)	0·093m²
1sq yd (yd²)	0·836m²
1 acre	4046·86m²
(4,840yd²)	

Metric	Imperial
1m²	10·76ft²
1m²	1·196yd²
1 hectare	2·4711 acres
(10 000m²)	

Approximate guide:
12yd² = 10m²

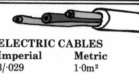

ELECTRIC CABLES

Imperial	Metric
3/·029	1·0m²
3/·036	1·5m²
7/·029	2·5m²
7/·036	4m²
7/·044	6m²

Use: Lighting, small power, ring power, cookers etc.

TEMPERATURE

Fahrenheit to Celsius (Centigrade)

$$C = F - 32 \times \tfrac{5}{9}$$

Celsius to Fahrenheit

$$F = C \times \tfrac{9}{5} + 32$$

Approximate guide:

Fahrenheit	32	40	50	60	65	70	75	80
Celsius	0	4·5	10	15·5	18	21	24	26·6

Approximately:
A difference of 10°F = difference of 5·5°C

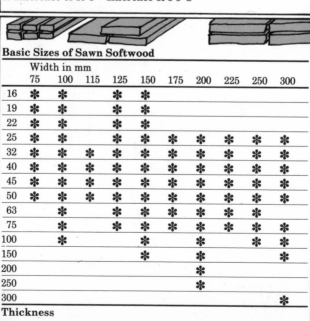

Basic Sizes of Sawn Softwood

	Width in mm									
	75	100	115	125	150	175	200	225	250	300
16	*	*		*	*					
19	*	*		*	*					
22	*	*		*	*					
25	*	*		*	*	*	*	*	*	*
32	*	*	*	*	*	*	*	*	*	*
40	*	*	*	*	*	*	*	*	*	*
45	*	*	*	*	*	*	*	*	*	*
50	*	*	*	*	*	*	*	*	*	*
63		*		*	*	*	*	*		
75		*		*	*	*	*	*	*	*
100		*			*		*		*	*
150					*		*			*
200							*			
250							*			
300										*

Thickness

BASIC LENGTHS OF SAWN SOFTWOOD

m	m	m	m	m	m	m	m
1·80	2·10	2·40	2·70	3·00	3·30	3·60	3·90
4·20	4·50	4·80	5·10	5·40	5·70	6·00	6·30

METRIC NOTE

			Symbol
Mega	means ×	1 000 000	M
Kilo	means ×	1 000	K
Hecto	means ×	100	h
Deca	means ×	10	da
Deci	means ÷	10	d
Centi	means ÷	100	c
Milli	means ÷	1 000	m
Micro	means ÷	1 000 000	μ

WEIGHT

Imperial	Metric
1 lb	0·4536 kilogrammes
1 ton	1·0161 tonnes

Metric	Imperial
1 kilogramme (1 000 grammes)	2·2046lb
1 tonne (1 000kg)	0·9842 ton

SHEET GLASS

Imperial	Metric
18oz is equivalent to	2mm
24oz is equivalent to	3mm
32oz is equivalent to	4mm
$\tfrac{3}{16}$in. is equivalent to	5mm
$\tfrac{3}{32}$in. is equivalent to	5·5mm
$\tfrac{1}{4}$in. is equivalent to	6mm

HEATING

The engineering industry is the last major one to change to metric, and imperial measurements may run parallel with metric until 1975. Both imperial and metric terms may be encountered as in the table below.

	Imperial Unit	Metric Unit
Pressure	inches water gauge (in wg) lb per square inch (lb/in²)	millibar (mbar) bar (bar)

1 N/m² (newtons per square metre) = 0·000 145 038 lbf/in² (lb force per sq in)

1 bar = 14·503 8 lbf/in²
(One bar equals 100,000 newtons per square metre)

Standard reference conditions for gas volumes

Temp.	60° Fahrenheit (60°F)	15° Celsius (15°C)
Pressure	30 inches of mercury (30″ Hg)	1013·25mbar
Sales unit	Therm	one hundred megajoules (100MJ)
Calorific value	British Thermal Units per ft³ (Btu/cu ft)	megajoules per cubic metre (MJ/m³)
Heat rate	British Thermal Units per hour (Btu/h)	kilowatt (kW)

OR, where information may be required to calculate running costs, megajoules per hour are used in addition to kilowatts — e.g. kW(MJ/h)

One kW is about 3,500Btu. To obtain the kilowatt equivalent in Btu/h, multiply kW by 3412 (exact equivalent). Thus, 4,000Btu equals 1·2kW (1,200 watts) and 100,000Btu is equivalent to 29·3kW. A therm equals 100,000Btu.

Heating and plumbing
Some, but not all, metric plumbing sizes are compatible with imperial. Tubes of ½in and 1in bore are interchangeable with the metric sizes 15mm and 28mm. Tubes of ¾in bore are not compatible with the 22mm metric size and a reducing set or adapter has to be used.

Tubes of 6mm and ¼in are also compatible; 10mm and ⅜in tubes are not and adaption is required.

Preparation of materials

Aluminium Thoroughly degrease, abrade with fine abrasive or etch with chromic acid. Wash in cold water and dry. Use caution.

Asbestos and fibreboards Abrade and remove dust. Use two coats of adhesive, dependent on porosity.

Brass and bronze Remove grease, abrade or etch with acid ferric-chloride. Wash and dry. Use caution.

Chromium Remove grease and abrade.

Concrete Abrade or chip up surface. Treat with PVA to seal pores.

Copper As for brass.

Oily wood Sponge with weak caustic soda solution and dry.

Polythene Remove grease and oxidize in flame or chromic acid. Caution.

Rubber Remove grease and dirt and abrade.

Mild steel Remove grease and abrade or etch with dilute phosphoric acid. Wash metal in cold water and dry thoroughly. Caution.

Stainless steel Remove grease and abrade or etch with hydrogen peroxide/formaldehyde solution. Extreme caution.

Wood Abrade and dry.

How to use this chart

Look across the top column to find the materials you wish to join. Then look down to the corresponding lines in the body of the chart until you find the symbols corresponding. From this point, follow the column across to find a suitable adhesive. There may be more than one adhesive satisfactory for the purpose.

If necessary, experiment to obtain the best results.

W = good water resistance.

For example, ceramic tiles (floor) can be joined to hardboard with contact adhesive, epoxy-resin, latex, PVA resin compound or synthetic rubber

Adhesive	Acetate Plastics (cellulose acetate)	Acetate Plastics (cellulose nitrate)	Acoustic Tiles (Fibre & Mineral)	Acrylic (Perspex)	Carpet (Not Foambacked)	Ceramic Tiles (Floor)	Ceramic Tiles (Wall)	Cork	Fabrics/Textiles	Flooring Thermoplastic Tiles	Flooring Vinyl Asbestos	Flooring PVC Backed	Flooring PVC Unbacked	Flooring Wood-block	Glass/china	Glass Reinforced Plastic (Fibreglass)	Hardboard	Leather	Leathercloth	Metal	Paper	Plaster (dry)	Plasterboard	Plastic Laminates	Polystyrene Expanded	Polystyrene Hard	Polythene	Rubber	Stone/Masonry	Thermoset Plastics	Wood
Acrylic plastic in solvent				●																											
Animal glue								●	●					●			●	●	●					●							●
Adhesive pads																	●						●	●							
Bitumen emulsion								●		●	●						●	●											●		●
Bitumen solution										●	●	●		●															●		
Bitumen rubber emulsion											●	●	●	●											●	●			●		●
Casein								W									W						W								W
Cellulose cement	●								●																						
Cellulose-water soluble																								●		●					
Cellulose nitrate in solvent		●																								●					
Clear general purpose	●								●						●			●	●		●					●					
Coal tar pitch			●			●																									
Contact			●		●	●	●		●		●						●	●	●					●					●		●
Cyanoacrylate			●		●	●		●												●											
Dextrine									●																						
Epoxy	W	W	W	W		W	W		W		W				W	W	W	W	W	W				W					W	W	W
Expanded polystyrene cement																									●						
Filled resin solution																															
Floor tile cement					●																	●							●		
Flour																						●	●								
Fuvane																															
Gum resin																	●														
Gypsum based																							●						●		
Latex			W		W	W	W	W	W		W						W	W	W	W						W					
Latex–Bitumen										●	●						●						●	●							●
Latex–Cement								●									●		●				●								
Melamine																															
Melamine formaldehyde																	●	●	●										●		
Natural rubber solution																	●	●	●					●							
Neoprene rubber solution																	●	●		●											
Phenol formaldehyde (PF)																	●	●		●											
Phenolic rubber																	●	●		●						●	●				
Polyurethane																				●											
Polyester																●	●	●													
Polystyrene in solvent																										●					
Polystyrene tile cement																	●					●									
Portland cement (thin bed)																							●						●		
Polyvinyl acetate (PVA)	●		●	●	●		●	●						●			●	●	●	●	●								●		●
PVA resin compound	●		●			●	●	●									●												●		
Resorcinol	W	W		W																W											W
Rubber solution																	●												●		
Rubber cement			●														●			●											
Silicone																											●				
Starch																	●														
Synthetic latex			●				●		●								●	●				●	●	●					●		
Synthetic rubber		●	●		●	●	●	●					●		●		●	●	●		●	●	●	●					●		
Synthetic rubber contact							●	●														●									
Urea formaldehyde (UF)																	W														W
Wallpaper paste																					●										
Wall tile cement							●															●							●		
Waterbased resin										●				●			●														
Product adhesive				●						●	●															●					●

1 French or round wire nail General carpentry, case making. Strong fixing, but unattractive, large head.

15	20	25	30	40mm
$\frac{5}{8}$	$\frac{3}{4}$	1	$1\frac{1}{4}$	$1\frac{1}{2}$in
45	50	60	65mm	
$1\frac{3}{4}$	2	$2\frac{1}{4}$	$2\frac{1}{2}$in	
75	90	100	115mm	
3	$3\frac{1}{2}$	4	$4\frac{1}{2}$in	
125	150	180	200mm	
5	6	7	8in	

2 Oval wire nail (oval lost or brad head) Joinery, unlikely to split wood if section follows grain. Head can be punched into wood.

20	25	30	40	45mm
$\frac{3}{4}$	1	$1\frac{1}{4}$	$1\frac{1}{2}$	$1\frac{3}{4}$in
50	60	65	75mm	
2	$2\frac{1}{4}$	$2\frac{1}{2}$	3in	
90	100	125	150mm	
$3\frac{1}{2}$	4	5	6in	

3 Round lost head Joinery. Head can be punched below surface leaving only a small hole.

15	20	25	30	40mm
$\frac{5}{8}$	$\frac{3}{4}$	1	$1\frac{1}{4}$	$1\frac{1}{2}$in
50	60	65	75mm	
2	$2\frac{1}{4}$	$2\frac{1}{2}$	3in	

4 Cut floor brad All-purpose carpentry nail. Strong holding, often replaced by oval and lost head.

20	25	30	40	45mm
$\frac{3}{4}$	1	$1\frac{1}{4}$	$1\frac{1}{2}$	$1\frac{3}{4}$in
50	60	65mm		
2	$2\frac{1}{4}$	$2\frac{1}{2}$in		
70	75mm			
$2\frac{3}{4}$	3in			
90	100	115mm		
$3\frac{1}{2}$	4	$4\frac{1}{2}$in		

5 Cut clasp General-purpose carpentry. Grips strongly.

25	30	40	50	65mm
1	$1\frac{1}{4}$	$1\frac{1}{2}$	2	$2\frac{1}{2}$in
75	90	100mm		
3	$3\frac{1}{2}$	4in		
115	125	150	180	200mm
$4\frac{1}{2}$	5	6	7	8in

6 Panel pin For light joinery and cabinet work. Fine gauge and head easily driven below surface.

10	15	20	25	30mm
$\frac{1}{2}$	$\frac{5}{8}$	$\frac{3}{4}$	1	$1\frac{1}{4}$in
40	50	65	75mm	
$1\frac{1}{2}$	2	$2\frac{1}{2}$	3in	

7 Veneer pin Very fine shank and head for small mouldings. In very fine work it is removed after adhesive has set.

10	15	20	25	30mm
$\frac{3}{8}$, $\frac{1}{2}$	$\frac{5}{8}$	$\frac{3}{4}$, $\frac{7}{8}$	1	$1\frac{1}{4}$in
40mm				
$1\frac{1}{2}$in				

8 Hardboard (deep-drive or diamond-point) pin Head is self-countersinking. 20mm ($\frac{3}{4}$in).

9 Screw nail For securing sheets of ply, hardboard or metal to timber, e.g. floors.

10	15	20	25	30mm
$\frac{1}{2}$	$\frac{5}{8}$	$\frac{3}{4}$	1	$1\frac{1}{4}$in
40	45	50mm		
$1\frac{1}{2}$	$1\frac{3}{4}$	2in		

10 Helical threaded nail For roofing, especially corrugated sheet. Thread gives some extra holding power. Usually used in conjunction with shaped washers.

40	45	50	60	65mm
$1\frac{1}{2}$	$1\frac{3}{4}$	2	$2\frac{1}{4}$	$2\frac{1}{2}$in
75	90	100mm		
3	$3\frac{1}{2}$	4in		
115	125	150	180	200mm
$4\frac{1}{2}$	5	6	7	8in

11 Plaster-board nail Has jagged sides to assist holding; 30mm, 40mm ($1\frac{1}{4}$ and $1\frac{1}{2}$in).

12 Clout nail (slate nail) Roofing, slating, fencing.

15	20	25	30	40mm
$\frac{1}{2}$, $\frac{5}{8}$	$\frac{3}{4}$	1	$1\frac{1}{4}$	$1\frac{1}{2}$in
45	50	65mm		
$1\frac{3}{4}$	2	$2\frac{1}{2}$in		
75	90	100mm		
3	$3\frac{1}{2}$	4in		

13 Extra-large head clout (felt nail) Roofing felt and external fabric.

15	20	25	30	40mm
$\frac{5}{8}$	$\frac{3}{4}$	1	$1\frac{1}{4}$	$1\frac{1}{2}$in

14 Pipe (chisel-point) nail Fixing drain pipes and gutters direct into masonry.

50	65	75	90	100mm
2	$2\frac{1}{2}$	3	$3\frac{1}{2}$	4in

15 Masonry nail Hardened steel to penetrate masonry and concrete. These pins must only be hit with a hardened engineer's hammer.

20	25	30	40	45mm
$\frac{3}{4}$, $\frac{7}{8}$	1	$1\frac{1}{4}$	$1\frac{1}{2}$	$1\frac{3}{4}$in
50	60	65mm		
2	$2\frac{1}{4}$	$2\frac{1}{2}$in		
70	75	90	100mm	
$2\frac{3}{4}$	3	$3\frac{1}{2}$	4in	

16 Chair nail Decorative upholstery work.

20	25	30mm
$\frac{3}{4}$, $\frac{7}{8}$	1	$1\frac{1}{4}$in

17 Cut tack Upholstery, carpets, canvas and other heavy fabrics.

5	10	15	20	25mm
$\frac{1}{4}$	$\frac{3}{8}$	$\frac{1}{2}$	$\frac{5}{8}$	1in
30mm				
$1\frac{1}{4}$in				

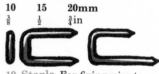

18 Sprig Headless tack for holding glass into wooden frames.

10	15	20mm
$\frac{3}{8}$	$\frac{1}{2}$	$\frac{3}{4}$in

19 Staple For fixing wire to wood. Made mostly from galvanised wire. Tenterhook has longer point on one side for easy fixing.

10	15	20	25mm
$\frac{1}{2}$	$\frac{5}{8}$	$\frac{3}{4}$	$\frac{1}{2}$in
30	40	50mm	
$1\frac{1}{4}$	$1\frac{1}{2}$	2in	

Better-nailing hints

Round wire nails–predrill hole to 80 per cent of shank diameter.

Drive nail through timbers and 'clench' (bend over) nail at angle to grain on reverse side.

Where possible use in conjunction with adhesive.

Dovetail nail in order of nailing shown below:

Nail through thinner material into thick. Do not nail in a straight line along run of grain, especially near ends of timber.

Nip off point of nail when nailing near timber ends, particularly on green wood.

When removing nails, always place a piece of scrapwood under the claw hammer or pincers and lever away from end of timber in direction of grain.

The nail for the job

Rough carpentry and heavy joinery	1, 2, 3, 4, 5
Light joinery and cabinet	2, 3, 6, 7
Wood sheet materials (hardboard, plywood, blockboard)	6, 8, 9
Plasterboard	11
Fixings to masonry	14, 15
Hard-roof coverings	10, 12, 13
Metal to wood	9
Fabric to wood	13, 16, 17
Roofing felt	13
Wire to timber or brickwork	19

Countersunk head (1) For general carpentry and joinery.

Roundhead (2) For fixing sheet material too thin to be countersunk.

Raised countersunk head (3) For use with ironmongery and screwcups where a high standard of finish is required.

Dome head For fixing mirrors and plastic panels. Head may be drilled and topped to take threaded shank of dome (4) or plastic snap-on fitting may be used (5).

Other drive methods **Phillips** and **Pozidriv** (7) heads both require special screwdrivers but the recessed cross-slots offer positive contact with the driver and less likelihood of drive-slip damage.

Clutch head (8) Non-removeable wood-screws; for security use.

Coach screws (9) Mainly used for heavy construction work. They are driven into prepared holes and given the final turns with a spanner. Use washers. Lengths: 18mm (¾in) up to 407mm (16in); thicknesses range from 4·76mm ($\frac{3}{16}$in) up to 12·7mm (½in).

Double spiral thread 'Twinfast' screws (10) are faster to drive, self-centering and have up to 25 per cent more holding power. Excellent for chipboard, blockboard and fibreboard.

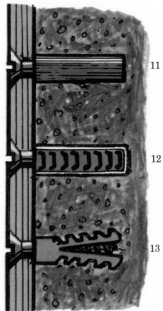

Wall fixings **Wall plugs** For inserting into masonry and concrete to give firm anchorage for wood-screwed fixings, fibre (11), alloy (12), plastic (13).

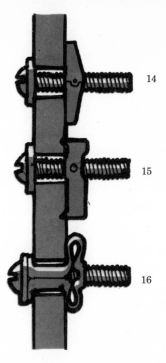

Cavity fixings For use in hollow walls: spring toggle (14) gravity toggle (15), plastic or metal collapsible anchor (16)

Heavy-duty bolts **Cup square, square carriage (or coach) bolt** (17) Lengths: 18mm (¾in)−407mm (16in) by 4·76mm ($\frac{3}{16}$in)−12·7mm (½in) thick.

Standard woodscrew sizes are not, as yet, metricated. The sizes shown are imperial sizes with metric conversions.

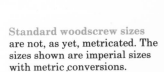

Screw and bolt accessories **Screw cups** Raised screwcups (18), countersunk screwcup (19).

Timber connector Double (20) and single-sided toothed plate. Placed between timber that are bolted together to stop twisting movement.

Generally preferred screw sizes

Length		Diameter 0	1	2	3	4	5	6	7	8	9	10	12	14	16	18	20	screw guage
in	mm	1·6	1·8	2·0	2·3	2·6	2·9	3·3	3·7	4·1	4·5	4·9	5·6	6·3	7·0	7·7	8·4	mm
¼	6·4	○	○	○	○	●												
⅜	9·5	○	○	●	●	●	●	●		○								
½	12·7		○	○	●	●	●	●	●	●	○	○						
⅝	15·9			○	○	●	●	●	●	●	○	○	●	○				
¾	19·1			○	○	●	●	●	●	●	●	○	●	○	○			
⅞	22·2				●	●	●	●	●	●	○	○	○					
1	25·4			○	○	●	●	●	○	●	●	●	●		○			
1¼	31·8				○	○	●	●	●	●	●	●	●	○	○			
1½	38·1				○	○	●	●	●	●	●	●	●	●	○	○	○	
1¾	44·5				○		●	○	●	●	●	●	●	●	○	○		
2	50·8				○		●	○	●	●	●	●	●	●	○	○	○	
2¼	57·2						●	○	●	●	●	○	●	●	○	○		
2½	63·5						●	○	●	○	●	●	●	●				
2¾	69·9							○		○		○	●	●	○			
3	76·2							○		●	○	●	●	●	○	○		
3¼	82·6											○	○	○				
3½	88·9									○		○	○	●	○	○		
4	101·6									○		○	○	○	○	○		
4½	114·3											○	○	○		○		
5	127·0												○	○	○	○		
6	152·4													○	○	○		

● Slotted and recessed head   ○ Slotted head

Tools for the job

Stripping and preparation tools

Blow lamp

Combination shave hook

Triangular shave hook

Stripping knife

Filling knife

Sand block

Pumice block

Finishing tools

Paint kettle

Paint brushes

13mm	25mm	38mm	50mm
½in	1in	1½in	2in
63mm	75mm	100mm	125mm
2½in	3in	4in	5in
150mm			
6in			

Cutting-in tool, used on window-frames and for painting straight lines

6mm	13mm	18mm	25mm

Radiator brush or crevice brush.

The right paint for the job

Interior Work

Surface	Paints	Primer and special preparations	Other qualities
Woodwork including high-density man-made boards	Emulsion paint two coats	For good-quality work. One coat lead-less primer after knotting	Thin with water; do not over-paint with oil paints
	Oil paint. One or two coats	Knot and prime (lead or lead-less); follow with at least one undercoat	Durable finish, easily cleaned. Withstands moisture. Thin with white spirit
	Plastic paints. One or two coats	Use knotting and primer on bare wood, otherwise rub well down. Follow maker's instructions	Non-drip (thixotropic). Dries quickly. Do not stir. Do not thin.
	Polyurethane. One or two coats	Follow maker's instructions	A very hard, good-quality finish. Thin as per instructions
Ceilings, walls and wall boards	Water paint (distemper). Two coats	Use coat thinned down as sealer for dusty or absorbent surfaces	Not washable or very durable. Cheap. Thin with water
	Oil-bound distemper. Two coats	Use coat thinned down as sealer for dusty or absorbent surfaces	Not washable or very durable. Cheap. Thin with water, but slightly more durable
	Emulsion paints. Two coats	Ensure surface is free from dust and loose particles	Washable. Not for use in high-condensation areas unless maker specifies. Thin with water
	Oil paint. Two coats	Ensure surface is free from dust and loose particles. Ensure surface is dry before applying undercoat	Washable. Do not use on plaster less than 6 months old. Thin with turpentine or white spirit
	Plastic paints. One or two coats	Thinned down leadless primer may be used as a sealer on dusty or absorbent surfaces	As for oil paint
Asbestos	Chlorinated rubber- or bitumen-based paints	Remove any loose particles and organic growth	Some oil-bound paints may be used but only if manufacturers recommend
Ferrous metals, e.g. iron	Oil paint. Two coats	Clean surface and use appropriate primer (usually a metallic suspension)	Easily chipped. Thin with turpentine or white spirit
Non-ferrous metals, e.g. copper, brass	Oil paint. Two coats	Clean surface with wire wool and white spirit. Use appropriate primer	Easily chipped. Thin with turpentine or white spirit
Walls	Cement paints. Two coats	Surface must be scrubbed free of loose particles and organic growth	Surface is liable to crazing
	Latex-based paints. One or two coats	Surface must be scrubbed free of loose particles and organic growth	Surface is excellent where movement is likely
	External quality emulsion. Two coats	Surface must be scrubbed free of loose particles and organic growth	Less durable than cement or latex-based paint
	Oil paint. Two or three coats	Surface must be scrubbed free of loose particles and dry. Use appropriate primer	Only suitable over rendered surfaces
Ferrous metals, e.g. iron	Oil paint. Three coats	Clean surfaces. Use special primer	Apply only in warm, dry weather

Exterior Work

Surface	Paint	Primers and special preparations	Other qualities
Woodwork	Oil paint. Three coats	Knot and prime (lead-based primer). Use two undercoats	Paint only in warm, dry weather. Ensure surface is dry
	Oleoresin or resin varnish. Synthetic varnish	Timber may be stained before varnish or scumbles may be used. Ensure no grease is present	Paint only in warm, dry weather. Ensure surface is dry
Fences	As for woodwork		
	Coal-tar paints paints and preservatives. Two–three coats	No special preparation needed	Most types cannot be painted over
	Water- or spirit-based preservatives	No special preparation needed	Most types cannot be painted over

Binding materials

Hydraulic lime Used to make lime-mortar. Will set under water and is, therefore, excellent for building thick walls which will retain moisture.

Non-Hydraulic lime For cement-lime (or gauged) mortar. Needs penetration of atmosphere to achieve proper set. Both types of lime are termed hydrated and are obtainable ground and slaked ready for use.

Portland cement So called because of its resemblance to Portland stone. Most general all-purpose building and concreting cement.

White portland cement Will provide an attractive finish to most decorative surfaces, e.g. decorative wall blockwork and grouting.

Masonry cement Is specially mixed without added lime to give a mortar of good plasticity and high bonding strength.

Coloured portland cement (Ready mixed). Strength is generally lower than ordinary Portland cement, and 10 per cent to 15 per cent more cement should be used. Colouring agents may be added to ordinary or white Portland cement.

High-alumina cement or ciment fondu Must not be mixed with other cements or limes; cleanliness is important when using this. It has very-high early strength, allowing early movement and use of castings. Good chemical resistance and heat-resisting properties; unsuitable for load-bearing usage.

Aggregates

Aggregates should be washed clean and be free of clay and vegetable matter.

Coarse aggregates

5mm to 20mm (washed, graded) shingle for foundations, lintels, drives, paths and floor slabs, 75mm thick and over.

5mm to 10mm (washed, graded) shingle for thin sections and screeds 36mm to 75mm thick; also suitable for decorative wall blocks, rough cast and pebble-dash rendering.

5mm to 10mm pea shingle Usually pea- or bean-shaped with no sharp edges. Good workability but little strength. Unsuitable as concrete aggregate other than for brushed-surface finish. It can be used for rough-cast and pebble-dash.

Fine aggregates

Sand is generally classified as pit or river sand. Seashore sand should never be used as its salt content causes excessive efflorescence. Pit sand is mainly used and it can be divided into two varieties–washed sharp and loamy. River sand is less suitable for brick-laying mortar than pit sand due to small amounts of salt.

Washed sharp sand for mixing with coarse concrete aggregates, or with cement alone, for use as screed or rendering. Builders' soft sand is not suitable for these purposes.

Builders' sand A mixture of sharp and loamy sand, suitable for all brick and block laying.

Other aggregates

All-in ballast Coarse and fine aggregates may be bought ready mixed; a drawback is that grading is not so accurate and volumes of coarse and fine aggregates are not accurately gauged.

Mixing cement and concrete

The best results are obtained if the amounts of each material used are gauged (measured) accurately. To this end a simple wooden gauge box should be constructed. The size is unimportant, but it should be easy to handle and not too heavy to carry when full.

Concrete and mortar additives

Waterproofers may be added to mixes to give water repellent properties.

Retarders reduce the setting time of concrete, thus allowing more time for placing and compacting.

Accelerators Particularly useful in low-temperature conditions.

Plasticiser gives greater workability by increasing plasticity to all forms of mortar. It should not be used with masonry cement.

Concrete and mortar mixes by volume

Materials		Hydrated limes				Light aggregates (A)			Coarse aggregates (A)		Combined all-in aggregates (B) — Alternatives to A & B		
Uses	Portland cement	Hydraulic lime	Non-hydraulic lime	Masonry cement	High-alumina cement	Sharp sand	Builders' sand	Vermiculite	20mm–5mm	10mm–5mm	20mm	10mm	Special considerations
Foundations, drives, floor slabs	1					2½			4		5		
As above but where moisture is excessive	1					2			3		3¾		
Paths, pools, steps, edgings and thin sections	1					2				3		3¾	
Setting in fence posts	1					2½			5		6½		Use as dry as possible
Insulating screed for floors	1							6					50kg cement to 2×110 litre bags vermiculite. Lay 36mm–50mm thick
Topping cement/sand screed for vermiculite floors	1					4							Do not lay plastic flooring until thoroughly dry.
Reinforced lintels and fence posts	1					2			3		2½		Choice depends on size of member. Allow one month per 25mm thickness of concrete screed
	1					2				3		2½	
Decorative blocks and paving slabs	1					2				4		4½	White or coloured cement may be used. Add 10–15% extra cement if coloured
Bedding for paving		1					3						
	1						8½						
Joints for paving	1						4						
Floor screeds	1					3							Use plasticizer
Path screeds	1					2				3		2½	
Load-bearing, engineering bricks retaining walls	1		¼				3						Any exposure
Sills and copings	1		½				4½						As above
	1						3						
Free-standing walls, work below DPC, unrendered parapets	1						3						As above
	1		1				5½						
				1			3						
External walls between DPC and eaves; unrendered parapets	1		1				5½						Severe weathering
				1			3½						
As above		1					2-3						For sheltered areas but should be pointed with stronger mix
	1		2				8-9						
				1			5						
Inner-leaf cavity walls	1		1				5½						
				1			4¼						
Internal walls	1		2				8½						
				1			6						
		1					3						
Where frost is likely during construction	1		2				8½						Plus plasticizer to entrain 8%–12% air
	1						7						
Rendering and plastering (internal)				1		4-6							
	1		2			9							
render and floating coats	1		1			6							
External rendering soft brick	1		1			6							or between two, dependent upon suction of background
hard brick	1		2			9							
Pargetting (liming) for open-fire flues	1		3			10							
Firebacks and barbecues					1		4-5						
Sealing gas-proof flue liners					1	3							
Flaunchings	1		1			6							
Pointing-mix engineering brick	1						2						
other brick	1		2				8						
Sealing stoneware sewer pipes					1	3							

Classification of Timber

Hardwood and Softwood

The division of timber into hardwoods and softwoods is based on botanical distinction and long usage rather than the relative hardness of the wood. (Parana pine, a softwood, is considerably harder than balsa or obeche, both hardwoods.)

Conversion

is the term applied to the way in which a log is cut up into smaller standard sized pieces.

Hardwoods belong to the broad-leafed class of timber, most of them being deciduous. They include oak, mahoganies and birches; also balsa. These are mainly used in high-quality joinery because of their strength, durability and good appearance.

Hardwood sizes

Length is as available. Some species of tree produce shorter lengths than others, but wood is charged to the next 100mm length if not already in multiples of 100mm.
Width 50mm, rising in stages of 10mm, depends on species.
Thickness 19mm, 25mm, 32mm, 38mm, 50mm, 63mm, 75mm and 100mm, rising thereafter in 25mm stages.

Softwoods are derived from narrow-leafed evergreen trees (conifers), which grow mainly in northern, temperate climates.

Softwood sizes

Standard metric lengths start at 1·8m and go up in increments of 300mm.
Planed softwood timber stock is referred to by its sawn (nominal) size; deduct 3mm from sawn sizes to allow for planing; thus 25mm × 50mm PAR (planed all round) is 22mm × 47mm in actual size, though this can vary slightly.

Planed softwood timber is not available as standard or commonly held stock in all sawn sizes.

Floorboards

Hard and softwoods are used for flooring. Redwood is used for ordinary good-quality work, whitewood and spruce for cheaper work and pitch pine and hardwoods (e.g. oak and maple) for top-grade work.

Boards of 25mm nominal thickness and less are only used when the joists are laid at 400mm centres or below.

Floorboards are planed on one side, laid planed side uppermost, and have two planed edges.

Commonly available softwood nominal floorings are:

mm	100	125	150	175
32			*	*
25		*	*	*
22	*	*	*	*
19	*	*	*	*

*Nearly always tongued and grooved (T & G).

Man-made boards

fall into three groups:

Laminated boards, such as blockboard, laminboard and plywood

Fibreboards, which covers hardboards, insulation boards and wall boards.

Particle boards, sometimes called compo board – woodchip boards

Datasheet Timber

Laminated boards

Blockboard and laminboards both consist of strips of softwood timber-core strips laid between timber veneer or lamins, the grain of which runs at right-angles to the core strips. Both types of board can have one or two facing lamins (3-ply or 5-ply) and either or both of the faces may be a hardwood, though commonly birch is used. Lamin board is less likely to warp than blockboard.

Decorative surfaces available include afromosia, ash, elm, mahogany, oak, teak, walnut, cherry, rosewood and pine.

Uses and grades of plywood

Marine	Waterproof, with two perfect sides	For boats and exterior work
Two clean faces	Both sides clear of knots	For general furniture and cabinet work
One clean face, plugged reverse	Knots on reverse side have to be taken out and plugged	Backings for furniture and for work requiring only one good face
One clean face, knotty reverse	Knots and splits on reverse	As above
Plugged both sides	Knots plugged on both sides	Work to be painted or veneered
Face side plugged knotty reverse		As above
Knotty both sides		A cheap grade used for backings where not seen. Will take plastic laminates

Hardboards

are available in a wide range of sizes and finishes. Some of these are:
Standard hardboard must have a density in excess of 880kg per m³.
Tempered hardboard has greater strength and improved moisture resistance. It is made by impregnating standard hardboard with oils or resins, then applying heat treatment.
Duo-faced hardboard Board which is smooth on both sides.
Pre-primed or sealed board Boards specially formed or treated after manufacture to obviate the need to prime and/or seal before painting.

Peg-board Hardboard perforated with circular, square or other holes.
Moulded hardboard The board is embossed with a pattern.

Plastic-faced hardboard
PVC faced A decorative sheet of PVC is bonded to the hardboard.
Melamine faced A resin-bonded, decorative-paper lamination is bonded to the hardboard and faced with melamine resin.
Wood-grain hardboard A melamine plastic laminate with a photograph of the wood grain in the surface or direct on to the hardboard.

Enamelled hardboard Hardboard lacquered or enamelled and usually stoved.
Others Other finishes on hardboard include flame retardant and true-wood veneered.

Maximum fixing centres to wooden frameworks:

Standard hardboard and tempered hardboard

3·2mm	405mm
4·8mm	510mm
6·4mm	610mm

Nails or screws should be applied at 100mm centres round the edges of the board and at 150mm–200mm along intermediate fixings.

Particle board

consists of compressed wood chips bound together with one of several resins. Wood chip board, as it is commonly called, has many uses, e.g. furniture making, flooring and partitioning.

Decorative chipboards are obtainable where the surfaces have been veneered, with either wood or plastic laminate, or treated with a painted melamine finish.

Thicknesses of unsurfaced wood chip boards: 12mm, 15mm, 18mm, 22mm, 25mm.

Sizes:	3660 (12′)	3050 (10′)	2745 (9′)	2440 (8′)
1830 (6′)		X		
1525 (5′)	X			
1220 (4′)		X		XO
610 (2′)				XO

Flooring grades are available in sizes marked O and may also be bought with T & G or grooved edges.

Datasheet Woodwork–Handtools

Planes, paring and shaping tools

4 Bench plane Most commonly used tool for preparing, trueing and smoothing the surface of timber. Sizes vary from 237mm × 44mm up to 550mm × 60mm. **Block plane** Small plane 156×41mm. (not shown).

Hammers

1 Pin hammer Has lightweight head for small pins and tacks.

2 Warrington hammer Like the pin hammer, it has a cross-piece for starting off small-headed pins. This hammer is most favoured by joiners and cabinet makers.

3 Claw hammer The claws are set for withdrawing nails; mainly used for rough and heavy work.

Chisels and gouges

5 Sash mortice or London pattern Very-heavy construction to allow for leverage when chopping across grain mortices; sizes 3mm-25mm.

Gouges For paring curves;

6 in-canal for concave curves;

7 out-canal for convex curves; sizes 3mm radius–150mm radius.

8 Firmer For heavy carpentry and joinery work, its strong construction makes it ideal for chopping out joints in heavy joist construction; sizes 6mm-75mm.

9 Bevel-edged Most favoured by cabinet makers also for fine joinery; Sizes 3mm-75mm.

Boring tools

10 Brace A tool used in association with various types of BIT for boring holes in wood.

11 Hand drill or Wheel Brace Used for holding smaller sized bits, both for wood and metal-work.
Bit Tool piece used with brace or hand drill.

12 Expansive bit adjustable; the 'set' of the thread varies dependent on use, i.e. for hardwood or softwood; 13-40mm or 16-75mm diameter.

13 Jennings-pattern auger bit smooth boring, preferred by cabinet makers; 5-40mm diameter.

14 Solid-centre auger bit general purpose; 5-40mm diameter.

15 Forstner-bit brace tang though expensive it is unequalled for fine work; it is unaffected by knots or grain; 5-50mm diameter.

16 New-pattern centre bit clean cutting of shallow holes especially plywood; 5-56mm diameter.

17 Rose-head countersink.

18 Screwdriver bit useful for removing stubborn screws.

19 Woodworking hand-drill bit for smaller sizes, use low-speed metal drills, but keep only for woodwork as timber has a ruinously dulling effect; 6-13mm diameter.

Screwdrivers or turnscrews Are available in many shapes and sizes. Sizes are measured by width of tip in relation to screw gauge and length e.g. No. 8 × 200mm. Common types are:

20 Pozidriv For use with Pozidriv cross-head screws which offer greater contact with tool tip than standard slotted screws; blades 75mm-15mm.

21 Engineer's or instrument has parallel tip. For small screws, invaluable when deep sunk; blades 150mm-450mm.

22 Cabinet pattern General-purpose tool; blades 75mm-300mm.

23 Spiral-ratchet Pump action enables rapid insertion of screws. Can also be locked rigid. Wide range of bit types and size including drill bits; closed lengths 120mm-500mm.

Tips from the trade

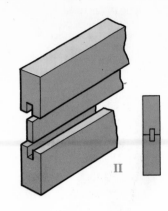

Tongued-and-grooved joints
for joining edges and particle board.

11 Tongued-and-grooved with loose tongue. The easiest tongued-and-grooved joint to make. The tongue may be made of plywood; the grooves must be deeper than half the width of the tongue.

II

Common joints used in carpentry and joinery

Halved and lap joints
for general framing, carcase and light structural work. All may be pinned or screwed and glued.

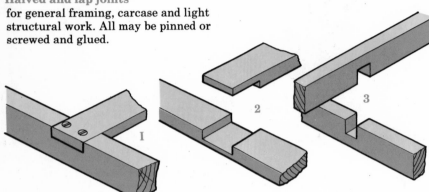

I2

Dowelled joint
for cabinet work.

12 Hidden-dowel joint. Most common furniture joint. If dowel extends through 'A' it is a through dowel; simple to make and dowel ends may make a design feature.

2

3

1 Full lap T-joint.

2 T-halving joint or T-half lap.

3 Cross halving joint and cross halving cut on edge.

4 Dovetail halving joint. Used where 'A' has to carry weight or, if 'B' is vertical, it is likely to splay.

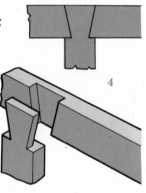

Mitred corner joint

13 Glued-and-pinned plain mitre. The simplest mitre joint most commonly used for picture framing.

4

I3

9 Simple, through-housing joint. For joinery and cabinet carcasing, e.g. shelving and stair treads.

10 Stopped housing joints; as 9 but has a neater finish.

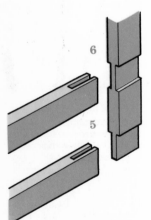

Rebate and housing joints
for neat, simple joinery.

7 End rebate joint; for carcasing e.g. bookcases.

8 Rebate housing or barefaced, tongued-and-grooved joints. General carcasing e.g. bookcases.

6

5

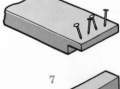

I0

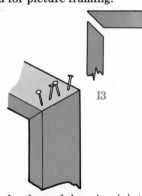

Bridle or open mortise joints
for framing and carcasing.

5 Corner-bridle joint; can be used for joining chair arms and legs.

6 Through-bridle joint gives a stronger finish than the halving joint.

7

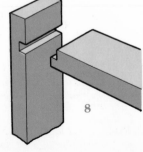

8

9

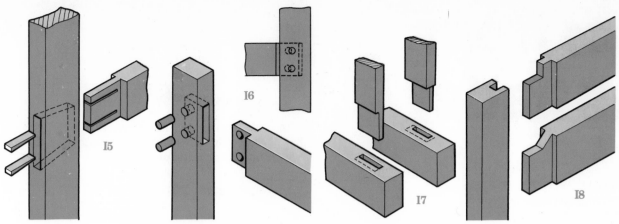

Mortise-and-tenon joints
the joint most commonly used where strength is required.

15 Wedged, through mortise and tenon. Tenon should extend 2mm beyond mortise to allow for trimming.

16 Stub mortise-and-tenon. In this case through dowelled. Note how holes are offset to allow dowels to draw up the tenon.

17 Barefaced tenon with single shoulders. Shoulders conceal any gaps in the work.

18 Haunched mortise-and-tenon and secret-haunched tenon; for furniture and high-class cabinet work.

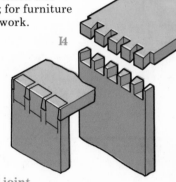

Dovetail joint
the strongest joint for corners.

14 Open-dovetail joint; most suitable for boxes, but if well cut, can be effective decoration.

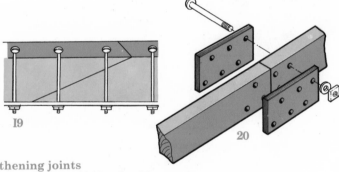

Lengthening joints
19 Simple scarf joint. May be glued for light work, otherwise it should either be screwed or bolted together with metal fish plates.

20 Fish-plate joint. A strong joint. Plates may be either plywood or mild steel.

Simple joints for man-made boards

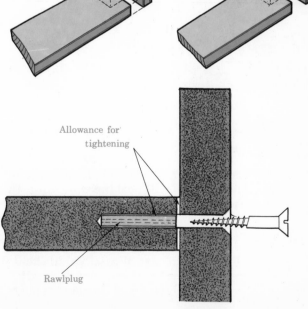

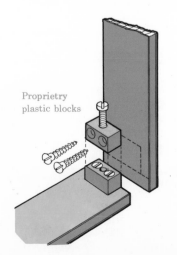

Proprietry plastic blocks

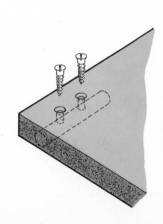

Allowance for tightening

Rawlplug

Tips from the trade

Nails

Use nails which are two to three times longer than the thickness of the timber they have to hold, and always nail light work to heavy.

To ensure strong joints, nails should be clenched. These are driven in from opposite directions and the

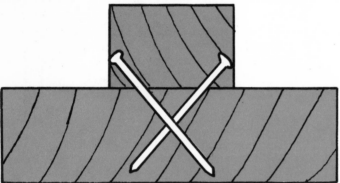

points are bent into the wood. Where joints meet at right angles, these should be skew-nailed (nailed at a right angle).

Dovetail nailing, with nails 'fanned' slightly

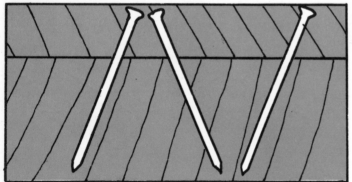

inwards, provides the best grip when nailing into the end grain.

Use a cramp to steady a frame when skew-nailing flat joints. The first nail will hold the work while the second is being driven in.

When nailing near an edge, if possible cut the wood overlength and then cut and plane to length after nailing. This will reduce the danger of timber splitting at the edges.

Avoid nailing into hardwood. If you have to nail, first bore guide holes slightly smaller than the nail shank and then hammer in the nails.

To prevent unsupported wood from 'bouncing' when being nailed, hold a stout piece of timber firmly against the unsupported side.

Secret nailing is a technique which does not show a nail or a nail hole. One method is to chisel up a

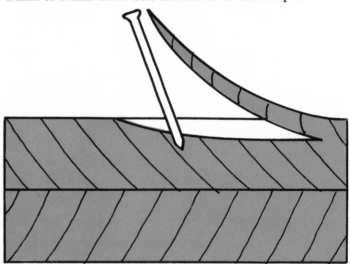

sliver of wood and drive a nail into the recess. Cut the sliver out carefully and take care not to bruise the surrounding timber when you nail. Drive the nail below the surface of the hole and then carefully glue the sliver back on top of it so that the nailing is concealed.

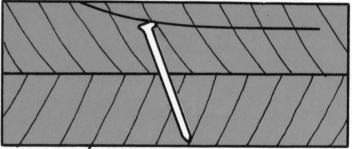

Secret nailing into tongued-and-grooved board is done by nailing at an angle through the tongue and shoulder of the board into the supporting joists or batten. The nail will not be seen when the next grooved section is fitted into place.

Small nail holes are best concealed by punching the nail below the surface of the timber with a nail punch and filling in the hole with a filler or stopping. Use a vegetable dye or ink to match the surrounding wood.

Tips from the trade

Screws

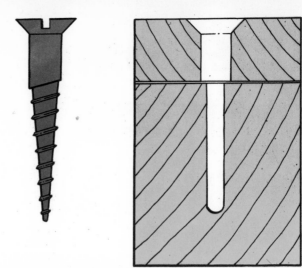

When screwing into end grain, screw fixings can be strengthened by driving the screws into a glued dowel, inserted across the grain.

If you are screwing into an awkward corner, use a drill bit in a spiral ratchet or an offset screwdriver. These will reach where a conventional screwdriver cannot.

Counterboring a joint enables you to fix thick wood to thin, using a shorter screw. Drill the counter-bore before drilling the clearance holes for the threads.

Chiselling out or boring a pocket in the workpiece is another way of counterboring. This method is used to fasten table or bench tops.

To ensure drilling accuracy, mark the position of a screw with intersecting lines. Bore the holes to the same diameter as the screw shank.

After countersinking, check that the depth is correct by making a trial insertion of the screw head. The depth of a thread hole should be half the length of the screw if fixing into softwood. It should be slightly deeper for hardwood. When tightening a series of screws, all should be tightened equally, or the surface may distort.

Depth of a thread hole should be half that of the screw length; fixing depth is slightly longer deeper for hardwood.

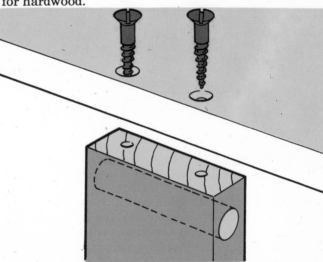

End-grain fixings are strengthened by screwing into a dowel inserted and glued across the grain.

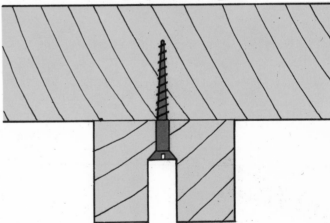

Thick timber can be fixed to thin by means of counter-boring before fixing. The counter-bore is drilled before thread clearance holes.

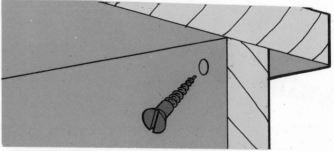

Counterboring can be done by first drilling or chiselling a pocket. This system is used to fix bench or table tops.

279

Tips from the trade

Wood fixings

When using a hammer clean the face frequently on a piece of fine or worn glasspaper. Greasy hammer heads can cause damage by bruising both wood and fingers.

A piece of hardboard or plywood under the head of a claw hammer or pincers will prevent damage to the work when pulling out nails.

Hit nail heads squarely with the hammer to prevent bending. A straight line of nails will weaken timber and cause splitting – always stagger them.

On a glued and nailed joint, punch the nail head slightly below the surface while the glue is still wet. This gives better cramping action and pulls the surfaces closer together making a stronger joint.

Use a nail punch which suits the size of the nail head to avoid unsightly holes.

Cut the head off a panel of veneer pin and use the shank in a hand drill to bore small holes. This is particularly useful when pinning fine beadings or picture frames as it will avoid splits in the timber. In hardwoods it will avoid bending the pins and causing damage.

A screw will be inserted much more easily if it is dipped in wax polish or soap.

When using brass screws, always insert a steel screw of similar size first. This will cut the thread for the brass screw and prevent it from twisting off or being left with a damaged head. This is particularly important in hardwood.

When putting in a number of screws, start them all with the slot pointing in one direction. They will all end up with the slots pointing the same way – giving a pleasant decorative effect.

A pair of dividers set to size will prevent a great deal of repetitive measuring with a ruler.

Always use an engineer's pattern type of hammer when knocking in hardened masonry nails. The face of a carpenter's hammer is too soft and could fracture, sending off a steel chip at high speed causing physical damage, perhaps to an eye.

To remove stubborn or rusted screws, place the screwdriver in the slot and bang the handle heavily with a hammer and mallet. This will jar the screw and in most cases release the grip of the wood on the screw thread.

A hot soldering iron or metal rod held on the head of the screw will cause it to expand. On contraction the grip of the screw on the wood will have been weakened.

When cutting sheet material use a chalk line to 'snap' a straight line across the surface of the material.

Always put a shallow groove in a dowel. This allows air and surplus glue to pass out as the dowel is driven in.

A coating of wax will prevent glue sticking where it is not required.

Tips from the trade

Woodwork

Test the quality of a hand saw by springing the blade into a curve. The curve should be regular and the blade perfectly straight when released.

Insert a wedge into the saw cut when ripping along a plank. This will prevent the saw from binding.

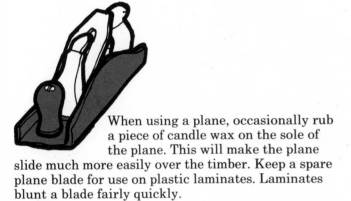

When using a plane, occasionally rub a piece of candle wax on the sole of the plane. This will make the plane slide much more easily over the timber. Keep a spare plane blade for use on plastic laminates. Laminates blunt a blade fairly quickly.

Hammering the point of a nail to make it slightly blunt will help to prevent it from splitting the wood when nailing close to the edge.

To fasten a panel pin into an awkward position where it is difficult to hold, push it through a strip of thin card or paper and use this to keep the pin in place when nailing.

When sawing veneered or faced boards always saw with the face side up. This will help to prevent splintering on the good side. Also to prevent splintering, cut the veneer on the reverse side of the saw cut with a knife and stick clear adhesive tape over the line.

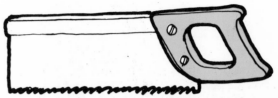

If you are boring a large hole in narrow timber, place a cramp across the width, to avoid splitting.

Where a saw cut is being made with the wood held in the vice, make sure that the wood is level or it will be difficult to saw to the line. When a cut is being made at an angle, adjust the timber so that the line appears to be vertical. The saw is then used in a vertical position.

A 'bruise' in wood may be lifted out with a damp cloth and a hot iron. An alternative method is to fill the dent with water and leave overnight. This will cause the grain to swell and the depression to disappear.

As most machine oils are too thick for use on oilstones, use a mixture of 50 per cent machine oil and 50 per cent paraffin when sharpening tools. A slightly hollow oil stone may be made flat by rubbing it on a sheet of plate glass covered in carborundum grinding paste.

A solution of oxalic acid will remove many stains from the surface of timber–but it is poisonous and must be kept away from children and be clearly labelled.

Never keep workshop solutions or preparations in bottles which children associate with drink. This could lead to serious accidents. Keep all such solutions high up or in a locked cupboard.

Waterproof Indian ink makes a good matt black stain for small items, such as picture frames.

Screw eyes will often make good shelf supports for small shelves.

A sticking drawer may be eased by rubbing candle wax on the bearing/running surfaces. Graphite will also do this.

Furniture finishing

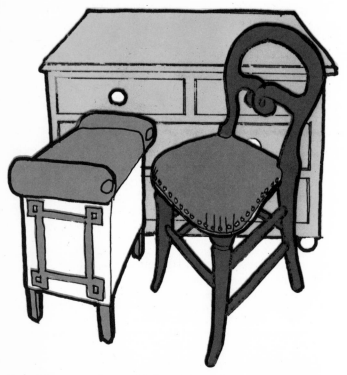

Scumbles, sometimes called graining colours, are generally used for hand-graining cheap woods to make them look expensive. Specially formulated to 'stay put' wherever they are applied, they do not flow out like orthodox oil paint–so enabling various designs to be made with a dry brush, a piece of cloth or a graining tool.

Scumbles may be bought in various colours from specialist stockists of decorators' materials.

You also need cellulose paint. As this dries quickly, do not brush it out. Just lay it on the surface with broad sweeps of a brush; you can also buy it in aerosol containers and spray it on. It can be thinned and applied with a spray gun.

Imitation gold leaf

A finish nearly approaching that of gold leaf is achieved by applying a sticky varnish, leaving it until it just starts to dry. Next, rub in fine bronze dust, using a lintless cloth, in a circular polishing motion. Bronze dust may be obtained from colour merchants and artists' sundries shops. This is used for picture frames, shelf edging and enriching reliefs.

Antique effect on picture frames

This process may be employed to make a new picture frame look old. After varnishing the surface, rub in bronze dust and leave for a few days to harden; paint on a dark-coloured scumble and, while this is still wet, rub off the highlights with a soft, lintless cloth–so leaving brightly burnished reliefs and dirty-look valleys.

An ordinary oil paint would also be suitable, provided it were well thinned and applied sparingly, so that the bronze underlay in the interstices slightly 'grins through'.

Crackle finish

Achieved by painting with a brush a short, brittle coat over a flexible undercoat–such as a hard, fast-drying oil paint over an ordinary undercoating, to which a little boiled linseed oil has been added to make it softer.

Another way is to apply a light-coloured scumble over a dark ground coat and then scratch on the pattern with a pointed tool. This will take longer, but it will enable you to control the position and extent of the 'crazing'.

In this case, scumble must be used; paint will flow out to fill the cracks as fast as you make them.

Using a spray gun or aerosol container, you can get a realistic crackle by spraying through plumbers' tow; this is first teased out and stiffened with glue size.

Another method using glue size is to coat the whole surface thickly with glue–relying upon the contracting property of the drying glue to craze the painted surface. Wash off the glue and then varnish the surface.

Ebonising

Where the substrate is oak, apply an iron-salt solution liberally. Iron salt is sulphate of iron dissolved in water. You can make it yourself by immersing bits of iron in vinegar for several days; or by leaving rusty nails in water for a week.

For other woods, treat the surface with tannic-acid solution which can be made by boiling oak galls, oak bark or scraps of oak in water. When the surface has dried, rub down and polish or varnish. In all cases, the black improves with time.

A good way to ebonise a staircase rail is to apply three or four coats of black cellulose paint, rubbing down between coats with fine abrasive paper. Leave for 48 hours and rub with fine steel wool moistened with soap.

Fumed oak

This is only a suitable treatment for small objects. Place the article on a grid over a pool of ammonia in a sealed box. Use care when opening the box as ammonia fumes are unpleasant.

If you wish to darken an oak fence, add oil-soluble nigrosine powder in a small quantity of naptha to creosote, and brush on. Another way, but not quite so good, is to add carbon black in white spirit to the timber.

Application should be made in warm weather when the timber is dry and its pores enlarged so that there will be adequate penetration.

Blackening steel

Clean with fine steel wool and household abrasive cleansing powder. Then mix the following, by volume, in this order: 125 parts of water, 15 parts of nitric acid (always add acid to water; never water to acid), 30 parts of alcohol, eight parts of copper sulphate. Apply the mixture and polish when dry.

Antique-leather effect

Applied over a rigid surface. Use a dark brown scumble over gold paint. If oil scumble is used, give a buffer coat of clear lacquer first.

Tips from the trade

Paperhanging

Seam rollering with safety Rollering the joins on wallpaper, particularly heavy varieties, ensures adequate adhesion of otherwise vulnerable edges; though, by laying

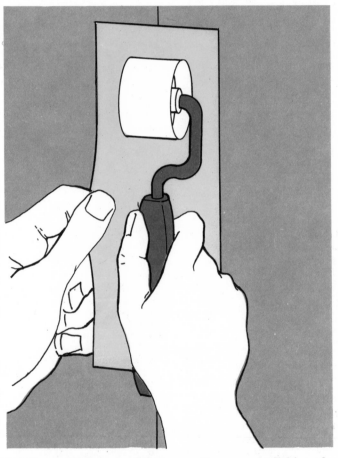

the fibres of the paper, rollering could cause a 'polish' mark to show. To prevent this, insert a strip of ordinary paper (toilet paper will do) under the roller.

Surmounting shading difficulties As you open rolls of paper and compare them, you may be disappointed in the difference in tone from edge to edge or from roll to roll. This is a fault of the printing process and, if pronounced, will show when the paper is hung. If the paper is plain or a random pattern you can often overcome the edge-to-edge difference by inverting every other length you hang. Where the difference is not from edge to edge but down the length – though not so likely – see if another roll has the same difference. If so, cut one length from one part of one roll and the adjoining length from the same part of the second roll.

Where half the rolls are printed on the light side and the remainder on the dark side, hang light-toned rolls on side walls and those that are darker on the wall facing the window. Light striking the latter will even out the tone and the difference at the corner of the room where the papers abut will not be noticed.

Crooked top edge No room is built with mechanical precision, and where the picture rail – or, if no picture rail, the angle between wall and ceiling – are considerably off horizontal, do not use a large-patterned paper because the design at the top of each length will accentuate the imperfection. Use a plain paper or one with a less-pronounced pattern.

When to size and seal If in doubt whether to size a surface before papering it, dampen a finger and press it to the wall. A surface that is 'hot' will soak up the moisture immediately and will require size. Never size an emulsion-painted surface because size has a contracting action which could loosen the bond between the emulsion and wall plaster. The adhesive of a paper would do the same damage. Seal the emulsion coating with an oil-penetrating primer or coat of oil paint, thinned with the same quantity of white spirit. Seal hardboard with hardboard primer before papering.

Awkward joins If your supply of paper runs short, use off-cuts over a door or under a window. People seldom look over the top of a door when leaving, and curtains and furniture will detract from the window area. In any case, it will be relatively shaded there and imperfections will not be readily seen.

Stains on a chimney breast Wall stains that 'bleed' through wallpaper should be sealed in with two coats of aluminium primer sealer before hanging the paper. Then add a small quantity of whiting or finely powdered pumice to the paste to give more grip to such an impervious surface. Where stains are very pronounced, metal-backed lining paper may have to be used.

Where not to use vinyl Where a wall is uneven or pitted and cannot easily be made good, use ordinary wallpaper, not vinyl, as the latter will show up every mark.

Papering new walls Allow several months to elapse for new walls to dry out before papering, because damp will bring forward alkali salts which interfere with the chemical constituents of adhesives and could also cause colour change of greens and blues, or even staining.

Adhesive problems A growing number of papers are prepasted. Where you have to do your own pasting, remember that cellulose pastes, though they may not stain the surface, do not soak papers so evenly as starch and flour pastes. Heavy papers should, therefore, soak for eight minutes and then be repasted with an almost dry brush and hung immediately; otherwise blisters may form. With lightweight papers, paste one length and put it on one side. Paste a second length and then hang the first.

Painting over old wallpaper Use emulsion, not oil paint, because oil causes the fibres in paper to disintegrate.

Patching up To patch over an indelible mark on a paper, place a small new piece over the mark, with patterns matching, and cut round it with a sharp knife, penetrating new and old papers, down to the substrate. Then scrape off the old paper up to the knife cut and the new piece will fit exactly.

Another way is to tear the patching piece away from the printed side to 'feather out' the edge. Treat a polystyrene lining that has been inadvertently damaged in stripping an old paper, by the first method.

Avoiding hazard Before hanging wallpaper, always fold pasted pieces inwards and put these under the pasting table, out of the way. Pasted paper is slippery and could cause a nasty accident.

ABC of terms

Carpentry and joinery

Tools are listed in the TOOLS Data Sheet. Screws, nails and fixings are similarly treated.

A

Abrasives Materials used for grinding or rubbing down to fine surfaces, e.g. sand, glass, garnet papers, wet and dry paper, emery cloth, sanding discs, pumice powder (used mainly in conjunction with French polish) and wire wool.

Architrave Mouldings surrounding a door or window.

Arris Sharp edge formed by the meeting of two surfaces. In brickwork and masonry the corners of bricks and stones are known as arrises.

Arris rail Triangular sectioned timber held between fence posts by means of galvanised brackets or mortice and tenon joints upon which is suspended fence boarding.

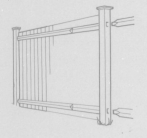

B

Balcony Balustraded platform projecting from an upper-storey window.

Baluster Vertical members of stair handrail.

Balustrade Coping or hand-rail supported by balusters.

Banister, Bannister Handrail running parallel to the incline of a staircase.

Barge-board Sloping board fixed to the end of a gable as a decorative finish, also called Verge or Gable board.

Barge-couple End pair of rafters which overhang a gable end.

Batten Term specifically used in the description of timber. Battens are from 50mm to 100mm thick × 125mm to 200mm wide. Slating and tiling battens are from 16mm to 32mm thick × 25mm to 100mm wide (usually 50mm × 25mm or 38mm × 19mm).

Beading A small timber or plastic moulding, used as decoration or finish.

Beam A long, heavy plank or bulk of timber; a long section of steel, light alloy or reinforced concrete used to support a load.

Bearer Section of material used to displace a load. See Beam, Joist, Lintel.

Bevel An angle which is not a right-angle, the slope on the edge of a mirror, a tool used for marking out with an adjustable blade.

Bezel The cutting edge of a plane iron, chisel or other cutting tool.

C

Cabinet making High-class joinery, as found in quality furniture.

Capillary action The movement or travel of a fluid by means of surface tension. See also Osmosis.

Capillary groove Horizontal groove on the underside of window-ledges to stop capillary action carrying water back to the brickwork.

Carcase construction System of construction based on a box system.

Carcasing The lowest grade of soft wood.

Carpentry Includes permanent structures such as floors, roofs, partitions and temporary work such as trench timbering. This is opposed to joinery, which covers lighter, but finer wood-craft, such as windows, stair-cases and panelling.

Casement Windows hinged on one vertical edge. See also Window.

Cavetto mould See Mouldings.

Ceiling joist Wooden ties between walls from which ceilings are suspended.

Centering Temporary wooden frame around which arches are built or from which plastering is scribed. (See also Folding Wedges.)

Chamfer Right-angled corner or bevel removed symmetrically, i.e. 45°.

Coach screw Screw with coarse pitched thread and square or hexagonal head.

Cross tie Transverse connecting piece.

Cubic metre Measurement of hardwood.

Cupola Small domed roof.

D

Deadwood Term applied to sub-standard redwood timber which has insufficient strength for building purposes.

Deal General term frequently applied to coniferous softwoods.

Death-watch beetle Insect whose grub bores into or out of timber.

Dote or Doatiness A form of decay showing as patches of grey stain speckled with black.

Dormer Vertical window in slope of pitched roof.

Double-hung Sash windows suspended by ropes or chains and counterweights over pulleys.

Dowel A straight-sided, circular-sectioned pin, used to hold two pieces of timber together.

Dragon beam Piece of timber to which a hip rafter is fixed. The dragon beam is in turn fixed to an angle tie.

Druxiness Timber decay appearing as whitish spots or streaks; a form of fungus.

E

Eaves The lowest over-hanging part of a sloping roof.

Elliptical bullseye An elliptically shaped window.

Escutcheon Metal plate surrounding or lining a keyhole.

Extension hinges Hinges used for hanging casement windows and doors, allowing them to open beyond the brick opening.

F

Face edge/side The first side and edge of a piece of timber to be trued. It is marked thus:

Fascia board Length of timber fixed vertically at the lowest end of rafters or spars.

Feather edge Boards cut to a thin wedge shape tapering from about 18mm or 25mm on one edge to 6mm on the other; usually used for fencing, cladding sheds and exterior walls.

Figured Pattern in timber caused by the effects of grain.

Fillister A rabbet (rebate) cut into window mouldings to receive glass and putty.

Firrings Wedge-shaped pieces of timber nailed to the horizontal joists of a flat roof to allow a 'fall', thus enabling water to run off.

Fixed sashes A window which cannot be opened.

Floor joists Structural or bearing timbers suspended between supporting walls upon which floorboards are laid. They must be sufficiently large to support safely the load the floor is required to carry.

Folding wedges used to hold an arch centre in position

Folding wedges

Folding wedges Wedge-shaped pieces of wood placed under temporary support. Two are used, one upon the other. Knocking them together forces the temporary support into a fixed position.

Formwork Demountable structure acting as mould for concrete.

Framed, ledged and battened door

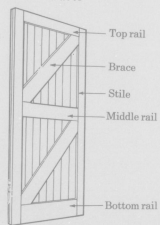

A common door construction for outhouses etc. When the stiles are not incorporated it becomes a ledged and braced door

Franked joint A joint where one moulded bar is cut into a moulded rail or stile in windows or doors.

G

Gable The triangular-shaped wall enclosed by the ends of a ridged roof or following the shape of a ridged roof above its level.

Glazing bar The wooden bars in a mullioned window.

Glazing bead Strips of timber used together with putty or chamois leather to hold glass within a frame.

Grain Surface pattern and texture of wood caused by the direction and composition of the fibres.

H

Herring-bone strutting Pieces of timber cross-braced between joists in continuous rows to make the joists more rigid. These comprise pairs of inclined pieces of timber tightly fixed between joists.

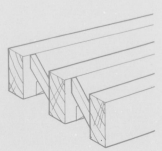

ABC of terms

K

Kerf The cut made by a saw.
King post Vertical support between a tie beam and the roof ridge incorporated within the framework of a roof.

L

Lantern light A box-shaped glazed skylight mounted on a roof.
Loose tongue Strip of timber or metal used to join the grooved edges of two boards.

Movement allowance Cut timber shrinks and expands, mostly across the grain, according to the ambient temperature and humidity. This movement is taken into consideration when, for example, setting in door panels, by allowing room for movement when cutting the grooves in which they sit.
Mullion A vertical member dividing windows.
Muntin Vertical members dividing the panels of a door.

Hips The line where two sloping edges of a roof meet. The rafter at this line is called a Hip Rafter and a roof of this type a Hip Roof.

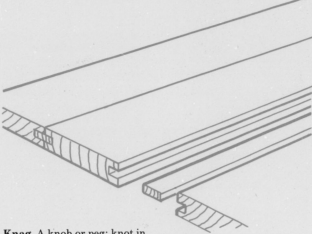

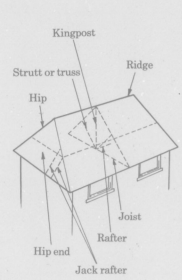

Knag A knob or peg; knot in wood.
Knot Round or oval-shaped, cross-grained piece within a sawn board, the result of a growing branch before the tree was felled.
Knuckle The line where the leaves of a hinge meet and fold round the hinge pin.

M

Matching Another name for tongued-and-grooved boards.
Meeting rails See **Sash windows**.
Mouldings

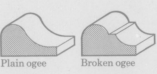
Plain ogee   Broken ogee

Ovolo

Astragal   Double astragal

Single

Reeded linen fold

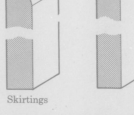
Double

Horns (or Joggles) The waste portions of timber left on the top and bottom of door stiles to give protection in transit. These are removed when the door is hung.

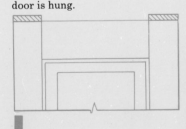

I

Internal spring-door hinges Spring-loaded hinges used for door hanging, which cause the door to close automatically.

J

Jack rafters Rafters of varying lengths running between the eaves and the hip rafter of a roof.
Jamb Vertical face inside a door or window opening; the vertical side members of doors or windows.
Jib-door Door whose face is flush with its surroundings decorated so as to camouflage it.
Joinery See **Carpentry**.
Joist Timber or steel beam supporting a floor or ceiling.

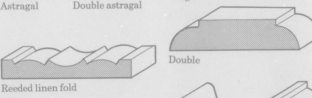
Scotia   Triangle

Skirtings

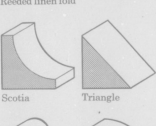
Hockey stick   Quadrant

Glass bead

Halfround   Cock bead   Parting bead
(with quirk)

Top rail

Muntin

Frieze rail

Muntin

Hinge stile   Closing stile

Mid or Lock rail

Muntin

Bottom rail

N

Neatsfoot oil Extracted from the hooves of cattle; it is the best lubricant for oilstones.
Newel Main supporting post for stairs and banisters (See **Stairs**)
Noggings Structural members in flooring or within a stud wall. (See **Studding**).
Nosing The overhanging portion of a stair tread. (See **Stairs**).

O

Ogee See **Mouldings**.
Oilstone A fine-grained stone used with a lubricant for sharpening tools. Among the finest is Arkansas but carborundum, India or Washita are acceptable.
Oilstone slip Small oilstones shaped to fit curved tools such as gouges.
Ovolo See **Mouldings**.

P

Parting bead See **Mouldings**, also **Sash windows**.
Patera Wood or metal covering to conceal a screwhead.
Pilot Screw Brass screws are liable to shear when used in hardwood. To overcome this problem, a steel pilot screw is inserted, then withdrawn, to make way for the brass screw.

ABC of terms

Carpentry and joinery

Planted Mouldings
See **Solid Mouldings**.

Plinth A low platform or base upon which a column or cupboard stands.

Pocket screwing A method of inserting screws when assembling a table or cupboard top.

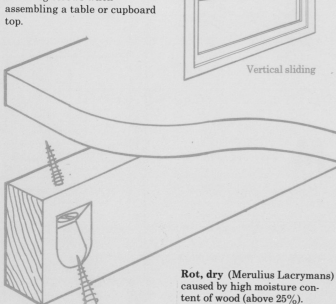

Purlin Horizontal roof member running at right-angles to the rafters along their mid-point.

R

Rafters Sloping timbers in a roof framework. (See **Hip**).

Rails Horizontal members of a door or table frame. (See **Muntin**).

Rebate (or Rabbet) Step cut along an edge of a piece of wood.

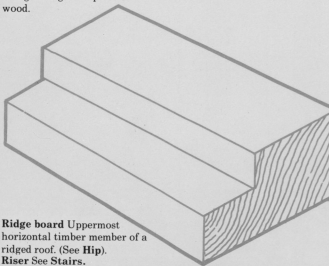

Ridge board Uppermost horizontal timber member of a ridged roof. (See **Hip**).

Riser See **Stairs**.

Rot, dry (Merulius Lacrymans) caused by high moisture content of wood (above 25%). Called 'dry rot' because of the dry and friable condition of affected wood.

Rot, wet (Coniphora Cerabella) caused by excessive moisture content of wood (optimum growth at 50–60%) combined with lack of ventilation.

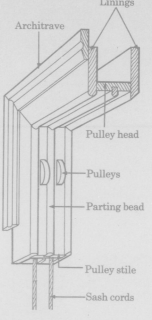

Architrave · Linings · Pulley head · Pulleys · Parting bead · Pulley stile · Sash cords

Vertical sliding

Access pieces to weights · Traditional timber sash window · Sill

S

Sapwood See **Timber Data sheet**.

Sash windows

Scantlings Term applied to timbers measuring from 50 to 100mm thick by 50 to 100mm wide. The stile timbers of sash window frames. (See **Sash windows**).

Seasoning The process of drying out timber to allow shrinkage to take place before the timber is used.

Shakes Splits which occur in timber during or after seasoning.

Sharpening angle The angle to which the *bezel* on cutting tools is honed on an oil stone. For general work this is 30°.

Sheradizing Process whereby steel is coated with zinc as a rust preventative.

Shingle Wooden roofing tile, used where weight considerations are important, usually oak or red cedar.

Skirt (Skirting board) Board running round the walls of a room, at floor level, to protect the plaster. Modern skirts may be plastic instead of wood.

Sole Plate See **Studding**.

Solid or stuck moulding Those worked ('stuck' means worked) into timber framing or panels in doors, as opposed to those fixed on by nails, i.e. planted moulding.

Stairs A series of steps joining one level to another.

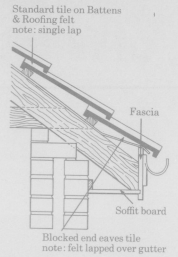

Soffit board Horizontal board fixed to the underside of overhanging rafter.

Standard tile on Battens & Roofing felt note: single lap · Fascia · Soffit board

Blocked end eaves tile note: felt lapped over gutter

Eaves detail Double pantile

Stiles Vertical members of a door, window frame or staircase. (See **Muntin**).

String (or Stringer) Side member of a staircase or ladder.

Studding Structural timber framework or skeleton within a dry, stud or framed partition wall.

T

Template (Templet) Metal, wood or card mould or outline, used as a guide when shaping materials.

Trenail Another name for a dowel peg.

V

Veneer Thin sheets of decorative timber, cut 730mm to 1·5mm thick, glued to a stable but uninteresting timber base. Veneers may be either knife or saw cut, the latter being almost unobtainable.

W

Wainscot Timber lining, frequently panelled, of the walls of a room.

Wallplate Length of timber, 100mm × 75mm, laid on brick wall, to which joists or roof members may be fixed.

Wane (or waney edge) Bark-covered edges of boards after they have been sawn from the log.

Winding A twist or kink in boards due to bad seasoning. Also a line of posts which are not vertical are said to be 'out of winding'.

Woodworm Loose generic term for wood-boring insects.

Wall string Main angled side member of a staircase nearest wall.

ABC of terms

Decorating

A

Acetate Salt, or ester of acetic acid, the base of several types of paint; clear plastic film.

Acetone Clear liquid solvent, particularly good for removing cellulose paints and adhesives.

Acrylic paint Emulsions of various acrylic esters and other polymers; generally hard wearing; available in most finishes.

Alkali Water-soluble compounds, such as soda, potash and ammonia, having caustic or corrosive action.

Alkali-resistant paints Porous surfaces – cement paint, lime wash, bitumen emulsions, some copolymer emulsions, acrylic emulsions. Impermeable surfaces – chlorinated rubber based, some hard gloss (check manufacturers' claims), bitumen solutions, chemically cured paints.

Agglomerates Collection of mass, e.g. agglomerates of pigment, i.e. lumps of undispersed pigment.

Aniline dye A chemical compound derived from coal tar.

Anti-condensation paints Used where limited condensation occurs; contain absorbent filler which makes small amounts of condensation inconspicuous.

B

Beaumontage A wood filler, comprising a solid stick of shellac which is melted; used mainly in cabinet and antique work.

Binder The residue left after the thinner or solvent has evaporated from paint, varnish, enamel or lacquer film.

Binding-down paint Contains large quantities of penetrating medium which bind down easily crumbled absorbent materials, such as old plaster surfaces or distemper.

Bituminous paint Paint composed of either emulsions or solutions of coal-tar bitumen; used where cheap, good resistance to water is required.

Brushing out The initial multi-directional application of paint with a brush to get maximum even coverage before LAYING OFF.

Burning in Application of beaumontage using a hot knife.

Burning off Method of removing old paint by causing it to soften and then blister by application of heat from a blow torch. Once blistered, the paint may be removed with a shave hook.

Butt-joining Joining wall coverings such as wallpaper and hessian so that there is no overlap.

C

Carnuba wax (or Brazilian wax) Hardest of all waxes, melting at 85°C, yellow in colour, particularly suitable for polishing turned work.

Casein Protein of milk used in the manufacture of certain paints and glues.

Catalyst An accelerator of changes brought about by chemical reaction.

Ceiling tiles A decorative application for ceilings, having sound- and heat-insulation properties. They can be made of expanded polystyrene, wood fibre or mineral fibre.

Cellulose Substance extracted from paints, but now mainly synthetic materials are used; the basis for some paints and fillers.

Cement paint Cement-based paint particularly suitable for painting direct on to new brick and masonry where no movement is likely.

Copal varnish A varnish based on hard fossilized gum resin.

Copolymer Correctly called condensation polymerisation, the process of making polymers with the formation of small, easily removed molecules, often water, for each step of the process. See POLYMERISATION.

Cork The product of the cork oak used for cladding walls, either in sheets or tiles.

Cove A shaped cornice made of plaster or expanded polystyrene.

Cross lining Method of hanging lining paper horizontally in order to disguise joins when the final paper is applied.

D

Dado The lower part of a wall when decorative treatment is different to the upper portion.

Damar A resin, softer than copal, used in the manufacture of varnish.

Distemper An obsolete paint based on colour pigment, whiting (finely ground chalk) and size.

Driers A catalytic substance added to paint to accelerate drying or hardening.

Drop The difference in position of motifs that make up an overall pattern on wall coverings.

Drying-out time The time taken for new plaster and brickwork to dry out. During this period paint should not be applied.

E

Efflorescence Natural salts within brick, mortar and plaster appearing on the surface; can cause paint to blister and flake off.

Emulsion A milky liquid in which is suspended oily or resinous particles.

Emulsion paint Can be sub-divided into copolymer, PVA (polyvinyl acetate), and acrylic. All may be thinned with water. All emulsion paints are suitable for use on plaster and masonry, but only acrylic emulsions are recommended for use on woodwork.

Enamel A general term for free-flowing pigmented varnishes or lacquers drying to a hard gloss or semi-gloss finish; usually characterized by absence of brush marks.

F

Fabric wall coverings Hessian Unmounted 1 830mm wide; on paper backing usually from 508mm to 534mm wide.

Felt Several different grades and a vast range of colours available, 1 830mm wide.

Silk Finely woven silk on a background of paper, 508mm to 534mm wide.

Filler
1 An inert substance, e.g. china clay, barytes, silica or whiting, mixed into paint to give it solidity.
2 A product, usually cellulose based, used for filling grain and cracks in timber, plaster and other painted surfaces.

Flock Shredded cloth fibres, applied to a tacky surface (either adhesive or paint) to form a cloth-like finish.

French polish Solution of shellac and industrial alcohol, applied in conjunction with raw linseed oil. French polish is agreed to be the highest form of polished finish for furniture.

Frieze Horizontal decorative band at the top of a wall between architrave and cornice, cove or ceiling.

G

Glaze Process of applying a coloured translucent paint or varnish over an opaque ground to give a quality of depth and lustre to the finish.

Grain varnish Imitates natural wood grains by applications of paint and varnish with special brush techniques.

Grout Decorative, waterproof filler used between ceramic tiles and mosaic.

Ground of colour Background of plain colour over which designs may be printed or painted.

H

Heat-resisting paint Contains variously silicone or butyl-titanate as heat-resistant mediums; used frequently in conjunction with aluminium pigment.

Hue The tonal quality or tint of colours.

J

Jelly (or **thixotropic**) **paint** Having the consistency of thick jelly, does not settle in the can and can be applied quite thickly without the likelihood of runs or sags. Jelly paints should not be stirred as this will dissipate the thixotropic quality.

K

Key Condition of workpiece enabling paint to adhere to a surface.

Knotting A shellac-based treatment, painted on to knots in wood to stop resins bleeding through subsequent layers of paint.

L

Laying off The action of the final brush strokes that give a painted surface a smooth finish.

Lead paint Lead used to be the base for most good-quality paints; now, with the exception of red lead and white lead primers, it has been almost totally replaced by synthetic resins.

M

Marbelling (marbling) Imitation of marble by special painting technique similar to grain and varnishing.

Masking tape A self-adhesive tape which may be stuck to a surface to prevent paint adhering.

Matt Dull, not glossy.

Medium Liquid vehicle for pigments in paint, e.g. oil, water.

Mordant Chemical to stop dyes fading, e.g. dichromate of potash.

Mosaic Decorative effect created by sticking pieces of glass, marble or ceramic on to background in form of pattern. Individual tiles used are called tessera(e).

N

Nitro-cellulose Extract of raw cotton mixed with nitric and other acids. The basis for many lacquers.

ABC of terms
Decorating

N

Non-lifting Term applied to a medium which has little or no solvent action upon previously painted surfaces.

O

Odourless Paint Has chemical additives which neutralize the 'medium' odours.
Oil paint Paint having oil as a medium or vehicle.

P

Parquet Wooden flooring consisting of hardwood blocks or veneers laid in geometrical patterns.
Paste Adhesive for wallpapers, formerly mixture of flour, water, borax and alum or washing soda; sometimes Scotch glue was added. These mixtures have been largely replaced by cellulose and PVA-based adhesives which, unlike flour pastes, do not discolour the paper.
Patina Quality of surface texture and colour, found on old polished furniture mellowing by time, usage and much polishing.
Pigment The finely ground substances added to paint medium to impart colour.
Polyurethane paint Synthetic resin based paint and varnish available mostly in 'one-pack' but also in 'two-pack' form. All one-pack polyurethanes are excellent for interior use though some are suitable for exterior use.
Polymerization The process whereby plastics, resins and rubbers are synthesized by uniting two or more molecules of a substance to form a molecule (polymer) with the same composition as the original substance (monomer).
Polyvinyl acetate A polymerized derivative of ethylene (a colourless gas) used as a base for glues, floor coverings, paint and fabrics.
Primer First coat of sealing paint or varnish applied to wood or metal in order that subsequent coats will adhere.
Putty A 'doughy' mixture of whiting and linseed oil used for filling blemishes in timber after priming: Also for holding glass within a frame.
PVA–Polyvinyl acetate.

Q

Quick-drying paint Paints based on highly volatile, usually alkyd, thinners and media, for use where time is short.

R

Resin Extract of timber, but also synthetics; soluble in alcohol or ether. Base of many paints.
Rubbing compound Fine abrasive powder for taking surface off paints.
Rust Loose particles on the surface of iron, formed by oxidization and due to exposure to water or air.
Rust inhibitor Paint primer for iron which excludes oxygen.

S

Screed A thin layer of plaster on a wall. A thin layer of concrete applied for the purpose of evening or levelling surface of floor.
Self-levelling screed. A resin-based screed in form of creamy liquid.
Sealers General term applied to a finish to bare wood or metal to close up the pores.
Selvedge The edge of cloth where it is woven to prevent unravelling; the waste edge of wallpaper, which is cut off before hanging.
Shellac Coloured resin produced on tree-bark by insects. The basis of varnish and polish.
Size Thin, liquid glue or paste used as a sealer on walls prior to hanging paper.
Skived ornament A form of Anaglypta; where individual three-dimensional motifs are stuck by their edges to a flat surface to make up an overall pattern.
Soda block Soluble abrasive block, containing soda and pumice, used with water, to clean down and abrade paint before redecorating.
Solvent Liquid capable of dissolving or softening other substances.
Spray painting Method of painting where paint is forced, by pressure of air or gas, through a small nozzle, causing it to fall evenly on a surface in a fine spray.
Stipple To drag the surface of tacky paint or plaster up into points to give a decorative effect.
Stopping Filler for surfaces prior to painting or polishing.
Strippers Various mixtures of chemical solvents applied to paint to ease its removal.
Stucco A fine-ground plaster used for wall decorations, particularly good for stipple and relief work.
Sugar soap A caustic substance, dissolved in water, for washing down dirty paintwork prior to redecorating.
Swedish putty A filler, mainly for external use, made by mixing oil paint and plaster of Paris or cellulose filler. Emulsion paint is sometimes used instead of oil paint.

T

Tears Dribbles of paint due to thick, uneven application.
Tesserae Small tiles used in mosaic work to make up a pattern.
Thinners Liquid, a solvent or water, mixed with paint to make it more workable.
Turpentine Volatile solvent, distilled from pine tree gum, used in the manufacture of certain paints and varnishes.
Turpentine substitute– White spirit.
Two-part paints Epoxy-resin based paints mixed with catalyst immediately before use. Mainly for exterior and marine use.

U

Undercoat A high-opacity keying paint which dries quickly.

V

Varnish A transparent or translucent finish. Traditionally consisting of resins such as shellac, linseed oil and turpentine.
Vehicle Liquid part of paint and other finishes.
Vinyl distemper Inexpensive form of emulsion paint having a high filler content. It is only suitable for dry conditions.

W

Wallpaper/_Anaglypta:_ An embossed material made from cotton fibre, resembling plaster. Good for covering badly cracked walls and ceilings. Patterns are three-dimensional; the material is sold in standard-length rolls and in panels of various sizes.
Wallpaper/_Embossed_ paper is best for disguising bad cracks or unevenness in walls or ceilings. This has the design pressed into it with a metal roller, so that it stands out in relief.
Wallpaper/_Flock paper:_ This has the appearance of velvet. Made by gluing silk, nylon or wool cuttings to the surface of the paper so that the design stands out in relief.
Wallpaper/_Hand-printed paper:_ Produced by block, screen or stencil printing.
Wallpaper/_Ingrain paper_ (or woodchip): An 'oatmeal' texture is given by the addition of small wood chips and sawdust to the paper pulp during manufacture.
Wallpaper/_Lincrusta:_ A putty-like material, made from linseed oil and fillers bonded to a flat backing paper. It is available in simulated wood panelling, or with textured effects.
Wallpaper/_Lining paper:_ Essential on some surfaces, but advisable before all papering where first-class results are required. Lining papers are available in several weights.
Wallpaper/_Machine-printed paper:_ The most common type of wallpaper. The design is printed on to the surface with rollers, in up to 20 colours. The cheaper papers, known as 'pulps', have the design printed directly on to the paper, while the better-quality and more-expensive papers are coated with a 'ground' of colour before the design is printed.
Wallpaper/_Moires:_ A watered silk effect, similar to moire material and achieved by means of a fine emboss.
Wallpaper/_Pitch-coated lining papers:_ Available for use on walls that are affected by dampness; should be pasted on the pitch-coated side.
Wallpaper/_Raised plastic prints:_ These papers have a raised surface but a flat back.
Wallpaper/_Washable paper:_ A transparent coating of synthetic resin protects this paper from penetration by water, making it suitable for use in bathrooms and kitchens.
Wallpaper/_Vinyl wall covering:_ Made from a layer of paper-backed PVC, which can either be printed or given a textured finish. This material is very tough and it will not tear when handled. It is also steam and water resistant.
Wet-and-dry paper Waterproof abrasive sheets used for rubbing down paintwork. Used in conjunction with water which acts as a lubricant.
White spirit Petroleum distillate used as a substitute for turpentine.
Wood-block-flooring Similar to, and cheaper than parquet; thinner strips of wood are used.

Y

Yellowing Term applied to white paint or coating which turns cream due to fault in composition.

Z

Zinc chromate Mixed with phosphoric acid as an etching primer for use on galvanized metal before applying zinc-chromate primer. Ordinary paint is then used.

ABC of terms

Electricity

A

Alternating current (AC) An eleric current which reverses (alternates) its direction of flow at a regular rate, generally 50 cycles a second. Most domestic supplies are **AC.**

Ampere (amp; A) The unit of electric current. It denotes volume of flow and may be compared with the number of gallons or litres flowing in a water pipe.

Armature The rotating coil of a dynamo or motor.

Auto-transformer A single-winding transformer in which the primary voltage (input) is applied to the whole winding and the secondary voltage (output) is taken from tappings on the winding (see shaver socket).

B

Ballast Equipment used with discharge lamps (fluorescent tube lights are a form of discharge lamp) to stabilize the current.

Bonded Term applied to pipes and other metalwork, connected together electrically to ensure a common potential; particularly applied to earthing.

Busbar A metal conductor which forms a common connection between several circuits. Found on consumer units.

C

Cartridge fuse Small fuse link used in plugs and fused connectors–13A coloured brown for appliances with over 750W load; 3A coloured red for appliances and lamps under 750W. Some consumer units also have cartridge fuses called HRC (high rupture capacity).

Ceiling rose An electric lighting point attached to a ceiling

Cleat Method of supporting or holding an electric cable.

Choke A device fitted to discharge lamps to give an initial starting boost or charge of electrical current. Sometimes called a 'starter'.

Current The movement or 'flow' of electricity measured in amperes.

Circuit-breaker A switch adapted for automatically closing. In the event of over-loading or a short circuit, the switch breaks contact.

Conductor A single wire or group of wires in continuous contact with each other.

Conduit A pipe, metal or plastic, for enclosing cables to protect them against damage.

Consumer board or unit Consumer's fuse board, usually incorporating an on-off switch.

Contact The part of an appliance or an accessory, such as a socket, plug or switch to which conductors are fixed. Also known as a terminal.

Core A conductor of a cable, including insulation, but not protective covering.

D

Dead Description of electrical circuits disconnected from any source of supply or live system.

Direct current (DC) An electric current which does not change its direction; usually from battery supply.

Discharge lamp A lamp in which light is produced by the passage of electricity through a metallic vapour or gas enclosed in a tube or bulb.

Double pole A switch in which the circuit is broken at both live and neutral poles simultaneously.

E

Earthed circuit A circuit connected to earth at some point.

Earth-continuity conductor The conductor, including any clamp, connecting to the earth lead or to each other, all those parts of an electrical installation which are required to be earthed. Earth wire is green or green-and-yellow sleeve.

Earth electrode A conductor providing a means of connection to the general mass of the earth.

Earthed Effectively connected to the earth mass.

F

Feeder Cable or other conductor used to supply electrical energy to a distribution system.

Final sub-circuit Any outgoing circuit connected to a consumer unit in order to supply electricity directly to a current-using appliance.

Fluorescent lamp A tubular discharge lamp producing a shadowless white or coloured light.

Fuse Deliberate 'weak link' to protect a circuit. Consists of thin wire, which melts when excessive current flows. Fused connector unit used on a ring main or spur to connect an appliance without the use of a plug.

H

Horse power (hp) The practical unit of mechanical power (one hp=746W).

I

Insulator (insulation) A non-conducting material used for enclosing, surrounding or supporting a conductor.

Inverter An inverted rectifier used for converting direct current (DC) into alternating current (AC).

J

Joint box A box that forms part of a wiring installation for joining two lengths of conductor together.

Junction box Similar to joint box, but used where three or more conductors join together.

K

Kilowatt (kW) Unit equal to 1.000 watts.

Kilowatt-hour (kWh) The amount of electricity used by an appliance is measured in kWh. This is 1,000W used continuously for one hour.

L

Live A conductor, circuit or appliance connected to a source of electrical potential; live wire is red or brown sleeved.

Load The power delivered by a machine or piece of apparatus.

Loop-in circuit Method of fitting lighting circuit.

Lumen (lm) The SI unit of luminous flux. Used in describing the total light emitted by a source or received by a surface.

Lux (lx) Unit of illumination: defined as the illumination produced by light emitted from one candle falling directly on to a surface at a distance of one metre.

N

Neutral conductor (Neutral wire) The black or blue sheathed conductor in a cable. flexes have blue conductor.

O

Ohm The unit of electrical resistance denotes the resistance of the wires to the passage of electricity. Ohms law is the basis of electrical calculations.

Open circuit A circuit in which flow of current is temporarily interrupted.

P

Pole The part of a magnet where the lines of force leaving or entering the iron are concentrated. One of the polarities of a supply, e.g. live or neutral.

Potential Electrical pressure is generally measured in volts.

Protective device Any device to protect electrical plant from the effects of abnormal conditions by automatically isolating the faulty part of the system.

Protective multiple earthing (PME) The continuation of metalwork associated with electrical apparatus to a conductor wire which is earthed at each consumer's installation and at other points.

R

Radial circuit A system of electrical distribution in which the circuit cables radiate from a consumer unit.

Relay A device, operated electro-magnetically by the current in one circuit, which causes contacts to close or open to control the current in another circuit.

Resistance (electrical) The resistance which a conductor or appliance offers to the flow of current when an electro-motive force is applied to it.

Resistance heating Heating by passing electric current through a body of high resistance.

Rheostat An adjustable resistance for current regulation.

Ring main A circuit arranged in the form of a ring which starts from and returns to the sub-circuit fuse or circuit breaker.

S

Shaver socket (see auto-transformer)

Short circuit A connection, accidental or otherwise, between two sides of a circuit.

Single phase Applied to a circuit or apparatus where a single alternating current is supplied by one pair of wires.

Single pole A cut-out, circuit breaker or fuse switch in which the circuit is broken in one pole only.

Socket-outlet The outlet for a plug. Modern sockets are 13A square pin, often fitted with an on-off switch single or in pairs.

Spur A branch cable attached to a ring circuit.

Storage heater Method of heating where electrical energy is converted to heat and stored in a suitable medium to be given off at other times.

Sub-circuit A branch of a main circuit supplied from a distribution fuse board.

Switch Device for breaking and making a circuit manually.

T

Terminal See CONTACT

Thermostat Device for controlling temperature, in order to maintain a constant predetermined temperature.

Two-way switch Method of wiring on a fixed light enabling control from two different points.

U

Unit The charge for electricity is based on number of 'units' used. A unit is 1,000 watts (lkW) of electricity used for one hour. See **Kilowatt.**

V

Volt (V) Unit for measuring the pressure or force which causes an electric current to flow in a circuit.

ABC of terms

Plumbing

A

Access bend A pipe bend for rainwater, soil or waste systems into which is fitted a sealable trap or access door. This door facilitates general cleaning.

Air lock Air trapped in pipework, causing interference with the flow of water.

Air vent There are two types:
1. key or hand operated;
2. automatic.
Type 1 is positioned at the highest point in pipe circuits and radiators.
Type 2 is located at the highest point in pipe circuits and generally used in pressure systems.

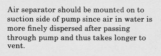

Air separator Both inlet and outlet are set at tangent to chamber, creating vortex which gives centrifugal action, forcing water to the wall and air to centre. Air rises to head of chamber and through orifice to vent.

Both types are for releasing air trapped in the system.

B

Back-drop (or entry) Entry of a pipe into an inspection chamber, cess-pit, septic tank or soakaway below ground level but above the level of the lowest point of the collection area. Frequently used to reduce the gradient of drains which are too steep.

Back- (or side-) inlet gully A drainage gully where entry is from the back or side below grating or cover level.

Balancing valve See valves.

Ball valve See valves.

Benching The protection of drainage, sewage or waste pipes with concrete stepping in concrete foundations.

Bend A change in direction of a pipe made with a tube-bending machine, bending spring or pipe fitting. An angled pipe fitting is also known as a bend and is similar to an elbow but has a much larger radius.

Bib tap (or cock) A screw-down tap with horizontal threaded inlet for fixing to a vertical surface.

Bidet A plumbed, WC-shaped pedestal basin; used for hygienic purposes.

Bleed valve See valves.

British thermal unit (BTU) One BTU is the amount of heat required to raise 1lb of pure water, at the temperature of maximum density, through 1°F. One BTU=1 kilojoule (kJ); about 100,000Btu=1 therm.

Bush This is a type of fitting threaded (metal) or plain (plastic) used for reducing the bore diameter of a fitting or connection in an appliance, i.e. cylinder or boiler.

C

Calorifier Inner heating coil in an indirect hot-water cylinder; immersion heater element; heat-exchanger element.

Capillary joint A method of joining copper pipe whereby solder is conducted, by capillary action, between the pipe and an exactly fitting copper sleeve. See solder and solderless (end-feed) joint.

Caulk To stop up a clayware pipe joint with a plastic or malleable substance, usually hemp soaked in pitch.

Cess-pit A subterranean storage pit for sewage. It has to be emptied at frequent intervals.

Cistern There are two main types for domestic use:
Storage–generally sited in the loft or roof space in a dwelling. Its function is to store the water for the indirect or low-pressure services in the household.

Flushing–used in conjunction with a WC. There are two types of these–the older 'ball' pattern and the modern piston-actuated type.

Close-coupled suite A WC system where the flushing cistern is adjacent to or an integral part of the WC pan.

Compression joint There are two types: In the manipulative type the pipe ends must be opened out and fitted to the rounded ends of a brass nipple. The tightening of two fly nuts forms the joint. In the non-manipulative type the ends are left as cut, the compression joint being formed by two olives held in place by the fly nuts.

Consumer pipe The section of water main between the water company's stopcock (or tap), usually situated near the property's boundary, and the rising-main stopcock (or tap) immediately inside the building.

Cross top A type of head on a tap in the form of a cross.

Crutch or bar top A type of head on a tap in the form of a straight bar.

Cylinder (or hot-water tank) Container for storing domestic hot water. Several types, e.g.: direct and indirect, the latter type has an inner cylinder or calorifier. Type used depends upon system in which it is to be installed.

D

Dead leg Pipes between the hot water cylinder and the draw-off points (i.e. taps) when these points are of considerable distance from the hot-water cylinder. This results in the heat of the water in the pipe being dissipated; hence a time lag when taps are opened, for hot water to arrive at the required point. The condition can be avoided by:
Ensuring that the pipe layout includes gravity circulation in the supply pipes;
Keeping the maximum length of pipe in which no circulation takes place to:
pipe dia. not exceeding 22mm–2·2m, pipe dia. exceeding 22mm but not 28mm–2·62m, pipe dia. exceeding 28mm–3·05m.

Diverter (or diverting) valve See valves.

Domestic hot water (DHW) Hot water used for washing and bathing facilities as opposed to heating.

Drains A pipe system for removing sink, toilet and WC effluent; also rainwater. In most modern buildings, rain-water disposal is separated from effluent either by a different drain system or by means of a rainwater soakaway.

E

Elbow Pipe fitting for connecting two lengths of pipe at a specified angle to each other–i.e. 90° 135°. The radius

of the change of direction of the elbow is the minimum permitted for the size of pipe for which it is to be used.

Electrolytic action The manufacture of electricity by passing water or other liquids across two dissimilar metals, e.g. copper and zinc. The chemical decomposition of the metals, caused by the ensuing electric action, is called electrolysis. Most likely to occur in hard-water areas.

F

Feed-and-expansion cistern This is required for some heating systems and is separate from the main cold-water storage cistern. Its purpose is to maintain the water level in the primary circuit and to accommodate the increases in volume due to the expansion of heated water. Water, raised in temperature from 0°C to 100°C expands by 1/23rd of its volume. In this way, the same primary circuit water is used repeatedly, thus avoiding wastage and the introduction of mineral deposits.

Female fitting Pipe fitting having a socket, plain or threaded, into which a tube or male fitting can be inserted.

Flue A vitreous metal, stainless steel, asbestos, glazed stone-ware or concrete duct for the removal of hot gases from a boiler; there are basically two types–conventional flues and balanced flues.

Gas volume Volume of gas is measured when the following conditions are present:
Temperature:
Imperial 60° Fahrenheit (60°F)
Metric 15° Celsius (15°C)

Pressure:
30ins of mercury (30″ Hg)
1013·25mbar

Moisture content:
saturated with water
dry.

G

Gate valve See valves.

Gland Sealing ring around the stem of taps, valves, and fittings to prevent leaking; generally adjustable.

Gravity circulation Occurs in a circuit, provided there is no obstruction to flow, when a heat source is applied to the low point of that circuit. Heated water becomes lighter and rises, forcing cold water downwards which, in turn, is heated.

Gully An opening to a drainage system to allow access of waste fluids. See also back inlet gully.

Gutter A metal, plastic or asbestos channel fixed to the lower edge of a roof to catch rainwater and convey it to a drainage system. The three most common sections are: half round, box and 'ogee'.

ABC of terms

H

Hand-wheel valve See valves.
Head The vertical height of a column of water between any lower point and the highest point in a heating system.
Header circuit A main supply pipe, making good heating-system water loss.
Heat-flow rate The quantity of heat produced in one hour measured in British Thermal Units per hour (Btu/h); the SI equivalent is joules per second (J/S) 1J/S=1 watt.
Holderbat A steel or iron clamp for fixing soil, waste or rainwater pipes to a masonry wall.

I

Immersion heater A metal-sheathed electric element inserted into a hot-water cylinder or tank to heat the water.
Index circuit The circuit with the highest resistance to flow.
Injector tee (or venturi) is a specially constructed tee-fitting usually connected into the gravity circuit of a combined gravity/pumped central-heating DHW system. When the heating circulating pump is switched on, the gravity flow is assisted or increased. This type of tee also reduces the number of tappings required on a heating appliance.
Inspection chamber (or manhole) A method of access to an underground drainage system, usually at a point where two or more drains meet.

K

Kilowatt/h (watts/h) The rate at which energy is supplied or consumed. The kW (1,000W) is normally the most convenient unit of measurement.

L

Lagging The protection of water pipes and tanks, by surrounding them with insulating materials such as glass fibre, vermiculite or expanded polystyrene.
Lockshield valve See valve.
Low-flush suite A WC and low-level, usually hip-height, flushing cistern.

M

Male fitting See female fitting.
Manhole See inspection chamber.
Manipulated fitting See compression joint.
Manometer A water-pressure gauge; used with sealed heating systems.
Minibore See Microbore.
Microbore A two-pipe hot-water system using 6mm, 8mm and 10mm bore pipes.
Mixer tap A combination tap whereby hot and cold water, individually controlled, enter separately and exit from one spout.

Mira dual-control shower mixer

Temperature control (selects more or less water from hot or cold supplies)

Flow control spindle

Inlet elbow

Flow control (operates piston movement via spindle)

Piston to open and shut off hot supply

Temperature control spindle

Hot supply

Cold supply

Piston to open and shut off cold supply

Outlet to shower

Mixing valves See valves.

N

Natural convection This occurs when a transmitting agent, such as air or water, is caused to move by a heat-source without any other influences.
Nipple A small valve which, when opened with a key, allows air to escape from a system. Also a fitting used in iron pipe-work, consisting of a short length of tube threaded on its outside diameter, throughout the entire length.
Non-manipulative fitting See compression fitting.

O

Olive/compression ring A small copper or brass ring used in non-manipulative compression fittings. When the fitting is tightened up, the 'olive' acts as a water seal. See also compression joints.
Overflow pipe A pipe, connected to any vessel capable of holding water, as a means of carrying any excess water from the vessel to a point of safety. The CSA of this pipe must always be larger than the total CSA of pipes and taps supplying water to the vessel (CSA= cross-sectional area).

P

Parallel branch connection A system of joining wastepipes into soil pipes whereby cross-flow between a WC branch and a waste water branch is avoided.

Pressure vessel A vessel which has its volume split into two sections by a rubber membrane. One side of the vessel is connected to the primary circuit and that side of it is filled with water. The other side of the vessel is filled with a gas, usually nitrogen or oxygen, to a predetermined pressure. The position of the membrane in the vessel, when it is in use, depends on the temperature and expansion volume of the water. The size and pressure of the vessel is directly related to the volume and temperature of the system.
Primary flow The movement of circulating water from the boiler.
Programmer A device for controlling the timing of domestic hot water and central heating automatically.
PTFE (Polytetra-fluorethylene) A tape or paste water-proofing compound used for pipe and fitting sealing.
Pumped primary The flow rate of water in a primary circuit, controlled by a circulating pump. Has the advantage over gravity flow that smaller-diameter pipes may be used; also much faster heat transference from heat source is obtained.

R

Radial circuit Any system, ducted air or water, where the heat-transference agent conducts the heat to the required site from a control point such as manifolds in a 'wet' system.
Rainwater (or hopper) head A hopper-shaped device, on the top of a rainwater pipe, acting as a collecting point for several rainwater pipes or spouts.
Reducing set A system of bushes fitted to the end of a pipe or fitting, thus enabling it to be connected to one of smaller or larger bore.
Rodding eye A small trap in a sewer, soil or wastepipe to enable the entry of a cleaning rod.

Choice of expansion vessel determined by: Total water content of installation; Its static head; Average selected water temperature.

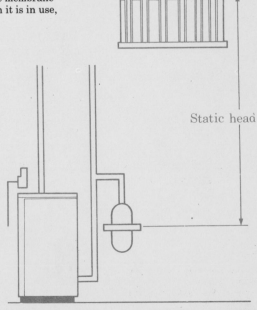

Static head

ABC of terms

Plumbing

S

Safety valve See valves.
Septic tank Similar to a cesspit but here effluent is broken down by bacterial action into a harmless fluid, which is then allowed to drain away naturally.

22mm and 28mm diameters and known as small-bore systems. There are two systems: single pipe and two pipe.
Single-pipe system Heat-exchangers (or radiators) are connected in series, or a 'loop'. Each heat exchanger has a 'by-pass' in the circuit, so it can be shut off without stopping the flow through the circuit.
Two-pipe system Heat exchangers are connected in parallel across two pipes, a flow and a return.
Soakaway Subterranean chamber of brick honeycomb construction; the hole is filled with non-organic hardcore.
Soil system Pipe system for the removal of effluent.

substance is the rate at which heat energy will be transferred through a substance to equalize the temperature on either side of that substance. This value is measured in wm²/°C (BTU/hr°F).

V

Valves A control for the flow of a liquid or gas.

Balancing valve A valve inserted in the section of a circuit which has the least resistance to flow, and adjusted to give uniform flow resistance throughout the system is called a balancing valve.

side of a heat exchanger; its function is to switch the exchanger on or off.
Lockshield valve Connected to the return side of a heat exchanger. This valve has the same internal construction as the handwheel valve. It is adjustable for water flow and used to balance each part of a heating system. However, the operating handle of the valve is replaced by a fixed protective cap, to prevent operation of the valve once set.
MT (empty) valve (or primary stop tap) Non-return valve in mains pipe adjacent to the boundary of a property.
Mixing valve A three-port (double entry single-exit) valve. The entry parts are connected to the hot and cold feeds; the function is to mix these feeds and supply water at a pre-determined temperature. This temperature can be controlled thermostatically or manually, dependent upon application.
Motorized valve A two-port motor-actuated on-off valve, usually controlled by a cylinder thermostat or programmer.
Non-return valve Automatic valve, normally held in closed position by a light spring, permitting water flow in one direction only. See also stopcock.
Safety valve Controlled by pressure; is set to open when pressure exceeds a set safe level.
Stopcock Hand-operated on-off valve, the internal construction of which permits water flow in one direction only and is, thus, a type of non-return valve. Its most common use is to separate the water board's supply from the consumer supply.
Thermostatic valve Similar to a thermostat, it opens and closes at set temperature levels, in order to maintain an even, required temperature.
Venting The act of letting air out of a system.
Vent pipe (VP) Part of a soil system which obviates the build up of natural gases in soil pipes and sewers.

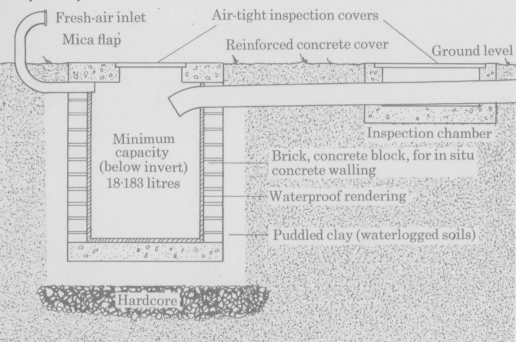

Scheme for septic-tank drainage

Labels: Fresh-air inlet · Mica flap · Air-tight inspection covers · Reinforced concrete cover · Ground level · Inspection chamber · Minimum capacity (below invert) 18·183 litres · Brick, concrete block, for in situ concrete walling · Waterproof rendering · Puddled clay (waterlogged soils) · Hardcore

Set back (night) A type of programming device, enabling a lower night temperature to be maintained in the home, reducing the amount of heat needed to top up temperatures in the morning.
Shoe The bent spout fitted at the base of a rainwater pipe.
Siphonic suite A more efficient WC pan than the normal wash-down type, improved emptying due to combined siphonic and wash-down action produces better soil-pipe discharge.

Small-bore system Central-heating systems relying upon smooth-bore tubes of 15mm,

Solderless or end-feed Capillary joint where solder is fed separately to fitting.
Solvent weld Used for joining plastic pipes. Volatile solvents temporarily soften two plastic surfaces, enabling these to be permanently joined together.
Stop cock See non-return valve.
Storage cistern See cistern.

T

Thermal capacity The amount of heat a substance will absorb and store.
Thermostat Device for maintaining a constant temperature by cutting and restoring heat supply as needed.
Thermostatic valve See valves.
Traps Sinks, WCs and gullies all have water traps to obviate smell rising from the drains. Sink traps are 'P' traps or 'S' traps.

U

'U' value The 'U' value of a

Ball (or float) valve Used to control the level of water in a cistern there are three types: Croydon, Portsmouth, or BSS patterns.
Bleed valve For evacuating (bleeding) air from a circuit.
Diverter valve Consists of a three-port two-way motorized valve, usually controlled by other heating controls. It is installed in the flow pipe from the boiler with the exit ports of the valve connected to the DHW cylinder and the heating circuit. It enables the total energy supply from the boiler to serve either part of the system as required. 'Proportional' diverter valves share the output between hot water and heating circuits.
Double (or twin) -entry valve Used to complete the termination of twin microbore tubes at a single entry on a radiator.
Gate valve A hand-operated on-off valve where the internal construction of the valve permits a water flow in either direction. Can be used for balancing (see balancing valve).
Hand-wheel or wheel-head valve Connected to the flow

W

Waste systems The arrangement of pipes and traps for the removal of water from sinks, showers and baths.
Water gauge A gauge for measuring gas and water pressures relative to surrounding atmosphere. Also unit of measurement used in determining the flow of water in a pipe.
Water hammer Repetitive knocking sound occurring when a tap is turned off quickly. The resulting shock-waves cause the stopcock jumper to oscillate. Water hammer may also be caused by the oscillation of a ball valve float, or exceptionally high mains pressure.

ABC of terms

Bricklaying and masonry

A

Abutment Sections of a wall supporting an arch (see arches).
Aggregate Materials mixed with binding or cementitious material to make mortars and concrete, e.g. sand, crushed brick, shingle, ballast.
Air-bricks Perforated brick let into walls to assist ventilation.
Alabaster Soft, white marble (sulphate of lime), used mainly for light ornaments. True material comes from Algeria, but similar materials are found elsewhere.
Aqueous Similar to, or containing water.
Arch Curved structure spanning a wall opening or room constructed in such a way as to carry the weight of materials above it and distribute them evenly to the supporting piers and abutments.

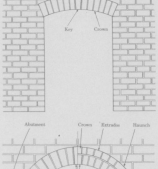

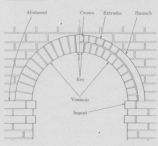

Architrave Mouldings surrounding a door or window.
Arris Sharp edge formed by the meeting of two surfaces. In brickwork and masonry the corners of bricks and stones are known as arrises.
Ash building blocks Constructed of kiln-dried, compressed furnace ash and cement or clay. Dimensions are such that they are easily handled. Although larger than standard bricks, the courses can be bonded into ordinary brick walls. They are a modern replacement for breeze blocks, being lightweight and having a high compression ratio. They are excellent for all forms of domestic building.
Ashlar Clean, wrought or worked building stone.

B

Asphalt Black, semi-solid substance made by adding sand or gravel to bitumen. Can be softened by heating and is used for roof coverings, pavings, and damp-proof membranes.

Balcony Balustraded platform projecting from upper-storey window.
Ballast Sand and shingle used as aggregate, available in various grades, most useful all-round one being 'three-quarter'.
Barge-course Course of bricks, edge laid across a wall next to a gable or as coping on a gable wall.
Bat Brick cut across – half-bat, quarter-bat, etc.
Batter or Butter To apply mortar to the ends or edges of bricks.
Beam A long, heavy plank or bulk of timber, a long section of steel, light alloy or reinforced concrete, used to support a load.
Bearer Section of material used to displace a load, see **Beam, Joist, Lintel.**
Bed Layer of fresh mortar on to which bricks or stones are laid.
Bed-rock Hard rock underlying surface soil or gravel.

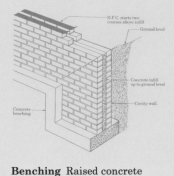

Benching Raised concrete steps in foundations in order to step the building or protect drains. The rounding off of corners and slopes at the bottoms of manholes.
Bitumen Mineral pitch, asphalt. Term covering numerous mixtures of these materials **Bituminous** containing bitumen.
Bond The way in which courses of bricks are laid to give strength to a wall.
Breast (Chimney) Projecting brick structure into a room, containing flue, hearth and fireplace.
Breeze (Blocks) Coarse building blocks of precast clinker concrete now largely replaced by other aggregate mixtures.
Brick Fired clay blocks used for building. Standard size 215mm by 102·5mm by 65mm. The most common bricks are general building bricks (*commons*): they are used for the main structure of brick-built buildings, on internal and external walls, where economy and practicability are more important than decorative

value: *facings* describes those bricks which as well as being durable and weather resistant, are used for their decorative qualities: *engineering bricks*, are practically impervious to moisture and very hard with a high load-bearing capacity. Better known types are Southwaters and Ruabons. Flettons are used as commons or facings as are stock bricks. With these more than any others the colours vary dependent upon the location of their manufacture.

Bricklaying and masonry tools

Bat gauge A stepped wooden board for measuring sections of brick when cutting them.

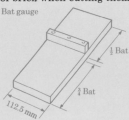
Bat gauge

Boaster A mason's chisel 50mm to 75mm wide, used for dressing and cutting stone.
Bolster (sometimes called Boaster) Bricklayer's chisel with 100mm to 125mm wide cutting edge, used for cutting bricks and 'chasing' plaster work.
Brick hammer Has a chisel edge for cutting and trimming bricks.
Brick Jointer A narrow trowel for finishing pointing.
Brick Trowel Varies in size from 150mm to 330mm in length and is used for laying mortar.
Broach A mason's pointed chisel.
Bubble Builder's slang for spirit level.
Club hammer Weighs 910 grammes to 2·03kg used in conjunction with boaster and bolster chisels.
Comb hammer or scutch Similar to the brick hammer but with serrations on the cutting edge.
Diamond saw Has teeth impregnated with diamond dust, used for cutting brick and masonry.
Float Steel trowel for finishing concrete and plaster work. Also slang term for spirit level.
Frenchman Hooked metal tool used for scraping out brick courses before pointing or repointing.
Gauging box Wooden box used for measuring out materials.
Gauging trowel Round-nosed trowel used for preparation of mortars.
Hawk Square metal plate on short handle, used for holding pointing mortars up to the work.
Hand board (See Hawk)
Mortar board Board 1m² in size, on which mortars are mixed or kept near the working position.
Pickaxe Metal tool on long

handle used for breaking up stone work, hard ground, when preparing foundations or demolishing old buildings.
Pitching tool (See Boaster)
Spot board (See Mortar board)
Spirit level Piece of wood or metal section with parallel sides in the middle of which is a glass phial containing a bubble in oil. This is used for testing the true level of brick courses. (Boat levels and line levels are smaller versions of this).
Tamper A flat, solid lump of iron to which is attached a long handle, used for compressing ground or hardcore.
Pointing trowel Small trowel 65mm to 140mm long used for pointing.
Brick-nogging Brickwork built up between the studs of a framed wooden partition.
Buff To polish or grind down by means of a revolving fabric or abrasive disc.
Building regulations Govern the construction and appearance of all structural building work.
Buttress Structural support for walls, constructed from brick, stone or timber.

C

Cantilever Pivoted beam or girder rigidly fixed at one end only.
Capillary action The movement or travel of a fluid by means of surface tension; osmosis.
Capillary groove Horizontal groove on the underside of window ledges and door ledges to stop capillary action carrying water back to the brickwork.
Cappings Topmost corbelled course of a chimney.
Capstone Coping stone.
Cavetto mould See illustration.

Cavity ties Metal ties of galvanised steel or wire bonded into brickwork to strengthen cavity walls. Coastal buildings should have bronzed or coppered ties to prevent corrosion.
Cavity wall Consists of two leaves, an outer wall half brick in thickness, and an inner wall of sufficient thickness to suit the type of building, being erected. These two walls separated by a continuous air space approximately 50mm wide. Each wall supports the other by means of metal wall ties. See **Cavity ties.**
Cellar Subterranean storage room.
Cement Powder made from burnt limestone and clay which hardens when mixed with water.

ABC of terms

Bricklaying and masonry

Cementation Method of supporting foundations by means of injecting liquid concrete.

Chimney bar Metal bar built into chimney breast to support brickwork above fireplace opening.

Chimney-stack Brickwork constructed to carry several flues.

Chuffs or Shuffs Badly cracked and misshapen bricks caused by moisture contact when hot. Should not be used.

Ciment fondu A high-aluminia or aluminous cement.

Closer A portion of an ordinary brick with the cut made longitudinally, (Queen closer) and usually having one uncut stretcher face. King closer is tapered from 102mm to 50mm.

Concrete A mixture of water, cement and aggregates which harden upon drying. Strength depends upon mixture.

Corbel Stone bracket projecting from a wall as a support for structural feature.

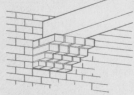

Coring hole Holes left at 1m centres (intervals) in the base of cavity walls directly above infill for clearing mortar droppings; are closed up when building is finished.

Crazing Formation of hairline cracks all over glazed or painted objects due to differing co-efficients of expansion. Similarly, hairline cracks over the surface of rendered and plastered brickwork, causing fabric to become pervious to water.

Crazy-paving Broken, irregular-shaped stone slabs laid at random to form a path or patio.

Creasing tile Tile with little or no camber and without nibs used for decorative effect in brickwork, particularly arches.

D

Damp proof course An impervious water barrier built into brickwork a minimum of 150mm above ground level. This can be slate, copper, zinc, lead and bitumous felts.

Injected silicone (polymerized compound of silicone and hydrocarbine radicals) and electro-osmosis (a proprietry wired-in damp course), are methods of inserting a DPC in old buildings.

Dentil course Where stretchers are inset from course below. Course above is in line with inset stretchers.

Diapers Bricks of a different colour from those mainly being used introduced into wall face to form pattern.

Dog-legged brick Used at corners and junctions in walls.

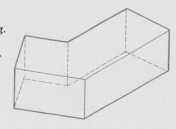

Double-breast fireplace Fireplace formed on the party wall back-to-back with another fireplace.

Drags Serrated steel chisel used to texture the surface of stone.

Drop arch A pointed arch which has its centre on the springing line.

Dry wall Wall constructed of stone but using no mortar, the stones being placed one on top of each other with the outer faces of the wall sloping in towards the top.

Dumpy level An optical measuring device used when setting out trench work prior to digging foundations.

E

Efflorescence White flakey salt deposits caused by moisture.

Electro-osmosis See DAMP-PROOF COURSE.

Embrasure A deep recess for window or door.

Entablature Masonry above a column including cornice, frieze and architrave.

Erosion Wearing away of soil or fabric by action of weather.

'Exmet' Trade name for type of expanded metal lathing.

Extrados External curve of an arch.

F

Face One side of a brick or stone, usually that which is mainly viewed.

'Ferrocrete' Rapid hardening or high-early-strength Portland Cement.

Ferro concrete Obsolete term for reinforced concrete.

Fire brick Bricks made of heat absorbent materials.

Fire clay Cement to which has been added heat absorbing materials.

Fireplace Opening in a room

for fire, above which is a flue for conducting away smoke and fumes.

Flag Slabs of stone used for paving.

Flint walling Walls made of flint and mortar, frequently reinforced by brick or concrete.

Flue lining Heat and damp resistant sections built into flues to obviate condensation causing damage to brickwork by penetrating damp.

Flush joints A flat joint finished flush with bricks on either side and left with a rough texture.

Folding wedges Two wooden wedges forced one against the other as an expanding locking piece to hold stays and supports in position.

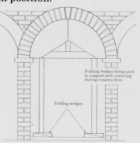

Folding wedges being used to support arch centering during construction

Folding wedges

Footings Brickwork foundations now replaced by concrete.

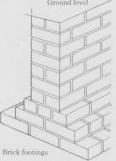

Ground level

Brick footings

Formwork Demountable structures acting as moulds for concrete.

Foundations Concrete base upon which buildings are erected.

Framed building Building consisting of a series of frameworks onto which all loads are spread.

Frame house Timber frame covered by weatherboards or shingles on the outer side, the inside being lined with plaster or fibre building boards.

Freestone Stone used for building in which the texture is so fine that it can be worked in any direction, there being no apparent grain.

Frog Hollow in the upper surface of brick which, when filled with mortar, helps to bond the brickwork.

Fungus Wet or dry rot, affecting timber. Can spread through porous brickwork to affect other timber. This is usually evident by what appear to be fine, sinuous webs over the brickwork.

G

Gable wall End wall of house supporting gabled roof.

Galvanize To coat steel with zinc, thus preventing rust.

Gargoyle Sculptured stone or metal pipe projecting from the eaves of buildings acting as drains or ventilators.

Gauged mortar A mixture of cement, non-hydraulic lime and sand.

Glass bricks Usually square, translucent, built into walls to allow light passage where windows would not be allowed by planning regulations.

Gravel A very useful aggregate providing impurities, such as clay, are removed by washing before use.

Grog Crushed brick and ceramic matter mixed with clay to allow clay-based materials to be fired to a high temperature.

H

Half-bat (See BAT).

Hangers Steel supports built into brickwork for the purpose of carrying joists.

Haunch The lower half of an arch.

Hardcore Broken brick, rubble or stone compressed to form a base upon which concrete can be poured. It is not used in foundations.

Headstone Central stone of an arch.

Honeycomb walls Are used below floors as supports for joists and are designed to allow free circulation of air. Similar constructions also found in drainage soakaways.

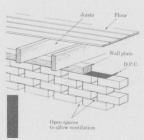

Joists   Floor

Wall plate

D.P.C.

Open spaces to allow ventilation

I

Impermeable Not porous.

Impervious Cannot be penetrated.

Insulating bricks Have heat insulating properties, mainly used in industrial furnaces, but also in certain types of domestic boiler and cooking range.

Irregate (DPC) See DAMP PROOF COURSE–Silicone.

J

Jamb Vertical support for a door or window.

Joggle Stone slabs held together by mild steel bars and molten lead.

K

Key Roughing a wall or surface to enable another material to adhere.

Keystone Central stone of an arch, without which it would collapse.

294

ABC of terms

Keenes cement A fine grain hard cement giving a smooth surface.
Kentish rag A sandstone used for building.
Knapp facing A textured finish to building stone.

L

Lacing course See ARCHES.
Laitance Liquid scum brought to the surface of wet concrete through excessive trowelling.
Lewis rag bolt A tapered fixing bolt used when fixing to masonry.
Level Dead horizontal. Spirit level.
Light-weight concrete Concrete using light-weight aggregate, e.g. clinker, foamed slag and pumice. Light-weight concrete is usually used where reduced weight and high insulation properties are desired.
Lime Slaked, burnt limestone; basically two types, 'hydraulic' and 'non-hydraulic'. The former is used for lime mortar, the latter for the making of cement-lime or gauged mortar.
Lintel Stone, timber or reinforced concrete beam spanning opening such as door or window. See BEAM
Load Weight carried by a structure measured in Newton's 'N/m' (foot/lb imperial).
Load-bearing wall Wall carrying the weight of superstructure, e.g. a second storey or roof.
Loggia Covered, but not enclosed extension to a house.

M

Maisonette Section of a house used as a self-contained dwelling.
Masonry Stonework. The craft of working stone in building.
Mastic asphalt Mixture of asphalt-rock or limestone impregnated with bitumen, or bitumen and siliceous grit. Supplied in blocks and heated to obtain plasticity. Used for horizontal and vertical DPCs, also roof coverings.
Matrix Binding material in mortar and concrete, i.e. Portland cement.
Metre Metric unit of length.
Mezzanine Intermediate storey.
Module Standardized unit of size in building design.
Modular bricks Bricks produced to fit architectural system of design–dimensional co-ordination–using standard components and dimensions to a 300mm module.
Mortar General term covering mixtures of cement and sand, lime and sand, cement, lime and sand.
Mullion Vertical division between windows either stone, metal or wood.

N

Natural foundation The ground or subsoil on which a building rests. Load-bearing capabilities vary according to its nature.
Nogging Brickwork infilling between wooden studding.

O

Offsets Narrow horizontal ledges caused by reducing the thickness of a wall (see FOOTINGS). Wide offsets may be used to support a floor.
Open or dry area Area surrounding a basement to allow passage of light and air.

P

Pad stone Block of stone or concrete surmounting a pier, pillar or column to support a beam or lintel and effectively distribute the load.
Pad foundation Concrete pad supporting an isolated pier.
Parapet Wall edging a balcony or bridge.
Parging Cement, lime and sand lining of old flues, now replaced by flue liners.
Party wall Dividing wall between two attached dwellings.
Pebble dash Wall surface consisting of fine gravel thrown on to soft mortar.
Penning See HARDCORE
Pilaster Square sectioned pillar projecting from a wall, sometimes fluted.
Pile Column of concrete or timber sunk into the ground as a foundation.
Plasticiser Mortar additive to make mix more workable.
Pointing Raking out soft mortar joints and filling them with a hard or decorative mortar mix.
Profiles Wooden boards and strings used to set out foundation trenches.
Purbeck Fine limestone.

Q

Queen closer Half brick cut lengthways.
Quicklime Unslaked lime.
Quoin External corner of a wall.

R

Raft-concrete A raft or slab of concrete laid over soft ground to form a foundation.
Rad See KENTISH RAG (Sandstone).
Rag bolt See LEWIS RAG BOLT.
Racking back The stepped section is higher than another.
Reinforced concrete Concrete reinforced with steel to give greater strength.
Render To apply cement mortar as a protective screed to external brickwork.
Retaining wall Reinforced or sloping wall built to support or retain higher ground.
Reveal The side of a window or door opening.
Rubbers Soft bricks which can be easily shaped with either a saw or carborundum stone, mostly used to form arches.

S

Saddleback coping This is sloped in such a way as to allow water to run off easily. Often, the coping overhangs its supporting walls, in which case, capillary grooves are cut into overhanging edges.
Sand A fine aggregate mixed both with mortars and concretes. In mortar, sand reduces shrinkage and obviates cracks. Soft builders' sand is used for bricklaying mortars, and strong sand is used for rendering or screeding.
Shuttering See FORMWORK.
Silicon Non-metallic element similar to carbon, a constituent of silicone.
Silicone Polymerized compound of silicon and hydrocarbon radicals used in lubricants and polishes. Also injected into walls to form a DPC.
Site concrete Concrete infill below lowest floor levels, but above exterior ground level, which together with DPC membrane, prevents damp and the growth of plant matter. Also called surface concrete.
Slate Natural stone used as DPC or roofing.
Sleeper walls A low wall, usually honeycombed, built below the centre of a ground floor as an extra support for the joists.
Slurry Any liquid plastic material, e.g. mortar.
Sneck (Sometimes CHECK) A small stone used in the construction of masonry walls.
Soldier course A course of bricks laid on end continuously.
Spade finish Finish applied in certain situations, e.g. site concrete, to concrete with the back of a spade or shovel.
Span Horizontal distance between two supports.
Spandril steps Steps with an almost triangular cross-section, being lighter than rectangular sectioned steps, also giving greater headroom.
Stepped foundation See BENCHING
Stop end The end of a wall where the courses finish flush.
Stretcher A brick laid with its sides in line with the wall-face.
Strike board A wooden tamping board rested across two shuttering boards used for levelling concrete.
Stucco Coat of fine plaster on a wall or ceiling, also light decorative relief.
Struck joint A decorative joint used only on interior brickwork. It has the advantage that it obviates shadows. If this joint is used on exterior walls, water would collect at the base of the joint and cause the mortar to break down, allowing the brickwork to become saturated.

T

Tamp Ram down.
Tanking A form of DPC where a continuous screed or membrane of DPC material, e.g. pitch/resin, is continued across the floors and up the walls. This treatment is common in basements and cellars.
Template (Sometimes TEMPLET) Wood or metal outline used for shaping or marking out prior to cutting.
Terracotta A brown-coloured clay which, when fired, produces a light red/brown earthenware.
Throat A narrowing in a chimney flue.
Tie bricks Bricks used to make the bond where two walls join.
Trench A long narrow hole cut into the earth.
Trench timbering Timber used to support the sides of a trench to stop cave-ins.
Turning piece Temporary timber support for arch while under construction.

U

Underpin To reinforce existing foundations or footings with concrete poured in sections.

V

Ventilation A free circulation of fresh air.
Voussoirs The individual stones or bricks used to form an arch.

W

Wall ties See CAVITY TIES
Waterproof membrane A horizontal membrane of DPC material, e.g. polythene or asphalt let into site concrete.
Weather pointing A mortar application to the joints in brickwork as a form of weather protection. Slope allows rain to run off and away from brickwork.
Withes The divisional wall between individual flues in a chimney stack.

Z

Zinc A hard grey-blue metal used in alloys, galvanizing and plumbing.

Index

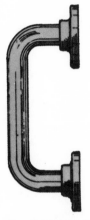
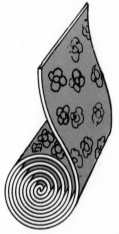

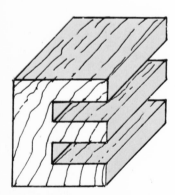

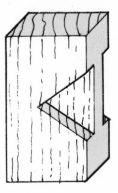

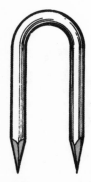
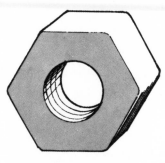

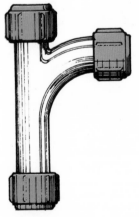

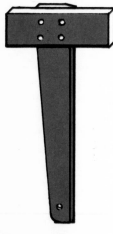

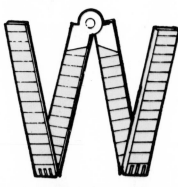